DR. CHARLES BEST SECONDARY

#	LAST NAME	YEAR
65775	Dean Floros	2004
72827	NICOLE KIRKLEY	2004

202174.

TWENTIETH CENTURY VIEWPOINTS

SECOND EDITION

An Interpretive History for the 21st Century

Lead Author
Don Quinlan

Graham Draper

Pamela Perry-Globa

Victor Zelinski

OXFORD
UNIVERSITY PRESS

OXFORD
UNIVERSITY PRESS

70 Wynford Drive, Don Mills, Ontario M3C 1J9
www.oup.com/ca

Oxford University Press is a department of the University of Oxford.

It furthers the University's objective of excellence in research, scholarship, and education by publishing worldwide in

Oxford New York

*Auckland Bangkok Buenos Aires Cape Town
Chennai Dar es Salaam Delhi Hong Kong Istanbul Karachi
Kolkata Kuala Lumpur Madrid Melbourne Mexico City Mumbai Nairobi
São Paulo Shanghai Taipei Tokyo Toronto*

Oxford is a registered trademark of Oxford University Press
in the UK and in certain other countries

Published in Canada
By Oxford University Press

Copyright © Oxford University Press Canada 2003

The moral rights of the author have been asserted

Database right Oxford University Press (maker)

First published 2003

National Library of Canada Cataloguing in Publication Data

Twentieth century viewpoints: an interpretive history for the twenty-first century / Don Quinlan ... [et al.]. — 2nd ed.

Includes index.
ISBN 0-19-541867-0

1. History, Modern—20th century. I. Quinlan, Don, 1947-

D421.T837 2003   909.82   C2003-900738-3

Printed in Canada

1 2 3 4 – 06 05 04 03

Acquisitions editors: Marian Marsh, Patti Henderson
Managing editor: Monica Schwalbe
Lead developmental editor: Tracey MacDonald
Developmental editors: Karen Alliston, Jessica Pegis
Copy editor: Susan McNish
Photo and permissions researcher: Paula Joiner
Production editor: Heather Kidd
Text and cover design: Brett Miller
Formatting: PageWave Graphics Inc.
Cartographer: Crowle Art Group

DEDICATIONS

To the readers of this text: May they learn from the lessons of the twentieth century as they shape their lives in the twenty-first century.
— Don Quinlan

With many thanks to Don, Spencer, Wallace, and McGee Globa.
— Pamela Perry-Globa

ACKNOWLEDGEMENTS

Oxford University Press would like to thank the following people for their valued contribution to the development of this text:

Craig Wallace, Sabha Ghani, Rich Winter, David Yoshida, David Mushens, Neil Pinder, Mark Shannon, Bob Johnston, Ray Verbeek, Wade Seymour, Donna McIntyre, Linda Mowatt, Dr. Rex Brynen, and Simon Rosenblum.

Cover photos
Main image: A couple take cover in Beijing as Chinese troops crush a pro-democracy demonstration in Tiananmen Square on 5 June 1989. Credit: AP/Wide World Photos. *Inset image:* "Wait for me, Daddy" — A child reaches out to his father as soldiers of the British Columbia Regiment march through New Westminster, BC, on their way to war in 1940. Credit: Claude P. Dettloff/National Archives of Canada/C-038723.

Since this page cannot accommodate all the copyright notices, pages 435-436 are considered extensions of this page.

Every possible effort has been made to trace the original source of text material contained in this book. Where the attempt has been unsuccessful, the publisher would be pleased to hear from the copyright holders to rectify any omissions.

Contents

Features

SKILL PATH

VOICES

VIEWPOINTS

About This Textbook

Twentieth Century Viewpoints: An Interpretive History for the Twenty-First Century is divided into four units. Unit One: 1900 to 1945 begins with a look at the world at the turn of the twentieth century and continues through the extended world conflict that began in 1914 with the First World War and ended in 1945 after the Second World War. There is a special focus in this unit on the inter-war period and the factors that can motivate nations to confrontation.

Unit Two: The Cold War focuses on the relationship between the two superpowers—the United States and the Soviet Union—from 1945 to 1990 and looks at the role of the United Nations in promoting peace, co-operation, and global security.

Unit Three: The Global Village highlights regional issues related to imperialism, economic development, and current trends and challenges. Specific national case studies help provide an in-depth look at each region.

Unit Four: The Contemporary World presents an overview of the world in the opening years of the twenty-first century. This unit focuses on the themes of progress and uncertainty in an age of conflict and co-operation.

Each unit opens with a detailed timeline of the specific period, while each chapter begins with an illustration (either a photograph or a painting) and a powerful quotation (or two) to introduce students to the era and the themes about to be studied. Each chapter also presents a Chapter Overview, a set of Focus Questions, and a series of additional features intended to add depth and interest to the main narrative text. These additional features include:

MAP STUDY

Large, clear maps provide important graphic information on themes and events central to the text. The maps are accompanied by a brief narrative text and a series of questions and activities designed to increase your understanding of the maps.

NETSURFER

This feature allows readers to delve deeper into specific topics through the use of relevant Internet sites. Because of the "in flux" nature of the Internet, site addresses given in this text may change over time. If you are unable to link to a site, use topical key words in your favourite search engine to try to locate the new address.

PROFILES

Profiles contain thumbnail biographies of key individuals who have helped shape historical events since 1900. Each Profile is supported with a brief series of questions.

Skill Path

History is not simply the accumulation of facts; it is also a vehicle for the exploration and mastery of important research, inquiry, and presentation skills. Skills are presented in a detailed step-by-step explanation and are integrated with the text through the use of examples taken from the content of the chapter. The "Practise Your Skill" activities included at the end encourage the immediate and relevant application of the skill into the ongoing study of the course.

Voices

Each Voices feature presents a number of direct quotations to represent a variety of opinions and comments on a particular topic.

In Review

Review questions, placed strategically throughout each chapter, reinforce the reader's understanding of the basic narrative. The features explained above, as well as many of the images, also provide questions and activities that foster a deeper understanding of the material under study.

Viewpoints

This feature presents conflicting readings in which expert authors argue for or against key issues or questions. A series of follow-up questions is included to help readers master the arguments of this more challenging material.

Chapter Analysis

Each chapter ends with a series of questions and activities—under the headings Making Connections, Developing Your Voice, and Researching the Issues—designed to increase comprehension and extend learning. There is also ample room for the reader to develop and present his/her own views and analysis.

Introduction

The study of history is much more than a stale recollection of past events: it should be an informed inquiry into the past. When we read history, we must work with two kinds of knowledge—the historical record of events, names, dates and places (usually termed the *facts*) and the *interpretation* of events from various points of view.

Historical facts can be proven by evidence. However, while it is important that we master the facts, there is much more to the study of history; the interpretation of events is perhaps a more significant and interesting form of historical knowledge.

Interpretations give us a sense of meaning. Historical interpretations are developed by people who try to explain events by discovering important relations (chronological ties, cause and effect, and similarities and differences) in the data studied. Unlike facts, these interpretations cannot be proven conclusively. Instead, the most that can be expected is that a consensus of opinion may be reached among most scholars and experts. Such a consensus then becomes the generally accepted understanding, or truth, about certain issues and events.

Interpretive knowledge is always subject to challenge and change, however, since historical accounts are written by people who analyse and evaluate past events in the context of their own time and place. This means they have their own viewpoints, biases, and perspectives. Thus, we must learn to assess the reliability of such knowledge.

Twentieth Century Viewpoints: An Interpretive History for the Twenty-First Century encourages an interpretive approach to the study of history. This approach is intended to help you develop a greater and more personal understanding of the central events of the twentieth century and the early years of the twenty-first century.

Each chapter in this text contains a Viewpoints feature, which introduces conflicting interpretations and points of view on specific topics. The authors of the readings contained in this feature are generally regarded as key players or experts in their field. As a result, you will be reading challenging but informed opinions from different sides of an issue. Do not assume that one opinion is wrong while the other must be right. Individuals who interpret evidence often arrive at very different conclusions. This kind of debate leads to a deeper and more comprehensive understanding of past events.

There are three steps to the interpretive approach used in this book. (For more detailed instructions and practise questions, please see the Chapter One Skill Path, "Analysing a Reading", on pages 14 and 15. It is recommended that you refer to this Skill Path for guidance before beginning a Viewpoints feature.)

1. *Understand the background to key events.* You need to know the basic facts, issues, and events before you can analyse and evaluate historical interpretations.

2. *Analyse and evaluate different interpretations of an event or issue.* You need to carefully separate fact from opinion and substance from rhetoric in order to identify the underlying reasoning of an argument as well as to determine if the argument is sound and logical. It is

> "Nothing is more likely to stunt the intellect than to have a knowledge of history unaccompanied by a sense of history."
> — Alden Nowlan

> "Any fool can make history, but it takes a genius to write it."
> — Oscar Wilde

important to assess and evaluate the viewpoints of others before forming your own opinions about important issues. It is also important to learn to identify over-simplified or exaggerated statements. As you analyse an interpretive reading, you must evaluate it—that is, make informed and reasonable judgements about the position taken in the reading. There are several Skill Path features that can help you learn the procedures needed to accomplish this. These include "Writing Thesis Statements" (page 166), "Recognizing and Analysing Bias in Information Sources" (page 195), and "Analysing a Current Issue" (page 352).

3. *Reach a decision by developing our own position on the issue.* This text is not designed solely to provide essential facts and differing historical interpretations. It is also aimed at encouraging you to develop *your* voice and to develop an informed analysis and evaluation of the past. Reaching a conclusion is not simply a matter of selecting one interpretation over another. You may decide to accept some aspects of an argument and reject others. Your conclusion might then be a unique composite and personal understanding based on your analysis of several different interpretations.

Additionally, over time, new information often becomes available, adding to the body of generally accepted facts. For instance, governments may release previously "classified" information that may have a significant bearing on our understanding of past events. It is also recognized that we may not be ready to make a decision on an issue and must, therefore, choose to remain undecided. As well, many issues may be developing and evolving, making it difficult to choose a definitive answer.

As you study the key events of the world from 1900 on, you will have the opportunity and the tools to critically analyse and evaluate the viewpoints that you have read. In so doing, you will develop your personal knowledge of history and your unique abilities as a creative, critical thinker. You can then apply your knowledge and understanding of history to current issues that confront you as a global citizen. Developing an informed opinion is an essential skill for all citizens in a democratic and diverse society.

Finding your own "voice" is critical to your personal growth and sense of self in an often confusing and chaotic world. Being capable of expressing your voice clearly and in a manner that reflects real understanding and respects the opinions of others is important. In this contemporary world of great progress coupled with considerable uncertainty, your voice and your viewpoints will be important in shaping the next years of this century.

"In truth, there is nothing in history like the problem of today."
— R.H. Coats

"History cannot give us a program for the future, but it can give us a fuller understanding of ourselves and of our common humanity so that we can better face the future."
— Rupert Warren

UNIT ONE

1900 to 1945

Learning Goals

By the end of this unit students will be able to:

- Analyse the motives for international confrontation
- Explain the basic features of various political ideologies, such as communism, fascism, and democracy
- Analyse the motives for international co-operation
- Explain the rise of dictators in Europe during the inter-war period
- Evaluate the role of security agreements in either maintaining peace between countries or promoting further conflict
- Understand how the nature of the Second World War changed both the nature of warfare and the balance of power in the world
- Create, interpret, and analyse timelines, graphs, concept maps, and charts
- Analyse a reading

	1900-1909	1910-1919
POLITICS / MILITARY	• Russia occupies Manchuria (1900) • Boxer Rebellion in China (1900) • End of Boer War (1902) • US acquires Panama Canal Zone (1903) • Britain and France form Entente Cordiale (1904) • Japanese victory in Russo-Japanese War (1905) • Britain, Russia, France form Triple Entente (1907) • Austria annexes Bosnia and Herzegovina (1908)	• Revolution in China (1911) • Assassination of Archduke Ferdinand; WWI erupts (1914) • British naval blockade of Germany (1915) • German submarine blockade of Britain (1915) • Italy joins war on Allied side (1915) • Sinking of *Lusitania* (1915) • Battle of the Somme (1916) • Conscription in Canada (1917) • US declares war on Germany (1917) • Battle of Vimy Ridge (1917) • Wilson outlines Fourteen Points (1918) • Second Battle of the Marne (1918) • Germany signs armistice to end WWI (1918) • Treaty of Versailles (1919) • Soviet Republic established in Russia (1919) • League of Nations born (1919)
CULTURE / SOCIETY	• Freud, *Interpretation of Dreams* (1900) • First Nobel Prizes (1901) • First gramophone recordings (1902) • Russell, *The Principles of Mathematics* (1903) • Picasso, *Les Demoiselles d'Avignon* (1907) • Exhibition of Cubist paintings in Paris (1907) • D.W. Griffiths shoots first film (1908) • Peary first to reach North Pole (1909)	• Amundsen reaches South Pole (1911) • 5 million Americans visit cinemas daily (1912) • *Rite of Spring* performance causes near riot in Paris (1913) • Griffiths, *Birth of a Nation* (1915) • Prohibition in US (1916) • Birth of Dadaism (1916) • Influenza epidemic (1918) • Labour unrest in Europe and North America (1919) • Bauhaus founded by Gropius (1919)
SCIENCE / TECHNOLOGY	• Planck's Quantum Theory (1900) • First transmission of human speech by radio waves (1900) • Marconi sends wireless signal across Atlantic (1901) • Wright Brothers make first airplane flight (1903) • First radio transmission of music (1904) • Einstein, Theory of Relativity (1905) • First dreadnought (1906) • Electric washing machine (1907) • Ford introduces Model T (1908)	• Creation of tank (1911) • First neon sign (1912) • Sinking of *Titanic* (1912) • Ford develops first assembly line (1913) • Wireless messages between ships at sea (1914) • Teletype machine invented (1914) • Panama Canal opened (1914) • Poison gas, flame-throwers on Western Front (1915) • First fighter aircraft built (1915) • First refrigeration of blood for transfusion (1916) • First use of mustard gas (1917) • Germans design bomber aircraft (1917) • Planck wins Nobel Prize for Quantum Theory (1918) • Rutherford splits atom (1919) • Alcock/Brown fly non-stop across Atlantic (1919)

1920-1929

- Prohibition across US (18th Amendment) (1920)
- First meeting of League (1920)
- American women win vote (1920)
- Lenin creates NEP in Soviet Union (1921)
- Stalin becomes Secretary-General in USSR (1922)
- Mussolini rules Italy (1922)
- Hitler's Munich Putsch (1932)
- Death of Lenin (1924)
- Hitler, *Mein Kampf* (1925)
- Civil war in China (1926)
- Stalin launches first Five Year Plan (1928)

1930-1945

- Japan occupies Manchuria (1930)
- Hitler in power in Germany (1933)
- Germany renounces Treaty of Versailles (1935)
- Japan invades China (1937)
- Munich Agreement (1938)
- Nazi-Soviet Pact (1939)
- German invasion of Poland (1939)
- WWII begins; Canada enters war (1939)
- Fall of France; Battle of Britain (1940)
- Germany invades USSR (1941)
- Japan bombs Pearl Harbor (1941)
- Germany and Italy declare war on US (1941)
- Germans defeated at Stalingrad (1942)
- Allies invade Italy (1942); fall of Mussolini (1943)
- Soviets drive into Eastern Europe (1944)
- D-Day invasion of Nazi-held Europe (1944)
- Germany defeated (1945)
- Yalta Conference (1945)
- United Nations formed (1945)
- Potsdam Conference (1945)
- US drops A-bomb on Japan (1945)

POLITICS / MILITARY

- Joyce, *Ulysses* (1922)
- KKK conference in US draws 200 000 (1923)
- Gershwin, *Rhapsody in Blue* (1923)
- First Winter Olympics (1924)
- First woman cabinet minister in Western government (Nina Bang, Denmark) (1924)
- Charleston dance craze (1923)
- Unemployment insurance introduced in Germany (1926)
- Disney studios open in Hollywood (1926)
- Great Depression (1929)
- BBC launches experimental TV (1929)

- World unemployment reaches 30 million (1932)
- Huxley, *Brave New World* (1932)
- Prohibition repealed in US (1933)
- Famine in USSR (1933)
- Gershwin, *Porgy and Bess* (1935)
- Berlin Olympics (1936)
- Picasso, *Guernica* (1937)
- *Hindenburg* destroyed by fire (1937)
- Hemingway, *For Whom the Bell Tolls* (1940)
- Britain applies conscription to women (1941)
- Welles, *Citizen Kane* (1941)
- *Maltese Falcon* (1942)
- Orwell, *Animal Farm* (1945)

CULTURE / SOCIETY

- Banting/Best isolate insulin (1922)
- Hubble shows galaxies beyond Milky Way (1923)
- Tuberculosis vaccine developed
- Ford makes 10 millionth car (1924)
- Baird transmits human image on TV screen (1923)
- Kodak makes first 16 mm film (1926)
- Lindbergh makes first solo flight across Atlantic (1926)
- Discovery of penicillin (1928)
- Teleprinter invented (1928)
- Einstein, Unified Field Theory (1929)

- Discovery of planet Pluto (1930)
- Beebe descends 900 m under sea in bathysphere (1934)
- Nylon invented (1935)
- First Volkswagen (1936)
- Jet engine tested in UK (1937)
- First ship equipped with radar (1938)
- First helicopter (1939)
- Blood plasma used in transfusions (1940)
- Manhattan Project launched (1941)
- US builds nuclear reactor (1942)
- First automatic computer built in US (1942)
- V1, V2 German bombs launch Missile Age (1944)
- Atomic bomb unleashes Nuclear Age (1945)

SCIENCE / TECHNOLOGY

CHAPTER ONE

The New World of the Twentieth Century

This painting, by August Mondlich, shows a street corner in Vienna, Austria, ca. 1900. Describe the details you see in this scene, for example, the style of dress, transportation, architecture, etc. What does this painting tell you about life at the turn of the twentieth century and the dramatic changes taking place at that time?

"Nothing recedes like progress."

— e. e. cummings (1894-1962), American poet

"Anyone desiring a quiet life has done badly to be born in the twentieth century."

— Leon Trotsky (1879-1940), a Russian revolutionary leader of the Bolshevik Revolution of 1917

Overview

In most of the world, life in the year 1900 was little different than it had been in 1800. The pace was slow and predictable. Most children grew up and followed in their parents' footsteps. The world scene was dominated by European nations—Britain, Germany, France, Russia, and Austria-Hungary. The economic and military powers of the United States and Japan were on the rise, but the principles of democracy were untested and distrusted in many countries. Women lacked many rights, including the right to vote. But as society moved into a new century, life began to change dramatically. Political violence erupted in many nations. The old ways were challenged and our systems of government, our habitats, our occupations, our entertainment, and our lifestyles embarked on a journey of remarkable transformation. The incredible adventure of the twentieth century was about to be unleashed. One thing was certain: the world would never be the same.

Focus Questions

1. What was Western society like at the turn of the century?
2. What issues fuelled the struggles of the women's suffrage movement?
3. What were some of the dominant political, cultural, and economic ideas of the time?
4. What were the relative strengths and weaknesses of the world's major imperial powers?
5. What conflicts erupted in the early years of the new century?

The World at the Turn of the Century

To illustrate the extent of change from the beginning of the century until now, let's picture our society as it was in 1900. Most people lived on farms or in rural areas. Homes did not have electricity and so there were no electric lights or refrigerators. Telephones were just coming into use. Movie theatres—or picture palaces, as they were called then—were beginning to show silent films with captions to explain the dialogue and piano music as accompaniment.

Horses provided much of the transportation, pulling carts, wagons, carriages, and even fire engines. In a few cities, electric tramcars transported people from place to place. And there were bicycles, trains, and boats. But new inventions were being developed that would revolutionize travel. Henry Ford founded the Ford Motor Company in 1903 and the classic Model T made its debut in 1908. The Wright brothers made the first successful airplane flight in 1903, remaining airborne for 59 seconds! Their accomplishment heralded the new era of flight.

Throughout the nineteenth century people had been migrating to the New World. By 1900, however, the wave of migration had reached unprecedented proportions. Immigrants flocked to North America, lured by the promise of prosperity. The west was opening up to settlement

Figure 1.1
New electric tramcars rolled alongside traditional horse-drawn carriages in downtown Toronto in 1910. Give an example today of an old technology coexisting with a new technology.

and cities and towns were growing rapidly. Opportunities abounded.

Despite the prosperity brought by industrialization, inequality between the rich and the poor was dramatic. The working class had almost no protection under the law in terms of wages, working conditions, and unemployment. Demands for social reform were mounting, and it was women who were leading the way. In demanding equality and the right to vote, the women's suffrage movement not only challenged long-standing ideas of male supremacy, but also shed light onto other social issues, such as unemployment and the plight of the middle classes and poor. It was a campaign that would not achieve its goals without a long and hard struggle. Much of the new century would be marked by the struggles of women across the globe.

CHANGES IN POPULATION AND OCCUPATION

In 1900, the world population was 1.6 billion. Over the course of the twentieth century it exploded to over 6 billion. But in spite of such a dramatic escalation, the distribution of people around the world then and now is similar. In 1900, out of every 1000 people, 570 lived in Asia, 260 lived in Europe and Russia, 75 lived in Africa, 50 lived in North America, 40 lived in Latin America, and five lived in Australia and New Zealand. Remarkably, these figures still reflect the world's population distribution today.

The turn of the century marked the beginning of important advances in controlling the spread of disease and improvements in medical care and sanitation. These led to a reduction in mortality rates in the early part of the century. This

MAP STUDY

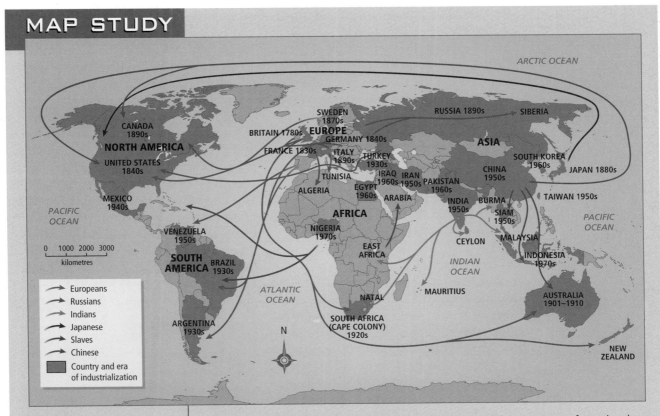

Figure 1.2

The Spread of Industrialization
and the Migration of Peoples,
Selected Countries

This map presents the chronology of industrialization and the movement of peoples during one of the greatest periods of human migration in history. Millions left the Old World in search of a better life in the New World.

Interpreting

1. Note three countries that "lost" migrating citizens.
2. Which nations in the world received most of these migrating peoples?
3. Which countries were the first and last to industrialize?
4. What impact has the date of industrialization had on their position in the world today?
5. Which nations might become the next industrial giants? Give reasons for your answer.

in turn spawned a surge in population growth in Europe despite a decline in actual birth rates. Global population growth and migration is still a central concern of leaders today.

In 1900, about 70 per cent of the world's population earned a living from farming, although this figure was lower in industrialized nations. In the United States in 1830, for example, 70 per cent of

the people were engaged in farming. By 1900 this figure had dropped to 38 per cent, and by 1980 it was a mere two per cent. Farming was of greater importance in the Canadian economy at the turn of the century as the pace of industrialization lagged behind that of the US. The rural population in 1900 was 62 per cent. But in the east, urbanization was spreading rapidly.

Western Europe and North America

were the most industrialized and urbanized regions on earth. In 1900, there were only 11 cities with a population of over 1 million, and seven of these were in the West. Three of them—New York, Chicago, and Philadelphia—were in the United States, which was quickly becoming the world's major industrial power. By 1913, the U.S. produced 36 per cent of all the world's manufactured goods. Germany followed a distant second at 16 per cent, while Britain accounted for 14 per cent. The industrialization of the Western economy was well under way.

IMMIGRATION

Increasing population, industrialization, urbanization, and unemployment combined to create conditions that inspired a huge wave of migration from Europe to the New World. Working class people crowded into steamships bound for North America, lured by offers of cheap passage and promises of new opportunities. The United States was a powerful magnet for immigrants hoping for a fresh start and a better future. Between 1861 and 1920, over 45 million Europeans emigrated, over half of them to the United States.

While Canada attracted far fewer immigrants than its southern neighbour, between 1900 and 1914 immigration soared as an average of 200 000 people arrived each year. In 1901, immigrants accounted for 13 per cent of the population. Half of these new arrivals headed west to the farmlands of the Prairies. In the first decade of the new century, the populations of Saskatchewan and Alberta more than quadrupled.

WOMEN'S SUFFRAGE

Inequality between the sexes at the beginning of the twentieth century was a long established way of life. Society was openly male-dominated. In most countries, women were treated as little more than the property of men. Men headed the household. Women were frequently treated more like children than responsible adults. The prevailing attitude was "a woman's place is in the home."

Educational and occupational choices for women were limited. Female roles were confined mainly to teaching and nursing. Few women managed to break into the world of business, except as typists and telephone operators. Working class women had no choice but to work, often as domestics or factory workers. These jobs yielded very little in terms of money and less still in terms of power.

To make positive changes in society and to gain control over their own lives,

Figure 1.3

Emmeline Pankhurst (shown here being arrested) and her daughter Sylvia were imprisoned for their participation in suffrage demonstrations. In one year, Sylvia engaged in numerous hunger strikes, which led prison authorities to feed her using a stomach tube. In your view, is the hunger strike an effective way to achieve change? Explain.

women first needed to obtain **enfranchise-ment**—the right to vote. The campaign began in earnest in the mid-nineteenth century, but the ensuing struggle was to take decades. Women's **suffrage** became the key objective for women's movements in Western countries. In Britain, the National Society for Women's Suffrage was founded in 1868; in the United States, the National American Women Suffrage Association was formed in 1890. Still, by 1910 only three countries—Australia, New Zealand, and Finland—had granted women the right to vote. Today the struggle for full female equality is being waged far beyond the narrow borders of Europe and North America.

Although the struggle took decades, in most Western countries women won the vote relatively peacefully. Not so in Britain, however, where resistance to giving women the vote was especially strong. The more extreme suffragists held public rallies, scuffled with police, chained themselves to fences, and threw objects through windows. Many were frequently arrested and jailed. In jail, the women went on hunger strikes. In 1918, the vote was finally granted to all women over 30. (Men could vote at the age of 21.) Ten years later women's voting age was reduced to 21.

In Canada, the Election Act stated that "No woman, idiot, lunatic, or criminal shall vote." Women across the country gathered to protest. In 1876, the Toronto Women's Literary Club met to discuss the status and rights of women and to organize the campaign for the right to vote. By 1883, the club was renamed the Canadian Woman Suffrage Association, and in 1886, the conservative yet powerful National Council of Women in Canada threw its support behind women's suffrage.

The Canadian suffrage movement was especially strong in the Prairies, where it

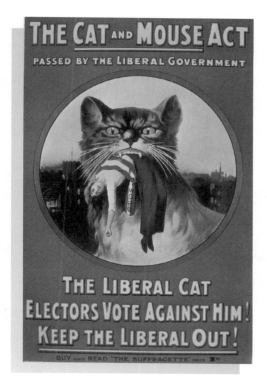

Figure 1.4

In response to the hunger strikes many suffragists staged while in prison, the British House of Commons passed a bill that allowed authorities to release women from prison when they went on hunger strikes and then re-arrest them as soon as they regained their strength. The bill was dubbed the "Cat and Mouse Act." In your view is this poster effective? Explain.

received greater support from men than it did in the east. Perhaps the harsh life of the prairie homesteader made men more inclined to view women as equal partners. Most western farmers, however, saw women's suffrage as a means of increasing the farm vote and strengthening their influence on provincial legislatures.

Nellie McClung led the movement in the west. Like other feminists of the day, McClung believed the only way to effect change throughout society was to enfranchise women. She fought for many social causes, including prohibition, compulsory education, prison and factory reform, and the rights of women and children.

> "We are not here to ask for a reform or a gift, or a favour, but a right—not mercy, but for justice."
> — Nellie McClung

Figure 1.5

Emily Davison said on one occasion, "The Cause [women's suffrage] has need of a tragedy." Davison was a member of the Women's Social and Political Union of England and later she joined the Workers' Educational Association. In 1913 she threw herself in front of King George V's horse at the Epsom Derby in England. She died of her injuries. A leading British suffragette, Christabel Pankhurst, daughter of Emmeline Pankhurst who founded the Women's Social and Political Union in 1903, said of Davison: "So greatly did she care for freedom that she died for it. So dearly did she love women that she offered her life as their ransom." What is your opinion of such actions in promoting the cause of the suffragettes?

The Enfranchisement of Women, Selected Countries*

1893	New Zealand	1937	Philippines
1902	Australia	1944	France, Jamaica
1907	Finland	1945	Croatia, Guyana, Italy
1915	Denmark, Iceland	1955	Cambodia, Ethiopia, Honduras
1917	Soviet Union; Netherlands	1963	Afghanistan, Congo, Fiji, Iran
1918	Canada (federal enfranchisement); Britain (women over 30)	1971	Switzerland
		1980	Iraq
1920	United States	1986	Liechtenstein
1928	Britain (women over 21)	1989	Namibia
1931	Chile, Portugal, Spain, Sri Lanka	1990	Samoa
1934	Brazil, Cuba, Portugal		

* Women's right to vote is still not universal.

Figure 1.6

In some nations, though women and men may have voting rights on paper, dictatorship, war, and corruption render this right meaningless. In what countries today are women still struggling for full political rights such as the right to vote and run for political office?

Profile Nellie McClung (1873-1951)

Figure 1.7
Nellie McClung

Nellie McClung was one of Canada's great social reformers. She played an instrumental role in securing women's right to vote in the early part of the twentieth century. As you read this profile and McClung's own comments, reflect upon whether or not her words still apply to our society today.

"The world has never been partial to the thinking woman…. Long years ago, when women asked for an education, the world cried out that it would never do. If women learned to read there seemed to be a possibility that some day some good man might come home and find his wife reading and the dinner not ready—and nothing could be imagined more horrible than that! That seems to be the haunting fear of mankind—that the advancement of women will sometime, someway, someplace, interfere with some man's comfort!"

— Nellie McClung, *In Times Like These*, 1915

"These tender-hearted gentlemen who tell you of their adoration for women cannot bear to think of women occupying public position. Their tender hearts shrink from the idea of women lawyers or women policemen, or even women

preachers; these positions would 'rub the bloom off the peach' to use their own eloquent words. They cannot bear, they say, to see women leaving the sacred precincts of home—and yet their offices are scrubbed by women who do their work while other people sleep…is there any pity for them? Not that we have heard of. It is the thought of women getting into comfortable and well-paid positions which wrings their manly hearts."

— Nellie McClung, *In Times Like These*, 1915

Born in Ontario and raised on a homestead in Manitoba, Nellie McClung began her career as a school teacher at the age of 16. After her marriage in 1896, she became an activist in the Woman's Christian Temperance Union.

It was in Winnipeg in 1911 that McClung first emerged at the forefront of the women's rights and social reform movement. McClung was an effective speaker winning audiences with her persuasive arguments wrapped in humour. She actively campaigned for the Liberal Party in Manitoba against the Conservative government, which had refused to enfranchise women. Moving to Alberta, McClung continued to campaign for female suffrage, prohibition, factory safety legislation, and other reforms. She gained increasing prominence through her speaking engagements across Canada, the United States, and Great Britain.

Nellie McClung was instrumental in gaining most women the right to vote in Canada in 1918 and in focusing attention on the need for women to gain economic independence. However, it was not a total victory. In Quebec, women did not have the provincial vote until 1940! Aboriginal women and many visible minorities did not yet have the right to vote or other rights of citizenship.

Responding

1. Explain why gaining the right to vote was considered to be the main key to advancing women's rights.
2. How might Nellie McClung view the lives of women today? Be specific.

Voices   The Rights of Women

The struggle for women's suffrage began to divide society at the end of the nineteenth and the beginning of the twentieth centuries. The idea that women were equal to men was simply not considered by most people at the time. For women to take part in acts of civil disobedience was totally unacceptable. In Britain, where the fight for equality was most fierce, outbursts of violence and hostility tore at the social and political fabric of the nation.

As you read the following quotations, consider whether any of these comments reflect current attitudes towards women.

GEORGE BERNARD SHAW, (1856-1950) PLAYWRIGHT

"Home is the girl's prison and the woman's workhouse." (*Man and Superman*, 1903)

VICTORIAN PROVERB

"Stay home, stay pure, stay busy."

FRANCES BEYNON, (1884-1951) CANADIAN SUFFRAGIST

"I consider it downright impertinence for a man on a farm to talk of supporting his wife. When she cooks his meals and sews and mends for him and his children from dawn to dark, what is she doing if not supporting herself?"

JUSTICE F.E. BARKER

"The paramount destiny and mission of women are to fulfil the noble and benign offices of wife and mother. This is the law of the Creator."

Responding

1. With which of the above statements do you most and least agree? Why?
2. Outline the views of a contemporary person whose views on the women's movement are considered important and note your reactions.

THE EMERGENCE OF THE GLOBAL VILLAGE

To people familiar with the Internet and the transfer of data almost instantaneously, it might be hard to comprehend that the world at the turn of the twentieth century was changing almost as rapidly. Significant changes were taking place in transportation and communications, increasing the speed at which these could take place. The movement of people and products around the globe was becoming relatively easy and it seemed that the world was shrinking. As it did so, the pace and stress of life was increasing.

Transportation

The refinement of steam power after 1870 revolutionized ocean transport. Huge ships could now sail the oceans without regard for wind or current. People could travel from one continent to another with relative ease and safety. Between 1901 and 1910, 11 million people boarded ships in Europe to find new lives in distant lands like Canada, the United States, and Australia. This massive flow of people resulted in a vibrant blending of languages, cultures, and ideas around the globe.

On land, steam power fuelled the great railways that chugged across the Western landscape during the last half of the nineteenth century. No longer was it an economic necessity to build towns and cities along waterways; trains could now provide the vital link between communities. In 1869, work was completed on the first transcontinental railway in the United

States when the Central Pacific and the Union Pacific lines met in Utah. The Canadian Pacific Railway completed its transcontinental line in 1885, linking Canada from sea to sea. In Russia, the Trans-Siberian railway was completed in 1905. These respective rail links enabled the settlement and economic development of the western provinces in Canada and of Siberia in Russia.

At the Paris Exposition in 1867, the world's first internal combustion engine was used for simple industrial purposes such as sawing wood and pumping water. But its usefulness in transportation was quickly recognized. The engine was gradually improved and eventually adapted to run on gasoline, thereby marking the emergence of oil as a valued resource. Soon the engine was ready for use in automobiles. By 1914, there were 1 million cars on American roads. American automobile manufacturers were producing more that 750 000 cars a year. The mass production of gasoline-powered vehicles was the single most important development in transportation and one that would dramatically shape the twentieth century.

Communications

New developments in communications were made possible by the long distance transmission of electric energy. The first invention to use electrical impulses to send messages was Samuel Morse's telegraph, patented in 1837. This invention was indispensable to the expansion of railways. Wireless telegraphs, developed in 1887, gained even greater importance because they could link ships at sea with stations on shore and with other ships.

In 1901, Guglielmo Marconi first established closer global links when he transmitted a signal on the wireless radio from St. John's, Newfoundland, across the Atlantic. Where a letter from Canada to England took several weeks, communication was now possible in a matter of seconds. The telephone, invented by Alexander Graham Bell in 1876, meant that verbal communication could be transmitted along a wire. Bell's first telephone call was made from his home near Brantford to Paris, Ontario, some 13 km away. By 1900 long distance telephone calls were common.

At the time few people were aware of these exciting new developments. As we look back on the twentieth century, however, we can see how important they were in changing our society and how they contributed to the **globalization** of the world.

Changes in transportation and communications were not simply a European or North American experience. In China, industrialization and railway building were advancing rapidly, though generally under the control of European imperial powers. The Chinese responded to this foreign control in a movement called the "100 Days", which involved radical reform and modernization programs. When the Empress Dowager of China put down the movement, the **Boxer Rebellion** was unleashed by the Chinese to remove foreign political and economic influence. However, the rebellion was crushed and China endured more domination and modernization of their industries by foreigners. In 1911, statesman Sun Yat-Sen led another (this time successful) rebellion aimed at modernizing and democratizing the vast nation. China would spend much of the twentieth century shaping itself into a more powerful, modernized industrial giant.

Japan too was rapidly modernizing, though under Japanese control. The island nation responded to the challenge of the Western Powers by turning to its military tradition for strength. Japan borrowed heavily from Western advances in transportation, communications, and industrial technique and rapidly became the first modern nation in Asia. Japan's aim was to extend control over areas held by its much larger but weaker neighbour, China, and included seizing territory in Korea and Manchuria. The Japanese soon exploited the resources of these territories by building large railway networks.

Much of Africa was being developed and modernized, though once again, under the control of Imperial powers. In particular, the rich resource wealth of the continent meant railway building boomed —an important step in developing mines and plantations in the interior. Ports faced expansion and development as raw materials were shipped to Europe and North America. The building of new facilities was usually a brutal experience for the indigenous populations. Slavery continued and workers often laboured under terrible conditions as they built modern infrastructure. The wonders of twentieth century technology and communications generally benefited imperial powers and only indirectly, if at all, the exploited populations.

Skill Path

Analysing a Reading

During the course of your studies, you may find yourself working with books, articles, and excerpts which were written by historians, politicians, professors, and others. At first glance, you may find yourself intimidated by these types of documents, which are often densely written and may appear complex. However, the message the writer is trying to convey can be decoded with a little extra effort and skill on the part of the reader.

The following steps will guide you in your analysis of two types of readings—position papers and research papers. In position papers, the author presents evidence to support a thesis or a specific point of view. In research papers, the author's goal is to communicate information by presenting facts and/or various views in an unbiased manner.

Step One: Orient Yourself to the Subject

Read the title, subtitle, and table of contents (if there is one) to help you orient yourself to the topic. Consider your prior knowledge about the topic. In your notebook, jot down any facts you already know, as well as any opinions you may hold.

Also read any biographical notes included about the author, as well as the date and place of publication. This information will allow you to set the piece in historical context and alert you to any possible biases the author may have, which could colour his or her interpretation of the facts.

Step Two: Identify the Specific Topic or Argument

Read the opening paragraph(s) of the piece. If it is a research paper answer the question: What is the main topic being presented by the author? Write it down in your own words in a clear, concise sentence in your notebook.

If the document is a position paper or an editorial, ask the following:

- What is the central issue being discussed by the author?
- What is the author's main argument? What is the main point of the thesis?
- Does the author argue for or against other interpretations?

You must identify and state in your own words the position the author plans to take on the issue. For example, in the Viewpoints feature on page 28, the question being discussed is whether or not the people of Britain should support the concept of imperialism. The author of the first piece, Cecil Rhodes, reveals his position clearly in the opening sentence, "I contend that we are the finest race in the world and that the more of the world we inhabit, the better it is for the human race." So, you might write a statement similar to the following in your notebook: "Cecil Rhodes supports imperialism because he believes the spread of British people around the globe will make the world a better place."

Step Three: Summarize Each Paragraph

As you continue to read the document, briefly summarize the information given or the argument being made in each paragraph and write it in your notebook. You could also list, in point form, any additional details on the topic or the pieces of supporting evidence.

Keep a dictionary beside you as you read and look up any words of which you are unsure. Note any references made by the author to historical people, places, and events that you do not recognize. You may decide to do a very light research of these on the Internet, in an encyclopaedia, or at the library so that you understand the point the author was making in using them. For example, some of the things you may want to research in the second reading on page 29 include the following: pax Britannia, financial juntos, and the South African War.

Step Four: Evaluate the Piece

Once you have finished reading and summarizing, ask:

- Do you agree or disagree with the main argument?
- Did the author present enough solid evidence to convince you of his or her point of view?
- Is the author's interpretation based on solid facts and sound reasoning?
- Are the arguments logical? Are there contradictions in the arguments?
- If it was a research paper, were you left with any unanswered questions on the content?
- Did the author present the facts in an unbiased manner? Were pertinent pieces of information overlooked?

Any deficiencies you note should be taken into account when you answer any questions related to the document or when you discuss it in a group.

Practise Your Skill

1. The following excerpt was written by Valerie Bryson in her book, *Feminist Debates: Issues of Theory and Political Practice*. State the author's topic in your own words and summarize the paragraphs. Be sure to define any difficult vocabulary or concepts as you read.

"As we enter a new millennium, many women throughout the world are campaigning, organizing and working together to improve their lives. Their aims, methods and interests are diverse in the extreme. Some are working in women's refuges, others are establishing professional networks; some are campaigning against pornography; some are setting up women-only organizations, others are being elected into political office; some are demanding total legal equality with men, others want improved maternity leave. The list goes on.

"These activities all share an underlying concern with improving the situation or furthering the interest of women. As such, they have all at times been described as 'feminist'. The status of feminism today is, however, highly ambivalent. In many countries today, young women see legal, economic, political, social, sexual and reproductive rights and freedoms as obvious entitlements (rights) rather than feminist demands."

Source: Excerpts from Valerie Bryson, *Feminist Debates: Issues of Theory and Political Practice*. (New York University Press: Washington Square), 1999. © 1999 NYU Press. All rights reserved.

2. Choose an article that interests you from a newspaper, magazine, or journal. Prepare notes analysing and evaluating the article employing the steps outlined above.

In Review

1. In your opinion, what was the most significant invention or development of the period covering the turn of the century? Why?

2. Who were the suffragists? Explain their goals.

3. What were some of the most important developments in the creation of the global village?

Politics, Economics, and Culture

As industrialization spread, there was a general feeling of optimism and confidence about the century that lay ahead. At the same time, however, there was growing criticism of national political goals and the dark underside that lay beneath the new prosperity. These conflicting views and values were reflected in the politics and culture of the era. Some were so unhappy with the world that they resorted to deadly violence to spark change.

THE POLITICAL ATMOSPHERE

The previous century had ushered in a period of significant political change. Massive revolutions in France and America presented new political ideas. **Liberalism**, a philosophy built on the ideas of equality, individual rights, and freedom of choice was gaining acceptance, particularly among the educated. For many, human progress and the possibility of improved living conditions for all was a matter of personal faith.

Democracy and civil liberties were the cornerstone of this new political process. The drift to more liberal forms of government was well underway at the turn of the century. However, much of the world in 1900 was still ruled by **authoritarian** regimes. In Russia, the czar wielded almost absolute power. In Germany, the kaiser ignored the weak *Reichstag* (parliament) at will. In Britain, while Queen Victoria had little political power, the royal family and the nobility maintained strong social influence. Most people in Asia and Africa were under the authoritarian rule of local monarchs, rulers, or European colonial powers. Ordinary citizens everywhere had few political or human rights. Obedience and respect for authority were paramount; individual liberty was rarely considered. Only in a few countries, such as Canada, Britain, France, Switzerland, and the United States, were political leaders elected by the people, and even here they were elected by a select group.

Few people thought about the concepts of equality and individual rights. Most believed it was natural that rulers should rule and the rest should obey. The nation was seen as a family and the ruler as its head. A small group of intellectuals challenged this view, but support for them and their ideas was minimal. Most people simply wanted a peaceful and orderly existence; they were not interested in the affairs of government. And those in power wanted to keep it that way. Most rulers opposed **universal suffrage.** They argued that uneducated farmers and labourers could not understand politics and so should not have the right to vote and influence governments. At the turn of the century, voting rights in many Western countries were restricted to men of property.

ECONOMICS

Change and progress emerged as important values in the first part of the twentieth century. These were expressed through the development and acceptance of new technology and the emergence of a new attitude affirming the importance of the individual. The American Revolution in 1776 and the French Revolution in 1789 had given birth to the ideals of democracy and individual freedom. The United States became known as "the land of the free." With its prosperous economy it also became known as "the land of opportunity." Millions of people were drawn to American shores in search of these ideals.

Capitalism, one of the most powerful

forces in the world, dominated economic life in the United States. This economic system featured private ownership, free enterprise, and the right to earn profits. Workers gave their labour for wages paid for by the assets of the owner. The owner then hoped to sell the goods or service for a profit in a free market. The risk was great but the rewards could be greater. The dizzying growth of industrialized nations often resulted in vast profits for the owners of business.

In the United States and Canada, the giants of industry and commerce—families like the Rockefellers, the Morgans, the Eatons, and the Masseys—wielded the power. In this new economic order, *what* you were was more important than *who* you were. One of the great attractions of America was the opportunity to go from "rags to riches." The opportunity was a reality for a few but became the dream of millions. This dream of wealth was a magnet for the poor and underprivileged of Europe.

Industrialization led to economic freedom. New inventions were transformed into successful business enterprises. Economic freedom led to political freedom as well. A class of wealthy and influential entrepreneurs emerged to challenge the traditional power of the aristocracy. By the early twentieth century, economic power had shifted from the land-owning aristocracy to the new business and manufacturing elite. In England, the factory owners controlled the money while the landowners held the titles. In time, money prevailed. The House of Commons, which represented ordinary citizens and the new business class, emerged as the real source of power, while the House of Lords declined to the position of a symbolic institution.

Capitalism has had many critics. The negative effects of industrialization, such

Figure 1.8
These children were photographed working in a vegetable cannery in 1912. At the turn of the century it was not uncommon for children to work in factories. What does this photo reveal about political and economic progress at the time?

as child labour, pollution, poverty, and slums, were being moderated in Britain, but they were just surfacing in nations still in the early stages of development. The notion of class became a powerful idea as wealth accumulated in the hands of a few capitalists while workers struggled in poverty. Rich capitalists also tended to wield political influence far beyond their numbers. Critics of the status quo became more vocal. Some became violent.

THE BIRTH OF MODERN CULTURE

The first decades of the twentieth century represent one of the most tumultuous periods in the history of art, culture, and philosophy. The sweeping advances made in science and technology, coupled with radical movements in art, literature, music, and theatre, created tension, optimism, and uncertainty.

Voices   The Clash of Ideas

As the new century dawned there was concern for the future of the human race. Three popular views caused great controversy. In time, these conflicting philosophies provided the basis for armed aggression.

Like many intellectuals of the nineteenth century, Herbert Spencer, an English philosopher, believed that science was the foundation of knowledge. He based an entire philosophy on Charles Darwin's theory of evolution, applying it not only to living things, but to government, economics, and society.

Brilliant but mentally unstable, Friedrich Nietzsche, a German philosopher, was one of the most controversial thinkers of his day. Unimpressed with nineteenth century society, particularly democracy and Christianity, Nietzsche proclaimed that a superior individual, a noble genius with a "master morality," must rise to lead and dominate the masses with their "slave morality." He believed that the Christian ideals of meekness and humility were weakening and crippling society. Instead, he envisioned a society in which the strong would lead, and the qualities of courage, strength, and beauty of character would be prized.

One of the most powerful voices in the struggle for international **socialism** was Rosa Luxembourg's. In 1892, Luxembourg helped found the Polish Socialist Party, and in 1898 she became leader of the German Social Democratic Party. Alone among socialists in Germany, she spoke out against German workers fighting in the First World War. War, she felt, benefited the owners of factories—the capitalist class—not the people who fought.

As you read these philosophical views, try to identify a specific situation in twentieth century history in which each was applied.

HERBERT SPENCER

"We have unmistakable proof that throughout all past time there has been a ceaseless devouring of the weak by the strong. This survival of the fittest which I have here sought to express in mechanical terms is that which Mr. Darwin has called 'Natural Selection' or the preservation of the favoured races in the struggle for life."

— Herbert Spencer, *Life as Struggle*, 1859

FRIEDRICH NIETZSCHE

"The herd seeks to perpetuate and protect one type of man while guarding itself on both flanks—against depraved and criminal members of society and against superior spirits who rise above its dead level of mediocrity. Morality in Europe today is herd morality."

— Friedrich Nietzsche, *The Geneology of Morals*, 1887

ROSA LUXEMBOURG

"The essence of a socialist society is that the great working mass ceases to be a ruled mass and instead lives and controls its own political and economic life."

"The fight against militarism cannot be separated from the socialist class war as a whole.... Wars are therefore inherent in capitalism."

— Rosa Luxembourg, *Family of Humankind*, 1910

Responding

1. Do Spencer's views apply to society today? Explain.
2. Do you personally accept the doctrine of "survival of the fittest" with respect to human beings? Explain.
3. What example of "herd mentality" can you find in history and the world today?
4. In a paragraph, explain what you think Luxembourg meant when she said, "Wars are therefore inherent in capitalism." Do you agree or disagree? Why?

Voices The Anarchists: Searching for a New Order

Not everyone accepted the status quo at the turn of the century. Many intellectuals and workers fought for a different world order. One group, the **anarchists**, believed governments were corrupt by nature and should be abolished; people would then live co-operatively with full political and social liberty. They fought against the growing powers of states that they felt were too powerful and against the interests of the people. They rejected the authority of the rich and powerful. Although mainstream anarchism is not violent, some fringe "anarchists" turned from philosophizing to outright revolt. The new century was witness to a wave of violence, including bombings, kidnappings, and political assassination. Interestingly, the power of most states is far greater today than at the opening of the twentieth century. The gap between the very rich and the very poor is also far wider. Review these quotations and indicate your personal reaction.

EMMA GOLDMAN (1869-1940), AMERICAN ANARCHIST AND FEMINIST

"Anarchism, then, really stands for the liberation of the human mind from the dominion of religion, the liberation of the human body from the dominion of property, liberation from the shackles and restraints of government."

"The strongest bulwark of authority is uniformity; the least divergence from it is the greatest crime."

MIKHAIL BAKUNIN (1814-1876), RUSSIAN FOUNDING FATHER OF ANARCHISM

"Anarchism is the spirit of youth against outworn traditions."

"The state is authority; it is force."

"Where all rule, there are no more ruled, and there is no state."

Responding

1. Why does anarchism often appeal to young people?
2. Is it possible to be free in a modern state?
3. Why do you think anarchism has remained a fringe belief, rejected by most people?

There are those who believe that art has a special capacity to reflect the essence of society. Others go further, believing that art has an important role to play in social protest. At the turn of the century, the arts were having a powerful impact on society. Audiences broke into riots at concerts and theatres where new and controversial compositions and plays were being performed. Igor Stravinsky's *The Rite of Spring* (1913) was equated with outright anarchy, so radical was its departure from accepted harmonic, melodic, and rhythmic concepts. (To later observers, the images created by *The Rite of Spring* foreshadowed the horrors that would engulf Europe during the First World War.)

Satirical farces by the French dramatist Alfred Jarry, which foreshadowed surrealism and the Theatre of the Absurd, caused equally extreme reactions. Ecstatic praise and vitriolic abuse greeted the works of contemporary artists such as Matisse and Picasso. From the insights of relativity and quantum theory to the striking canvases of the group of French impressionist painters known as *Les Fauves* (The Wild Beasts), the new era of the twentieth century promised change and conflict.

"The mission of art is simply to inspire the vision of a new social dawn."

– French artist and anarchist Grandjouan (1875-1968)

Profile   Pablo Picasso (1881-1973)

Figure 1.9

This painting, *Woman in an Armchair*, was done by Picasso in 1910. Judging by this painting, what would you say are the defining characteristics of cubism?

Many feel that Spanish artist Pablo Picasso revolutionized the visual arts in the twentieth century, demonstrating versatility, imagination, and technical brilliance. As you read about this artist, consider why you might agree or disagree with this assessment.

"I paint objects as I think them, not as I see them."

— Pablo Picasso, in John Golding's *Cubism*, 1959

"Everyone wants to understand art. Why not try to understand the song of a bird? Why does one love the night, flowers, everything around one, without trying to understand them? But in the case of a painting people have to understand…. People who try to explain pictures are usually barking up the wrong tree."

— Pablo Picasso, in Dore Ashton's *Picasso on Art*, 1972

The art of Pablo Picasso first began to earn acclaim during his Blue Period (1901 to 1904), in which the artist combined representational form with emotional subject matter. His subjects were poor social outcasts and the paintings were dominated by cold blue tones. In the Rose Period (1905 to 1906) the blue tones gave way to pinks and greys and the mood was less sombre. His subjects now were dancers and acrobats.

In 1906 and 1907, Picasso created *Les Demoiselles d'Avignon*, which critics have proclaimed as the single most important landmark in the evolution of modern painting. At the time many other artists considered the work incomprehensible. In fact, so revolutionary was *Les Demoiselles d'Avignon* that it was not publicly exhibited until 1937. But this work heralded the beginning of the most influential artistic movement in the twentieth century, **cubism**.

From 1910 to 1916, Picasso worked closely with Georges Bracque developing and exploring cubism. In creating abstract images from nature, Picasso and the cubists released their art from simply imitating reality. The movement established the idea that art exists as an object in its own right.

Later Picasso's work became increasingly filled with a mood of foreboding. He became preoccupied with scenes of despair and turmoil. This period culminated with his second pivotal work, *Guernica* (1937). It symbolically depicts the horrors of war following the bombing of the Basque town of Guernica by German planes during the Spanish Civil War.

Picasso continued to create art throughout his life, exploring a wealth of themes in a variety of styles. His vast array of work is his legacy as one of the most influential visual artists of the twentieth century.

Responding

1. Do you find Picasso's *Woman in an Armchair* to be incomprehensible? Explain.
2. How might cubism reflect the other changes taking place at the turn of the century?
3. In your view, does art have an important role to play in society? Explain.

Political Violence at the Turn of the Century

With revolutionary changes in art, commerce, and transportation, it should not be surprising that politics was also changing dramatically. The pace, scope, and energy of all this economic, cultural, technological, and political change was difficult to contain or direct. Some were totally opposed to the existing order. The world soon faced a disturbing reality: the spectre of political violence and terrorism. Bombings, riots, and political assassinations became a more prominent part of the existing order. Some who opposed governments and policies were prepared to use violence to effect change or spark revolution. This brutality was to continue throughout the century. In a few short years, President Carnot of France, King Umberto of Italy, and President McKinley of the United States were but a few in the wave of assassinations that marked the new century. Revolutions erupted in Turkey and China. Imperial wars swept nations and territories in Africa and Asia. If the new century was born in progress and change, it was born in violence as well. This tension was also reflected internationally.

IMPERIALISM AND INTERNATIONAL RELATIONS

As the nineteenth century drew to a close, Europe was at the pinnacle of its power. A newly energetic **imperialism** dominated national policies. Imperialism is the process by which powerful nations extend their influence and control over other nations for the benefit of the more powerful nation. The urge to create empires was rooted in the search for "Gold, Glory, and God." Gold referred to the rich raw materials that could be seized and exploited. Glory came to those victorious soldiers who triumphed over weaker opponents in far-off places. The reference to God indicated the urge to impose Christianity on other peoples, regardless of their own faiths and belief systems. Much of the rest of the world seemed ready for the taking. The nations of Asia and Africa were treated as prizes or jewels to be owned. By 1895, imperial powers controlled over 90 per cent of Africa.

The European nations were in a race with one another for colonies, mainly in Africa and Asia, and the increased trade, markets, and raw materials these would bring. Britain, France, Germany, Holland, Belgium, Portugal, and Italy all had colonies in Africa. Britain, France, Holland, and Russia were enlarging their spheres of influence in Asia. To defend and extend what they saw as their possessions, these European nations built larger armies and navies. As jealousies and tensions mounted, international relations became increasingly hostile. Among a range of "flashpoints," two stand out.

Flashpoint: The South African War (1899-1902)

In 1900, Britain was the world's leading power, controlling an enormous empire stretching from Canada to Africa to India to Australia. So vast was Britain's reach that it was said that "the sun never sets on the British Empire." By the turn of the century, however, Britain's domination was being challenged. The result was armed conflict. In the South African, or Boer War of 1899 to 1902, hostilities erupted between the Boers (settlers of Dutch descent) and the British. The political catalyst for the war was the Boers' refusal to grant equal rights to British immigrants. But essentially the conflict was about imperial domination and the riches this would bring—control

Figure 1.10

The Boer War between the Dutch and British settlers in South Africa was the first of many armed conflicts in the twentieth century. More than 7 360 Canadians served in South Africa during this war. Shown are troops of the Royal Canadian Regiment storming a hill in 1900. Revealingly, the interests of the indigenous peoples of the region were never considered. What is the political status of South Africa today?

Figure 1.11

The Boer War was one of the first in the twentieth century to divide people around the globe and even within Britain and its empire. Better communications and a growing mistrust of the power of the state led to real debate and division. Look at these two political cartoons and note the different messages presented. One of these is British, the other is French. Can you tell which is which? Which is most effective in your opinion? Why?

of the vast gold and diamond deposits of the Transvaal. It took half a million troops for the British to prevail. The British even had troops from Canada and Australia. In 1902, the Boer republics of the Transvaal and the Orange Free State were defeated and annexed as British Crown Colonies.

> **"I would annex the planets if I could."**
>
> — Cecil Rhodes,
> British imperialist and
> business magnate

MAP STUDY

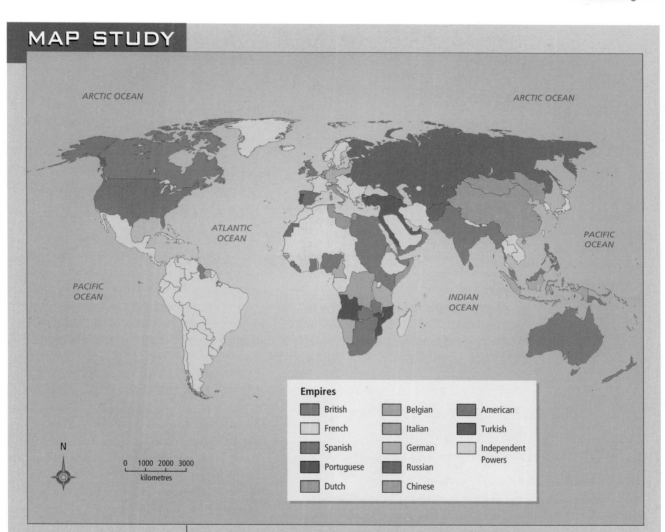

Empires

British	Belgian	American
French	Italian	Turkish
Spanish	German	Independent Powers
Portuguese	Russian	
Dutch	Chinese	

Figure 1.12
Empires of the World, 1900

At the turn of the twentieth century, European nations and the United States believed in building vast empires. Little concern was shown for the peoples actually inhabiting these conquered lands.

Interpreting

1. In 1900, which region of the world was least affected by European empires?
2. Which of these empires is still intact today?
3. Which areas of the world have since gained full independence and political freedom?
4. In your view what are the major arguments for and against the notion of "empire"?

Flashpoint: The Russo-Japanese War (1904-1905)

As a new century dawned, so too did a new force of imperialism. In Asia, Japan, like Britain, was a small island nation with limited resources. And Japan, like Britain, embarked on its own campaign to become a great military and industrial power.

Japan's leaders believed the only way to defend against Western imperialism was to learn the ways of the West. Japanese observers were sent to England to study financial and naval affairs, to France to learn about law and government, and to Germany to study military organization and strategy. They began to develop a strong industrial base. This in turn led to the need to secure raw materials. The Japanese saw how Europeans had pursued their imperialist goals in Asia. If the Europeans could do it, why not the Japanese?

Japan's aspirations in Asia were destined to clash with the imperialist ambitions of other nations. From 1894 to 1895, Japan successfully invaded China and advanced north into Manchuria. There they encountered the Russians as they moved south. This collision of interests finally led to the outbreak of war between Russia and Japan from 1904 to 1905. Most of the world expected that Russia would win a smashing victory. However, the Japanese forces crushed and humiliated Russia on land and on the seas.

For the first time, a non-European state had defeated a European power and had exposed as myth the notion of Western invincibility. The victory also gave Japan confidence in its power and influence in Asia. The year 1905 thus marked the beginning of a long and hard struggle to liberate Asia from European colonial control. The repercussions of the war between Japan and Russia would be felt for many decades.

AMERICAN IMPERIALISM

The turn of the century saw the emergence of the United States as an imperial power. As a former British colony, the US had traditionally opposed imperialism. The Monroe Doctrine of 1823 had essentially warned the European powers to stay away from the Western Hemisphere. But by the end of the nineteenth century, the US was ready to take a more aggressive stand. New territories like Alaska and Hawaii had been acquired, either by direct purchase, annexation, or war. American business interests dominated Latin America economically. The expansion of US imperialism marked the beginning of American economic and military domination throughout the world. It was to be a central theme of the new century.

> "To innovate by imitation."
>
> — Japanese motto

> "We are a conquering race—we must obey our blood and occupy new markets and if necessary new lands."
>
> — Albert Beveridge (1862-1927), US Senator

NETSURFER

WWW.RUSSOJAPANESEWAR.COM

The Russo-Japanese War Research Society maintains an excellent site for more detailed study of the Russo-Japanese War. The site provides detailed commentary, biographies, excellent images and detailed maps of the various campaigns and battles for this almost "forgotten war". Visit it for personal or class research.

Imperial Powers of the Turn of the Century

Country	Reasons for Imperialist Expansion	Spheres of Influence
Britain	• the world's leading power in 1900 • colonial acquisitions provided Britain with an abundance of raw materials as well as markets for its finished products • supported by a large and powerful navy	• empire included 25 per cent of earth's land surface • stretched from Canada to Australia and included India, New Zealand, and parts of Africa and Asia • led to the phrase "the sun never sets on the British Empire"
France	• rivalled Britain as an imperial power • did not need raw materials but desired prestige and power • competition with Britain over colonial territories led to many conflicts and disputes	• empire covered 12 per cent of earth's land surface • controlled one-third of African continent, a large part of South East Asia, and some islands in the South Pacific
Germany	• new German Empire emerging as dominant power on European mainland • desire to increase German power beyond Europe to rival Britain and France • need to access a warm water port for the navy	• challenged France for control of Morocco • seized interests in Asia • prepared to challenge Britain and France on land and at sea
Russia	• need to access a warm water port for the navy	• Trans-Siberia Railway established link to Pacific and access to northern China
Japan	• need to secure raw materials for rapidly developing industrial base • part of new Japanese motto "innovate by imitation" • desire to keep Asia for Asians rather than European imperialists	• occupied Korea and moved north into Manchuria • in Manchuria, collided with the Russians, leading to Russo-Japanese War of 1904
United States	• opposed European imperialism in Western Hemisphere • desire to expand commercial interests • "vital interest" in the Panama Canal	• US economic and military power dominated Latin America • Purchase of Alaska in 1867 • Annexation of Hawaii • Obtained control of former Spanish possessions such as Cuba and the Philippines following Spain's defeat in war of 1898 • Controlled 40 per cent of Mexico

Figure 1.13

Review this table and note what appear to be the common reasons for the national desire to create global empires.

MAP STUDY

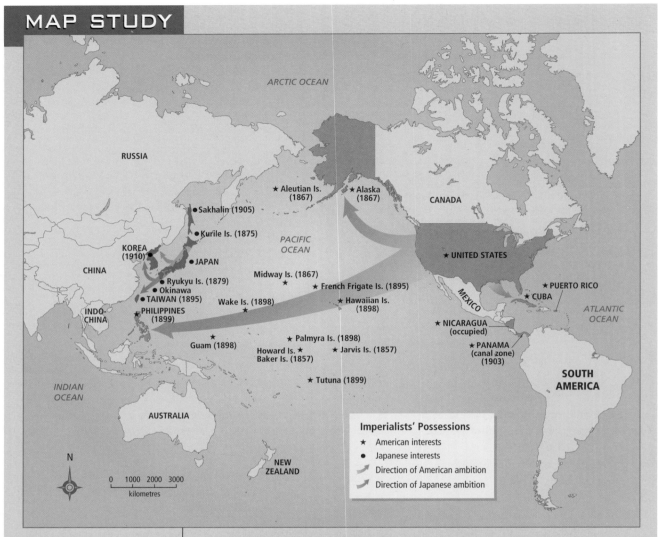

Figure 1.14

The New Imperialists, Japanese and American Possessions, 1910

As the twentieth century opened, the rising nations of Japan and America were on a collision course in the Pacific. The Japanese defeated China during the Sino-Japanese War (1894 to 1895) and the Americans gained the Philippines in the Pacific after their defeat of Spain in the Spanish-American War of 1898.

Interpreting

1. In your opinion, why was the Pacific Ocean so important to the U.S. and Japan?
2. What evidence is there that this imperial competition and national clash of interests would turn violent?

In Review

1. What were the conflicting views and values of Western society at the beginning of the twentieth century? How were these reflected in politics and culture?

2. In a chart, compare the strengths and weaknesses of the following nations at the turn of the century: Britain, France, Germany, Russia, Japan, and the United States.

3. "We do not desire to put anyone else in the shade, but we want our place in the sun." (Prince Bernhard von Bülow, German Chancellor, 1900-1909). What does this statement tell you about imperialism and the attitudes of the European powers at the turn of the century?

4. What evidence is there that the twentieth century would likely be a violent period? In your view will the twenty-first century be violent too? Explain.

Summary

At the dawn of the twentieth century, Europe was the centre of world politics, economics, and culture. The British Empire stood at the zenith of its power. The interests of nations and peoples in Asia, Africa, Latin America, and other parts of the world seemed to carry little weight. It was a moment of European triumph. Nations such as Japan and the United States were just beginning to flex their political, military, and industrial muscles.

Forces for change were everywhere. New technologies, ideas, and energy were exploding across a shrinking globe. The old order was being openly challenged. However, except for some minor skirmishes, peace had reigned for almost 100 years. The interlude of King Edward VII's reign after the long Victorian age camouflaged the tremendous forces waiting to erupt into the cataclysm of the First World War.

The nineteenth century had somehow been able to contain the forces of imperialism and democracy, liberty and authority, individualism and collectivism, science and religion. The twentieth century would witness the explosion of these forces into open conflict.

To many historians, the First World War marked the true beginning of the twentieth century. It foreshadowed an era of war, revolution, and tremendous social, political, and technological change. These realities would characterize much of the new century.

Viewpoints

ISSUE: Is it possible to justify imperialism?

Background to the Issue

Much of the nineteenth and early twentieth century witnessed a rampant imperialist spirit among the nations of Europe. The rising powers of the United States and Japan seemed to share this world view as well. For most people, the benefits of imperialism were obvious. Some even felt that they were in fact bringing "civilization" to indigenous peoples by conquering them and exploiting their resources. There was little criticism of the motives and successes of the imperialist powers at the turn of the century.

Cecil Rhodes was a fervent supporter of British imperialism. He was instrumental in establishing and extending the British presence in southern Africa. He was inspired to write a "Confession of Faith" that summed up his views of British imperialism.

John Atkinson Hobson is also British but he had a much different view of the imperial spirit so beloved by many of his fellow citizens and practised freely by the major powers. He led a powerful and biting attack on the values held so dearly by people like Rhodes. Read these two viewpoints carefully and answer the questions that follow. (You may want to refer to the Skill Path "Analysing a Reading" on page 14 for guidance before you begin.)

Cecil Rhodes

I contend that we are the finest race in the world and that the more of the world we inhabit, the better it is for the human race. Just fancy those parts that are at present [not inhabited by the English], what an alteration there would be if they were brought under Anglo-Saxon influence. Look again at the extra employment a new country added to our dominions gives. I contend that every acre added to our territory means in the future birth to some more of the English race who otherwise would not be brought into existence. Added to this, the absorption of the greatest portion on the world under our rule simply means the end of all wars...

The idea gleaming and dancing before one's eyes like a will-of-the-wisp at last frames itself into a plan. Why should we not form a secret society with but one objective; the furtherance of the British Empire and the bringing of the whole uncivilized world under British rule for the recovery of the United States, for the making the Anglo-Saxon race but one empire. What a dream, but yet it is probable, it is possible.

Put your mind into another train of thought. Fancy Australia discovered and colonized under the French flag....We learn from having lost, to cling to what we possess. We know the size of the world; we know the total extent. Africa is still lying ready for us—it is our duty to take it. It is our duty to seize every opportunity of acquiring more territory, and we should keep this one idea steadily before our eyes that more territory simply means more of the Anglos-Saxon race, more of the best, the most human, most honourable race the world possesses...

Source: Cecil Rhodes "Confession of Faith" (1877), quoted in Marvin Perry, ed. *Sources of the Western Tradition, Volume II: From The Scientific Revolution To The Present*, pp.178-179. Copyright © 1987 by Houghton Mifflin Company.

John Atkinson Hobson

...The decades of Imperialism have been prolific in wars; most of these wars have been directly motivated by aggression of white races upon "lower races," and have issued in the forcible seizure of territory. Every one of the steps of expansion in Africa, Asia, and the Pacific has been accompanied by bloodshed; each imperialist Power keeps an increasing army available for foreign service. Rectification of frontiers, punitive expeditions, and other euphemisms for war are in incessant progress. The pax Britannica, always an impudent falsehood, has become of recent years a grotesque monster of hypocrisy; along our Indian frontiers, in West Africa, in the Soudan, in Uganda, in Rhodesia fighting has been well-nigh incessant. Although the great imperialist Powers have kept their hands off one another, save where the rising empire of the United States has found its opportunity in the falling empire of Spain, the self-restraint has been costly and precarious. Peace as a national policy is antagonised not merely by war, but by militarism, and even graver injury. Apart from the enmity of France and Germany, the main cause of the vast armaments, which are draining the resources of most European countries, is their conflicting interests in territorial and commercial expansion. Where thirty years ago there existed one sensitive spot in our relations with France, or Germany, or Russia, there are a dozen now. Diplomatic strains are of almost monthly occurrence between Powers with African or Chinese interests, and the chiefly business nature of the national antagonisms renders them more dangerous, in as much as the policy of Governments passes more under the influence of distinctively financial juntos....

...It is not to the interest of the British people, either as producers of wealth or as tax-payers, to risk a war with Russia and France in order to join Japan in preventing Russia from seizing [K]orea; but it may serve the interests of a group of commercial politicians to promote this dangerous policy. The South African war [the Boer War, 1899 to 1902], openly fomented by gold speculators for their private purposes, will rank in history as a leading case of this usurpation of nationalism. ...

...The industrial and financial forces of Imperialism, operating through the party, the press, the church, the school, mould public opinion and public policy by the false idealisation of those primitive lusts of struggle, domination, and acquisitiveness which have survived throughout the eras of peaceful industrial order and whose stimulation is needed once again for the work of imperial aggression, expansion, and the forceful exploitation of lower races. For these business politicians, biology and sociology weave thin convenient theories of a race struggle for the subjugation of the inferior peoples, in order that we, the Anglo-Saxon, may take their lands and live upon their labours; while economics buttresses the argument by representing our work in conquering and ruling them as our share in the division of labour among nations, and history devises reasons why the lessons of past empires do not apply to ours; while social ethics paints the motive of "capital imperialism" as the desire to bear the "burden" of educating and elevating races of "children." Thus are the "cultured" or semi-cultured classes indoctrinated with the intellectual and moral grandeur—or Imperialism. For the masses there is a cruder appeal to hero-worship and sensational glory, adventure and the sporting spirit...

...The condition of the white rulers of these lower races is distinctively parasitic. They live upon these natives, their chief work being that of organising native labour for their support. The normal state of such a country is one in which the most fertile lands and the mineral resources are owned by white aliens and worked by natives under their direction, primarily for their gain. They do not identify themselves with the interests of the nation or its people, but remain an alien body of sojourners, a "parasite" upon the carcass of its "host," determined to extract wealth from the country and retire to consume it at home. All the hard manual or other severe routine work is done by natives...

Source: John Atkinson Hobson, "Imperialism" (1902) quoted in Marvin Perry, ed. *Sources of the Western Tradition, Volume II: From The Scientific Revolution To The Present*, pp.186-188. Copyright © 1987 by Houghton Mifflin Company.

Analysis and Evaluation

1. Some of the language used in these two turn-of-the-century readings is considered racist according to modern thinking.

    a) Make a list of all the terms and phrases you consider biased and explain why you feel they are.

    b) What does this type of language reveal about the attitudes and knowledge of these authors?

2. What is Rhodes' dream?

3. List and explain, in your own words, the reasons Rhodes gives to justify the colonization of other lands around the globe.

4. According to Hobson, what has been the result of the decades of imperialism in the world?

5. How is imperialism promoted according to Hobson?

6. Why are the white rulers seen as "parasitic"?

7. Decide which of the viewpoints you tend to support and explain why. If you support neither, state your position on the issue and explain it. Be sure to use specific information from this textbook, the readings, and other sources to support your position.

Chapter Analysis

MAKING CONNECTIONS

1. Compare how you might spend a typical day living in 1900 with a typical day today. Which would you prefer and why?

2. In your opinion, what impact does culture have on Canadian society today? Describe the art form you believe has the most powerful influence on Canadians.

3. Compare the ways the roles of men and women in the home and in the workplace have changed from the turn of the century to today.

DEVELOPING YOUR VOICE

4. Organize a class debate on one of the following topics:
    - Imperialism today is dead.
    - Women have made only modest gains in equality with men since 1900.
    - Technology has enslaved, not liberated, the world.
    - The new century will usher in a new era of peace.

5. Role-play one of the major figures presented in this chapter and be interviewed by members of the class.

6. Create a poster in support of an idea or personality in this chapter.

RESEARCHING THE ISSUES

7. Research the suffragist movement in Canada. Identify some of the key personalities and events in the movement.

   a) What factors contributed to the movement's success?

   b) Are there any lasting influences of the suffragists on women's groups today?

8. Research European imperialism at the turn of the century in either Asia or Africa and write a brief report of your findings.

9. Research Kabuki Theatre and describe how this traditional Japanese art form has changed from its creation to its present form today. How are the changes that took place in Kabuki theatre a reflection of changes in Japanese society?

10. With a partner or in a small group, brainstorm the ways in which life in North America has changed since 1900. After completing your list, select what you consider to be the three most important changes and explain your choices. Present your selection to the class.

CHAPTER TWO

The First World War: 1914-1918

Over the Top was painted by Canadian war artist A. Bastien. Look closely at this image. What does it suggest about the nature of the First World War? What feelings are inspired in the viewer?

"Europe, in her insanity, has started something unbelievable. In such times one realizes to what a sad species of animals one belongs."

— Albert Einstein, (1879-1955), physicist and winner of the 1921 Nobel Prize for Physics

"The lamps are going out all over Europe; we shall not see them lit again in our lifetime."

— Edward Grey (1862-1933) British Foreign Secretary on the eve of the First World War

Overview

In the early 1900s, the clouds of war were beginning to form over Europe. Stimulated by rising nationalism and the growth of imperialist rivalries, nations sought protection against each other. Most of the major European powers entered into strategic alliances and began rebuilding their armies and navies. By 1914, Europe had divided into two heavily armed camps, ready for conflict.

Yet while many of Europe's leaders saw war as inevitable, no one envisioned the four years of slaughter and horror that were to follow. The treaty that ended the war failed to bring either a just or a lasting peace. In reality, the First World War brought to an abrupt end a century of relative peace and stability and introduced a century of conflict, uncertainty, and change.

Focus Questions

1. What were the underlying causes of the First World War?
2. How did technology change the nature of warfare during the war?
3. What were the major outcomes of the First World War?
4. What were the terms of the Treaty of Versailles? Was the Treaty of Versailles a just peace settlement?

The Causes of the First World War

There were at least four underlying causes of the First World War: nationalism, economic rivalry, the arms race, and the alliance system. Within the context of conditions in 1914, these causes help to explain why war broke out. An atmosphere of fear and suspicion among nations had developed. People began to believe war was necessary.

NATIONALISM

Nationalism is an intense feeling of loyalty to a nation. It can be positive, but at the turn of the twentieth century nationalism often meant hostility to other nations and feelings of superiority. Nations often felt war was a test of strength and worth.

The French region of Alsace-Lorraine, alongside Germany's western border, had an abundance of coal and iron ore deposits and a thriving textile industry. When France was defeated in the Franco-Prussian War of 1871, it surrendered Alsace-Lorraine to Germany. The region became important to Germany's naval and military power. But German control spawned bitter resentment among the largely French-speaking population. The region became a focus for French nationalism and anti-German sentiment. On the larger stage, France attempted to restore national pride and prestige by focusing on acquiring an empire. Thus France joined the scramble among European nations for colonies in Africa.

German nationalism was stimulated by politics, economics, and a desire to become an imperial power. There was a new pride and optimism after the unification of the German states in 1871. Following unification, German technology, industry, and trade developed rapidly. Intense competition for markets contributed to its growing economic nationalism. But Germany's imperialist ambitions went unfulfilled. By the time Germany entered the race for colonies, Britain, France, and other European powers had already established distant empires that included the most desirable territories. Germany's inability to acquire important new colonies was a source of great frustration. From the German point of view, Britain and France were conspiring to prevent their nation from expanding.

In Austria-Hungary, **ethnic nationalism**—a form of nationalism based not on the nation-state but rather on a particular religious, linguistic, or cultural identity—was fragmenting the country. The old Austro-Hungarian Empire that had once dominated middle Europe was in a state of inner decay. The empire contained many nationalities, including Serbs, Croats, Slovaks, Czechs, and Poles. In 1914, local wars erupted throughout the Balkans as each group fought for its own interests. These conflicts did not go unnoticed by neighbouring powers. Russia saw an opportunity to increase its influence in the region and possibly gain control of the Dardanelles. Russian nationalists called on the Slavic people in the Balkans to unite under their leadership. Within this movement known as **Pan-Slavism**, Russia was supporting the Slavic state of Serbia in its efforts to break free of Austria-Hungary.

Britain was the major economic and imperial power in the world. The country's nationalism was intricately linked with pride in the British Empire. A sense of noble destiny permeated British society.

In middle-class England, belief in king and country was intertwined with the concept of duty. Young men enlisted in the army, believing that a **Pax Britannia**, or British peace, was the proper order of things in the world and that it was their duty to maintain this order. As the dominant world power, Britain was eager to maintain the status quo. Its leaders were suspicious of aggressive new nations—Germany and Japan—that sought to increase their territories and power in competition with the British Empire.

ECONOMIC RIVALRY

In an age of rampant imperialism, as discussed on pages 21-26 in Chapter One, Germany and Britain were keen economic competitors. Imperialism was not simply about military and political competition. Leaders understood that economic strength was the true foundation of military and political power and so **economic rivalry** was intense.

The unification of Germany and the annexation of Alsace-Lorraine enabled the German economy to flourish. By 1900, many German industries had surpassed those in Britain and in 1914 were producing twice as much steel. Because Germany had become industrialized later than Britain, its manufacturing industry enjoyed newer factories with equipment that incorporated the latest technology. British factories, on the other hand, were older and becoming less efficient. In addition, the excellent German education system, with its concentration on science and technology, produced the engineers and scientists needed to foster Germany's developing technology. While the British and French economies continued to grow after 1900, they could not keep pace with Germany. This economic competition increased tensions in Europe.

THE ARMS RACE

One of the consequences of nationalism, imperialism, and economic rivalry in the decades preceding the First World War was a determined **arms race** to win military superiority, usually through sheer size of military forces and/or the control of advanced weaponry. The new German monarch, Kaiser Wilhelm II, grandson of Britain's Queen Victoria, wanted to extend German influence as far as possible. He hoped to increase German military and economic power to equal that of Britain. As the world's dominant power, however, Britain was not about to relinquish its favourable balance of power. Both countries, afraid that the other would gain an advantage, embarked on large-scale armament programs.

The Naval Race

Britain depended on its navy for defence and to guarantee the security of its colonies. As a result, the British navy was twice the size of any other power. After 1898 Germany launched a naval build-up designed to rival Britain's fleet. Forty-one battleships and sixty cruisers were planned for the next two decades. From the British point of view, Germany's naval expansion posed a threat to Britain's naval supremacy and constituted a direct challenge to the nation's security.

The British responded by launching their own naval expansion. In 1906 a new class of battleship, the **dreadnought**, was introduced, intensifying the race for naval supremacy. By 1914 Britain numbered 29 battleships of this class, while Germany had 18.

What was the major significance of the naval race? Until 1900 Britain's closest ally on the European continent had been Germany. Since the days of Napoleon, France had traditionally been Britain's enemy and imperial rival. But

Figure 2.1

In 1906, the British introduced a new class of battleship, the heavily armoured dreadnought (literally "fear nothing") equipped with deadly, high calibre guns. However, Germany responded quickly launching its first dreadnought in 1908. Why do arms races often end in war?

German naval expansion alarmed British leaders and aroused suspicions about their ally's ultimate goals. Rather than face a potential enemy in isolation, Britain sought alliances with its former rivals, France and Russia.

Economic and Military Potential of the Powers, 1913 to 1914

	Great Britain	France	Russia	Germany	Austria-Hungary	United States
Population (millions)	45.6	39.7	175.1	66.9	52.1	97.3
Military and naval personnel*	532 000	910 000	1 352 000	891 000	444 000	164 000
Warships tonnage*	2 714 000	900 000	679 000	1 305 000	372 000	985 000
Total industrial potential (UK in 1900 = 100)	127.2	57.3	76.6	137.7	40.7	298.1
% shares of world manufacturing output	13.6	6.1	8.2	14.8	4.4	32.0

* Compiled from Kennedy, Paul. *The Rise and Fall of the Great Powers*. London: Unwin Hyman Ltd., 1988.

Figure 2.2

Which nations appear to be stronger in terms of military power? Which nation appears to have the greatest potential? Why?

[handwritten margin notes:]
• Germany
• Austria-Hungary
• Italy

Triple Entente
• France
• Russia
• Britain

A SYSTEM OF ALLIANCES

Otto von Bismarck, the powerful German chancellor who had brought about the unification of Germany, engineered an alliance system in the 1880s that provided Europe with the illusion of peace and stability. Behind the scenes, however, tensions were mounting.

Bismarck's diplomacy had been aimed at isolating France. In 1879, he signed the Dual Alliance with Austria-Hungary. Three years later, in 1882, he negotiated the **Triple Alliance** that drew Italy into the pact. Then in 1887, he persuaded Russia to sign a secret Reinsurance Treaty in which both countries agreed to remain neutral if the other was attacked by a third power. Bismarck avoided conflict with Britain by refusing to pursue a colonial empire and by resisting German naval expansion.

After the death of Wilhelm I in 1888 his successor, Wilhelm II, embarked on very different policies. The new kaiser decided to act as chancellor himself and dismissed Bismarck in 1890. In the same year he allowed the Reinsurance Treaty with Russia to lapse. Feeling cast aside by its former ally, Russia turned to France. In 1891, the two countries negotiated an understanding, and in 1894 they entered into a military alliance. This marked an important shift in European alignments as France and Russia had been enemies since the French invasion of Russia in 1812 during the Napoleonic Wars.

These changes in Europe were a source of concern for Britain. Its leaders were distrustful of the new alliance between Russia and France and uneasy about Germany's growing economic power and increasing imperialism. But of even greater importance was Germany's new policy of naval expansion. Growing insecurity caused Britain to end its century-old policy of "splendid isolation" from alliances with continental powers. By 1907, Britain had joined France and Russia to form the **Triple Entente**.

Europe was now divided into two rival camps—the Triple Alliance of Germany, Austria-Hungary, and Italy against the Triple Entente of France, Russia, and Britain. From this point until the outbreak of the First World War in 1914, the arms race intensified, armies multiplied in size, navies expanded their fleets—and international tensions grew. All that was lacking was a spark to set off a deadly chain of events.

MAP STUDY

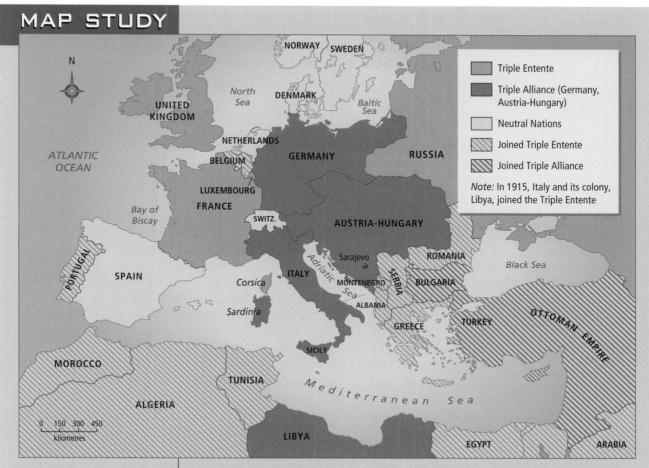

Figure 2.3
Europe in 1914

As the new century opened, most nations in Europe were drawn into two armed camps: The Triple Alliance and the Triple Entente. Although naval power was important, the First World War was still primarily a land war.

Interpreting
1. Identify the members of each alliance.
2. Review the map and note what you see as the relative strengths and weaknesses of each alliance in geographic terms.
3. Which nation changed sides during the war?

In Review

1. Summarize the four major underlying causes of the First World War.

2. In your opinion, which of these causes was most important? Why?

3. Which, if any, of these causes of the First World War still exist in our world today? Explain.

The Road to War

As 1914 approached, the international power struggle became more intense. One incident followed another and each contributed to the mounting tension and hostility between the European powers.

TENSION IN THE BALKANS

The humiliation of defeat in the Russo-Japanese War in 1905 refocused Russian interests on Europe, particularly the Balkan states. The Balkans included Bosnia, Herzegovina, Serbia, Bulgaria, and part of Greece. They became a focus for European nationalism and imperialism as Turkey, Russia, and Austria-Hungary had conflicting interests there.

In 1908, Austria-Hungary annexed the states of Bosnia and Herzegovina from the Turks. This act of aggression infuriated Serbia because these two states held large numbers of Serbs. In addition, the annexation effectively cut Serbia off from the Adriatic Sea. Serbia hoped that Russia would intervene on its behalf, but Russia, aware that Germany would back Austria-Hungary, decided not to become involved in the conflict.

In 1912 the situation changed dramatically. A Balkan league was formed under the leadership of Serbia. It declared war on Turkey and succeeded in defeating the Ottoman Turks, thereby reducing Turkish influence in the region. The rise of Serbian power concerned Austria-Hungary. These fears were heightened in 1913 when another Balkan war erupted. After the battles, Serbia had almost doubled its size. Afraid of Austro-Hungarian aggression, Serbia turned to its ally Russia for protection. The situation was becoming increasingly volatile. As Russia and Austria-Hungary took opposite stands in the Balkan conflicts, their allies watched with growing apprehension.

THE MAJOR POWERS IN 1914

Britain

In the decades preceding the First World War, Britain was overtaken industrially by both the United States and Germany. Where the British empire had been the foremost colonial power of the nineteenth century, by the twentieth century it was facing intense competition in its commercial and colonial interests. Still, Britain remained the leading power in the world, even if its domination was in decline. The greatest challenge for Britain at this time was to maintain the status quo, or at least to maintain a strong level of control over the unfolding of events. British foreign policy was often ambiguous. Britain's leaders were reluctant to form a military alliance with Germany in 1889 and again from 1898 to 1901, or against it from 1906 to 1914.

Germany

In the years leading up to the First World War, Germany was an industrial power led by an authoritarian monarch. Unlike the British monarch, the German Kaiser exercised enormous power. His personality, views, and beliefs shaped German foreign policy. The Kaiser challenged the existing order. He directed Germany to flex its muscle, and thereby dramatically alter the European balance of power.

Russia

By 1914, Russia had a rapidly expanding population several times larger than that of either Britain or Germany. The size of its standing army was enormous, with 1.3 million troops and up to 5 million reserves. In addition, Russia had become the fourth largest industrial power. Other European nations were concerned about Russia's emerging might. But this picture of Russian power was misleading. Most of Russia's industrial development was in textiles and food processing, not equipment or armaments. Its status as an industrial power ranked well behind the United States, Britain, and Germany. Russia was still a peasant society, with 80 per cent of its population deriving their livelihood from agriculture.

France

By the eve of the First World War German industry was eclipsing France's industrial development. By 1914, France ranked fifth as an industrial nation among the European powers. Its population growth was almost stagnant compared to that of Germany. Between 1890 and 1914 Germany's population surged by 18 million while the population of France rose by only 1 million. These factors served to increase Germany's power while France's relative position declined. This was a particularly bitter pill for the French given the history of conflict between the two countries.

MAP STUDY

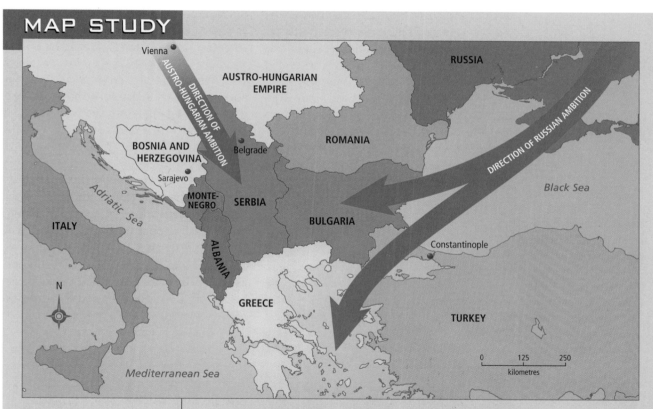

Figure 2.4
The Balkans in 1914

Unrest in the Balkans became a serious issue for the major European powers. Great powers such as Austria-Hungary and Russia had competing interests in the increasingly volatile region.

Interpreting

1. What alliances did Austria-Hungary and Russia represent?
2. Why might the region be considered so important to European politics?
3. Which Balkan nation was most significant? Why?

THE BALKAN CRISIS

The Balkans are deeply divided by geography, history, religion, language, and culture. Historically, Germans, Hungarians, Slavs, and Muslims have made war upon each other. Among the Slavs, several nationalities—Croats, Serbs, Bulgarians, and others—have fought for dominance.

The Ottoman Turks had ruled the Balkans from the late fifteenth century, but Turkish rule had been ineffective and revolts were frequent. In the nineteenth century, the Turkish Empire was weakening and other European powers—Austria-Hungary, Germany, and Russia—began taking an active interest in the Balkans.

At the beginning of the twentieth century, Serbia was expanding and wanted to unite all Serbs under one great nation, including those in Austrian-controlled Bosnia-Herzegovina. Russia, the great Slavic nation to whom Slavs looked for protection, encouraged Serbia in its goals.

Figure 2.5

The assassination of the Austrian heir to the throne and his pregnant wife set in motion forces that would soon engulf much of the world in war. Why is this bloody event not considered the actual cause of the war, but rather a "spark"?

The juggling for power in the Balkans intensified deep divisions and hatreds. Observers often noted that the region was like a powder keg ready to explode. The explosion, when it came, not only rocked the Balkans but also Europe and the world.

The incident that ignited the First World War occurred on 28 June 1914. Archduke Franz Ferdinand, heir to the Austro-Hungarian Empire, was assassinated in Sarajevo, the capital of Bosnia. A young Bosnian Serb, Gavrilo Princip, was the assassin. Princip belonged to a secret Serbian nationalist organization known as the **Black Hand**, which was dedicated to obtaining Bosnian independence from the Austro-Hungarian Empire. Friedrich von Wiesner, an Austrian investigator on Serbia's involvement in the assassination of the Archduke, concluded, "There is nothing to show the complicity of the Serbian government in the direction of the assassination or its preparations in supplying of weapons. Nor is there anything to lead one even to conjecture such a thing. On the contrary, there is evidence that would appear to show that complicity is out of the question." However, Austria-Hungary used the assassination as an excuse to re-establish control in the region by insisting the Serbian government was to blame for the attack.

Germany had promised to support Austria-Hungary. With this pledge and the belief that Russia would not intervene, on July 23 Austria-Hungary presented Serbia with a forty-eight-hour **ultimatum**. This ultimatum was a poorly designed attempt to force war on Serbia. Among the list of Austrian demands included a call to Serbia to put an end to all nationalist hatred against Austria-Hungary and punish all who were active in the assassination plot. Serbia was prepared to accept most of the ultimatum except the term calling for Serbia to allow

The Steps to War, 28 June to 4 August 1914

June 28: Archduke Ferdinand of Austria assassinated in Bosnian city of Sarajevo by Bosnian Serb nationalist.

July 23: Austrian government gives Serbia 48-hour-ultimatum. Serbia does not agree to all terms and begins to mobilize.

July 28: Austria-Hungary declares war on Serbia; Serbia turns to Russia for help.

July 29: Czar Nicholas agrees to help Serbia and mobilizes army.

July 30: Germany sends Russia ultimatum to halt mobilization; Russia refuses.

August 1: Germany declares war on Russia; France mobilizes army.

August 2: Germany invades "neutral" Belgium as part of Schlieffen Plan for attacking France.

August 3: Germany declares war on France; Britain gives Germany an ultimatum to halt invasion of Belgium.

August 4: No reply from Germany; Britain declares war on Germany; Canada automatically at war as part of British Empire; US declares neutrality.

Figure 2.6

In your view was the outbreak of the First World War inevitable? At what point might the rush to war have been halted? What lessons can be learned from this uncontrolled series of events?

Austrian officials into Serbia itself to crush the Black Hand.

This set off a chain of events that directly involved the European powers. Russia intervened on behalf of Serbia, demanding that Austria-Hungary guarantee Serbia's independence. In keeping with their mutual defence agreement, France then declared its support for Russia. But even to this point, the situation appeared to be under control. Serbia had agreed to all but two of Austria-Hungary's demands. But as a precaution, Serbia mobilized its troops to protect its borders from a possible invasion. Now the mechanisms for war were in motion and events began to spiral out of control. On July 28 Austria-Hungary mobilized its armies and declared war on Serbia. Russia responded by declaring war on Austria-Hungary. Within a month, most of Europe was at war.

THE MOOD OF 1914: A SHORT BUT NECESSARY WAR

Leaders of both alliances gradually came to believe that war was necessary, but that it would be over quickly. The German Kaiser assured the *Reichstag* (parliament) that victory would be won "before the leaves fall"; in Britain, Winston Churchill spoke of a short "cleansing thunderstorm."

In his book *The Origin of the First World War*, historian James Joll claims that "long-term patterns of education, the rhetoric of the inevitability of war, invasion scares, and downright fear all contributed to the mood of 1914." It was a mood that was in part a revolt against the liberal values of peace and rational problem-solving. According to Joll, this "mood of 1914" made the outbreak of war acceptable to the general populations on both sides. Thus, he notes, when war finally broke out there was a sense of relief, even celebration. The British ambassador to Austria described the mood in Vienna when it was announced that relations with Serbia had been broken: "[There was a] burst of frenzy of delight, vast crowds parading the streets and singing patriotic songs till the small hours of the morning."

Meanwhile, across the ocean in Canada, a similar view emerged.

Skill Path   Interpreting Graphs and Timelines

Some people may think of history as a mainly textual subject, heavy on written descriptions and explanations. However, it is often possible to present historical overviews and bits of data visually as well, in the form of graphs and timelines. For example, an author could write ten pages explaining the various major events in the First World War. Such a presentation would give the reader lots of detailed information. But, a well-drawn timeline included with the explanation provides a visual snapshot of the sequence of events that may be quickly interpreted by the audience. Likewise, topics such as increased militarism, the rise of fascism, and the casualties of both world wars may all be explained in great detail by an author, but they may also provide data for pie graphs, line graphs, and bar graphs to succinctly summarize the information.

Graphics such as timelines and graphs are especially useful in oral reports, Powerpoint presentations, and displays because of the visual punch and clarity they provide.

Timelines

Step One: Determine the Organizational Structure

A timeline's purpose is to provide a linear view of chronological events. This does not mean, however, that all timelines appear as one straight line—these graphics can be organized into many different formats. Each of the Units in this text is preceded with an extensive timeline, and we will use the first one (found on pages 2-3) as our example.

First, read the title and any headings. This will tell you how the author has organized the information. In the case of the Unit One timeline, events are broken down into three categories: Politics, Technology, and Culture. The time periods—running across the top of the timeline, in this case—are broken into four columns. Note that the first three are nine-year intervals, while the last column represents a period of 15 years. It is important to notice details such as this, and then ask yourself about their significance. In this case, the first column covers the pre-war years at the turn of the century, the second covers the First World War, the third covers the beginning of the inter-war period, and the fourth covers the Great Depression and the Second World War. Knowing this will allow you to place each of the events in their proper context.

Step Two: Analyse the Information

Timelines can simply be read as a chronological series of events. However, depending on their organization, you may also be able to identify trends, hypothesize about the cause-and-effect relationships among events, and make comparisons between time periods. The organization of the Unit One timeline allows the reader to compare different categories of events across the time intervals. For example, the reader can see what types of technological advances were being made at the turn of the century in comparison to those made directly prior to and during the two World Wars. The structure will also allow the reader to make links between cultural movements and the state of the world economy. Analysis of events in all three categories may allow you to develop a sense of the reasons for the escalating tensions that led to the two World Wars.

Graphs

Step One: Identify the Type of Graph

A graph is a type of diagram used to show relationships between two or more quantifiable variables, but as mentioned in the introduction to this skill, there are many different types of graphs, each of which may be better suited to different kinds of data. Learning to identify the type of graph you are dealing with will help in understanding how the information has been organized. The following are descriptions of the most commonly used graphs.

Bar Graph: These are useful when you would like to compare information about different topics or places at one point in time. (See example in Figure 3.9 on page 81.)

Line Graph: Useful for comparing change over a period of time, for one topic or one place. (See example in Figure 3.8 on page 81.)

Pie (or circle) Graph: Useful for showing the percentage that parts of a topic make up when compared to the whole. (See example in Figure 11.7 on page 355.)

Pictograph: These graphs use symbols to represent statistics or quantities.

Consider Figure 2.2, Economic and Military Potential of the Powers, 1913 to 1914 (on page 36). If required to convert this information to graphic format, which type of graph would you use? You could compare population with military and naval personnel for each nation using a bar or line graph. You could use pictographs to describe warship tonnage per nation. A circle/pie graph is useful when conveying data in percentages of a whole—you could use this type of graph to attribute "Percentage shares of world manufacturing output."

Step Two: Understand What the Graph is Showing

Start your examination of a graph by reading the title and the legend. These will tell you exactly what relationship the graph is showing. For example, look at Figure 3.9 (on page 81). The title is "Nazis at the Polls, 1928 to 1933". The legend indicates that the election results for three parties—Nazis, Communists, and Social Democrats—will be shown for each election. The results for the rest of the parties who ran are lumped together under title "Others". The bottom of the graph shows the five elections that were chosen and the total number of representatives who ran in each.

Step Three: Analyse the Data

Study the graph to determine its significance. Is it meant simply to relay information in an unbiased way, or has the author chosen to present the data in such a way as to make a strong point? In Figure 3.9, the mustard-coloured bars show that the Nazi Party experienced a dramatic, though inconsistent, gain in the approval of the German people from 1928 to 1933. However, if you calculate the number of elected Nazis as a percentage of the total number of seats, one might interpret the data to indicate that even at the height of their popularity, the Nazis never achieved a clear majority (more than 50 per cent of the seats).

When you are analysing a graph, also try to keep in mind what the graph does not show. In the case of Figure 3.9, the number of elected representatives from each party is given, but the graph does not give the actual percentage of votes received by each party.

Practise Your Skill

1. Choose one of the five most powerful nations that participated in the First World War. Using a computer or a hand-drawing, develop a chronological timeline of events in which that nation was involved, from 1914 through 1919. (You may have to do some research on the Internet or at the library to fill in the events.)

2. Make a graph to show the number of soldiers killed from each of the major countries involved in WWI.

"With the British declaration of war on Germany on August 4, Canada was then automatically at war as well, and most Canadians heartily approved of this arrangement. It was thought that the war would be over and won in short order, would in fact be something of a glorious adventure.... There was much display of patriotic fervour as young men... flocked to join up. Everywhere in the Dominion people greeted the war with enthusiasm; crowds sang patriotic songs in the streets."

Source: Roger Graham, Canadian historian, quoted in Andrew H. Malcolm, *The Canadians* (Markham, ON: Fitzhenry and Whiteside, 1979).

Why were so many prepared to accept war? Each side came to see a need for war in order to settle their differences, since it appeared that diplomacy alone could not resolve competing and conflicting national goals. Russia wanted to extend its influence in the Balkans, while Austria-Hungary saw Russian goals as a direct threat to its own plans to bring Serbia under its control. Germany wanted to break the powerful Triple Entente that was blocking its emergence as a world power. France wanted to maintain and increase its power but felt threatened by Germany. Meanwhile, Britain, as the strongest power, wanted to maintain the status quo, with no nation dominating European affairs.

The hard choice for these competing nations was between going to war or accepting compromises that could be viewed as diplomatic defeat and humiliation. Given this choice, a short war seemed acceptable. It was, in hindsight, a tragic miscalculation.

"This country has gone wild with joy at the prospect of war with Serbia."

– British Ambassador in Vienna, 1914

Voices Pre-War Germany and Britain: A Clash of Values

The First World War was not only a clash of armies, it was a conflict of different beliefs and values. Britain and its empire represented the most powerful and successful nation in the world; they looked to the past, to traditional values, and to maintaining the status quo. Germany represented a nation on the rise. Germans looked to the future—to a new world in which German power could expand and be recognized. As you read these statements, compare the beliefs and values of the two societies. In what ways might the differences between the two contribute to rivalry and conflict?

GERMAN ATTITUDES TO THE WAR BEFORE 1914

"War was regarded, especially in Germany, as the supreme test of spirit and as such, a test of vitality, culture, and life. 'War,' wrote historian Friedrich von Bernhardi in 1911, was a 'life-giving principle.' It was an expression of a superior culture. 'War,' wrote a contemporary of Bernhardi's, was in fact 'the price one must pay for culture.' In other words, whether considered as the foundation of culture or as a stepping-stone to a higher plateau of creativity and spirit, war was an essential part of a nation's self-esteem and image."

Source: Modris Eksteins, historian, *The Rites of Spring: The Great War and the Birth of the Modern Age* (Toronto: Key Porter © 1989).

BRITISH ATTITUDES TO THE WAR BEFORE 1914

"If a situation were forced upon us in which peace could only be preserved by the surrender of the great and beneficent position Britain has won by centuries of heroism and achievement, by allowing Britain to be treated, where her interests were vitally affected, as if she were of no account in the Cabinet of Nations, then I say emphatically that peace at that price would be a humiliation intolerable for a great country like ours to endure."

— David Lloyd George,
British politician and prime minister
(1916-1922) in 1911

"For the Germans this was a war to change the world; for the British this was a war to preserve a world. The Germans were propelled by a vision, the British by a legacy."

— Modris Eksteins,
The Rites of Spring

Responding

1. Do you accept either of these views of war? Explain.
2. In your opinion, is war ever justifiable? Explain.

The Schlieffen Plan

German leaders based their military strategy on the quick victory promised by the **Schlieffen Plan**. General Schlieffen believed that a long war was impossible in the modern age where "the existence of nations is based on the uninterrupted progress of trade and commerce." Like many European leaders, he assumed that the enemy would quit rather than risk a long, destructive war.

The Schlieffen Plan called for the concentration of almost the entire German army on one decisive assault. The goal was the knockout blow. Timing was critical since Germany had to defeat the French army before the Russians attacked from the east. To succeed, France had to be defeated in just six weeks.

MAP STUDY

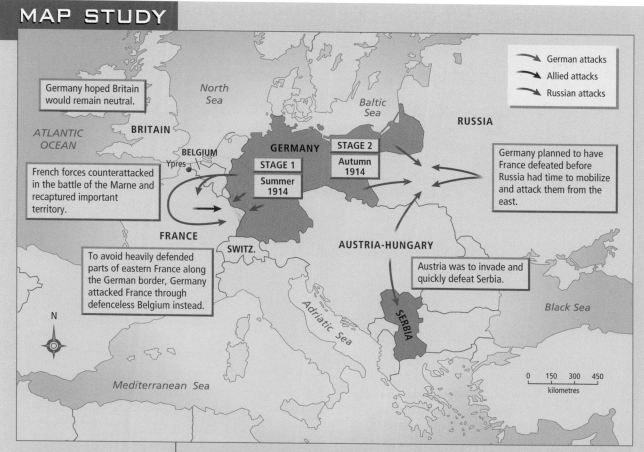

Germany hoped Britain would remain neutral.

French forces counterattacked in the battle of the Marne and recaptured important territory.

To avoid heavily defended parts of eastern France along the German border, Germany attacked France through defenceless Belgium instead.

Germany planned to have France defeated before Russia had time to mobilize and attack them from the east.

Austria was to invade and quickly defeat Serbia.

Legend:
- German attacks
- Allied attacks
- Russian attacks

Map labels: North Sea, Baltic Sea, RUSSIA, ATLANTIC OCEAN, BRITAIN, BELGIUM, Ypres, GERMANY, STAGE 1 Summer 1914, STAGE 2 Autumn 1914, FRANCE, SWITZ., AUSTRIA-HUNGARY, SERBIA, Adriatic Sea, Black Sea, Mediterranean Sea, N, 0 150 300 450 kilometres

Figure 2.7
The Schlieffen Plan and Ensuing Battles

- The Schlieffen Plan called for the German army to avoid the heavily armed and defended French-German border to the east. The Germans instead attacked France through defenceless Belgium. The objective was to smash across the French border in a rapid hammerhead blow and surround Paris, the capital. The French would be taken by surprise from behind.
- However, the Belgians fought valiantly. The British sent troops into France and German troops were sent to the border with Russia. The German hammerhead slowed.
- French forces made a desperate counterattack in the Battle of the Marne and blunted the German advance.
- Germany moved to capture the towns of Calais and Boulogne but they battled British forces for six weeks at Ypres.
- The German dream of a swift victory was shattered. The war became a deadly struggle of increasingly bloody battles over hundreds of metres of battle-scarred fields. Europe was split by a wall of barbed wire and trenches that snaked across half a continent.

Interpreting

1. In your view what were the key strengths and weaknesses of the Schlieffen Plan?
2. What was the chief result of the German failure to launch a knockout blow?

Plan XVII

The French knew of the Schlieffen Plan prior to 1914, but they doubted Germany's ability to execute it because of the huge army that would be required. They had developed their own "short-war" plan, called Plan XVII, which called for a rapid and devastating attack on Alsace-Lorraine. After recapturing these two provinces, they would move at high speed to Berlin. The German army, caught between the French army in the west and the huge Russian army in the east, would be crushed. Part of France's plan included military assistance from Britain. However, both of these "short war" victory plans resulted in a long and increasingly bloody war that would destroy the youth of a European generation.

In Review

1. Using the following headings, explain why the First World War broke out in 1914.
    - Intense nationalism
    - Imperialism and economic rivalry
    - Arms race
    - Growing tension in the Balkans
    - The alliance system
    - Assassination of Archduke Ferdinand

2. Compare and contrast British and German attitudes to the war. Outline your personal reaction to these attitudes.

3. What were the objectives of the Schlieffen Plan and Plan XVII? How might the existence of these plans have affected the likelihood of war breaking out in Europe?

4. Why was Canada involved in the war?

The Course of War

When war broke out, each side hoped that the other would quit after the first major battle. Most people were convinced that everything would be over by Christmas. Young men rushed to enlist, afraid that the war would end before they reached the front. No one could have predicted that the battles would rage for four years, and that when it ended a whole generation of young men would be lost forever.

THE WESTERN FRONT

On the night of 4 August 1914, the Germans launched the Schlieffen Plan, crossing the neutral frontier of Belgium without warning. Belgium fell swiftly. The German army pushed south into France, sending French and British troops into retreat. In early September, an Allied line of defence was established along the River Marne north of Paris. The Germans advanced to within sight of the French capital. But in the critical Battle of the Marne that ensued, the Allied forces held and launched a counterattack. This surprised the German army and stalled their offensive. At Ypres in Belgium, British and Indian troops held back the Germans as they tried to seize control of ports on the English Channel.

By October 1914, both sides had dug a line of trenches from the North Sea to the Swiss frontier. The Allies and the Central Powers now faced each other across mud and barbed wire and the tragic stalemate of trench warfare began. During the four brutal years that followed, the line of trenches remained virtually stationary, in spite of the massive battles fought. Both sides suffered tremendous losses in this cruel war of attrition. As millions died, millions more were conscripted or enlisted to take their place. When the war on the western front ended on 11 November 1918, the opposing lines were at almost the same position as they had been when they were first established in 1914.

The Royal Newfoundland Regiment and the Battle of the Somme

The British-inspired Somme offensive in July 1916 was designed as a smashing breakthrough of German lines. Instead, it turned into a horrific killing field where hundreds of thousands of young soldiers were sacrificed for a few metres of mud. The fate of one regiment, the Royal Newfoundland, after the first day's assault on enemy lines near Beaumont-Hamel on the Somme was a savage reminder of how hopeless the war had become for rank and file soldiers. As you read about the devastating Battle of the Somme, consider the question of moral responsibility of sending young troops to certain death in a hopeless mission.

In his H.Q. dug-out, Lieut-Col. Hadow, the English officer commanding the battalion, received his orders by phone from the brigade commander. These were simple. The Newfoundlanders were to leave their present position as soon as possible and advance to the German front line.

The Newfoundlanders had to go 300 yards before reaching the British front line and then a similar distance across

'No Man's Land.' As soon as they appeared in the open, the German machine-gunners spotted them and opened fire. They concentrated their fire on the 752 Newfoundlanders advancing over the open ground less than half a mile away. Before the men could even get into "No Man's Land," they had to pass through several belts of British barbed wire. As they bunched together to get through the narrow gaps in this wire, the German machine-gunners found their best killing ground. Dead and wounded men soon blocked every gap, but those still not hit struggled on, having to walk over their comrades' bodies.

Those who survived to reach 'No Man's Land' continued toward the German trenches, but they had no chance. Only a handful of Newfoundlanders reached the German wire. There they were shot.

The attack had lasted forty minutes. Of those who had attacked, 91 per cent had become casualties—26 officers and 658 men. What had this battalion, which had sailed with such high hopes from St. John's a year and a half earlier, achieved? It is probable that not a single German soldier was killed or wounded by their attack and no Allied unit had been helped to improve its position.

Source: Excerpts reprinted from *The First Day on the Somme* by Martin Middlebrook. Copyright © 1972 by Martin Middlebrook. Reprinted by permission of Curtis Brown Ltd.

NETSURFER

HTTP://COLLECTIONS.IC.GC.CA/GREAT_WAR/

There are innumerable sites devoted to the First World War on the Internet. This particular site is excellent in that it provides a combination of videos, audio, and text articles revolving around Newfoundland's role in the Great War. The site is maintained by the Canadian government. Click on "Articles" and read about how the Newfoundland regiments fought in Europe.

MAP STUDY

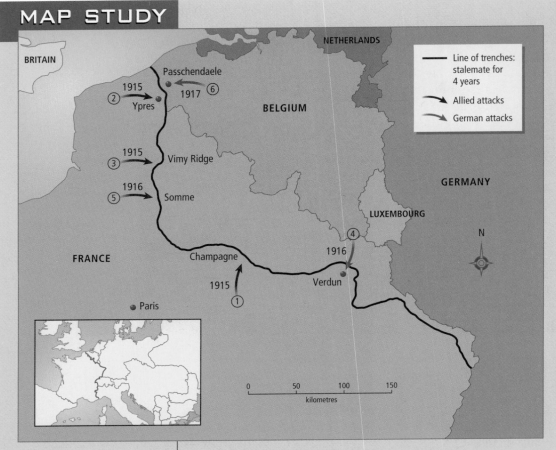

Figure 2.8
The Western Front, 1915 to 1918

1. French troops advance at Champagne, 1915.
2. Second Battle of Ypres, 1915; Germany advances.
3. French troops advance at Vimy Ridge, 1915.
4. Battle of Verdun, 1916; in 6-month battle Germans fail to take Verdun, but French losses total 360 000 dead.
5. Battle of the Somme, 1916; British and French troops advance; death toll exceeds 1 million.
6. Third Battle of Ypres (Passchendaele), 1917; British troops defeat German attack.

The casualty rates for the First World War break down as follows: British Empire, 900 000; France, 1.5 million; Germany, 1.75 million; Austria-Hungary, 1.25 million; Italy, 600 000; Russia, 1.75 million; Turkey, 300 000; and the Balkans, 450 000.

Interpreting

1. What was the result of the stalemate on the casualty rate during the First World War?
2. Why do you think conscription (compulsory enlistment for military service) became such a vital necessity for all countries during the war?
3. Why do you think that a breakthrough was so hard to achieve for both sides during the war?

Figure 2.9

In November 1917, Canadian troops at Passchendaele held the line in the waterlogged landscape of trenches. How would these difficult conditions affect soldiers physically and psychologically?

THE EASTERN FRONT

August / 1914

On the eastern front, the line was much more mobile. Nevertheless, conditions were deplorable. In August 1914, at the Battle of Tannenberg in Prussia, the Germans out-manoeuvred a much larger Russian force and won a major battle. The Russian supply system had failed, leaving the troops exhausted and half-starved after their long march. Russian communications had broken down, and the Russian high command, unaware of German troop movements, made fatal mistakes regarding the deployment of Russian armies. As a result, the Second Russian Army was surrounded and destroyed. The Germans killed at least 30 000 Russians, took 100 000 prisoners, and captured a vast supply of guns at Tannenberg. The Russian commander, General Samsonov, unable to face his men or the czar, shot himself.

In early September, the Germans took another 125 000 prisoners at the Battle of the Masurian Lakes. The Russians fell back across the border, confused and demoralized. Within the first two months of the war, Russia had lost two armies.

The Russian army was ill-equipped. Russia did not have a strong munitions industry, and arms could not be shipped by its allies, Britain and France, because Germany controlled access to the Black and Baltic seas. Russian soldiers frequently ran out of weapons and ammunition and at times had to fight with pitchforks and swords. It is estimated that one in three Russian soldiers was sent to the front without a weapon. There they waited for someone to be killed or injured and then took his weapon and fought on.

For the next three years, the Russians

Germans won
Sept 1914
Masurian Lake

MAP STUDY

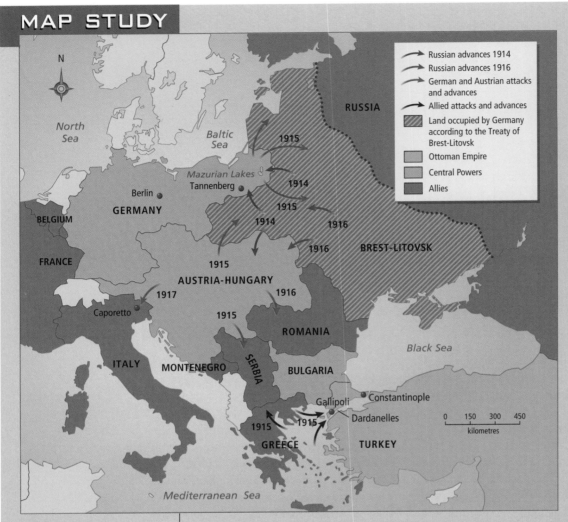

Figure 2.10
The Eastern Front and the Treaty of Brest-Litovsk, 1914 to 1917

Conditions on the eastern front were different. Here there were large-scale battles with considerable movement and huge casualties. The trench system was not nearly as formidable. German forces won tremendous victories against the Russian forces.

By the Treaty of Brest-Litovsk, Russia ceded this territory (green stripes) to Germany and allowed German troops to enter and occupy it, including the rich wheat lands of the Ukraine. Thus the German army was more powerful because it had a rich new food supply and entire armies could now be transferred to the Western Front to fight the final battles of the war. For the first time since 1914, Germany was able to concentrate its forces on one front.

Interpreting

1. Why were the Russians unable to contain the German attacks?
2. Why was the Treaty of Brest-Litovsk so important to German hopes of victory?
3. How do you think the Allies regarded the new Bolshevik government of Russia? Why?

fought bravely. But by the beginning of 1917, 3 million Russian soldiers were dead or captured. Within Russia the constant defeats, combined with crushing poverty and unbridled corruption, led to a loss of confidence in the czarist regime. Protest groups marched through the streets of St. Petersburg and Moscow demanding food, an end to the war, and economic reforms. Finally in March 1917 the people revolted (see pages 69-70). The czar was forced to abdicate his throne and a more moderate reform government was established. Russia was prepared to continue the war against the Central Powers, but the new government was unable to satisfy the needs of its own people never mind continue a savage war against a much more powerful foe.

In November 1917, the moderate government of Alexander Kerensky was toppled by the **Bolsheviks**, a radical socialist group of workers and soldiers led by Vladimir Ilyich Lenin. The Bolsheviks, who would become the Russian Communist Party the following year, opposed the war. Once they had established a revolutionary government they proceeded to negotiate an armistice with the Central Powers. The **Treaty of Brest-Litovsk**, signed in March 1918, ended Russia's involvement in the war. But the terms were harsh. Russia lost one-third of its population and agricultural land and almost all of its coal reserves. For the time being, Germany now dominated eastern Europe.

The Russian armistice was a devastating blow to the Allies. It meant that Germany could relieve food shortages caused by the naval blockade by using the agricultural products of Ukraine. It also allowed Germany to concentrate its forces on the western front against France and Britain. The war was now hurtling towards its final great battles.

Technology and the First World War

As war clouds gathered and even during the fighting, advances in technology were feverishly applied to a new industry—armaments. The types of weapons and the enormous quantities turned out by European, and later American, industries between 1900 and 1918 not only made the war longer and bloodier, but they changed the nature of war.

The world was shocked by the frequent use of weapons of mass destruction such as gas. As early as 1914, gas was employed on the battlefield. The main types of gas were chlorine and mustard gas. Chlorine gas produced violent choking and death while mustard gas left horrible internal and external burns. Even those soldiers who survived gas attacks were often left with disfiguring scars or damaged lungs that often resulted in an early death.

In Canada's first major battle at Ypres, Belgium, in 1915, Canadians distinguished themselves by extending and holding their lines in the midst of a gas attack that sent French colonial troops fleeing. The Canadians' courage cost 6000 lives. Troops were seen "to roll about like mad dogs in their death agonies." Gas attacks were blunted by the advent of good gas masks and the fact that using gas was dangerously unpredictable as a shift in the wind could send the gas back to kill the force unleashing the weapon.

Although machine guns had been developed earlier, they were perfected as brutally effective killing machines of the First World War. This marriage of industrial technology and the mass citizen armies resulted in millions of casualties along the killing fields of Europe. Placed in an entrenched position, defenders using a weapon such as the Vickers Mark I could fire 5550 rounds per minute at the densely packed and exposed waves of troops coming forward. Soldiers referred to this weapon as "the coffee grinder" because it ground to pieces waves of attacking troops.

In September 1916, the battlefields were altered forever when the British introduced the first tanks at the Battle of the Somme. Initially the tanks (primitive by modern standards) were ineffective because the crews were inexperienced and the slow, cumbersome vehicles were frequently caught in the quagmire of the muddy battlefields. Later versions in 1917 and 1918, however, were more effective.

Aviation technology was still in its infancy when war broke out. Military planners saw little use for the weak and unreliable aeroplanes that were available at the time, except for occasional reconnaissance flights. Nevertheless, military aviation technology made rapid advances over the course of the war, and planes became more numerous, durable, and powerful.

Aerial reconnaissance gained importance in the static warfare of the trenches. Aerial photographs of enemy defences were carefully studied before an attack was launched. Planes were used for observation of enemy movements and artillery, but by 1915 they were taking a more offensive role. The first fighter planes in 1915 were one- or two-seaters armed with forward-firing machine guns. Both sides carried out strategic aerial bombing, although it had little serious impact on events. By the end of the war, however, there were dog-fights in the air and regular bombing missions. Air power had become a significant military factor. Aviation added a new dimension to the battlefields of war.

On the seas, there were no full-scale naval battles between British and German fleets until the Battle of Jutland in the North Sea in 1916. At the end of May, the British had sailed towards Denmark to intercept the German fleet. The British enjoyed superior naval strength; Germany

[handwritten margin note: Battle of Jutland British & Germany]

Figure 2.11

Tank warfare: a British tank carrying troops over an embankment. Why was the tank likely to be such an effective weapon in the First World War?

could only hope to gain victory by isolating part of the fleet and destroying it. This they failed to do. But the British also failed to destroy the German fleet and suffered the greater losses. Although the Battle of Jutland ended in a draw, both sides claimed victory. But Germany never again directly challenged the might of the British navy. In the end, the British retained control of the North Sea and the Germans remained confined to the Baltic Sea for the rest of the war.

German submarines, on the other hand, were successful in many of their attempts to destroy British shipping. In retaliation for a British blockade that prevented Germany from obtaining goods from overseas, Germany announced in 1915 that any Allied merchant ships entering British waters would be sunk by German **U-boats**, or submarines. By October 1917, the Germans had destroyed 8 million tonnes of shipping. Britain was in danger of losing its lifeline to the United States and the colonies of the British Empire. Eventually, the submarine war brought the United States into the conflict.

Figure 2.12
This painting illustrates a "dog fight" typical to World War One. How did the use of planes aid military intelligence?

The United States Enters the War

The United States was determined to remain neutral, viewing the war as the imperialist ramblings of ageing European nations. While the war raged on, the United States became increasingly rich and powerful, shipping produce and manufactured goods, including war materials, across the ocean. The Americans expected the warring nations to respect the "freedom of the seas" and protested against both British and German blockades. Between 1914 and 1918, American exports rose from $2 billion to $6 billion annually, largely due to supplying goods to war-ravaged Europe. When the war was over, European countries owed $10 billion to the United States for goods bought on credit.

In 1915, Germany declared the waters around Britain a war zone. They warned that Allied vessels would be torpedoed and the safety of neutral vessels would not be guaranteed. On May 7, a British ocean liner, the *Lusitania*, was torpedoed by German U-boats. Among the 1198 victims were 128 Americans. The incident shocked the United States and served to turn public opinion against Germany. US President Woodrow Wilson warned Germany that another such act would be interpreted as "deliberately unfriendly."

Germany, not wishing to draw the United States into the war, loosened the blockade for two years. In February 1917, however, Germany began a campaign of unrestricted submarine warfare. The German high command hoped that, with supplies cut off, Britain would be forced into a quick surrender before the United States was able to mobilize and send troops. The United States broke off diplomatic relations with Germany and began arming its freighters. During February and March, several American ships were sunk by U-boats. On 6 April 1917, the United States declared war on Germany.

The American entrance into the war ensured a fresh supply of soldiers and materials to the Allied war effort. But the United States was unable to recruit, train, and equip a substantial number of troops to send to Europe until almost a year later. As a result, 1917 was a year of untold hardship and loss for the Allies in Europe.

In the spring of 1918, the armies of both sides were battered and exhausted. Only six divisions of American soldiers had arrived by March. The German army, hoping for a decisive victory before American troops arrived in strength, began a huge offensive on the western front. In March, April, May, and July the Germans attacked Allied troops and advanced to positions not held since 1914. But the casualties on both sides were staggering.

On July 18, just as the Germans had begun their fourth offensive, the Allies began their counter-offensive, the second Battle of the Marne. The Allies, with French light tanks leading the way and bolstered by eight American divisions, pushed the German lines back over the Marne. That day marked the turning point of the war. From then on the Allies would have the initiative.

In August, Germany suffered its greatest defeat. British, Canadian, and Australian troops launched a surprise attack on the German army near Amiens. The Germans were unable to defend themselves. In one day—called *Der Schwarze Tag* (The Black Day) by Germany—the Allies took 16 000 prisoners. Germany had run out of reserves. Those soldiers who were still fighting were exhausted, ill equipped, and demoralized. The Allied forces, on the other hand, were now physically and psychologically bolstered by the constant arrival of American troops. Germany's collapse was only a matter of time.

In September, at the Battle of Saint-Mihiel, the Americans won their first independent victory. September and October saw more Allied victories from Ypres to Verdun as the Allies kept pressuring the retreating Germans with tanks, aeroplanes, heavy artillery, and infantry. By October, the Allies had advanced to the German border. On October 28, the German fleet mutinied at Kiel. The morale of the German forces was cracking.

One by one, Germany's allies bowed out of the war. On October 4, Germany and Austria-Hungary asked US President Wilson to begin negotiations for an armistice. On November 4, Austria-Hungary surrendered to the Allies, and on November 7, the German Kaiser abdicated and fled to Holland. The "war to end all wars" came to a close at eleven o'clock on the eleventh day of the eleventh month of 1918 when Germany accepted peace based upon Wilson's terms. In the words of T.S. Eliot, the end came "not with a bang but with a whimper." But not without a horrendous price: more than 9 million soldiers dead and civilian losses unknown.

In Review

1. Why did the young men from Newfoundland suffer such horrible casualties at the Battle of the Somme?

2. a) Briefly describe the nature of the war from a soldier's viewpoint.

   b) How does this reality compare with the image presented at the outset of war?

3. Describe the impact of weapons such as tanks, aeroplanes, and submarines on the course of the war.

4. In your view, should Canada have been involved in the First World War? Explain your answer.

5. What was the significance of the US entry into the war?

6. Outline the major reasons for Germany's defeat.

The Search For Peace

Ending the First World War had been a long and difficult struggle. President Wilson looked to a new world body—The League of Nations—to provide **collective security**, that is, a system to ensure world peace with the support and action of the world's nations and to prevent future conflicts. Designing a fair peace proved to be equally challenging. The Allies had the difficult task of redrawing the map of Europe and establishing the conditions for a lasting peace. But the process seemed doomed from the start. The new communist government in Russia was refused representation at the talks. Decision-making power rested in the hands of three governments—Britain, France, and the United States.

The Paris Conference, convened on 18 January 1919, was the largest and most important diplomatic gathering since the Congress of Vienna in 1815. Thirty Allied nations were given seats at the conference. The defeated nations were not given any status at the negotiations, so their fate would be decided for them. While all present had

a voice in the terms of the peace treaty, the real decision-making power lay with the three leading victorious nations.

The damage the war had inflicted was horrendous. Ten million lives had been lost. The direct financial costs were estimated at $180 billion, with another $150 billion in indirect costs. Four great empires had crumbled: Hohenzollern Germany, Habsburg Austria-Hungary, Romanov Russia, and Ottoman Turkey. The task that lay before the peacemakers was to establish political and economic stability in Europe and to ensure that the First World War was, in US President Woodrow Wilson's words, truly "the war to end all wars."

The United States was regarded with great hope by millions of war-weary Europeans. President Wilson offered a vision for a new world order along with the moral authority and economic power to get things done. Wilson joined the American peace delegation in Paris. His personal participation in the peace process and his pledge "to make the world safe for democracy" was welcomed in Europe with great hope and enthusiasm.

WILSON AND THE FOURTEEN POINTS

Wilson believed that war was caused by three major factors: secret diplomacy among nations; the tendency of dominant nationalities to oppress ethnic minorities; and autocratic governments ruled by elites. He believed that these causes of war had to be removed if the world was to have lasting peace. Wilson's **Fourteen Points**, announced on 8 January 1918, addressed these key issues.

Wilson hoped the Fourteen Points would be the basis for a new world order, but as the hard realities of negotiations proceeded, these principles gradually receded to the background. Key decisions were made in secret by the big powers. Revenge and power politics dominated. In time, the high public expectations based on Wilson's idealistic statements would be shattered.

THE PARIS PEACE CONFERENCE: DIFFERENT EXPECTATIONS

The major powers had different expectations at the Paris Peace Conference that began on 18 January 1919. The United States was determined to establish a new international order based on Wilson's Fourteen Points. Added to this idealism was the practical desire to resume the free flow of trade so that American business could continue to prosper. Britain, too,

Wilson's Fourteen Points

I. Open covenants of peace, openly arrived at, after which there shall be no private international understandings of any kind but diplomacy shall proceed always frankly and in the public view.

II. Absolute freedom of navigation upon the seas, outside territorial waters, alike in peace and in war.

III. The removal, so far as possible, of all economic barriers and the establishment of an equality of trade conditions among all the nations consenting to the peace and associating themselves for its maintenance.

IV. Adequate guarantees given and taken that national armaments will be reduced to the lowest point consistent with domestic safety.

V. A free, open-minded, and absolutely impartial adjustment of all colonial claims, based on the principle that in determining all such questions of sovereignty, the interests of the populations concerned must have equal weight with the equitable claims of the government whose title is to be determined.

VI. The evacuation of all Russian territory and... assistance of every kind that she may need and may herself desire.

VII. Belgium... must be evacuated [by the Germans] and restored.

VIII. All French territory should be freed and the invaded portions restored, the wrong done to France in the matter... of Alsace-Lorraine... should be righted.

IX. A readjustment of frontiers of Italy should be effected along clearly recognizable lines of nationality.

X. The people of Austria-Hungary, whose place among the nations we wish to see safe-guarded and assured, should be accorded the freest opportunity of autonomous development.

XI. Romania, Serbia, and Montenegro should be evacuated... Serbia accorded free access to the sea.

XII. The Turkish portion of the present Ottoman Empire should be assured a secure sovereignty, but the other nationalities which are now under Turkish rule...[should be allowed] autonomous development.

XIII. An independent Polish state... should include the territories inhabited by indisputably Polish populations...[and should] be assured a free and secure access to the sea.

XIV. A general association of nations must be formed under specific covenants for the purpose of affording mutual guarantees of political independence and territorial integrity to great and small states alike. "The world must be made safe for democracy."

Figure 2.13

For each of Wilson's points, indicate whether you agree or disagree. Be prepared to explain your choices. In your opinion, which point is the most important? Why?

was eager to establish a peaceful atmosphere in which business could flourish. France, where the northern provinces had been a vast battlefield and where the dead numbered over 1 million, wanted assurances that it would be able to rebuild without threat from neighbouring Germany. Thus each country had different expectations of the peace treaty.

The United States was a new player in the affairs of Europe. The long tradition of American diplomacy had been one of isolation. Essentially, the Americans were eager to revert to that policy. Their greatest national interest in the peace process was to maintain their robust economy. To that end, the US placed pressure on Britain and France to repay their war loans. These war allies in turn decided to pass on this financial burden to Germany.

French Objectives

France had two basic goals at the peace conference: national security and financial **reparations** (payments). To ensure national security, France wanted to remove the threat from German military power. In the pre-war years, Germany had developed into a powerful military and economic nation. To keep Germany in check, France had forged an alliance with Russia. Now, with Russia in the hands of the Bolsheviks, France had to find other guarantees of security. France demanded the return of Alsace-Lorraine, which had been seized by Germany following the Franco-Prussian War of 1870. The Allies accepted this without question. But France also demanded the German Rhineland to serve as a buffer zone between the two countries. Seizure of this territory clearly violated Wilson's principle of **national self-determination**, which called for individual nationalities to have their own state and protected

borders, and the demand was rejected. However, if France could not have the Rhineland, it demanded that the region be neutralized. The compromise was a **demilitarized zone**. Germany was prohibited from placing troops or fortifications within 50 km of the east bank of the Rhine River. As insurance, the Allies would occupy the west bank for 15 years. This settlement, combined with other military restrictions and a pledge of immediate military assistance from Britain and the United States in the event of German aggression, satisfied France's security concerns.

The other French goal was to gain financial compensation for losses during the war. Northern France had been devastated after four years of German occupation. Furthermore, the German army had destroyed what was left of the region when they withdrew in 1918. Mines were flooded, railways destroyed, and fields torn apart by shells and trenches. To make up for the German destruction of French coal mines, France was awarded coal rights in Germany's Saar Valley until 1935.

French premier Georges Clemenceau demanded that Germany pay full reparations for war damages. The Americans felt that reparations should be limited to what Germany could afford to pay in 30 years. But the French disagreed, demanding that Germany pay whatever damages were assessed with no time limit. Eventually Clemenceau agreed to the 30-year limit on the condition that it be

NETSURFER

WWW.BBC.CO.UK/EDUCATION/MODERN/VERSAILL/
VERSAHTM.HTM

The BBC's Modern World History pages are an excellent source for more information, documents, visuals, etc., on the Treaty of Versailles. This is a very helpful source for initial research for projects or assignments. Scroll down the homepage to learn about each of the leaders who attended the peace conference.

extended if necessary. In 1921, Germany was presented with a reparations bill of more than $30 billion, of which the French share was 52 per cent. It was impossible for Germany to pay this amount, and by 1922 the country had already fallen behind in its payments. The German economic crisis soon turned to political crisis.

British Objectives

The key British objective at the conference was to ensure the security of the sea lanes to its empire. This meant that German sea power had to be crippled. This was achieved by reducing the German navy to a token force of six warships, prohibiting German submarines, and redistributing German colonies to the Allies. Britain was not prepared to support French demands for huge reparation payments or territorial gains. If Germany were forced to pay massive reparations to France, the result would be a weak Germany and a strong France. In 1919, Britain was beginning to fear the spread of Bolshevism more than it feared the rise of Germany. Both British Prime Minister Lloyd George and Liberal Party colleague Winston Churchill felt that if Germany were weakened too much, it could fall into the hands of communist Russia. So Britain began to soften its stand on reparations.

THE PEACE OF PARIS, 1919

When the Allies established the terms of the **Treaty of Versailles**, Germany was invited to Versailles for the formal signing on 18 June 1919. Germany signed the treaty, but only under protest. The Germans

---

The Main Terms of the Treaty of Versailles

1. Territorial Changes

a) Alsace-Lorraine to be returned to France

b) Belgium, Poland, and Czechoslovakia to receive German border areas

c) Poland re-established as an independent state with access to the Baltic Sea (the Polish Corridor to Danzig)

d) Danzig to be a free city under the League of Nations

e) Germany to give up all overseas colonies to the League of Nations; mandates for administering former German colonies assigned to Britain, France, and Japan

2. Military Terms

a) German army reduced to 100 000 troops

b) Germany forbidden to have an airforce

c) Most German naval vessels, including the submarine force, to be handed over to the Allies

d) Germany forbidden to have heavy military frontier fortifications

3. Admission of War Guilt

a) Germany forced to accept responsibility for starting the war

4. Reparations

a) Germany to pay war reparations to France and Belgium for damages caused during the war

b) Germany to pay reparations for shipping damages by turning over part of its merchant marine fleet

5. Other Terms

a) Germany to cede Saar coal mines to France for fifteen years

b) Allied troops to occupy the Rhineland for fifteen years

c) East bank of Rhine to be demilitarized

Figure 2.14

The Treaty of Versailles was one of the most important documents of the twentieth century. Its failure helped shape global politics for decades to come. Review the terms of the treaty and indicate which terms you support, which ones you reject, and why.

were particularly incensed by the War Guilt clause that stipulated that Germany accept sole responsibility for the war: "The Allied and Associated Governments affirm and Germany accepts the responsibility of Germany and her allies for causing all the loss and damage to which the Allied and Associated Governments and their nationals have been subjected as a consequence of the war imposed upon them by the aggression of Germany and her allies." It was a clause that would have serious repercussions in the years to come.

In the months following the signing of the Treaty of Versailles, separate treaties were signed with Austria (the Treaty of St. Germain, 1919); Bulgaria (the Treaty of Neuilly, 1919); Turkey (the Treaty of Sevres, 1920); and Hungary (the Treaty of Trianon, 1920). Seven new countries were created from the former Russian, Turkish, and Austro-Hungarian empires, including Latvia, Estonia, Lithuania, Finland, Czechoslovakia, and Poland. Millions of ordinary people found themselves living as minorities in new countries or in different countries after the boundaries were redrawn. The new Europe became a breeding ground for political tension and unrest. Europe needed stability to heal the wounds of war but turmoil was its destiny.

The League of Nations

The League of Nations came into being with the signing of the treaty. This international organization of nations was part of Woodrow Wilson's vision of a new world order. Ironically, the United States Senate rejected the treaty and along with it the League of Nations. Even without American membership, however, the League was a step towards the establishment of an international arbitrator of disputes, although it came to be seen as a European rather than a world body.

Figure 2.15
The "Big Three"— British Prime Minister David Lloyd George, French Prime Minister Georges Clemenceau, and American President Woodrow Wilson—shaped and signed the Treaty of Versailles. In your opinion should the defeated nations have had any input into the treaty? Explain.

EVALUATING THE TREATY

The Treaty of Versailles created controversy that continues even to this day. German colonies across the globe were taken away. The territorial, military, and economic terms infuriated and humiliated Germany. Later German leaders used the hated treaty to illustrate how unfairly the world was treating Germany. Instead of resolution, the treaty encouraged revenge.

MAP STUDY

Figure 2.16

The Price of Defeat: Germany's Losses by the Terms of the Treaty of Versailles

The Treaty of Versailles redrew the map of Europe and parts of the globe. Compare this map with the map of Europe in 1914 (see page 37).

1. All German overseas colonies lost. Displaced Germans returned to Germany.
2. Saar coalfields placed under French rule for fifteen years.
3. Union between Austria and Germany forbidden.

Interpreting

1. What evidence is there that the principle of national self-determination was violated?
2. What new nations were created in Europe?
3. What impact might this have on political stability in the region? Explain.
4. In your view, were German losses justified? Explain.

Reparation payments were blamed for Germany's staggering inflation and economic collapse. To make these payments, the government printed paper money until the currency was worthless. By 1923, the German economy was in ruins. Furthermore, the military restrictions imposed on Germany were seen as harsh and humiliating. Thousands of demobilized German troops, resenting the terms of the treaty and disgruntled with a political system that had been incapable of striking a better deal in Paris, joined right-wing political groups. The treaty provided fertile ground for propaganda against the Allies' treatment of Germany and it was employed with great success. German violations of the treaty grew bolder and more flagrant until finally Adolf Hitler and the Nazi Party effectively killed the Treaty of Versailles in the early 1930s.

In Review

1. What were the key objectives of France, Britain, and the United States at the Paris Peace Conference? In your opinion, which country was most successful in achieving its objectives? Explain your answer.

2. Why did Wilson's idealism not gain much support at the peace conference?

3. In your opinion, do Wilson's Fourteen Points have any relevance in today's world? Explain.

4. How would you have changed the Treaty of Versailles and why?

5. In general, what do you think should be the central purpose of a treaty that ends a serious conflict?

6. How did the Treaty of Versailles help the rise of Hitler and the Nazi Party?

Summary

When war broke out in 1914, the mood was almost festive. Most people believed it would be a short war that would solve many of the problems of the competing nations. As the war dragged on, it became a battle of attrition: who could continue to supply soldiers and weapons in order to outlast the others.

The war cost Europe dearly in terms of human lives and almost ruined the continent economically. The cost of feeding and equipping the military forces was staggering. The destruction left vast areas of Belgium and France in ruins. But while the economies of both the victors and the vanquished in Europe were severely damaged, the American economy was strengthened by the war. Even though most European countries recovered by 1924, they faced a new order in which the international economic **balance of power** had shifted from Europe in favour of the United States.

Viewpoints

Background

Under the Treaty of Versailles in 1919, the victorious allies imposed the conditions of peace upon Germany. The key players drafting the treaty were American president Woodrow Wilson, British Prime Minister David Lloyd George, and French Prime Minister Georges Clemenceau. The expectations were that a just and fair treaty based on the idealism of Wilson's Fourteen Points would emerge from the Paris Peace Conference. To many observers, however, the true spirit of the Fourteen Points was sacrificed and replaced with a series of tough measures designed to cripple Germany.

Economist John Maynard Keynes was a delegate at the peace conference. He abandoned the proceedings in protest over the harsh and unrealistic demands of the treaty. In his famous book *The Economic Consequences of the Peace*, Keynes denounced the treaty.

Twenty years after the Treaty of Versailles, the world was engulfed in the Second World War when historian Paul Birdsall published his review of the Paris Peace settlement. In it, he praised Woodrow Wilson and his idealism as well as the overall peace settlement he had inspired. Read each of these viewpoints carefully and complete the questions that follow. (You may want to refer to the Skill Path "Analysing a Reading" on page 14 before beginning.)

John Maynard Keynes

There are two separate aspects of the peace which we have imposed on the enemy—on the one hand its justice, on the other hand its wisdom and its expediency.

Its justice

The nature of the terms which we were entitled in justice to impose depends, in part, on the responsibility of the enemy nations for causing so tremendous a calamity as the late war, and in part on the understanding on which the enemy laid down his arms at the time of the armistice. In my own opinion, it is not possible to lay the entire responsibility for the state of affairs out of which the war arose on any single nation.

But I believe, nevertheless, that Germany bears a special and peculiar responsibility for the war itself for its universal and devastating character, and for its final development into a combat without quarter for mastery or defeat. A criminal may be the outcome of his environment, but he is none the less a criminal.

Even so, however, it was our duty to look more to the future than to the past, to distinguish between the late rulers of Germany on the one hand and her common people and unborn posterity on the other, and to be sure that our acts were guided by magnanimity and wisdom more than by revenge or hatred.... Above all, should not the future peace of the world have been our highest and guiding motive?...

The treaty's wisdom

With these brief comments I pass from the justice

of the treaty, which can not be ignored even when it is not our central topic, to its wisdom and its expediency. Under these heads my criticism of the treaty is double. In the first place, this treaty ignores the economic solidarity of Europe, and by aiming at the destruction of the economic life of Germany it threatens the health and prosperity of the Allies themselves. In the second place, by making demands the execution of which is in the literal sense impossible, it stultifies itself and leaves Europe more unsettled than it found it. The treaty, by overstepping the limits of the possible, has in practice settled nothing.

Indemnity demands

I believe that it would have been a wise and just act to have asked the German Government at the peace negotiations to agree to a final settlement, without further examination of particulars. This would have provided an immediate and certain solution, and would have required from Germany a sum which, if she were granted certain indulgences, it might not have proved entirely impossible for her to pay. This sum should have been divided up among the Allies themselves on a basis of need and general equity.

The blank check

No final amount is specified by the treaty itself, which fixes no definite sum as representing Germany's liability. This feature has been the subject of very general criticism that is equally inconvenient to Germany and to the Allies themselves that she should not know what she has to pay or what they are to receive. The method, apparently contemplated by the treaty, of arriving at the final result over a period of many months by an addition of hundreds of thousands of individual claims for damage to land, farm buildings and chickens, is evidently impracticable, and the reasonable course would have been for both parties to compound for a round sum without examination of details. If this round sum had been named in the treaty, the settlement would have been placed on a more businesslike basis.

Source: John Maynard Keynes, "The Peace of Versailles," *Everybody's Magazine*, 1920 (September) pp. 36-41.

Paul Birdsall

The simple thesis of those who oppose the treaty is that the doctrinaire and unrealistic program of Wilson collapsed under the impact of the power politics of Europe. Nationalist aims triumphed over his principles. There was division of the spoils of war... in defiance of his principles of self-determination. Keynes in his disillusionment has fixed the legend of a Carthaginian Peace* in Wilsonian disguise.

This is caricature, not history, but like most successful caricature it has enough verisimilitude [truth] to be plausible.... The 'Reparation' chapter of the Treaty of Versailles, besides being a clear violation of the Pre-Armistice Agreement with Germany, proved in the outcome to be the most disastrous section of the treaty.

The prosaic [sad] truth is that elements of good and bad were combined in the treaties. There were Carthaginian features like the Reparation settlement and Wilsonian features like the League of Nations. The territorial settlement in Europe was by no means the wholesale, iniquitous, [unfair] and cynical perversion of Wilson's principles of self-determination which has been pictured. The populations of central Europe are hopelessly mixed and, therefore, simple self-determination is impossible.

The treaty was essentially a compromise between Anglo-American and French conceptions of a stable international order. On the one hand, immediate French concern for military security was taken care of by the limitation of German armaments, demilitarization of the Rhineland area and Allied military occupation for a fifteen-year period, and—finally—an Anglo-American treaty of military guarantee. They represented the minimum price which English and American negotiators had to pay for French abandonment of their traditional policy of entirely dismembering Germany. They were a realistic concession to French needs without violating the Fourteen Points in any important particular.

The Reparation settlement was the chief stumbling block, partly because of impossible financial demands. In both financial and political results it proved disastrous. The Reparation issue emphasized more than any other the necessity of continuing Anglo-American cooperation to make effective Anglo-American conceptions of a world order.

The defection of the United States destroyed the Anglo-American preponderance which alone could have stabilized Europe. It impaired the authority and prestige of the League at its birth and it precipitated an Anglo-French duel which reduced Europe to the chaos from which Hitler emerged to produce new chaos. Practically and immediately, it destroyed the Anglo-American treaty of military guarantee which was to have been one of the main props of French Security.

English sentiment was already developing the guilt-complex about the whole Treaty of Versailles which, among other factors, paralysed English foreign policy from Versailles to Munich. It would be interesting to speculate as to how much that guilt-complex was the result of the brilliant writing of John Maynard Keynes. Devastatingly accurate and prophetic in its analysis of the economic aspects of the treaty, his *The Economic Consequences of the Peace* included the whole treaty in one sweeping condemnation as a "Carthaginian Peace," and his caricatures of the leading negotiators at Paris immediately fixed stereotypes which still affect much of the writing about the Paris Peace Conference.

Only too late did British and French leaders observe that Hitler was less concerned about rectification of the "injustices" of the *Diktat* of Versailles than with the conquest of Europe. The muddle and confusion in liberal and democratic communities about the real character of Versailles contributed to the stupidity of Allied policy from Versailles to Armageddon.

Source: Paul Birdsall, *Versailles Twenty Years After*, (1941), in I.J. Lederer (ed.), *The Versailles Settlement: Was It Foredoomed to Failure?* (Boston: D.C. Heath and Co.), 1960.

*Carthaginian Peace refers to the complete destruction of the city state of Carthage by Rome in 202 BCE and 146 BCE. A "Carthaginian peace" is one where the enemy is completely destroyed and unable to rebuild.

Analysis and Evaluation

1. What does Keynes believe should have been the guiding motive when the Allies designed the treaty? Do you agree? Explain.

2. How would Keynes have settled the issue of German compensation for the war?

3. According to Birdsall what was the result of the fact that the US did not join the League?

4. What blame does Birdsall lay on Keynes' criticism of the treaty? Is this fair in your opinion? Explain.

5. Decide which of the viewpoints you tend to support and explain why. Be sure to use specific information from this textbook, the readings, and other sources to support your position. If you do not agree with either author, explain your own view.

Chapter Analysis

MAKING CONNECTIONS

1. Review the major causes of the First World War. Identify similar issues that appear to be alive and well in the world today.

2. Compare and contrast the tension in the Balkans in the period before the First World War and in the early 1990s.

3. Identify a modern pro or antiwar song. Present some of the lyrics and discuss their meaning.

4. a) Describe the political relationship that existed between Canada and Britain at the turn of the century. If Britain went to war, did Canada also go to war? Why?

   b) Describe the political relationship that exists between these two countries today. If Britain goes to war today, would Canada also be obliged to go? Why or why not?

DEVELOPING YOUR VOICE

5. Organize a class debate on one of the following topics:
   • The First World War—Whose Responsibility?
   • Should Canada have been involved in the First World War?
   • Treaty of Versailles: An Unjust Peace?

6. Assume you are a soldier or battlefield nurse during the war. Write a letter home outlining your experiences, hopes, fears, etc.

7. Write a letter to the editor of a local newspaper as if it were 1919 and comment on the Treaty of Versailles from the point of view of a soldier from one of the following nations: Britain, Canada, France, Germany, or the United States.

8. Write a brief speech stating your views on the First World War to be delivered during a Remembrance Day assembly.

RESEARCHING THE ISSUES

9. Select a major battle of the First World War and prepare a presentation or display showing:
   a) the objectives of the opposing armies;
   b) the basic strategy used by both sides; and
   c) the outcome of the battle.
   You might include maps and statistics.

10. Research the career of one of the key personalities of the First World War or the Treaty of Versailles and write a brief biographical profile of this individual in the "Profile" format used in this book.

CHAPTER THREE

Change and Conflict Between the Wars: 1919-1939

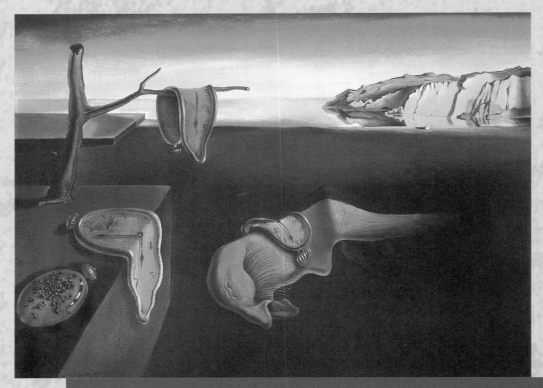

Salvador Dali (1904-1989) was one of the most famous members of the Surrealist group of painters. Surrealism was a revolutionary art form that stressed the bizarre and the irrational. This is perhaps Dali's most recognized work, *The Persistence of Memory*. Dali was later rejected by the surrealists for his support of the fascist General Franco of Spain. What is suggested in this painting? Can you find the self-portrait that Dali included in this work?

"This is not peace. It is an armistice for twenty years."

— Marshal Ferdinand Foch (1851-1929),
French Commander of the Allied Armies, speaking on
28 June 1919, the day the Treaty of Versailles was signed

"Whoever can conquer the street will one day conquer the state, for every form of power politics and any dictatorially-run state has its roots in the street."

— Joseph Goebbels (1897-1945),
Hitler's minister of propaganda

Overview

The impact of the Treaty of Versailles was hardly what the Allies had intended. Instead of an agreement for peace, the treaty seemed more like an armistice—a brief respite before the renewal of war.

Democracies, new and old, were challenged by the rise of powerful ideologies (fascism, communism), strut-

ting dictators (Mussolini, Franco), and economic crisis including the onset of a global depression. The dream of a League of Nations soon became a nightmare as the world drifted slowly towards yet another global conflict. The failure to produce a lasting peace would scar the rest of the twentieth century.

Focus Questions
1. What was the impact of communism on the peoples of Russia and Europe?
2. Why did fascism gain such appeal in Europe during the inter-war years?
3. What factors led to the Great Depression?
4. What accounted for the failure of the League of Nations?

International Confrontation

Idealists such as American president Woodrow Wilson hoped that the terrible lessons of "The Great War" or "The War To End All Wars" (it was not yet called the First World War, since no one suspected another horrible conflagration would erupt) would result in a new international order based on honesty and co-operation. The new League of Nations provided hope, and more importantly, an ongoing structure to resolve international issues through diplomacy. However, the nations of the world, particularly the powerful nations of Europe, were soon divided by old rivalries, nationalism, desires for revenge, and shaky new frontiers.

Many of the states created or reshaped by the Treaty of Versailles were weak and unsteady politically and economically. These difficult divisions were sharpened by the rise of new ideologies and political philosophies. Dictatorial regimes arose in war shattered states and soon challenged democracies both young and old. The new world order of 1919 rapidly descended in a spiral of radical politics, revolution, and rearmament.

THE POLITICS OF THE EXTREME RIGHT AND THE EXTREME LEFT
The terms *right* and *left* are commonly used in describing political parties. Right, in general, refers to people or parties with more conservative, traditional views; and left refers to people or parties that hold more liberal, less traditional views. These political labels derive from the French Revolution. In the seating plan of the French National Assembly, those who wanted greater democracy tended to sit on the left while those who preferred to maintain a strong monarch sat on the right. Those in the centre were more willing to compromise. Those further to the

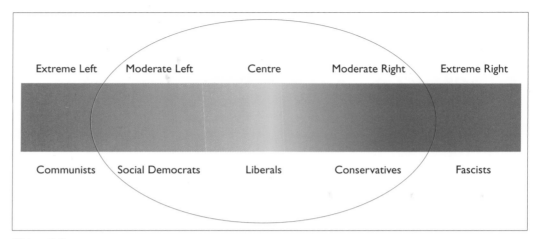

Figure 3.1
The political spectrum is a conceptual tool used by observers to classify political parties, ideologies, and even individuals. Like a light spectrum, it attempts to show the "political colours" or range of belief systems in an organized manner. It can only be used in a general sense, since people and parties are seldom right or left on all issues, all the time. The more a society becomes polarized (i.e. with strong parties at the edges, rather than the centre) the more unsteady, divided, and sometimes violent the political system is likely to be.

right or left tended to hold more extreme views and were less willing to compromise their beliefs.

At both ends of the spectrum (as seen in Figure 3.1) are extreme parties or individuals that are less democratic and more open to revolution and dictatorship. The centre includes conservatives as a party of the moderate right, **social democrats** as a party of the moderate left, and liberals as a party of the centre. Although these parties may differ widely on important social, economic, and political issues and policies, they refrain from political violence and support democratic means to achieve their goals. However, in the outer parts of the spectrum are two parties with extreme views that are distinct from others in that they reject the values of the centre— democracy and freedom—in favour of totalitarian beliefs.

Totalitarianism is a political ideology that is generally opposed to democracy and personal freedom. The emphasis is on rigid and dictatorial control on all aspects of society from the ruler down. Freedom

is chaos in a totalitarian regime, and chaos will be suppressed by any means necessary—including violence. In this sense, **fascism** is a rightist totalitarian party and **communism** a leftist totalitarian party.

Politics is most simply described as the pursuit and exercise of power. In the aftermath of the First World War, a host of new parties arose to claim the leadership of their nations. In the confusion, chaos, and confrontation of the post-war years, two movements on the radical extreme, communism and fascism, moved to the forefront of this struggle. As the compromise politics of the centre collapsed, the extremes seized power and helped edge the world to yet another global war.

THE CHALLENGE OF SOVIET COMMUNISM

Well before the outbreak of the First World War, Russia was a nation teetering on the edge of revolution. In fact, in 1905, after the humiliating defeat of Russia by the forces of Japan (see page 24), the

Russian government came close to collapse as the state was besieged by a series of urban riots, peasant uprisings, military mutinies, and nationalist uprisings.

The Russian peasantry was destitute and needed land reform. The economy was in shambles and the difference in lifestyle between the rich and the poor was growing. On a day that came to be known as "Bloody Sunday," a peaceful parade of workers, led by a priest, attempted to present a list of moderate demands to the czar. They were gunned down by czarist soldiers. For many Russians, the image of their czar as a benevolent figure who cared about his people was forever swept away in the carnage of that day.

THE SEEDS OF REVOLUTION

Russia entered the First World War with great hopes of victory over Germany. However, when the czar led his nation into the cataclysm, he exposed his long suffering people to a series of bloody defeats that revealed too clearly the backwardness of the regime, the economic weakness of the state, and the incompetence of the leadership. By 1917, Russian soldiers had lost the will to fight and Russia was on its knees.

During the war, Grigori Rasputin, a peasant monk who claimed mystical powers, appeared to exert powerful political influence over the czar's German-born wife. While Czar Nicholas was away at the front, Russia fell into anarchy. Rasputin was brutally murdered but his personal excesses and ties to the monarchy further destroyed the image of the czar in the eyes of his people and provided much gossip for his critics.

At home, starving citizens began to riot for an end to the war and the desperate poverty. An expanding middle class felt it had little future and railed against the feudal and autocratic features of the czarist regime. Many of these people were well-educated and young. They wished to modernize Russia and usher in a period of political freedom, economic progress, and social justice.

Meanwhile, peoples in nations that had been conquered by Russia over centuries prior to the Great War were eager to claim their independence. National revolts were a continuing theme in Russian history. Most revolts were ruthlessly repressed, but the urge to throw off the Russian yoke was undying.

A REVOLUTION IN TWO STAGES

In 1917, Russia experienced two revolutions. They are known as the February Revolution and the October Revolution. In February, armaments workers in Petrograd went on strike. They were soon joined by workers in other cities. Army units also went on strike. The unrest spread quickly and the czar was forced to abdicate. This left the fate of the country in the hands of the Duma (the Russian parliament) and workers councils called "Soviets" that were formed in the major cities. This was an uneasy alliance and soon fell apart under the pressure of war, political and economic chaos, and deep mistrust.

When the Duma decided to continue the unpopular war, the split with the Soviets was wider and deeper. Alexander Kerensky took power in July of 1917, but was unable to reverse war losses or deal with the rising revolts among Russia's destitute peasantry.

Soon the Soviets fell under the control of a small band of highly organized Bolsheviks, led by Vladimir Lenin—a brilliant Marxist theoretician and tough minded political leader. He had spent much of his life in exile waiting for this moment to strike. Lenin, a master slogan-writer, promised "peace, bread, and power" to the Soviets. Brushing aside objections and fears, Lenin bullied and inspired his small party to seize power and create the first communist state on the face of the earth.

The Bolsheviks struck in October, 1917. This seizure of power was the first modern revolution and became a template for future revolutions during the twentieth century. With scarce resources and no real popular support, the Bolsheviks decapitated the Russian government by seizing the instruments of state power such as the telegraph and telephone offices, the railway stations, newspaper offices, and government institutions. Although Lenin and his associates were in power, the revolution had yet to spread beyond a few cities and a few vital buildings.

One of Lenin's first tasks was to end Russian involvement in the war. In March 1918, Russia was so desperate to leave the battle fields that it felt it had no alternative but to sign the Treaty of Brest-Litovsk. This Treaty forced Russia to acknowledge the independence of Ukraine, Poland, Finland, Latvia, Estonia, and Lithuania and to agree to substantial reparation payments. This treaty cost Russia over 30 per cent of its population and 75 per cent of its coal and iron ore. But with Germany's defeat later that year, the treaty became little more than a piece of paper.

Russian Civil War: War Communism 1917-1921

After the collapse of both the czar and the Russian Duma, an intense civil war erupted across Russia. Soviet historians refer to the period between 1917 and 1921 as the period of **War Communism**. This was a time of desperate struggle for the soul and soil of Russia. Dozens of factions battled each other for many different reasons. In general, the belligerent forces were identified as Red (Communist) or White (anti-Communist). The Red army was led

by Leon Trotsky, who built a dedicated and powerful military force. The Whites included a broad range of groups, including former czarist officers and units, rebellious nationalities such as Finns, Poles, and Estonians eager to throw off Russian control, and provincial warlords. This diversity made the White forces larger and more widespread but also unwieldy, disorganized, and undisciplined. The White Army was aided somewhat by the arrival of Allied forces including British, French, American, and Canadian forces. These former allies of Russia were keen to keep Russia in the war against Germany and to seal the fate of the Communist state.

Red Victory

The Red Army eventually triumphed due to the lack of coordinated leadership of their foes. When the Allied forces left in 1919, the Whites were weakened. Peasants in White territories were frustrated by the lack of land reform. On the other hand, Trotsky worked tirelessly to transform the Red Army into an organized, motivated, and effective fighting force. The Reds controlled the major cities and had easy access to supplies. A special secret police force called the *Cheka* unleashed a brutal attack on anti-communist elements. This "Red Terror" was a key element in the Red victory.

By 1921, the civil war was over. Although some peoples such as the Estonians, Latvians, and Lithuanians had gained independence, the vast territories of czarist Russia were now firmly under the control of the new Communist regime. The lasting result of the civil war and Allied intervention was a deep distrust on the part of the Communists toward all Western powers. The atmosphere of hostility and fear would permeate Russian attitudes about the Western nations for the next 70 years.

Profile Vladimir Ilich Lenin
(1870-1924)

Figure 3.2
Vladimir Ilich Lenin

Vladimir Ilich Ulyanov, or Lenin, the revolutionary name by which he was known, was the architect of one of the greatest political revolutions in the twentieth century. Lenin's story reveals the profound impact that one human being can have on the course of world history.

Lenin was born in 1870 to a family of the lower Russian nobility. His older brother Alexander was arrested, tried, and executed for plotting the assassination of the czar when Lenin was still a teenager. Lenin joined a group of Marxist revolutionaries. (Marx had argued that all history was the history of class struggle and that eventually the poor, oppressed workers would rise up and destroy their capitalist masters, the **bourgeoisie**. He foresaw a world where no classes would exist and all people would live and prosper in communal harmony and freedom.) Lenin was arrested and exiled to Siberia, where he married another revolutionary, Nadezdha Krupskaya.

In 1900, with his term of exile completed, Lenin and Krupskaya travelled to Western Europe to continue their underground revolutionary activities. In 1903, the Russian Marxists held a congress in Brussels and London to unify Russian Marxism. Instead, the congress served to split the Marxists into two groups—the **Mensheviks** and the **Bolsheviks**. Lenin headed the Bolsheviks.

When the First World War erupted, Lenin believed the end of czarist Russia was imminent. Under mounting pressure from military defeats and internal economic and political chaos, the czar abdicated in March 1917. Lenin and other exiled revolutionaries hurried back to Russia.

Lenin skilfully won support for the Bolsheviks with slogans promising peace, land, and bread. In the political chaos of the months following the czar's abdication, Lenin knew the time was ripe for action. "History will not forgive us if we do not act now," he urged. When the Bolsheviks did strike, in November 1917, they were victorious.

Consolidating the victory would take years. In 1918, thirty different groups claimed to rule Russia. However, Lenin, with unwavering support from Leon Trotsky and Joseph Stalin, and backed by the Red Army, defeated all rivals. Bourgeoisie, reactionaries, moderate socialists, and proletarians alike were eliminated to establish the communist regime. The czar, his wife, and five children were murdered in 1918 to prevent counter-revolutionary forces from rallying behind the monarchy.

In 1918, an attempt was made on Lenin's life when a member of a rival left-wing socialist group shot and seriously wounded him. The would-be assassin, Fanny Kaplan, and her collaborators were executed. A few years later, Lenin suffered a series of debilitating strokes, and in 1924 he died. His death set the stage for the emergence of Stalin and a far bloodier chapter in the history of the new communist nation.

Responding

1. What conditions allowed Lenin to seize power in Russia?
2. Although Lenin had been born into nobility and economic advantage, he subscribed to Marxist philosophy—a world without social classes. What do you think this says about Lenin's personality and values?

THE NEW COMMUNIST STATE

The First World War, the civil war, and Western intervention had a severe impact on the new communist state. Agricultural regions, particularly Ukraine, had been a battleground for years, resulting in a collapse of food production. Industry was completely disrupted; most factories lay idle. Mines had been destroyed and iron production had dropped to three per cent of 1913 figures.

The policies of state control introduced by the communist government almost paralysed the economy. The government assumed ownership of many aspects of the economy, such as mines, banks, and the oil industry, as well as any business employing more than ten workers. Foreign trade dried up; transportation broke down. Dissatisfaction spread. Strikes and protests added to the chaos. The government requisitioned all surplus food to feed the people in the cities. This in turn antagonized the peasants, who retaliated by growing only enough food for their own needs. A severe drought ushered in the great famine of 1921 to 1922 in which between 4 and 5 million people died.

By 1921, Lenin realized that the success of the communist revolution was threatened. It was necessary to build in incentives for workers, farmers, and industrial leaders to work harder and more efficiently. Thus the **New Economic Policy**, which incorporated capitalist practices, was introduced in 1921.

THE NEW ECONOMIC POLICY (NEP), 1921-1928

"Two steps forward, one step backward." Lenin realized that to save communism, it was necessary to temporarily step backwards and introduce aspects of private ownership and personal profit—that is, capitalism. Lenin announced at the Communist Party Congress in 1921 that the country would move backward towards a mixed economy—socialism blended with capitalism. Under the NEP, some ownership of small industries was permitted. Farmers could once again sell part of their produce for personal profit. With the reinstatement of these rights of private ownership, foreign investment in Russian industries was invited. As a result, agricultural production gradually increased, although not fast enough to prevent the devastating famine of 1921 to 1922. Industrial production also increased and in the period up to 1927 the Russian standard of living gradually improved. The easing of some of the economic hardships made the new government more acceptable to the people.

What was Russia like during this period? The following are points taken from Lenin's writings.

Religion and Ethics:

- Our program necessarily includes the propaganda of atheism. Religion is one of the forms of spiritual oppression, which everywhere weigh upon the masses who are crushed by continuous toil for others, by poverty and loneliness.
- We say that our morality is entirely subordinated to the interests of the class struggle.

Education:

- Give me four years to teach the children and the seed I have sown will never be uprooted.

The Press:

- The press should be not only a collective propagandist and a collective agitator, but also a collective organizer of the masses.

In 1922, the Communist Party created the Union of Soviet Socialist

Republics. The new Soviet Union at first consisted of the Russian, Ukrainian, White Russian, and Transcaucasian Soviet Socialist Republics (Georgia, Armenia, and Azerbaijan). Theoretically this was a voluntary federation of autonomous Soviet republics. In fact, the federation was dominated by the Russian majority and their Communist Party leaders.

In 1924 Lenin died just as his revolution was taking firm hold. Power was eventually seized by Joseph Stalin, who created a ruthless dictatorship that rapidly transformed the Soviet Union.

THE FIVE-YEAR PLANS

Beginning in 1928, the government embarked on a series of Five-Year Plans to greatly increase industrial production. If the USSR was to be strong enough to resist foreign attack, it would have to catch up with the rest of the industrial world. Goals were set and priorities established to increase production—more machinery was needed along with greater steel production, new factories, more oil production, and more electrical power plants. The policies were initially successful and the economy began to return to pre-war production levels. However, famine once again threatened the country. In January 1928, the government experienced a serious shortfall in the amount of grain needed to feed urban populations, due in part to hoarding by farmers.

In Stalin's view, several problems were emerging. First, the success of the NEP had created a new class of successful farmers—the **kulaks**, who were thriving under a semi-capitalist system and who had no use for a communist society. Second, Stalin recognized the potential danger from foreign intervention or invasion. Throughout Russian history, whenever Russia had been attacked by outside forces, its main weakness had been

Figure 3.3

In the Russian famine of 1921 to 1922, despite some government emergency relief, millions of people died of starvation.

technological inferiority. In order to preserve the only communist state in the world, the Soviets would have to increase their industrial and military power. The existing rate of industrial expansion was too slow; rapid, large-scale industrialization was needed. But where would Russians get the investment capital? They could not rely on foreign investors, and there was not sufficient revenue being generated within the USSR. Stalin concluded that the capital must come from agriculture; therefore, agriculture must be totally restructured for maximum efficiency and the profits expropriated for industrial development.

The Results of the First Two Five-Year Plans (1928-1938)

Stalin's attempt at creating a **command economy**—one in which all production decisions are made by a small group of political leaders—yielded two opposing results. The first was the collapse of Soviet agriculture as farmers who resisted the attempts at **collectivization** were eliminated. This led to the complete eradication of the wealthier peasants called kulaks. Agricultural production dropped sharply. The situation was further aggravated by the famine of 1933.

The policy of forced collectivization completely shattered the agricultural economy. Hardest hit was the Ukraine, once known as "the breadbasket of Europe". The loss of life was estimated at between six and seven million. Output began to recover slowly in the late 1930s with the help of improved farm machinery, an army of agricultural scientists, and strict control of the collectives.

The second result was more positive.

The Soviet Union was able to invest heavily in industrial development as well as in science, education, and the military. The number of people employed in agriculture declined sharply while educational opportunities expanded. As a result, there were more trained and educated professionals. New power plants and manufacturing facilities developed, spurring on the country's surge towards industrialization. The rapid transformation from a peasant agricultural society to a modern industrialized one was unprecedented. By the late 1930s Russia's industrial output exceeded that of France, Italy, and Japan. A new power arose from the ashes of the old czarist Russia.

Figure 3.4

In Stalin's Russia, his picture was prominently displayed everywhere. Why do you think dictators often ensure that their images are shown widely?

In Review

1. What were the major weaknesses of the czarist regime in Russia?

2. Summarize the terms of the Treaty of Brest-Litovsk. Do you support or reject Lenin's decision to withdraw Russia from the First World War? Explain your answer.

3. Summarize the problems faced by Russians during the period of War Communism (1918 to 1921).

4. How did the New Economic Policy attempt to revive the Russian economy?

5. What were the objectives and results of the first Five-Year Plans (1928 to 1932 and 1933 to 1938)?

6. In your opinion, was the economic progress made under Stalin worth the price paid by the Russian people? Explain.

The Rising Tide of Fascism

THE ORIGINS OF FASCISM

Fascism, an extreme but popular philosophy that still has adherents in the world today, spread across Europe in the turmoil of the post-war world and gained renewed life in the chaos of the Great Depression. It has been argued that its appeal lies in its simple answers to complex questions and in its strategy of finding and attacking scapegoats for the problems of millions.

The name, Fascism, originated in Italy and refers to the bundle of rods (called fasces) that were symbols of power in Ancient Rome. First used by Mussolini in Italy, the term came to describe a new political movement that professed an extreme right-wing ideology. In addition to Mussolini, it had adherents across the globe including Adolf Hitler in Germany and Francisco Franco in Spain. There were similar movements in most European countries and the fascist philosophy found believers in Britain under Oswald Mosley and in Canada under Adrien Arcand.

Principles and Policies

Although there was no international fascist organization, and different nations and leaders expressed varying beliefs and policies, there are a number of features that most fascist parties then and now exhibit. These include:

- **Extreme nationalism**
  Far beyond loyalty or love of country, fascist parties and leaders demand unquestioning loyalty and service to the nation-state. They tend to see the world in terms of good and evil and they are ostensibly on the side of good. There is a clear sense of superiority to others, which often involves returning a failed nation back to the glories of the past. For example, Mussolini constantly fanned belief in the greatness of Ancient Rome.

- **Racial purity**
  Closely allied to the sense of extreme nationalism is the concept of racial purity. Many fascists believe that intermarriage and ideas such as multiculturalism weaken and corrupt a nation. They promote separation of races and cultures.

- **Violence and war**
Fascists believe pacifism is a weakness and belligerence a virtue. Conciliators, moderates, and parliamentarians are generally despised as weak and lacking in courage and principles. Fascists have only disdain for the principles of democracy. Although willing to use democratic freedoms in order to win power, fascist regimes quickly move to shatter democratic political structures immediately after.

- **Devotion to a leader**
Fascist parties promote the cult of the leader and absolute obedience to that person's wishes. They swear loyalty to one person who becomes the voice of the nation and represents the entire power of the nation. Hitler became *Der Führer* (The Leader), Mussolini proclaimed himself *Il Duce* (The Leader), and Franco in Spain was lionized as *El Caudillo* (The Leader). Most fascist states and parties are organized into a rigid hierarchy in which everyone knows his/her place and duty.

- **Creation of Scapegoats**
Tragically, much of fascism's appeal is based on the identification, hatred, and oppression of "scapegoats," that is, people and groups unjustly blamed for a nation's ills or failures. The defeat of Germany in WWI was often blamed on communists, Weimar politicians, and Jews. Mussolini blamed socialists, communists, trade union leaders, and democrats for Italy's weakness after the First World War, and Franco attacked those who believed in the Republic rather than the old monarchy of Spain. This political strategy was to result in the deaths of millions of innocents and the unleashing of the horrors of the Holocaust (pages 123-127).

Italian Fascism:
"The rods represent the power of corporal punishment and the axe represents the power of capital punishment."

Spanish Fascism:
"The crossbow and arrows was adapted from the Spanish coat of arms and represented military might."

Figure 3.5

Symbols of fascism. Are you aware of any current political movements in Canada or abroad that seem to follow fascist principles?

WHY WAS FASCISM SUCCESSFUL?

The politics of 1920s Europe became increasingly polarized between communism on the left and fascism on the right. Many of the new nations created by the Treaty of Versailles had little experience with democratic politics. People looked to simple solutions and dramatic leaders. The depressed economic conditions in the aftermath of the First World War led to pessimism about the future. People were impatient with moderate policies that did not seem to deal effectively with important issues. In Britain, the Liberal Party faded as a political force in 1924; the Labour Party, a left-wing coalition, took power the same year. In Germany, while the Social Democrats remained strong, the forces of the right were gaining power. The most dramatic change, however, occurred in Italy where the extreme right, under Benito Mussolini, swept aside all democratic institutions and established a dictatorship in just a few years.

Post-War Italy

When the guns of war died down, Italy was on the victor's side but with little to show for having changed sides from the Triple Alliance to the Triple Entente. The Treaty of Versailles did not give much to Italy. The country was impoverished and in chaos. **Inflation** (an increase in prices and decrease in the value of currency) was only second to the **hyperinflation** that so ravaged Germany. Parliament was unstable and radical political movements fought in the streets. Benito Mussolini was to rise from the chaos and institute the first fascist regime in history. He would be a role model for a young Adolf Hitler dreaming of similar glory.

Benito Mussolini was born into a poor blacksmith's family in rural northern Italy. Although a capable student, he was often violent and twice was expelled from school when he stabbed other boys. As a young man, he dreamed of re-creating the might and glory of the ancient Roman Empire.

In 1914, as editor of a socialist newspaper, *Avanti*, he opposed Italy's entry into the First World War. But the next year he joined the popular pro-war movement and served as a soldier until wounded. In the chaos that followed the war, his star began to rise. He founded a right wing, paramilitary organization called the *Fasci di combattimento* (battle squads) in 1919. Members saluted, carried blackjacks (leather-covered lead batons) and knuckle dusters, and wore black shirts. This unofficial army burned the offices of left-wing newspapers and unions, broke up strikes,

and beat people at the political meetings of opponents.

Mussolini's opposition to communism won him the support of industrialists and wealthy landowners who feared a communist revolution similar to that in Russia. His claim to be "of the people" and his promise to restore order and greatness to Italy appealed to the working class. Those who opposed the Fascists were beaten and in some cases murdered. Before long the **Blackshirts**, Mussolini's unofficial army, dominated Italy's politics. As Italy faced the threat of more chaos and even civil war, Mussolini and 25 000 Blackshirts travelled across the country in the "March on Rome". He was then offered the prime ministership.

Once Mussolini had accepted King Victor Emmanuel's invitation to become Italy's prime minister in 1922, he wasted little time eliminating the opposition through intimidation and violence. In 1924, Giacomo Matteoti, leader of the United Socialist Party, was murdered. Mussolini later accepted responsibility. By 1925, he had control of the press, the police, and the government. No other political parties were allowed. Strikes and lockouts were illegal. Mussolini moved to halt Church disapproval of his regime by negotiating the **Lateran Treaties**, which recognized Roman Catholicism as the state religion of Italy and the Vatican City as an independent state within Italy itself. *Il Duce* was the unquestioned dictator of Italy. It was a dictatorship that would last for 21 years.

Under Mussolini, Italy did experience some economic recovery. Unemployment was reduced by public works schemes in housing, hydroelectric power, highways, and land reclamation. However, after 1929 the Great Depression hit Italy as it did most of the world, causing unemployment and hardship. It was a situation that gave

Figure 3.6
Benito Mussolini ruled Italy for 21 years: 1922 to 1943. He became an inspiration for the young Adolf Hitler. What is suggested about Mussolini by this photo?

Mussolini justification for total state control of the economy. With the rise of Hitler, Mussolini's international stature rose, as Hitler was a strong supporter of Mussolini. In 1945 Mussolini was executed by Italian partisans. His rule resulted in economic stagnation, political dictatorship, and military humiliation for the Italian people.

THE NAZI PARTY IN GERMANY

In Germany, even more than in Italy, fascism found mass support and flourished. Adolf Hitler, who led the German movement, initially admired Mussolini and incorporated many of the principles of Italian fascism into his Nazi doctrine. Like the Italian Fascists, the Nazis denounced democracy, liberalism, capitalism, and communism. They called for a powerful German state, strengthened by unity of purpose and decisive action. At every opportunity, they attempted to increase fear of communism and decrease confidence in democracy and the existing government.

Democratic Failure in Germany: The Weimar Republic

In 1918, the Kaiser was overthrown by German politicians eager for an end to the First World War. The monarchy was replaced with a **republic,** a state in which power rests with the people or their elected representatives, as opposed to a monarch or dictator. So weak was the support for the new regime that it had to be centred in Weimar, away from the turmoil of the former capital of Berlin. For some Germans, the Weimar government was forever tainted with the smell of defeat as it reluctantly signed the Treaty of Versailles. It was often referred to as "a democracy without democrats." Even though Germany was reeling from military defeats and economic collapse, a myth grew up that Weimar politicians had "stabbed Germany in the back." The birth of democratic rule had promised hope for Germany and peace for Europe, but the new government had little time to establish deep roots or enjoy the flowering of political success.

Threats to Weimar

The Treaty of Versailles: Few Germans supported the Treaty of Versailles. The "war guilt clause" seemed insulting to a nation that had suffered so much. The loss of territory, colonies, and national pride was a bitter experience. For a time, Germans suffered the dismemberment of their armed forces and occupation of parts of their country. In 1924, when the government was unable to make the huge reparation payments demanded by the treaty, French and Belgian forces occupied the Ruhr Valley, Germany's industrial heartland. For many, it seemed as if the new government was unable to protect German borders or German pride. This defeat and humiliation bred a thirst for revenge among some Germans.

Economic Instability: The stability of the new government was threatened by the enormity of the post-war task—the rebuilding of a devastated nation. The economy was in ruins; huge war debts and reparations payments overwhelmed the new treasury. In the early years, a wave of hyperinflation left the German mark almost worthless. The economy was so poor that in 1922 people resorted to the barter system to avoid paying a literal truckload of deutschmarks for a bottle of milk. Families used some of the bundles of worthless money as fuel. Children made kites out of the banknotes. The life savings of many people were wiped out and those on pensions, including many former soldiers, were reduced to poverty. The economic crisis turned to distrust, even hatred of the Weimar regime.

Political Instability: Germans did not have a long experience with democracy. Although some voting rights existed before the First World War, in general, the government was in the hands of a wealthy elite, led by a hereditary monarch. The shift to adult suffrage with dozens of new political parties was for some exhilarating, but for the majority, it was confusing and disappointing. Governments rose and fell with depressing regularity. Elections often descended into brutal propaganda campaigns and fist fights. New more radical parties such as the communists and fascists broke into open battle in the streets of the major cities. Political maneuvering left many citizens with a lack of respect for democracy and elected politicians. Too many political leaders seemed more concerned with their own welfare and presented few successes to the average German. Frustration and intrigue resulted in outright rebellions, often led by hordes of former soldiers disenchanted with their fate.

A Ray of Hope

In spite of all the massive challenges facing the Weimar regime, it would be wrong to see it as a doomed experiment in democracy. There was hope and promise and, for some years, measurable progress. The new government also found friends and helpers from the United States and other former enemies. When hyperinflation crushed the value of the German currency in the early 1920s and the nation could not continue its reparations payments, a team of financiers led by American banker Charles Dawes authored the **Dawes Plan**. This plan made it easier for Germany to make the repayments and even extended loans to help bolster the troubled currency. In 1929, in a new economic crisis, another American initiative called the **Young Plan** was devised to lower Germany's reparations payments by 75 per cent. Only one payment was made before Hitler cancelled all payments entirely.

Figure 3.7

The worthless German deutschmarks were used as cooking fuel, wallpaper, and even kites. What effect would this economic instability have had on the people's morale?

Internationally, Germany slowly became an accepted member of the world community. In 1925, Germany was invited to join the League of Nations after signing the **Locarno Pact**, a series of agreements to guarantee the borders of former combatants such as Germany, France, and Belgium. (Although Germany did not fully accept the borders with Poland and Czechoslovakia, it did promise to pursue any changes peacefully.) In 1928, it signed the **Kellogg-Briand Pact**, an agreement that outlawed war among the signatories.

Germany made particular progress economically and within the world community under the leadership of Gustav Stresemann. Stresemann served in a variety of positions in the Weimar period, including foreign minister and chancellor. His efforts to rebuild Germany economically and to establish a true peace earned him the Nobel Peace Prize. Tragically, he died in 1929 at the outset of the world depression that would sound the death knell for the young German Republic.

The Fall of Weimar

The hard-won but fragile progress of the Weimar republic was shattered by the unforeseen onslaught of the **Great Depression** that erupted from the United States, the world's wealthiest and most powerful nation. Within months, the German economy was reeling. Business failed, industries closed their doors, and unemployment levels soared. Political tensions rose and the electorate looked for an end to a seemingly endless series of crises. Elections produced street battles and minority governments. Depression, social collapse, international humiliation, and political chaos destroyed the fabric of the new democracy. The final blow was delivered by Adolf Hitler, once one of the millions of unemployed former

soldiers wandering the streets of the failed republic. Within a dozen years, Hitler would lead Germany to an even greater defeat in the Second World War.

THE RISE OF HITLER

Adolf Hitler was not born in Germany, but in a small town in Austria. His early years were marred by the deaths of his brother and sister and the abuse of a drunken, overbearing father. He was a failure at school and left as a drop-out. Afterwards he became a vagrant, working at menial jobs. He was a bitter, desperate young man with a bleak future.

When the First World War broke out, Hitler rushed to join the Austrian military, but was rejected as unfit. He moved to Germany where he successfully enlisted in the army. For Hitler, the war was a great adventure. He had a good war record, earning medals for his service. But the return to civilian life meant a return to poverty and obscurity. At the time, Germany was boiling over with discontent and revolutionary fervour. Hitler threw himself with vigour and determination into this political storm. He joined a tiny political party of other disenchanted, ruthless young men and soon found an outlet for his energy and ideas.

As leader of the **National Socialist German Workers Party (Nazi)**, Hitler skilfully and purposefully brought his movement into the forefront of German politics. He provided organization, discipline, and a clear political program. He vilified the German democrats as spineless traitors. He attacked the hated Treaty of Versailles and boldly promised to shred it to pieces. Hitler preached about the **Aryans** (Caucasians not of Jewish descent; usually described as blonde with blue eyes), a "master race" destined to rule "inferior" peoples. His hatred included visible minorities, people with disabilities, and homosexuals. However, he unleashed his most vitriolic attacks on Jews. Building on long-standing European prejudices, he blamed the Jewish population for all of Germany's problems, from disease to defeat in the First World War.

Hitler was a powerful orator able to hold his audiences entranced for hours. His speeches drew larger and larger crowds and the Nazis began to hold spectacular rallies and marches. Many German youths were attracted to the Nazis, who provided a little food, some shelter, an impressive uniform, and pocket money.

Many Germans feared that rising communist strength, strikes, and revolts would lead to a Bolshevik Revolution like that in Russia. The Nazis were the only political party to boldly confront communism. Hitler seemed to be a safe bulwark against the communist threat.

The popularity of the Nazi Party rose as the Great Depression quashed any hopes of a post-war German recovery. Blaming everything on the Jews, communists, democracy, and Versailles, Hitler gathered increasing attention—and votes. The electoral gains were stunning: in 1928, 12 seats; in 1930, 107 seats; in 1932, 230 seats. In the growing confusion and polarization of German politics, Hitler made strategic alliances with elements in the army and big businesses that were eager to crush the "red menace" and rebuild German might.

By 1933, Adolf Hitler was the leader of the most powerful political force in Germany, but still not the leader of a majority party. In the political chaos of the time, no one seemed capable of running the government. In 1932, two chancellors tried and failed to command a majority in the Reichstag. The chancellorship of Germany seemed too important to go to such a radical upstart as Hitler. But by skilful negotiation with the

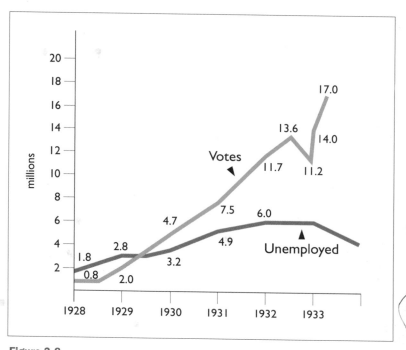

Figure 3.8

The Relationship Between Unemployment and Votes for the Nazis. What appears to be the relationship between the employment rate and support for the Nazis?

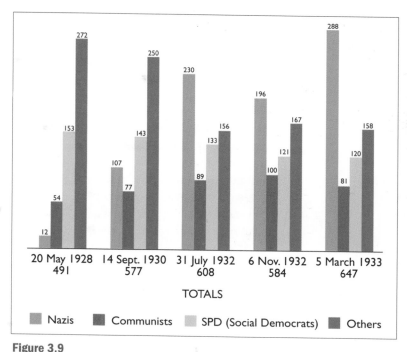

Figure 3.9

Nazis at the Polls, 1928 to 1933. Study the graph carefully and describe any patterns you see.

aging President Hindenburg, Hitler, as leader of a coalition of right wing parties, had himself appointed chancellor. After all, he did lead one of the most successful parties in the Reichstag. Most political observers felt that Hitler would soon prove to be a weak leader or be controlled by the business and military elite. They were wrong. It was the end of democracy in Germany.

HITLER'S GERMANY

After becoming Chancellor in January 1933, Hitler took immediate steps to establish a totalitarian state. Within two months, after failing to win an absolute majority in the last free elections, the Reichstag passed the **Emergency Decree** and the **Enabling Law**. These laws allowed Hitler to suspend the Weimar constitution and rule by decree, as opposed to parliamentary consent. As a result, Hitler had virtually unlimited power. All political parties, except the Nazis, were abolished. When President Hindenburg died, Hitler combined the offices of president and chancellor. In 1934 during the "Night of the Long Knives" Hitler turned on his friends and associates and murdered those he felt might be rivals or challengers. A secret police force—the **Gestapo**—was created. Concentration camps were set up to hold prisoners and "undesirables". The judiciary and civil service were purged of possible dissidents. Jews were removed from the universities and public service. Anyone could be arrested without charges and imprisoned without a trial.

Nazi Persecution of the Jews

As Hitler's power was consolidated, the Nazis launched their campaign of persecution against Jews. The **Nuremburg Laws** of 1935 deprived Jews of German citizenship and outlawed marriage between Jews and Aryans. Jews were not permitted to practise law or medicine or to perform music. Many Jewish shops were closed, synagogues were shut down, and properties were confiscated.

The situation escalated on 7 November 1938, after a German diplomat in Paris was assassinated by a Jewish youth. Two nights later, on November 9, Jewish communities across Germany were attacked. This night of terror became known as **Kristallnacht**—the night of broken glass. Synagogues, homes, and shops went up in flames. Jews were arrested, beaten, and even murdered. The Jewish community was forced to pay an atonement fine to repair the damages that resulted from *Kristallnacht*. They could no longer own stores or businesses or engage in trade of any kind. Jewish children were banned from attending school. Places of public entertainment, culture, and sports were off limits. Driving licences were revoked. All Jews were forced to wear yellow stars, symbolizing the Star of David, on their clothing as identification. Thousands were arrested and imprisoned. Still more were forced into **ghettos**, and then ultimately into the Nazi death camps.

Hitler's Economic Policies

At the time Hitler rose to power in 1933, Germany was in the midst of the Depression. World trade was at a standstill and the American loans that had allowed Germany to make reparation payments had ended. Hitler immediately set to work to eliminate unemployment and make Germany economically self-sufficient. Vast public works and rearmament programs absorbed the unemployed. German factories started manufacturing war materials; housing programs were begun; highways were built across the country; and, after 1935, the armed forces were greatly increased through conscription. Strict government control aimed at minimizing imports and maximizing exports substantially strengthened the economy. Working to reduce Germany's need to import raw materials, German scientists developed synthetic rubber, plastics, and textiles. These decisive policies and the positive results they yielded won Hitler many supporters, both inside and outside of Germany.

Foreign Policy

In 1936, Hitler announced his ultimate goal: to mobilize the armed forces and the economy for war within four years. State control of industry, commerce, and the military made sure these aims were implemented.

Hitler's foreign policy was geared towards the destruction of the Treaty of Versailles, rejection of the new League of Nations, the annexation of all German areas in Europe into Germany, expansion to the East, and the destruction of communism. His foreign policy rested on full-scale rearmament that would lead to German supremacy on the battlefields. The stage was set for another world war.

Voices Fascism in Germany

Adolf Hitler has been called many things— "the greatest demagogue in history," "a madman." Whatever the reality, he had a tremendous effect upon the history of the twentieth century. His voice was mesmerizing, strident, and all too prophetic. Hitler was to be the touchstone that unleashed forces that ultimately led to the deaths of 50 million people. As you read these quotations, consider how a person like Hitler could rise to power. Was it due to events and desperate times or personal charisma?

"One truth which must always be borne in mind is that the majority can never replace the man."

—Adolf Hitler, *Mein Kampf*, 1925

"The great masses of the people... will more easily fall victims to a big lie than to a small one."

—Adolf Hitler, *Mein Kampf*

"The importance of physical terror against the individual and the masses... became clear to me."

—Adolf Hitler, *Mein Kampf*

"The Marxists taught—if you will not be my brother, I will bash your skull in. Our motto shall be—if you will not be a true German, I will bash your skull in."

—Adolf Hitler, 1933

Responding

1. What ideas seem to dominate Hitler's thinking?
2. How might opponents have countered Hitler's message?
3. Do Hitler's views have any appeal today? Explain.
4. What qualities do you think would make a leader attractive to the general population? Why do you think certain speakers seem to have an uncanny ability to captivate and influence their audience?

Skill Path

Creating Concept Maps

When visiting a large city you have never been in before, it is easy to become inundated by information: new street names, buildings, people, sounds and transit systems, not to mention local customs and procedures with which you may not be familiar. All of this can be very disorienting, as well as distressing. You may feel a similar sort of disorientation when you are studying a new history topic—one rich with personalities, place names, events and, of course, dates. One method of gaining your bearings and keeping this information straight in your mind is by using a map.

Concept maps are organizers that graphically link ideas in a logical way. You could use a concept map when a question asks you to criticize or judge a topic or issue. Justifying and proving require a visual display of your reasoning towards a conclusion you have reached. When you are asked to relate ideas, you must show connections between things—how one influences the other.

These maps can help you both in the short term to understand and analyse a topic, and in the long term to prepare for your exam. Creating concept maps is more effective than simply reading your notes because it forces you to interact with the material and discover how it all ties together.

Step One: Decide on Your Objective

After reading about a topic in history, decide on what you want to accomplish through the use of a concept map. Do you want to define a certain element or idea? Analyse a problem or issue? Or, organize various elements of the topic in a logical structure? A different type of concept map can be used to help you accomplish each of these goals. The following diagrams will give you a basic outline for each.

A) A concept map as a defining tool (using the example, Fascism)

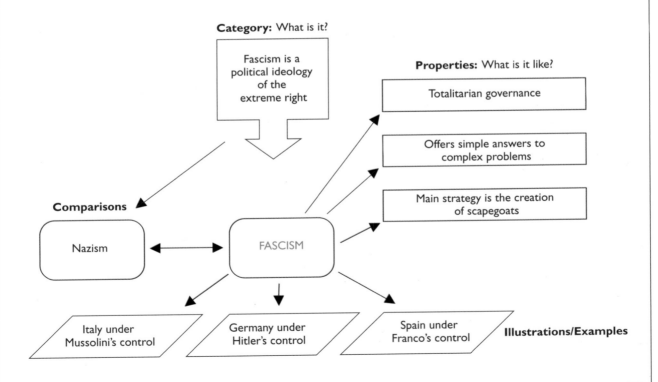

B) A concept map as an outline for problem solving

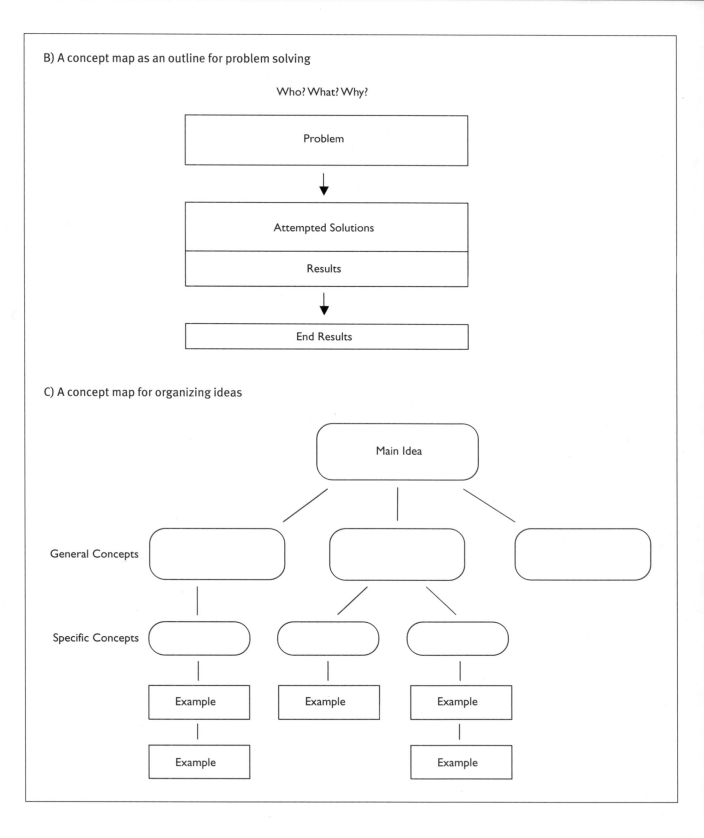

C) A concept map for organizing ideas

Step Two: Identify the Central Idea or Issue

No matter what your purpose is in creating a concept map, you must start by identifying the central idea or issue. This main idea should be worded very concisely. Print it in capitals or highlight it in some way on the page so that you are constantly reminded of it as you are filling in the rest of the map. For example, say you want to define the ideology of fascism. Write this word in capitals at the top of a blank sheet of paper and draw a box around it. Next, from memory, or by referring back to your notes or textbook, begin drawing an arrow out from that main box to a new box or circle containing a simple definition.

Step Three: Expand Your Links

A concept map is used to link boxes in an organized way so that each bit of information expands on the previous link. So, for the example, try brainstorming comparisons to other ideologies you've learned about. You might add on more arrows and boxes to give examples of fascist countries. From there you could expand the information to include such details as the names of the leaders of each of these fascist states and the dates during which they ruled. More branches could outline the indigenous characteristics of fascism in various countries.

Step Four: Apply Emphasis

As you are adding links, you may also want to highlight the most pertinent boxes and arrows. You could do this with colour, or different types of fonts, etc. Also, consider adding pictures or drawing graphics if they will help you make a point. Such emphasis will provide visual clues to help jog your memory later, when you use the map to study for exams.

Practise Your Skill

1. Use a concept map to explain one of the following situations based on material studied in this chapter.
- An evaluation of Stalin's Five-Year Plans
- Analysis of the fall of the Weimar Republic
- Comparison of Hitler and Mussolini as fascist dictators
- The causes and results of the Great Depression
- An assessment of the League of Nations and collective security

2. In what way is the political spectrum presented on page 68 a concept map? How effective is it in your opinion?

In Review

1. Summarize the central beliefs of the Fascists.

2. What factors explain the rise to power of Mussolini in Italy and Hitler in Germany?

3. How did the Emergency Decree and the Enabling Law prepare the way for a totalitarian state in Germany?

4. What measures did Hitler take to tighten his grip on Germany?

5. How did the Nazis persecute the Jewish citizens of Germany?

6. What were the results of Nazi economic policies in Germany?

7. In your opinion, how should the world have regarded the rise of the Fascists?

The United States in the 1920s and 1930s

THE RETURN TO ISOLATIONISM

One of the great disappointments in Europe following the peace of 1919 was the American return to **isolationism**. While Woodrow Wilson was optimistically forging the League of Nations in France, his support at home was crumbling. Americans were eager to return to peace and prosperity and did not wish further entanglements with European nations.

This desire for isolation was due in part to the fact the United States was a nation of immigrants, many of whom had emigrated in order to escape the corruption and hostilities of Europe. There was also a long-standing American suspicion about the under-handed politics of the Old World. Membership in the League of Nations was perceived as a permanent tie to the complicated affairs of Europe. Consequently, the United States Senate refused to ratify the Treaty of Versailles and rejected the bill to join the League of Nations.

In the US elections of 1920, Warren Harding and the Republican Party won by a landslide. Despite the fact that he won the Nobel Prize for Peace that year, President Wilson was not even re-nominated to lead the Democratic Party in the election.

THE STOCK MARKET CRASH OF 1929

September 13, 1929 was a day to remember on the New York Stock Exchange. It was the last good day for the booming stock market of the 1920s. Over the next month stock prices fluctuated drastically. No one knew why or what to do about it. Then, on October 24—"Black Thursday"—the stock prices collapsed as some 13 million shares were sold. Panic set in as everyone wanted to get out of the market before it dropped even lower. The following Tuesday—October 29—another record was set as 16 million shares were sold and prices dropped even further. The stock market had crashed. Millions of people who had gone from "rags to riches" in the new industrial economy found that the process was indeed reversible.

Causes of the Great Depression

Although the stock market crash got the headlines, it was only one of a number of factors that led to the Great Depression. Although the world's biggest economy had largely benefited from the First World War, the boom of the "Roaring Twenties" was misleading. America had serious problems that were to burst the illusory "bubble" of progress. These problems included:

- **Unequal distribution of wealth**: It is estimated that only five per cent of Americans owned nearly 33 per cent of the nation's wealth. Nearly 70 per cent of the population was at or below the level of a decent living wage. Few people could purchase the goods streaming from the factories.
- **Over-production of goods and services**: People seemed to think that rapid growth would go on forever. As a result, factories and businesses expanded quickly and without restraint in an attempt to increase their capacity to make more and more. The problem was that they were producing more goods than could realistically be sold or consumed.
- **Debt fuelled the growth of businesses**: Individuals also took out loans for purchases. Much of the stock market boom was made "on margin" or with loans. High levels of credit "busted" companies and individuals when the economy slowed down and the debt collectors came knocking.

- **Drought**: In North America's western regions, unprecedented drought and grasshoppers destroyed much of the agricultural economy. Farmers lost their farms and headed for an uncertain future in the cities where unemployment was soaring.
- **International tariffs**: High tariffs between nations created barriers to trade. As each nation faced an economic downturn, it rushed to raise trade barriers to protect its own industries and workers. This strangled economic growth even further.
- **Government inaction**: At first, few governments were prepared to intervene in the economy. They preferred to let the market provide the answers. This probably prolonged the Depression. In some European nations, the Depression led to the rise of more radical parties, such as communists and fascists who demanded an end to the economic crisis and promised immediate relief. Although the United States did not follow this path, the American President, Franklin Delano Roosevelt, won an election on the promise of very forceful and dramatic government intervention.

The effect of the stock market crash was devastating. Thousands of businesses went bankrupt, putting countless people out of work. With rising unemployment and no unemployment insurance, people could not buy goods; consequently, other businesses suffered. As profits shrank, more companies laid off workers, and a vicious downward economic cycle resulted. By 1932, unemployment reached 25 per cent; 15 million American workers were without jobs.

In 1933, Franklin Roosevelt was sworn in as president, reassuring the American public that "The only thing we have to fear is fear itself…. I am prepared to recommend the measures that a stricken nation in the midst of a stricken world may require." He proceeded to enlist the services of the best minds in the country to find a way out of the Depression. During his first term in office, Roosevelt announced the **New Deal**—a comprehensive program of "relief, recovery, and reform" for Americans. Included in the New Deal was legislation dealing with public welfare, agriculture, public utilities, housing, industry, and transportation. Ultimately, however, it was the Second World War and the need for armaments that actively stimulated the economy and brought an end to the Great Depression.

In Canada, where the economy depended mainly on exports of farm products and raw materials, the Depression hit extremely hard. Wheat prices plunged, markets shrank, and the economy of the prairies collapsed. The situation was made even worse by drought, dust storms, and crop failure. In Saskatchewan, two-thirds of the population was forced to go on welfare. Across Canada, farms and homes were lost and businesses were closed. Soup kitchens and relief camps were common. Men "riding the rails" on the tops of freight cars became a familiar sight, travelling from one part of the country to another in search of work that wasn't there.

WORLD DEPRESSION

The economic recovery of Europe after the First World War was largely spurred by the strong American economy. The crash of 1929, therefore, had international repercussions. In the mid-1920s the United States had only three per cent of the world's population. Yet it accounted for 46 per cent of the world's industrial output, 70 per cent of the world's oil, and 40 per cent of the world's coal.

When this powerful engine of growth slowed down, the effects were felt around the world. The most immediate impact was an end to foreign lending and pressure to call in existing loans. Between 1931 and 1938 American banks received $6.6 billion from Europe. This massive withdrawal of funds had a negative impact in Europe. The political implications of the economics of the 1930s were seen in the rise of fascism and the movement toward war.

Profile Franklin D. Roosevelt
(1882-1945)

Figure 3.10
Franklin D. Roosevelt

Franklin Delano Roosevelt (FDR) was one of the most popular presidents in American history. He struck a powerful chord with Americans from all walks of life, and his years in office resulted in sweeping changes.

"I pledge you, I pledge myself to a new deal for the American people."

— FDR in his acceptance speech at the Democratic Convention in Chicago, 2 July 1932

Roosevelt was born into a wealthy old American family. While in university, he married Eleanor Roosevelt, a niece of former president Theodore Roosevelt.

Money and family connections soon drew Roosevelt into politics, first as a state senator, then as Assistant Secretary of the Navy. His promising career was almost finished in 1921, however, when he contracted polio. Although he recovered, he was never again able to stand or walk without support.

Roosevelt won the governorship of New York state in 1928. Four years later he won the Democratic presidential nomination. In 1933, during the dark days of the Depression, Roosevelt was sworn in as president of the United States, and he moved swiftly to deal with the economic crisis. He had pledged a New Deal with relief programs, job creation, and financial assistance. He maintained an approachable, down-to-earth image, despite the fact that he came from a world of wealth and affluence. His famous radio "fireside chats" endeared him to large segments of the American public.

Increasingly, he was drawn to the events unfolding in Europe. As war loomed, he had to balance his country's traditional isolationism against his own convictions that the United States was a great power with global interests and responsibilities. With the outbreak of the Second World War in 1939, Roosevelt promised to help Britain with "all aid short of war." When Japan attacked the American naval base at Pearl Harbor on 7 December 1941, the United States was drawn directly into the conflict. America declared war on Japan. On December 11, Germany and Italy declared war on the United States. Roosevelt was now free to unleash America's industrial and military power on its enemies.

The strain of the war and the pressures of holding down the presidency for an unprecedented 12 years ultimately proved to be too much. In 1945, Roosevelt died suddenly of a cerebral hemorrhage. Roosevelt's leadership in the Depression and the Second World War contributed greatly to the United States' new superpower status in the world community in 1945.

Responding

1. What was the secret of Roosevelt's popularity?
2. How did he influence American foreign policy?

THE TREATY SYSTEM VS. COLLECTIVE SECURITY

One of the most important political issues following the First World War was how to maintain world peace. Most European leaders maintained a nationalist point of view. They argued that each nation was best able to pursue and protect its own national interests and that **national security** could best be achieved through individual military power or the forging of powerful alliances. Thus the big powers of Europe would act as a world police force to keep the smaller nations in line.

Signs of Progress

After the First World War, Woodrow Wilson's idealism resonated for many who survived the horrors of 1914 to 1918. Many people resolved to make the world a better place and to end the scourge of war.

Figure 3.11

What treaty is represented by the 'Treaty of Peace'? What is the main point of the cartoon?

Pacifism, the belief that disputes should be settled by peaceful means, grew as an international movement against warfare. Diplomacy resulted in a broad range of agreements designed to reduce tension and promote peaceful resolution of international issues. For example, the Dawes Plan and the Young Plan (as discussed on pages 79-80) were aimed at helping Germany regain economic stability, while the Locarno Pact and the Kellogg-Briand Pact (also known as the Pact of Paris), were attempts at international peace and non-violent border negotiations.

There were also encouraging steps along the difficult road to disarmament. For example, the League of Nations Disarmament Conference of 1932 invited 60 nations to find ways to disarm.

THE LEAGUE OF NATIONS

Woodrow Wilson believed that global collective security should be an international responsibility maintained under the auspices of the League of Nations. The underlying assumption was that the world is inter-dependent and that national self-interest must give way to the common interests of all nations. Security for individual nations would be achieved through group solidarity. In theory, no nation would dare to attack another because that would violate international law, resulting in punishment or sanctions.

While this argument seemed theoretically sound, in practice there were problems. Perhaps the biggest was the question of enforcement. Who would send troops to stop an attack or enforce a punishment? The League of Nations was a collection of independent states, not an independent body with specific laws or a police force to enforce those laws. The only power it held was the power allocated to it by its members. And how much power would they be willing to give? The League had three types of **sanctions** in its arsenal for world peace.

1. **Moral Sanctions** — World opinion might be used to encourage nations to follow League decisions or refrain from aggressive activity. In the end, this meant talk rather than action.

2. **Economic Sanctions** — In theory, the threat of being cut off from supplies and trade by members of the League was a powerful non-violent way to bring pressure on nations to amend their ways. However, these were seldom effective. When a Canadian diplomat suggested using oil sanctions to halt Mussolini, he was not supported by his own government. Mussolini himself declared "Oil means war!" The League talked but did little. During the Depression, few nations were prepared to take any actions that would weaken trade and commerce further.

3. **Military Sanctions** — Potentially the most powerful international weapon to stop aggression, military sanctions—which involve monitoring and restricting the importing of weapons and military-related technology— were never used by the League. Since many nations were not in the League, it was difficult to mobilize the forces required. The idea of sending an international force across the globe was still new. With the brutal memories of the First World War still fresh in so many minds, it is perhaps understandable why few leaders would be prepared to actually initiate yet another war.

The absence of the United States, the Soviet Union, and later Japan and Germany from the League of Nations meant that there was more power *outside* the international organization than inside. Without the major powers to back its decisions, the League had little clout. Nations determined to expand their territory found it easy to ignore the League and simply forge ahead with their plans. This perceived weakness only encouraged Adolf Hitler in his expansionist plans.

Soon after the First World War ended, the new League of Nations was faced with solving international disputes. The League experienced some success but without powerful nations such as the US and USSR, it was difficult to control dictators such as Mussolini and Hitler. When the League failed to prevent Italy's attack on Ethiopia and Japanese aggression in China, the stage was set for yet another global confrontation.

The China Incident: Manchuria 1931

Manchuria, in northern China, had an abundance of rich mineral and timber resources that Japan wanted to exploit. In September 1931, Japanese troops guarding the South Manchurian Railway alleged that Chinese saboteurs had attempted to blow up a section of the track. On the pretext of protecting the railway, they seized control of the nearby cities of Mukden and Changchun. Within a few months, the Japanese army, acting on its own initiative, had captured all the main cities of Manchuria.

The Chinese leader, Jiang Jie Shi (Chiang Kai-shek), appealed for help from the League of Nations. In 1933, after a lengthy investigation, the League recommended that Japan withdraw from Manchuria. But while the League condemned Japan it did not act, and Japan simply withdrew from the League. The militarist element in Japan gained great prestige from this successful and profitable gamble. As a result, expansion by conquest became a preferred Japanese policy.

Mussolini's Seizure of Ethiopia 1935-1936

Mussolini dreamed of rebuilding the might of the ancient Roman Empire. Part of this dream was to capture new territories in Africa. He settled on the ancient kingdom of Abyssinia (Ethiopia). Italy had invaded this land before in 1895 and met defeat. Mussolini wanted to avenge that defeat. In 1935, Italian forces poured into Abyssinia from Italian colonies in Africa. A modern army of tanks and aeroplanes savagely hurled itself against people equipped with old weapons and spears. Much of the world was outraged by this blatant aggression. The Emperor of Ethiopia, Haile Selassie, visited the League of Nations and begged for help. The League threatened economic sanctions against Italy. When Mussolini refused to withdraw and even threatened war if sanctions on oil imports were imposed, the League backed down. Although the people fought a desperate battle against overwhelming odds, by 1936, Ethiopia was swallowed up by Italian forces. Later Mussolini admitted, "If the League had extended economic sanctions to oil, I would have had to withdraw from Abyssinia within a week."

This last failure was, for many, the final nail in the League's coffin. The dream of world peace and collective security was dead.

In Review

1. Why did Americans reject the League of Nations and return to isolationism?

2. Explain the major causes of the Great Depression. In your view, which was most important? Why?

3. How did the collapse of the US economy affect the world economy and the drift toward war?

4. Explain the main ideas behind the internationalist and nationalist view of maintaining world peace. Outline your reaction to these ideas.

5. Explain the important League failures that helped encourage aggressive leaders and nations.

Summary

As the dust settled on the European landscape following the war, many nations began or continued intense internal struggles over political ideologies. Leaders from all points on the political spectrum battled for power.

The low morale in many nations was compounded by the desperation of the Great Depression, and these factors helped the rise of dictators such as Stalin in Russia, Hitler in Germany, and Mussolini in Italy. Although these leaders claimed to have all the solutions to their country's woes, the majority of people continued to suffer as tensions rose. It wasn't long before defeated and humiliated Germany turned to revenge and began a series of aggressive acts, which threatened world security.

So, after a failed attempt at international peace through the signing of the Treaty of Versailles and the establishment of the League of Nations, the all-too-brief respite from fighting came to an end. Countries in Europe, Asia, and North America began to drift once again towards world conflict.

Viewpoints

ISSUE: Was Stalin a builder or a destroyer?

Background

As dictator, Stalin embarked on a dramatic policy of rapid economic reform. He cast aside Lenin's NEP policies and centralized all economic and political power in himself, using it to transform the Soviet Union within a few years. However, change came at a terrible price. Those who resisted Stalin's reforms were eliminated. The Soviet Union became a state characterized by repression, fear, torture, threats, mass trials, imprisonment, and execution. Millions died as a result of Stalin's **purges**—Bolsheviks, government leaders, army and police officers, even members of Stalin's own family. No group escaped the terror.

The first document below is a speech given by Stalin to a group of industrial managers responsible for the success of his Five-Year Plans. In this important speech, Stalin outlines his goals and why he feels they are necessary. He reveals his views on why Russia must be strong. The second reading is by George F. Kennan, an American diplomat and academic. Kennan focuses on the violent methods Stalin used to achieve these goals and reforms, and the impact this had on the Soviet people. Consider how Stalin's aspirations for his country should be judged in view of his methods for attaining them. On the whole was he a champion of the Soviet people or a destroyer?

Read these two viewpoints carefully and answer the questions that follow. (You may want to refer to the Skill Path "Analysing a Reading" on page 14 before beginning.)

Stalin on the industrialization of Russia

It is sometimes asked whether it is not possible to slow down the tempo somewhat, to put a check on the movement. No, comrades, it is not possible! The tempo must not be reduced! On the contrary, we must increase it as much as is within our powers and possibilities. This is dictated to us by our obligations to the workers and peasants of the USSR. This is dictated to us by our obligations to the working class of the whole world.

To slacken the tempo would mean falling behind. And those who fall behind get beaten. But we do not want to be beaten. No, we refuse to be beaten! One feature of the history of old Russia was the continual beatings she suffered because of her backwardness. She was beaten by the Mongol khans. She was beaten by the Turkish beys. She was beaten by the Swedish feudal lords. She was beaten by the Polish and Lithuanian gentry. She was beaten by the British and French capitalists. She was beaten by the Japanese barons. All beat her because of her backwardness, military backwardness, cultural backwardness, political backwardness, industrial backwardness, agricultural backwardness. They beat her because to do so was profitable and could be done with impunity. Do you remember the words of the pre-revolutionary poet: "You are poor and abundant, mighty and impotent, Mother Russia." Those gentlemen were quite familiar with the verses of the old poet. They beat her, saying: "You are abundant; so one can enrich oneself at your expense. They beat her, saying: "You are poor and impotent '" so you can be beaten and plundered with impunity. Such is the law of the exploiters-to beat the backward and the weak. It is the jungle law of capitalism. You are backward, you are weak-therefore you are wrong; hence, you can be beaten and enslaved. You are mighty-therefore you are right; hence, we must be wary of you.

That is why we must no longer lag behind.

In the past we had no fatherland, nor could we have one. But now that we have overthrown capitalism and power is in our hands, in the hands of the people, we have a fatherland, and we will defend its independence. Do you want our socialist fatherland to be beaten and to lose its independence? If you do not want this you must put an end to its backwardness in the shortest possible time and develop genuine Bolshevik tempo in building up its socialist system of economy. There is no other way. That is why Lenin said on the eve of the October Revolution: "Either perish, or overtake and outstrip the advanced capitalist countries."

We are fifty or a hundred years behind the advanced countries. We must make good this distance in ten years. Either we do it, or we shall be crushed.

Source: J. V. Stalin, *Problems of Leninism*, (Moscow: Foreign Languages Publishing House, 1953) pp. 454-458.

George Kennan, historian and diplomat

…We know pretty well today what at one time we could only suspect; that this was a man of incredible criminality, of a criminality effectively without limits; a man apparently foreign to the very experience of love, without pity or mercy; a man in whose entourage no one was ever safe; a man whose hand was set against all that could not be useful to him at the moment; a man who was most dangerous of all to those who were his closest collaborators in crime… he liked to be the sole custodian of his own secrets…. We are confronted with a record beside which the wildest murder mystery seems banal. I cannot attempt to list the man's crimes. Trotsky seriously charged that Stalin poisoned Lenin…. He evidently either killed his young wife in 1932, or drove her to suicide in his presence. There is every probability… that it was Stalin himself who inspired the murder of his Number Two in the Party, S.M. Kirov, in 1934. How many others… died as a result of Stalin's malignant ministrations, we can only guess. There are at least half a dozen… the writer Maxim Gorky…. That the man who split Trotsky's skull with an axe in Mexico City in 1940 did so at Stalin's instigation is beyond question. By way of response, apparently, to what seems to have been some opposition to his purposes on the part of the seventeenth Party Congress in 1934, Stalin killed, in the ensuing purges of 1936 to 1938, 1108 out of a total 1966 members of the Congress. Of the Central Committee elected at that Congress and still officially in office, he killed 98 out of 139—a clear majority, that is, of the body from which ostensibly he drew his authority. These deaths were only a fraction, numerically, of those which resulted from the purges of those years. Most of the victims were high officials of the Party, the army, or the Soviet government apparatus.

All this is aside from the stupendous brutalities which Stalin perpetrated against the common people; notably in the process of collectivization, and also in some of his wartime measures… [deaths run] into the millions. But this is not to mention the broken homes, the twisted childhoods, and the millions of people who were half-killed; who survived these ordeals only to linger on in misery, with broken health and broken hearts.

Source: *Russia and the West Under Stalin and Lenin* by George F. Kennan. Copyright © 1960 by James Hotchkiss, Trustee. By permission of Little, Brown and Company.

Analysis and Evaluation

1. According to Stalin, why could the Soviet Union not afford to slow the tempo of change?
2. What did Stalin mean by the "jungle law of capitalism"?
3. Evaluate Stalin's views. Are his goals attainable?
4. Why does Kennan accuse Stalin of criminality?
5. In your view, is Kennan fair to Stalin? Explain.
6. Is political violence ever justified in your opinion? Explain.
7. Decide which of the viewpoints you tend to support and explain why. If you support neither, explain your opinion on the issue. Be sure to use specific information from this textbook, the readings, and other sources to support your position.

Chapter Analysis

MAKING CONNECTIONS

1. What evidence is there that fascist principles and leaders still exist in the world? Offer specific examples.

2. Why do economic difficulties often propel people towards leaders and parties with extremist views? Note any current examples of this reaction.

3. Give a current example of peoples suffering persecution similar to that faced by Jews in Germany? Explain the situation.

4. Does today's world economy reveal any similarities with the economy that led to the Great Depression? Explain.

5. Do some research either on the Internet or at the library on the United Nations to find out about this organization and its mission. In your view, why would the UN be more successful at establishing peace than the League of Nations? Explain.

6. a) What actions might the League have taken in response to aggression by Japan and Italy?

   b) How might the League have been made a more powerful body for world peace?

   c) In your view, should international organizations try to "police" individual nations?

7. a) Explain the term "collective security" in your own words.

   b) Describe how it was used in the inter-war period.

   c) In your opinion, should international organizations today be used to achieve global collective security?

DEVELOPING YOUR VOICE

8. a) Review the political spectrum on page 68. Where would you place Canada?

    b) Write a paragraph explaining whether you would like to see more or less government intervention in the lives of Canadians.

9. Assume you are a young student in Hitler's Germany. In your diary, note reasons why you might be attracted to, or repelled by, Hitler.

10. Assume you are a Jewish citizen living in Nazi Germany. Write a letter to friends in North America about your experiences with the Nazis.

RESEARCHING THE ISSUES

11. Do further research and write a one- to two-page "Profile" on the main ideas and influences of one of the following:

    — Karl Marx

    — Leon Trotsky

12. Do some research on the Internet or at the library on the living conditions in Canada during the Depression. List some of the ways people coped with the hardships.

13. Prepare a detailed report either on the failure of the League of Nations to solve aggression in Manchuria or in Abyssinia. Was it possible to solve the dispute peacefully?

CHAPTER FOUR

The Second World War: 1939-1945

This painting by famous Canadian artist Alex Colville is entitled *Infantry Near Nijmegen* (Holland). What is suggested in the faces of these soldiers? How does this image of infantry differ from that shown in the popular media?

> "When Hitler attacked the Jews I was not a Jew, therefore I was not concerned. And when Hitler attacked the Catholics, I was not a Catholic, and therefore I was not concerned. And when Hitler attacked the unions and the industrialists, I was not a member of the unions and I was not concerned. Then, Hitler attacked me and the Protestant church—and there was nobody left to be concerned."
>
> — Martin Niemöller (1892-1984), German pastor imprisoned for preaching against the Nazis, in the *Congressional Record*, 14 October 1968

Overview

In Europe, the Second World War began on 1 September 1939 when Germany invaded Poland. But the war clouds had been building for several years, perhaps since the signing of the Treaty of Versailles in 1919. In this truly global war, both the east and the west were swept into strife that would last for six years.

War between China and Japan had been smouldering and flaring up throughout the 1930s. Japan had been expanding its economic control and territory in Asia. In 1937, it launched all-out war against China. The United States, Britain, and Holland, all of which had interests in Southeast Asia, supported China. Most experts expected the conflict to remain localized. However, on 7 December 1941, the Japanese attacked the American naval base at Pearl Harbor, Hawaii. Attacks on the Philippines, Singapore, and Hong Kong followed. Declarations of war rang out from continent to continent. A global war had begun.

By the time the guns of war had been silenced in 1945, a new and potentially even more dangerous era had begun—the nuclear age. The spotlight now shifted to the fundamental differences between the two new superpowers, the United States and the Soviet Union.

Focus Questions
1. What were the major steps on the road to war between 1930 and 1939?
2. What were the key events of the Second World War?
3. What were the major results of the war?
4. What are some of the major interpretations of the basic causes of the Second World War?
5. What were the origins of the Cold War?

Hitler's Aims and Foreign Policy

The rise of Hitler and the Nazi Party signalled the beginning of a new age for Germany and Europe. Upon becoming chancellor in 1933, Hitler quickly consolidated power as the undisputed dictator of Germany. He then turned his attention to the goal of establishing Germany as the dominant power in Europe. To achieve this, it was necessary to violate the Treaty of Versailles, which Hitler viewed as humiliating and designed to maintain a weak German state. Hitler embarked on this objective in 1935 by rearming Germany. At the same time, he began to gather personal control of Germany's military and foreign affairs.

Hitler was encouraged in his expansionist foreign policy by the failure of the League of Nations to create international peace and order following the First World War. Weakened by the worldwide economic depression and a lack of commitment and resolve on the part of its members, the League was powerless to prevent aggression anywhere in the world. In 1931-1932 Japan occupied Manchuria without challenge. In 1935-1936 Italy conquered Abyssinia (Ethiopia) with little protest. In the Spanish Civil War (1936-1939), Spanish fascist forces, aided by Mussolini and Hitler, overthrew an elected government in a brutal war with a million casualties. There, the Spanish fascist Generalissimo Franco led a military revolt against a democratically elected government. Spain was torn apart by political chaos.

In some ways, the Spanish Civil War became a rehearsal for the Second World War. The dictators, Hitler, Mussolini, and Stalin, sent forces and supplies to the wartorn nation. Hitler used his air force to practise the bombing techniques that would prove so effective during the Second World War. While the League of Nations and most democratic governments stood by, individual citizens from 50 nations volunteered and went to Spain to fight in "International Brigades"; they included Canadians, who formed the Mackenzie-Papineau Battalion or "Mac-Paps." The Spanish Republic collapsed because of internal disagreement and massive pounding by the militarily superior fascist forces. Hitler learned many lessons from the war and observed that the threat of international action against aggression was virtually non-existent. Interestingly, the victorious Franco continued to rule Spain for another 35 years, long after Hitler and Mussolini had been swept from power.

In Hitler's vision, a great Germany meant an expanded Germany, and this new territory was to be obtained through conquest. The fact that the areas Hitler wanted belonged to other nations was of no concern to him. He believed in the principle of "might is right"—those who are fit survive, while those who are weak perish. According to Hitler's outlook, the Germans were a superior Aryan (defined by Nazis as Caucasians not of Jewish descent) race that should subdue and control "lesser" races such as the Slavic peoples in eastern Europe. As for the Jews, Hitler felt it was his mission to banish them as well as all homosexuals, people with physical and mental disabilities, and visible minorities from Europe by whatever means necessary.

Hitler believed that Germany needed more *lebensraum* (living space) for its expanding population of pure-blooded Aryans. To encourage an increase in the birth rate of Aryans, Hitler dismissed women from jobs in industry, exhorting them to devote themselves to *kinder, kirche, kuche* (children, church, kitchen).

Hitler also wanted Germany to be self-sufficient. Trade was not the answer because that would make Germany dependent on others. In order to obtain rich agricultural land and other valuable natural resources, Germany would have to expand into eastern Europe.

THE REOCCUPATION OF THE RHINELAND

The Treaty of Versailles had established a demilitarized zone in the Rhineland between Germany and France. (See Figure 4.3 on page 103.) In March 1936, Hitler ordered the army to move into the Rhineland and reclaim it for Germany. This was a clear violation of the Treaty of Versailles and the spirit of the Locarno Pacts. The move was risky. Hitler's military leaders opposed the action, fearing it would precipitate war with France—a war for which Germany was simply not ready. As a precaution, German troops were ordered to retreat at the first sign of French resistance. Hitler, however, had gambled that there would be no such resistance. He was right.

ANSCHLUSS

Anschluss (the union of Germany and Austria) was one of Hitler's long-standing dreams. While the union would be an important military advantage, for Hitler it was more personal. He wanted to annex Austria so that he and his fellow Austrians would be officially German. The fact that Anschluss was forbidden under the terms of the Treaty of Versailles was of little consequence.

Still, there were other obstacles in Hitler's way. First he had to persuade the Italian dictator Mussolini, who had signed a treaty with Austria guaranteeing its independence, to renege on that commitment. Hitler came up with a simple solution: he offered German support to Mussolini, whose troops had just occupied Abyssinia, if Italy would ignore its commitment to Austria.

Next, Hitler pressured Austria to legalize the Nazi Party and appoint a Nazi supporter as Minister of the Interior. Once legalized, the Austrian Nazi Party became increasingly vocal, demanding union with Germany. However, the Austrian Chancellor, Kurt von Schuschnigg, convinced that Austrians would vote for independence, decided to hold a **plebiscite**. Hitler was furious. Under the threat of German invasion, Schuschnigg was forced to resign. The leader of the Austrian Nazi Party assumed the office of Chancellor.

Figure 4.1

Hitler led a victory parade in Vienna following Germany's occupation of Austria in 1938. Look at the photo closely. What evidence of security concerns is there? What reaction might ordinary Germans have to this photo? Why?

He invited the German troops massed along the border to enter the country and restore order. As German forces marched into Vienna, the union of Austria and Germany was officially proclaimed. The first step in Hitler's plan was now complete.

WHY ENGLAND AND FRANCE SLEPT

In hindsight, Germany's march of aggression in the 1930s seems obvious. Why, then, wasn't Hitler stopped? Why were Britain and France so timid in their response to Hitler's demands and his territorial conquests? The answers are complex.

In the 1930s, the horrible slaughter of the First World War was still fresh in the memories of most Europeans. A mere 15 years before, a whole generation of young men had died on the fields of France and Belgium. Most leaders wanted to avoid a repetition of that senseless bloodshed. They believed that another world war would be even more devastating.

Furthermore, the Western world was caught in the Great Depression. Most countries lacked the funds needed to support their unemployed citizens and deal with the social problems arising from the economic crisis. Rearmament and war preparations would only further drain already depleted economies.

Political opinion in Britain and France was deeply divided between the conservative forces of the right and the labour and social democratic forces of the left. Many people of the right were suspicious of the growth of communism in the USSR and feared communist expansion in the rest of Europe. To some, the strong anticommunist rantings of Hitler and Mussolini were a counterforce to the spread of communism. Thus some were prepared to support fascism simply to contain communism. For others, communism seemed to be the movement of the future, a means of overthrowing the oppressive capitalist forces. These conflicting views tended to split nations, and they made it difficult for governments to establish a strong foreign policy. The result, for both Britain and France, was political paralysis. Where fascist actions did not conflict directly with their interests, the Western powers were prepared to follow a policy of **appeasement**. In practice, this meant trying to calm international tensions by making concessions. Unfortunately, fascists viewed appeasement not as reasonable compromise but as weakness. If given an inch, they were quite prepared to take a mile.

CZECHOSLOVAKIA AND THE MUNICH PACT

In April 1938, Hitler issued his directive on his plans for expansion into Czechoslovakia: "It is my unalterable decision to smash Czechoslovakia by military action in the near future." Hitler's plan was to isolate Czechoslovakia from its allies, then launch a short but decisive attack. He believed that a massive show of power and a quick victory would discourage outside military intervention. But before Hitler could launch his attack, Neville Chamberlain, the British prime minister, and the French premier, Édouard Daladier, announced that they would agree to give the predominantly German-speaking Sudetenland region of Czechoslovakia to Germany in order to avoid war. They pressured Czechoslovakia to give in to Hitler's demands.

The matter was decided at a conference in Munich in September 1938. Czechoslovakia was not represented. Hitler, Chamberlain, Daladier, and Mussolini signed the **Munich Pact**, giving Germany the Sudetenland in return for agreeing to make no further demands.

> "We must always demand so much that we can never be satisfied."
>
> – Hitler on his strategy during negotiations at Munich

Figure 4.2

When Neville Chamberlain returned from Munich, he confidently declared "peace for our time." Why was Chamberlain so tragically wrong in his assessment?

> "In spite of the hardness and ruthlessness I thought I saw in his [Hitler's] face, I got the impression that here was a man who could be relied upon when he had given his word."
>
> — Neville Chamberlain, prior to the Munich Conference

Czechoslovakia thereby lost the fortified border the Sudetenland provided; the country was now defenceless. Meanwhile, the exclusion of the Soviet Union from the Munich Conference raised Stalin's suspicions that Britain and France, by appeasing Germany, hoped to turn Hitler's attention away from them and to the east—and the USSR.

Following the Munich Conference, Chamberlain returned to England and proclaimed to a cheering crowd, "I believe it is peace for our time." To Hitler, the agreement signified the willingness of the West to let him have his way in order to avoid armed conflict. Now there would be no stopping Germany.

In March 1939, despite Hitler's assurances in Munich, German troops occupied the rest of Czechoslovakia. Not a shot was fired. Hitler was clearly contemptuous of the Allies. Once again, he had gambled and won. Few people in Germany would dare speak out against such obvious success. Now more than ever, Hitler believed that his genius and superior will would enable him to achieve any objective.

MAP STUDY

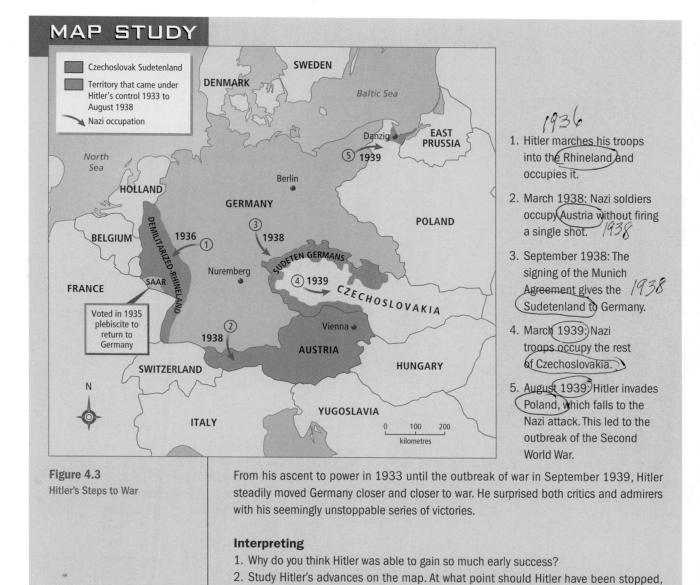

Legend:
- Czechoslovak Sudetenland
- Territory that came under Hitler's control 1933 to August 1938
- Nazi occupation

(handwritten annotations on map region labels: 1936)

1. Hitler marches his troops into the Rhineland and occupies it.

2. March 1938: Nazi soldiers occupy Austria without firing a single shot. *1938*

3. September 1938: The signing of the Munich Agreement gives the Sudetenland to Germany. *1938*

4. March 1939: Nazi troops occupy the rest of Czechoslovakia.

5. August 1939: Hitler invades Poland, which falls to the Nazi attack. This led to the outbreak of the Second World War.

Map labels: SWEDEN, DENMARK, Baltic Sea, North Sea, HOLLAND, BELGIUM, FRANCE, DEMILITARIZED-RHINELAND, SAAR, Voted in 1935 plebiscite to return to Germany, Nuremberg, GERMANY, Berlin, Danzig, EAST PRUSSIA, 1939, POLAND, SUDETEN GERMANS, CZECHOSLOVAKIA, Vienna, AUSTRIA, HUNGARY, SWITZERLAND, ITALY, YUGOSLAVIA, 1936, 1938, 1939, kilometres 0 100 200

Figure 4.3
Hitler's Steps to War

From his ascent to power in 1933 until the outbreak of war in September 1939, Hitler steadily moved Germany closer and closer to war. He surprised both critics and admirers with his seemingly unstoppable series of victories.

Interpreting

1. Why do you think Hitler was able to gain so much early success?
2. Study Hitler's advances on the map. At what point should Hitler have been stopped, in your opinion? Why?

THE POLISH GAMBLE

Hitler's successful foreign policy achievements encouraged him to gamble for increasingly higher stakes. Poland was his next target.

The specific dispute between Germany and Poland was over the free port city of Danzig (later renamed Gdansk) and the Polish Corridor, both of which had been part of Germany prior to 1919. Danzig had become a free city by the terms of the Treaty of Versailles, and Poland had been given special trading privileges there. The Polish Corridor, created to give Poland access to the Baltic Sea, cut East Prussia off from the rest of Germany. The predominantly German population in the Polish Corridor clamoured to be reunited with their homeland. Hitler exploited this instability and ordered his generals to develop plans for a Polish invasion. Could Hitler win Poland by bluster and bluff, as he had won Czechoslovakia, or would this gamble lead to war? Now there was a new ingredient in the mix: Britain and France, realizing they had been fooled at Munich, no longer trusted the Nazi leader. Chamberlain reacted to Hitler's manoeuvres by pledging support to Poland. It was a warning that further expansion would be opposed.

Figure 4.4
What does this cartoon suggest about the character of the Nazi-Soviet Non-Aggression Pact of 1939? What does the corpse represent? Refer to the Skill Path "Interpreting Political Cartoons" (page 122) for help.

THE GERMAN/SOVIET PACT

For years Hitler had proclaimed that the Soviet Union, as a communist nation, was the major enemy of Germany. Suddenly, in August 1939, Germany and the USSR announced an **agreement of mutual non-aggression**. The world was shocked by this agreement. However, both countries had secretly co-operated for years when they were outside the League of Nations. Since the West seemed unwilling to rein in Hitler, Stalin made his own deal with his rival. In truth, the agreement simply bought both implacable enemies time before their almost inevitable clash to come. Germany was now free from the danger of fighting a war on two fronts. One week later, on 1 September 1939, Germany unleashed its crushing military might on Poland. The Second World War had begun.

"England has been offered a choice between war and shame. She has chosen shame and will get war."
— Winston Churchill, in opposition to Chamberlain's policy of appeasement, September 1938

In Review

1. What were Hitler's foreign policy objectives?

2. What foreign policy victories did Hitler win between 1936 and 1939?

3. Why did England and France "sleep" while Hitler marched toward war?

4. Outline the results of the Munich Pact.

5. What was appeasement and why was it ultimately unsuccessful?

6. What was the importance of the pact between Germany and the Soviet Union?

7. What lessons might future leaders learn from the drift to war in the 1930s?

The Outbreak of War

THE NATURE OF THE SECOND WORLD WAR

The speed, scale, and destruction of the Second World War were unprecedented in human history. This was no war of the eighteenth and nineteenth centuries in Europe, in which colourfully dressed professional soldiers met on isolated fields of battle. This was **total war**, much like the First World War, except that the killing machines were more efficient and more deadly. This was a war where civilians at home were just as much a part of the conflict as the uniformed soldiers at the front. For some, the human tragedies of the war would reveal the bloody, brutal nature of humanity at its absolute worst.

The Second World War was characterized by **blitzkrieg**—lightning war! The principle behind blitzkrieg was that the best way to defeat an enemy was to cut them off from all supplies and communication. This would require swift, massive strikes from the air, coupled with rapid tank invasions on the ground. Hitler successfully employed blitzkrieg tactics to expand Germany's territorial control in the early stages of the war.

THE PHONEY WAR

On 1 September 1939, the German army invaded Poland. Using blitzkrieg tactics, it defeated Poland by the end of the month. Soviet troops moved in to occupy eastern Poland, in accordance with the secret terms of the Nazi-Soviet Pact signed on August 23. With the eastern front secure, Hitler turned his attention to the West.

From October 1939 to April 1940 there was little fighting. During this lull in the action, known as the "phoney war," the German army refined its attack plans and trained its troops for the battles that lay ahead. The Allies seemed content to improve their defences and wait for Hitler's next move. French troops waited behind the massive Maginot Line while British forces and the French 1st and 7th armies took up positions along the Belgian border where an anti-tank ditch had been prepared and fortified. To the north and west, German troops massed along the Siegfried Line.

THE FALL OF FRANCE

The phoney war came to a sudden end on 9 April 1940, when, without warning, Germany attacked Norway and Denmark, both neutral nations. While Denmark fell immediately, Norway, with the help of the Allies, continued to resist until June.

On May 10, Germany attacked Holland, Belgium, Luxembourg, and France. Relying on blitzkrieg tactics, the German army conquered Holland in one week and Belgium in three. The main thrust of the attack took place in France as the Germans swarmed into the country through the Ardennes forest. Their position drove a huge wedge between the bulk of the French army stationed behind the Maginot Line and the Allied forces in Belgium.

The Germans then pushed straight for the sea, forcing British and French forces to retreat to the west. In a mighty sweep, the Germans encircled the retreating French troops to the south and the British Expeditionary Force (BEF) to the north, pinning them on the beaches of Dunkirk in northern France. (See Figure 4.5 on page 106.)

Hitler's victory could have been even more devastating. But while the German ruler fussed over whether the air force or the army should have the honour of completing the victory, an amazing rescue by the British navy and thousands of

april 1940

may 1940

MAP STUDY

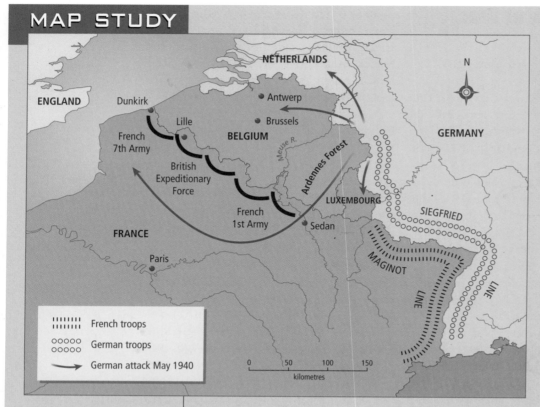

Figure 4.5
The Fall of France

The French front was static in the early months of the war as French and German troops faced each other along the Maginot and Siegfried Lines. This "phoney war" suggested the earlier trench experience of the First World War. The British Expeditionary Force (BEF) and the French 1st and 7th armies massed along the border of neutral Belgium to guard against the possibility that the Germans might strike there. On May 10, the German forces unleashed a terrible blitzkrieg against the Netherlands, Belgium, Luxembourg and France. Within weeks, all had fallen to German speed and armour.

Interpreting

1. In what way was the German approach similar to that employed in the early days of the First World War?
2. What advantages did the Germans have over the Allied forces?

ordinary citizens was underway at Dunkirk. Tugs, barges, fishing boats, yachts, lifeboats, and naval vessels crossed the English Channel to evacuate the Allied troops on the beach. This heroic effort resulted in the rescue of more than 330 000 troops. While heavy arms and equipment were destroyed or abandoned, the British army escaped to fight again.

The German forces continued to press southward, taking Paris by mid-June. On June 17, the newly appointed French premier, H. Philippe Pétain, requested an armistice with the Germans. The agreement was signed on June 22. France had fallen in just over a month.

THE BATTLE OF BRITAIN

The defeat of France was a severe blow to the Allies. Now continental western Europe was in Hitler's hands. Only the English Channel and the powerful British navy separated Britain from Hitler's empire.

Hitler was convinced that Britain would now have no choice but to seek peace. But the success of the rescue at Dunkirk had made Britain determined to fight to the end. In frustration, Hitler gave orders to launch Operation Sea Lion, the invasion plan for Britain. First, however, the *Luftwaffe* (the German air force) had to gain control of the air to ensure the safe passage of the German army across the English Channel.

On 10 July 1940, the Luftwaffe began air raids over Britain in preparation for invasion along England's southern coast. The Royal Air Force (RAF) airfields, British ships in the English Channel, and harbours in the south were targeted for destruction by German aircraft. The air assault continued throughout the summer and into the fall. Never before had bombing from the air been so intense.

Although German bombers and fighter planes outnumbered those of the British by four to one, the RAF had great success against the Luftwaffe, losing only one plane for every two German planes. A new invention—radar—allowed the British to detect German bombing missions in advance and to prepare to defend themselves.

In September, Hermann Goering, the commander of the Luftwaffe, decided to change his tactics. Instead of bombing RAF bases, the Germans began bombing industrial and port centres in the hope of breaking British morale. Cities such as London and Coventry were heavily bombed. In London, explosives and incendiary bombs rained down night after night, destroying huge sections of the city. The centre of Coventry was obliterated. But the bombing campaigns only made British civilians more determined to resist defeat. They also meant fewer attacks were made on British airfields scattered throughout the countryside.

German losses were so heavy in September that in October the Luftwaffe changed tactics again, switching to night bombing. Although this was much less effective from a military standpoint, the dark of night hampered Britain's defensive plans. This siege, which lasted from July 1940 until May 1941, was known as the **Blitz**.

While German bombs were laying much of Britain to ruins, British bombers were causing similar destruction in German cities. Air raids on centres like Hamburg, Dresden, and Berlin were leaving masses of rubble and debris in their wake. The scale of civilian destruction was unprecedented. The Second World

> "We shall defend our island, whatever the cost may be. We shall fight on the beaches, we shall fight on the landing-grounds, we shall fight in the fields and in the streets, we shall fight in the hills. We shall never surrender."
>
> — Winston Churchill, 1940

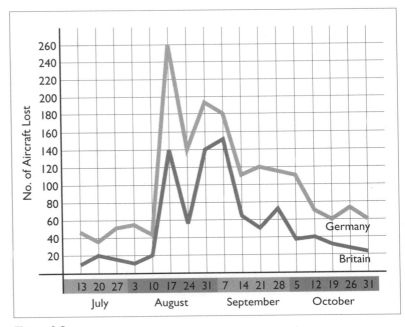

Figure 4.6

The Battle of Britain. This graph compares the number of aircraft lost by Britain and Germany each week during the Battle of Britain. When was the climax of the battle? Why were German losses so high? Why was this battle so important?

War was clearly a "total war" from the early months onward.

By October 1940, Hitler realized that the Battle of Britain was lost. He postponed his invasion plans and began to refocus his attention eastward toward Russia. In 1941, he launched Operation Barbarossa, his fateful invasion of Russia, and began a savage campaign that would eventually devastate the German army. He was now fighting a war on two fronts.

GERMAN INVASION OF RUSSIA

In June 1941, led by heavily armoured panzer units, the German army poured over the Soviet borders and drove hard and fast deep into the heart of Russian territory. It was a three-pronged attack aimed like a dagger at the cities of Leningrad and Moscow, at the agricultural riches of Ukraine, and at the oil-rich Caucasus region. Victory came easily at first; the German army moved 80 km a day and swept up entire cities and collapsing Soviet forces. By December, Hitler's forces were in possession or in sight of all their objectives. Then came Russia's oldest ally—winter. The season that had crushed the legions of Napoleon returned to halt the Nazi forces in their tracks. With impossibly long supply lines, soldiers freezing in summer uniforms, and vehicles unable to move in the cold, the Soviet Union gained an important respite from the Nazi onslaught. For the first time, the Nazi forces seemed vulnerable.

In 1942, the Germans returned to the attack and met with some early victories,

Figure 4.7
The Battle of Stalingrad from September 1942 until January 1943 ended Germany's success on the Eastern Front. What were some of the problems facing the German forces?

MAP STUDY

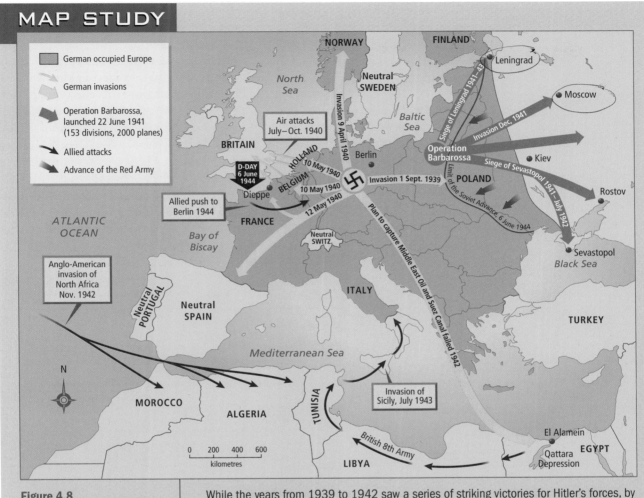

Figure 4.8
The War in Europe, 1939 to 1945

While the years from 1939 to 1942 saw a series of striking victories for Hitler's forces, by 1942 the tide was beginning to turn. The combined muscle of Britain, the USSR, the US, and the British Commonwealth (including Canada) was simply too much for Axis forces. In the end, they were stretched very thin and outgunned and outnumbered. Hitler's ruthless ambitions were simply too much for the German army to achieve.

Interpreting

1. Write a paragraph briefly outlining the tactical movements of each army and the battles that ensued as shown on this map.
2. In your view, which campaign was most important to the overall war effort? Why?

but by the end of the year the Soviets roared back. In February of 1943, the Germans suffered a humiliating defeat at Stalingrad. In July 1943, at the historic Battle of Kursk, Soviet forces led by Marshal Zhukov slaughtered the German army, resulting in the loss of 70 000 military personnel and 1500 tanks. The Germans would never regain the initiative. By the end of 1943, Leningrad was relieved and Soviet forces were gaining strength, poised to drive Hitler's forces from Mother Russia, push through Eastern Europe, and then strike deep into Germany itself.

The war on the Eastern Front was characterized by sweeping savagery, soaring casualty figures, and massive numbers of soldiers and munitions. Some observers credit the Soviet forces for ripping the heart out of the German army and dealing a death blow to Hitler's ambitions.

WARTIME CONFERENCES

While the battles raged on in Britain, Russia, and other parts of the world, the major Allied leaders (Churchill, Roosevelt, and Stalin) realized some degree of co-operation was needed among their nations. The many years of global warfare demanded that they meet in conferences to discuss strategy and work out difficulties among their very different nations. They not only negotiated the path of the war, but went a long way toward defining the shape of the postwar world.

The following chart outlines some of the more important conferences attended by the Allied leaders and the issues that were discussed.

Allied Conferences

Location	Date	Leaders Present	Issues
Newfoundland, on the battleship *Prince of Wales*	August 1941	Churchill, Roosevelt	Created Atlantic Charter, a declaration on the purposes of the war against fascism
Washington	December 1941	Churchill, Roosevelt	Created unified military command
Casablanca	January 1943	Churchill, Roosevelt	Worked on war strategy. Demanded unconditional surrender from the Axis nations
Cairo	November 1943	Churchill, Roosevelt, Jiang Jie Shi (Chiang kai-shek, Chinese leader)	Plotted strategy against Japan
Teheran	November/December 1943	Churchill, Roosevelt, Stalin	Discussed invasion of Europe, setting up of United Nations, and Russian help against Japan
Quebec	a) August 1943 b) September 1944	Churchill, Roosevelt	Planned D-Day and naval war against Japan
Moscow	October 1944	Churchill, Stalin	Discussed postwar Europe
Yalta	February 1945	Churchill, Roosevelt, Stalin	USSR pledged to join war against Japan, agreement on United Nations, discussed plans for postwar Europe, including occupation of Germany
Potsdam	July/August 1945	Churchill/Atlee, Stalin, and Truman	Details of German occupation, Polish borders

Figure 4.9

Review the chart above and note which nations appear to have had closer political ties. Which nation clearly gained power as a result of the war? Do leaders of powerful nations still meet regularly today?

THE ALLIED VICTORY IN EUROPE

In 1945, the Allied forces bombed, torpe-doed, and marched their way to victory in Europe. The German forces were out-numbered and outgunned by the vast Allied armies that now swept across the continent. Hitler's empire was crumbling against the pounding from Russian forces in the east and American, British, and Canadian forces in the west. Allied con-trol of the air and seas made victory inevitable. While German soldiers fought desperately and valiantly in defence of their own soil, Hitler refused calls for surrender. With Allied troops about to capture Berlin, Hitler finally committed suicide in an underground bunker in the bombed-out ruins of the city in May 1945. Germany soon surrendered uncon-ditionally. The war in Europe was over.

Figure 4.10

All that remained of Hitler's dream of glory and a thousand-year empire were cities of rubble and ash, such as Berlin shown here, and millions of civilian and military casualties.

Figure 4.11

American, British, and Canadian soldiers stormed the beaches of the French coast directly into fire from Nazi defenders in the D-Day invasion. Canadian forces made the deepest inroads on the first day, and the Allies soon began the drive to Berlin and the liberation of Nazi-occupied Europe.

Profile Sir Winston Churchill
(1874-1965)

Figure 4.12
Sir Winston Churchill

"I expect that the Battle of Britain is about to begin. Upon this battle depends the survival of Christian civilization. Upon it depends our own British life and the long continuity of our institutions and our Empire. The whole fury and might of the enemy must very soon be turned on us. Hitler knows that he will have to break us in this island or lose the war. If we can stand up to him all Europe may be free and the life of the world may move forward into broad, sunlit uplands; but if we fail then the whole world, including the United States, and all that we have known and cared for, will sink into the abyss of a new dark age made more sinister, and perhaps more prolonged, by the lights of a perverted science. Let us therefore brace ourselves to our duty and so bear ourselves that if the British Commonwealth and its Empire lasts for a thousand years, men will still say 'This was their finest hour.' "

—Winston Churchill, to the House of Commons
when the invasion of Britain seemed imminent,
18 June 1940

Long before the twentieth century was even half over, Sir Winston Churchill was being lionized as "the greatest living Englishman" and "one of the greatest figures of the twentieth century." World leader, author, prime minister, soldier, war correspondent, painter—Churchill played all these roles.

As you read about Churchill, consider why he played such an important role in the British resistance.

"We have before us an ordeal of the most grievous kind. We have before us many, many long months of struggle and of suffering. You ask, what is our policy? I will say: It is to wage war, by sea, land, and air, with all our might and with all the strength that God can give to us: to wage war against a monstrous tyranny, never surpassed in the dark, lamentable catalogue of human crime. That is our policy. You ask, what is our aim? I can answer in one word: Victory, victory at all costs, victory in spite of all terror; victory, however long and hard the road may be; for without victory there is no survival."

—Winston Churchill, upon becoming
British prime minister, 13 May 1940

Winston Churchill was a member of one of England's most illustrious noble families. He was educated at the prestigious institutions of Harrow and Sandhurst and could have lived a life of ease and comfort, but his pugnacious personality and the events of the twentieth century were to provide nearly a century of adventure, challenge, and singular achievement.

In 1900, Churchill entered Parliament and embarked on a dramatic political career that saw the independent-minded politician switch parties—twice! During the First World War, Churchill served as First Lord of the Admiralty, where he used navy funds to develop a new weapon, "the land battleship"—the modern tank.

After the First World War, Churchill served in a variety of cabinet positions. During the 1930s, he became increasingly alarmed by the spread of fascism and the rise of Adolf Hitler. But his dire warnings found few listeners in a world preoccupied with economic depression.

As the Second World War ignited, Churchill was once again admitted to the British cabinet as First Lord of the Admiralty. In the wake of successive Nazi victories on the continent, Chamberlain resigned as British prime minister. In May 1940, Churchill took his place. While much of the world was stunned by the speed and power of the Nazi blitzkrieg, Churchill seemed defiantly confident and unwilling to buckle under to the Nazi war machine. As prime minister, Churchill came to symbolize the indomitable will of the British people and their allies to survive and defeat Axis aggression. His leadership provided the inspiration England needed to face Nazi Germany while he forged a powerful alliance with the United States and the Soviet Union to defeat the Axis Powers.

In 1945, Churchill was defeated at the polls but he returned to office from 1951 to 1955, finally retiring as Conservative Party leader at the age of 80. However, he did not leave politics even then, but served as a Member of Parliament for nine more years. He also found time to write the six-volume *The Second World War*, which earned him the Nobel Prize for Literature in 1953.

When Churchill died in 1965, a grateful nation gave him a grand state funeral. This man, with such a powerful sense of self, history, and destiny, had his own explanation for his perceived greatness: "I have never accepted what many people have kindly said, namely that I inspired the nation. It was the nation and the race dwelling all around the globe that had the lion's heart. I had the luck to be called upon to give the roar."

Responding

1. Why has history been so kind to Winston Churchill?
2. In your opinion, do great leaders make events, or do events make great leaders? Explain.

TECHNOLOGY AND WAR

Scientists joined forces with military strategists to create a range of new weapons for use in the Second World War. On both sides of the battle front, thousands of researchers applied scientific techniques to the special problems of war. In the United States alone, 30 000 scientists and engineers were employed in the development of new weapons and machines, as well as new medical techniques.

Breaking the Codes

Science played a key role in breaking German and Japanese secret communications codes. The British were able to crack the German code in April 1940. They used this knowledge to help the RAF during the Battle of Britain and throughout the war. The Americans were successful in breaking the Japanese secret codes, which helped them locate and track the Japanese fleet. As a result, the Americans were able to win critical naval battles and begin the destruction of the Japanese navy.

In 1938, a Polish mechanic working in a factory in eastern Germany discovered that the plant was secretly manufacturing signalling machines for the German army. The man carefully observed the parts being made and turned over the information to a British agent in Warsaw. With help from the Polish secret service, he was smuggled out of Poland to Britain. There he created a model of the machine, called Enigma, from memory. British scientists realized that Enigma was the key to breaking the German communications code. The Polish secret service stole a complete working machine from the factory, then British scientists began the complicated task of solving the puzzle of Enigma. By April 1940, the code was broken. For the rest of the war the Allies were able to read secret German messages.

Medical Technology

New or improved drugs and medical techniques made an important contribution to the war and saved the lives of one out of every two wounded soldiers. In the war in the Pacific, malaria was a constant threat to the troops. The principal source of the traditional cure—quinine—was the island of Java. When Java was captured by the Japanese in 1942, the Allies successfully developed a synthetic form of quinine. This new drug was critical to the success of Allied troops in both the Middle East and Asia.

Radar

Radar is used to detect the nature, position, and movement of an object. Electromagnetic waves are beamed out, reflected from the target, and picked up by the radar unit, which then converts the signals into images on a screen. This technology was being developed by Britain, Germany, and the United States prior to the war, but it was the British who made the most rapid progress. Radar provided them with an early warning system for the German air raids and played an important role in winning the Battle of Britain.

Jet Planes

Germany produced the first jet airplane in 1939. By 1941, the Germans had developed a jet fighter plane. These jet planes could fly at speeds much greater than propeller-driven aircraft and would have given Germany air superiority. But when Hitler was presented with the new plane in November 1943, he demanded that it be adapted for bombing. This delayed production of the aircraft until the fall of 1944; as a result, the plane was ready too late to play an important role in the German war effort. The Allies were also developing their own jet planes and had their fighters ready for use in Belgium by 1945.

Rockets

As the Allies invaded France and Russian forces moved against Germany from the east, Hitler announced that the German people would be saved by new "miracle inventions." The first of these, the V-1 (Vengeance), was a pilotless monoplane that carried an explosive warhead. Almost 10 000 of these **buzz-bombs** (so called because of the noise they produced) were fired at British cities beginning in 1944. But while the V-1 inflicted serious damage, the more advanced V-2 rockets that followed gave Britain cause for far greater concern. The V-2 flew at supersonic speed, giving no warning and offering no opportunity for defence. Fortunately, British intelligence discovered where these bombs were being developed. An Allied bombing raid on the production plant in August 1943 delayed its manufacture until the following year. In September 1944, however, V-2s were fired on Britain. Still, the delay was an important one for Britain. Had the V-2 been available to the Germans earlier, it might have changed the course of the war.

The Atomic Bomb

In 1939, Albert Einstein, a physicist who had emigrated from Germany to the United States in 1933, wrote a letter to President Roosevelt advising him that German scientists were working on an atomic bomb that would be capable of mass destruction. In response to this German threat, Roosevelt established the **Manhattan Project** to develop an atomic bomb for American use. Robert Oppenheimer led a group of American and Allied scientists in developing the bomb. Following its successful testing in New Mexico in July 1945, the United States was ready to use the ultimate weapon of destruction.

In Review

1. What was the blitzkrieg? What effect did it have on German success in the early years of the Second World War?

2. Briefly describe the campaigns waged by Hitler against England and France.

3. Why was Hitler unable to conquer Britain?

4. What impact did the Russian campaign have on German fortunes?

5. In your opinion, what was the most significant technological invention of the Second World War?

6. Develop arguments for and against the following statement: "War encourages technological improvements for society."

7. Why do you think Hitler's early successes did not lead to ultimate victory? What is the most important reason for the defeat of Germany in the Second World War?

The Asian Pacific Conflict

As an industrialized nation, Japan needed raw materials and export markets. With the economic crisis of the 1930s, international trade with the West was drastically reduced. The strong militarist element in Japan believed that if Japan had a colonial empire, it would have access to raw materials and could control its own markets. The more liberal element, composed of industrialists and bankers, felt that Japanese trade should be carried out peacefully. They worried that acquiring territory by force would result in trade reprisals from the West.

With Manchuria conquered by 1932, expansion in Southeast Asia was the next goal. But first Japan needed to secure its northern flank from a possible attack by the Soviet Union. This was achieved through the Anti-Comintern Pact Japan signed with Nazi Germany in 1936. Germany and Japan agreed to co-operate against the **Comintern** (the world communist movement led by the Soviet Union). With this agreement, the USSR was threatened on two fronts—by Japan in the east and Germany in the west.

WAR WITH CHINA

In the summer of 1937, the Japanese launched an all-out attack against Beijing, Shanghai, Nanking, and much of the coastal areas. They soon occupied most of China. As it had in the Manchurian conquest, the League of Nations condemned Japan, but took no action.

In 1939, the United States announced its intention to cancel its commercial treaty with Japan, which had been in effect since 1911. This allowed the US to impose trade restrictions against Japan, which seriously affected industries that depended upon American petroleum, steel, iron, copper, and industrial machinery. While the Japanese government pondered the problems the trade restrictions created, events in Europe provided new opportunities. The German invasion of

Poland focused the attention of the European powers and the United States on Germany. Japan took advantage of the situation by occupying the northern part of French Indochina in 1940. Now Japan posed a direct threat to the British naval base at Singapore and the vast oil supplies in the Dutch East Indies.

Britain and Holland were fully embroiled in the war in Europe and could not send ships to defend their Pacific colonies. The United States, although not yet directly involved in the war, issued repeated warnings to Japan against further aggression. In May 1940, it reinforced these warnings by stationing its Pacific Fleet in Pearl Harbor, Hawaii. In 1941, Roosevelt imposed further economic sanctions in the form of an embargo on aviation fuel, iron, and scrap metal. This was a serious blow to Japan's economy.

Refusing to buckle to US pressure, in July 1941 Japan announced a new foreign policy. Called the Greater East Asia Co-prosperity Sphere, the policy was designed to eliminate Western influence in Asia. The plan called for Japanese control of the natural resources of Southeast Asia; in return, Southeast Asia would become the market for Japanese manufactured goods. In effect, it was the blueprint for a Japanese empire.

In July 1941, Roosevelt froze all Japanese assets in the United States. All trade between the two nations was now terminated. Japan was faced with a tough choice: to fight or negotiate. But as a condition to any negotiations, the Americans insisted that Japan must withdraw from all the territories it had seized. The Japanese government, now firmly controlled by the militarists led by General Tojo Hideki, chose war.

THE ATTACK ON PEARL HARBOR

Japan intended a quick and decisive victory over the United States. In a long war, American industrial power would crush Japan. The most obvious target for the Japanese was the American fleet stationed at Pearl Harbor, Hawaii. With this fleet eliminated, Japan would have naval supremacy in the western Pacific Ocean. Plans for a surprise attack were engineered by Japan's brilliant naval commander and military strategist Admiral Yamamoto Isoroku.

On 7 December 1941, Japanese bombers took off from aircraft carriers positioned north of Hawaii. They caught the American navy completely off guard, and the fleet suffered severe damage and a staggering loss of life. A total of 19 ships were destroyed or disabled, 150 planes were lost, and 2400 military personnel and civilians were killed. That evening, the Japanese officially declared war on the United States.

Japanese hopes that the attack on Pearl Harbor would be the first step toward establishing a lasting empire in the

Figure 4.13
The USS Shaw exploded during the Japanese raid on Pearl Harbor, 7 December 1941. Why were the Japanese victorious at Pearl Harbor?

MAP STUDY

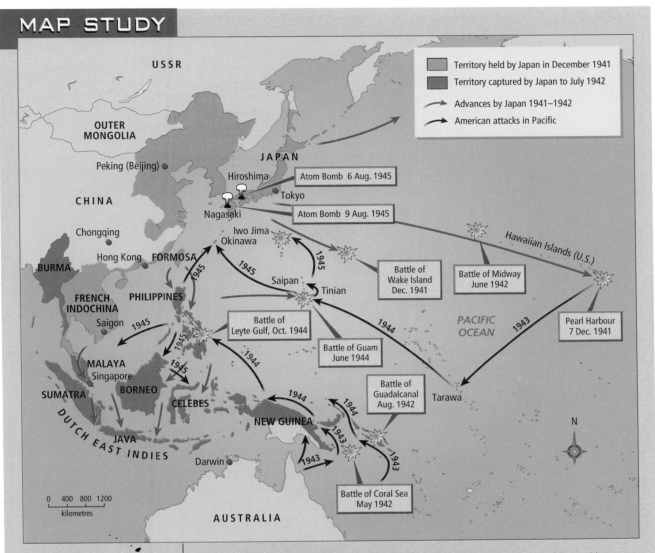

Figure 4.14
Asian Pacific Theatre,
1941 to 1945

The Japanese won a stunning surprise victory at Pearl Harbor and followed it up with sweeping advances throughout the Pacific and Asia. However, the massive military and industrial might of the United States was soon aimed at destroying the Japanese war machine. In less than a year, the tide was turning against the Japanese. The Americans pushed Japanese forces back and prepared the most powerful weapon the world had ever seen.

Interpreting

1. As you view the map, what appear to be the major strengths/weaknesses of the Japanese forces with respect to the United States?
2. How might American industrial strength help the US defeat the Japanese Empire?

Pacific were short-lived, however. The US navy recovered quickly. Within a year almost all of the vessels damaged in the raid were back in service and in action against the Japanese. The size of the American fleet and the number of personnel, combined with more advanced technology and a faster rate of production, helped the Americans drive the Japanese from their possessions in the Pacific. The massive destruction by American bombing culminated with the dropping of atomic bombs over Hiroshima and Nagasaki. In August 1945, Japan unconditionally surrendered. The Second World War was finally over.

Figure 4.15
In the Battle of Midway Island in June 1942, low-flying Japanese torpedo planes bombed US aircraft carriers but the Japanese suffered heavy losses in ships, planes, and soldiers. With four Japanese aircraft carriers sunk, the war in the Pacific turned in favour of the United States.

Figure 4.16
In the Battle of Iwo Jima in February 1945, US marines secured the tiny island in order to mount bombing offensives against Japanese cities. The bloody battle resulted in 23 000 Japanese casualties. US casualties exceeded 20 000.

In Review

1. Describe the goals of the militarists and liberal groups in Japan. Which predominated?

2. What were the results of the Japanese invasion of China?

3. Why did Japan decide to attack the United States?

4. What were the results of the attack on Pearl Harbor in 1941?

5. What accounted for the defeat of Japan in the Second World War?

The Tragedies of War

The Second World War resulted in scenes of brutality on a scale rarely seen in world history. War was brought ever closer to civilians, and atrocities were all too common. It would take much of the last half of the century for leaders and governments to design strategies to prevent and punish these new "crimes against humanity."

SOVIET PRISONERS OF WAR

The German invasion of the USSR in 1941, called Operation Barbarossa, resulted in millions of prisoners of war as entire Soviet divisions were overrun by the blitzkrieg. Nazi propaganda presented these defeated soldiers as evidence of Slavic inferiority in contrast to German superiority. Photographs of Soviet prisoners of war, in which the captives were described as untermensch (subhuman) were distributed throughout Germany. One booklet concluded with the shrill warning "The *untermensch* has risen to conquer the world.... Defend yourself, Europe!" Routinely, Russian prisoners were starved, beaten, and worked to death. Many were murdered outright. By the time the war ended, 2 500 000 Soviet prisoners of war had died.

THE KATYN FOREST MURDERS

The Katyn Forest, located near the Polish city of Smolensk, was the site of a grisly discovery in June 1941. The German army reported finding mass graves containing over 10 000 Polish officers. The Germans claimed this was a Soviet atrocity; the Soviets, in turn, denied responsibility, claiming the murders were the work of the Germans. It was not until an investigation was conducted in 1951-1952 that the Soviets were charged with the crimes. Evidence indicates that when the Soviet army occupied part of Poland from September 1939 to June 1941, they sent Polish officers and intelligentsia to Russian prison camps. Later, under Stalin's orders, the prisoners were murdered. Although the exact reasons for the massacre are uncertain, it is possible that Stalin wanted Poland's military and intellectual leaders eliminated in order to weaken Polish nationalism and military capability after the war.

THE ALLIED BOMBING OF DRESDEN

The massive Allied bombing of the historic German city of Dresden on 13 February 1945 resulted in nearly 100 000 civilian deaths. The city was a railway distribution centre overcrowded with refugees, but it was of little strategic value. The strategy behind the Allied bombing of German cities was to break civilian morale. After the war, however, many people questioned the morality of destroying cities that were of minor military significance and inflicting such human suffering during the last months of the war.

ALLIED PRISONERS IN ASIA

Cultural differences may explain in part Japan's harsh treatment of civilian and military prisoners. The Japanese believed that surrender was dishonourable; those who surrendered were held in contempt. Japanese soldiers themselves were expected to die rather than surrender. Hundreds of Japanese pilots volunteered for **kamikaze** (suicide) missions, flying planes laden with explosives directly into American ships. In Japanese culture, to die in combat was glorious.

The Japanese also wanted to dispel the myth of white superiority. These two factors led to harsh treatment of Allied prisoners. In the Philippines, 70 000 soldiers were force to march 100 km under a blazing tropical sun with almost no food or water. Only 54 000 survived. Prisoners of war were frequently used as slave labour; it is estimated that 13 000 POWs died building the Burma-Siam Railway.

THE CANADIAN DEFENCE OF HONG KONG

In the autumn of 1941, Japanese armies were routinely defeating poorly equipped Chinese forces. North of Hong Kong, Guangzhou had been taken by the Japanese. Would Hong Kong be next?

Some British leaders believed that Hong Kong could not be defended in the event of a Japanese attack, therefore it would be pointless to station additional troops there. Others argued that reinforcing the base at Hong Kong would provide

moral support for the Chinese and act as a deterrent to invasion by the Japanese.

In September 1941, Churchill made the controversial decision to ask Canada to provide the troops needed to increase Allied military presence in Hong Kong. On November 16, two battalions—Quebec's Royal Rifles and the Winnipeg Grenadiers—arrived in Hong Kong to begin their first mission. On December 7, the Japanese attacked, first from the air and two days later from the ground. On Christmas Day, with no air force, no navy, and heavy casualties, the British commander surrendered.

Nearly 300 of Canada's 2000 troops were killed in the battle. The rest were sent to Japanese prisoner-of-war camps, where more than 260 died, some from malnutrition and disease, others from the harsh living conditions. Canadian veterans and historians have questioned why unprepared Canadian troops were sent into a dangerous war zone to protect what many had acknowledged was a defenceless position.

THE ATOMIC BOMBING OF HIROSHIMA AND NAGASAKI

The devastation of atomic war was clearly demonstrated in August 1945. On August 6, the United States dropped the newly developed atomic bomb on Hiroshima, Japan. The impact was devastating: 80 000 people died instantly; 100 000 people were injured; another 60 000 died within a year. When Japan failed to surrender, a second bomb was dropped on Nagasaki on August 9, killing another 40 000 people.

American president Harry S. Truman justified the use of the A-bomb by arguing that it would force an end to the war, thereby saving American and Allied lives. Casualties were heavy in the Pacific. The Japanese aversion to surrender meant that many battles were literally fought to the last soldier. Based on such strong resistance, Allied military leaders estimated that half a million to a million troops would be lost in an invasion of Japan by ground forces.

The decision to use atomic weapons on civilians continues to cause controversy. There are those who believe that the bombings were carried out for political rather than military reasons. They argue that the bombs were really intended to intimidate the Soviet Union, which was taking a hard line at the peace negotiations at the Potsdam Conference (see page 130). Others believe that the bombings were racially motivated, arguing that atomic force would never have been used on a European city. While it is impossible to settle this debate with any certainty, one point seems clear: the atomic bomb achieved its goal. Five days after the bombing of Nagasaki, Japan unconditionally surrendered.

Figure 4.17
The dropping of the atomic bombs on Hiroshima and Nagasaki in August 1945 resulted in nearly 200 000 dead and led to Japan's unconditional surrender. These two photos show the city of Nagasaki before and after the dropping of the bomb. In your view, was the use of such a powerful and horrendous weapon justified? Explain.

Skill Path

Interpreting Political Cartoons

Finding "the message in the medium," in other words, identifying purpose and meaning in visual images such as political cartoons, is an important skill to develop if you are interested in understanding the atmosphere surrounding current and historical events. Political cartoons are satirical illustrations that not only poke fun at people and situations, but also show distinct perspectives on issues. A quick glance at the cartoon on the editorial pages of your favourite newspaper can deliver an immediate take on the topic of the day, not to mention the occasional chuckle.

A University of Virginia Web site dedicated to the history of political cartoons points out that, for the most part, they are editorial statements composed of two elements: caricature, which parodies the individual, and allusion, which creates the situation or context into which the individual is placed. The following steps will help guide you through the process of interpreting these elements.

Step One: Find the Facts

Read the cartoon's caption or title and any other text within the frame. Identify the people, objects, and/or symbols in the cartoon. Look at the setting and determine if it is historical, imaginary, or current. Answering these questions may require some background reading if you are unaware of the issue being illustrated.

In the example below, the appearance of the American flag and the desk tells us this scene is taking place in the present-day White House. The two objects above the desk are rockets with their destinations written on them. In the second frame we see the same political office, but note the name on the desk is Truman. So, we know that the period at the end of the Second World War is likely the setting for this frame. The two mushroom clouds are labelled Hiroshima and Nagasaki, representing the atomic bombs dropped on Japan in 1945.

Figure 4.18
This political cartoon was created in August 2002.

Step Two: Interpret the Cartoonist's Message

After identifying the objects and the setting of the cartoon, try to figure out the point of view being illustrated. Asking the following questions will help you do this.

- To what current event or issue is the cartoon related?
- Why might the cartoonist have deliberately used the title or caption, people, objects, symbols, and setting that were employed?
- Who has been caricatured? At its best, caricature suggests the subject's inner nature by humorously exaggerating their prominent physical features. What physical features have been emphasized, and why?
- What view of the event or issue is presented? Does this view ridicule by showing contempt? Does it use sarcasm to mean the opposite of what is being said? Does it employ irony to demonstrate disparity between what happens and what is expected to happen?

Step Three: Evaluate the Cartoon

Once you thoroughly understand the context of the cartoon and the point of view being illustrated, consider how effective the cartoonist was in conveying his or her message. For example, do you think the cartoon would be readily understood by an "average" reader? What techniques did the cartoonist use to create humour? Were they effective?

What could the cartoonist have added, emphasized, or changed to improve the effectiveness of the message?

Finally, ask yourself whether you agree or disagree with the cartoonist's view of the event or issue. Consider the reasons for your answer.

Practise Your Skill

1. Interpret and evaluate the cartoon in Figure 4.18 using steps 2 and 3 outlined in this feature.

2. Choose an issue or event from this unit and create your own political cartoon to illustrate your point of view. Post the cartoons around the classroom and evaluate one another's work.

3. The Internet hosts a variety of Web sites that contain political cartoons about both historic and contemporary events and issues. Browse the sites listed below and choose a cartoon you feel is especially effective. Print the cartoon and explain your reasons for selecting it.

> cagle.slate.msn.com
> lcweb.loc.gov/rr/print/swann/herblock/sand.html
> zone.artizans.com/browse.htm?cat=7
> www.mackaycartoons.net/huh2002-06-18.html
> www.syndicam.com/cartoons/2001_frameset.html

THE HOLOCAUST

During the Second Word War, the Nazis set out to eliminate all Jews—about 11 million people—from Europe. The process began in the 1930s when Jewish citizens were stripped of their rights and possessions. Eventually, Jews were forced to live in urban ghettos and then in **concentration camps**. In January 1942, Hitler gave orders to apply "the **final solution** of the Jewish question"—the systematic extermination of all Jews under German control.

At first, firing squads carried out the mass murders. Later, other techniques were used. Jews were transported by railway cattle cars and trucks from all over Nazi-occupied Europe to death camps such as Treblinka, Auschwitz, Belsen,

Dachau, and Buchenwald. At the camps, those who could work were spared the gas chamber temporarily. Then, along with thousands of other Jews who arrived at the camps daily, they were herded to their deaths in the gas chambers. By 1945, six million Jews had been murdered in the death camps—over 65 per cent of the Jewish population of Europe.

When the Allied armies arrived to liberate the camps, the true horror of Hitler's final solution was revealed to the world. While rumours had circulated during the war, many people believed a policy of **genocide** (the deliberate extermination of a group of people) was inconceivable in the "enlightened" atmosphere of the twentieth century. Now, with the horrific evidence before them, they realized—too late—that genocide had been all too real. Official photographs and films were taken at each camp as proof of Nazi atrocities for the war crimes trials that would follow and as permanent reminders of the extent to which hatred begets tragedy.

In the Nuremberg Trials following the war, 22 high-ranking Nazi officers were charged with various crimes, including crimes against humanity. Twelve were condemned to death. Seven received prison sentences. Three were found not guilty. The trials continued until July 1949, as 99 other defendants were tried and sentenced to prison. Many Nazi war criminals escaped, however. Some were eventually captured and brought to trial. Others managed to hide from their pasts and never had to answer for their actions. The search for war criminals continues to this very day. As late as 2002, one war criminal known as "The Butcher of Genoa" was sentenced in Italy for the slaughter of prisoners of war.

The Extermination of Jews

	Country	Previous number of Jews	Losses Lowest estimate	Losses Highest estimate	
1	Poland	3 300 000	2 350 000	2 900 000 = 88%	
2	USSR	2 100 000	700 000	1 000 000 = 48%	
3	Romania	850 000	200 000	420 000 = 49%	
4	Czechoslovakia	360 000	233 000	300 000 = 83%	
5	Germany	240 000	160 000	200 000 = 83%	
6	Hungary	403 000	180 000	200 000 = 50%	
7	Lithuania	155 000	—	135 000 = 87%	
8	France	300 000	60 000	130 000 = 43%	
9	Holland	150 000	104 000	120 000 = 80%	
10	Latvia	95 000	—	85 000 = 89%	
11	Yugoslavia	75 000	55 000	65 000 = 87%	
12	Greece	75 000	57 000	60 000 = 80%	
13	Austria	60 000	—	40 000 = 67%	
14	Belgium	100 000	25 000	40 000 = 40%	
15	Italy	75 000	8 500	15 000 = 26%	
16	Bulgaria	50 000	—	7 000 = 14%	
17	Denmark	—	(less than 100)	—	—
18	Luxemburg	—	3 000	3 000	—
19	Norway	—	700	1 000	—
	Total		4 194 200 app.	5 721 000 = 68%	

Figure 4.19

Outline your personal reaction to these statistics. In your view, how should nations respond to these kinds of war crimes? (Source: Hans Jacobsen, *Der Zweite Weltkrieg*, 1965)

RESPONSIBILITY FOR WAR CRIMES

The Nuremberg Trials were based on the principle, affirmed by the United Nations, that "the fact that a person acted pursuant to the order of his government or a superior official does not relieve him from responsibility under international law...."

The decision to prosecute individuals for war crimes was a historic event. It brought into focus the competing values of personal and public responsibilities. The trials made it clear that individuals cannot avoid personal responsibility for their actions. Soldiers who shot civilians or herded them into death camps could not deny their personal responsibility by claiming they were simply following orders.

Many suspected Nazi war criminals were hunted down by famous Jewish concentration camp survivor Simon Wiesenthal. In 1961, Adolf Eichmann, the infamous Nazi leader directly responsible for implementing Hitler's final solution, was captured in Argentina and brought to trial in Israel. After a trial that lasted four months, Eichmann was convicted of crimes against humanity and sentenced to death. Some feel that the victors also committed war crimes and have gone unpunished because, as victors, they made the rules. Critics point to the decisions to firebomb Dresden and to drop the atomic bomb on Japan as evidence of war crimes that have gone unprosecuted.

In Canada, the Criminal Code was amended in 1987 to allow trials in this country for war crimes committed by individuals elsewhere. By 1992, there were 45 cases of suspected Nazi war criminals under review for possible prosecution. However, by 2002, only one had been extradited and two deported for their crimes. It is likely that the vast majority of war criminals will die unpunished for their crimes.

Figure 4.20

More than six million Jews were deliberately and systematically killed as part of Hitler's final solution. This figure is based on the carefully kept records of the SS officers who ran the death camps. What other occurrences of genocide have taken place in the world since the Second World War?

FORCES OF RESISTANCE

There are many examples of people who risked their lives to try to help the Jews escape the Nazi onslaught. Their stories lend support to the idea that individuals can make a difference and resist the forces of darkness.

Raoul Wallenberg

A Swedish diplomat stationed in Hungary during the war, Raoul Wallenberg worked tirelessly and fearlessly to help 95 000 Hungarian Jews escape the death camps. Through bribes, threats, bluffs, and false passports, he confounded the local fascist authorities, often risking confrontation with armed soldiers. He was later arrested by the USSR as a spy and died in a Soviet prison camp. For his courage, he was made an honorary citizen of Canada, the US, and Israel.

Sempo Sugihara

As Japanese consul in Lithuania, Sempo Sugihara defied his own government, which was allied with Germany. In a dramatic 19-day period in 1940, he bravely signed exit visas allowing Jews to find transit out of Lithuania, a few steps ahead of the rapidly advancing German forces. Some historians credit Sempo Sugihara with saving 600 lives personally; others note that up to 25 000 may have left using his forged visas. Although forced to resign from the diplomatic service, many years later Sugihara was praised by the government of Japan for his "courageous and humanitarian act."

NETSURFER

WWW.HOPESITE.CA/VHRES/VHRES_DESCRIP.HTML

The tragedy of the Holocaust is carefully documented on many Internet sites. Visit the Victoria Holocaust Remembrance and Education Society site at the above address and see over 400 pages dedicated to "breaking down walls of prejudice and intolerance through education and remembrance of the Holocaust." Consider writing a reflective piece on how the information you uncover at this site affects you personally.

Oskar Schindler

Not all Germans were Nazis. Even those who had co-operated with the Nazis and profited from their activities sometimes found the courage to change their course. Early in the war, Oskar Schindler used forced Jewish labour in Poland to ring up huge profits working on behalf of the Nazi war machine. As the atrocities increased, Schindler had a change of heart and began to use his own money and cunning to save Jews. He purchased a list of 1100 Jewish workers to take to a new factory in Czechoslovakia where they could survive the Nazi killing machine. He and his wife Emilie stopped the Nazis from sending a trainload of 120 starving Jews to the infamous Auschwitz death camp. His actions are all the more remarkable because he had been a willing collaborator with the Nazis and had profited handsomely from his connections. Schindler's story was presented in the powerful film *Schindler's List*.

Voices   The Horror of the Death Camps

The horror of the Nazi death camps has been recorded and preserved for the historical record. Testimony during the Nuremberg Trials presented the grim details of the Nazis' plan for the genocide of all European Jews. These quotations present vivid descriptions of the death camps, from opposing perspectives—that of a commander and that of a survivor. As you read these descriptions, reflect on the question of individual responsibility in carrying out crimes against humanity.

RUDOLF HOESS, NAZI COMMANDANT

"I was ordered to establish extermination facilities at Auschwitz in June 1941. At that time there were already three other extermination camps [in Poland]. I visited Treblinka to find out how they carried out their extermination. The camp commandant at Treblinka told me that he had liquidated 80 000 in the course of half a year. He was principally concerned with liquidating all the Jews from the Warsaw ghetto. He used monoxide gas and I did not think that his methods were very efficient. So when I set up the extermination building at Auschwitz, I used Zyklon B, which was a crystallized prussic acid which we dropped into the death chamber from a small opening. It took from three to fifteen minutes to kill the people in the death chamber.... We knew when the people were dead because their screaming stopped. We usually waited about a half hour before we opened the doors and removed the bodies. After the bodies were removed our special commandos took off the rings and extracted the gold from the teeth of the corpses.... I estimate that at least 250 000 victims were executed and exterminated there by gassing and burning, and at least another half-million succumbed to starvation and disease."

— From the Nuremburg Trials

ELIE WIESEL, HOLOCAUST SURVIVOR

"We did not yet know which was the better side, right or left, which road led to prison and which to the crematory. But for a moment I was happy, I was near my father. Our procession continued to move slowly forward.

"Another prisoner came up to us."

" 'Satisfied?' "

" 'Yes,' someone replied."

" 'Poor devils, you're going to the crematorium.' He seemed to be telling the truth. Not far from us, flames were leaping from a ditch, gigantic flames. They were burning something. A lorry drew up at the pit and delivered its load—little children. Babies! Yes, I saw it—saw it with my own eyes... those children in the flames.... I pinched my face. Was I still alive? Was I awake? I could not believe it. How could it be possible for them to burn people, children...and...my father's voice drew me from my thoughts: 'It's a shame...a shame that you could not go with your mother.... I saw several boys of your age going with their mothers....' "

"My forehead was bathed in cold sweat. But I told him that I did not believe that they could burn people in our age, that humanity could never tolerate it.... 'Humanity? Humanity is not concerned with us. Today, anything is allowed. Anything is possible, even these crematories.' "

Source: Excerpt from NIGHT by Elie Wiesel, translated by Stella Rodway. Reprinted by permission of Hill and Wang, a division of Farrar, Straus, and Giroux. LLC.

Responding

1. How can seemingly normal, educated people commit acts of such brutality?
2. How should nations and individuals ensure that nothing like the Holocaust happens again?

In Review

1. What lessons can all societies learn from the tragedies of war you have read about here?

2. Who should be held responsible for atrocities committed in war—the person issuing the orders? the person carrying them out? both parties? Why?

3. Read the quotation by Martin Niemöller (page 97). What was his message? Does it have meaning for you today in your community, in Canadian society, or in the world?

4. Sometimes when people have a problem they "pick on" someone less powerful than themselves. This is called **scapegoating**.
   a) In what way did the Nazis use the Jews as scapegoats in Germany in the 1930s?
   b) Describe another historical situation in which a person or group has been made a scapegoat.

The Beginning of the Cold War

The ashes of war had hardly cooled when the former allies the United States and the Soviet Union began to look warily at each other as they moved to establish their place in the new world order. The atmosphere of suspicion, distrust, rivalry, and hostility between the superpowers became known as the **Cold War**. An era of tense rivalry between the two countries emerged with the spectre of nuclear war casting a new shadow over the globe.

THE SUPERPOWERS: FROM FRIEND TO FOE

Although the Cold War began after the Second World War, its origins lie earlier in the century. The swift and effective communist takeover in Russia in 1917 shocked the Western democracies. After the First World War, many allies, including the United States and Canada, sent a small number of troops to help the White Russian forces overthrow the new communist regime. This intervention was not forgotten by the victorious Soviet communists.

In the 1920s and 1930s, the West feared that communism would spread throughout Europe. As a result, the Soviet Union was politically isolated by the Western powers. No Soviet representatives were invited to participate in the peace talks at Versailles. The United States refused to recognize the Soviet government until 1933. And the Soviet Union was not invited to join the League of Nations until 1934.

During the 1930s, while the rest of the industrialized world was mired in economic depression, the Soviet Union was forging a new industrial order. Under Stalin's reforms, sweeping social and economic changes were transforming the country. The West watched with a great deal of uneasiness.

BITTER ALLIES

The Soviet Union suffered terrible losses in 1941-1942. The Soviets appealed to the Allies to open a second front in Western Europe to divert some of the German forces and relieve some of the pressure on the Soviet Union. Promises of an Allied invasion of Europe were made but not kept. In June 1943, Stalin was told by Roosevelt that the second front had been postponed until 1944. Stalin suspected the Allies were deliberately delaying a European invasion to give the Nazis and the Soviets more time to destroy one another.

The Battle of Stalingrad (1942-1943) ended with a decisive victory for the Red Army. It marked a turning point in the war and the beginning of the German defeat. But fighting on the Eastern Front remained intense. Throughout 1943 and well into 1944, 75 per cent of Germany's ground troops were engaged there.

As the Soviet army steadily advanced westward in 1943, the Allies began to worry about a new scenario in which the Soviet Union would liberate not only Eastern Europe but possibly Western Europe as well. German occupation of the continent would then be replaced with Soviet domination. With the opening of the second front in June 1944 in Normandy, the Allies began to move west to meet the Soviet army. As the Soviets forced the Germans back from the east, the Allies fought their way to Germany from the west. In a sense, this became a race to capture Europe.

YALTA

At the Yalta Conference in February 1945, Churchill, Roosevelt, and Stalin met to decide the fate of postwar Europe. They agreed that, once defeated, Germany would be temporarily divided into three zones, with Britain, the United States, and the Soviet Union each controlling one zone. The former German capital of Berlin, although deep within the Soviet zone, was also to be divided. It would prove to be a prime flashpoint of the Cold War.

The key issue of the conference was the future of Eastern Europe, particularly Poland. Soviet troops already occupied most of the region and Stalin was determined that the Eastern European states would have pro-Soviet governments. His position reflected the long Russian tradition of establishing a buffer zone along its extensive border. This zone included Poland, Czechoslovakia, Hungary, and Romania. In the Soviets' view, countries they recaptured from the Germans should remain under their control. Twice within 30 years, Russia had been attacked via Poland. As soon as Soviet troops had liberated Poland, Stalin installed a pro-Soviet government there.

Roosevelt and Churchill were reluctant to allow Poland to fall under the Soviet umbrella. After all, Britain had entered the war to guarantee Poland's independence. With the fall of Poland, a government-in-exile was formed in London—the so-called "London Poles"—which claimed to be the legitimate government of Poland. Clearly Poland was a test case: American and British recognition of Soviet control would signal their recognition of Stalin's right to establish a **sphere of influence** in Eastern Europe. Churchill strongly opposed the spread of Soviet influence and he urged the American president to be firm. Roosevelt, however, favoured a global approach to world peace. He proposed a co-operative undertaking, with China, the Soviet Union, the United States, and Britain acting as international enforcers in their own spheres of influence. The Soviets conveniently interpreted this plan to mean that they would police Eastern Europe, thereby effectively establishing their much-desired sphere of influence.

Churchill also favoured the sphere of influence approach to world security. Unknown to Roosevelt, Churchill had already reached an understanding with Stalin. In a meeting in Moscow in October 1944, Churchill and Stalin unofficially—and secretly—agreed on the division of the Balkans after the war. Churchill wrote his "percentage agreements" on a piece of paper and gave it to Stalin. Stalin had the paper translated, then placed a large checkmark on the paper. The deal was done. The Soviet Union would control 90 per cent of Romania and 75 per cent of Bulgaria. Britain would control 90 per cent of Greece. Yugoslavia and Hungary would be divided up fifty-fifty.

Figure 4.21

Churchill, Roosevelt, and Stalin determined the fate of postwar Europe at Yalta. Notice that Roosevelt does not look well. He died in April, shortly after this conference, and was replaced by his vice-president, Harry Truman.

At the insistence of Roosevelt and Churchill, Stalin pledged that free elections would be held in the Eastern European states as soon as possible. This promise was given great significance by Roosevelt and Churchill. But, in reality, when Stalin left Yalta he believed that Soviet domination in Eastern Europe would not be challenged.

TRUMAN TAKES OFFICE

In April 1945, Roosevelt died. Harry S. Truman, vice-president for little more than a year, assumed the presidency. On the international scene, Truman was a relative unknown. Most observers believed he would quietly serve out FDR's term and then fade from the political scene. But Truman was determined to take a hard line with the Soviet Union. He angrily rebuked Soviet Foreign Secretary V.M. Molotov for breaking the Yalta agreement on Polish self-determination. Truman demanded a new government for Poland. But in June 1945 he was forced to accept a compromise when the Soviets agreed to install a few pro-Western Poles in the government. Truman's "get tough" policy was hardening Soviet resistance. His belief that the Soviets would yield to American pressure was a critical misperception.

POTSDAM

Between 17 July and 2 August 1945 another conference was held, at Potsdam outside Berlin. Two of the key players had now changed: Truman represented the US and, partway through the conference, Clement Atlee replaced Churchill as Britain's leader. Stalin still presided over the Soviet delegation.

The Potsdam Conference, although marked by arguments and accusations, began the long process of cleaning up after the war. To establish peace treaties with Italy, Romania, Bulgaria, Hungary, and Finland and to finalize boundaries, the powers agreed to establish a Council of Foreign Ministers. As for Nazi Germany, several conditions were established. It was agreed that all Nazi institutions would be dismantled and Nazi war criminals would be tried and punished. Reparations would be paid in machinery and equipment, with the Soviets having the right to take what they wanted from the eastern sector of Germany and 35 per cent from the western sector. The Allies could not agree on the future of Germany so the "temporary arrangement" to divide Germany and Berlin remained in effect.

The question of Poland, however, continued to be hotly debated. The West wanted to reinstate the "London Poles." Stalin, however, would recognize only the pro-Soviet government—the "Lublin Poles"—already in place and backed by the Red Army. The Western powers finally backed down and accepted Soviet control of Poland.

The conflicts, arguments, and misunderstandings of the Yalta and Potsdam conferences provided a glimpse into the Cold War to come. The American perception was that Soviet control of Eastern Europe was temporary. The Soviet perception was that Eastern Europe was now its sphere of influence. With the defeat of Japan in August, the need for co-operation between the Soviet Union and the West evaporated and the Cold War began in earnest.

In Review

1. What is meant by the term "Cold War"?

2. What were some of the background causes of the Cold War?

3. How did the Second World War both unite and divide the Soviet Union and the West?

4. State the key areas of agreement and disagreement between the Soviet Union and the Western Allies at (a) Yalta and (b) Potsdam.

5. What change of attitude did Truman bring to these negotiations?

6. Contrast the opposing views about the future of Poland held by Churchill and Stalin.

Summary

The short time between the First and Second World Wars was a missed opportunity to create a better and more peaceful world. The failure of the League of Nations and the rise of dictators such as Adolf Hitler led to yet another global confrontation. Appeasement proved to be an empty, hopeless policy. When war broke out in Europe and Asia, it lasted for years, was increasingly brutal, and resulted in at least 50 million deaths.

Out of the ashes of unparalleled destruction a new category of criminal activity was identified. "Crimes against humanity" revealed the bestial nature of modern warfare, the overwhelming power of weaponry, and the need to find a new world order to promote peace and progress.

The world that emerged from the ashes of Berlin and Hiroshima was radically different from that which had gone to war in 1939. Europe was no longer the centre of the world. A bipolar world dominated by the United States and the Soviet Union had emerged after the first half of the twentieth century. The second half of the century would be dominated by the Cold War between these two new superpowers in which every crisis could mean the total destruction of human society.

Viewpoints

ISSUE: Was Hitler responsible for the outbreak of the Second World War?

Background

The conventional historical interpretation is that Hitler and Nazi Germany bear the primary responsibility for the Second World War.

In his controversial book *The Origins of the Second World War*, British historian A.J.P. Taylor challenged this traditional view. Taylor claimed that Hitler did not plan to go to war but was simply a politician trying to solve the historic German problem of security and to right the wrongs of the Treaty of Versailles. Taylor's viewpoint is countered by historian H.R. Trevor-Roper. He argues that Taylor's analysis and interpretation of the events leading to war are historically false. Read these two viewpoints carefully, and answer the questions that follow. (You may want to refer to the Skill Path "Analysing a Reading" on page 14 before beginning.)

A.J.P. Taylor

Most people think that the Germans wanted international equality—a state free from all restrictions on its armed forces and including all Germans. This is correct. But the inevitable consequence of fulfilling this wish was that Germany would become the dominant state in Europe. Again, many people, including many Germans, said that Germany merely wanted to reverse the verdict of the First World War. This also is correct. But they misunderstood what was implied. They thought that it meant only undoing the consequences of defeat—no more reparations, the recovery of the European territory and the colonies lost by the Treaty of Versailles. It means much more than this: not only that things should be arranged as though Germany had not been defeated, but that they should be arranged as though she had won.

We now know...what the Germans would have arranged if they had won the First World War. It was a Europe indistinguishable from Hitler's empire at its greatest extent, including even a Poland and a Ukraine cleared of their native inhabitants. Hitler...was a gambler in foreign, as in home, affairs; a skilful tactician, waiting to exploit the opportunities which others offered to him. His easy successes made him careless, as was not surprising, and he gambled steadily higher....

I fear I may not have emphasized the profound forces. Of course there was a general climate of feeling in Europe of the nineteen-thirties, which made war more likely. In particular, military men—in Great Britain and France as much as in Germany—treated war as inevitable. This was quite right from their point of view. It is the job of military men to prepare for war and indeed to assume that it is coming. But their talk washed over on to the politicians, as it still does, and they, too, began to regard war as inevitable....

We do right to ask: why did war seem likely in the nineteen-thirties? But wars, however likely, break out at a specific moment and presumably over some specific issue. On 1 September 1939 the German armies invaded Poland. On 3 September Great Britain and France declared war on Germany. These two events began a war, which subsequently—though not until 1941—became the Second World War.... I think we are entitled to ask: why did Hitler invade Poland when he did? why did

Great Britain and France declare war on Germany? These questions may seem trivial, but historians spend much of their time on trivialities, and some of them believe that only by adding up trivialities can they safely arrive at generalizations....

Source: Reprinted from *Past and Present* (April 1965), by permission of the author and *Past and Present* (Article: "War Origins" p.110).

H.R. Trevor-Roper

The thesis of [A.J.P. Taylor's book *The Origins of the Second World War*] is perfectly clear. According to Mr. Taylor, Hitler was an ordinary German statesman in the tradition of [chancellors] Stresemann and Bruning, differing from them not in methods (he was made chancellor for 'solidly democratic reasons') nor in ideas (he had no ideas) but only in the greater patience and stronger nerves with which he took advantage of the objective situation in Europe. His policy, in so far as he had a policy, was no different from that of his predecessors. He sought neither war nor annexation of territory. He merely sought to restore Germany's 'natural' position in Europe, which had been artificially altered by the Treaty of Versailles: a treaty which, for that reason, 'lacked moral validity from the start.' Such a restoration might involve the recovery of lost German territory like Danzig, but it did not entail the direct government even of Austria or the Sudetenland, let alone Bohemia. Ideally, all that Hitler required was that Austria, Czechoslovakia and other small Central European states, while remaining independent, should become political satellites of Germany.

Of course it did not work out thus. But that, we are assured, was not Hitler's fault. For Hitler, according to Mr. Taylor, never took the initiative in politics. He 'did not make plans—for world conquest or anything else. He assumed that others would provide opportunities and that he would seize them.' And that is what happened.... The last thing [Hitler] wanted was war. The war of nerves was 'the only war he understood and liked.'...

Do statesmen really never make history? Are they, all of them, always 'too absorbed by events to follow a preconceived plan'? Certainly Hitler himself did not think so. He regarded himself as a thinker, a practical philosopher, the...evil creator of a new age of history. And since he published a blueprint of the policy which he intended to carry out, ought we not at least to look at this blueprint just in case it had some relevance to his policy? After all, the reason why the majority of the British people reluctantly changed, between 1936 and 1939, from the views of Neville Chamberlain and Mr. Taylor to the views of Winston Churchill was their growing conviction that Hitler meant what he said: that he was aiming... at world conquest.

Let us consider briefly the programme which Hitler laid down for himself. It was a programme of Eastern colonisation, entailing a war of conquest against Russia. If it were successfully carried out, it would leave Germany dominant in Eurasia and able to conquer the West at will. In order to carry it out, Hitler needed a restored German army which, since it must be powerful enough to conquer Russia, must also be powerful enough to conquer the West if that should be necessary.

Now this programme, which Hitler ascribed to himself, and which he actually carried out, is obviously entirely different from the far more limited programme which is ascribed to him by Mr. Taylor, and which he did not carry out. How then does Mr. Taylor deal with the evidence about it? He deals with it quite simply either by ignoring it or by denying it as inconsistent with his own theories about statesmen in general and Hitler in particular: theories (one must add) for which he produces no evidence at all.

I think Mr. Taylor's book utterly erroneous. In spite of his statements about 'historical discipline,' he selects, suppresses and arranges evidence on no principle other than the needs of his thesis; and that thesis, that Hitler was a traditional statesman, of limited aims, merely responding to a given situation, rests on no evidence at all, ignores essential evidence, and is, in my opinion, demonstrably false."

Source: E.M. Robertson (ed.), *The Origins of the Second World War: Historical Interpretations*, 1978, Macmillan Press Ltd., pp.83-104 reproduced with permission of Palgrave Macmillan.

Analysis and Evaluation

1. According to Taylor, what did Germany appear to want before the outbreak of war?

2. What kind of Europe does Taylor think Germany wanted?

3. How does Trevor-Roper refute the idea that Hitler was just another German statesman?

4. What criticism does Trevor-Roper make of Taylor's book?

5. Decide which of the viewpoints you tend to support and explain why. If you agree with neither, state the position you do support and explain it. Be sure to use specific information from this textbook, the readings, and other sources to support your position.

Chapter Analysis

MAKING CONNECTIONS

1. How was the world that emerged from the Second World War different from the world that entered it?

2. What current evidence is there that the brutality revealed during the Second World War is still a part of life today? Offer specific examples.

3. Should Canada continue to prosecute suspected Nazi war criminals? Explain your answer.

4. Briefly describe the current relationship of the US and the new Russian federation.

DEVELOPING YOUR VOICE

5. Select one student to take the role of US president Harry Truman. The rest of the class should prepare brief arguments for and against the dropping of the atomic bomb on Japan. Organize a council to debate the issue. The final decision rests with the president.

6. Working in small groups, rank the following in terms of their responsibility for the tragedies of war: (a) government; (b) military leaders; (c) society; (d) the nature of war; (e) specific individuals; (f) other (specify). Discuss your ranking with the class.

RESEARCHING THE ISSUES

7. Select a major battle of the Second World War. Research the battle and prepare a presentation for the class. Include: the objectives and tactics of the battle, the key factors that affected the outcome of the battle, the significance of the battle to the outcome of the war.

8. View the CBC videotape *The Valour and the Horror*, particularly Part III, which examines the role of bombing raids in the Second World War. What questions does this program raise about the Allied and Axis bombing raids?

9. Research the Manhattan Project. Look particularly for details about Canada's contribution. Prepare a written report of your findings.

UNIT TWO

The Cold War

Learning Goals

By the end of this unit students will be able to:
- Describe the shift in the global balance of power resulting from the realignment of nations during the Cold War
- Analyse the structure, procedures, and role of the UN in promoting peace
- Examine the challenges faced by the Soviet Union and Eastern Europe and the reasons for the collapse of the USSR
- Demonstrate an understanding of the nature of the world's power structure at the end of the Cold War
- Recognize and analyse bias in different sources of information
- Evaluate information from a variety of sources and use them effectively to support a point of view

	1946-1959	1960-1969
POLITICS / MILITARY	• Churchill's "Iron Curtain" speech (1946) • Nuremberg Trials (1946) • Truman Doctrine (1947) • Marshall Plan (1947) • First Arab-Israeli War (1948) • UN signs Declaration of Human Rights (1948) • Gandhi assassinated (1948) • Independent state of Israel declared (1948) • Berlin Blockade (1948) • NATO formed (1949) • Communists win civil war in China (1949) • Newfoundland joins Canada (1949) • Korean War begins (1950) • Korean War ends (1953) • Warsaw Pact (1955) • Soviets crush Hungarian Revolution (1956) • Egypt seizes Suez Canal (1956) • W. European nations launch EEC (1957) • Castro becomes leader of Cuba (1959)	• Soviets shoot down US spy plane (1960) • Sharpeville massacre in South Africa (1960) • Berlin Wall built (1961) • US Bay of Pigs invasion (1961) • Eichmann trial in Jerusalem (1961) • Cuban Missile Crisis (1962) • US establishes military presence in Vietnam (1962) • Nuclear Test Ban Treaty (1963) • Assassination of JFK (1963) • US enters war in Vietnam (1964) • PLO formed (1964) • US begins bombing of North Vietnam (1965) • Americans walk in space (1965) • Arab-Israeli Six-Day War (1967) • Canada's Centennial Year (1967) • European Community formed to promote political unity (1967) • Soviets invade Czechoslovakia (1968) • Tet offensive in Vietnam (1968)
CULTURE / SOCIETY	• Spock, *The Commonsense Book of Baby and Childcare* (1946) • Robinson first black player in US baseball (1947) • *Diary of Anne Frank* (1947) • Orwell, *1984* (1949) • First credit card (1950) • Salinger, *Catcher in the Rye* (1951) • Contraceptive pills introduced (1952) • First scaling of Mt. Everest (1953) • Tolkien, *Lord of the Rings* (1954) • Rock 'n' roll (1955) • Disneyland opens (1955) • Galbraith, *The Affluent Society* (1958) • Stereophonic records introduced (1958)	• Freedom riders test racism in southern US (1961) • Thalidomide tragedy – deformed babies worldwide (1962) • The Beatles become international sensation (1963) • Martin Luther King leads civil rights campaign in US (1963) • Kodak Instamatic camera (1963) • Thousands arrested in US race riots (1964) • Colour TV widely enjoyed (1966) • Rise of black power in US (1967) • 100 million telephones in US (1967) • Worldwide student unrest (1968) • Woodstock music festival (1969)
SCIENCE / TECHNOLOGY	• ENIAC the first computer (1946) • Yeager breaks sound barrier (1947) • Invention of the transistor (1947) • Land develops Polaroid camera (1947) • LP record invented (1948) • Soviets detonate their first atomic bomb (1949) • First commercial jet (1952) • US launches first nuclear submarine (1952) • Watson-Crick decode DNA structure (1953) • USSR explodes H-bomb (1953) • Salk develops anti-polio vaccine (1955) • First use of atomic-generated power in US (1955) • USSR launches first satellite (1957) • US produces first ICBM (1958) • USSR lands satellite on moon (1959)	• France explodes its first nuclear bomb (1960) • Yuri Gagarin (USSR) first person in space (1961) • Britain and France agree to build world's first supersonic airliner (1962) • Telstar satellite (1962) • Valentina Tereshkova (USSR) first woman in space (1963) • First compact disc (1963) • China explodes A-bomb (1964) • American doctors use plastic heart to keep patient alive (1966) • First heart transplant (1967) • US astronauts on the moon (1969) • First human egg fertilized outside of woman's body (1969)

1970-1979

POLITICS / MILITARY

- National Guard in US fires on student demonstrators at Kent State (1970)
- People's Republic of China enters UN (1971)
- US détente with China (1971)
- US and China establish diplomatic relations (1972)
- Great Britain joins Common Market (1973)
- Arab-Israeli Yom Kippur War (1973)
- Arab oil embargo (1973)
- Watergate scandal forces Nixon to resign (1974)
- Vietnam falls to communist forces (1975)
- Egypt's Sadat visits Israel (1977)
- Carter pardons American draft dodgers (1977)
- Vietnam conquers Cambodia (1979)
- Thatcher first woman PM in UK history (1979)
- SALT II signed in Geneva (1979)
- Soviets invade Afghanistan (1979); end of détente

CULTURE / SOCIETY

- Huge wave of American student protest against war in Vietnam (1970)
- Billie Jean King first female athlete to earn $100 000 in a year (1971)
- US army ends draft (1972)
- Global energy crisis (1973)
- Airlift of Vietnam refugees to US (1975)
- Japan introduces the first video game (1975)
- Start of punk rock (1977)
- Cardinal Karol Wojtyla first non-Italian Pope in 450 years (1978)
- Nobel Peace Prize to Mother Teresa (1979)

SCIENCE / TECHNOLOGY

- Boeing 747 jumbo starts service (1970)
- First heart pacemaker (1970)
- Discovery of two new neighbouring galaxies (1971)
- Leakey discovers 2.5 million-year-old fossil (1972)
- US Skylab space mission (1973)
- India sixth nation to explode A-bomb (1974)
- US and Soviet craft link up in space (1975)
- *Viking I* lands on Mars (1975)
- *Viking II* orbits Mars (1975)
- First solar-powered calculator (1977)
- World's first test-tube baby born (1978)

1980-2002

POLITICS / MILITARY

- Solidarity formed in Poland
- US invades Grenada (1983)
- USSR and Eastern bloc boycott LA Olympics (1984)
- Gorbachev elected Soviet General Secretary (1985)
- Canada-US Free Trade Agreement (1988)
- Berlin Wall falls (1989)
- Collapse of E. European communist regimes (1989)
- Unification of East and West Germany (1990)
- Gulf War (1991)
- START Treaty on Nuclear Disarmament (1991)
- Dissolution of Soviet Union (1991)
- UN peacekeepers sent to former Yugoslavia (1992)
- European Union (1992)
- Czechs and Slovaks divide Czechoslovakia (1993)
- Mandela wins first free elections in S. Africa (1994)
- NATO air strikes on Serbia (1999)
- September 11 attacks on World Trade Center and Pentagon (2001)
- Euro currency becomes legal tender for EU (2002)
- UN arms inspectors sent to Iraq (2002)
- 1972 US-Soviet ABM Treaty expires (2002)
- US announces new anti-ballistic missile defence system (2002)

CULTURE / SOCIETY

- Rubik's Cube craze (1981)
- AIDS identified (1981)
- Wall Street stock market crash (1987)
- Hawking, *A Brief History of Time* (1988)
- UN ranks Canada as best country in world in which to live (1994)
- Outbreak of Ebola virus in Africa (1995)
- Mother Teresa dies (1997)
- Princess Diana dies in auto accident (1997)
- First two *Lord of the Rings* movies released (2001, 2002)
- Enron, seventh-largest US corporation, declares bankruptcy (2001)
- Canadian men's and women's hockey teams win Olympic gold medals (2002)

SCIENCE / TECHNOLOGY

- Stealth bomber deployed by US (1980)
- US launches first space shuttle (1981)
- Nuclear accident at Chernobyl (USSR) (1985)
- Space shuttle *Challenger* explodes (1986)
- Hargreaves first woman to scale Everest alone, without oxygen cylinders (1995)
- US space probe, Pathfinder, reaches Mars (1997)
- Molly, an adult sheep, cloned in Scotland (1997)
- Human Genome DNA project completed (2001)
- Canada signs Kyoto Accord (2002)

CHAPTER FIVE

The Cold War: 1945-1990

The Bikini Atom Bomb Explosion of 1946, similar to the one dropped on Nagasaki, Japan, was used by the US navy to test its destructive power. The bomb destroyed five ships, heavily damaged nine, and caused various degrees of damage to 45 others. Apart from the two bombs dropped on Japan, were any other nuclear weapons ever used in war?

"This war is not as in the past; whoever occupies a territory also imposes on it his own system as far as his army has power to do so. It cannot be otherwise."

— Joseph Stalin (1879-1953), Soviet leader (1929-1953)

"They've got to draw in their horns and stop their aggression, or we're going to bomb them back into the Stone Age."

— American Air Force General Curtis LeMay (1906-1990) during the Vietnam War (1965)

Overview

With the end of the Second World War, a new and even more dangerous era began—the **nuclear age**. The spotlight now focused on the fundamental differences between the two new superpowers, the United States and the Soviet Union. The threat of an all-out nuclear war clouded the new dawn that followed the Second World War.

The hostility and tension between the two heavily armed superpowers were based on fear, rivalry, and distrust. The period became known as the Cold War, and it shaped much of the last half of the twentieth century. The term aptly described the hostile atmosphere that developed between the superpowers following the Second World War: while they were not making war, neither were they making peace. The superpowers often played a dangerous game of **brinkmanship**, a risky practice of taking an issue to the very edge of war before turning back at the last moment. The Cold War sometimes erupted into open conflict involving third parties. These **flashpoints** brought the United States and the Soviet Union to the brink of direct confrontation and possible nuclear war.

Focus Questions
1. What events led to the hardening of positions between the superpowers?
2. What roles did ideology and nuclear weapons play in the development of the Cold War tensions between the superpowers?
3. What were some of the major flashpoints of the Cold War?
4. How did the rivalry between the superpowers affect international conflict and co-operation in the last half of the twentieth century?

The Cold War Declared

The deterioration of Soviet-American relations in 1945 was little known outside official government circles in Moscow and Washington. The citizens of the Soviet Union were preoccupied with the enormous task of restoring their country after enduring the ravages of war. The Americans were content to return to their traditional isolationism. After their victories in two theatres of war, they felt secure in the knowledge that they possessed, in the words of President Harry S. Truman, "the greatest strength and the greatest power" the world had ever known.

Washington's attention, however, was riveted on Moscow. Every Soviet move was viewed with suspicion, every utterance from the Kremlin analysed for hidden meaning. The countries occupied by the Soviet army were becoming increasingly entrenched in communism, and further expansion of the Soviet sphere of influence seemed likely.

Many American politicians considered the US monopoly of atomic weapons a deterrent to Soviet expansion and a lever against Soviet domination of Eastern Europe. The atomic bombs dropped on Japan ended the war. They also had the effect of demonstrating American power to the Soviet Union. Between 1945 and

1949, Truman used American atomic power as a threat against the mighty Soviet army. This contributed to deteriorating American-Soviet relations and hastened Soviet development of their own atomic weapons. By 1949, the Soviet Union evened out the playing field by exploding its own atomic bomb.

THE OPENING SHOTS OF THE COLD WAR

Two speeches in 1946 alerted the world to the mounting tensions between the West and the Soviet Union. In February 1946, Joseph Stalin addressed voters in Moscow, predicting that, because of "the unevenness of development of the capitalist countries," they would split into "two hostile camps," with war the inevitable result. He exhorted the Soviet people to prepare for a situation similar to that of the 1930s by sacrificing consumer goods in favour of industrial production. He warned that the future would bring neither internal nor external peace. In Washington, Stalin's words were interpreted to mean that war with the West was inevitable.

Churchill's "Iron Curtain" Speech

Winston Churchill had always been distrustful of Stalin's intentions. He took the threat of communist expansion seriously. At Truman's invitation, Churchill travelled to the United States to warn the Americans of the Soviet threat and the need for an "association of the English-speaking peoples" acting outside of the United Nations to re-order the world. His "Iron Curtain" speech, which received massive press coverage, had a great impact on American public opinion. It convinced many Americans that Truman's "get tough" approach to the Soviets was the right one.

Stalin reacted angrily to the speech. He accused Churchill of embracing racial theories not unlike Hitler's and of wanting English-speaking people to "rule over the remaining nations of the world." Labelling Churchill a "firebrand of war," Stalin reminded him that the Allies had agreed to the Polish settlement in Potsdam. If communism was expanding, it was because "[c]ommunists have showed themselves to be reliable, daring, and self-sacrificing fighters against Fascist regimes for the liberty of peoples."

THE TRUMAN DOCTRINE

A year after Churchill's Iron Curtain speech, on 12 March 1947, Truman delivered his declaration of Cold War. He called on the nation to resist communism throughout the world:

Figure 5.1
In a speech in Fulton, Missouri, Churchill warned that "a shadow has fallen" over the Allied victory in the Second World War. What was the effect of this speech on the American public? How did Stalin react?

MAP STUDY

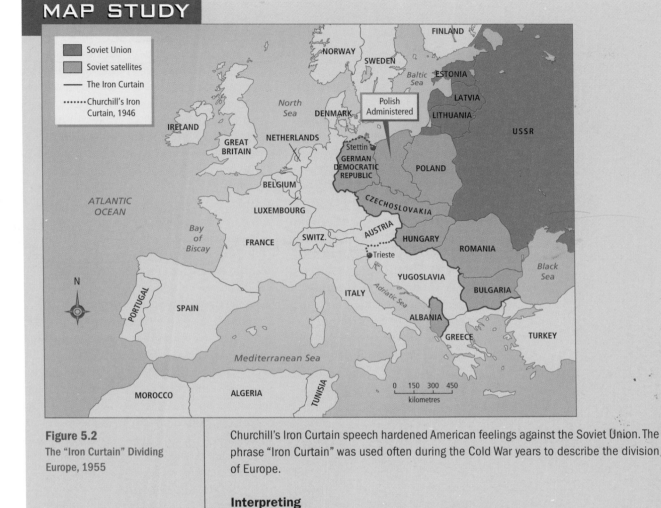

Figure 5.2
The "Iron Curtain" Dividing Europe, 1955

Churchill's Iron Curtain speech hardened American feelings against the Soviet Union. The phrase "Iron Curtain" was used often during the Cold War years to describe the division of Europe.

Interpreting

1. List the Eastern European countries behind the Iron Curtain.
2. Why would the Soviet Union want these countries as buffer states under its control?

"I believe that it must be the policy of the United States to support free peoples who are resisting attempted subjugation by armed minorities or by outside pressures.... I believe that our help should be primarily through economic and financial aid which is essential to economic stability and orderly political processes.... The free peoples of the world look to us for support in maintaining their freedoms. If we falter in our leadership, we may endanger the peace of the world—and we shall surely endanger the welfare of our own nation."

Truman's speech was designed to garner support for an American pledge of hundreds of millions of dollars to prevent the spread of communism in Europe. Greece was in the throes of a civil war in which rebel forces, including communists, were challenging the pro-Western government. Britain could no longer afford to provide military aid to Greece. Although the rebels were supported by Yugoslavia, not Moscow, Truman feared that without Western military support Greece would fall to communism. In reality, however, Stalin recognized Britain's position in Greece; he went so far as to warn Yugoslavia not to provoke a confrontation with the West. For Truman, however, in order to win congressional approval for $400 million in aid, the communist threat had to appear overwhelming.

The policy of fighting communism around the world became known as the **Truman Doctrine**. In the years that followed, American aid was extended to a host of regimes, including right-wing dictatorships, in an effort to block communist takeovers. Thus the United States committed itself to sacrificing money and lives to halt the growth of communism anywhere in the world. It was a policy that would have serious implications for the entire world.

THE POLICY OF CONTAINMENT

George Kennan, a prominent American diplomat and respected expert on Soviet affairs, warned Washington in 1946 that the combination of "the traditional and instinctive Russian sense of insecurity" with communist ideology, secretiveness, and conspiracy would inevitably create an explosive situation. He argued that Stalin's policies were shaped by a communist ideology that called for revolution in order to overthrow capitalist governments. Since the collapse of capitalism was inevitable, according to communist theory, Moscow would be in no hurry. The Soviets would slowly chip away at the capitalist world.

Kennan believed that if the United States could contain the spread of communism, the Soviet system would eventually crumble. He did not advocate military confrontation; his was strictly a defensive strategy. His ideas formed the basis for the new American **policy of containment**.

While Kennan was realistic about the establishment of spheres of influence by both the Soviets and the Americans, Truman's administration was not prepared to tolerate a Soviet sphere of influence in Eastern Europe. Consequently, Kennan's strategy of "firm" containment, when incorporated with Truman's "get tough" policy, lost its defensive character. It was replaced with an aggressive anticommunist policy that called for reducing Soviet influence around the world rather than simply containing it.

AMERICAN FOREIGN POLICY

By 1947, and for the next 25 years, American foreign policy was founded on the fear of communism around the world and within the United States itself. Intervention in the affairs of independent nations was considered justified if the forces of communism were seen as a threat. Anyone challenging the legitimacy of such intervention could be conveniently branded a communist sympathizer.

The assumption in most of official Washington was that *any* action by the Soviet Union was aimed at expanding world communism. Yet there were some who disagreed. They believed that Soviet determination to control Eastern Europe and the Black Sea region was a traditional Russian goal aimed at ensuring national security, an objective that dated back to czarist Russia. They suggested that Stalin wanted to control the countries on the USSR's western frontier to provide a buffer zone against German aggression. But in the suspicious atmosphere of the Cold War, simplistic assumptions about superpower conduct were more readily embraced than more complex political realities.

The prevailing attitude in Washington was that the activities of all communist governments were controlled from Moscow. This was certainly true in the satellite countries of Eastern Europe, where Soviet occupation armies guaranteed that any new leaders would be favourable to Moscow. However, in other parts of the world, such as Vietnam and China, communist governments operated independently. Foreign policies in these states reflected nationalist ambitions and frequently differed from policies Moscow might have imposed.

THE MARSHALL PLAN

In 1947, Western Europe was in the midst of a postwar depression. Governments lacked the capital and resources to revive their wartorn economies. Widespread unemployment and social unrest in Europe caused concern in Washington. If Western European states were to remain outside the orbit of the Soviet Union,

they would have to regain their economic and political strength. American financial aid was the key. Yet there was another reason for placing European economic recovery on the American agenda. As an exporting nation, the United States depended on a prosperous Europe to purchase its products. There was widespread concern that if the European economies did not recover quickly, the United States might also sink into a depression.

On 5 June 1947, US Secretary of State George Marshall announced a new European recovery program that became known as the **Marshall Plan**. The plan offered American economic aid to all countries devastated by the war. The offer was not without conditions, however. Countries seeking aid had to open their economic records to American scrutiny, make their financial needs public, and present a plan for the allocation of funds. The Marshall Plan was open to all countries, including those of the Soviet bloc.

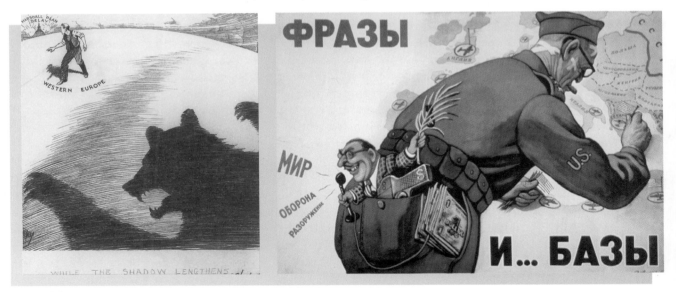

Figure 5.3

These cartoons show how the superpowers viewed each other. How does the Soviet cartoon portray the motives behind the Marshall Plan? What does the American cartoon say about Soviet intentions?

Vyacheslav Molotov, the Soviet foreign minister, was willing to explore the possibility of accepting aid under the Marshall Plan. He met with British and French officials, but refused to accept the joint approach to economic reconstruction that these former Allies proposed. Perceiving the plan to be an extension of the Truman Doctrine and a tool of American economic imperialism, Molotov finally rejected it. He warned Britain and France that the plan would divide Europe, create a strong Germany, and give the United States control over European affairs.

To counterbalance the Marshall Plan, Molotov created a recovery scheme for the Soviet bloc. Czechoslovakia, Hungary, and Poland, which had shown interest in the US plan, were obliged to reject it in favour of the **Molotov Plan**. Lacking the funding of the Marshall Plan, Molotov's scheme was founded on bilateral trade agreements within the Soviet bloc. Eventually, 70 per cent of all trade of the Soviet bloc nations was among the bloc.

In the fall of 1947, 16 Western European countries, including Germany, agreed to a four-year recovery plan. As a leading industrial power before the war, Germany was the key to restoring a healthy economy in Western Europe. And with its strong anticommunist tradition, Germany could provide a counterforce to Soviet expansion.

THE IMPACT OF THE MARSHALL PLAN

More than $13 billion was allocated to the Marshall Plan between 1948 and 1952. As a result, industrial growth in Western Europe flourished. While the plan enhanced economic and political stability, it also produced tangible benefits for the United States. Millions of dollars worth of American goods were sent to Europe. This stimulus to the American economy led to a period of unprecedented growth in the 1950s.

In response to the success of the Marshall Plan, Stalin moved to tighten his political and economic hold on Eastern Europe. In the fall of 1947, coalition governments were abandoned. All non-communist parties were dissolved, paving the way for complete communist control of Poland, Bulgaria, Romania, and Hungary. Non-communist leaders fled their countries or faced imprisonment, even assassination.

Cominform

The Communist Information Bureau (**Cominform**) was established in September 1947 under Moscow's direction. Together with the Molotov Plan, the purpose of the Cominform was to help consolidate the position of the Soviet Union in Europe and bring the Soviet bloc countries closer together. The Cominform co-ordinated the work of Communist parties across Europe, including democracies like France and Italy, where communist supporters were ordered to provoke strikes and use labour unions to mount opposition to the Marshall Plan. Their efforts were unsuccessful and the Cominform was disbanded in 1956.

Comecon

In January 1949, the Soviet Union established the Council for Mutual Economic Assistance (Comecon) as a direct economic response to the Marshall Plan. The intent of Comecon was to form an integrated economic bloc of communist nations. Joint companies were created, and trade arrangements were made to ensure economic control of the Eastern European countries. However, this control led to dissatisfaction and economic stagnation because the Eastern European countries were forced to buy Soviet products and raw materials at high prices. They also had to provide specific products and materials at low prices set by the Soviets. Thus, while the Western European economies grew, Eastern Europe remained poor throughout the 1950s and 1960s.

Pressure from consumers within the Soviet bloc to open markets to the West finally forced the Soviet leadership to more openness in the 1970s. Under Leonid Brezhnev's leadership, Comecon became irrelevant as the doors were opened to a flood of Western products, technology, and investment into Eastern Europe.

THE COMMUNIST COUP IN CZECHOSLOVAKIA

After the Second World War, Czechoslovakia returned to a democratic government under the liberal leadership of President Edvard Benes. But in elections in 1946, the Communists won 38 per cent of the vote, more than any other single party. A coalition government was formed under Communist leader Klement Gottwald.

Czechoslovakia, located along the dividing line between Eastern and Western Europe, had maintained a neutral position in the early stages of the Cold War. Stalin, however, wanted to ensure that the Czechs would be firmly positioned on the Soviet side. In December 1947, in a five-year trade deal, the Soviet Union agreed to supply Czechoslovakia with much-needed wheat and cotton. In February 1948, with active Soviet support, Gottwald and the Communist Party took control of the government, expelling all non-communists and eliminating all other parties. Czechoslovakia was now a single-party dictatorship and a firm Soviet satellite.

The takeover of Czechoslovakia shocked the West. Only 10 years earlier in Munich the Allies had handed Czechoslovakia over to Germany. Now the country threatened to be the spark that would ignite new hostilities. Believing that war was possible, Truman called for a resumption of the military **draft**. In June 1948, he signed the **Selective Service Act**, which ordered all males between the ages of 18 and 25 to register for service in the armed forces. The Cold War was beginning to heat up.

THE BERLIN BLOCKADE AND AIRLIFT

Until 1948, the Cold War had not drawn the two superpowers into open conflict. There had been a war of words, and policies and promises had been made to woo or coerce individual nations into one camp or the other. Still, they had managed to avoid direct confrontation. The crisis in Germany was about to change all of that.

The partitioning of Germany and Berlin into occupied zones was supposed to be a temporary measure. But the fragile state of relations between the Soviets and the West prevented any permanent solution. The stalemate caused severe economic hardship in Germany. To spearhead an economic recovery, the United States, Britain, and France established economic co-operation and currency reform in their zones. Plans to establish a constitutional assembly that would lead to an independent West German state were set in motion. The Soviet Union responded to the West's actions by establishing a blockade of all rail, canal, and road links into and out of West Berlin and by cutting off electric power from East to West Berlin. Since Berlin was located within the Soviet sector of Germany, the 2.1 million inhabitants of West Berlin were left isolated and helpless.

Stalin's motives for blockading West Berlin puzzled the West. On the surface, the blockade appeared to be a protest against the currency reform. But it was more than that. Stalin wanted to prevent the West from establishing a West German state. He wanted the whole of Germany eventually reunified as a communist state under Moscow's control. Stalin may also have been gambling that the West would allow West Berlin to be absorbed into the Soviet sector rather than risk armed conflict. The success of the coup in Czechoslovakia had suggested to Stalin that a gamble might pay off. But it was not to be this time.

Britain and the United States responded to the blockade with a massive airlift. Twenty-four hours a day, thousands of tonnes of supplies were flown into West Berlin. Air space over Germany was open to all the Allies. Had the Soviet

Union tried to block the airlift, it would clearly have been an act of war, and war was not what the Soviets had intended. In fact, the blockade, rather than damaging the West's ties to West Berlin, served to reinforce them. Moreover, a counter-blockade imposed by the British and Americans on Western goods being shipped to the Soviet zone severely damaged the East German economy.

The Berlin Airlift lasted 11 months. Finally, in May 1949, accepting that the blockade was futile, Stalin reopened surface access to West Berlin. As a precaution, however, the airlift continued until September.

In May, the three occupation zones of the Western Allies became the German Federal Republic (West Germany), with its capital in Bonn. The following October, the Soviet zone of occupation officially became the German Democratic Republic (East Germany), with its capital in East Berlin. Germany would remain divided until 1990.

RIVAL ALLIANCES: NATO AND THE WARSAW PACT

The Truman Doctrine and the Marshall Plan were economic strategies designed to foster the reconstruction of Europe. But events like the coup in Czechoslovakia and the Berlin Blockade suggested to the Americans that economic intervention was not enough to contain communist expansion. A greater military deterrent was needed. The policy of **deterrence** is based on the idea that a strong military force, including better nuclear weapons and other military technology, can ensure that the other side will not attack.

NATO

The **North Atlantic Treaty Organization** (NATO) was established on 4 April 1949. It brought together 12 countries—the

Figure 5.4

An American airlift plane approaches the Berlin airport in May 1949 as jubilant Berliners wave welcome. Why were American planes allowed to fly over Soviet-controlled air space?

United States, Canada, Britain, France, Belgium, the Netherlands, Denmark, Norway, Iceland, Italy, Portugal, and Luxembourg. (Greece and Turkey joined in 1952, Spain in 1982.) The purpose of the alliance was to counter the perceived military threat from the Soviet bloc countries. It indicated the West's intent to meet Soviet expansion with collective resistance and to prevent war through collective defence. By signing the treaty, the United States agreed to rearm Western Europe and it assumed a leadership role in the defence of the Western world. NATO represented a big step for the US. Never before had the Americans joined an alliance in peacetime.

To the West, the formation of NATO seemed all the more justified when, in August 1949, the Soviets exploded their first atomic bomb. This marked the beginning of the biggest threat in the Cold War—the **nuclear arms race**. Truman promptly ordered the development of a new super weapon—the hydrogen bomb.

In 1955, West Germany was allowed to join NATO. The decision was a momentous one. As a member of the alliance, it meant that Germany would be rearmed. France and Britain were especially uneasy about German rearmament. But since they did not have the military power to defend West Germany from a Soviet attack, they had little choice. As a precaution, however, German forces were placed under American control.

The Warsaw Pact, 1955

Five days after West Germany joined NATO, the Soviet Union met in Warsaw with representatives of seven Soviet satellites—Albania, Bulgaria, Czechoslovakia, East Germany, Hungary, Poland, and Romania—to sign the **Warsaw Pact**. Modelled after NATO, it set up a military alliance in which members pledged to assist one another in the event of attack. It also established a unified military command, with headquarters in Moscow. The military alliances of the two superpowers, created in order to maintain a **balance of power** between them, were now complete.

Other Military Alliances

NATO was only one part of the new strategy of international organizations and military alliances designed to contain communism. In 1948, the **Organization of American States** (OAS) was established to achieve "peace and justice and to promote American solidarity." Initially, however, it was an American-dominated vehicle designed to resist communism and limit relations with the Soviet Union.

Another alliance, the **Southeast Asia Treaty Organization** (SEATO), was created in 1954. This pact included the United States, Australia, New Zealand, the Philippines, Thailand, Pakistan, Britain, and France. SEATO was created to stop communist expansion in Southeast Asia and was used to justify American intervention in Vietnam. A key provision of the pact provided for mutual action in the event of an external attack or from internal subversion. Thus, the existence of any local communist group labelled "subversive" could justify US intervention as part of the American policy of containment.

In 1955, the United States and Britain engineered the Baghdad Pact, renamed the **Central Treaty Organization** (CENTO) after one of the signing members, Iraq, left the alliance in 1958. Initially, CENTO offered mutual assistance between members—Turkey, Iraq, Iran, Pakistan, and Britain (with the US as an associate member)—in the event of aggression. But increasingly the pact sought to provide a mutual defence policy against the Soviet Union.

MAP STUDY

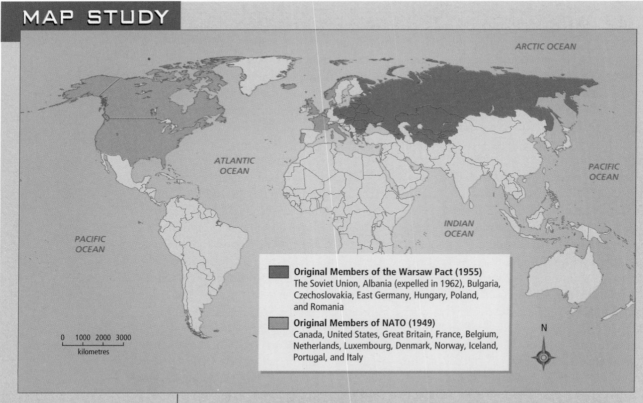

Original Members of the Warsaw Pact (1955)
The Soviet Union, Albania (expelled in 1962), Bulgaria, Czechoslovakia, East Germany, Hungary, Poland, and Romania

Original Members of NATO (1949)
Canada, United States, Great Britain, France, Belgium, Netherlands, Luxembourg, Denmark, Norway, Iceland, Portugal, and Italy

Figure 5.5
NATO and Warsaw Pact Nations

NATO was formed under US leadership to stop further Soviet expansion in Europe. The Warsaw Pact simply formalized existing Soviet military control of the Soviet bloc countries.

Interpreting

1. Why was it important for the Western European nations to include the US in NATO?
2. Why was the US interested in joining NATO?
3. What NATO action prompted the Soviet Union to form the Warsaw Pact in 1955?

WWW.WEBLEARN.CA

This site was developed by the Centre for Military and Strategic Studies at the University of Calgary in collaboration with the Calgary School Boards. Click on the "NATO" module. This module contains information and activities on topics such as:

- Formation of the NATO Alliance
- Cold War Methods
- Assessing NATO's Role in the Cold War
- NATO Crossword Puzzle
- Cartoon Analysis

In 1957, Canada and the United States joined together to create the **North American Air Defence Command** (NORAD). Canada and the United States knew that Soviet bombers would likely fly over Canada's Arctic en route to their targets in the United States. It was essential that the US gain sufficient warning time of any Soviet bomber raid, since its own strategic bombers would need time to launch a strike at targets in the Soviet Union. The agreement established nuclear tracking, warning, and control stations across the northern Arctic. Eventually, surface-to-air missiles with nuclear warheads were introduced. In 1981, NORAD changed its name to the **North American Aerospace Defence Command** (NAADC).

The USSR and Eastern Europe were almost surrounded by military alliances or mutual defence treaties backed by American arms. The United States was now committed to the defence of 42 nations around the world.

THE SPREAD OF COMMUNISM IN ASIA

Civil War in China

China had been embroiled in civil war since 1927. It began when Jiang Jie Shi (Chiang Kai-shek), the leader of the Chinese Revolutionary National Party (the **Kuomintang**) attempted to eradicate the Communist Party. In a three-year purge known as the "White Terror," communists, suspected communists, and communist sympathizers were murdered. Despite the heavy loss of life, the communists, under the leadership of Mao Zedong, continued to be a powerful force. They established a stronghold in northwest China, where they launched repeated attacks against the Kuomintang. The civil war was suspended when China was attacked by Japan in 1937. During the Second World War, the warring sides co-operated long enough to defeat the Japanese. (See Chapter Ten for a more detailed history of the Kuomintang and the Communists.)

When the Second World War ended, the United States attempted to mediate an end to the civil war by negotiating a coalition government between Jiang and Mao. But the attempt failed and civil war resumed in 1946. Substantial American aid in the form of arms, money, and military advisors was provided to Jiang to bolster his fight against communism. Between 1945 and 1949, more than

$3.5 billion was invested in the Nationalist forces in an attempt to stop the communists. Ironically, Stalin also aided Jiang as part of an earlier agreement with Franklin D. Roosevelt in 1945 before the defeat of Japan. But he had other motives as well. Stalin did not want to see a strong, united China that might oppose Soviet ambitions in Asia, and Soviet leadership in the world Communist movement.

Mao's policies of land reform and peasants' rights had strong appeal for the large majority of Chinese people. The Communist army was disciplined and had gained respect for its dedicated defence of China against Japan. By 1946, Mao's policies were beginning to make steady inroads. Jiang, on the other hand, headed a corrupt regime and was seen in China as an American puppet. Jiang represented a return to the past and was uninterested in reform. Areas controlled by the Kuomintang were poorly run and

Figure 5.6

Mao and Jiang toast their success against Japan in the Second World War at a dinner held in the fall of 1945. This friendship was short-lived, since the two enemies resumed their civil war immediately after the surrender of Japan.

corrupt. Toward the end of the civil war, many Nationalist soldiers deserted to the Communist side.

By 1948, it was apparent that the Communists would win. Washington now faced a difficult decision: to withdraw support of Jiang, thereby losing face as well as the enormous Chinese market, or to embark on full-scale military intervention, creating resentment on the part of the Chinese people and condemnation by the American public. Reluctantly, Truman decided to halt the flow of aid to the Kuomintang.

In Beijing, on 1 October 1949, Mao proclaimed the People's Republic of China. Jiang, along with the remnants of his Nationalist army, fled to the island of Taiwan, where he set up the Republic of China. In the years that followed, Taiwan was supported through foreign aid and was protected by the US navy. The American government recognized Taiwan as the sole legitimate government of China in the naive hope that Jiang would eventually liberate the mainland from the Communists.

The United States blocked the People's Republic of China from admission to the United Nations. It insisted that Jiang's tiny Republic of China hold the UN seat for all of China. As a result, over 25 per cent of the world's people were not represented in the UN. It was not until 1971 that the People's Republic of China (mainland China) was admitted to the UN, replacing the Republic of China in Taiwan. In 1978, the United States finally recognized the People's Republic as the sole legal government of China.

The Korean Conflict

The Cold War turned hot in 1950 with the outbreak of the Korean War. This conflict marked the first face-to-face confrontation between Communist troops and Western forces. The Americans led a UN-sponsored army into combat against the Communist forces of North Korea, who were supported by Chinese troops. The guns fell silent in 1953, but no lasting peace was achieved. UN forces continued to patrol the border between North and South Korea. (The Korean conflict is discussed in greater detail in Chapter Six.)

COLD WAR POLITICS

The atmosphere of suspicion and fear escalated in the 1950s. The United States and the Soviet Union were increasingly distrustful of each other's motives and actions. This was clearly exhibited by the continual wrangling at the United Nations.

But fear and mistrust were evident within the two countries as well, not only in the totalitarian Soviet Union, but in the democratic United States. Dissent or disagreement with government policies was frequently viewed as suspicious or subversive. In the United States, this led to the anticommunist crusade of Senator Joseph McCarthy. From 1950 to 1954, McCarthy and the House Un-American Activities Committee searched for communists everywhere in American society. Often with little or no substantial proof, they accused fellow legislators, civil servants, Hollywood actors, newspaper publishers, US army officers, and even the 1952 Democratic presidential candidate, of communist activities. **McCarthyism**, as it became known, destroyed the lives of many innocent people. By 1954, McCarthy's colleagues in the Senate had denounced him and stripped him of his power. But the anxiety and antagonism that was reflected in and intensified by McCarthyism affected American policy for decades and prevented a balanced American appraisal of Soviet aims and Communist leaders.

In Review

1. What was the Truman Doctrine? What was its impact on the Cold War?

2. Explain the policy of containment. Do you think this was an effective way to deal with the Soviet Union? Explain.

3. Briefly explain the objectives, terms, and results of the Marshall Plan.

4. What was the impact of the following events on the course of the Cold War: (a) the coup in Czechoslovakia; and (b) the Berlin Blockade and Airlift?

5. In your opinion, could the Cold War have been avoided? Explain.

6. Compare the origins, membership, and goals of (a) NATO, (b) the Warsaw Pact, and (c) NORAD.

7. Why were Mao and the Communists able to gain victory in China?

8. Explain the purpose and results of McCarthyism in the United States.

Cold War Flashpoints

A series of international incidents between the late 1950s and the 1980s caused the Cold War to heat up. Each of these flashpoints added to the antagonism between East and West and heightened fears of a Third World War.

FLASHPOINT: THE HUNGARIAN REVOLUTION, 1956

Stalin's death in March 1953 opened the door to new leadership and opportunity for the Soviet Union. When Nikita Khrushchev finally emerged as the new leader, he openly criticized Stalin's legacy in a policy of "de-Stalinization" that proved popular at home and around the world.

Khrushchev's speeches at the Twentieth Communist Party Congress in 1956 denouncing Stalin unleashed a great deal of hope in the world and raised expectations for nations in the communist bloc. Khrushchev called for greater individual liberty and denounced the role of the secret police. He also questioned Stalin's belief that the Soviet Union was the centre of communism. This suggested that the satellite nations could experiment with their own brand of communism, as Marshal Josip Broz Tito in Yugoslavia had been doing since 1948 (see Chapter Seven).

Hardline Stalinists in Soviet bloc nations felt threatened by Khrushchev's new approach and its effects. In Poland, for example, the Stalinist leader, Boleslaw Bierut, was replaced by the popular leader, Wladyslaw Gomulka. Gomulka had been imprisoned by the government in 1951 because he favoured social and economic reforms to reduce Soviet control of his country. Khrushchev confronted Gomulka in a dramatic face-to-face meeting in which the Polish leader stood firm while promising to remain within the Warsaw Pact and friendly to the USSR. Khrushchev analysed the situation and agreed. Gomulka could stay, and Poland was given elbow room to develop its own national brand of communism.

Inspired by the success of Poland, the people of Hungary began to call for similar

Figure 5.7
Rebels wave the Hungarian flag from a Soviet tank captured in the main square in front of the houses of parliament in Budapest on 2 November 1956.

changes. Intellectuals demanded more freedom and a return to true socialist values and ideals. Workers wanted better wages and working conditions. Hungarian nationalists railed against Soviet domination and influence. A wave of resentment rose against the brutality, incompetence, and corruption of the Hungarian Communist regime.

On 23 October 1956, 50 000 Hungarians gathered in front of the Polish embassy in their capital city, Budapest. Their new prime minister, Erno Gero, spoke to the crowd. The throng was expecting some statements about change and freedom, but Gero lectured them instead. The mob became enraged, destroying a large statue of Stalin and battling with the police. As the situation deteriorated and violence spread, Prime Minister Gero was replaced by Imre Nagy,

who was much more sympathetic to change. Pushed by events, and misreading the extent of support from the US, Nagy made the fatal error of announcing that Hungary would withdraw from the Warsaw Pact to become a neutral, multiparty democracy. This was a step too far for the Soviet Union. On November 4, Soviet tanks and troops moved into Budapest to crush the revolution.

Soon the world was faced with images and reports of savage fighting in the streets of Budapest. Hungarian freedom fighters, the hated secret police, and Soviet soldiers all committed acts of cruelty and brutality. Corpses hung from lampposts, soldiers were burned alive in their vehicles, and civilians were cut down in crossfires. Some Hungarian freedom fighters were little more than children waging a hopeless war against heavily armed, seasoned soldiers and tanks. The revolution was soon smashed; Nagy, the Communist rebel, was executed, and a pro-Soviet government was restored under Janos Kadar.

All of this took place with little response from the West or the United Nations. Hungary's calls for assistance went largely unheeded. The West was in the middle of the Suez Crisis and was focused on the Middle East. Also, many in the West considered this a distant internal battle among communists.

The use of force in Hungary was seen by many in the West as proof of Soviet aggression. The Soviet Union, meanwhile, claimed that it had been invited by Hungarian Communists to intervene. The Soviets were not deterred by American power from crushing Hungary. They had acted to make sure that a buffer state stayed friendly. Hungary was in their sphere of influence, and the fact that the US was not prepared to fight over Hungary signalled acceptance of that reality.

FLASHPOINT:
CZECHOSLOVAKIA, 1968

On 19 November 1956, reflecting on the recent brutal end of the Hungarian revolution, journalist Milovan Djilas wrote, "The Hungarian revolution blazed a path which, sooner or later, other communist countries must follow." These prophetic words came true 12 years later in the nearby country of Czechoslovakia. While the time and place were different, the issue was the same: Can Soviet bloc nations break free of Soviet control? And, as in the Hungarian revolution, the answer was no.

The crisis in Czechoslovakia had its roots in the bitter Sino-Soviet dispute of the 1960s. When China became a communist state in 1949 it was not prepared to simply be a member of the Soviet bloc. For example, China wanted the atomic bomb, but the Soviets insisted on joint controls, which the Chinese refused. Then, as Khrushchev consolidated his power and offered détente to the West (see page 168), Mao became suspicious. Was the Soviet Union secretly forming an alliance with the West against China? The final straw was their conflicting policies toward Tibet. In 1959 China was denounced by the West for brutally crushing a pro-independence rebellion in Tibet. China was greatly annoyed to find the Soviets offering symbolic public support for Tibet. By 1960 the Sino-Soviet dispute escalated into a series of serious border confrontations that continued into the 1970s.

The Sino-Soviet rift gave nations in the Soviet bloc an opportunity to play one side against the other. Albania and Romania openly condemned Soviet policy and joined the unofficial Chinese communist bloc. The Soviets did not act, however, since these countries maintained strongly repressive communist regimes. But when Czechoslovakia challenged Soviet control, the revolution was crushed. Czechoslovakia crossed the line by offering liberal communism and national independence.

Czechoslovakia was led by an old Stalinist, Antonin Novotny, until he was overthrown by Alexander Dubcek in January 1968. While claiming allegiance to Moscow, Dubcek announced a policy of "socialism with a human face." He promised the people a less repressive and more efficient government where workers would have a greater say in running their factories. The Soviets were willing to accept moderate changes, but the people of Czechoslovakia began to demand more freedoms. In the spring, Dubcek presented an action program that included freedom of speech, a free press, free elections, and closer ties with the West. This program resulted in what became known as the "Prague Spring" as people begin to exercise their new rights. Unlike other Eastern European countries, Czechoslovakia had been a democracy from 1918 to 1938, and this apparent return to democracy was a dream come true for the population. Small and large groups gathered to celebrate and debate the future of their country.

It was clear that the Communist Party in Czechoslovakia would not win in a free election and that a non-communist government would want to leave the Soviet bloc. This in turn could cause a ripple effect on the other East European countries. The Soviet press began to criticize the Czech leadership, demanding that they act against the "enemies of socialism." On 20 August 1968, Leonid Brezhnev ordered 500 000 Warsaw Pact troops into Czechoslovakia on the basis of what became known as the **Brezhnev Doctrine**. This doctrine stated that intervention was justified by communist bloc forces in any communist country threatened by internal or external forces "hostile to socialism."

Unlike in the Hungarian revolution, there was little organized resistance to this overwhelming force. Dubcek was removed from office and assigned a minor role in the government.

Figure 5.8
Soviet tanks move in to occupy downtown Prague in August 1968.

In Review

1. What is meant by "de-Stalinization"?

2. What caused the Soviet intervention in Hungary?

3. Why didn't the West send in troops to help win freedom for Hungary?

4. In what way did the Sino-Soviet dispute encourage dissent within the Eastern European Soviet bloc nations?

5. In what ways were the Czechoslovakian and Hungarian revolutions the same? In what ways were they different?

FLASHPOINT: THE CUBAN MISSILE CRISIS, 1962

The island of Cuba, 150 km off the Florida coast, had long been an American military, political, and economic stronghold. By 1945, Americans owned 90 per cent of the country's mineral wealth, 80 per cent of its utilities, and 40 per cent of its sugar cane fields. The island was ruled by the corrupt dictatorship of Fulgencio Batista until a young socialist revolutionary named Fidel Castro succeeded in ousting the regime in 1959.

When Castro took power he promised free elections, but none were ever held. Instead, Castro set out to contain all opposition to his regime through government control of the media, the trade unions, and the University of Havana. Those who opposed Castro's government had three alternatives: silence, imprisonment, or exile.

Castro also moved quickly to rid the country of foreign interests and regain control of Cuba's economy. Economic policy was centralized under a planning authority controlled by Castro. Private businesses, which were mostly foreign-owned, were **nationalized.** Some US$1 billion in property owned by Americans was confiscated. In order to redistribute property to the poor, all large estates were expropriated and divided into plots for small landowners. Extensive public housing projects were undertaken, and education and health care were made available to all Cubans at government expense. In time, Castro's regime succeeded in creating a first-class health care system and an education system unequalled in Latin America. His socialist policies, however, pitted the island nation against the United States.

American investors and their government were outraged at the confiscation of American property. In retaliation, President Dwight Eisenhower imposed a trade embargo on Cuba (an embargo that continues to the present day [2003]). American goods could not be exported to Cuba, nor could Cuban goods be imported to the United States. In need of economic and political support, Castro found a willing ally in the Soviet Union, which saw an opportunity to gain an outpost close to the United States. The USSR bought huge quantities of sugar from Cuba and gave large sums of money for the purchase of equipment. The Soviets also began to ship military weapons and personnel to the Caribbean island. Threats and economic pressure from the United States only served to push Castro closer to the Soviets and to embrace communism more fully. Finally, in 1961, Eisenhower severed diplomatic relations with Cuba.

It wasn't long before armed confrontation between the superpowers was ignited in Cuba. The Central Intelligence Agency (CIA) had trained a small army of Cuban exiles; their mission was to overthrow Castro. On 17 April 1961, 1500 exiles landed in Cuba at the Bay of Pigs. The invasion was a disaster as Cuban troops quickly rounded up the invaders.

The Bay of Pigs incident embarrassed the United States and its new president, John F. Kennedy. Perhaps more significantly, however, the abortive invasion strengthened Cuba's ties to the Soviet Union. Soviet weapons were deployed to defend Cuba from another invasion. But between August and October 1962, American intelligence sources and spy plane photographs revealed that something much more sinister was being shipped to Cuba. On October 22, Kennedy announced that the United States had proof that Cuba was building missile sites that could be used to launch Soviet nuclear weapons at the US. Kennedy took a firm stand. He ordered a naval blockade of

"It shall be the policy of this nation to regard any nuclear missile launched from Cuba against any nation in the Western Hemisphere as an attack by the Soviet Union on the United States requiring a full retaliatory response upon the Soviet Union."

– John F. Kennedy, in an address to the nation, 22 October 1961

Cuba. No ships would be allowed into or out of Cuban ports.

Ready to launch a nuclear war, the two superpowers were poised, as Kennedy said, at "the abyss of destruction." This was a classic example of brinkmanship.

The Soviets called the American reaction a "crude form of blackmail" and warned that "if the aggressors unleash a war, the Soviet Union will strike a mighty retaliatory blow." But in reality the Soviets were in a difficult position. The missile sites had been discovered before they were completed and so posed no real threat to the United States. The Americans would have the advantage,

while the Soviets would be caught in a fight far from home on the enemy's doorstep. Their plan had backfired. But now what were they to do about it?

At first, Khrushchev threatened retaliation. But behind the scenes, Kennedy's brother Robert, the US Attorney General, met with the Soviet ambassador to the US on October 27 to present an ultimatum: remove the missiles by the following day or the US would remove them by force. In return, Kennedy guaranteed that the US would not invade Cuba and assured the Soviets that the US had already decided to remove its missiles from Turkey.

In response, Khrushchev wrote directly to the president to negotiate a settlement. He offered to withdraw the missiles if the Americans guaranteed they would not invade Cuba. For Khrushchev it was a face-saving measure. Each side could now withdraw with honour. The missiles were removed and the crisis ended.

While each side claimed success, American Secretary of State Dean Rusk expressed the situation accurately when he said "We were eyeball to eyeball, and I think the other fellow just blinked." The crisis had shown the perils of courting catastrophe. Both sides knew there could be no victory in a nuclear war.

The Cuban Missile Crisis highlighted the need for closer international communications. In response, the famous **hotline** was established between the leaders of the two superpowers. In the event of another major crisis, the two leaders would be able to talk to each other immediately and directly.

Figure 5.9
The world was on the brink of nuclear war when the Soviet Union attempted to establish a nuclear missile base in Cuba. US aerial reconnaissance shows Soviet missiles aboard a ship bound for Cuba. To find out how the US was able to get pictures of the missile sites, go to www.weblearn.ca and click on the "NORAD" module then open the "1960s" reading.

MAP STUDY

Figure 5.10
US Missile Sites in Turkey

Figure 5.11
Range of Cuban Missile Sites If Built

These maps show the range of nuclear missiles in Turkey and Cuba. The location of the missile sites directly threatened the superpowers.

Interpreting

1. The withdrawal of missiles from Turkey was downplayed in the US and given prominence in the USSR. Explain why you think this was the case.
2. Compare the proximity of Turkey to the USSR, and Cuba to the US, in Figures 5.10 and 5.11. Do you think the Soviets were justified in trying to place missiles in Cuba?
3. Estimate the distance from the blockade line to Cuba in Figure 5.12. Do you think Kennedy would have authorized the destruction of the Soviet fleet if it had crossed the line? Do you think both leaders were guilty of pursuing a policy of brinkmanship in this conflict?

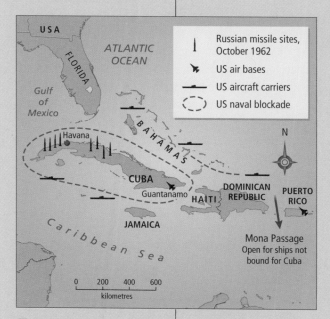

Figure 5.12
US Naval Blockade of Cuba
During the Missile Crisis

Profile   John F. Kennedy (1917-1963)

Figure 5.13
John F. Kennedy

John Fitzgerald Kennedy was elected the 35th president of the United States. Although he served only 1000 days before an assassin's bullet ended his life, his presidency offered a new vision of freedom and social justice. The impact of what came to be known as the "Camelot" years extended beyond the effects of the administration's legislative achievements.

"Let the word go forth from this time and place, to friend and foe alike, that the torch has been passed to a new generation of Americans—born in this century, tempered by war, disciplined by a hard and bitter peace, proud of our ancient heritage—and unwilling to witness or permit the slow undoing of those human rights to which this nation has always been committed, and to which we are committed today at home and around the world....

"And so my fellow Americans: ask not what your country can do for you—ask what you can do for your country."

— John F. Kennedy, inaugural address, 20 January 1961

John F. Kennedy was the second of nine children born to a wealthy Irish family in Boston. He graduated from Harvard University in 1940 and joined the US navy. During the Second World War, the torpedo boat he was commanding was hit and sunk in the Solomon Islands. Kennedy helped his crew to escape despite his own personal injuries, and he was awarded a medal for gallantry.

After the war, JFK won a seat in Congress; he was elected to the Senate in 1952. In 1960 he became the Democratic nominee for president and narrowly defeated his Republican rival, Richard Nixon. At the age of 44, Kennedy became the youngest man to be elected president of the US.

Kennedy's youth and energy created a spirit of hope and enthusiasm. Together with his young and elegant wife Jacqueline, JFK brought a sense of glamour to the White House and created a new image for the American public.

In 1961, as a direct challenge to the successful Soviet space program, Kennedy announced his intention that an American would land on the moon "before this decade is out." Congress enthusiastically approved appropriations for Project Apollo and the space race was on. As JFK had hoped, an American took the first steps on the moon in 1969.

During his term as president, Kennedy enjoyed increasing popularity. But his time in office was not without problems. The Bay of Pigs fiasco in 1961 was a personal humiliation. His leadership was challenged again in 1962 during the Cuban Missile Crisis. This time, however, Kennedy took control and skilfully manoeuvred the situation through the threat of nuclear war.

Kennedy's assassination in Dallas on 22 November 1963 is engraved in the minds of many people.

Responding

1. Why did Kennedy appeal to younger voters?
2. What were Kennedy's main achievements?
3. In 1964, JFK's younger brother Robert ran for president. Research his life, and write your own profile, comparing his life with John's.

Profile   Nikita Khrushchev (1894-1971)

Figure 5.14
Nikita Khrushchev

Nikita Khrushchev, as Soviet leader, sought to effect internal reform while maintaining parity with the United States. Although he rose to power under the wing of Stalin, he also transformed Soviet politics, ridding the system of the worst Stalinist excesses.

> *"Anyone who believes that the worker can be lulled by fine revolutionary phrases is mistaken.... If no concern is shown for the growth of material and spiritual riches, the people will listen today, they will listen tomorrow, and then they may say: 'Why do you promise us everything for the future? You are talking, so to speak, about life beyond the grave. The priest has already told us about this.'"*

— Nikita Khrushchev, 19 September 1964

> *"We say this not only for the socialist states, who are more akin to us. We base ourselves on the idea that we must peacefully co-exist. About the capitalist states, it doesn't depend on you whether or not we exist. If you don't like us, don't accept our invitations and don't invite us to come to see you. Whether you like it or not, history is on our side. We will bury you."*

— Nikita Khrushchev, 18 November 1956

Born into a poor mining family in Kalinovka, Russia near the Ukraine border, Nikita Khrushchev received a sporadic education. In 1918, he joined the Bolsheviks and served in the Red Army during the First World War. By 1935 he had become first secretary of the Moscow region, and by 1939 he was a member of the Politburo.

During the Second World War, Khrushchev saw active duty at Stalingrad. Shortly before the war's end he returned to Ukraine, where he assumed the position of first secretary. With Stalin's death in 1953, Khrushchev emerged as leader of the Soviet Communist Party. In 1956, he launched an attack on the extremes of Stalinism and the "cult of personality" during the Twentieth Party Congress.

In 1958, Khrushchev became premier of the Soviet Union. He introduced dramatic schemes to transform and modernize Soviet industry and agriculture. The challenge of the space race was launched, and the Soviets enjoyed great early success. Internationally, Khrushchev alternately heated up and cooled down the Cold War. He clashed with the US over Berlin and brought his nation to the brink of nuclear war in the Cuban Missile Crisis. Yet he also instigated the notion of peaceful co-existence, travelling to the US, Western Europe, China, and other foreign countries on goodwill missions.

By 1964, Khrushchev's image was tarnished within the Soviet Communist Party. His aborted confrontation with Kennedy during the Cuban Missile Crisis cost him both popularity and credibility at home. Poor harvests and economic stagnation seemed to signal a failure of his domestic policies. In 1964, Khrushchev was forced to resign.

Responding

1. In what way did Khrushchev's background make him an ideal and popular Soviet leader? In what ways is his background quite different from that of John F. Kennedy?
2. List the ways in which Khrushchev added to Cold War tensions and to the prospects of peace with the West.

FLASHPOINT: THE WAR IN VIETNAM

The French had controlled the colony of Indochina (Vietnam, Laos, and Cambodia) since the 1860s. During the Second World War, however, nationalism swept through this corner of Southeast Asia. The British and Dutch reluctantly accepted the inevitability of their colonies gaining independence. The French, on the other hand, were determined to keep theirs and to fight the local nationalist forces.

The Indochinese were led by Ho Chi Minh, a popular nationalist and communist leader who had been seeking Vietnamese independence for more than 25 years. He led his forces using classic **guerrilla warfare** tactics against the French: controlling the countryside, fighting small hit-and-run battles, using sabotage, and winning the support of the local people. In 1954, the main French forces were surrounded at Dienbienphu and forced to surrender. This marked the end of French control in the region. But it would prove to be far easier to win a victory on the battlefields than to create a lasting peace.

Following the Vietnamese victory, a peace conference was held in Geneva, Switzerland. It was agreed that Vietnam would be divided temporarily at the 17th parallel and that elections to reunite the country would be held by 1956. North Vietnam, under Ho Chi Minh, established a communist state. With American support, the South established a government under Ngo Dinh Diem, an ardent anticommunist and willing puppet of American policy. Diem refused to allow the elections to be held, and Vietnam remained divided into two separate and hostile states.

North Vietnam realized that an invasion of the South would provoke foreign intervention, as had happened in Korea in 1950. So instead of invading, North Vietnam began to actively support the Viet Cong communist opposition groups in the South. By 1959, the Viet Cong guerrilla forces were launching major attacks throughout the South.

American Intervention in Vietnam

At first, the Americans stayed on the sidelines of France's Indochina conflict. However, the communist victory in China, the strengthening of the communist regime in North Korea, and tensions with the USSR in Europe led the Americans to adopt a more aggressive stance. In 1954, President Eisenhower proposed the **domino theory** to explain the spread of communism. According to this theory, the fall of one nation to communism leads to the fall of the adjacent country, and so on, like a row of dominos. Thus, it was feared that if the US allowed Vietnam to fall to communism, Laos, Cambodia, and other nations in the region would follow.

In 1960, the US sent 800 military advisors to help the South Vietnamese army. Under Kennedy, the number of personnel was expanded to 16 000. However, the South Vietnamese army was still unsuccessful in containing the communist forces.

With Kennedy's assassination on 22 November 1963, Lyndon Johnson assumed the presidency. Johnson did not want to be accused of being "soft" on communism, nor did he want to be the only American president to lose a war. He was determined to take a hardline approach. In 1964, American naval vessels in the Gulf of Tonkin were allegedly fired upon by the North Vietnamese. (Recent documents indicate that American naval forces may have provoked the incident.) Johnson used the Gulf of Tonkin incident as justification "to take all necessary measures to repel

MAP STUDY

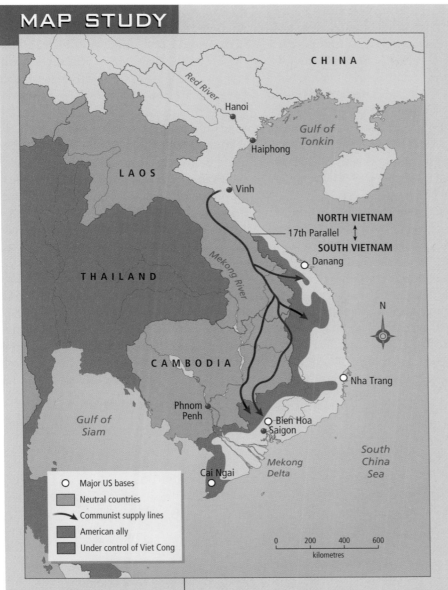

Figure 5.15
Vietnam War, 1960 to 1973

> "As Ed Murrow once said about Vietnam, anyone who isn't confused doesn't really understand the situation."
>
> — Walter Bryan,
> *The Improbable Irish*, 1969

Note that the North Vietnam forces used the neutral countries of Laos and Cambodia for their supply lines. American bombing of these neutral countries to stop the flow of supplies caused international condemnation.

Interpreting

1. Note the locations of the major US bases. What reasons can you suggest for these locations?
2. Compare the American and North Vietnamese strategies for fighting the war. Which strategy proved more successful?

armed attack and to prevent further aggression." From the American perspective this was a **limited war**; that is, a war that did not involve the total effort of the nation, as did, for example, the Second World War. In fact, no formal declaration of war was ever issued, although the conflict gradually escalated into a full-scale war in all but name. By 1965, more than 500 000 American troops were in Vietnam, accompanied by squadrons of helicopters, fighters, and bombers.

The North and South Vietnamese forces were not evenly matched. Typical of other puppet regimes, South Vietnam was hindered by corruption and the lack of popular support. It was never able to mount an effective fighting force. The North Vietnamese, however, were trained and equipped by China and the Soviet Union. The Viet Cong were backed by troops from the regular North Vietnamese forces. Massive American bombing raids on the North killed some two million civilians, but they could not stop the flow of troops and equipment southward along the Ho Chi Minh Trail. When the Viet Cong lost large numbers of fighters in the Tet Offensive in 1968, North Vietnamese regular troops assumed a larger role in the fighting. In spite of their losses, North Vietnam was determined to continue the fight, believing time was on its side.

In the end, the United States, the most powerful military force in the world, lost the war in Vietnam. The reasons lie in the nature of the conflict. Ho Chi Minh and his followers were fighting a traditional war of liberation. They had fought the Japanese, the French, then the Americans. They were fighting for their homeland and their culture. They appealed to the people, who supported them as defenders from yet another group of foreigners. The Americans, on the other hand, were fighting for the abstract idea of "stopping communist

> "Television brought the brutality of war into the comfort of the living room. Vietnam was lost in the living rooms of America—not on the battlefields of Vietnam."
>
> — Marshall McLuhan, Canadian communications theorist and cultural critic

Figure 5.16
North Vietnamese president Ho Chi Minh (right) sought and received aid from Communist China's leader Mao Zedong.

aggression." Technically, the American soldiers were there simply to help the South Vietnamese troops defend their country from the North. Some critics called the US involvement a "**war by proxy**" because the South Vietnamese forces were used to achieve American goals.

American Division Over the War

The American people were divided over the Vietnam War. Many simply didn't understand why US troops were in Vietnam in the first place. They found it hard to believe that the American way of life was somehow threatened by a small country thousands of kilometres away.

It was evident that the conflict in Vietnam would not be resolved quickly or easily. As the war escalated, so too did the anti-war protests at home. Sit-ins at army recruiting offices and demonstrations at military bases often turned violent. Demonstrators burned their draft cards and the American flag. Police were pelted with rocks and bricks; often they used clubs and tear gas to control the crowds. Organized marches like that in October 1967 on the Pentagon brought hundreds of thousands of protesters into riotous confrontations with police and National Guard troops. (See Chapter Nine for more information on the protest movement.)

Tens of thousands of Americans fled the country as **draft dodgers**, many settling in Canada. Others chose to go to jail rather than serve in Vietnam. Those who did fight felt betrayed and discarded by Americans at home. The war in Vietnam was taking its toll on American society at large.

The Costs and Consequences of Vietnam

In 1973, the United States joined North Vietnam in signing the Paris Peace Accords. They called for a withdrawal of

Figure 5.17
Anti-war protesters march through the streets of San Francisco, ca. 1968. Identify and explain the significance of the message on the woman's placard. To avoid going to jail, many protesters fled to Canada as draft dodgers. In 1977, President Jimmy Carter announced a general amnesty for all draft dodgers.

all American troops, the exchange of all prisoners of war, the withdrawal of foreign forces from Laos and Cambodia, and consultations between North and South Vietnam regarding general elections. The two Vietnams were left to determine their own destinies. In 1975, North Vietnam occupied South Vietnam and reunited the country by force of arms.

What did Vietnam cost the world? Most people would say it cost far too much. Over three million American military personnel served in Southeast Asia; 57 000 were killed in action, 300 000 were wounded, and 2500 were listed as "Missing in Action" and have never been accounted for. Tragically, an estimated

> "I regard the war in Indochina as the greatest military, political, economic, and moral blunder in our national history."
>
> — George McGovern, Democratic candidate for the US presidency, 1972

Voices   The Debate Over Vietnam

The war in Vietnam deeply divided the American people. Many of the younger generation denounced the war and even their own country. But most Americans supported military action as a concrete way to fight communism.

In 1964, US Senator William Fulbright observed that "in a contest between a hawk and a dove the hawk has a great advantage, not because it is a better bird, but because it is a bigger bird with lethal talons and a highly developed will to use them." As you read the following quotations, identify the arguments of the "hawks" and the "doves."

RONALD REAGAN, CANDIDATE FOR CALIFORNIA GOVERNOR, OCT. 1965

"We should declare war on North Vietnam. We could pave the whole country and put parking stripes on it and still be home by Christmas."

HANSON W. BALDWIN, JOURNALIST, 1965

"The reasons we must fight for Vietnam have little to do with making Saigon safe for 'democracy' or 'freedom.' There has been far too much cant on this point, far too much effort devoted to trying to establish a politically legitimate South Vietnamese Government after our own image. Nor does it do much good to argue the past, debating whether or not we should have become involved in Vietnam in the first place. The facts are that Communist expansionism in Asia has been consistent, related, and progressive, that the end of the Korean war, without a simultaneous settlement in Vietnam, gave Peking and North Vietnam's Ho Chi Minh the opportunity in South East Asia they have so well exploited….

"Vietnam is a nasty place to fight. But there are no neat and tidy battlefields in the struggle for freedom; there is no 'good' place to die. And it is far better to fight in Vietnam— on China's doorstep than fight some years hence in Hawaii, on our own frontiers."

Source: *New York Times Magazine*, 21 Feb. 1965. Copyright © 1965 by The New York Times Company. Reprinted by permission.

US SENATOR MIKE MANSFIELD, 1964

"The conflict in Vietnam remains a Vietnamese conflict, and in the end it must be resolved by the Vietnamese themselves. We have given extraordinary support to two successive governments in Vietnam. We can do no more and should try to do no more for a third. We have teetered for too long on the brink of turning the war in Vietnam which is still a Vietnamese war into an American war to be paid for primarily with American lives."

US SENATOR WAYNE MORSE, 1963

"So I would have the United States get out of South Vietnam and save the American people the hundreds upon hundreds of millions of dollars that our Government is pouring down that rat hole—and I use the descriptive phrase 'rat hole' advisedly.

"On the basis of the present policies that prevail there, South Vietnam is not worth the life of a single American boy…. [I]… will not vote to continue to sacrifice the lives of American boys in South Vietnam."

Responding

1. What do the terms "hawk" and "dove" mean?
2. Which of the arguments from the hawks makes the most sense to you, and why?
3. Which of the arguments from the doves makes the most sense, and why?
4. After reading both sides of this question, which side do you support—the hawks' or the doves'? Give reasons to support your decision.

50 000 American Vietnam veterans have committed suicide since their return from the war; even larger numbers still battle the substance abuse problems or psychological wounds they brought back from Vietnam. In material terms, the US spent over $150 billion on the war effort.

Among the Vietnamese on both sides, the losses were even more staggering, although more difficult to verify. Certainly more than a million Vietnamese were killed; half the dead were civilians. Hundreds of thousands of uprooted people sought refuge in other, often unfriendly, countries. The economies of both North and South Vietnam were drained. Agriculture, forestry, and fishing industries were devastated.

American involvement in Vietnam did not contain communism in that country or anywhere else in Southeast Asia. In fact, the war proved that the policy of containment through the use of force was unworkable and that American military power was not invincible. Furthermore, American prestige, popularity, and support were diminished in the eyes of many nations around the world.

But perhaps the most serious consequences for the United States were experienced within the country itself. The astronomical defence expenditures distorted the American economy, making it heavily dependent on defence contracts for jobs and profits. With the end of the war, the economy slid into recession and high inflation. The war transformed the vision many people held of themselves as a nation, and it undermined their trust in government, in politicians, and in their country.

FLASHPOINT: WAR IN AFGHANISTAN

Afghanistan occupied a strategic position between the Soviet Union, Pakistan, and Iran. For nearly a century before the Second World War, the British Empire competed for influence in the region, first with imperial Russia and later with the USSR. In the process, Afghanistan was invaded many times. But no foreign power ever succeeded in controlling the fervently independent people of Afghanistan for long.

> "What America lost in Vietnam was, to put it in one word, virtue."
>
> – Barbara Tuchman, American historian

Figure 5.18

Refugees from the 1979 Soviet invasion of Afghanistan crossed mountain passes into Pakistan. In 2001, refugees were again on the move trying to get out of the way of the American-led war on terrorism.

Skill Path

Writing Thesis Statements

Events and people from the past are often the subject of discussion and debate. Joining such a debate by writing a position paper can help you learn more about a particular topic and develop fact-gathering and analysis skills.

The first step in writing a position paper is developing a **thesis statement** (declaration of the point of view you intend to support on an issue). Establishing your thesis statement before you begin to write your position paper will help you to logically develop your stance throughout the paper. You will be better able to organize your paragraphs and defend your position. The following steps will help you to formulate your thesis statement.

Step One: Do Preliminary Research

Since it is always easier to write convincingly about an issue you care about, leaf through this textbook (or any other twentieth-century history book) and find a topic that interests you. Locate books, magazine articles, encyclopedia entries, or television documentaries about your topic to gain background knowledge and broaden your understanding of the issues involved. For example, doing some preliminary research on the Vietnam War will fill you in on the terminology specific to the topic, the chronology of the events, the social, political, and economic circumstances surrounding those events, and the individuals and/or groups who participated.

Step Two: Identify the Issues

Ask yourself what potential controversies or issues you see evolving, and write them down in the form of questions. For example, "Was the US involvement in Vietnam justified?" If you are finding it difficult to formulate at least one question, you may need to do a little more research to clearly recognize different points of view or contradictory evidence about your topic.

Step Three: Write Your Thesis

If you formulated several questions, choose one and answer it with at least two alternative positions. You may want to take one of these positions as your own thesis. Or, you might take certain aspects of each position to produce a balanced point of view. For example, for the question

"Should national leaders be judged by their accomplishments or their methods?" you could answer, "Some people believe that national leaders should be judged by their accomplishments. Others believe that leaders should be judged by their methods." A qualified position would take the stance that "Still other people believe that national leaders should be judged by both their accomplishments and their methods."

Formulating your thesis statement requires careful thought. Your wording must be specific and accurate. Try to keep your thesis statement to one sentence. Your statement must include a clear intent as to what will be demonstrated, proven, or resolved. Here are three examples of effective thesis statements:

- Nation states should pursue self-determination in order to maintain their culture and language.
- Powerful nations should intervene in other countries' civil wars only when their own security is threatened.
- Every nation has a moral obligation to contribute to global collective security.

Next, try to determine if you have enough evidence to support your thesis. Your preliminary research may help you determine this, but you will probably have to do additional research. Strategies that you can use to locate the resources you need are the subject of the Skill Path feature in Chapter Seven (see page 235).

Practise Your Skill

1. Work with another student to compose thesis statements. Collaboration will give each student an audience as you think out loud and draft examples. Here are several issues that you might consider:

- To what extent should nation states be allowed to pursue nationalistic goals?
- To what extent should powerful nations intervene in other countries' civil wars and ethnic conflicts?
- Should nations pursue isolationist policies?

2. Decide what is wrong with the following thesis statement, and then revise it so that it meets the criteria discussed above: "The US got involved in Vietnam as a result of the domino theory."

Between 1945 and 1978, Afghanistan had been first a monarchy and then, following a coup, a republic. Both governments were dependent on Soviet aid, but they also sought ties with pro-Western governments in Iran and Pakistan. The government of Mohammed Daoud, from 1973 to 1978, was dictatorial and repressive. It was strongly opposed by factions on both the political right and left.

In 1978, the Communist Party in Afghanistan seized control and banned all other political groups. The Soviet Union immediately recognized the government and sent in 85 000 troops to support the new state. But the Communist government was unpopular, partly because of its radical reform policies, which alienated small landowners and offended the religious beliefs of the Muslim Afghans. While rival factions among the communists struggled for supremacy, non-communist rebels launched a revolution in the surrounding mountains. Units of the Afghan army began to join the rebels. It became clear that the Afghan communists could neither control the rebellion nor be relied upon to follow Moscow's orders.

The Soviets invaded the country in December 1979 and promptly installed their own choice for leader, Babrak Karmal. At the time, Islamic fundamentalists were sweeping into power in Iran and Pakistan. The Soviets were concerned that these neighbouring countries would offer support to Islamic fundamentalists in Afghanistan, which might create instability in the southern republics of the Soviet Union, where more than 50 million Muslims lived. They also considered the People's Republic of China a potential rival and wanted to preserve their domination of the area.

For the next 10 years, anti-government *Mujahidin* ("fighter in a holy war") guerrillas waged war against Afghan troops armed with and supported by Soviet tanks, aircraft, and equipment. In 1982, the Soviets launched a massive attack against the rebels, but with little success. The Soviet Union sent hundreds of thousands of troops into the country in a futile attempt to put down—or at least outlast—the rebellion. While Soviet troops controlled the country's few cities, the Mujahidin controlled most of the countryside. The conflict became known as the Soviet Union's Vietnam.

The war in Afghanistan renewed tensions between the Soviet Union and the West. The United States unofficially supported the rebels, and by 1986 had provided more than $3 billion in military aid. In protest against the Soviet's intervention, the US cut grain exports to the USSR and, along with Canada and more than 30 other countries, boycotted the 1980 Olympic Games in Moscow.

By the late 1980s, the new Soviet president, Mikhail Gorbachev, initiated a dramatic change in Soviet foreign policy. With growing opposition to the war at home, and with domestic problems mounting, Gorbachev announced that the Soviet Union had no desire to impose its policies on its neighbours and that Soviet forces would be withdrawn from Afghanistan. The Communist government in Afghanistan was quickly overthrown by the rebels, and the country was left to sort out its long-standing religious, ethnic, and political conflicts on its own. After the Soviet withdrawal, Afghanistan fell under the control of the Taliban—Islamic fundamentalists—who were strongly opposed to Western ideas and culture. The Taliban regime provided shelter and support for a wide range of terrorist groups, including al-Qaeda, the group that masterminded the 11 September 2001 attack on the World Trade Center and the Pentagon (see Chapter Twelve).

In Review

1. Why did the Soviets try to install missile bases in Cuba?

2. What measures did Kennedy use to force removal of the missiles?

3. How was the Cuban Missile Crisis settled?

4. Why did the United States become involved in Vietnam?

5. Why was it difficult for the United States to win a military victory in Vietnam?

6. a) Why were Americans so deeply divided over Vietnam?

   b) What role did young people play in opposing the war?

7. Why did the Soviet Union deploy troops to Afghanistan?

8. To what extent can the Soviet Union's role in Afghanistan be compared with the United States's role in Vietnam? Explain your answer.

Détente

Soviet-US relations were not all bad. Under Brezhnev's leadership, the Soviet Union showed a willingness to resolve several key issues with the West. Along with the US, the Soviet Union finally agreed in 1973 to admit East and West Germany as separate countries into the UN. Brezhnev also agreed to accept the US proposals for arms limitation talks if the US accepted Soviet proposals for a European Security Conference (CSCE). This resulted in the SALT I agreement in 1972 and the CSCE Helsinki Accords of 1975. These achievements in the 1970s are examples of **détente**—a French word meaning "to take it easy."

Détente did not end the Cold War, for the Americans and Soviets continued their competition for supremacy around the world. The key difference, however, was the determination to avoid major confrontations between the superpowers, such as the Cuban Missile Crisis in 1962. During this period the United States and the Soviet Union opened the lines of communication, held important summit conferences, and signed a number of significant treaties, particularly in the area of arms control. There was also a tacit acknowledgement of respect for each other's sphere of influence.

Complementing the political and military détente was an informal "economic détente." Brezhnev and the Soviet leaders were well aware of mounting consumer demand for Western products in the Soviet bloc, and so they opened the doors to an influx of foreign products and investment. West German and French banks invested heavily in Eastern Europe. Italy opened a Fiat automobile plant in Russia, and by the late 1970s the US and Canada became the largest foreign suppliers of grain to the Soviet Union.

THE ARMS RACE AND ARMS CONTROLS

The Cuban Missile Crisis taught the Soviets that they were far behind the United States in terms of naval strength. The Soviet navy had retreated from a confrontation over Cuba. The Red Army was

Highlights of a Decade of Détente

Year	Treaty	Terms/Description
1971	People's Republic of China Enters UN	• US agrees to bring mainland China into UN with a seat on the Security Council
1972	Beijing and Moscow Summits	• Nixon travels to Russia and China and establishes new spirit of détente
1972	SALT I	• Nixon and Brezhnev agree to a Strategic Arms Limitation Treaty (SALT I) • first arms limitation agreement since start of Cold War • restricted number of missiles held by superpowers • paved way for more arms limitations talks
1973	East and West Germany Enter UN	• Soviet-American co-operation paves way for "two Germanys" to take their place in UN
1975	Helsinki Conference	• 35 European nations plus Canada, the US, and the USSR sign pact on European security and co-operation 30 years after end of WWII • recognizes Europe's postwar boundaries (Soviet demand) • Soviets pledge support for greater freedoms and human rights (American demand) • increased co-operation in trade, science, and technology
1979	SALT II	• renewal and expansion of landmark SALT I agreement • return of Cold War tensions after Soviet invasion of Afghanistan leads US Congress to refuse final ratification

powerful, but it was mainly in Europe. The USSR did not have a powerful navy or air force, nor did it have the nuclear missiles to match American power and capability. In response, the Soviets adopted two strategies, one diplomatic and the other military. On the diplomatic front, the USSR promoted détente to avoid another direct confrontation with the Americans. On the military front, over time, the Soviets set out to establish greater power at sea and in the air.

The lesson of the Cuban Missile Crisis for the United States was quite different. The Americans were convinced that the Soviets were extremely powerful. The firing of a Soviet **intercontinental ballistic missile** (ICBM) and the launching of the *Sputnik* satellite in 1957 supported this myth. But the reality was that the Soviets were unable even to shoot down the American U-2 spy planes that regularly scrutinized their country at 25 000 m. In four years, only one plane was shot down (in 1960) and that was only after it developed engine trouble and lost altitude. It is uncertain why American intelligence failed to gain an accurate assessment of Soviet military strength. However, the **military-industrial complex** used the threat of superior Soviet power as an effective selling point for increases in military spending.

Figure 5.19

How many of the agreements listed here controlled the use or development of nuclear weapons?

Voices   Two American Views of the Soviet Union

In the 1980s, there was a growing difference of public opinion over the Cold War and efforts at détente. On one side were the traditional hardliners who believed that military might was essential in maintaining stable relations with the Soviet Union. On the other side were those who sought a more conciliatory approach to the tensions that plagued the world.

As you read these two points of view, consider which person you believe had a better understanding of the complex relationships among nations.

GEORGE F. KENNAN, AMERICAN INTERNATIONAL RELATIONS ADVISOR

"In this day...when the image of the Soviet leaders has replaced that of Hitler in so many Western minds as the centre and source of all possible evil.... [l]et us not repeat the mistake of believing that either good or evil is total. Let us beware, in future, of wholly condemning an entire people.... Let us remember that the great moral issues, on which civilization is going to stand or fall, cut across all military and ideological borders, across peoples, classes, and regimes.... No other people, as a whole, is entirely our enemy."

Source: *Russia and the West Under Lenin and Stalin* by George F. Kennan. Copyright © 1960 by James Hotchkiss, Trustee. By permission of Little Brown and Company.

RONALD REAGAN, PRESIDENT OF THE UNITED STATES

"Soviet leaders have openly and publicly declared that the only morality they recognize is that which will further their cause, which is world revolution.... Morality is [for them] entirely subordinate to the interests of class war....

"Well, I think the refusal of many influential people to accept this elementary fact of Soviet doctrine illustrates a historical reluctance to see totalitarian powers for what they are. We saw this phenomenon in the 1930s. We see it too often today.

"Let us pray for the salvation of all those who live in totalitarian darkness....

"I urge you to beware the temptation of...blithely declaring yourselves above it all and label both sides equally at fault, to ignore the facts of history and the aggressive impulses of an evil empire, to simply call the arms race a giant misunderstanding and thereby remove yourself from the struggle between right and wrong and good and evil...."

Source: Reprinted with the permission of Simon & Schuster Adult Publishing Group from AN AMERICAN LIFE by Ronald Reagan. Copyright © 1990 by Ronald W. Reagan.

Responding

1. Whereas Kennan warned against "wholly condemning an entire people," Reagan called the Soviet Union an "evil empire" and the fight against the Soviets a "struggle between good and evil." Do you think the people of any country should be called evil? Which of the two statements would you support? Explain your answer.

The Cold War in the 1980s: The Reagan Era

Ronald Reagan was elected president of the United States in 1980. He had little faith in the spirit of détente, preferring to meet the Soviet challenge from a position of overwhelming strength. His administration pursued a policy of strengthening America's military might.

In Reagan's first three years in office, military spending increased by 40 per cent. In 1982 the defence budget was $182 billion; by 1985, the budget was almost $300 billion—bigger than the entire GNP of many poor nations and larger than Canada's entire federal budget. Reagan launched a massive high-tech campaign to develop a *Star Wars*–type defence system to permanently ensure American military superiority over the Soviet Union.

This system, called the Strategic Defense Initiative (SDI), was supposed to provide a shield of laser weapons in space that would shoot down any incoming Soviet missiles. The concept was appealing, but totally impractical. For example, it would not work against the low-flying **cruise missile**—a self-guided nuclear missile launched from an aircraft and programmed to hit a specific target. Also, there were hundreds of missiles hidden in submarines that could deliver a lethal blow. After billions of dollars were spent trying to make the system work, the project was quietly dropped.

Reagan's years in power were also marked by interventions in Latin American countries. Just as the Soviets kept a firm hand on Eastern European countries to ensure co-operative communist regimes, the US was greatly concerned with keeping communism out of the Western Hemisphere.

LATIN AMERICA

In the late nineteenth century, the governments of Latin America sought to modernize their countries. Lacking the financial resources to do so on their own, they encouraged foreign investment from the industrialized nations of Europe. Foreign companies gained control of large segments of the Latin American economy. Their economic clout enabled them to dictate development policies and projects that benefited their interests rather than those of the host country or its people. In the early twentieth century, political imperialism in Latin America had been replaced by **economic imperialism**.

Frustrated by the failure of both democratic governments and military **juntas** to bring about change, new rebel guerrilla movements emerged throughout Latin America in the 1960s. The rebels demanded sweeping reforms, including the nationalization of natural resources

Figure 5.20

American military intervention in Latin American countries like Grenada (in 1983) has been a source of controversy. Why did the United States send troops to this small island nation?

"All people in this
hemisphere are
entitled to a decent
way of life. Those
who make peaceful
revolution
impossible will make
violent revolution
inevitable."

— John F. Kennedy, 1961

and land redistribution. During the Cold War, many of the left-wing rebel groups were backed militarily and/or financially by the Soviet Union. The United States viewed any Soviet influence in the region as a threat to American security and interests. The loss of Cuba to Soviet influence raised fears of the spread of communism to all of Latin America.

In 1961, US president John F. Kennedy initiated the **Alliance for Progress**, a multi-billion-dollar program aimed at fostering democracy and promoting economic development in Latin America. Initially, the program showed modest progress in building schools and hospitals. But the economic development side of the plan gradually lost its momentum, and in the 1970s the program concentrated on American military aid to help governments fight left-wing guerrilla

insurgents. American military aid continued throughout the 1970s and 1980s. Generous supplies of arms were shipped to countries such as Honduras, El Salvador, and Nicaragua. The United States also engaged in many direct interventions in Latin America, including the invasion of Grenada in 1983 to depose the Marxist government there, and the arrest of Panama's dictator Manuel Noriega in 1989.

Nicaragua

Nicaragua is an example of how small Latin American countries were used by the superpowers as pawns in the Cold War. In 1979, Nicaragua's right-wing dictator, Anastasio Somoza, was overthrown by the left-wing Sandinistas. The Sandinistas named themselves after a popular anti-American rebel leader, Cesar Sandino, who was killed in 1934. Since

Figure 5.21
This cartoon deals with President Reagan's secret funding of Contra rebels in Nicaragua even after the US Congress cut off all official funding. Reagan was determined to end what he viewed as the Communist threat in that country.

the Somoza regime was a corrupt dictatorship, US President Carter did not show much concern. But his political rival in the 1980 US presidential election, Ronald Reagan, claimed this was a "Marxist Sandinista takeover" and pledged support for the "efforts of the Nicaraguan people to establish a free and independent government." Reagan won the 1980 election and immediately began a program to overthrow the Sandinista government. The deliberate use of American military and economic power to stop the spread of communism in Latin America became known as the **Reagan Doctrine**.

At first, the US tried diplomacy to force the Sandinista government to change. They hoped the threat of military intervention and the promise of aid would lead Nicaragua to reduce its ties to the Soviet Union. However, the US approach quickly hardened in favour of a military solution. By the fall of 1981, military aid was flowing to anti-Sandinista rebel groups called the **Contras**.

Throughout the 1980s Nicaragua was in a state of turmoil. In 1984 the Sandinista government under Daniel Ortega won a free and fair election with a large majority. That, however, did not stop the US and the Contra forces from continuing the fight to overthrow the government. Finally, in 1990, a loose coalition of opposition parties, the United Nicaraguan Opposition (UNO), won a stunning victory over the FSLN Sandinista government. The UNO victory was due in part to an estimated $26 million provided by the US to help fight the election.

In Review

1. What was meant by détente in the context of the Cold War?

2. List three major highlights that illustrate détente.

3. With reference to the budget for military spending, describe Reagan's strategy for dealing with the Soviet Union.

4. What is the difference between political imperialism and economic imperialism in Latin America?

5. What was the Alliance for Progress? How did the goals of the Alliance change in the 1970s and 1980s?

6. Why was the US concerned about the Sandinista government in Nicaragua?

Summary

By 1950, the world had split into two hostile camps, divided by ideology and armed with nuclear weapons. Over the next 40 years, the superpowers confronted each other indirectly, as in Vietnam and Afghanistan. At other times, they confronted each other directly, as in the Cuban Missile Crisis. Détente created a more conciliatory atmosphere between the superpowers, yet the possibility of nuclear annihilation was always present. The knowledge that the Third World War would leave few survivors was never far from the minds of the superpower leaders.

Viewpoints

ISSUE: Was the United States responsible for the development of the Cold War?

Background

Following the end of the Second World War, the victorious Allies faced a new world. The European powers were replaced by two new superpowers, the United States and the Soviet Union. The fundamental differences between the two former allies quickly gave rise to misunderstanding and friction.

What caused the rapid deterioration of relations between the two superpowers? Did the Americans provoke the Soviets to take an aggressive stance, or were they provoked by the Soviets? The following viewpoints shed some light on this question. In the first reading, John Lewis Gaddis argues that unilateral behaviour by the Soviets was the cause of the Cold War and that the United States was reactive and defensive. In the second reading, Thomas G. Paterson argues that the United States was to blame as it first exaggerated the Soviet threat and then launched the policy of containment against the USSR. Read these two viewpoints carefully and answer the questions that follow. (You may want to refer to the Skill Path "Analysing a Reading" on page 14 before beginning.)

The sincerity of the Americans' alarm

Wartime lack of concern over the powerful position the Soviet Union would occupy in the postwar world had been predicated upon the assumption that the Russians would continue to act in concert with their American and British allies....

Estimates of Moscow's intentions ... consistently discounted the possibility that the Russians might risk a direct military confrontation within the foreseeable future. Several considerations contributed to that judgment, not least of which was the damage the Soviet Union itself had suffered during the war and the still relatively primitive character of its air and naval forces....

But these estimates also suggested that the Russians would not need to use force to gain their objectives, because of the ease with which war-weakened neighbors could be psychologically intimidated....

It was the psychological implications of an extension of Soviet influence over Europe that probably most concerned American leaders. Although the term "domino theory" would not come into currency for another decade, administration officials worried deeply about the "band-wagon" effect that might ensue if the perception became widespread that the momentum in world affairs was on the Russians' side. And despite the United States' own history of isolationism, despite its relative self-sufficiency, there was a very real fear of what might happen if the nation were left without friends in the world. In one sense, this fear grew out of the tradition of American exceptionalism: the United States had always viewed itself as both apart from and a model for the rest of the world....

Soviet historians have argued with unsurprising consistency through the years that the United States over-reacted to the "threat" posed by the USSR in the wake of World War II. During the late 1960s and early 1970s, a number of American students of the early Cold War expressed agreement with that conclusion, though not with the methods that had been used to arrive at it.... These accounts portrayed official Washington as having in one way or another fabricated the myth of a hostile Soviet Union in order to justify its own internally motivated drive for international hegemony. The difficulty with this argument was the impossibility of verifying it, for without access to Soviet sources there could be no definite conclusions regarding its accuracy.... The intervening years have brought us no nearer to a resolution of that problem, but they have witnessed the emergence of several new lines of historical interpretation that appear to call into question the thesis of American "over-reaction."

History, inescapably, involves viewing distant pasts through the prism of more recent ones. The incontestable fact that the United States over-reacted more than once during the subsequent

history of the Cold War to the perceived threat of Soviet and/or "communist" expansionism has, to an extent, blinded us to the equally demonstrable fact that in the immediate postwar years the behaviour of the Russians alarmed not just Americans but a good portion of the rest of the world as well. How well-founded that alarm was—how accurately it reflected the realities that shaped Soviet policy—are issues upon which there are legitimate grounds for disagreement. But to deny that the alarm itself was sincere, or that Americans were not alone in perceiving it, is to distort the view through the prism more than is necessary. Fear, after all, can be genuine without being rational. And, as Sigmund Freud once pointed out, even paranoids can have real enemies.

Source: THE LONG PEACE: INQUIRIES INTO THE HISTORY OF THE COLD WAR by John Lewis Gaddis, copyright © 1987 by John Lewis Gaddis. Used by permission of Oxford University Press, Inc.

The exaggeration of the Soviet threat

Presidents from Eisenhower to Reagan have exalted President Harry S. Truman for his decisiveness and success in launching the Truman Doctrine, the Marshall Plan, and NATO, and for staring the Soviets down in Berlin during those hair-trigger days of the blockade and airlift.... Some historians have gone so far as to claim that Truman saved humankind from World War III. On the other hand, he has drawn a diverse set of critics.... Many historians have questioned Truman's penchant for his quick, simple answer, blunt, careless rhetoric, and facile analogies, his moralism that obscured the complexity of causation, his militarization of American foreign policy, his impatience with diplomacy itself, and his exaggeration of the Soviet threat....

To study this man and the power at his command, the state of the world in which he acted, his reading of the Soviet threat, and his declaration of the containment doctrine to meet the perceived threat further helps us to understand the origins of the Cold War. Truman's lasting legacy is his tremendous activism in extending American influence on a global scale—his building of an American "empire" or "hegemony." We can disagree over whether this postwar empire was created reluctantly,

defensively, by invitation, or deliberately, by self-interested design. But few will deny that the drive to contain Communism fostered an exceptional, worldwide American expansion that produced empire and ultimately, and ironically, insecurity, for the more the United States expanded and drove in foreign stakes, the more vulnerable it seemed to become—the more exposed it became to a host of challenges from Communists and non-Communists alike....

Why did President Truman think it necessary to project American power abroad, to pursue an activist, global foreign policy unprecedented in United States history? The answer has several parts. First, Americans drew lessons from their experience in the 1930s. While indulging in their so-called "isolationism," they had watched economic depression spawn political extremism, which in turn, produced aggression and war. Never again, they vowed. No more appeasement with totalitarians....

Another reason why Truman projected American power so boldly derived from new strategic thinking. Because of the advent of the air age, travel across the world was shortened in time. Strategists spoke of the shrinkage of the globe....

Airplanes could travel great distances to deliver bombs. Powerful as it was, then, the United States also appeared vulnerable, especially to air attack....

These several explanations for American globalism suggest that the United States would have been an expansionist power whether or not the obstructionist Soviets were lurking about. That is, America's own needs—ideological, political, economic, strategic—encouraged such a projection of power. As the influential National Security Council Paper No. 68 (NSC-68) noted in April 1950, the "overall policy" of the United States was "designed to foster a world environment in which the American system can survive and flourish." This policy "we would probably pursue even if there were no Soviet threat."

To Truman and his advisers, the Soviets stood as the world's bully, and the very existence of this menacing bear necessitated an activist American foreign policy and an exertion of American power as "counterforce."

But Truman officials exaggerated the Soviet threat, imagining an adversary that never measured up to the galloping monster so often depicted by alarmist Americans. Even if the Soviets intended to dominate the world, or just Western Europe, they lacked the capabilities to do so. The Soviets had no foreign aid to dispense; outside Russia Communist parties were minorities; the Soviet economy was seriously crippled by the war, and the Soviet military suffered significant weaknesses.... A Soviet *blitzkrieg* invasion of Western Europe had little chance of success and would have proven suicidal for the Soviets, for even if they managed to gain temporary control of Western Europe by a military thrust, they could not strike the United States. So

they would have to assume defensive positions and await crushing American attacks, probably including atomic bombings of Soviet Russia itself....

Why then did Americans so fear the Soviets? Why did the Central Intelligence Agency, the Joint Chiefs of Staff, and the President exaggerate the Soviet threat? The first explanation is that their intelligence estimates were just that—estimates. The American intelligence community was still in a state of infancy, hardly the well-developed system it would become.... So Americans lacked complete assurance that their figures on Soviet force deployment or armaments were accurate.... When leaders do not know, they tend to assume the worst of an adversary's intentions and capabilities....

American leaders also exaggerated the Soviet threat because it was useful in galvanizing and unifying American public opinion for an abandonment of recent and still lingering "isolationism" and support for an expansive foreign policy.... The military particularly overplayed the Soviet threat in order to persuade Congress to endorse larger defense budgets....

The story of Truman's foreign policy is basically an accounting of how the United States, because of its own expansionism and exaggeration of the Soviet threat, became a global power.... He firmly implanted the image of the Soviets as relentless, worldwide transgressors with whom it is futile to negotiate. Through his exaggeration of the Soviet threat Truman made it very likely that the United States would continue to practice global interventionism years after he left the White House.

Source: MEETING THE COMMUNIST THREAT: TRUMAN TO REAGAN by Thomas G. Paterson, copyright © 1988 by Thomas G. Paterson. Used by permission of Oxford University Press, Inc.

Analysis and Evaluation

1. According to Gaddis, what role did fear play in the origin of the Cold War? What is meant by "American exceptionalism"?

2. According to Paterson, what role did President Truman play in the development of the Cold War?

3. Why did Truman pursue such an activist foreign policy?

4. Why did the Americans exaggerate the Soviet threat?

5. Decide which of the viewpoints you tend to support and explain why. If you agree with neither, state the position you do support and explain it. Be sure to use specific information from this textbook, the readings, and other sources to support your position.

Chapter Analysis

MAKING CONNECTIONS

1. Compare the major flashpoints in this chapter using an organizer with the following headings: Dates; Causes; Events; Key Personalities; Results.

2. Working with a partner, list the major conflicts threatening world peace today. Is our world today more, or less, peaceful than at the time of the Cold War? Explain.

DEVELOPING YOUR VOICE

3. Debate the topic: Be It Resolved that the Cold War was started by the USSR.

RESEARCHING THE ISSUES

4. With a partner, prepare a set of questions you would use to interview one of the following people:

   a) Joseph McCarthy

   b) Nikita Khrushchev

   c) John F. Kennedy

   d) Fidel Castro

   e) Ronald Reagan

5. Using this textbook and other sources, collect 10 to 15 quotations by key figures in the Cold War that illustrate their views on various issues and events at the time. Display your quotations in a collage on a class bulletin board.

6. Working in groups, design three "Cold Warrior" trading cards. For each person you select, write a brief biography, perhaps with important quotations or relevant statistics, and some illustrations.

CHAPTER SIX

The United Nations

The entrance to the United Nations headquarters in New York features the flags of the member nations. This office tower houses some of the 15 000 employees working for the UN worldwide. The UN was formed on 24 October 1945 with 51 members. How many members does the UN have today?

"We have our last chance. If we do not devise some greater and more equitable system, Armageddon will be at our door."

— General Douglas MacArthur, United States Army, 1945

"At the UN everybody wins a few, loses a few, settles for half a loaf. No one, not the US, not the USSR, not Japan, not China, not India, can get away with playing the Big Bully or the Lone Ranger."

— Natarajan Krishan, India's Ambassador to the UN, 1985

Overview

After 1945, two new superpowers, the United States and the Soviet Union, emerged from the wreckage of the Second World War to dominate international relations. The two of them set out to carve up the world into new alliances in an effort to find security for themselves and their allies. Caught in the middle of their struggle for power was the United Nations, an organization created to maintain peace.

The superpowers often used the UN as a tool for their own agendas, but over the years the UN gradually began to chart its own course. This chapter will trace the efforts of the UN to achieve collective security for all nations during and after the Cold War.

Focus Questions

1. Why was the United Nations created?
2. How has the UN met the challenges to world peace and security?
3. How effective is the United Nations as a peacekeeper and peacemaker?
4. What is the humanitarian role of the UN?

Creating the United Nations 51

Amidst the confusion of the new world order, the United Nations was founded on 24 October 1945. Fifty-one nations joined together to establish the United Nations Charter calling for international peace, security, and co-operation. Their efforts mark one of the great collaborative achievements of humankind.

One of the Allies' goals during the Second World War was to create an international organization to ensure **global collective security** in the postwar world. Collective security is the protection of individual nations by the large worldwide group of nations. The Allies realized that they needed an effective organization that could deal with belligerent countries, such as Nazi Germany and Japan in the 1930s, and prevent small conflicts from escalating into another world war.

US president Franklin Roosevelt wanted to avoid repeating the tragic failure of the League of Nations. He declared, "This time we shall not make the mistake of waiting until the end of the war to set up the machinery of peace." Long before the guns were silent, the foundations for a new world order were being laid. In a series of meetings between Roosevelt and Britain's Winston Churchill, and later with Soviet leader Joseph Stalin and Chinese leader Jiang Jie Shi (Chiang Kai-shek), the Allied powers built a consensus for an international organization to ensure lasting peace.

The League of Nations had been too weak to stop aggression by the Axis powers. Roosevelt realized that the lack of American participation was one of the main reasons for that weakness. He was determined to make the United Nations a strong organization by ensuring that all the major powers—especially the United States—were actively involved. To ensure ongoing American commitment to the UN, it was decided that the headquarters would be in the United States. A gift of prime land on the Hudson River, from American entrepreneur J.D. Rockefeller, helped determine the UN site in New York City.

THE STRUCTURE OF THE UNITED NATIONS

The creation of the United Nations was an exercise in compromise and negotiation. The lessons learned from the failure of the League of Nations were applied to the new organization. The key issue was how to accommodate the realities of national self-interest of both large and small powers. What was required was a formula that would give the major powers a greater role in the direction of the UN while still recognizing the need for all countries to have their voices heard. The solution was to divide the UN into two parts: a **General Assembly** in which each country had one vote, and a **Security Council** controlled by the major powers. In addition, the Secretariat, the Economic and Social Council, the Trusteeship Council, and the International Court of Justice were created to address other areas of concern to the international body.

THE GENERAL ASSEMBLY

The General Assembly is the forum for all member states. It holds an annual session in September, but meets throughout the year for emergency debates. The Assembly is a meeting place where world leaders or their representatives, from nations large and small, present their positions on various issues.

The General Assembly divides its responsibilities among six standing committees. Reports from the committees are presented to the Assembly for debate. Most decisions are reached by a simple majority vote; resolutions on questions of peace and security, expulsion of member states, and approval of the budget require a two-thirds majority. The Assembly appoints the **Secretary-General** and elects a president to preside over Assembly meetings.

Some critics dismiss the General Assembly as an ineffective "talk shop" where nations simply play politics. Others argue that such a forum, in which all nations are recognized and given the opportunity to express their views, serves a valuable purpose. It provides an opportunity for the peaceful resolution of conflicts and provides a stage on which to focus world opinion.

Figure 6.1
Prime Minister Jean Chrétien addresses the UN General Assembly in 2002. The UN has five official languages: Chinese, English, French, Russian, and Spanish. Simultaneous translations are provided for the delegates.

THE SECURITY COUNCIL

The real power behind the United Nations lies in the Security Council. The Council is made up of two groups. One group consists of five permanent members—China, France, Britain, the United States, and Russia—each of which has **veto power**. The other group consists of 10 non-permanent members (the number was originally six, but it was increased to 10 in 1966), which are elected for a two-year term. The major responsibility of the Security Council is to maintain peace and security. It can order a ceasefire, impose economic sanctions, and authorize the use of military force against an aggressor.

Matters of peace and security were originally placed exclusively in the hands of the Security Council. Since the Korean War in 1950, however, the General Assembly has also been empowered to address these issues. Permanent members of the Security Council have direct control

Figure 6.2

Name the world leaders depicted here at the formation of the UN in 1945. Which country with a veto in the Security Council is missing? What is British cartoonist David Low's view of the conflicting interests of the major powers in the UN?

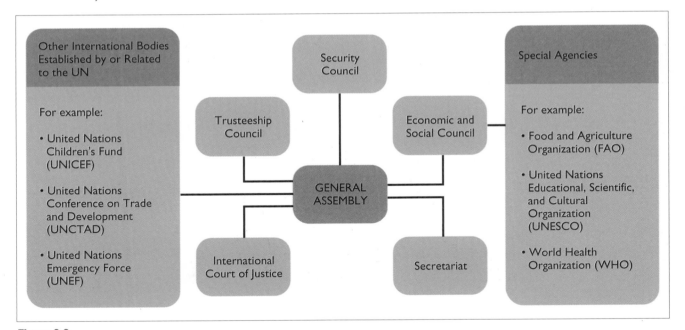

Figure 6.3

The United Nations Organization. The UN has greatly expanded its humanitarian role since 1945. Give one example of an organization shown in the chart that's responsible for security and one that's responsible for humanitarian work. Access the UN Web site at www.un.org for a detailed description of the UN humanitarian agencies.

over UN intervention in any conflict. But, with their individual veto power, any action considered not to be in a member's national interest may be blocked. This has often led to deadlock in the Security Council and provides a ready target for those who question the UN's effectiveness. But it is the power of the veto that ensures the continuing support and commitment of the major powers.

THE ECONOMIC AND SOCIAL COUNCIL

The Economic and Social Council (ECOSOC), with a membership of 54 nations elected by the General Assembly, is entrusted with the **humanitarian** role of the UN. This includes the UN's international economic, social, cultural, educational, and health responsibilities. The work of the Economic and Social Council

has become the most important and enduring of all the UN's achievements. The Council co-ordinates the programs of organizations such as the Food and Agriculture Organization (FAO), the World Health Organization (WHO), the International Labour Organization (ILO), the United Nations Children's Fund (UNICEF), and the United Nations Educational, Scientific, and Cultural Organization (UNESCO).

THE TRUSTEESHIP COUNCIL

This council provides for an international trusteeship to protect the interests of those territories that are not fully self-governing. These trust territories remain under the council's protection until such time as they become independent. The Trusteeship Council consists of the United States, China, France, Russia, and Britain.

Figure 6.4

UNICEF textbooks are handed out to girls in Kabul, Afghanistan. The first textbooks for Kabul schoolchildren began to roll out of the capital's distribution centre on 12 March 2002 as the nationwide "Back to School" campaign began. The campaign, which is led by the Afghan Interim Administration and supported by UNICEF, aims to equip more than 1.5 million primary school age children in over 4000 schools.

THE INTERNATIONAL COURT OF JUSTICE

The International Court of Justice forms an integral part of the United Nations Charter, and all UN members are automatically parties to the Statute of the Court. The Court is composed of independent judges who possess the necessary qualifications to preside over the high courts of their home countries or who are recognized for their expertise in international law. Fifteen judges are appointed to the Court. They are elected by the Security Council and the General Assembly. In 1993, the UN set up a war crimes tribunal—the first international court of its type since the Nuremberg Trials that were established after the Second World War. The tribunal's purpose is to bring to justice those who had been involved in genocide, mass murder, or other crimes against humanity. The first trials were held at The Hague, Netherlands, for those accused of committing atrocities in the former Yugoslavia. The following year, the court was also brought to the African nation of Rwanda, where the ethnically motivated killing of hundreds of thousands of people had taken place in 1994. A Canadian, Louise Arbour, was appointed chief prosecutor for the tribunal in 1996. By the time her term ended in 1999, Arbour had successfully indicted 67 people.

THE SECRETARIAT

The chief executive officer of the United Nations is the **Secretary-General**. With what has been described as the most important public service job in the world, the Secretary-General is the top-ranking administrator and diplomat in the UN. The Secretariat supports a staff of more than 15 000, which is larger than the civil services of many small countries, from more than 140 nations. The Secretary-General reports to the General Assembly, asks the Security Council to deal with matters that threaten international peace and security, and acts as a mediator in international disputes. In addition, the Secretary-General must maintain complete independence, free of any influence by any member of the UN.

Choosing a Secretary-General is a complex process. The candidate must be acceptable to the members of the UN and cannot be too closely identified with a particular country or region. This position has been filled by a variety of leaders from different regions of the globe: Trygve Lie of Norway (1946-1952); Dag Hammarskjöld of Sweden (1953-1961); U Thant of Burma (now Myanmar) (1961-1972); Kurt Waldheim of Austria (1972-1982); Javier Pérez de Cuéller of Peru (1982-1991); Boutros Boutros-Ghali of Egypt (1992-1997); and Kofi Annan of Ghana (1997).

Figure 6.5

At the International Court of Justice, Judge Arbour announces the indictment of Serbian leader Slobodan Milosevic in 2002 (see page 232).

The Purposes and Principles of the United Nations

Purposes

1. To maintain international peace and settle disputes

2. To develop the principle of equal rights and self-determination of peoples

3. To solve international social, economic, and humanitarian problems and promote human rights and fundamental freedoms

4. To be a centre for harmonizing the actions of nations to achieve these common goals

Principles

1. The Organization is based on the "sovereign equality" of all members.

2. All members are expected to fulfil "in good faith" all UN obligations.

3. All members should settle their international disputes by peaceful means so that "international peace, security, and justice are not endangered."

4. All members are to refrain from the threat or use of force against any state.

5. All members are to assist the UN in any actions taken and are not to assist any state against which the UN is acting.

6. The Organization seeks to ensure that non-member states act in accordance with these principles to promote peace and security.

7. Nothing in the Charter authorizes the UN "to intervene in matters essentially within the domestic jurisdiction of any state."*

* Ironically, principle 7, which prevents UN intervention within any state, limits purpose 3, which aims to promote human rights and freedoms. In many cases it is the state government itself that violates human rights and freedoms. **Apartheid**, or absolute racial segregation, in South Africa, was a case in point. This was an official policy of the white government from 1948 until 1991. While many nations demanded UN action against apartheid, the South African government argued that apartheid was an internal matter and therefore outside the jurisdiction of the UN.

Figure 6.6
Do you think the UN should have the authority to overrule national laws that it considers unacceptable?

THE UNITED NATIONS AND THE COLD WAR

The world after 1945 was increasingly **bipolar**; that is, made up of two opposing blocs, one formed around the US and the other around the USSR. The United Nations was caught in the middle. The Security Council became an arena in which the two blocs competed for influence and undermined each other. The Western democracies brought their Cold War battles to the UN and tried to mobilize world opinion on their side. Nations of the Soviet bloc charged that the UN was dominated by the United States and its allies. They had a point, since a majority of UN members until the 1960s were pro-American. To protect their interests, the Soviets began to use the veto on a regular basis. This paralysed the Security Council, preventing it from making decisions or taking effective action in times of crisis.

THE CHANGING FACE OF THE UNITED NATIONS

The early years of the United Nations were decidedly preoccupied with Cold War issues. By the mid-1950s, however, pressures for decolonization of Africa and Asia pushed the organization to broaden its focus. As former colonies became independent and joined the UN, it changed from a body dominated by European and American members to an organization representing more than 160 diverse countries, many of them developing nations. As membership changed, the UN took on a new form. Organizations under the UN umbrella, such as the Food and Agriculture Organization (FAO), the United Nations Educational, Scientific, and Cultural Organization (UNESCO), and the World Health Organization (WHO), began to take on more prominent roles on the international scene.

Conflicting Cultural Values

In 1948, the United Nations passed the Universal Declaration of the Rights of Man. Known today as the **Declaration of Human Rights**, it is a cornerstone of UN policy. This all-encompassing document calls for universal human rights, including the right to fair government and freedom to vote, equal rights for men and women in marriage, the right to fair employment, the right to protect children, the right to freedom to travel, and the right to private ownership of property. But these human rights are primarily a Western ideal. Some of these principles are not shared by non-Western nations. They may conflict with cultural traditions and religious values or with other political, economic, and legal systems. Where reality clashes with ideals, establishing a universally accepted standard of human rights is not a straightforward task.

It is also important to remember that the West has not always embraced the concept of universal human rights. In 1946, both the United States and Britain opposed the establishment of the UN Commission on the Status of Women as well as Article 8 of the UN Charter guaranteeing both women and men the right "to participate in any capacity and under conditions of equality" in all UN organizations. The Western nations, including the United States and Canada, bear the scars of sanctioned injustices against many people throughout their histories. Social values will continue to change over time.

In spite of its cultural biases, the United Nations has developed an important moral and humanitarian leadership role in the world. It has improved world health, economic and social welfare, and education, and it has addressed many important issues, such as those concerning refugees and disarmament. Through its humanitarian efforts, the UN has helped to create a better life for millions of people.

Figure 6.7
Access the UN Web site at www.un.org and find two or three other organizations not listed here. Identify the purpose and achievements of these organizations.

Key UN Agencies

Organization	Date	Purpose
Food and Agriculture Organization (FAO)	1945	To raise levels of nutrition and standards of living; to improve the production and distribution of food and agricultural products; and to eliminate hunger
World Bank	1945	To provide loans to member governments for economic development
United Nations Educational, Scientific, and Cultural Organization (UNESCO)	1946	To promote collaboration among nations through education, science, and culture in order to further universal rights and freedoms
United Nations Children's Emergency Fund (UNICEF)	1946	To provide development assistance aimed at improving the quality of life for children and mothers in developing countries
World Health Organization (WHO)	1948	To obtain the highest levels of health for all the world's citizens through improved health services, the eradication of diseases, improved health training and education, and safe working conditions
International Monetary Fund (IMF)	1947	To promote international monetary co-operation and international trade and to offer monetary assistance
General Agreement on Tariffs and Trade	1948	To establish a common code of conduct in international trade and trade relations and to provide a forum for trade negotiations and the reduction of trade barriers
International Labour Organization (ILO)	1946	To formulate international standards of labour conventions

Profile

Eleanor Roosevelt (1884-1962)

Figure 6.8
Eleanor Roosevelt

Eleanor Roosevelt, the wife of US president Franklin Roosevelt, has been called one of the great women in history. As you read this profile, consider why she was known to many as the "conscience of America."

"When we look upon the failures of the United Nations, we should not be disheartened, because if we take the failure and learn, eventually we will use this machinery better and better. We will also learn one important thing, and that is, no machinery works unless people make it work.

"And in a democracy like ours, it is the people who have to tell their representatives what they want them to do. And it is the acceptance of the individual responsibility by each one of us that actually will make the United Nations machinery work. If we don't accept that, and if we don't do the job, we may well fail—but it lies in our hands. And I think that is the main thing for us to remember today."

— Eleanor Roosevelt, 1946

"When will our consciences grow so tender that we will act to prevent human misery, rather than to avenge it?"

— Eleanor Roosevelt, 1948

The niece of President Theodore ("Teddy") Roosevelt, Eleanor Roosevelt endured an unhappy childhood. Both parents died before her tenth birthday. As a teenager, she was sent to study abroad. In 1905, at the age of 21, Eleanor married a distant cousin, Franklin Delano Roosevelt.

After her husband was stricken with polio in 1921, Eleanor Roosevelt assumed a more active role in his political career. At the same time, she forged an independent course for herself as a champion of the underprivileged. Her confidence and public stature blossomed. During the Depression in the early years of FDR's presidency, she became an inspiration for millions of Americans. Throughout her years in the White House she transformed the traditional role of a political wife and established a remarkable career for herself as champion of social causes. Roosevelt was actively involved in the administration of subsidized housing. She promoted female equality and succeeded in having FDR appoint the first woman to the federal cabinet. During the Second World War she visited Allied forces around the globe, offering her personal support and encouragement.

When FDR died in 1945, Roosevelt's political and social activism rose to even greater heights. She was a delegate to the first meeting of the United Nations General Assembly. In 1946, she was appointed to chair the UN Human Rights Commission. Shepherding 18 nations in the chilling atmosphere of the Cold War, Roosevelt led the group in drafting what she termed "a magna carta for mankind." After long, tedious, and contentious meetings, the United Nations passed the Universal Declaration of the Rights of Man in 1948. This landmark document has been the foundation for human rights around the world. Roosevelt continued to serve in the UN until 1952, and again from 1961 until her death the following year.

Responding

1. List examples of Roosevelt's commitment to women's rights and the underprivileged.
2. What was her major contribution to the UN?

In Review

1. Why was the United Nations created?

2. How was the role of the major powers in the UN different from their role in the failed League of Nations?

3. Describe the work and membership of the General Assembly and Security Council. Which has the most power to ensure peace? Why?

4. Why has the Security Council often been unable to take effective action?

5. What is the main task of the Secretary-General? Why might this position be viewed as an "impossible" job?

6. Rank the seven principles of the UN in order from most important to least important. In point form, list your reasons for your ranking.

7. Summarize the intentions of purpose 3 and principle 7 of the UN Charter, and explain how one can be used to limit the other.

8. To what extent are many human rights issues based on Western values? List examples of human rights that reflect a Western bias.

The Role of the UN in Peacemaking and Peacekeeping

In the 1950s, two crises emerged to threaten the world's security. The United Nations was put to the test in bringing peace and order to these explosive situations. The first conflict was the Korean War, in which the UN acted as **peacemaker** through direct military action. The second incident was the Suez Crisis, in which the UN assumed a new role as **peacekeeper**.

The key difference is in the purpose and nature of the intervention. Peacemaking occurs when an outside force (such as the UN, US, or NATO) intervenes in order to stop a conflict. This kind of operation usually requires a massive military intervention. Peacekeeping, on the other hand, occurs when both sides of the conflict agree to stop fighting and accept a token force to monitor the ceasefire agreement. Since peacekeepers are there by agreement of the combatants, their presence is mainly symbolic and therefore they are not heavily armed.

THE UN AS PEACEMAKER: THE KOREAN WAR, 1950-1953

From 1910 to 1945, Korea had been a Japanese colony. At the conclusion of the Second World War, the USSR declared war on Japan, attacking on several fronts, including northern Korea. With the defeat of Japan, Soviet troops held the northern half of Korea while American troops occupied the south. As with the "temporary" partition of Germany, the Allies agreed to divide Korea, in this case at the 38th parallel. The two Koreas were to be reunited following a peace settlement. But, as with the two Germanys, the Cold War intervened and Korea remained divided.

In 1947, when the United States was unable to obtain Soviet co-operation to hold a general election in Korea, the issue was turned over to the United Nations. The General Assembly voted to establish a commission to oversee a free election and to assist officials in setting up a unified and independent government. The Soviets, however, held their own "election" in the north and established the Democratic Republic of Korea under Kim Il Sung. The Americans did the same in the south and formed the Republic of Korea under President Syngman Rhee.

Both governments claimed to speak for all Korea. Each of the leaders had ambitions to unify the country under his own rule by force of arms. Neither North nor South Korea was able to gain admission to the UN because each was vetoed by the opposing superpower. Instead of moving toward unification, North and South Korea became even more deeply divided, and increasingly hostile. By 1950, tensions had reached a boiling point. War erupted on June 25 when Northern forces crossed the 38th parallel and invaded South Korea.

The Outbreak of War

Once US President Harry Truman learned of the attack he ordered his military commander, General Douglas MacArthur, who was stationed in Japan, to send supplies to the South Koreans. At the same time, the United States Seventh Fleet was dispatched to protect Taiwan from possible Chinese invasion. The following day, Truman pledged American military intervention against any act of communist expansion in Asia.

At the UN Security Council, the United States introduced a resolution branding the North Koreans as the aggressors and demanding that they withdraw their troops from the South. There was no Soviet veto because the Soviets were boycotting the UN over American refusal to allow the People's Republic to take

China's seat in the organization. (In 1949, the defeated Chinese Nationalist government of Jiang Jie Shi had been allowed to keep China's seats in the Security Council and the General Assembly. The Soviets argued that the seat should be held by Mao's new Communist government of the People's Republic of China. In protest, they refused to participate in any UN sessions for six months.) With the USSR out, the UN Security Council approved military action against North Korea. Under US leadership, the UN embarked on its first major test of global collective security.

At first the military campaign went well for the Communist forces. By September 1950, they controlled all of Korea except a small area around Pusan in the southeast. Then, on September 15, MacArthur executed a daring attack on Inchon, splitting the North Korean army in half. (See Figure 6.9.) North Korea lost 35 000 soldiers. What had seemed like an easy victory was turning into a disaster.

With the North Koreans in retreat, MacArthur and President Rhee decided to take advantage of the opportunity to conquer North Korea. Rhee pressured MacArthur to cross the 38th parallel in pursuit of the enemy. But the conflict was still a UN operation. Coalition members, including Canada, questioned the ultimate goals of the operation. The UN resolution had called for the restoration of South Korea; it did not include the right to invade North Korea. Sensing a total victory was at hand, however, a confident Rhee declared: "Where is the 38th parallel? It is non-existent: I am going all the way to the Yalu [River] and the United Nations can't stop me."

The UN forces crossed the 38th parallel early in October and advanced rapidly toward the Yalu River. MacArthur even proposed pursuing the Communists

MAP STUDY

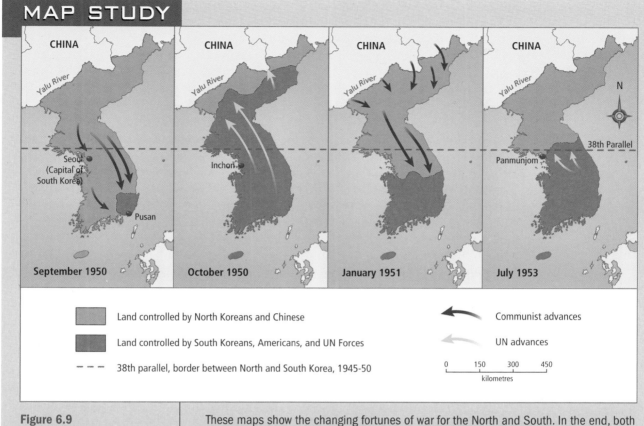

Land controlled by North Koreans and Chinese

Land controlled by South Koreans, Americans, and UN Forces

- - - 38th parallel, border between North and South Korea, 1945-50

Communist advances

UN advances

0   150   300   450
kilometres

Figure 6.9
Korean War, 1950 to 1953

These maps show the changing fortunes of war for the North and South. In the end, both sides settled on the 38th parallel, where they began.

Interpreting

1. What is the significance of Inchon in the second map?
2. What do the small arrows indicate about the attack in 1951?
3. Why were the UN forces reluctant to cross the Yalu River?

into China, bombing the bridges, and laying nuclear waste along the river to prevent the enemy from using China as a safe base of operations. MacArthur believed that the Americans should invade mainland China, defeat the Communists, and restore Jiang Jie Shi to power. However, Truman was not prepared to launch a third world war over Korea, and he ordered the troops to halt at the Yalu. As a concession to MacArthur, he allowed limited bombing of the bridges, but "only on the Korean side." This mixed message convinced MacArthur that, for all his tough talk, Truman was actually "soft" on communism.

At the same time, Truman had received a message from the Chinese government, through the Indian Ambassador via the British, that if UN troops joined the South Koreans in combat north of the 38th parallel, China would intervene. Truman's objective in Korea was a limited victory—to repel the North Korean invasion, thereby demonstrating the effectiveness of collective action by the UN. MacArthur's objective, on the other hand, was to defeat Asian communism. With their objectives clearly incompatible, a showdown between the two was inevitable.

China Enters the Conflict

As the Americans and the United Nations debated the course of action, the People's Republic of China mobilized half a million troops on the Korean border. In late October 1950, UN and South Korean units advancing toward the Yalu River were halted by Chinese forces. Yet just as suddenly as they had appeared, the Chinese troops vanished. Then, on November 25, the day after the Americans and South Koreans resumed their offensive, six Chinese armies counterattacked. Within a month, they pushed the surprised UN coalition troops back beyond the 38th parallel into South Korea.

For several months the battle lines shifted back and forth. A stalemate was developing. MacArthur urged an all-out war, including the use of nuclear weapons. Truman refused, and MacArthur was forced to obey his commander-in-chief. This setback did not stop MacArthur's political interference, however. He continued to clash with Truman over military policy until finally, on 10 April 1951, he was fired. Truman was determined to enforce one of the basic principles of the American Constitution—that the government sets policy while the military carries it out. American policy was now officially to secure a unified and independent Korea by "political, as distinguished from military, means."

Throughout June 1951, behind-the-scenes contacts between American and Soviet diplomats at the UN finally resulted in a ceasefire. Peace talks officially began on 10 July 1951. Yet, throughout the negotiations, sporadic outbursts of fighting continued. A truce between North and South Korea was finally reached on 27 July 1953. In total, between 3 and 4 million casualties resulted from this "limited" war. Of the dead, wounded, and missing, more than half were Korean civilians. In the United Nations Command, 94 000 soldiers were killed.

Was the effort in Korea an American or a UN military operation? In spite of the immediate American response to lend air support to the South Koreans, Truman intended to use the United Nations to stop communist aggression. Sixteen nations sent combat forces to the war zone; 30 others provided medical units, hospital ships, food, and other supplies and equipment. But, as Figure 6.10 shows, the majority of the forces in the Korean conflict were American.

United Nations Forces in Korea

	USA	Other UN*	South Korea**
Ground force	50%	10%	40%
Naval force	86%	7%	7%
Air force	93%	2%	5%

*Includes Canada and 14 other countries; Canada contributed 25 583 personnel and the casualties were 1 642 of which 406 died

**South Korea was not admitted to the UN until 1991

Figure 6.10

Given these figures, should this conflict be described as a US or a UN peacemaking operation?

The Lessons of the Korean War

The Korean War demonstrated the United Nations' strength and limitations as a peacemaking organization. The UN was directly involved in Korea only because the United States had decided it should be and the Soviet Union had not been in a position to use its veto. So it was more by luck than design that the Security Council was able to authorize military action in Korea. The conflict also highlighted the disadvantages of relying on voluntary military assistance. Technically, all UN members are obliged to provide military forces. But in Korea only 16 nations participated in actual combat, and these were all friends of the United States.

The enduring legacy of the UN experience in Korea was the **Uniting for Peace resolution** passed in November 1950. This gave the General Assembly responsibility for dealing with international aggression should the Security Council be deadlocked. It was passed by the Security Council during the Soviet boycott as a means of countering future Soviet vetoes. Once the Soviet Union returned to the Security Council, it used its veto 103 times while the United States used its veto once. But because of the Uniting for Peace resolution the UN was able to take action in a variety of hot spots around the globe. For example, when Iraq invaded Kuwait in 1991, it was the Uniting for Peace resolution that enabled the UN to launch a massive attack to drive the Iraqi troops out of Kuwait.

THE UN AS PEACEKEEPER: THE SUEZ CRISIS

The Korean War demonstrated that the United Nations could be a military peacemaker, but as in any war, a high price was paid in human life. In addition, although the shooting had stopped, Korea was no closer to peace than it had been before the armed conflict began. Many middle and small powers were not keen to be pawns in conflicts stage-managed to promote the interests of the major powers. It was clear that if the UN was to succeed, a new and more flexible formula for peacekeeping was needed. It was the Suez Crisis of 1956 that brought about the first multinational, voluntary peacekeeping force in the history of international relations.

Nasser and the Emergence of Egypt as an Arab Power

Colonel Gamal Abdel Nasser emerged as the leader of Egypt following the Arab defeat in the 1948 Arab-Israeli war. Nasser had two main goals: to create an independent Egypt free from colonial rule and to destroy the newly formed nation of Israel.

To achieve his goals, Nasser needed money, and lots of it. The fastest way to obtain funds was to let the superpowers bid for Egypt's allegiance. Nasser had no ideological preference for dollars or rubles. He accepted both American and Soviet aid in the form of cash, military equipment, technical expertise, and food.

Egypt needed a modern army to destroy Israel, so Nasser's long-term solution was to industrialize. The first requirement was electricity. Nasser announced ambitious plans to expand the Aswan Dam on the Nile River as a power source. He opened negotiations with both superpowers for financing of the project. In 1955, Nasser signed an arms deal with Czechoslovakia, a Soviet bloc nation. By 1956, he was ready to conclude an agreement with the United States to help finance and build a $1.3 billion dam at Aswan. It appeared that Nasser had successfully manoeuvred the Soviets into supplying arms and the Americans into supplying money and technical expertise. But this delicate balancing act was soon to crumble.

> "We want independence for our country. We want to preserve our nationalism and our dignity."
>
> — Gamal Abdel Nasser, 1956

Nationalizing the Suez Canal

The Americans were concerned about Nasser's brand of non-aligned nationalism. The continued conflict with Israel, which had close ties to the US, also cost Nasser Western support. Contrary to international and UN agreements, Egypt stopped Israeli ships, and all other ships bound for Israeli ports, from using the Suez Canal. When the United States refused financial and technical aid for the Aswan Dam project, Nasser's reaction was immediate and dramatic: on 26 July 1956 he seized control of the Suez Canal and turned to the Soviets for help in building the dam. This accomplished two goals. It signalled the end of Egypt's colonial status and provided funds for building the Aswan Dam and modernizing Egypt.

Nasser's takeover of the canal was a peaceful one; the British and French were offered compensation at the July 25 market value and full use of the facility. Nevertheless, the sudden expropriation increased global tensions. Only two years before, Egypt had assured the UN that international management of the canal would continue. The British and French were determined to regain their 97 per cent share of the canal's profits and reassert their status as major powers in the Middle East. Their military leaders plotted with Israel to recapture the Suez and bring about Nasser's downfall in the process.

Britain and France devised an elaborate scheme. Israel was to attack Egypt as part of the ongoing Arab-Israeli dispute. Britain and France would land troops at the canal zone on the pretence of protecting international shipping during the conflict. The plan would allow Britain and France to repossess the Suez Canal and enable Israel to expand its territory; Nasser would be overthrown and replaced with a leader more favourable to Anglo-French interests. But the conspirators miscalculated the reaction of the United States and the world community.

The United Nations' Response

On 29 October 1956, Israel attacked Egypt. Britain ordered the Egyptians and Israelis to withdraw from both sides of the Suez Canal. Egypt refused; but five days after the Israeli attack the fighting had already stopped. Even so, Anglo-French paratroops and commandos landed as planned, attacking Egyptian positions along the western side of the canal and securing the canal itself. The invasion stunned the world. The Soviet Union threatened to launch missiles on Paris and London. The United States was outraged. How would the UN deal with this act of aggression by two of the permanent members of its Security Council?

The day after the attack, the US introduced a resolution in the Security Council. It called for Israel to withdraw its troops and for all members to "refrain from the use of force." But France and Britain used their vetoes to kill this motion along with a Soviet proposal that the Americans and the Soviets jointly intervene. Deadlocked, the Security Council considered taking the matter up in the General Assembly. Only Britain and France voted against the motion. Since the veto does not apply in procedural matters, the motion carried and the Suez issue was brought before the General Assembly.

On November 2, an American resolution calling for a ceasefire and UN action to ensure international passage through the Suez Canal was passed. Only five nations (Israel, France, Britain, Australia, and New Zealand) opposed; six others (including Canada) abstained. On November 4, Canada's UN representative, Lester B. Pearson, proposed that the Anglo-French force in the canal zone be

> "Imperialism is the great force that is imposing a murderous, invisible siege upon the whole region."
>
> — Gamal Abdel Nasser, 1956

Profile   Gamal Abdel Nasser (1918-1970)

Figure 6.11
Gamal Abdel Nasser

Gamal Abdel Nasser was an important spokesperson for the Arab nationalism that swept through the Middle East after the Second World War. Although unpopular with Western leaders, in the Arab world Nasser was viewed as a hero. As you read about his life, consider why this might be so.

> *"[The Egyptian revolution] has brought about the evacuation of British imperialism and the independence of Egypt. It had defined Egypt's Arab character and brought about a profound change in the Arab way of life. It has affirmed the people's control of their resources and the product of their national action....*
>
> — Gamal Abdel Nasser, 1952

Gamal Abdel Nasser was one of 11 children. As a student, he protested against British domination of Egypt. Eventually his actions landed him in jail before he joined the military.

Arab pride and Egyptian nationalism sparked growing criticism of Egypt's monarchy, widely viewed as corrupt and repressive, under King Farouk (himself a Turk rather than an Egyptian). Egypt's defeat by Israel in the war of 1948 caused humiliation among Egyptian soldiers. Pledging to restore Arab pride and dignity, Nasser and others formed a Free Officers movement aimed at ousting the old regime and driving out foreign powers. In 1952, army officers revolted, forcing Farouk to abdicate. The monarchy was abolished and a new republic proclaimed. Nasser became prime minister of Egypt in 1954 and president in 1956.

Nasser had several objectives. He wanted to free the Arab world from foreign influence. He hoped to weld all Arab peoples into one great Arab movement. He knew that the redistribution of wealth and land was critical if he was to improve the lives of the peasants. He hoped to initiate a vast program of public works and industrialization to provide money and muscle for the Arab revival. Finally, he pledged to restore Palestine to the Palestinians and destroy the state of Israel.

Britain and France viewed Nasser as a dangerous revolutionary and warmonger. Egypt's takeover of the Suez Canal only reinforced their suspicions. But Nasser was celebrated in Egypt and throughout the Arab world for standing up to the Europeans.

In his years as leader of Egypt, Nasser tried to forge pan-Arabian alliances. He brought Soviet influence into the country as a counterbalance to the West. The Egyptian education and health systems were expanded and reformed, and there was some redistribution of land and wealth. By modernizing and enlarging the Egyptian army, Nasser continued Arab pressure against Israel.

In 1967, Nasser demanded the withdrawal of the United Nations Emergency Force, which had been present since the Suez Crisis. At the same time he pledged a new war of extermination against Israel. In the Six Day War that ensued, Egypt suffered massive losses of territory. Nasser tried to resign, but his offer was rejected. He spent his final years struggling to rebuild Arab confidence and unity.

Responding

1. What evidence is there that Nasser was both a nationalist and socialist?
2. What was Nasser's attitude toward the state of Israel?

replaced by a peacekeeping force charged with protecting the canal and keeping Israel and Egypt apart. Pearson's diplomatic skills succeeded in getting the motion passed unanimously, with nine nations abstaining.

The Significance of the Suez Crisis

The lasting significance of the Suez Crisis was the establishment of an international police force, the UNEF. Since 1956, UN peacekeeping forces have been called into service around the world. Unfortunately, they are not always the solution for maintaining international peace and security. The reason is **national sovereignty**—the right of independent nations to control their territory. Thus, when nations request peacekeeping troops, they come as invited guests of the host nation. When Nasser agreed to accept the UNEF on Egyptian soil in 1956, it was on the condition that the force would leave whenever, in the opinion of the Egyptians, its work had been accomplished. Eleven years later, the UNEF was unceremoniously kicked out of Egypt and a new Arab-Israeli war promptly followed. An international police force can be effective only if the nations involved agree that peace should be maintained.

UN Peacekeeping

Since the Suez Crisis, the United Nations has continued its role as peacekeeper. UN forces have had a variety of forms and purposes: as unarmed observers monitoring ceasefires (Kashmir, 1965-1966); as armed forces overseeing the withdrawal of belligerent forces (Afghanistan, 1988); and as enforcers of free elections (Nicaragua, 1989). Sometimes, lightly armed troops have not only had to keep the opposing sides apart or prevent the renewal of battles (Lebanon, 1978), but have acted as a police force to maintain law and order (Cyprus since 1964). On a few occasions, UN land and air forces have had to fight, not only to prevent civil war but to save their own lives under attack (the Congo, 1960-1964, and Rwanda, 1993-1996). Peacekeeping forces have been as small as a few hundred and as large as several thousand.

Peacekeeping forces have been drawn primarily from small and middle powers like Canada. Canada, for example, has contributed to almost every UN peacekeeping mission. The United States, Britain, France, and the other major powers have occasionally sent troops, but most often they have provided transportation, equipment, and funds.

Financing peacekeeping operations is becoming increasingly difficult. With the decline in defence spending, Canada and other smaller nations can no longer afford to take on new assignments or even to maintain existing forces. Some peacekeeping operations, like that in Cyprus and several in the Middle East, have continued for decades.

NETSURFER

WWW.UN.ORG

This is the official site of the United Nations. It is available in six languages and contains a great deal of information on the work of the UN. On the English-language home page, click on the "Peace and Security" link, and follow the links for "Peacekeeping," "Current Operations," "Africa." List the current UN operations in Africa. What is the current status of the following UN operations listed on the map on page 199: UNAMSIL (Sierra Leone), UNMEE (Ethiopia and Eritrea) and MONUC (Democratic Republic of Congo)? (If the operations are no longer listed in this group, check under "Past Operations.")

WWW.WEBLEARN.CA

Go to www.weblearn.ca and open the UN module then click on the reading "A Day in the Life of a Peacekeeper". Read the stories, and select a peacekeeper you would like to meet if you could. Write down several questions you would ask that person if you had a chance to meet.

The Effectiveness of Peacekeeping

Is peacekeeping successful? It is true that in almost every part of the world to which peacekeeping forces have been dispatched, sooner or later there has been renewed fighting. This does not mean that peacekeepers have failed to do their job. It does indicate, however, that the process of creating a lasting peace requires a variety of strategies. The key contribution of peacekeepers is to minimize confrontations and uphold cease-fires and truces while diplomats and politicians attempt to negotiate a permanent end to the hostilities.

The peacekeepers' successful role in this larger process has been recognized outside the UN. In awarding the 1988 Nobel Prize for Peace to UN peacekeeping forces, the Nobel committee declared that these forces "represent the manifest will of the community of nations to achieve peace through negotiations and the forces have, by their presence, made a decisive contribution toward the initiation of actual peace negotiations."

In Review

1. How did the Cold War hostilities affect the work of the UN?

2. What were (a) the underlying and (b) the immediate causes of the Korean War?

3. Was the Korean conflict more a UN or a US military operation? In what way was Canada involved? What was the outcome of the conflict?

4. What was the Uniting for Peace resolution? What purpose did it serve?

5. Why is the Korean War considered an example of UN peacemaking?

6. What was the national interest of each of the following nations in the Suez Crisis: Egypt, Israel, Britain, France?

7. What critical role did Lester Pearson play in helping to end the Suez Crisis?

8. What was the lasting significance of the Suez Crisis?

9. Should Canada continue to participate in peacekeeping and/or peacemaking operations? Explain your answer.

Skill Path

Recognizing and Analysing Bias in Information Sources

People understand the world around them based on their beliefs, attitudes, values, and ideologies. Each of us develops preferences that can easily become biases: we preconceive outcomes, we predict behaviours, and we are predisposed to take a certain stand on an issue. **Bias** exists when only one side of an issue is considered, or when facts are used to defend one particular viewpoint only.

Biased sources of information can distort one's understanding and influence readers unfairly. In order to take a balanced approach, it's important to seek information from a variety of sources. You must also be able to recognize bias within each of your sources. You can still use the ideas in clearly biased source materials, as long as you state what these biases are.

Step One: Consider the Circumstances

The social, political, and economic climate during which a source of information was created can influence its content. Consider the date it was created and whether new knowledge has since emerged that would make the material presented obsolete or invalid.

Also consider the intended audience. Has the information been shaped to conform to or influence the viewpoints held by a particular group of people? Consider, too, whether the author is closely tied to the subject he or she is writing about and whether this might colour the information. You may want to do some research to find out the author's background, area of expertise, political affiliations, and reputation.

Step Two: Evaluate the Information

a) *Explicit or implicit bias.* Bias can be explicit. Authors will announce their position, usually within the thesis statement or opening paragraphs, to leave the reader in no doubt about their perspective. For example, in the statement "Adolf Hitler was evil incarnate and individually responsible for the Second World War" the writer declares her point of view that Hitler, and Hitler alone, was an evil man without whom World War II would not have happened.

More difficult to detect is bias that is implicit—not directly stated. "Many Nazi war criminals escaped, and some were eventually captured and brought to trial. Others managed to hide from their pasts and never had to answer for their actions." Implicit in this statement is the condemnation of those who went unpunished for war crimes.

b) *Emotionally charged words or visuals.* Emotionally charged words and phrases, photographs, or videos can be used to present information favourably or unfavourably. **For example, if a politician is described as "spewing forth" opinions or "trotting out" arguments, then these opinions and arguments are presented in a negative light.** Exaggeration and over-generalization reflect bias in written materials: words such as "always," "never," and "none" are absolutes and should be noted by the reader. Images can be especially powerful tool for influencing an audience. **For example, while an automobile advertisement might depict a solitary car on an open country road,** an article on global warming might feature a photograph of a city traffic jam with cars emitting exhaust fumes. Even the background music used in videos or on radio programs can affect the tone and mood of a piece and thus sway the listener to a particular point of view.

c) *The use of facts versus opinion.* Facts are verifiable pieces of information, whereas opinions are personal interpretations, which may or may not be based on facts. Opinion pieces based solely on emotion may be of little use to someone writing a research or position paper. Even if the information is based on facts, the author may oversimplify the issue by presenting only one perspective (**e.g., the US should attack Iraq to free Iraqi citizens from an oppressive regime**), without acknowledging contradictory facts or alternative positions (**e.g., such an attack may destabilize the region and do more harm than good**).

Step Three: Find Corroborating Evidence

If you are uncertain whether the author has presented biased information or whether the facts are simply inaccurate, you could find corroboration for the information you would like to use. This means finding other references that agree with the facts presented by the author.

Because it is easy for anyone to publish information on the Internet whether they have expertise on a topic or not, corroboration of facts becomes especially important when you are considering using information found on Web sites.

Practise Your Skill

1. Read two or three newspaper editorials about world events. Choose one of these editorials that you think may contain bias.

a) List the beliefs and attitudes expressed in the editorial.

b) Do you detect any indications of bias? These may include the following:

- emotionally charged words and phrases
- exaggeration
- overgeneralization
- missing facts
- oversimplification

c) Now write a summary of why you think the editorial may be biased, and list your reasons.

Profile · Lester Pearson (1897-1972)

Figure 6.12
Lester Pearson

Canada's commitment to the development and expansion of the UN was mirrored in the career and philosophy of Lester Bowles Pearson, perhaps Canada's greatest diplomat. During the early challenges of the UN, Pearson laboured tirelessly to protect and enhance the goals of international order and co-operation. In what ways do you think Pearson's work earned Canada international recognition and trust?

> *"Diplomacy is letting someone else have your way."*
>
> — Lester B. Pearson, 1957

> *"I've seen more common sense expressed around the table in a farm house than I have around the table in the United Nations committee room."*
>
> — Lester B. Pearson, 1974

Lester B. Pearson was born and raised in southern Ontario, the son of a Methodist parson. Pearson served in the medical corps during the First World War. At war's end, he completed his education at the University of Toronto and at Oxford, England. After trying business, law, and teaching, Pearson found his niche in the Department of External Affairs.

In 1928, he began a brilliant career as an international diplomat, serving in London and Washington and representing Canada at many conferences, including the one that founded the United Nations, in 1945. As deputy Minister of External Affairs, Pearson exhibited great diplomatic skill and expertise in building the foundations of this organization.

In 1948, Pearson was elected to Parliament and appointed Secretary of State for External Affairs. He continued to be involved in the UN, serving as President of the General Assembly in 1952. Pearson believed that military alliances during the Cold War were essential. But he continued to push for non-military solutions and preferred that the will of the United Nations rather than the interests of the United States should be the determining force in world affairs.

The Suez Crisis in 1956 stunned the world. Britain and France were condemned by the UN as well as the United States. Amidst the turmoil, Pearson developed a bold plan to end hostilities, reduce tensions, and reaffirm the purposes and principles of the United Nations.

He developed the idea of a multinational force of peacekeepers from the middle and smaller powers to serve as a United Nations "police force." Pearson skilfully persuaded UN members to endorse this United Nations Emergency Force (UNEF). It was a radical new approach to keeping the peace among nations. Pearson was awarded the Nobel Prize for Peace in 1957, the only Canadian ever to be so honoured.

Upon retiring from service at the United Nations, Pearson was elected leader of the Liberal Party in 1958 and served as prime minister from 1963 to 1968. In 1967 Pearson presided over nationwide celebrations of Canada's Centennial Year.

Pearson retired from politics in 1968 and died four years later. He is remembered by many as a person who combined the realism, practicality, and flexibility of a politician with the highest ideals of humanitarian principles.

Responding

1 Why was Pearson awarded the Nobel Prize for Peace?
2. Describe Pearson's idea of a UN peacekeeping force.

Voices   The UN: Keeping the Peace

When he was elected as Secretary-General in 1992, Egypt's Boutros Boutros-Ghali envisaged a more active and powerful United Nations. He produced a document, "Agenda for Peace," in which he called for permanent peace enforcement units designed for rapid deployment to world hot spots. Boutros-Ghali firmly believed that the UN should be prepared "to take coercive action against cease-fire violators."

This vision of a more forceful UN was not shared by all. Critics felt the cost in personnel and armaments would be too high. Some felt the UN was acting like a world government and trampling national sovereignty. Whatever the objectives, however, the UN has been increasingly involved in crises around the globe. In fact, the UN entered into more operations in the first five years after the Cold War ended than it had undertaken in its first 40 years. Boutros-Ghali was clearly prepared to pursue a more activist international role and challenge old ideas about the UN.

Toronto Star columnist Richard Gwyn interviewed Boutros-Ghali in 1993. As you read the following excerpts from the interview, consider whether international authority should take priority over national sovereignty, and if so, under what circumstances.

"Q: Is the UN not now trying to do too much in too many places?

A: During the Cold War, the UN suffered a crisis of credibility. Today, we are suffering a crisis of an excess of credibility…. We are over-stretched, overloaded. But we cannot refuse to respond, any more than a hospital can refuse a patient.

Q: Does this mean the UN is beginning to become a kind of quasi-world government long before it in fact is ready to be one?

A: We are in a transition period and we are trying to find new concepts on which we can build our actions.

Q: In this trend for the UN to become a quasi-world government, is the key to it the globalization of human rights so that what a national government does to its citizens is no longer its affair alone but the world's?

A: Human rights is one case and an important one. But so is the environment. Or that you have AIDS spreading all over the world. Or the international traffic in drugs. You will have more and more global problems and global problems can only be solved by an international forum.

Q: In the corridors here you'll get people who'll say all this 'global' stuff is just rhetoric. That in reality it's the US that runs the UN. True?

A: That is not the reality, it is an exaggeration. I assure you that decisions are taken by consensus and that is often not easy to reach."

Source: Excerpted from "We Need New Concepts, A New Approach," by Richard Gwyn, *Toronto Star*, 23 March 1993, A17. Reprinted by permission of the Toronto Star Syndicate.

Responding

1. What response did Boutros-Ghali give to the question about world government?
2. Does this interview suggest that Boutros-Ghali believes the UN should become a kind of world government? Do you think nations would agree to give up their sovereignty? Do you think that is a good idea?

MAP STUDY

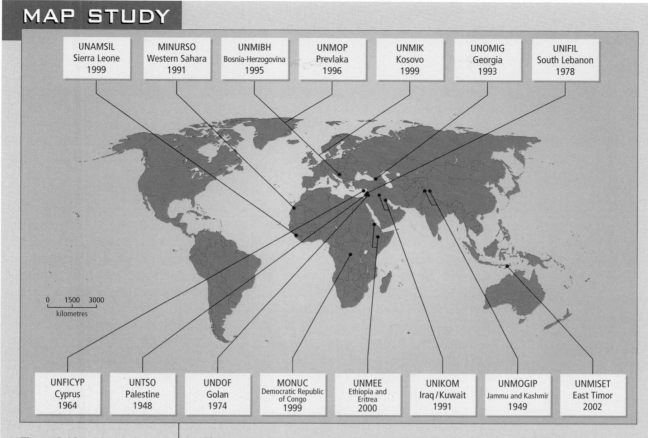

UNAMSIL
Sierra Leone
1999

MINURSO
Western Sahara
1991

UNMIBH
Bosnia-Herzegovina
1995

UNMOP
Prevlaka
1996

UNMIK
Kosovo
1999

UNOMIG
Georgia
1993

UNIFIL
South Lebanon
1978

UNFICYP
Cyprus
1964

UNTSO
Palestine
1948

UNDOF
Golan
1974

MONUC
Democratic Republic
of Congo
1999

UNMEE
Ethiopia and
Eritrea
2000

UNIKOM
Iraq/Kuwait
1991

UNMOGIP
Jammu and Kashmir
1949

UNMISET
East Timor
2002

Figure 6.13
UN Peacekeeping Operations in 2002

These are the ongoing peacekeeping operations of the UN as of May 2002.

Interpreting
1. Which operation is the longest-running and which is the most recent?
2. Access the UN Web site at www.un.org/Depts/cartographic/map/dpko/4000e.pdf to find the most recent changes.

Evolving Approaches to Peacemaking and Peacekeeping

Despite its many peacemaking and peacekeeping efforts, the United Nations had little expectation of making or keeping peace in conflicts that directly involved the United States or the Soviet Union. The Security Council could do little about crises involving the Soviets in Eastern Europe (the Berlin Blockade, 1949; Hungary, 1956; Czechoslovakia, 1968), and the Americans have had a free hand in Latin America (Guatemala, 1954; the Bay of Pigs, 1961; Grenada, 1983). Nor did the United Nations override the principle of non-intervention "in matters essentially within the domestic jurisdiction of any state" (Britain's crisis in Northern Ireland; China's conflict with the Soviet Union over Tibet).

After the embarrassment of Britain

and France in the 1956 Suez Crisis, the major powers were left to sort out their own disputes through diplomatic and political means. But when these efforts did not produce the desired results, the superpowers were willing to fall back on military intervention, as the US did in Vietnam and the USSR did in Afghanistan.

In the 1980s, however, the patterns of peacemaking and peacekeeping began to change. The Soviets accepted UN observers to monitor their withdrawal from Afghanistan in 1988. In 1989, for the first time since the Monroe Doctrine of 1823, the United States co-operated with foreign observers in Central America through the Organization of American States (OAS). Other regional alliances began playing a role more consistent with UN peace initiatives in the late 1980s.

A more fundamental change emerged in the United Nations' reaction to Iraq's attacks upon its Kurdish and Shiite Muslim minorities after the Persian Gulf War of January and February 1991. The Security Council declared that the masses of refugees fleeing the region constituted a threat to international peace and security. As the *New York Times* reported on 6 April 1991: "Never before has the United Nations Security Council held that governments threaten international security if their actions force thousands of their citizens to flee to other lands."

Since the end of the Cold War in the 1990s, peacemaking has replaced peacekeeping as the dominant feature of UN interventions. In 1991, the United Nations authorized the use of military force to drive Iraqi invaders out of Kuwait in the Gulf War. (See page 351.) In 1992, for the first time, the UN authorized the use of massive military force to ensure that humanitarian aid reached the people of Somalia. It sent a smaller force for the same purpose to Bosnia-Herzegovina.

(See page 230.) In 1994, the UN struggled to contain the overwhelming human misery resulting from civil war in Rwanda, but played almost no role in ending the fighting. (The UN's role in Somalia and Rwanda is examined in more detail below.)

In 2001, the UN was dragged into a US-led NATO operation in Afghanistan in the "war on terrorism," which is covered in detail in Chapter 12. Then, in 2002, the US decided that Iraq was also a terrorist state and should be disarmed. As with Afghanistan, the US felt that the Iraqi leader, Saddam Hussein, should be overthrown by a US-led, UN-sanctioned military operation. The UN, however, preferred negotiations and the resumption of weapons inspections in Iraq. Faced with a clear lack of enthusiasm in the UN, US President George W. Bush bluntly threatened to attack Iraq with or without UN sanction.

Canada was caught in the middle trying to show support for the US as our neighbour and ally yet preferring to follow the UN. However, given the poor state of Canada's military forces, our role is more symbolic than real. David Pratt, Chairman of the Commons defence committee, stated bluntly that our forces are "essentially tapped out" and "would not be significantly adding anything to the allied forces".

THE LESSONS OF SOMALIA AND RWANDA

With the defeat of Soviet communism, the US developed a new role as a kind of world police force. Trouble spots anywhere in the world that touched on American interests became targets for intervention. International peacekeeping and peacemaking operations, which normally come under UN jurisdiction, now relied very heavily on US support. In

How badly does the US need the UN? As a practical matter, the US wants and needs allies. UN approval confers legitimacy that even a superpower can't claim by itself, and such approval is essential in the Middle East.

— *Time* magazine, 14 October 2002

most cases, this close relationship between UN moral leadership and US military power worked well. In other cases, however, such as Somalia, the US-led UN operations became confused and ineffective. What started out as UN peacekeeping operations in some countries soon turned into peace*making* operations. As casualties began to mount, individual nations, including the US, began to reconsider the missions and withdraw support. This left the UN with token peacekeepers caught in the middle of active civil war zones. The main lesson from these conflicts was that peacekeeping and peacemaking operations are very different, and one should not be confused with the other.

Somalia

The Republic of Somalia was created in 1960 by unifying the former British Somaliland Protectorate and the Italian Trusteeship Territory of Somalia. Nine years later, in a bloodless military coup, the Marxist Somali Revolutionary Socialist Party took power and renamed the country the Somali Democratic Republic.

For more than 20 years the nation was ruled by the dictatorship of General Muhammed Siad Barre. His government led to the elimination of Somalia's fledgling democracy, nationalization of industries, drastic deterioration of the Somali economy, human rights abuses, and terrorism of the populace. For two decades, various independent Somali clans opposed Barre's regime and fought the military.

Civil war broke out in the drought-stricken land in 1988 between government forces and rebel groups such as the prominent Somali National Movement (SNM). The fighting forced UN staff and other aid workers in non-governmental relief organizations to abandon the nation in May 1989. Struggling to survive

famine, disease, and insurgency, one-third of the Somali population became internal refugees. Others fled the warring factions to neighbouring Djibouti and Ethiopia.

By 1991, Barre and the Somali National Front (SNF) proclaimed a new Somaliland Republic in the north. A new provisional government was then set up in the south, but clan-based guerrilla groups and militias competed for political power. By the end of the year, part of Mogadishu was under the control of the 5000 fighters of interim president Mahammad (Abgall clan). The other part was held by General Muhammad Aidid (Habar Gidir clan) and his 10 000 guerrillas.

The report of a 1991 United Nations–sponsored mission to Somalia suggested that hope for settlement of the civil war lay in international support. Instead, the UN tried to negotiate with the clan warlords to resolve the conflict. However, this only added to the power and prestige of the warlords.

Conditions in Somalia deteriorated as famine spread, and 300 000 to 500 000 people died. Thousands of people fled to Mogadishu, but the warlords controlled the distribution of food and other essential items. They used food as a weapon by providing it only to those Somalis who supported their particular clan. They also opposed the idea of any UN military forces entering the nation.

A ceasefire agreement mediated by the United Nations came into effect in March 1992. At that time, the only UN agency at work in Somalia was UNICEF, and its work was restricted to the capital city of Mogadishu. A few voluntary relief agencies—the international Red Cross and Save the Children—were able to offer humanitarian aid to a limited number of rural Somalis. Despite their best efforts, food supplies destined for famine victims continued to be looted and used by those engaged in fighting the civil war. By June 1992, 6 million people faced starvation.

In 1992, with Operation Restore Hope, the UN authorized the use of massive military force to ensure that humanitarian aid reached the people of Somalia. Budgeted at US$1.5 billion per year, it was the most expensive humanitarian aid effort ever undertaken. In December, a US-led coalition force arrived in Somalia to begin land-based intervention, which put UN soldiers in direct confrontation with the warring factions. In 1993, 18 US soldiers were killed in an operation in Mogadishu and their bodies were dragged through the city's streets.

More than 30 000 UN troops were sent to Somalia, but the humanitarian mandate of the UN mission changed to demobilizing the warlord factions. At least 6000 people died in clashes between UN forces and rival Somali factions, including dozens of UN peacekeepers. The United Nations was unable to maintain a ceasefire, and so

the mission ended in failure. UN troops were withdrawn by March 1995.

In July 2000 an interim 245-member Transitional National Government was established in Mogadishu under UN supervision. It has a three-year mandate to create a new constitution and hold elections to form a permanent national Somali government.

Rwanda

In the central African country of Rwanda, the predominant ethnic group is Hutu. The Hutus make up about 85 per cent of the population, while Tutsis make up the remaining 15 per cent. Since the 1600s, hereditary Tutsi kings ruled Rwanda. In 1959, seeking equality for all groups in Rwanda, the majority Hutu tribe overthrew the Tutsi monarchy. After four years of war, Rwanda was declared a republic, and in 1962 the nation gained its independence.

The majority Hutus formed a new government under President Gregoire Kayibanda, and held power until a coup in 1973. Supported by the Rwandan military, General Juvenal Habyarimana became president and instituted a new constitution, which limited the presidency to members of the Hutu tribe. The politically empowered Hutus forced about 150 000 Tutsis into exile. The Tutsi exiles formed the Rwandan Patriotic Front (RPF) and invaded Rwanda in 1990.

The Rwandan Patriotic Front continued its campaign of hostilities until 1993, when the government of Rwanda and the RPF signed the Arusha Peace Agreement. This agreement gave the United Nations a broad role to play as a Neutral International Force (NIF). The force would supervise the implementation of the agreement during a transitional period, which was to last 22 months.

A UN delegation, which was sent to Rwanda to investigate the possible role of

Figure 6.14
US troops in Mogadishu. US troops entered Somalia with high hopes, but the ambush and death of American soldiers had a negative impact on US public opinion for such UN-sponsored peacemaking operations.

Figure 6.15
This display of human skulls is all that remains of some 5000 Tutsis massacred in the Ntarama Church compound in April 1994. Could the UN have prevented this kind of mass slaughter?

the NIF, argued for the rapid deployment of an international force and swift establishment of transitional institutions. The delegation warned that any delay might lead to the collapse of the peace process.

Once in Rwanda, Canadian General Romeo Dallaire, commander of the UN peacekeeping mission in Rwanda (UNAMIR), advised the UN that tensions between the Hutus and Tutsis were increasing. He requested more troops and a mandate to use force in response to crimes against humanity, such as executions and attacks on displaced persons or refugees. He told the UN that weapons distribution among the Hutus was escalating, terrorist activities were increasing, and death squad target lists were being drawn up. The commander warned of catastrophic consequences, but his requests for additional UN forces and changes to

the rules of engagement were denied. Instead, he was told that he had not provided conclusive or compelling evidence to support his plea.

The April 1994 assassinations of President Habyarimana of Rwanda and the Hutu president of neighbouring Burundi unleashed Hutu fury. As civil unrest erupted, UNAMIR troops tried to offer some protection. Belgian peacekeepers, for example, who were trapped within the presidential compound as they tried to prevent the assassination of the Rwandan prime minister, had to operate on orders not to fire until fired upon. The prime minister and 10 Belgian peacekeepers were executed, and the Belgian contingent of UNAMIR left Rwanda.

Unable to achieve a ceasefire, and denied the mandate to address the widespread massacres and chaos, the entire

UNAMIR operation was nearly suspended. Most of the UN peacekeepers from various countries were evacuated. Over a 13-week period, the Hutu-dominated army (Rwandan Armed Forces) and armed civilians killed more than 800 000 Tutsis. It became clear that extremist Hutus intended a genocide of the entire Rwandan Tutsi population.

After a May 1994 Security Council resolution, 5500 UN peacekeepers were sent to Rwanda in June. These forces were followed by 2000 French troops, who were sent on a humanitarian mission to create a "safe zone" for refugees in southwestern Rwanda. Although the UN forces struggled to contain the overwhelming human misery, they played almost no role in ending the fighting. The Tutsi Rwandan Patriotic Front, along with tens of thousands of Tutsis from Burundi, eventually won military control in Rwanda and implemented a ceasefire. By March 1996 all UN forces had left Rwanda.

While civil strife between the two tribes has continued, there is a sense of reconciliation. In 2002, Rwanda's national government was led by President Paul Kagame (Tutsi) and Prime Minister Bernard Makuza (Hutu). An International Criminal Tribunal for Rwanda was established to judge the key leaders, and more than 120 000 prisoners were put on trial for crimes arising from the 1994 genocide.

In its *1999 Report of Independent Inquiry into the Actions of the United Nations During the 1994 Genocide in Rwanda*, the Inquiry identified 18 fundamental failures. It concluded: "While the presence of United Nations peacekeepers in Rwanda may have begun as a traditional peacekeeping operation to monitor the implementation of an existing peace agreement, the onslaught of the genocide should have led decision-makers in the United Nations—from the Secretary-General and the Security Council to Secretariat officials and the leadership of UNAMIR—to realize that the original mandate, and indeed the neutral mediating role of the United Nations, was no longer adequate and required a different, more assertive response, combined with the means necessary to take such action." In other words, this was a peacekeeping mission that turned into a peacemaking mission, and the UN was not able to adjust to the change.

Although the report cast blame on the "leadership of UNAMIR," what is missing is any explanation as to why the repeated requests for military assistance by Dallaire were ignored. Part of the reason can be found in the disastrous UN mission in nearby Somalia. The US was in no mood to send additional troops to Rwanda after 18 of their soldiers had died in the Mogadishu ambush in 1993. The US-led UN failure in Somalia was the biggest background reason for the reluctance of any nation, particularly the US, to commit more troops to Rwanda.

CHALLENGES TO THE UN

As the world political scene changes, so too will the role of the United Nations. New questions on old issues will be raised. Should the UN take an aggressive role in fulfilling its mission of peace and security and solving social, economic, and humanitarian problems throughout the world? Can the UN gather sufficient forces to undertake major peacemaking and peacekeeping missions?

The key question for the near future, however, is whether the US will continue to work with the UN or simply ignore it. The US was willing to lead UN-sponsored operations in the Gulf War and the war on terrorism in Afghanistan. However, in 2002 the US made it clear that it would invade Iraq with or without UN support.

What can the UN do if the US is the aggressor nation in a conflict? The problem for the UN is that it needs the US more than the US needs the UN. A rift between the US and UN could have serious implications for the future.

This problem also exists with respect to the humanitarian role of the UN. The US has opposed many recent UN initiatives on the grounds they could interfere with national sovereignty and American interests. Since the UN represents the world community, differences between the US and UN can add to the developing sense of the US standing alone against the world.

In 1945 the UN was formed to provide peace and security in the world. It was located in the US to ensure that the US would remain committed to the ideals and operations of the UN. Only the future will tell if the UN grows and remains effective or suffers the same fate as the League of Nations.

In Review

1. Why did people rebel against the government of General Barre in Somalia?

2. How did the warlords in Somalia use food as a weapon?

3. Using point-form notes, create a timeline that details UN involvement in the Somali civil conflict.

4. What were the origins of the conflict between the Hutus and the Tutsis in Rwanda?

5. What caused Canadian commander Romeo Dallaire in Rwanda to petition the UN for more soldiers and an expanded mandate for action? How did the UN respond?

6. What was the conclusion of the 1999 report on the UN operation in Rwanda?

7. What was the main lesson learned from the UN operation in Rwanda?

Summary

The United Nations was created with a General Assembly to represent all nations, and a Security Council that gave powerful nations a dominant role. With the development of the Cold War, the Security Council became deadlocked and matters of peace and security became more difficult to manage. In the Korean War, the principle of military peacemaking was applied as the United States led a coalition of UN forces to fight North Korean aggression. In the Suez Crisis, the UN was successful in providing a forum for discussion and resolution of the problem. One major outcome of the Suez Crisis was the establishment of a UN peacekeeping (as opposed to peacemaking) force. Canada's role as an important peacekeeper and middle power was established. Lester Pearson's proposal for the UNEF, which was introduced at Suez, has been the model for UN peacekeeping activities since then.

As Cold War tensions have subsided, there has been renewed interest in the United Nations. Increasingly, the UN has become more active in conflicts and humanitarian work around the globe. The organization appears willing to use both its peacekeeping and peacemaking options in a still troubled world.

Viewpoints

Background

The United Nations has been the subject of debate since its inception in 1945. Since that time the UN has changed. As the nations of Africa and Asia gained independence, they joined the UN and gave greater representation to the developing countries of the world. The United Nations has broadened its commitment to the medical, social, cultural, and educational welfare of the developing world. UN peacekeeping and peacemaking missions have increased in number and size.

The viewpoints presented here examine two perspectives on the UN. Professor Gerald Segal believes that, while the UN is flawed, it is generally a useful organization that provides a valuable forum for the poor and weak nations of the world. Ted Carpenter claims the United Nations has many basic faults and needs to accept a much more limited role in the world. Read these two viewpoints carefully, and answer the questions that follow. (You may want to refer to the Skill Path "Analysing a Reading" on page 14 before beginning.)

Useful roles of the UN

To be sure, there is much that is very wrong with the UN. It is often out of touch with reality, unwieldy and run by incompetents. But, as the most universal of the proliferating international organisations ... it continues to serve useful, if mundane functions....

The ritual incantations of support for the UN have roots in the odd mixture of idealism and realism that existed when the organisation was created. The idealism was rooted in the horror of the Second World War and the carnage that followed the failure of the previous world organisation, the League of Nations, to confront the aggression of Japan, Italy and Germany. The UN was supposed to overcome these failings by operating a system of collective security where aggression would be repelled by the common action of a concerned world. What is more, to help prevent conflict breaking out at all, the UN would take an active role in furthering economic and social progress....

[The] rapid increase in members not only wrested the control of the UN from the United States; it also raised the second major issue for the organisation—North-South relations. The UN had been an early participant in the decolonisation process.... But when North-South relations moved beyond the broadly popular issue of ending colonial rule, the UN became the setting for the damaging, extremist rhetoric of North-South relations. The South demanded various "new orders", meaning the transfer of resources from North to South.... It was no wonder that the United States (by far the largest backer of the UN) responded by cutting back its funding and began decrying the one-state-one-vote principle in the UNGA that had given it so much power back in the 1950s.

But, for all its obvious excesses, the UN has its good points. First, its various types of peacekeeping have all been useful. By now we are familiar with the strange mixed-race, multi-lingual, blue-helmeted soldiers, lightly armed and operating in squalid or remote places under bewildering acronyms like UNFICYP, UNIFIL, or ONUC. They have to carry out difficult, if not impossible, tasks because the UN itself is rarely sure about what it is doing and does not give its forces much authority. These soldiers have been described as "false teeth" or an umbrella taken away the moment it rains....

Second, UN-organised international co-operation has also been evident in the various moves ... to impose sanctions on Rhodesia (later Zimbabwe) and latterly on South Africa. Third, the UN serves a passive role as a venue for traditional diplomacy. In the more obscure, smoky corridors or small back rooms, enemies can meet, signals can be sent and talks can begin. Even in a shrinking world of modern communications, there is still a need for face-to-face contacts.

Fourth, the UN has established a wide range of specialised agencies and associated organisations that are of practical use. The World Bank and the International Monetary Fund (IMF) are perhaps two of the best-known suppliers of funds to states in economic need. The UN International Children's Emergency Fund (UNICEF) and the High Commission for Refugees (UNHCR) provide essential help for individuals in need. The International Telegraph Union (ITU) and International Civil Aviation Organisation (ICAO) assist modern means of communication....

Finally, the UN is simply a place where the poor and weak, in a world so dominated by the Superpowers and the developed states, can feel they are being heard. To be sure, this has too often deteriorated into absurd and outrageous proposals, childish antics and shrill speeches. The impotent may feel better for upbraiding the powerful but their actions only undermine the ability of the UN to act effectively. The UN has become much more an arena for conflict than co-operation. Clearly the organisation can do better but that is no reason simply to ignore or deride the place. If the UN did not already exist it would certainly have to be invented.

Source: Excerpted from Gerald Segal, *The Stoddart Guide to the World Today*, Stoddart Publishing Co. Limited. Don Mills, Ontario, 1988.

Limitations of the UN

A blizzard of hype and excuses from the UN's cheerleaders cannot disguise the organization's numerous faults. Its record in the realm of conflict resolution has been unimpressive. The nation-building project in Somalia (which was to be the model for rehabilitating failed states) produced a bloody fiasco. The UNPROFOR mission in Bosnia, essentially an attempt to manage a civil war, fared no better. Even the UN's much-touted achievement in ending the long civil war and fostering democracy in Cambodia has unravelled.

To be fair, the UN has not been without successes. The organization played a constructive role in helping to end the armed conflicts in El Salvador and Mozambique and in supervising elections that brought independence and democracy to Namibia. Nevertheless, the failures are decidedly more spectacular than the successes and serve to emphasize the UN's inherent limitations.

On non-military matters the UN's performance has been dreadful. The organization is plagued by problems of mismanagement and corruption. Much of the UN's energy and funds has been devoted to pushing such pernicious measures as the Law of the Sea Treaty and holding pretentious summits on the environment, world population, and other issues. Delegates to those gatherings habitually embrace the discredited notion that more government intervention and regulation are the solution to any problem.

Ultimately, the United States needs to re-examine its enthusiasm for the entire concept of global collective security. We should no longer accept on faith that it is either feasible or wise to attempt to "globalize" civil wars and minor cross-border conflicts.

America ought to have a restrained and somewhat skeptical relationship with the United Nations. The belief that the UN was mankind's last best hope for peace was erroneous when the organization was established in 1945 and it is erroneous today. The United Nations is neither the guardian of global peace nor the institutional conscience of humanity. (The recent investigation of U.S. prisons by a UN functionary to ferret out alleged human rights violations is precisely the kind of overreaching and gratuitous meddling that justifiably infuriates Americans.)

The UN has limited utility as an international forum for different points of view and a mediation service to resolve quarrels. It also can play (and indeed has played) a useful role in coordinating humanitarian relief efforts. But the notion of the United Nations as a powerful global security body is unrealizable and undesirable.

The United Nations is merely an association of the world's governments—not, it should be emphasized, the world's peoples. As such, it is, and should be, only a marginal player on the global stage.

Even the more limited version of an activist United Nations, with a standing military force and a mandate to rebuild "failed states" around the planet, would constitute a dangerous entanglement for the United States. Not only is it dubious wisdom to make parochial conflicts a matter of global concern and intervention, but the lives of American military personnel should be put at risk only to defend America's vital security interests. Their lives should never be sacrificed for the abstract and illusory goal of global collective security.

Source: Adapted from Ted Galen Carpenter, "Pruning the United Nations," 18 November, 1997.

Analysis and Evaluation

1. Briefly note the five useful aspects of the UN stated by Segal.

2. In your opinion, which aspect of the UN is most important? Explain.

3. What spectacular failures of the UN does Carpenter suggest?

4. What does Carpenter think of the UN on non-military matters?

5. Decide which of the viewpoints you tend to support and explain why. If you agree with neither, state the position you do support and explain it. Be sure to use specific information from this textbook, the readings, and other sources to support your position.

Chapter Analysis

MAKING CONNECTIONS

1. Contact your local legion or military base and, if possible, invite a local peacekeeper to your class to talk about his or her experiences in a peacekeeping operation.

2. Compare the roles played by the UN and the results it achieved in (a) the Korean War, (b) the Suez Crisis, (c) Rwanda, and (d) Somalia.

3. What powers would the UN need to become a world government? Consider the following basic powers normally held by nations: taxation, police/military forces, making laws, territory.

DEVELOPING YOUR VOICE

4. Organize a small-group discussion on one of the following topics:

    a) Should Canada continue to participate in UN peacekeeping operations?

    b) Should the UN expand its role to use military force for peacemaking?

    c) Is the world at the beginning of the twenty-first century any safer than it was at the beginning of the twentieth century?

5. If possible, invite a member of a local UN association to visit your class for a presentation/interview session.

6. Write a letter to your MP or the Minister of Foreign Affairs expressing your views on Canada's future role in the UN.

RESEARCHING THE ISSUES

7. Identify a current example of a UN peacekeeping operation and a UN peacemaking operation. In what ways do these operations differ? What is the justification for these interventions? How do the national interests and the domestic problems of the disputants affect the ability of the UN to make peace or to keep it?

8. Write a brief biography of one of the UN Secretaries-General.

CHAPTER SEVEN

The End of the Cold War and Beyond

Germans break down the infamous Berlin Wall in November 1989, while the once-feared East German troops look on. When and why was the Berlin Wall built? Why is its destruction considered the symbolic end of the Cold War?

"It is given to very few people to change the course of history. But that is what Gorbachev has done. Whatever happens today, his place in history is secure."

— British prime minister John Major, commenting on Gorbachev's resignation, 26 December 1991

"The era of the bipolar division of the world is over.... The old orders are falling apart, and it is our task to build new ones."

—Václav Havel, president of Czechoslovakia, 1990

Overview

This chapter will begin with the dramatic developments over six short years that literally changed the world. The main agent of change was Mikhail Gorbachev, who assumed leadership of the Soviet Union in 1985 and initiated a series of reforms that resulted in the dissolution of the USSR in 1991 and the end of the Cold War.

The end of the Cold War began with Gorbachev's announcement that the people of Eastern Europe were free to choose their own political and economic systems. By 1990, free elections were the order of the day, the Berlin Wall fell, and the two Germanys were reunited. With the collapse of communism in Eastern Europe, the communist system in the Soviet Union also started to unravel. Once the process began, it continued at a dizzying pace. One by one the Soviet republics declared their independence, and the political map of Europe was redrawn almost overnight.

The end of the Cold War was not all positive. A period of disintegration followed as various nations and ethnic groups emerged from Soviet control to demand their own freedom. In some cases, as with the former Ukrainian Soviet Socialist Republic, the transition to independence was easy and joyous. In others, however, such as Yugoslavia, the transition degenerated into open warfare among the various ethnic groups.

Focus Questions

1. What caused the collapse of the Soviet Union?
2. What was the impact of Gorbachev's policies on the Soviet Union and Soviet bloc countries?
3. How has Russia changed since the collapse of communism?
4. What factors led to the disintegration of Yugoslavia?

The Gorbachev Revolution

The sweeping changes in the Soviet Union were remarkably peaceful and rapid—so rapid, in fact, that the West was caught off guard. After 40 years of rivalry and hostility the West was reluctant to put much faith in the promises of the new Soviet leader, Mikhail Gorbachev. Was this just another period of détente or was this a fundamental change? As Gorbachev proposed one peace initiative after another, the United States cautiously tried to understand these new Soviet policies. The traditional Cold War attitudes expressed by US president Ronald Reagan and his successor, George Bush, no longer seemed appropriate. The Soviet Union was no longer the enemy and the world was no longer divided into two armed camps. Co-operation seemed to be the new order for Soviet-American relations.

PEACE INITIATIVES

At 54, Gorbachev represented a younger, better educated, and more progressive generation of Communist Party officials. Upon assuming the leadership of the

Soviet Union in March 1985 he began a series of radical peace initiatives. Until then, the typical Soviet-American approach to international security had been to talk about peace while both sides continued to prepare for war. Gorbachev seriously challenged the West to stop the arms race.

The Soviet Union had practical economic reasons for trying to end the arms race. Under President Reagan's leadership in the early 1980s, the US had raised its level of military spending by 40 per cent. The strength of the US economy allowed for this kind of massive increase. The Soviets, on the other hand, were already directing up to 25 per cent of their gross domestic product (GDP) toward military spending, and this was causing severe economic hardship. If Gorbachev was to provide a better life for the Soviet people he had to reduce military spending.

At the United Nations, Gorbachev announced the unilateral reduction of Soviet armed forces, including a substantial number in Eastern Europe. Then, in 1988, the Soviet Union began to withdraw its troops from Afghanistan. The war in Afghanistan has been called the Soviet Vietnam because the conflict dragged on for years without any hope of a clear victory. The Soviet army faced local guerrilla forces, armed by the US, that blended in with the local population. Afghanistan had become a military and political disaster for the USSR, and Gorbachev decided to get out.

Arms talks that had begun in 1986 now led quickly to agreements. The United States and the Soviet Union signed a treaty agreeing to destroy all their intermediate- and short-range nuclear missiles. In 1990, Warsaw Pact and NATO members signed the Conventional Forces in Europe Treaty, which substantially reduced their military forces in Europe.

ECONOMIC REFORM

As revolutionary as Gorbachev's peace initiatives were, his program of reform did not end there. When he took office in 1985, Gorbachev was faced with a rapidly deteriorating economic situation. The Cold War emphasis on military strength had drained the Soviet economy. This financial burden threatened the stability of the Soviet Union. It became clear to Gorbachev that the main threat to Soviet security was economic collapse, not invasion from the West.

The deteriorating economic situation was made worse by the communist system

Figure 7.1

In 1988, the Soviet Union pulled its troops out of Afghanistan as Gorbachev reduced Soviet military forces. This event was considered a sign of important changes in Soviet foreign policy. Why was this war dubbed the "Soviet Vietnam"?

itself. Its program of guaranteed employment combined with a lack of incentives did little to encourage technological innovation, competence, or efficient management. In the agricultural sector, for example, government officials, most of whom lacked any agricultural background or expertise, made the decisions. As a result, the industry was unproductive. A comparison of private plots versus collective farms revealed that the private plots produced 25 per cent of the country's total crop output on only 4 per cent of the land. It was clear that the private agricultural operations were performing significantly better than the government-operated farms.

In 1986, Gorbachev announced to the 27th Communist Party Congress that the country was facing economic disaster. Gorbachev argued that the present system was too inefficient and inflexible to meet the needs of domestic consumers or to allow the Soviet Union to compete in the global marketplace. The remedy was **perestroika** (economic restructuring). For Gorbachev, economic restructuring meant moving away from **state socialism** toward a freer market economy. Farmers, for example, could own some land and sell their products for profit in open markets. Similarly, entrepreneurs could start their own businesses and sell products based on consumer demand. However, this meant the removal of government subsidies on food products and consumer goods—a measure that was not popular with the Soviet people, who had grown accustomed to the low food prices.

Moving from a state-controlled economy to a free market economy in the former Soviet Union proved to be much more difficult than expected. In spite of Gorbachev's initiatives, by 1990 little headway had been made in establishing a freer market system with private ownership.

This was partly because of fierce opposition to the reforms by conservative Communist officials and in part because of the sheer magnitude of the changes. There was widespread dissatisfaction and frustration with the slowness of the reform program and with the soaring inflation that accompanied perestroika. Strikes, which had been forbidden under communism, were now common occurrences as people protested their poor working and living conditions. In this time of economic hardship and instability, food became one of the most valuable commodities and it was used to trade for other goods.

Boris Yeltsin, president of the Russian Soviet Socialist Republic, became Gorbachev's chief political rival. He favoured a much faster pace for change than did Gorbachev. Yeltsin wanted Russia to move directly to a free market economy as quickly as possible. The Russian people needed food, housing, and medical supplies, and Yeltsin used these shortages for his own political agenda against Gorbachev.

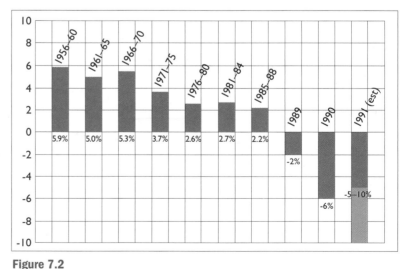

Figure 7.2

The Decline in the Rate of Growth of Soviet GNP (Gross National Product) to 1991. Why did the Soviet economy drop so quickly? (Source: Paul Kennedy. *Preparing for the 21st Century*. Copyright 1993 by Paul Kennedy. Published in Canada by HarperCollins Publishers Ltd.)

Figure 7.3
Food rationing in the Soviet Union resulted in long lineups for limited supplies. Why did the situation get even worse under the economic reforms of Gorbachev and Yeltsin?

In 1991, industrial production had fallen a further 20 per cent, famine was threatening many northern regions, and inflation was increasing by 2-3 per cent a week. Gorbachev was forced to approach the Western industrial nations for help in rescuing the deteriorating Soviet economy. The United States and Germany were willing to extend credit and aid, but the political situation was so unstable within the USSR that they decided to deal with some of the Soviet republics on an individual basis.

SOCIAL PROBLEMS IN THE USSR

As the Soviet economy deteriorated, so too did social conditions. Everything that contributed to the quality of life seemed to be in decline. Corruption increased and a crime wave swept the country.

The health care system began to unravel, and, with it, the standards of public health. Infant mortality rates began rising and life expectancy started to decline. Staggering pollution levels were creating health hazards for much of the Soviet population. High levels of industrial waste, toxic chemicals, and radioactive waste—the result of the Communists' demand for economic growth at all costs—had created serious environmental problems.

For example, in April 1986, a reactor at the nuclear power complex at Chernobyl broke down, bringing the facility to the brink of a nuclear meltdown. The explosion, fire, and resulting radioactive debris caused hundreds of deaths and injuries. The causes of the disaster were identified as faulty design and inadequate staff training. This highly publicized disaster exposed Soviet backwardness in technology and was a blow to Soviet prestige. By 1993, 8000 people had died from radiation-induced diseases, and a million cases of serious illness had been diagnosed.

The consumption of vodka, a traditional drink in Soviet culture, was becoming a serious problem. Between 1970 and 1980, alcohol became the third most common cause of death and a contributing factor in the escalating divorce and crime rates. Gorbachev campaigned to control alcohol consumption by reducing production and sales of vodka. These measures made him even more unpopular with producers and consumers alike.

The deteriorating social conditions in the Soviet Union created even greater hardships for women. While communist ideals always supported gender equality, women's pay averaged only about 65 per cent of men's, a figure comparable to that in most capitalist democracies. As in the West, most women worked outside the home, but traditional roles had not really changed. Women were still responsible for most domestic chores and child care. Their problems were compounded as the

Profile Mikhail Gorbachev (1931-)

Figure 7.4
Mikhail Gorbachev

Mikhail Gorbachev's years in power from 1985 to 1991 transformed the Soviet Union and inspired much of the West.

"The use or threat of force no longer can or must be an instrument of foreign policy…. All of us, and primarily the stronger of us, must exercise self-restraint and totally rule out any use of force."

— Mikhail Gorbachev, in a speech to the UN, Dec. 1988

"It is…quite clear to us that the principle of freedom of choice is mandatory. Its nonrecognition is fraught with extremely grave consequences for world peace."

— Mikhail Gorbachev, in a speech to the UN, Dec. 1988

Mikhail Gorbachev was born into a peasant family in the Russian province of Stavropol in 1931. Clever and ambitious, he entered Moscow University in 1953, where he studied law and joined the Communist Party. Upon graduating from university, Gorbachev returned to Stavropol and began his political career. To broaden his education and to increase his chances of promotion within the Communist Party, he earned a college degree in agronomy by correspondence.

He returned to Moscow in 1978 as agriculture secretary.

From 1982 to 1985, a succession of old and progressively weaker Soviet leaders died: Leonid Brezhnev in 1982; Yuri Andropov in 1984; and Konstantin Chernenko in 1985. Gorbachev was named the new Soviet leader (officially, the General Secretary of the Communist Party) in 1985. He promptly embarked on a new era in Soviet politics, introducing radical social, economic, and political changes. Two words came to symbolize the new Soviet Union—*perestroika* (restructuring) and *glasnost* (openness).

In 1986, Gorbachev demonstrated his commitment to disarmament and world peace by proposing a plan for the elimination of nuclear arms by the year 2000. His proposals culminated in the historic Soviet-American arms control treaty in 1987 and effectively ended the Cold War.

Believing that a communist monopoly of power in the Soviet Union obstructed the reform process, Gorbachev introduced free elections to the Supreme Soviet (national parliament) in 1989. He created the new position of president of the USSR so that the country would be run by an elected government rather than by a communist dictatorship. He did not oppose the dismantling of communist regimes in Eastern Europe. To revive the failing Soviet economy, Gorbachev encouraged the gradual development of a free market system. Criticism of Gorbachev and his reforms within the Soviet Union mounted. In 1991, after the failure of a conservative communist coup, Gorbachev resigned as leader of the USSR.

Gorbachev moved international relations beyond détente and brought an end to the Cold War. For this enormous contribution he won the 1990 Nobel Prize for Peace. He was in office for only six years but is considered by many to be one of the most important political leaders of the twentieth century.

Responding

1. What reforms did Gorbachev introduce to the Soviet Union?
2. Why was Gorbachev awarded the Nobel Peace Prize? Do you think he deserved the award?

economy worsened. Women now found themselves spending long hours after a full day's work waiting in food lines for the few commodities available.

Gorbachev's policy of **glasnost** (openness) was intended to reform Soviet life by making society more open, stimulating, and rewarding. By opening up the channels of communication, more information would be available, making informed dialogue possible and, ultimately, leading to a better society. Removing censorship to allow freedom of information and giving the media the right to criticize authority were major steps taken under Gorbachev's leadership. Because of glasnost, the works of previously silenced dissident writers resurfaced, the policies and actions of former leaders were examined, and social issues such as homelessness, unemployment, drug and alcohol abuse, and prostitution were openly discussed by the media. In addition, Gorbachev ended the ban on Western broadcasting, allowing the Russian-language broadcasts of the Voice of America and the BBC to be heard by Soviet citizens. Ironically, this openness also encouraged the formation of all kinds of opposition groups critical of the government.

In Review

1. a) What did Gorbachev believe to be the basic problem in the Soviet Union?

    b) What was his strategy for remedying these problems?

    c) What do the Russian words "perestroika" and "glasnost" mean?

2. List some of the social problems the Soviet Union faced. In what ways did these problems contribute to the slow rate of reform?

3. What did Gorbachev hope to achieve with glasnost?

The Dismantling of an Empire

POLITICAL REFORM

In a radical departure from the one-party rule of the Communist Party, Gorbachev called for free elections to the Supreme Soviet in 1989. His hope was that the Communist Party would be seen as a party of reform and would appeal to the people. But the electoral results resembled a tidal wave as Communist officials were swept out of office and new reform-oriented candidates from other parties were voted in.

For the satellite states of Eastern Europe, events in the Soviet Union came to mean the destruction of the communist system. Eager to seize the opportunity, the countries of Eastern Europe asserted their independence after more than 40 years of tight Soviet control. Free to decide their own destinies, Hungary, Czechoslovakia, and Poland rejected communism and introduced democratic reforms. Romania, Bulgaria, and Albania chose to retain a communist system of government. Yugoslavia rejected communism but was immediately plunged into a devastating civil war as ethnic rivalries escalated into violence (see page

The Soviet Satellite States Achieve Independence

Country	Date	Key Events
Poland	1989	Free elections held after a series of strikes in 1989 by labour movement Solidarity. Solidarity forms the government under Lech Walesa.
East Germany	1990	Communist hardliner Erich Honecker is forced out of office in 1989. Free elections are held in 1990 and East Germany is unified with West Germany.
Hungary	1990	New leadership liberalizes laws and allows multi-party elections. Communists defeated in free elections and coalition government formed.
Czechoslovakia	1990	Mass demonstrations and a general strike force Communist government to agree to multi-party rule. Václav Havel becomes president. Free elections held and Communists defeated. Ethnic divisions lead to division of Czechoslovakia into two states, the Czech and Slovak Republics.
Bulgaria	1991	Mass demonstrations bring down the Communist government.
Romania	1991	Mass demonstrations and economic pressures topple Communist dictatorship of Nicolai Ceauçescu. Free elections held.
Baltic states (Part of USSR)	1990-1991	Mass demonstrations in Latvia, Estonia, and Lithuania. Free elections defeat Communist governments. Baltic states secede from Soviet Union.

Figure 7.5

In each case, free elections toppled the totalitarian communist regimes. Communist parties must now run for office like any other political party.

228). But perhaps nowhere were events more dramatic at the time than in East Germany.

THE UNIFICATION OF GERMANY, 1990

The Berlin Wall long symbolized the division of the world into opposing Cold War camps. On 10 November 1989 the world was captivated by the sight of Berliners from east and west perched atop the wall celebrating its dismantling. At points throughout Berlin, sledgehammers were busy reducing the wall to rubble. This event more than any other signified the symbolic end of the Cold War.

The division of Germany had always been a central issue of the Cold War. The Soviet Union had held East Germany firmly in its grip since the end of the Second World War. After 1985, however, the Soviet Union withdrew its military support for satellite communist governments. This raised East German hopes for reunification with West Germany. Demonstrations calling for reform became more and more common in East Germany. Government officials paid little heed to these demands, however, and ignored Gorbachev's calls for glasnost and perestroika.

In 1989, a tide of East German people flowed to the West, travelling through Hungary and crossing the newly opened border into Austria and then into West Germany. As discontent in East Germany spread, Communist Party chief Erich Honecker, a hardliner devoted to maintaining the status quo, was forced out of office. He was replaced by a reform-minded

"In every border post there's something insecure

Each one of them is longing for leaves and for flowers.

They say the greatest punishment for a tree

is to become a border post...."

– Excerpt from a poem by Evgenii Evtushenko that appeared in a Soviet literary magazine in September 1985

government that opened the borders and eased travel restrictions for East German citizens. This led to the dismantling of the Berlin Wall in November. While this contained the emigration exodus somewhat, thousands of East Germans continued to flee the country. West German chancellor Helmut Kohl proposed a unification plan that was conditional on East Germany holding free elections. Demonstrators in East Germany took up the call for "one Germany," but the East German Communist government was lukewarm to the idea. By December, however, the Communist Party in East Germany could no longer maintain power, and free elections were set for the following year.

Amidst all of these changes massive demonstrations for unification accelerated. When free elections were held in March 1990, the people voted for a government that supported reunification. In July, Kohl met with Gorbachev to ensure Soviet support for a united Germany. West Germany even agreed to pay US$9.5 billion to finance the withdrawal of 370 000 Soviet troops from East Germany. On September 12, the four nations that had participated in the division of Germany at the end of the Second World War—Britain, France, the United States, and the Soviet Union—signed a reunification treaty. East and West Germany were reunited on 3 October 1990.

Figure 7.6

Germans celebrate reunification in October 1990, as East Germany, a Soviet bloc nation, unites with West Germany. Why was the reunification seen as the symbolic end of the Cold War?

PROBLEMS OF REUNIFICATION

The new united Germany faced serious domestic problems. There were huge discrepancies between the standards of living in the two parts of the country. While the economy was prosperous in the west and the people enjoyed a high standard of living, in the east, consumer goods were in short supply and businesses were obsolete, overstaffed, and mismanaged after four decades of centralized planning. Most of the eastern businesses could not compete, and up to 35 per cent fell into bankruptcy. By 1992, 30 per cent of workers in the former East Germany were unemployed or underemployed. Wages were purposely set at 60-70 per cent of those in the west to encourage investment and to reflect the lower productivity of the region.

East Germans faced a unique set of problems. On unification, West Germany's laws and practices were applied to the whole country, including banking, the welfare system, taxes, and environmental standards. Gone were many aspects of the communist system the East Germans had come to enjoy, such as guaranteed employment and subsidized food prices. There was a new and disorienting insecurity for the East German people.

Many West Germans were unhappy with the new united nation as well; many resented that an estimated US$775 billion would be needed over five years to improve the infrastructure in the east.

ETHNIC TENSION AND VIOLENCE

Between 1989 and 1991, 2.5 million immigrants and refugees arrived in Germany. These non-Germans were seen by many as an additional burden. Incidents of violence began to erupt, at first in the former East Germany, where unemployment was highest, but then throughout the country. Most often the attackers were young, right-wing **skinheads** who adopted Nazi jargon and insignias as symbols of hatred and rebellion. These neo-Nazis, though small in number, were responsible for thousands of brutal assaults on immigrants and refugees, many of which resulted in death.

In response to the actions of the skinheads, hundreds of thousands of Germans took part in marches, rallies, and candlelit vigils to condemn the violence and demand that the government put a stop to it. In November 1992, on the anniversary of *Kristallnacht*, the night of violent Nazi attacks against Jews in 1938, 300 000 people protested in Berlin. By 1993, however, the German government was forced to bow to pressure from the right. The country's liberal asylum laws for immigrants were revoked, stemming the flow of refugees.

Figure 7.7
Neo-Nazis have resurrected Hitler's racist slogans and the Nazi salute. Why did the rise of the neo-Nazi movement create concern both in Germany and the world community?

Voices   The New Germany

The reunification of Germany profoundly affected the political and economic character of Europe. Read the two opinions expressed here about the possible threat posed by a reunified Germany. Ten years after these statements were made, which viewpoint turned out to be more accurate?

MADELAINE DROHAN, JOURNALIST

"West Germany developed a powerhouse economy and became a responsible member of the new world order through its membership in the North Atlantic Treaty Organization, the European Community and the G-7.

"Then the world order changed. The Berlin Wall came down. The Cold War ended. And West Germany became enmeshed in the unexpectedly expensive and troublesome unification with East Germany that has left both sides feeling sour....

"Former British Prime Minister Margaret Thatcher put into words what many other Europeans feel when she warned, 'With the collapse of the Soviet Union and the reunification of Germany, the entire picture has changed. The problem of German power has again resurfaced.'"

Source: Excerpted from Madelaine Drohan,
The Globe and Mail, 4 July 1992. Reprinted with
permission from The Globe and Mail.

FLORA LEWIS, JOURNALIST

"The most important difference now dividing Germans from their allies and neighbors is that while most everyone else talks of projection of a greater new German strength from the center of the continent, the Germans feel suddenly weak and uncertain. No one foresaw the emotional, psychological and political problems that unification would bring, let alone the staggering economic and social difficulties that are still only beginning to be understood.... The more they advance with the totally unexpected task...the more they discover they must do.... At this point they feel overwhelmed, not rambunctious; burdened, not burdensome."

Source: Reprinted from Flora Lewis,
"A European Germany or a German European?"
New Perspectives Quarterly, Winter 1993, by permission.

Responding

1. How does Madelaine Drohan describe the unification of East Germany with West Germany? Is she positive or negative about the union?
2. Why do you think Margaret Thatcher considered the unification of Germany as a "problem"?
3. What is Flora Lewis's view of German unification? Does she think Germany will be a problem in the future?
4. Which of their views is more accurate today?

In Review

1. a) What key factors led to the dismantling of the Berlin Wall?

   b) In what way did the dismantling of the Berlin Wall mark the symbolic end of the Cold War?

2. What were some of the problems facing Germany following reunification?

3. Who were the German skinheads in the early 1990s and what was their agenda?

Rivalry and Crisis in the Soviet Union

POLITICAL RIVALRY

One of the ironies of Gorbachev's leadership was that he was more popular in the West than in his own country. With his wife, Raisa, he toured the world, charming the public and winning the admiration of the press. To the West, Gorbachev represented new hope for a peaceful world. His decision in 1988 to withdraw Soviet troops from Afghanistan, where they had been locked in conflict for eight years, was a convincing demonstration of his commitment to world peace.

Gorbachev's reputation as a progressive leader was undisputed outside the Soviet Union, but at home there was growing criticism of the slow pace of his reforms. By 1991, many people felt he was trying to slow down the process of reform rather than lead it, while Communist hardliners felt he had already gone too far. Leaders of the individual Soviet republics, such as Boris Yeltsin, did not hesitate to exploit Gorbachev's vulnerable position for their own advantage.

Gorbachev's main rival was Boris Yeltsin. Both men were committed to a program of reform, but their approaches were different. Gorbachev aspired to introduce major reforms within the Soviet Union by reforming the communist system. Yeltsin, on the other hand, believed that the communist system was the source of the problem and that communism itself had to be abolished. Reforms, he argued, must be quick and radical.

As president of Russia, the largest of the Soviet republics, Yeltsin was able to move swiftly with reforms to create a market economy. But a "war of laws" broke out when Gorbachev tried to block Yeltsin through legislation. Yeltsin countered by legislating that Russian laws took precedence over Soviet laws.

In 1991, Yeltsin was elected president of the Russian republic by popular vote in a democratic election, winning a landslide victory over his Communist Party rival. Yeltsin now had the support of the Russian people. Gorbachev, on the other hand, had not been elected by the people. His rise to power had been through the Communist Party. Furthermore, he had lost popularity because of the declining economy and his inability to improve living standards. Politically, he lost favour. The conservatives claimed he had sold out to the radicals, while the radicals claimed he had sold out to the conservatives. It was clear that reconciliation of the two sides was impossible. Gorbachev would have to move to one side of the political spectrum or the other. The political appointments he made in the first half of 1991 signalled that his position had shifted toward the conservative hardliners.

THE MOSCOW COUP

For one week in August 1991, dramatic events unfolded in Moscow and the world was on edge awaiting the outcome. A small group of hardline Communists—all of them in powerful positions—attempted a coup to overthrow Gorbachev and the reform movement.

It began on Sunday, August 18. Gorbachev was placed under house arrest at his Crimean *dacha* (vacation home) by the Communist leaders of the coup. Realizing they would also have to eliminate the radical reform group headed by Yeltsin, the hardliners ordered army tanks to roll through the streets of Moscow and surround key buildings, including the Russian parliament where Yeltsin and his supporters had taken refuge. Before a violent confrontation

> "Your dearest wish is for our state structure and our ideological system never to change, to remain as they are for centuries. But history is not like that. Every system either finds a way to develop or else collapses."
>
> – Aleksandr Solzhenitsyn, excerpt from his Letter to the Soviet Leaders, 1973

Profile Boris Yeltsin (1931-)

Figure 7.8
Boris Yeltsin

Boris Yeltsin emerged as a leader of the Russian people at a critical moment in Russian history. Just as Soviet communism began to self-destruct, Yeltsin boldly offered a radical alternative that appealed to the Russian people desperately looking for change.

"Yeltsin's destruction of the Soviet State looks less like a revolution than a palace coup."

— Lilia Shevtsova, *Current History*, October 2000

Boris Yeltsin was born in 1931 in Sverdlovsk, USSR. He trained as an engineer and worked on various construction projects from 1955 to 1968. He didn't join the Communist Party until he was 30 years old. In 1985, Mikhail Gorbachev, the new general secretary of the Communist Party, brought Yeltsin to Moscow for the post of the first secretary of the Moscow City Party Committee (similar to city mayor).

Yeltsin eagerly aligned himself with the Gorbachev-led reformist wing of the Communist Party and threw himself into an attack on the entrenched party machinery. His abrasive and domineering attitude made him many enemies. But what got him into real trouble was his impatience with the pace of reform—Gorbachev's "perestroika." On 21 October 1987,

Yeltsin shocked the assembled Communist Party Central Committee by resigning his posts because economic reform was proceeding too slowly. This public dispute was a deliberate challenge to Gorbachev.

Yeltsin quit the Communist Party in 1990, and on 12 June 1991 he became president of the Russian Federation. He created the Commonwealth of Independent States (CIS) on 8 December 1991, bringing to an end Gorbachev's efforts to preserve the USSR.

As the leader of the new independent state of Russia, Yeltsin faced a number of problems. His personal popularity plummeted when he introduced a radical reform plan intended to move Russia toward a market-based economy. In December 1994, Yeltsin sent Russian troops to invade the Muslim minority region of Chechnya to quell a separatist rebellion. The bloody conflict became an ongoing humiliating problem for Russia.

Yeltsin was not expected to do well in the presidential election of June 1996. He had suffered two heart attacks and a huge drop in popularity as a result of the war in Chechnya and the hardship caused by his economic reforms. Still, he refused to quit. He hired American political consultants, or "spin doctors," who used US-style political marketing techniques to influence the Russian voting public. It worked, and won the election.

Yet, Yeltsin's drinking problem began to affect his work. He embarrassed friends and foes alike by arriving at many official functions quite drunk. Toward the end of his second term as president, his health problems became more serious. Commenting on Yeltsin's life, Lilia Shevtsova observed that "from a once-powerful charismatic leader, Yeltsin gradually degenerated into a powerless, pitiful old man." Vladimir Putin replaced Yeltsin in December 1999.

Responding

1. Why did Yeltsin quit the Communist Party?
2. Do you agree or disagree with the statement that Yeltsin was a better revolutionary leader than president? Why?

could take place, however, Yeltsin emerged from the building and climbed up onto one of the tanks. In a bold stroke of public image-making, he stared defiantly at the soldiers and militia around him and announced that the army supported the people and would not attack the defenders of democracy. The tank crews then broke ranks and disbanded.

The hardliners' tactics signalled a return to the repressive style of the Stalinists. In protest, thousands of people rallied in front of the Russian parliament. For two days, unarmed Soviet citizens who supported Yeltsin and democracy faced down heavily armed riot troops. Finally, the coup leaders lost their nerve and the coup collapsed.

Gorbachev returned to Moscow on Thursday, August 22. But his power had been seriously undermined by the week's events. Now it was Yeltsin who was the real leader in the eyes of the people. He took control of the situation immediately, praising those who had defended democracy and promising punishment for those who had aided the coup. Yeltsin laid the blame for the coup squarely on the Communists and announced measures to remove Communist influences from Russia, including replacing the Soviet flag with the traditional Russian flag. On the streets, the overjoyed crowds chanted Yeltsin's name.

Betrayed by his own party, Gorbachev announced his resignation as General Secretary on Saturday and recommended the dissolution of the Communist Party.

Figure 7.9
The people of Moscow took to the streets during the attempted coup in August 1991, pleading with army soldiers to retreat with their tanks. How did the soldiers respond?

Figure 7.10
Following the failed coup, Gorbachev presented a proposal to the Congress of Peoples' Deputies (the Duma) to transform the Soviet Union into a loosely knit confederation. However, the coup attempt was a fatal blow to his leadership. What were some other effects of the Moscow coup?

THE EFFECTS OF THE MOSCOW COUP

The effects of the August coup attempt were dramatic. Prior to the coup, conservative Communist leaders had been intent on blocking the new Union Treaty, due to be signed on August 20. Gorbachev had reasoned that the only way to keep the Soviet Union together was to give the republics much more authority and put an end to centralized power in the Kremlin. The conservative Communists opposed this relinquishing of power for fear of weakening the Soviet Union. But the coup attempt exposed the weakness of the central government and unleashed a flood of nationalism in many of the republics. By the end of August most of the republics had declared their independence from the Soviet Union.

The coup also undermined the central government of the USSR. Gorbachev had lost the confidence of the people and had been betrayed by his own party. Yeltsin emerged as the hero, having defied communism and successfully defended democracy. He wasted no time capitalizing on the opportunity to discredit Gorbachev. More than any other single event, the coup brought about the end of Soviet communism, the Soviet Union, and Gorbachev's leadership.

THE COMMONWEALTH OF INDEPENDENT STATES

On 7 December 1991, Yeltsin met with the leaders of Ukraine and Belarus in the Belarus capital of Minsk. The next day the three leaders declared that the Soviet Union no longer existed and that in its place would be the new Commonwealth of Independent States (CIS). On December 21, 11 republics signed an agreement to become members of the CIS; Georgia and the three Baltic republics of Estonia, Latvia, and Lithuania declined to join. (In October 1992, Azerbaijan voted against remaining in the Commonwealth.) The Soviet Union was officially dissolved on 1 January 1992.

The CIS helped to prevent the former Soviet Union from collapsing into complete economic and political chaos. It could also be seen as an example of Russian **supranationalism**—the transcending of national boundaries in order to link people to ideas or movements. Officially, the CIS was formed as a loose federation to maintain economic and military relationships while permitting national groups to run their own governments. Problems quickly arose over conflicting interests among the various religious, ethnic, and national groups. The smaller states were caught between the huge Russian magnet and the desire for **self-determination**—the ability to determine their own future. While most republics were more than happy to embark on independent nationhood, there was also the sobering reality that they would no longer be an integral part of a mighty superpower.

LIFE AFTER COMMUNISM

All of the newly independent states, including Russia, faced three serious challenges: political reform, economic stability, and ethnic relations. The overthrow of communism led to demands for democracy and expectations of a higher standard of living. But after 70 years of communist totalitarian control, the problems encountered in putting democracy into practice and establishing a market economy were enormous. In Russia, a wide split developed between Yeltsin and the old Communist parliament.

In addition, the Russian people had no experience with competitive capitalism. The rapid and sweeping changes involved in introducing a market economy caused economic chaos. The introduction of a market system resulted in spiralling inflation, escalating unemployment, and widespread poverty. Accustomed to the security of subsidized prices, a controlled market, and guaranteed employment, some people rejected the new capitalist system. The majority, however, did not want to return to communism, believing the long-range promise of a higher standard of living was worth the short-term suffering.

ETHNIC DIVERSITY AND CONFLICT

The former Soviet Union consisted of 50 different nationalities speaking 100 different languages, using five different alphabets, and practising many different religions. Many of these groups were small, but their cultures dated back hundreds and even thousands of years. For the most part, they were encouraged by the Soviet government to speak their own language and maintain their cultural identity. Their political rights, however, were restricted, and separatist activities were repressed by the centralized Russian-dominated Communist government.

Once Gorbachev was in power and the policy of glasnost was implemented, minorities throughout the Soviet Union became more vocal. In the late 1980s, as

MAP STUDY

Figure 7.11
The Former Soviet Union

This map shows the beginning and end of communism in the 15 republics in the former Union of Soviet Socialist Republics (USSR). These republics, or soviets, were controlled by the Russian Soviet and the central Soviet government in Moscow. The Russian republic was by far the largest and most dominant. Today, the former Soviet republics are independent states. Russia, however, still remains the major power in the region.

Interpreting

1. When did Soviet communism end in Russia?
2. How many republics continued with the communist system after the dissolution of the Soviet Union?
3. Use an encyclopedia or atlas to find out which republic is the largest in population and geographic size after Russia.
4. Can you think of circumstances in the future in which Russia might decide to regain direct political control of these former republics?

the control of the Communist Party and the Kremlin loosened, local national groups were encouraged to seek independence. Power struggles and territorial disputes broke out between rival groups in many parts of the Soviet Union.

With the dissolution of the Soviet Union, disputes over boundaries, language rights, and a host of other problems threatened the peaceful co-existence of these ethnic groups. In some areas, such as Chechnya in the southern part of Russia, ethnic rivalries and hostilities degenerated into civil war and the direct intervention of the Russian army.

RUSSIA TODAY

Russia was formally established as a nation with the dissolution of the Soviet Union on 1 January 1992. Since then, Russia has faced enormous political, economic, and social problems. The country has always been poorer than Western countries, but the disparities of wealth and poverty became even more obvious. There are now (2002) 57 McDonald's restaurants in Moscow, but many ordinary people can barely afford to buy a meal. The free market provides all the luxuries one could possibly want, but only the rich do the buying. It is estimated that 40 per cent of Russians live below the poverty line.

Russia, once a military superpower, is now much like a developing nation. Vladimir Putin was named Prime Minister in 1999. In 2000, Putin estimated that if Russia could maintain an annual growth rate of 8 per cent for 15 years, that would put the country on the same level as Portugal—the poorest nation in the European Union. The current GDP for Russia is only slightly larger than that of Ontario.

Russia can claim some specific progress in the years since the collapse of

WWW.SALON.COM

This site contains interesting articles and essays on current international conflicts. It is updated daily with news stories and opinion pieces on world events. It also archives its articles so that you may view past opinion pieces.

Select a current international conflict to investigate in the site's archive. For example, if you type in "Chechnya" in the search box, you will call up a list of article titles, with a brief description of each article along with the date it appeared. Choose at least two articles listed under the topic of your choice, and write a summary of each one. What is each writer's view of the conflict? Do the opinions of the individual writers differ, and, if so, how? What is your opinion of the writers' views?

Figure 7.12
Vladimir Putin with Jean Chrétien at the June 26-27, 2002 G-8 Summit in Kananaskis, Alberta. When asked about the ongoing economic problems in Russia, Putin said, "There are no reasons for us to be dizzy with success...we have only managed not to fall further behind other countries." In what way do these high-profile meetings help Russia maintain its status as a world power?

communism. Elections continue to be free and reasonably fair. There are laws in place for the private ownership of property, an income tax has been set to generate revenue, and there is a free press. As part of the long-term strategy to improve life in Russia, Putin has moved to develop closer ties to the West. He is pursuing membership in the World Trade Organization and has already accepted an active role with NATO and the G-7 club (now known as the G-8).

In Review

1. What kinds of reforms did Gorbachev introduce when he took over the leadership of the Soviet Union in 1985?

2. What was the impact of Gorbachev's reforms on the following?
   a) the Soviet government
   b) the Soviet economy
   c) ethnic minorities in the former Soviet Union
   d) the communist states of eastern Europe
   e) relations with the West
   f) the Cold War

3. Why did Gorbachev decide to loosen the Soviet Union's tight control of the Soviet bloc republics in Eastern Europe? How did the republics respond to this action? What was the result?

4. What did the leaders of the Moscow coup hope to accomplish? In what ways did the coup bring about the end of the Soviet Union?

5. What have been some of Russia's problems and accomplishments since the collapse of communism?

Yugoslavia: A Nation Divided

The end of the Soviet Union created a power vacuum in Eastern Europe. Most newly independent nations remained relatively intact after the fall of Soviet communism. In other cases, for example Czechoslovakia, the nation voted for partition and peacefully divided. Yugoslavia, however, was different. There, ethnic and nationalist forces exploded into violence.

Yugoslavia was created following the breakup of the Austro-Hungarian Empire at the end of the First World War. The new nation was formed by amalgamating the Balkan provinces of Croatia, Dalmatia, Bosnia, Herzegovina, Slovenia, and Vojvodina, and the independent state of Montenegro. In 1941, Hitler invaded Yugoslavia, but the Nazi forces encountered a strong resistance movement led by Josip Broz Tito, the head of the Yugoslav Communist Party. Tito's success in resisting the Nazis earned him the popularity and support to lead the new Yugoslav government after the war. He was the nation's dictator for 35 years, from 1945 to 1980. Tito's Yugoslavia was made up of six republics: Bosnia, Croatia, Macedonia, Montenegro, Slovenia, and Serbia.

Tito also unified his people by resisting Soviet efforts to control Yugoslavia.

MAP STUDY

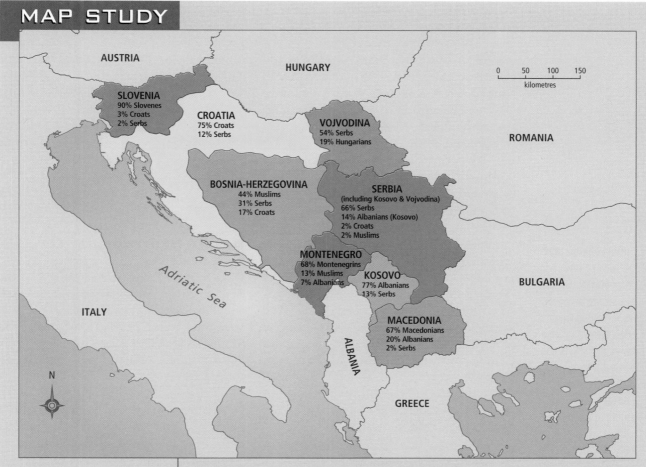

Figure 7.13

The New States of the Former Yugoslavia, with Ethnic Breakdown Before the 1990 Civil War

Yugoslavia's ethnic diversity was further complicated by religious differences. Approximately 9 per cent of Yugoslavs were Muslims, living mainly in Bosnia and Herzegovina; 30 per cent, mostly Croats and Slovenes, were Roman Catholic; and about 50 per cent were Eastern Orthodox Catholics.

Interpreting

1. All states but one have a majority ethnic population. Which state does not?
2. Why might Kosovo want to become part of Albania?
3. Which state has the highest percentage of Muslims?

Unlike his neighbours in Eastern Europe, he stood up to Stalin and refused to allow the country to become a satellite of the Soviet Union. Tito's popularity and power was such that even Stalin was reluctant to force a military confrontation. In 1948, Tito expelled Soviet military advisors and, in return, the Soviet Union expelled Yugoslavia from the Cominform.

When Tito died in 1980, Yugoslavia was prosperous, peaceful, and independent. The Olympic Games in Sarajevo in 1984 were considered a showpiece to mark the nation's entry into the global mainstream.

CROATIA, SLOVENIA, AND SERBIA

Despite relative independence from Soviet control, the disintegration of the USSR in the late 1980s had a profound impact on Yugoslavia. The collapse of Soviet communism triggered the fragmentation of the Yugoslav federation into competing ethnic and political groups.

After Tito's death in 1980, Yugoslavia's various ethnic and religious groups began raising their nationalist voices to demand greater **autonomy**. Without Tito's strong leadership, the Communist Party was unable to contain the discord. Meanwhile, charismatic leaders in the republics, such as Slobodan Milosevic, the president of the Serbian Republic, were convinced that their interests were not being well served by the Yugoslav federation. The collapse of communism in Poland and the Soviet Union hurt the Communist Party in Yugoslavia. In 1990, multi-party elections were held in the republics and the communists were defeated everywhere except in Serbia and Montenegro.

The breakup of Yugoslavia began in late 1990, when Croatia adopted constitutional reforms proclaiming the republic as a sovereign state of the Croats. No mention was made of the 12 per cent of the population that was Serbian. In response, the Serbs in Croatia seized control of small areas and declared these **enclaves** as autonomous Serb territory. They were supported by the government in Serbia, which applied economic and military pressure on the Croatian government, including the use of the Yugoslav army in Croat-Serb clashes within Croatia. The Serbs demanded that the boundaries of the two republics be redrawn so that Serbian enclaves in Croatia would become part of the Serbian Republic.

In June 1991, both Slovenia and Croatia unilaterally declared themselves independent. The Serbian-dominated Yugoslav army attempted to prevent the separations, but they were defeated by the Slovenian forces in a 10-day war. The Yugoslav army retreated into Croatia, where fighting between the Serbs and the Croats intensified. In the breakaway republics, militias were formed to defend the newly proclaimed nations. Various ethnic communities armed themselves and dug into defensive enclaves. The fighting raged throughout 1991, killing thousands of soldiers and civilians.

BOSNIA-HERZEGOVINA AND SERBIA

By the end of 1991, it was clear that the Serbian government had failed to prevent the disintegration of Yugoslavia. It had won only token protection for Serbs in Slovenia and Croatia. The Serbs were determined to prevent the separation of Bosnia-Herzegovina.

The population of Bosnia was 44 per cent Muslim, 31 per cent Serbian, and 17 per cent Croatian, with the remainder being of other ethnic and religious backgrounds. The Muslims and Croats voted overwhelmingly in favour of independence in a referendum in February 1992. Unwilling to see the largest group of Serbs outside Serbia become a minority within a new country, the government of the Serbian Republic, under Slobodan Milosevic, launched a full-scale assault on Bosnia. Serb forces moved into Serbian enclaves in Bosnia-Herzegovina in an attempt to eliminate all Muslims and Croats from these regions. People were driven out of their homes, and houses were systematically burned down to prevent the return of the expelled Muslim or Catholic residents. This policy of forcing ethnic groups out of a region became known as **"ethnic cleansing."** By its nature, ethnic cleansing was directed at civilians.

"In the region that used to be Yugoslavia, war is becoming a way of life. Values have been turned upside down. Criminals are turned into heroes and patriots. Adolescents are taught to be killers."

— Helsinki Citizens Assembly, "Appeal to Stop the War in Yugoslavia," *HCA Newsletter*, Prague, 1992

The tragedy of Yugoslavia began to attract world attention and intervention. The European Community recognized the independence of Bosnia-Herzegovina on 5 April 1992. The United Nations demanded an end to the violence, but was ignored. Both the EC and the UN imposed harsh economic sanctions against Serbia. In the media battle for world opinion, particularly in the US, Serbia became the villain in the conflict. Russia offered token moral support for Serbia but was not willing to alienate the West. UN peacekeeping forces were established in Bosnia to keep the airport in Sarajevo operational and to protect the limited civilian relief shipments. These forces had neither the mandate nor the military capability to impose peace.

Through 1992 the fighting in Bosnia escalated. Ceasefires were negotiated, but they lasted only a few days. By September, Yugoslavia (now the combined republics of Serbia and Montenegro) was expelled from the United Nations. By the spring of 1993, Serb forces had continued to make inroads into Muslim territory. The security of the UN peacekeeping forces stationed in the region was threatened, and the West began to talk of military intervention by NATO.

A peace proposal, which would have divided Bosnia into three ethnic regions, was rejected by Bosnian Muslim leaders, and this added to the push for a military solution. Serbian offensives were met with NATO ultimatums to withdraw. After considerable arm-twisting by the US, NATO members agreed to participate in military intervention in Yugoslavia. This decision was controversial because NATO was formed as a defensive alliance against the spread of Soviet communism in Europe. Now NATO was in the middle of a Serbian civil war and involved in a peacemaking operation, normally reserved for the UN.

In February 1994, NATO launched its first combat mission since its inception in 1949 with a limited bombing raid against a Serbian stronghold. Throughout it all, UN peacekeeping forces tried to fulfill their dangerous mission of protecting civilians and keeping supply lines open. Yugoslavia became a confusing mix of NATO peacemaking and UN peacekeeping operations—and both failed to provide lasting peace in the region.

Throughout 1994 and 1995 the conflict continued. No peace proposal satisfied all groups, since each proposal was viewed as giving up too much territory to a rival group. In 1995, Milosevic participated in negotiations for a peace settlement at Dayton, Ohio. These meetings culminated in the Dayton Accord. The accord concluded the three-year Boznia-Herzegovinian war by acknowledging a Serb republic and a Muslim-Croat federation within the state's existing borders.

> "Countries don't give their troops to the UN in trust to be killed trying to implement a really lousy cease-fire agreement arranged by a bunch of diplomats and politicians. That's what is happening in Yugoslavia."
>
> – Major-General Lewis Mackenzie, former officer in command of UN forces in Bosnia, in the *Toronto Star*, 30 January 1993

Figure 7.14
Canadian members of the NATO-led stabilization force patrol the western Bosnian town of Drvar in May 1998.

Profile   Slobodan Milosevic (1941-)

Figure 7.15
Slobodan Milosevic

Slobodan Milosevic was the Serbian leader of Yugoslavia caught in the turbulence of the Soviet Union's collapse. He used brutal measures to try to hold on to the remnants of Yugoslavia under Serbian control. Milosevic became the key villain of the Yugoslav tragedy in the West, lost his power, and was finally arrested as a war criminal.

> *"As prosecutor, I bring the accused, Milosevic, before you to face the charges against him. I do so on behalf of the international community and in the name of all the member states of the United Nations, including the states of former Yugoslavia…the search for power is what motivated Slobodan Milosevic. They were not his personal convictions, even less patriotism or honor, or even racism or xenophobia, which inspired the accused, but the quest for power, and personal power at that."*

— Carla Del Ponte, UN Chief Prosecutor, International Criminal Tribunal, February 2002

Slobodan Milosevic was born in 1941. His early years were influenced by the desertion and suicide of his father, the eventual suicide of his mother (a Communist Party official), and by his only close relationship—with his future wife, Mira Markovic. While studying law at the university in Belgrade, he became deeply involved in the Communist Party, the only route to power in Tito's Yugoslavia.

Milosevic was elected first secretary of the Serbian Communist Party in 1987. Regarded as a champion of the Serbian cause, he won the May 1989 presidential election in Serbia. In 1992-1993, Milosevic organized the intervention of the Yugoslav army in opposition to Slovenian and Croatian declarations of independence. Ethnic Serbs in Croatia and Bosnia were encouraged by Milosevic to pursue the dream of a "greater Serbia". In December 1992, Milosevic was returned to power as president of the Serbian Republic with 55 per cent of the vote amidst charges of voting irregularities. Reaching the end of the legal term limit for his presidency in 1997, Milosevic changed his title to president of the Yugoslav Federation (formerly a ceremonial role) and continued to govern unilaterally. He was ousted as Yugoslav president by reformers in 2000, and then arrested as a war criminal in April 2001.

At his war crimes trial at The Hague, Milosevic was charged with pursuing a policy of ethnic cleansing against Kosovar Albanians in 1999, killing dozens of people in villages and forcing 800 000 from their homes to refugee camps beyond Serbia's borders. He was also charged with sanctioning genocide in Kosovo, Bosnia, and Croatia. Milosevic denied his individual guilt and questioned the validity of the trial.

Responding

1. As leader of Yugoslavia, Milosevic wanted a "greater Serbia." Why would this concern the other ethnic groups?
2. As leader, do you think Milosevic was correct in trying to prevent the various provinces of Yugoslavia from seceding (breaking away)?
3. Why was he tried for war crimes? Research his trial and prepare a short report updating the latest developments.

Kosovo

In 1989, Milosevic, the Serbian president and ardent Serb nationalist, revoked the autonomy of the Serbian province of Kosovo. Kosovo's major ethnic group, the Albanians, protested with mass demonstrations. During the demonstrations the Serbian police killed 23 Kosovars. Over the next nine years, tensions and violence escalated between the Serbs and ethnic Albanians. In 1998 civil war broke out between the Serbian forces and the ethnic Albanians' Kosovo Liberation Front (KLF).

Serbian security forces killed thousands of ethnic Albanians as they implemented the policy of ethnic cleansing in Kosovo. This created an exodus of more than one million refugees and led to an international outcry and a call to end the violence in Kosovo.

The massive humanitarian crisis worsened with the increasing flood of ethnic Albanian refugees into Albania, Macedonia, and Montenegro. Some Kosovars were air-transferred out, but an estimated 800 000 struggled to survive in refugee camps.

In March 1999 the US-led NATO bombing campaign of Serbia began. More than 3500 missions were flown by NATO forces before the Serbian government withdrew its troops from Kosovo on June 10. During the conflict the Serbian government accused NATO of deliberately bombing civilian targets. NATO admitted to some mistakes but accused the Serbs of using civilians to protect their troops.

The devastation of Kosovo was captured by the media around the world as ethnic Albanians returned to the rubble of destroyed tracts of land and property. However, the defeated Serbs in Kosovo now fled to avoid revenge attacks and reprisals by the Albanians. NATO forces supervised the refugees' return and tried to keep the peace between the two groups,

Figure 7.16
Ethnic Albanians returning to rubble where their homes used to be after NATO forces cleared the way for them to return to Kosovo. Canadian peacekeeping troops participated in the UN mission to keep the peace between the Albanians and Serbs. Check the UN Web site for an update on the UN peacekeeping operation in Kosovo.

while the UN's World Food Program airlifted food and supplies into the area. The European Union and NATO began the enormous process of reconstruction to restore housing, municipal services, and civil and judicial administration.

Many sanctions against Serbia by the international community were lifted after the Serbian people removed Milosevic from power and elected a democratic government. Peace and security for the region will be hard to restore, however. Ethnic hatreds have a long history in the Balkans, and many fear that NATO's military intervention could provoke a wider conflict involving Russia and militant Muslim groups in the region.

In Review

1. After the Second World War, Yugoslavia was made up of six republics with a mixture of ethnic groups and religions. What percentage of Yugoslavs were Eastern Orthodox Catholic, Roman Catholic, and Muslim? Match the predominant ethnic groups with each religion.

2. Why was Yugoslavia relatively peaceful under Tito's leadership?

3. What effect did the dissolution of the Soviet Union have on most Soviet bloc nations? What effect did it have on Yugoslavia?

4. What is meant by the term "ethnic cleansing"? Give examples of how this policy was applied in the various conflicts in the former Yugoslavia.

5. Why did NATO intervene against the Serbs? Why was this a controversial decision?

Demilitarization

Like its American counterpart, the military-industrial complex in the Soviet Union was extremely powerful. Some 10 million people were employed in military-related industries, accounting for 25 per cent of the Gross National Product. In the Russian republic, almost 50 per cent of all manufacturing was for the military. With the breakup of the Soviet Union, however, this powerful sector of the Russian economy collapsed, creating more economic chaos in its wake.

The Red Army had some four million troops, about half of them from Russia. Soviet troops had begun to withdraw from the satellite nations of Eastern Europe in 1988 and they continued to do so until 1994. This was an enormous undertaking because of the sheer numbers of troops, weapons, and materials involved. Many of these troops returned home, not to the country they had left, the Soviet Union, but to their newly independent republics.

Absorbing these troops back into civilian life presented difficulties for these new and changing societies. Upon their return, many soldiers found themselves competing for housing and jobs. The resettlement of such large numbers of military personnel placed an additional burden on already fragile economies.

The collapse of communism in Eastern Europe and the Soviet Union effectively disbanded the Warsaw Pact. Its Western counterpart, NATO, began to search for a new role. With the Cold War over, Canada and the United States questioned the need for their troops to remain in Europe as part of the NATO commitment. Canada gradually removed its troops from Europe, and the United States made major reductions in its forces. However, NATO did not disband. It found a new mission in Kosovo as a peacemaker for the world, and began to enlarge its membership to include former communist adversaries.

Skill Path

Developing Research Strategies

Locating and extracting precise information is an invaluable skill. And with unlimited amounts of data literally at our fingertips, developing strategies to find information is especially important. Finding and choosing the right information can make all the difference when you are trying to support a particular point of view in a position paper.

Asking yourself informed questions is one of the best ways to begin gathering information for a position paper. There are several different kinds of questions, each of which will produce different kinds of information.

- *Factual questions.* These concern the who, what, when, where, why, and how of your topic. For example, for the thesis statement "NATO should be enlarged to take in former Warsaw Pact nations" (one of the views expressed in the Viewpoints feature on page 239 of this chapter), you may want to ask such factual questions as "What nations currently want to join NATO?" and "How have their governments changed since they were members of the Warsaw Pact?"

- *Interpretive questions.* These delve deeper into the meaning of the uncovered facts. For example, the question "What are the characteristics of a genuine democratic society?" may have different answers, although you should make sure that the author of each has supported his or her interpretation with reliable evidence.

- *Inquiry questions.* These questions look for connections between facts to draw together arguments in favour of a particular viewpoint. For example, "What would be the advantages to global collective security if NATO were expanded?"

Step One: Formulate Research Questions

Once you have decided on your thesis statement, begin by formulating the factual, interpretive, and inquiry questions that will guide your research. Once you have composed these questions it will be easier to judge the type of sources you should consult for the answers. Keep in mind that as your research progresses, your list of questions may grow or change in response to the material you uncover.

Step Two: Begin with General Sources

You may have already answered all the fact-based questions on your topic before composing your thesis statement. However, if you are still unsure about some facts, general sources—such as encyclopedias, textbooks, and broad-based Web sites and documentaries—are good places to start. For the NATO thesis, you could use the keywords "NATO expansion" when searching the indexes and contents of general sources. The facts you uncover in these sources may lead you to other sources and on to more probing questions.

Step Three: Focus In

To answer interpretive questions you will need to consult focused sources. These include historical journals, magazines, and content-specific books and Web sites, as well as knowledgeable individuals or organizations. Use keywords again at this stage to locate information, but make them more specific. You could type in "NATO expansion + [name of country]," for example, to find out about particular countries that are currently seeking membership in NATO.

The various research tools available to you include the following:

- *Library electronic catalogues.* Many libraries are equipped with computer terminals that can be used to track down content-specific books by title, author, or subject. In some cases, the software also allows you to connect from one book to other books on the same topic or to books by the same author. If your local library does not have computers, use its card cataloguing system and search by subject. Once you find an appropriate book, check its bibliography to find additional sources on that specific topic.

- *Periodical indexes.* Most scholarly journals and magazines are catalogued in indexes by subject to make the articles easier to find. These indexes are often in electronic format at the library or on the Internet, but they can still usually be found in print format as well.

- *Web sites.* Find content-specific sites on the Internet using search engines that allow you to narrow your parameters with "advanced" searches. Use a complex search string, which will bypass sites that aren't directly related to your topic. Remember to be especially cautious when evaluating material found on the Internet, since it is much easier to post biased and inaccurate information on-line than it is to do so in a published book or magazine. Suffixes in URL addresses will give you a clue as to the creator of the site and, thus, whether it can be considered reliable.

  .gov   a government site

  .edu   an educational site (usually a college or university)

  .org   an organization or advocacy group

  .com   a commercial site

  .ca   a Canadian site

  ~   a personal Web site

- *Individuals and organizations.* Excellent sources include instructors, historians, and other experts as well as individuals who were or still are directly involved in events and issues related to your topic. Heads of organizations can also be very helpful by supplying information or by recommending specific source material. You can conduct interviews with these people over the telephone, via e-mail, or in person.

Practise Your Skill

1. Choose one of the following topics:
- Soviet communism as a stabilizing force in Eastern Europe
- The effect of the forces of nationalism on Yugoslavia
- The role of the US in policing the world
- NATO peacemaking and the goals of collective security

a) Formulate factual, interpretive, and inquiry questions that would help you to guide your research.

b) Find two general sources and three specific sources that would help you to answer your research questions.

NUCLEAR CONTROL AND DISARMAMENT

The most serious question facing NATO in the aftermath of the Cold War was the control of the nuclear weapons amassed by the former Soviet Union. Somewhere in this vast region were some 27 000 nuclear warheads. NATO had hoped that Yeltsin, as leader of Russia, would concentrate all nuclear weapons and keep them under Russian control. But at least four of the former Soviet republics—Russia, Ukraine, Belarus, and Kazakhstan—initially kept their nuclear weapons. Ukraine in particular was reluctant to turn over its nuclear arsenal to Russia. In fact, Ukraine inherited enough Soviet nuclear weapons in 1991 to make it the third largest nuclear power in the world. However, in 1995 Ukraine formally signed a treaty to eliminate all nuclear weapons.

The Nuclear Club, 2003

Nuclear Nations	Working on Nuclear Weapons	Believed to Have Nuclear Weapons
United States	North Korea	Israel
France	Iran	
China	Iraq	
Russia	Libya	
United Kingdom		
India		
Pakistan		

Figure 7.17

This chart shows the spread of nuclear weapons to a variety of nations. As nuclear technology improves, it is likely that more nations will join the nuclear club. Have any other nations joined the club since 2003?

The development of national armies has increased the possibility of conflict among former Soviet republics. There is also the question of what might happen if cash-strapped republics decide to sell their nuclear weapons to the highest bidder. The prospect of nuclear missiles falling into the hands of terrorists or countries with territorial ambitions remains a major concern for NATO and the world.

Another problem is the high cost of destroying nuclear weapons. The former Soviet republics do not have the money to dismantle the warheads. Even if all parties agreed to the destruction of nuclear weapons, the West would have to pay to

MAP STUDY

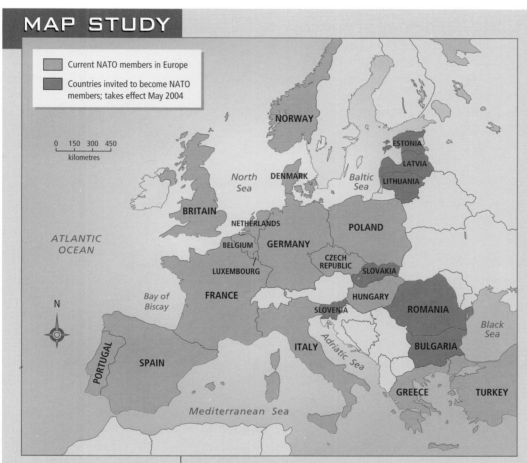

Figure 7.18
NATO Expansion Plans

On 22 November 2002, at the Prague Summit, NATO announced its plans for further expansion by inviting seven new members to join in 2004. These countries were former members of the Warsaw Pact.

Interpreting
1. What countries were Slovakia and Slovenia part of during the Cold War?
2. Why do you think former Soviet bloc nations like the Czech Republic and Poland were interested in joining NATO?

get the job done. As a result, the United States has continued to work toward further arms control agreements with Russia. One of the most important, START II, was signed in January 1993. It provided for the destruction of two-thirds of the nuclear arsenal held by the US and the former USSR, but was cancelled in 2002.

On 24 May 2002, Russian President Putin and US President Bush signed an arms control treaty to reduce the number of deployable nuclear warheads in both countries by two-thirds. The two nations have some 6000 deployable nuclear warheads, and this number must be reduced to 2200 by 2013. The presidents issued a statement pledging a "new strategic relationship." As evidence of this new relationship, NATO announced the formation of the NATO-Russia Council, which gives Russia full access to NATO without formally joining the organization.

Russia wants to continue as a world player in the war on terrorism (see Chapter 12) and to co-operate in other military matters such as restricting the spread of nuclear, biological, and chemical weapons. Russia's co-operation with NATO clears the way for more members from the former Soviet bloc to join. By the end of 2002, NATO had expanded to 19 members. Seven additional countries from the Soviet bloc have been invited to join in 2004: Bulgaria, Estonia, Latvia, Lithuania, Romania, Slovakia, and Slovenia.

In Review

1. What problems did the withdrawal of Soviet troops from Eastern Europe create?

2. What was the challenge facing NATO after the Cold War? Describe the new role for NATO.

3. a) How has the breakup of the Soviet Union complicated the problem of the nuclear arms stockpile?

   b) What are the dangers associated with the nuclear arms stockpile?

4. What is the objective of the START II agreement?

Summary

Gorbachev's reform policies and the collapse of the Soviet Union had a profound impact on the world. At first the dizzying pace and scope of change behind the Iron Curtain spurred sweeping optimism about peace, global security, and world prosperity. But the early euphoria was subdued and overshadowed by the rise of political, economic, ethnic, and military conflicts. The newly liberated and democratic nations of Eastern Europe found economic and political progress to be slow, painful, and at times divisive. Most countries made the transition peacefully; except for Yugoslavia, where extreme nationalism and ethnic clashes led to all-out civil war. Because Russia, the traditional stabilizing force in the Balkans, was not willing to act, NATO took the extraordinary step of intervening. Russia suffered greatly under the economic reforms of Boris Yeltsin, but gradually recovered to make some economic progress under Putin.

Viewpoints

ISSUE: Should the NATO alliance be enlarged to include Russia and other former Warsaw Pact nations?

Background

With the end of the Cold War, NATO had to redefine its role and purpose. Should it disband like the Warsaw Pact or enlarge by inviting former Warsaw Pact nations to join?

The viewpoints presented here examine two opposing perspectives on NATO. Jane Sharp argues in favour of opening up NATO to former communist nations in Eastern Europe to help them develop along Western standards. David Law argues that NATO should not expand. Read these two viewpoints carefully and answer the questions that follow. (You may want to refer to the Skill Path "Analysing a Reading" on page 14 before beginning.)

The case for opening up NATO to the East

Today, former adversaries in Western Europe never even contemplate settling disputes between themselves by force. This is the state of affairs we should strive for throughout the continent, by gradually bringing into the fold all those European states that achieve genuine pluralistic democracy, market economies, and a healthy respect for the rule of law. No one advocating the opening of NATO to the new democracies claims that the process will be trouble-free, but this does not undermine the case for spreading the benefits of the Western security community eastwards. As German Defence Minister Volker Rube put it in October 1993: "If we don't export stability we shall import instability." Western Europe cannot put up a barrier between itself and the former Communist states; it must open up its institutions to those striving to meet Western standards.

One obvious benefit of signalling in 1994 that NATO was prepared to take in new members has been the dramatic modification in behaviour since then among those states that aspire to join. Some have accelerated civilian controls over military forces, others have peacefully settled long-standing disputes over minority rights—and borders. In January 1997 the Czech government gave a formal "expression of regret" for the expulsion of Sudeten Germans from Czechoslovakia in 1945 and 1946. Over a number of years Hungary and Romania transformed their relationship with each other, as did Romania, Ukraine, and, to a lesser extent, Hungary and Slovakia. In March 1997 the Polish government sacked a general who was unwilling to accept civilian control over Polish military forces. Estonia and Latvia both softened their attitudes towards their Russian minorities, not least to make themselves more acceptable partners to the West. These actions reflect real progress towards democracy and deserve recognition.

Far from aggressively expanding eastwards as some have charged, until 1994 most NATO states were reluctant to take in new members, some because they feared provoking Russia, others because they were not yet ready to provide security throughout Europe. The initiative for enlargement came not from NATO but from the former Warsaw Pact states, who in 1991 felt themselves in a security vacuum as violence erupted in the former Yugoslavia and the former Soviet Union. Initially, NATO offered two outreach programs but fell short of offering membership. In December 1991 NATO established the North Atlantic Cooperation Council (NACC) for all former Warsaw Pact states including all the former Soviet Republics, and in January 1994 it offered the Partnership for Peace (PFP) to the European neutrals as well as to NACC members.

It was Germany's interest in stability on its eastern border that finally drove the Alliance to consider accepting new members. Germany also felt, more strongly than the other allies, a heavy responsibility to right the wrongs of Yalta and to bring back into Western Europe those pre-war democracies on whom Moscow had imposed Communist governments in 1945. The other European allies acquiesced, realizing that if NATO did not provide security in Central Europe, sooner or later either Germany or Russia would—thereby taking us back to the uncertainties of the 1930s.

Source: Jane Sharp, "The Case for Opening Up NATO to the East." In Charles-Philippe David and Jacques Levesque (Eds.) *The Future of NATO: Enlargement, Russia, and European Security.* McGill-Queens University Press, Montreal & Kingston. (Published for the Centre for Security and Foreign Policy Studies and The Teleglobe+Raoul-Dandurand Chair of Strategic and Diplomatic Studies). 1999.

Why Spain should have been NATO's last member

Lest the title mislead, [I do] not take the view that NATO should go out of business. On the contrary, notwithstanding the sea of change that has taken place in the strategic environment that gave rise to its founding fifty years ago, the organization remains irreplaceable. NATO binds the two North American democracies to Europe in a way that none of its sister institutions can replicate, and in a way that brings benefits that none of them can provide. It is the only multilateral security institution capable of dealing with anything other than the most minor of military contingencies in Europe, and for that matter—and if it were so inclined—anywhere else in today's troubled world. It is the Western democracies' main instrument for their ongoing effort to shore up the security of the transition countries of post-Communist Europe. Beyond that, NATO remains indispensable as a pacifier of bilateral relationships among its traditional members. However, it does not follow, as the champions of NATO enlargement hold, that for others to partake of such benefits, the Atlantic Alliance needs to expand its membership. NATO enlargement, like so much else in life, is too much of a good thing.

As the author and many other observers have argued, NATO's projected expansion of membership does not make good strategic sense—and this for three reasons in particular. First, enlargement is not fair because, as it has been conceived, it brings into the Alliance first those countries least needing a security umbrella and leaves to later—or leaves out altogether—those needing it most. Second, enlargement is *not stabilizing*, for at the very least it complicates the delicate process of reordering security relationships in post-Cold War Europe—and not just between the West and Russia. But it also runs the risk of engendering substantially more security problems—for new, non-, and old members alike—than the architects of enlargement claim it can resolve. Third, enlargement is in reality *not necessary*, because NATO has a more efficient and effective way of addressing the security problems of today's and tomorrow's Europe, namely, through further development of the already quite impressive security arrangements organized under NATO's Partnership for Peace (PFP).

If enlargement is so strategically flawed, how do we explain why the project got off the ground in the first place? In actual fact, the enlargement process was not launched within the Alliance as the result of any serious debate on the strategic imperatives of the times. The enlargement process was initiated because the United States and Germany thought it made political sense, and because they thought that if it made political sense to them, it would by definition make political sense to others—as had almost invariably been the case during the Cold War.

Since the end of the Cold War, defence budgets have been downsized worldwide. In the United States, the amount spent on procurement in 1996 was only half as much as it was ten years earlier. Production lines have shrunk and there is increased competition for markets both at home and abroad. At the same time, weapons systems have become much more expensive to develop. This has led to far-reaching consolidation in the US defence industry. The number of players has been significantly reduced and unemployment in the industry is down almost half relative to the mid-1980s.

In an effort to keep costs manageable, the defence industry has attempted to maximize economies of scale. For example, to maintain the costs of the latest, state-of-the-art, joint fighter aircraft at the level of $30 million per plane—roughly the cost of the F-16 developed the 1970s—it is planned to have a production line of 2900 planes and to this end, to customize models for several countries and services. The bottom line is basically this: the longer the production line, the lower the cost.

It is not difficult to imagine how certain interests within the American military-industrial complex may have concluded that NATO enlargement would be better for defence sales than the PFP. In the PFP there has been little peer pressure to modernize and standardize. NATO membership, on the other hand, has been associated with a high degree of interoperability of weapons systems. In its 1997 report to the Congress on NATO enlargement, the State Department provided a lengthy list of the kinds of military restructuring new members' militaries might be expected to undergo. This included training of various kinds, ground-force modernization, surface-to-air missile procurement, and air-force modernization, including the procurement of one squadron of refurbished Western combat aircraft per new member.

It is this kind of numbers that may have convinced US defence manufacturers in the run-up to the 1994 NATO summit to attempt to build support among Democrats and Republicans alike for membership expansion.

Source: David Law, "Why Spain Should Have Been NATO's Last Member." In Charles-Philippe David and Jacques Levesque (Eds.) *The Future of NATO: Enlargement, Russia, and European Security.* McGill-Queens University Press, Montreal & Kingston. 1999 (Published for the Centre for Security and Foreign Policy Studies and The Teleglobe+Raoul-Dandurand Chair of Strategic and Diplomatic Studies).

Analysis and Evaluation

1. According to Sharp, what are some of the benefits of opening up NATO to other states?

2. Why has NATO even considered accepting new members?

3. According to Law, why does NATO expansion not make sense?

4. What economic reality appears to be behind the expansion of NATO?

5. Decide which of the viewpoints you tend to support and explain why. If you agree with neither, state the position you do support and explain it. Be sure to use specific information from this textbook, the readings, and other sources to support your position.

Chapter Analysis

MAKING CONNECTIONS

1. Compare the impact of Gorbachev and Yeltsin on ending the Cold War. Which one would you consider to be more important and why?

2. Debate the issue: Be it Resolved that the world is a safer and more secure place now than during the Cold War.

DEVELOPING YOUR VOICE

3. In December 1991 Ivan Laptev, a Gorbachev associate, said, "He opened the dam and hoped he could control the water flow. Instead, the dam burst." Using the information in this chapter, explain why this is a true statement about Gorbachev's efforts to reform the USSR.

4. From the perspective of the twenty-first century, will Gorbachev be seen as a valiant reformer or as an inept politician? Give reasons for your opinion.

RESEARCHING THE ISSUES

5. Select one of the 15 former Soviet republics (see map on page 226) and research and write a report on its transition from communism. Use the following questions to guide your research:

   a) When did the country abolish communism? Are new governments now established through democratic elections? Are the governments stable?

   b) Is the country moving toward a market economy? Is this causing problems?

   c) Are there ethnic rivalries and conflicts? Are these handled peacefully?

   d) Are the people generally better off now than before the fall of communism?

6. Select one Eastern European country and prepare a current affairs update on events in the country since the collapse of the USSR.

7. On 1 January 1992, Czechoslovakia ceased to exist as a nation. Prepare a report on the rise and fall of Czechoslovakia from 1945.

8. Should NATO get involved in peacemaking operations such as the one in Kosovo? As a starting point for your research, review the purpose of NATO and its evolving role in Chapter 5, and the Kosovo conflict in this chapter. State and defend your position on the issue.

UNIT THREE

Global Village

Learning Goals

By the end of this unit students will be able to:
- Identify individuals who facilitated political change in Europe, Asia, and Africa after 1945
- Examine different models of regional co-operation such as the European Union and NAFTA
- Analyse the movement from colonization to independence in Africa and Asia
- Identify barriers to development in Africa
- Summarize the main events involved in the end of apartheid in South Africa and the struggle for civil rights in the United States
- Analyse economic and political changes in China and other Asian nations
- Demonstrate an understanding of the role of religious fundamentalism in the Middle East
- Describe the roots of conflict between Israel and Palestine and the ongoing peace talks
- Connect historical events to present circumstances
- Use appropriate inquiry models to answer questions about interactions between nations

	Europe	Africa
1940s	• Second World War ends (1945) • United Nations formed (1945) • Churchill, "Iron Curtain" speech (1946) • Nuremburg Trials (1946) • Marshall Plan (1947) • NATO formed (1948) • Berlin Blockade begins (1948)	• Apartheid system established in South Africa (1949)
1950s	• Stalin dies (1953) • Hungarian Revolution (1956) • Six European countries sign Treaty of Rome creating Common Market (1957)	• Mau Mau rebellion in Kenya (1952-56) • Ghana gains independence (1957)
1960s	• Berlin Wall (1961) • UN peacekeeping forces in Cyprus (1964) • European Community formed (1967) • Czechoslovakian revolt brutally suppressed (1968)	• 31 countries become independent (1960-69) • Sharpeville massacre in South Africa (1960) • African National Congress banned; Nelson Mandela imprisoned (1960) • Organization of African Unity founded (1963)
1970s	• Britain imposes direct rule on Northern Ireland (1972) • Ireland, Great Britain, and Denmark join Common Market (1973) • Worldwide inflation brought on by rapidly rising fuel costs (1974) • Margaret Thatcher becomes prime minister of Britain (1975)	• 5 countries become independent (1970-79) • Idi Amin establishes himself ruler of Uganda (1971) • Fierce fighting between Ethiopian troops and rebels from Eritrea (1975)
1980s	• Soviet Union invades Afghanistan (1980) • Polish government cracks down on unions (1981) • Soviets withdraw from Afghanistan (1988)	• 2 countries become independent, ending colonial era in Africa (1980-89) • Famine threatens millions of Ethiopians (1984) • State of emergency declared in South Africa (1986)
1990s	• East and West Germany unified (1990) • Civil war breaks out in Yugoslavia (1991) • Czechs and Slovaks form separate countries (1992) • Maastricht Treaty creates European Union (EU) (1993) • Austria, Finland, and Sweden join EU (1995) • Treaty of Nice begins integration of Eastern European countries into EU (1997) • Euro becomes official currency (1999)	• South Africa liberalizes apartheid and frees Nelson Mandela (1990) • South Africa holds first non-racial elections; Mandela elected president (1994) • Civil war in Rwanda (1994) • Report of South Africa's Truth and Reconciliation Commission released (1998)

Asia	Middle East	
• Second World War ends (1945) • Elected assembly replaces emperor in Japan (1946) • India partitioned into India and Pakistan (1947) • Gandhi assassinated (1948) • Communist Chinese takeover mainland China (1949)	• Second World War ends (1945) • League of Arab Nations established (1945) • Jewish state of Israel established (1948) • First Arab-Israeli war (1948-49)	1940s
• Start of Korean War (1950) • Korean War ends (1953) • Communist forces defeat French in Vietnam (1954)	• Egypt becomes a republic (1954) • Nasser seizes Suez Canal; Israeli troops invade the Sinai Peninsula (1956) • Israeli forces withdraw from the Sinai; UN peacekeeping forces established (1957)	1950s
• US military advisors to South Vietnam (1960) • Indira Gandhi becomes prime minister of India (1966) • Mao's Cultural Revolution (1966-68)	• OPEC formed (1960) • Six-Day War resulted in Occupied Territories (1967) • Arafat elected leader of the PLO (1969)	1960s
• Mainland China admitted to the UN (1971) • War between India and Pakistan (1971) • US withdraws from Vietnam (1973) • Communist forces overrun South Vietnam (1975) • Shah of Iran deposed by Islamic republican government (1979)	• Yom Kippur War (1973) • OPEC oil embargo (1973) • Israeli-Egyptian peace treaty (1979) • Islamic revolution in Iran (1979)	1970s
• Indira Gandhi assassinated (1984) • Bhutto elected first female prime minister of Pakistan (1988) • Tiananmen Square massacre (1989)	• Iran-Iraq War (1980-88) • Israel invades Lebanon (1982) • Israel withdraws from Lebanon (1985) • Violent rioting by Palestinians marks beginning of first *Intifadah* (1988)	1980s
• Chinese Communist Party adopts capitalist ideas to socialist ideologies (1992) • Afghan guerrillas defeat government forces (1992) • China regains possession of Hong Kong (1997)	• Iraq invades Kuwait (1990); Gulf War (1991) • Arab states and Israel agree to peace conference (1991) • PLO recognizes Israel's right to exist (1993) • Self-rule to Palestinians in Gaza and Jericho (1994) • Israel's settlement of Occupied Territories resumes (1997) • Beginning of second *Intifadah* (2000)	1990s

CHAPTER EIGHT

Regional Co-operation: The European Union and NAFTA

The futuristic Palais de l'Europe is located in the city of Strasbourg, France, on the French-German border. Strasbourg is one of the capitals of the European Union and a symbol of the new, united Europe. Why do you think the European nations wanted to unite when doing so meant giving up their sovereignty and creating a new layer of government?

> "Integration is ... the only way for Europe to retain any semblance of world stature and significance."
>
> — Richard P. Ahlstrom, "The European Community Faces 1992," *Current History*, November 1991

> "The policy of European integration is in reality a question of war and peace in the 21st century."
>
> — German chancellor Helmut Kohl, 2 February 1995

Overview

Immediately following the Second World War, Europe lay in ruins. Millions were dead and cities and farms were levelled. Yet as early as the 1960s, much of Europe had begun to enjoy a new prosperity, fuelled by the European Recovery Program, or the Marshall Plan. This plan involved billions of dollars in US aid to help European nations rebuild their economies.

Aid was not the only factor in recovery. The devastation of two wars had set Europe on a new path toward unity. For many, economic co-operation seemed to assure long-term peace. For others, it provided the means to compete in the new international reality—a world dominated by the United States and the Soviet Union. The **European Union** (EU) evolved over 45 years of diplomacy and negotiation, and produced a highly integrated economic and political entity. Only six nations of Western Europe shared the original vision of the EU. By 2002, 15 nations had joined, and many more—including nations from Eastern Europe—were candidates for membership.

North America looked with interest on these developments. If Europe could find a way to overcome division and foster co-operation, then regional integration might work in other parts of the world. In 1989, Canada and the United States opened the door to co-operation with the successful negotiation of the Free Trade Agreement. In 1994, Mexico joined to complete the regional integration of North America, creating the largest free trade zone in the world.

Young people in Europe and North America now face an almost borderless world. Travel and work among the nations of Europe and North America is easier than perhaps ever imagined. Yet the benefits of international co-operation and regional integration have yet to be determined. Will co-operation work in the long run, or will nations fall to age-old antagonisms and new conflicts? Can regional co-operation be extended across the globe? Will it benefit everyone or just a few? As the twenty-first century opened, these questions had yet to be answered.

Focus Questions

1. Why did Europe evolve toward a European Union?
2. What was Britain's response to joining the EU?
3. What issues do Eastern European countries create for the European Union?
4. What challenges does the new Europe face in the twenty-first century?
5. In what ways is the European Union similar to and different from trade blocs such as NAFTA?

Toward a European Union

Two destructive wars had raged through Europe in the first half of the twentieth century. While both had cost thousands of lives, the world was no safer after the wars than before them. The escalating nuclear arms race after 1945 threatened world peace and security even more than had Nazi aggression.

Nationalism had played a key role in both wars, and continued to fuel hostilities in postwar Europe. Some leaders in Western Europe, such as Winston Churchill, believed that the time had come to set aside nationalist interests and to support the economic and political integration of European states. Believing that a strong, united Europe could deter Soviet expansion, the United States supported calls for European unity. The Marshall Plan, which provided American financial aid for postwar reconstruction in Western Europe, stimulated trade and interdependence.

In 1949, Churchill helped to form the Council of Europe. It had no legislative power but provided a forum for leaders to discuss common European values and goals. The first step toward European economic and political unity was taken in 1952 with the formation of the European Coal and Steel Community (ECSC). The organization pooled coal, iron, and steel production, eliminated tariffs on these industries, and created a free labour market among the participants. While West Germany, France, Italy, Belgium, Luxembourg, and the Netherlands all signed on to the ECSC, Britain refused to join, preferring not to relinquish any of its sovereignty.

The **European Economic Community** (EEC), or **Common Market**, was created in 1957. Tariffs and trade restrictions among members were abolished, and common trade policies and tariffs were required toward all non-members. The EEC also allowed for the free movement of people, capital, and services among members and set a common agricultural policy. Britain opposed the EEC because it meant giving too much economic control to the Community and loosening historic ties with the **Commonwealth**. Once the EEC was operating successfully, however, Britain felt isolated, and negotiated an economic alliance with other countries that remained outside the EEC.

Between 1958 and 1964, trade between EEC members increased by 98 per cent. While Britain had established satisfactory economic ties with other nations, it began to view EEC membership as highly desirable. In the 1960s, Britain submitted its application for EEC membership—a move blocked by French president Charles de Gaulle. De Gaulle believed that Britain was too closely allied with the United States and that American influence would weaken European integration. When de Gaulle resigned in 1969, French opposition decreased. In 1973, Britain, Denmark, and Ireland joined the **European Community** (EC). Greece joined in 1981, and Spain and Portugal became members in 1986, bringing the total membership to 12.

MAP STUDY

GREENLAND
(Common Market
1973–1985)

N

0 150 300 450
kilometres

Legend:
- Original six of the Common Market, 1957
- EFTA, 1959
- Countries joining the Common Market, 1973
- Countries joining the Common Market later (with dates)

* Following the reunification of Germany

NORWAY

SWEDEN

IRELAND

GREAT BRITAIN

North Sea

DENMARK

NETHERLANDS

EAST GERMANY 1990*

BELGIUM

WEST GERMANY

LUXEMBOURG

ATLANTIC OCEAN

Bay of Biscay

FRANCE

SWITZ.

AUSTRIA

PORTUGAL 1986

SPAIN 1986

ITALY

Adriatic Sea

GREECE 1981

Mediterranean Sea

Figure 8.1
Western European Economic Co-operation, 1957 to 1991

This map shows the progress of European economic co-operation from 1957 to 1991, starting with the formation of the Common Market in 1957.

Interpreting

1. Using the map, suggest reasons why the original six members of the Common Market might have sought economic integration.
2. Why was Great Britain less eager to become integrated with the other nations of Western Europe?
3. Why might Greece have wanted to be part of the Common Market?

Figure 8.2
In 1969, Britain was invited to join the EEC, much to the annoyance of France's Charles de Gaulle. Britain's prime minister was Harold Wilson. Why do cartoonists often focus on facial features?

"P-s-s-s-s-s-T . . !"

Economic Co-operation Since 1940

Year	Treaty/Organization	Aims	Members
1949	Council of Europe	To achieve greater co-operation and unity of 10 member states	Belgium, Denmark, France, Ireland, Italy, Luxembourg, Netherlands, Norway, Sweden, Britain; later joined by Austria, Cyprus, Greece, Iceland, Malta, Switzerland, West Germany, Turkey
1952	European Coal and Steel Community (ECSC)	To create an integrated market for coal and steel	France, West Germany, Italy, Belgium, Netherlands, Luxembourg
1957	Treaty of Rome: European Economic Community (EEC), the Common Market	To create an integrated economy for member states	France, West Germany, Italy, Belgium, Netherlands, Luxembourg
1960	Stockholm Convention: European Free Trade Association (EFTA)	To establish a rival economic free trade community led by Britain	Britain, Austria, Denmark, Norway, Portugal, Sweden, Switzerland; Iceland and Finland joined later; Britain, Denmark, and Portugal left to join EC
1967	EEC and ECSC combine to form European Community (EC)	To evolve toward greater economic and political unity among members	France, West Germany, Italy, Belgium, Netherlands, Luxembourg; Britain, Denmark, and Ireland joined in 1973; Greece joined in 1981; Spain and Portugal joined in 1986
1991	European Economic Area (EEA)	To merge the EC and the EFTA	EC and EFTA members; Austria, Sweden, Finland, Norway applied for full EC membership
1993	European Union (EU)	To create a unified community with economic and political unity	Twelve members of EC, with Austria, Finland and Sweden joining in 1995
1997	Treaty of Nice	To work toward integration of Eastern European countries	Negotiations began with Poland, Czech Republic, Hungary, Estonia, Slovenia and Cyprus; in 1999, further invitations were extended to Latvia, Lithuania, Slovakia, Romania, Bulgaria and Malta

Figure 8.3
Review the sequence of events shown in this figure and suggest what might be the next stage in European co-operation.

THE EUROPEAN UNION

A significant step toward "a Europe without frontiers" took place in 1991 when EC members agreed to a summit at Maastricht in the Netherlands. At this meeting, members explored the feasibility of common technical and pollution standards and allowing capital to flow more freely. While these objectives were uniformly accepted, others—such as a central monetary policy and banking system, a common military force, and agricultural subsidies—stirred up great controversy. The Maastricht Treaty set a timetable for the adoption of a common currency, introduced policies regarding workers' rights, and paved the way for Eastern European countries to join a united Europe. In effect, the EU was an example of supranationalism, which means that citizens are loyal to something bigger than their own nation. However, many people had difficulty seeing themselves as "European" (as opposed to "British" or "French"), and many rejected the idea of the EU.

Each member nation had to ratify the Maastricht Treaty before it could be implemented—no simple task. Maastricht faced fierce opposition in Denmark, France, and Britain, where politicians protested that it would centralize too much authority. In France, the treaty passed with a bare majority in 1992. Denmark ratified the treaty only after it was revised to exempt that country from using a common currency and supporting a common defence policy. In May 1993, the British House of Commons voted in favour of the treaty, clearing the way for Britain to join the Union.

On 1 November 1993, after two years of political wrangling in 12 countries, the European Union came into effect. On 1 January 1995, three other countries— Austria, Finland, and Sweden—joined the Union, bringing the total membership to 15.

Figure 8.4

Demonstrators in Copenhagen, Denmark, clashed with police during protests against the Maastricht Treaty. What aspects of the treaty would cause such outrage?

THE STRUCTURE OF THE EUROPEAN UNION

The European Union is a remarkable entity, and citizens living in one of its member states have many advantages. They can easily move to any other member state, pursue employment, and work under exactly the same conditions as the citizens of that country. They even qualify for social security benefits, since it is illegal for EU members to confine their social security benefits to nationals. They can also vote in the elections of any member state, and stand as candidates for the European Parliament. People with physical disabilities can look ahead to some of the most forward-thinking anti-discrimination legislation ever proposed as the EU enthusiastically paves the way for a "barrier-free Europe." These and other opportunities exist because of a carefully structured network of institutions, each with different functions (see Figure 8.5).

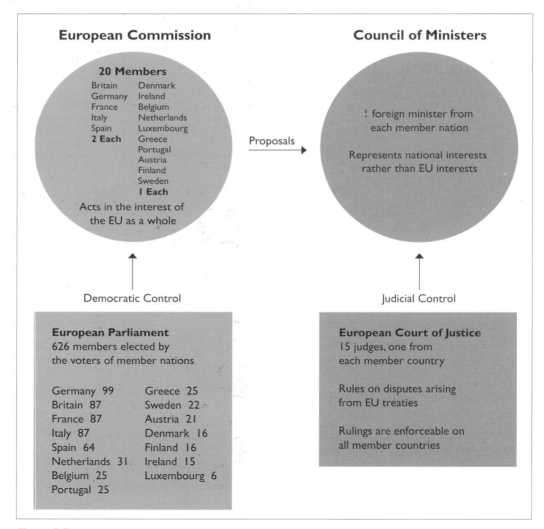

European Commission

20 Members

Britain	Denmark
Germany	Ireland
France	Belgium
Italy	Netherlands
Spain	Luxembourg
2 Each	Greece
	Portugal
	Austria
	Finland
	Sweden
	1 Each

Acts in the interest of the EU as a whole

→ Proposals →

Council of Ministers

1 foreign minister from each member nation

Represents national interests rather than EU interests

↑ Democratic Control

↑ Judicial Control

European Parliament
626 members elected by the voters of member nations

Germany 99	Greece 25
Britain 87	Sweden 22
France 87	Austria 21
Italy 87	Denmark 16
Spain 64	Finland 16
Netherlands 31	Ireland 15
Belgium 25	Luxembourg 6
Portugal 25	

European Court of Justice
15 judges, one from each member country

Rules on disputes arising from EU treaties

Rulings are enforceable on all member countries

Figure 8.5

European Institutions, 2002. The European Union is structured in a way that balances the needs of individual members with the needs of the Union. What mechanisms try to deliver a balance of power?

The Council of Ministers

The Council of Ministers is the major decision-making body of the EU. It is made up of heads of state or important ministers of member nations. Its task is to protect the interests of individual nations while furthering European integration. One minister represents each country, although the representative may change depending on the topic being discussed. For example, ministers of agriculture represent their countries to discuss farm subsidies, while defence ministers usually attend meetings to discuss international security. Countries with larger populations do have more votes than smaller states. The Council adopts proposals from member states and issues directions to the European Commission.

The European Commission

The European Commission conducts day-to-day business by creating and implementing policies to meet the direction provided by the Council, and by managing the financial affairs of the EU. They meet in Brussels and are appointed by the member states for five-year terms. Commissioners have a good deal of power. Because they are appointed rather than elected to their positions, they are sometimes charged with being "unaccountable."

The European Parliament

The European Parliament is made up of 626 representatives who are elected in each of the member countries. It conducts its affairs in 11 official languages. Its job is to oversee the activities of the European Commission, acting in an advisory or consultative role. This body has the power to reject budgets put forward by the Commission, and it can remove the Commission through a vote of no confidence. The European Parliament does not, however, have any ability to control the Council of Ministers.

Figure 8.6
On 28 October 2002, Valéry Giscard d'Estaing, the chairman of the European Convention, held an Internet chat with the citizens of Europe about the institutions and legal structures of the EU. The theme of the chat was "Time to Take Stock."

NETSURFER

WWW.EUROPARL.EU.INT/FACTSHEETS

This site includes a number of fact sheets about the European Parliament. Under "how the European Community works," scroll down to "European Institutions and Bodies" for information on the history, powers, and operation of the European Parliament. Choose one fact sheet and summarize a portion of it in your notebook.

EUROPA.EU.INT

For all the latest news about the European Union, its institutions and members, visit this official site of the EU. Try visiting the site every few weeks for a period of several months and make note of some of the new developments reported or forecasted.

The European Court of Justice

The European Court of Justice is the judicial arm of the European Union. Each member country appoints one judge to the European Court of Justice. The Court of Justice establishes laws for the EU and the member states, but has no direct link to national courts and cannot control how they apply the laws. Laws made by the Court of Justice supersede national laws, often bringing the Court into conflict with local decisions. For example, in 1998, the Court of Justice effectively banned certain types of antibiotics in animal feed. The ban applies to all the member nations of the EU.

A COMMON CURRENCY

The Maastricht Treaty proposed a common European currency, one that would replace all of the national currencies. Those who supported the EU argued that a single currency was needed to establish economic unity and to align members' monetary policies. A single currency would also help with more practical matters, such as the inconvenience of currency conversion and currency fluctuations. Supporters of the single currency—and the monetary union that was implied—claimed it was necessary for a united Europe. The euro became an official currency on 1 January 1999.

Not all EU members were excited about the monetary union and single currency. Britain, Sweden, and Denmark opted out of the monetary union, claiming that such integration among the member states would shackle their autonomy and prevent them from protecting their own interests. Greece also resisted at first, but then joined the monetary union in 2000.

Figure 8.7
The euro as a financial security blanket—just one of many images created to promote the benefits of a single European currency. What is the message of this photo?

Adopting the Euro

1 January 1998
- European Central Bank is open for business

1 January 1999
- Euro is the currency for the 11 member nations of the EU
- Conversion rates are set for national currencies

1 January 2001
- Greece adopts the euro

1 January 2002
- Euro bank notes and coins are put into circulation
- Cash transactions are reported in euro denominations
- Withdrawal of national currencies begins

28 February 2002
- National currencies are withdrawn from circulation

Figure 8.8
What day-to-day disruptions do you think Europeans experienced when the EU member countries switched over to the euro?

In Review

1. a) On a timeline, plot the key economic changes in Europe since 1945.

    b) In your opinion, which changes were most instrumental in shaping postwar Europe?

2. What did the countries of Europe expect to gain from the European Union?

3. What were key concerns for those opposed to the European Union?

4. Briefly describe the four main bodies of the European Union and the function of each.

5. What were the advantages and disadvantages of the euro as seen by member states of the EU?

Britain and the European Union

Following the Second World War, successive governments in Britain tried to plot a new economic course for the nation but produced few positive results. Britain's economic performance remained sluggish and lagged behind that of many other European nations. While the 1950s and 1960s brought prosperity to much of the industrialized world, Britain seemed to stand on the sidelines. Voters blamed the government, but economic analysts suggested a variety of explanations, including ever-changing government policies and industries mired in old technologies.

In an effort to improve trade, Britain joined the European Community in 1973. However, this was not enough to turn its economy around. The economic chaos that resulted from the 1973 oil embargo by OPEC (the Organization of Petroleum Exporting Countries) dealt a sharp blow to the British economy. The embargo raised the price of crude oil by 200 per cent. This in turn caused inflation to skyrocket. At the same time, unemployment was on the rise and strikes by labour unions continued to plague the nation. With the Labour Party unable to solve Britain's economic woes, voters turned to the Conservative Party and its new leader, Margaret Thatcher, in 1979.

Thatcher recognized the importance of the European Common Market and the need to eliminate trade barriers within Europe. But she was opposed to expanding Britain's political and economic integration in the new European Union if it meant transferring authority to the international body. She favoured a decentralized union that would be expanded to include other European nations. Consequently, she resisted even her own party's efforts to achieve greater European integration. As a result, Thatcher was ousted as leader in November 1990.

> "[T]he average British citizen is suspicious of everything to do with the EU ..."
>
> — Sir Timothy Gardens, Professor, University of London, March 2001

Profile   Margaret Thatcher (1925-)

Figure 8.9
Margaret Thatcher

Margaret Thatcher was Britain's first female prime minister, serving from 1979 to 1990—longer than any British prime minister in the postwar era. She rose from a modest background and served with a determined, uncompromising style that gained the respect of some and the indignation of others. Trained in chemistry and law—but keenly interested in politics—Thatcher ran for her first seat in Parliament in 1950. In 1959, she was elected to the House of Commons. Her aggressive style and thorough understanding of the issues gained her attention in the media and in the House.

"I am extraordinarily patient, provided I get my own way in the end."

— Margaret Thatcher, in the *Observer*, 4 April 1989

Thatcher became the Minister for Pensions and National Insurance in 1962, a junior position in the cabinet. Over the next few years she fine-tuned her political image both as a cabinet minister and as an opposition critic. She also drew notice within her party. While the Conservatives clung to social welfare policies in the hopes of gaining the support of the unions and the voters, Thatcher proposed cutting back on the welfare system and giving more freedom to the private sector. She felt that the welfare state discouraged independence, initiative, and the work ethic. She envisioned a society in which people were self-reliant, worked hard, and took risks—what she called an **enterprise culture.**

Thatcher led the Conservatives to victory in 1979 on a platform of reducing inflation and limiting government spending. Two more terms followed, making her the first prime minister in 160 years to be elected to a third consecutive term. As the decade drew to a close, however, her critics became more vocal. Thatcher privatized a number of nationalized industries, sold off public housing to tenants, proposed limits on the national health plan, and introduced an unpopular poll tax. She was often accused of sacrificing the public good and destroying British institutions for the sake of efficiency and private profit, although she did not, in fact, introduce sweeping reforms to the social welfare system.

Thatcher's reservations about Britain's role in the EU eventually brought her into conflict with other Conservatives, who wanted Britain to integrate fully into the new union. In November 1990, after 11 consecutive years as prime minister, Thatcher resigned as leader of the party and took a seat as a government backbencher.

Responding

1. What were the qualities that made Margaret Thatcher a strong leader?
2. Which of her characteristics would likely cause others to dislike her?
3. What are the characteristics that you like to see in a leader? Make a list of at least five characteristics and then compare your list to a classmate's. Discuss the differences in your lists.

Thatcher was replaced by John Major, a politician of more moderate views who had no reservations about full participation in the European Union. Proclaiming that he wanted Britain to be at the heart of Europe, Major led the Conservatives into a fourth term in April 1992. The government then set out to formally link Britain's economy to that of the EU.

Major faced a challenge almost immediately. In September 1992, pressure on the British pound forced him to withdraw from the European Monetary System and to devalue the British currency. The move further delayed Britain's plans to ratify the Maastricht Treaty that would create the European Union. It was not until May 1993 that the House of Commons voted in favour of a modified Maastricht agreement that exempted Britain from the monetary system.

Although the economy of Britain continued to prosper under the leadership of John Major, voters elected a new government in 1997. Not that Britons disliked Major, but someone new had caught their attention. Tony Blair had become leader of the Labour Party in 1994. Educated at private school and armed with a law degree from Oxford University, Blair represented a new face of socialism. He began to move the party closer to the political centre, carefully distinguishing the new Labour Party from its union-oriented past. He was so successful in moving his party's policies to the centre that observers soon labelled him "Tony Blur." In 1997, the new Labour Party won 418 out of 659 seats, taking even Margaret Thatcher's old riding. Blair became the youngest prime minister of Britain elected in the twentieth century. Once in power, Blair developed warmer relations with the United States and carried on the Conservative resistance to joining the European monetary union.

Figure 8.10
On 6 May 1994, Britain took another historic step toward unity with Europe when the Channel Tunnel (the Chunnel) linking Britain with the continent was officially opened. The Eurostar passenger train—pictured here in London's Waterloo Station—whisks people between London and Paris via the Channel Tunnel in just over two hours. In what ways might this technological change have an impact on British-French relationships?

In Review

1. Identify some characteristics about Britain that would make it resist full integration in a European Union. Identify other characteristics that would encourage it to integrate. What observations can you make about Britain's commitment to the European Union?

2. Was Margaret Thatcher's character an important factor in determining her stand on integration with Europe? Explain.

3. What compromise was needed in order for Britain to ratify the Maastricht Treaty?

The European Union and Eastern Europe

The world order was shattered when the Soviet Union collapsed in 1991. One by one, the communist dictatorships of Eastern Europe crumbled and fell. Free elections installed new leaders committed to democracy and the free-market system. But even as the political reform was well underway, their economies were not recovering.

Moving from a centralized economy to a market economy proved to be a slow and difficult process. Almost immediately, the new democracies of Central and Eastern Europe experienced severe economic hardships. Inflation and unemployment reached record levels. Food and other essential goods were often in short supply. For many people, especially older citizens who had lived within the communist system most of their lives, democracy appeared to offer few benefits. Unlike the younger generation, who saw the hope for economic prosperity once the transition was complete, many older people believed they would never be as well off as they had been before. The effects of the economic hardships began to be reflected at the polls. In 1994, several former Communist Party members were elected in Hungary, Poland, Romania, and Slovenia.

In spite of these setbacks, the momentum toward democracy and capitalism was too strong for Central and Eastern European states to resist. By the middle of the decade, democratic political systems were reasonably well established in most of the formerly communist countries in that part of the continent, and economic reforms were well underway.

The leaders of the European Union were faced with the tough question of how best to deal with these changing economies. To ignore them completely—to create a "fortress Europe"—could result in a new east-west schism that could threaten Europe's peace. Moreover, such an approach made little sense economically, as these nations offered their own business opportunities. On the other hand, EU members did not want to jump too quickly into a type of partnership that could obligate them to make costly trade and security agreements. Some leaders argued that the EU needed better unity among existing members—on issues such as monetary policies, farm subsidies, and immigration—before any form of expansion took place. Other members voiced concern over the practical challenges of managing a much larger organization. Expansion into Eastern Europe carried the prospect of communicating in as many as 22 official languages!

"Poland, 10 years. Hungary, 10 months. East Germany, 10 weeks. Czechoslovakia, 10 days. Romania, 10 hours."

— Prague graffiti describing the end of communism

Figure 8.11
By 2000, some Eastern European countries, such as Poland, had already survived the worst of the disruption as they shifted to a capitalistic system. The members of the European Union could not ignore these developing nations, if only for the sake of peace in the long term.

There were doubts among the candidate nations as well. Promises of European integration made by their leaders had been widely exaggerated, and citizens had become suspicious of any talk on the subject. Their economic circumstances were simply too grim to inspire confidence in future partnerships. In some sense, the political and military Iron Curtain of the previous era had been replaced by a new socio-economic Iron Curtain.

In the end, the EU opted for a controlled integration of Central and Eastern European nations, beginning with those nations that were most stable and most likely to complete the transformation to capitalism successfully. In 1997, Poland, the Czech Republic, Hungary, Estonia, Slovenia, and Cyprus were invited to begin negotiations and, in 1999, the candidate list was expanded to include Latvia, Lithuania, Slovakia, Romania, Bulgaria, and Malta. Turkey was also readmitted to candidate status at this time. (In 1997, Turkey's request to join the EU had been rejected. Its human rights record, particularly with respect to the Kurds, was cited as the main reason.) Negotiations were expected to lead to an expanded EU by 2005.

Candidate Countries for EU Membership, 2002

Candidate Country	Population (millions)	GNP/capita (US$)	Exports (millions US$)	Imports (millions US$)
Bulgaria	8.3	1 220	5 542	5 671
Cyprus	0.8	11 920	4 127	4 703
Czech Republic	10.3	5 150	33 817	34 610
Estonia	1.4	3 360	4 149	4 651
Hungary	10.1	4 510	23 814	25 037
Latvia	2.4	2 420	3 053	3 899
Lithuania	3.7	2 540	5 071	6 348
Malta	0.4	10 100	n/a	3 259
Poland	38.7	3 910	36 718	42 931
Romania	22.4	1 360	9 801	13 037
Slovakia	5.4	3 700	12 965	15 239
Slovenia	2.0	9 780	11 068	11 351
Turkey	65.5	3 160	49 229	56 129

Figure 8.12
Not all the candidate countries have the same chance of being invited to join the EU. Which countries do you think are most likely to be invited? Why? (Source: World Guide 2001/2002, New Internationalist Publications. © Copyright 2002 New Internationalist Publications Ltd. All rights reserved.)

MAP STUDY

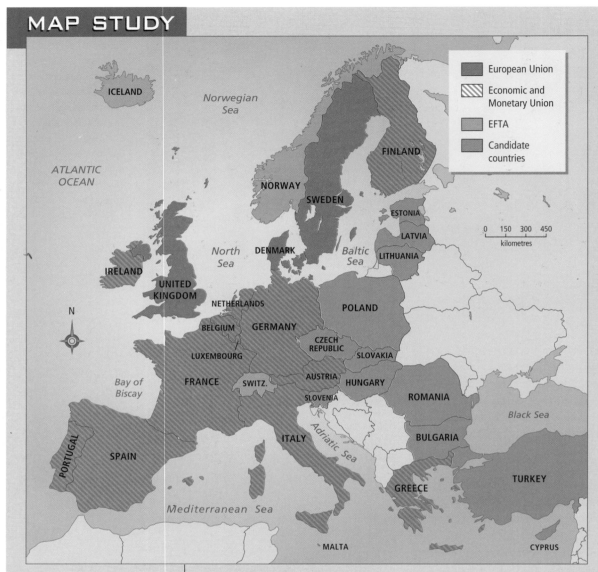

Legend:
- European Union
- Economic and Monetary Union
- EFTA
- Candidate countries

ICELAND

Norwegian Sea

ATLANTIC OCEAN

FINLAND

NORWAY

SWEDEN

ESTONIA

LATVIA

North Sea

DENMARK

Baltic Sea

LITHUANIA

IRELAND

UNITED KINGDOM

NETHERLANDS

POLAND

BELGIUM   GERMANY

LUXEMBOURG

CZECH REPUBLIC

SLOVAKIA

AUSTRIA

HUNGARY

Bay of Biscay

FRANCE   SWITZ.

SLOVENIA

ROMANIA

Black Sea

ITALY

Adriatic Sea

BULGARIA

SPAIN

PORTUGAL

TURKEY

GREECE

Mediterranean Sea

MALTA

CYPRUS

N

0   150   300   450
kilometres

Figure 8.13

The European Union in early 2003

This map shows the members of the EU, and highlights the 13 countries that are preparing to join.

Interpreting

1. Using an atlas, identify some countries that have not been invited to join the EU. Offer some reasons why these countries have not been invited to apply for membership.
2. Suppose all the candidate countries eventually are admitted to the EU. What might be some implications for non-EU countries in Europe?

In Review

1. What are some issues surrounding the integration of Central and Eastern European nations into the European Union?

2. Write an advertisement recommending the integration of Eastern European countries into the organization (or recommending against integration). Your advertisement should offer reasons for or against integration.

The European Union and Other Trade Blocs

The integration of the 15 European economies into the European Union provoked much analysis and comment around the world. However, it was not the only instance of integration. The North American Free Trade Agreement (NAFTA) was signed in 1992 and came into effect in 1994. An expansion of a previous free trade agreement between Canada and the US, this agreement tied together the economies of Mexico, Canada, and the United States into a continental trade bloc. Not to be outdone, two international trade blocs—Mercosur and the Andean Community—were created in South America. These three trade organizations differ significantly in structure from the European Union.

THE STRUCTURE OF NAFTA

The core of NAFTA is the Free Trade Commission, a body composed of the trade ministers from each of the three member countries. They meet annually or as required by pressing issues. Their job is to oversee the more than 25 committees and working groups that are implementing the agreement—full implementation is expected by 2008. The Commission receives reports from the committees and

then instructs officials on implementation directions.

The day-to-day work of implementing the trade agreement is done by the three levels of committees and groups. They are co-chaired by an official from each of the three countries and are staffed

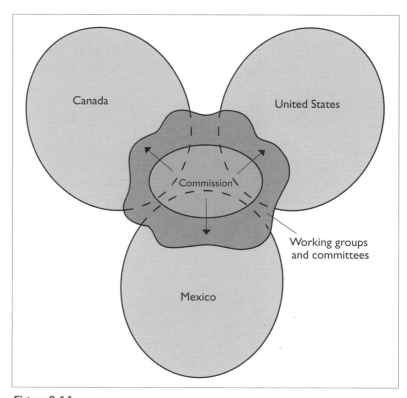

Figure 8.14

The Structure of NAFTA. Under NAFTA, directions determined by the Free Trade Commission are carried out by officials in each country. What might be one disadvantage of this system?

by representatives from the agencies and ministries of the three countries according to the issues being considered, for example, agriculture, transportation, immigration, and the environment.

The Commission and committees and groups are supported in each country by a national NAFTA Secretariat. These organizations administer the dispute resolution processes that are built into NAFTA and work toward settling disputes.

Figure 8.15
Under NAFTA, a dispute mechanism allows one country to challenge another country's adherence to the overall principles and rules of the agreement. For example, the United States questioned the use of stumpage fees in Canada, claiming that they were a form of subsidy for the forest industry, an action that led to heavy taxes on Canadian lumber being sold in the United States.

The Member States of NAFTA

Country	Population (2000)	GDP/capita (US$)	Imports (US$ billion)	Exports (US$ billion)
Canada	31 281 100	23 300	242.4	271.9
Mexico	100 349 800	8 500	158.4	148.4
United States	275 562 700	33 900	1 200.0	767.0

Figure 8.16
Examine the figures given for each nation. What potential problems with integration do these figures suggest?

COMPARING THE EU AND NAFTA

Both the European Union and the North American Free Trade Agreement represent the move toward an unrestricted global trading system. The trade agreements remove trade barriers such as tariffs (a form of trade tax), equalize standards, and allow the free movement of goods and capital among member countries. However, the European arrangement represents a deeper form of integration. It goes beyond removing trade barriers to coordinating common economic, political, social, and military policies for the member states. For example, the EU has its own currency while Canada, the US, and Mexico maintain their own currencies.

Many critics argue that the NAFTA model fails to significantly address "behind the border" issues—problems such as low environmental standards, labour inequalities, and human rights issues. These problems are still addressed at the national level, sometimes poorly. Mexico, for example, has often been rebuked by opponents of free trade for its lack of labour and environmental regulations. Foreign-owned plants in Mexico are sometimes located in areas with the laxest standards and the lowest wages. However, in recent years, Mexico has been more serious about enforcing its new environmental legislation, taking away the incentive for foreign-owned firms to locate there because of a lack of regulations.

Failure to resolve such issues can compromise the economic success of the country and the trade bloc. The assumption behind NAFTA is that prosperity generated by improved trade opportunities will lead to a better living standard, more opportunities, and greater social security for everyone. But there is no verdict yet on whether this will actually occur. The European Union, on the other hand, has used its deep integration to take action on social issues, such as unequal wages. Weaker member states such as Portugal, Spain, and Greece can ask for financial support to develop workers' skills, reduce unemployment, and help poorer areas transform their economies to more growth-oriented sectors. The goal of these programs is to promote regional stability by distributing incomes and opportunities equitably throughout member countries.

Figure 8.17

Faces of NAFTA: A woman earns better-than-average wages assembling television sets at a Samsung factory in Tijuana, Mexico, while an Illinois man tells reporters that local broom-making businesses have been destroyed by NAFTA. Do you think that these two views balance each other out?

The lack of integration has meant that NAFTA members have not been able to co-ordinate their policies on a wide range of topics other than trade. Subsequent agreements on the environment and labour policies have only partly solved the problem. Deeper harmonization of policies on such controversial topics as cultural industries is difficult without such a broad framework.

COMPARING THE EU TO SOUTH AMERICAN TRADE BLOCS

Other trade blocs were created in the 1990s in order to develop trade among their members and compete with the European Union and the North American Free Trade Agreement. Two of these blocs are in South America. Mercosur, or the Southern Common Market, is an agreement among Argentina, Brazil, Paraguay, and Uruguay, while the Andean Community joins Bolivia, Colombia, Ecuador, Peru, and Venezuela in a regional organization. All nine of these countries have relied on high trade tariffs in the past to protect their industries from foreign competition. However, the pressures from globalization forced them to begin to open their markets.

Members in both trade organizations are working to co-ordinate their trade policies and to harmonize their industries through such actions as removing trade and investment barriers. For example, Brazil reduced its intra-regional tariffs from an average of 32 per cent in 1990 to 14 per cent by 1997. In comparison with the European Union, these trade blocs are limited in scope, neither integrating widely (i.e., having many members), nor deeply (i.e., going beyond trade to other issues such as environmental and social issues). They require only modest concessions in autonomy on the part of their members.

Critics of the South American trade organizations suggest that the trade picture has not improved as a result of these arrangements. Economic growth, they argue, has come in sectors where the countries are not internationally competitive. The countries are simply trading among themselves, with their industries protected by tariffs that keep out competitors from non-member nations. In the critics' view, the trade agreements have created "fortresses" that discourage investment in industries that could be internationally competitive.

NETSURFER

WWW.JHU.EDU/~SOC/LADARK.HTML

For more information about Latin American development and trade, visit this site. Under working papers, select a paper that interests you and use it as a reference source in an upcoming project.

The Trade Blocs of South America

Country	Population (2000)	GDP/capita (US$)	Imports (US$ billion)	Exports (US$ billion)
Mercosur				
Argentina	35 955 200	10 000	25.4	27.1
Brazil	172 860 400	6 150	57.3	52.7
Paraguay	5 585 800	3 650	3.7	1.2
Uruguay	3 334 100	8 500	3.5	2.4
Andean Community				
Bolivia	8 152 600	3 000	1.9	1.2
Colombia	39 685 700	6 200	11.5	13.0
Ecuador	12 920 100	4 300	3.4	4.8
Peru	27 012 900	4 400	8.8	7.0
Venezuela	23 542 600	8 000	16.3	29.5

Figure 8.18

Based on the figures in this table, which countries would seem most able to compete in a hemispheric trade bloc? Why? Which countries could have the hardest time competing with countries like the United States and Canada? Why?

MAP STUDY

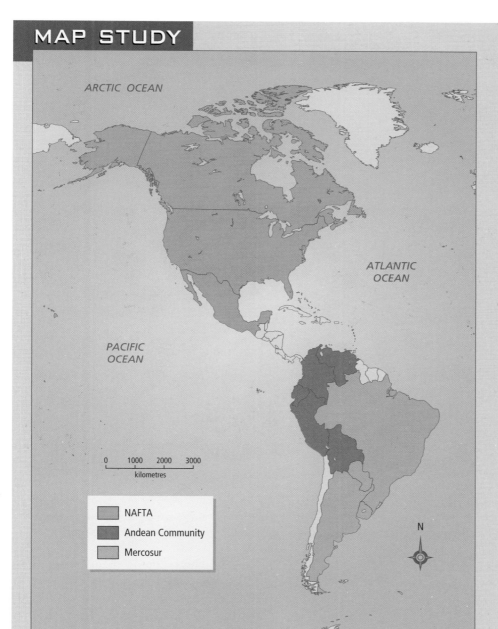

Figure 8.19
Trade Blocs of North and
South America

This map shows the extent of the free trade zones in North and South America.

Interpreting

1. What advantages might there be in creating trade blocs with neighbouring countries?
2. Speculate on some reasons why two trade blocs were created in South America.
3. What do nations that do not belong to a trade bloc have in common? Explain your answer.

Figure 8.20

At a Summit of the Americas in Quebec City in 2001, protesters from all countries in the hemisphere signalled their unhappiness with negotiations on a free trade agreement. What might have been some of their concerns?

For many analysts, the real opportunities will come with a hemispheric trade arrangement—a Free Trade Area of the Americas (FTAA). Negotiations are underway to begin integrating most of the economies of North, Central, and South America. However, while most South American nations want access to North American markets, the details have yet to be worked out. Mercosur and the Andean Community are important first steps in tearing down barriers to trade and in encouraging these nations to become successful members of a much larger trading community.

Skill Path

Writing a Position Paper

Everyone forms opinions about news events reported in the media. It is an instantaneous process, and one you may take for granted. However, it would be a mistake to say that such opinions are truly *positions*. A position paper provides the writer with an opportunity to go beyond superficial observations and reach a deeper level of understanding. Position papers involve gathering, analysing, and interpreting facts in order to justify a viewpoint. This is a useful skill in almost any area of professional life.

Skill Path features in earlier chapters of *Twentieth Century Viewpoints* (pages 166, 195 and 235) outlined the first steps of creating a position paper. These are writing a thesis statement; developing research strategies; and recognizing and analysing bias in information sources. The following steps outline how to use the information gathered to structure an argument.

Step One: Organize Your Evidence
Study your research findings to determine the strongest evidence for the argument proposed in your thesis statement. For example, if your thesis states that Britain should not adopt the euro, you might look for evidence showing that it would disadvantage Britain economically or that Britons would heartily resist adopting another currency. You might even want to arrange your pieces of evidence into separate physical piles, each of which could represent a paragraph in the body of your essay. You should be able to determine at this point if there are any major holes, or lack of evidence in your findings. Were you able to collect enough information to support your thesis? If not, more research is required before you begin writing.

Step Two: Outline Your Rough Draft
Create an outline to structure the whole paper, including the introduction, the body paragraphs, and the conclusion. Include specific information in point form under each heading in your outline. The following blueprint will help you organize your paper:

Introduction
- Reflect upon the importance of the issue.
- Explain the complex nature of the issue.

- Specify fundamental and immediate causes of the problem that are addressed in the issue.
- Identify alternative positions on the issue, citing the main beliefs and values that would be held by advocates of each position.
- State your position/thesis.

Note that an effective paper does not just mention each of the above in the introductory paragraph(s); an effective paper reiterates these features, when appropriate, throughout body and concluding paragraphs.

Body Paragraphs
- Main Points: The main paragraphs of the paper should present the material you have gathered to justify your particular point of view. Open each paragraph by forcefully presenting an argument, or claim, that supports your thesis. Build your paragraphs to locate your strongest material early. Make sure you also cover views that are at odds with your own, and explain why the argument you propose is stronger.
- Examples: Support each main argument with at least one example—two examples are preferable. For example, if you argue that Britons would simply refuse to use the euro, you must find evidence to support that claim. Such evidence is found in a variety of sources, including first- and second-hand accounts found in newspapers, magazines, reputable Internet sites, scholarly journals, and documentaries.

Conclusion
- Point out weaknesses you found in contrary points of view.
- Restate your position.
- Summarize the strengths of your position.
- Make a closing remark significant to your thesis.

Step Three: Write Your Rough Draft
Start filling in each point in your outline using the evidence you collected. Consider including examples from published case studies, powerful quotes from experts, and solid facts to flesh out your arguments.

Certain strategies can help you create emphasis in your writing. Key words or phrases may be occasionally italicized, boldfaced, capitalized, underlined. (The watchword is *occasionally*—don't overdo this device.) Tell your reader that something is important by using words such as "especially," "particularly," "primarily," "above all," and so forth. Vary your sentence structure and length by alternating short sentences with longer ones, or by inserting rhetorical questions. Interrupt the progression of a sentence by the use of a word, phrase, or clause. Repeat key words.

Once you have finished, set the paper aside for at least a day. Then read it with a fresh and critical eye. Ask yourself whether your audience will have any trouble discerning your thesis statement. Did you include enough evidence to support each of the arguments in the body of your paper? Does the paper flow logically? Is the writing style inviting, yet professional? Does the conclusion restate your thesis? Then make any necessary changes and/or additions.

Proofread your final draft by reading slowly. Ensure that you have spelled everything correctly, that you have included a variety of sentence lengths and structures, and that the text makes grammatical sense.

Step Four: Cite Your References

You must cite all the sources you used to write your paper, whether you quoted them directly or not. This step is extremely important because it not only tells the reader that you did your research, but also allows you to properly acknowledge the authors whose ideas and words you borrowed. To not do so would be considered plagiarism.

Your teacher may have given you special instructions on the style to use for your citations. If not, two widely accepted styles you could use are the MLA (Modern Language Association) and the APA (American Psychological Association). To learn how to apply these styles, you could do a search for each on the Internet or consult one of the many writing manuals available, including the following:

Publication Manual of the American Psychological Association, 4th ed. (Washington DC: APA, 1994).

MLA Handbook for Writers of Research Papers, 5th ed. (New York: Modern Language Association, 1999).

The chart below gives a few comparisons between how the APA and the MLA handle different types of citations.

Source	MLA	APA
Books	Last name, First name. *Source title.* Place of publication: Publisher, Year.	Last name, Initial(s). (Date) <u>Source Title</u>. Place of publication: Publisher.
Newspaper articles	Last name, First name. "Title of article." *Newspaper* day month year: page number.	Last name, Initial(s). (year, month day). Article title. <u>Newspaper</u>, page number.
Periodical or magazine	Last name, First name. "Title of article." *Magazine* month/year: page number.	Last name, Initial(s). (year, month). Article title. <u>Magazine</u> page number.
Internet	Last name, First name. *Site name.* Home page. Updated day month year. <www.worldwar1.com/armo06.htm>	Last name, First name. *Site name.* Home page. Updated day month year. www.worldwar1.com/armo06.htm

Practise Your Skill

1. Develop a thesis with three supporting arguments for a view with which you disagree. Locate one example of evidence to support each of your arguments. For each example, briefly explain why you think the source is a good one. At the end of the assignment, debrief. What did you learn from the exercise that you could apply to your next position paper?

2. Develop two arguments for the following thesis: The EU offers more advantages to citizens than does NAFTA. Tip: Write down the statement and follow it with the word "because" to begin developing your arguments. What specific examples might you search for to back up your arguments?

In Review

1. Identify three ways that NAFTA is similar to the European Union, and three ways that it is different.

2. Mexico's per capita GDP is roughly one-third of Canada's and one-quarter of the US figure. In what ways might this be a problem in a continental trade agreement? In what ways might it be an advantage?

3. Explain why the larger nations of South America could not avoid linking themselves to a regional trade agreement.

Summary

The twentieth century was a remarkable era of turmoil and change in Europe. For most of the century, the continent was divided by war. Following the Second World War, Europe began to rebuild and to see the advantages of co-operation among European states. The new quest for unity resulted in the European Union in 1993—a union limited to the Western European nations. For the nations of Eastern Europe, a difficult path lay ahead as they tried to rebuild their political institutions and their economies following the demise of communism. As stability returned, these nations wanted to join the EU as well.

The nations of North and South America have also looked for new ways to enhance economic co-operation. The 1994 North American Free Trade Agreement (NAFTA) brought together the economies of Mexico, Canada, and the United States into one huge trade bloc. Other international trade blocs, such as Mercosur and the Andean Community, have been created in South America. While these trade organizations differ in structure from the EU, they both represent regional agreements to create advantages for members.

Viewpoints

ISSUE: Should the European Union enlarge to include Central and Eastern European countries?

Background

By 2002, there were 15 countries in the European Union (EU). The long-range plan to expand the EU includes the addition of up to a dozen countries from Central and Eastern Europe by the year 2010. However, these countries must meet the standards set for joining by the EU. These nations are much poorer than the nations of Western Europe and have a very different political and economic history. Will these countries truly benefit from joining the EU? Can they meet the standards for entry? What impact will these poorer countries have on wealthy members of the EU?

The first reading has been reprinted from Europa, the official Web site of the European Union. It lists many of the benefits that would come from an expanded EU. The second reading, by John Hall, Professor of Economics and International Studies at Portland State University, and Wolfgang Quaisser, senior research fellow at Osteuropa-Institut in Munich, Germany, gives qualified support for enlargement. These authors argue that enlargement is a "win-win situation" but that many serious problems could stand in the way of success. Read these two viewpoints carefully, and answer the questions that follow. (You may want to refer to the Skill Path "Analysing a Reading" on page 14 before beginning these articles.)

Enlargement: Frequently asked questions

Why is the EU extending to include new countries?
Enlargement of the European Union is a historic opportunity to unite Europe peacefully after generations of division and conflict. Enlargement will extend the EU's stability and prosperity to a wider group of countries, consolidating the political and economic transition that has taken place in Central and Eastern Europe since 1989.

By enhancing the stability and security of these countries, the EU as a whole can enjoy better chances for peace and prosperity. After the terrorist attacks of 11 September, 2001, a strong and united Europe is more important than ever before to ensure peace, security and freedom.

This round of enlargement, like previous ones, will add to the Union's strength, cohesion and influence in the world. The extension to include new members will put the Union in a better position

to take up the challenge of globalisation, and to strengthen and defend the European social model. Enlargement is thus a continuation of the EU's original purpose of healing Europe's divisions and creating an ever-closer union of its peoples. By welcoming new members who respect our political criteria, the Union is re-stating the fundamental values that underpin it.

Enlargement will present significant economic opportunities in the form of a larger market. Adding the applicant countries to the EU's Single Market of over 370 million inhabitants will create the biggest economic area in the world. A market of this size can be expected to give a boost to investment and job creation, raising levels of prosperity throughout Europe, in both new and old member countries.

In joining the EU, the new members will

reinforce their economic integration with the existing members. Consumers will reap the benefits of wider choice and lower prices, and European businesses across the continent will share a common set of rules and benefit from increased trade, greater efficiency and more competition.

Is the EU sufficiently prepared for enlargement?

The European Council in Nice in December 2000 reached agreement on a new Treaty that paves the way for enlargement. With the ratification of the Treaty, the EU will be ready to welcome new members.

The Treaty includes important changes to streamline decision-making in an enlarged Union:

- extension of majority voting to more policy areas in the Council of Ministers, in place of decision-making by unanimity;
- new weighting of votes of member states in the Council, to take account of the arrival of new members;
- new allocation of seats in the European Parliament;
- increased authority for the President of the European Commission, in relation to Commissioners and their portfolios.

Source: Europa: The European Union Online, March 2002. <europa.eu.int/comm/enlargement/faq/index.htm#Why> © European Communities, 1995-2002.

Europe's eastern enlargement: Who benefits?

The European Union is preparing to take a quantum leap eastward. For the EU, previous rounds of enlargement meant adding tens of millions of West Europeans. In contrast, its current plan for enlargement means adding between 100 million and 200 million new citizens from central, eastern, and southeastern Europe.

Fifteen countries currently (2001) compose the EU. Its eastern enlargement means bringing in as many as 12 more countries, likely entering as two or three groups spaced over time. If all goes as scheduled, just after 2010 the population of the EU should approach 500 million. Its population will be significantly larger than that of the United States.

In recent decades the EU has allowed a small number of countries—Ireland, Spain, Portugal, and Greece—with per capita incomes well below the EU average to join. Ireland, Spain and Portugal have made significant strides in converging toward the EU per capita GDP average.

But eastern enlargement poses a more formidable challenge. Could the vision of Europe's elite leaders backfire, threatening and even undermining hard-earned prosperity by extending the EU too far eastward? Citizens to the east ponder: Is the European Union's current scheme for enlargement as virtuous as purported? Is this in reality a quickly spun stop gap measure to shore up security risks along a newly formed eastern border created by the Soviet Union's unexpected demise? The historical experience of the East European countries is to dance to the tunes played by regional powers to their west and to their east. Is this just one more round, with Brussels choreographing the show now, rather than Vienna, Berlin, or Moscow?

The European Commission provides criteria for judging a country's preparedness for accession. The Brussels-based commission annually evaluates countries to determine if each has fulfilled the "Copenhagen Criteria" regarding the establishment of stable institutions guaranteeing pluralistic democracy, the rule of law, and respect for human rights, including protection of national minorities. Its economic criteria presuppose the existence of a functioning market economy.

What makes the EU's eastern enlargement so challenging economically? Foremost are the systemic changes candidate countries confront at home as they abandon legacies of failed communist experiments and embrace the West European model based on democracy and a liberal market economy. The second challenge is the unprecedented scale and speed of the anticipated expansion. In addition, vast differences exist in the levels of economic development and economic performances between the prospective CEECs [Central and Eastern European Countries] and the advanced members of the EU.

Which CEECs will be invited to join the "rich man's club," and when? The stakes are high. Those invited can expect to prosper, since they will benefit from the EU's agricultural and structural funds—transfers that could be as large as 4 percent of their GDPs. These transfers could continue to flow in for decades, as they have for Ireland. In addition, those chosen will benefit from insider access to the largest single market on earth.

What keeps the dream of eastern enlargement moving forward? The obvious answer is that eastern enlargement can be considered an essential aspect to fulfilling a political vision. Europe's unification was spelled out as a goal in the 1957 Treaty of Rome. Also, at least two major studies suggest that existing EU members can expect modest growth in output resulting from integration.

On the down side, EU members have started to show signs of divisions that will likely deepen over time as countries estimate their prospects for future gains and losses associated with eastern enlargement.

Since trade in goods and services, as well as capital flows, is not likely to lead to an equalization of incomes among the current 15 members of the EU and the CEECs in the short term, gaps in wages between regions are expected to persist for some time.

Labor migration will, over the short term, have greater effects on the EU's labor markets than will trade and investment. Sharing contiguous (common) borders with some of the CEECs, and in relatively close proximity to others, Austria and Germany can expect to absorb the lion's share of eastern migrants. Of the predicted annual net migration of close to 300,000 workers, 200,000 are expected to head for Germany.

The balance sheet

From an economic standpoint, eastern enlargement appears to be a win-win situation. CEEC economies are comparatively small, together generating an output that is only 4 percent of the EU-15, and eastern enlargement is not expected to generate significant benefits or costs for Western Europe over the short term. In contrast, the CEECs are expected to gain disproportionately and significantly upon accession.

Friction will occur in the intense power play that will emerge between net payers and net receivers of Brussels's budgetary funds. In addition, the power play could cause the formation of at least two camps firmly at odds with one another. Austria, Germany, Sweden, and the Netherlands apparently will be counting their gains, while France, Spain, Portugal, Greece, and Ireland will be mourning their losses.

Source: Adapted from John Hall and Wolfgang Quaisser, "Europe's Eastern Enlargement: Who Benefits?" *Current History*, November 2001, pp. 389-393. Reprinted with permission from *Current History* magazine (November 2001), © 2001, Current History, Inc.

Analysis and Evaluation

1. Why would you expect to see an argument in favour of expanding the EU on the Europa Web site? Explain whether you think Europa is or is not a reliable source of information on this issue.

2. What do Hall and Quaisser mean by the statement, "The historical experience of the East European countries is to dance to the tunes played by regional powers to their west and to their east"?

3. Decide which of the viewpoints you tend to support, and explain why. If you agree with neither, state the position you do support and explain it. Be sure to use specific information from this textbook, the readings, and other sources to support your position.

Chapter Analysis

MAKING CONNECTIONS

1. Outline the important forces that shaped both Eastern and Western Europe in the second half of the twentieth century.

2. Describe the ways in which the European Union integrates its member countries. Consider social, political, and economic ties.

3. a) Use a comparison chart to compare the structure and functioning of the European Union to the structure and functioning of NAFTA.

   b) In your view, which organization does a more effective job, as seen from the perspective of an average citizen of Western Europe or North America? Explain your opinion.

DEVELOPING YOUR VOICE

4. In 1991, Belgium's foreign minister, Mark Eyskens, remarked that Europe "is an economic giant, a political dwarf, and a military worm."

   a) What do you suppose Eyskens meant by this comment?

   b) What might be the implications for the rest of the world if this comment is accurate?

5. Do you think that the nations of Europe should form a United States of Europe? Give reasons for your position.

6. Design a logo for the European Union. In a paragraph, describe the symbols you have created and give reasons for your choices.

RESEARCHING THE ISSUES

7. Research one country in Europe, focusing on how it has responded to either the creation of the European Union or the disintegration of the Soviet Union.

8. Research how five individual nations in Europe have responded to one of the issues below. Before you begin, prepare a research organizer in which you list topics and subtopics that may be important to the issue. Present your conclusions to the class.
   - terrorism
   - the environment
   - refugees and immigration
   - AIDS
   - illegal drugs

9. How successful has an integrated European community been? Compile statistical information to document the economic, political, and social changes since 2000. Determine whether or not the expansion of this trade bloc with the Maastricht Treaty has been beneficial to the member countries.

10. Conduct research to find one area of conflict among the NAFTA members. Describe the conflict, summarize the issues, and point out what is being done to improve the situation.

CHAPTER NINE

Africa: After Independence

Crowds cheer Nelson Mandela as he campaigns for the presidency in South Africa. Supporters cheer from the top of a billboard. What do nations look for in their leaders? How does this leader exemplify those qualities?

"Westerners have aggressive problem-solving minds; Africans experience people."

— Kenneth Kaunda, president of Zambia (1964-1991)

"The time has come for South Africa to take up its rightful and responsible place in the community of nations."

— Nelson Mandela, "South Africa: Future Foreign Policy," *Foreign Affairs,* Vol. 72, No. 5, 1993

Overview

Nationalism swept across the African continent following the Second World War. One by one, the European colonies in Africa launched campaigns for independence. For some, it was a peaceful transition. For others, the road to independence was one of violent confrontation. In 1945, when the United Nations was founded, only four members were African states. By 2003, 53 African nations sat in the General Assembly, comprising more than 28 per cent of UN membership.

The nations of Africa have developed in distinct ways. Yet perhaps no nation symbolizes the struggle to overcome the destructiveness of colonialism more than South Africa. This nation was torn by turmoil as the black majority struggled to obtain equality in a society dominated by white rule. Its story illustrates many of the issues and challenges facing the people of this continent. Here too the UN played a role. For half a century, its Universal Declaration of Human Rights, recognizing "the inherent dignity and... equal and inalienable rights of all members of the human family" was a signpost for those fighting against racism and injustice in South Africa and elsewhere.

Focus Questions

1. What were the conditions in colonial Africa before the Second World War?
2. What factors led to the colonies of Africa gaining independence?
3. What are some benefits and problems resulting from independence?
4. How did the people of South Africa end apartheid and white rule?
5. What is the future for South Africa in the twenty-first century?

From Colonialism to Independence

Europeans knew little of the interior of Africa before the middle of the nineteenth century. They had travelled the coast of the continent for hundreds of years, relying on African traders to bring them the ivory, spices, minerals, and slaves they sought. All this changed during the era of European imperialism when the nations of Western Europe extended their authority throughout Africa. In the process, local economies and traditional African cultural, social, and political systems were pulled apart and reshaped to meet the needs of the imperial powers.

Between 1870 and 1914, most of the continent of Africa was controlled by Europe. Britain, France, Portugal, Belgium, Spain, Italy, and Germany partitioned Africa in their scramble for territory. The motives behind colonial expansion were threefold.

First, the European powers wanted to establish new supplies of natural resources to fuel their developing industries. In return, they expected the nations of Africa to buy their manufactured

Figure 9.1

This painting, made in 1897, shows officials of the Imperial British Africa Company and members of the Kikuyu people of (what is today) Kenya making a treaty.

goods. When a nation's economy prospered, it had more international power and prestige. Second, colonial expansion was fuelled by the atmosphere of rivalry that existed among European nations. Colonial holdings symbolized international power and provided military outposts to help the European empires maintain their positions in the world order. Finally, the notion of **racial superiority** was an underlying motive behind European imperialism. Many people in Europe believed the racist notion that Western civilization was superior to all others, and that it was their duty to spread it around the world.

THE EFFECTS OF IMPERIALISM

The imperial powers controlled all aspects of life in their colonies. They moulded the economy, government, law, education, and social institutions to conform to Western standards and values. In some cases, large numbers of Europeans settled in the colonies, thereby reinforcing the imperial power's control and changing the face of Africa forever.

The colonial powers also regulated all economic activities in their African territories. Cash crops destined for European markets were grown on sprawling plantations. Mining and logging operations provided an abundance of valuable raw materials for the industrial processing plants of Europe. While the Africans supplied most of the labour, working long hours under harsh conditions for little pay, the Europeans owned and controlled the businesses and collected most of the profits. Much of what the Africans did earn was paid to the colonial government in the form of taxes. These were used to offset the high cost of the soldiers and administrators sent to the colonies, and for roads, railways, and other facilities that primarily benefited the colonists.

Most Europeans did not value the traditions and customs of the African societies. Instead, they imposed their own beliefs through schools, courts, businesses, and government, a process known as **colonial domination**. Some Africans, impressed by the wealth and power of the Europeans, rejected their traditional lifestyles in favour of Western ways. Colonialism led to a breakdown of traditional African values and village life. African ideas of identity and nation were replaced with vastly different European concepts.

MAP STUDY

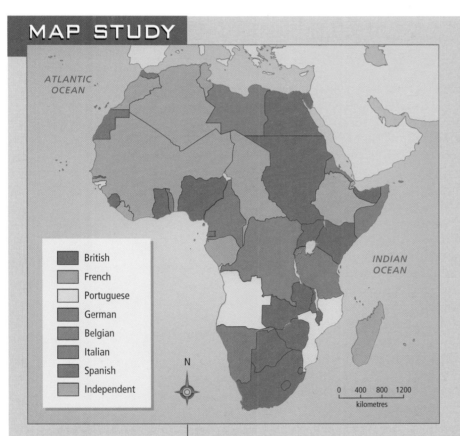

Figure 9.2
Imperialism in Africa, 1914

This map shows which imperial powers held colonies in Africa at the start of the First World War.

Interpreting

1. Which imperial countries had the largest influence in Africa in 1914?
2. Some imperial powers controlled colonies that bordered on the oceans, while other powers ruled large interior parts of the continent. What factors might have encouraged the expansion into the centre of Africa?
3. What might be some implications of dividing Africa in the manner shown in the map?

THE RISE OF AFRICAN NATIONALISM

The seeds of African nationalism are actually found in colonial rule itself. Since the early days of colonial domination there had been sporadic revolts and local organized resistance in many colonies. Most of the leadership at this level came from local chiefs. But sustained and effective opposition to the powerful European interests required a different kind of leadership. Ironically, the colonial powers themselves provided the training for a new generation of African leaders.

During the 1930s and 1940s, large numbers of African intellectuals, writers, artists, and professionals returned home from universities in France, Britain, the United States, and other Western countries. Armed with a Western education and experienced in the ways of Western culture, this new generation was prepared to lead their countries to independence. Some members of this group emerged as leaders of a host of newly independent states after the Second World War. Other nationalist leaders prepared for their roles through the colonial military or police forces. Key personnel were frequently trained abroad. There they learned European military practices—methods they would later apply against the Europeans. In this way, the colonial system played an important part in the events that ultimately led to its own destruction.

From 1945 through the 1950s, African leaders emerged at the head of political parties and armed resistance groups. These organizations united and directed the actions of a widespread and diverse membership. Political organizations such as the Rassemblement Democratique Africain, founded in 1946 in the French colonies, and insurgent groups such as the Mau Mau in British Kenya, which was active between 1952 and 1960, challenged colonial rule.

In 1963, the **Organization of African Unity** (OAU) was established at Addis Ababa in Ethiopia. The goals of the organization were to promote African unity and solidarity, to co-ordinate political, economic, defence, and social policies of all members, and to eliminate colonialism in Africa.

Leaders in the Fight for an Independent Africa

Leader	Region of Africa
Idi Amin	Uganda
Nnamdi Azikiwe	Nigeria
Ibrahim Babangida	Nigeria
Hastings Banda	Malawi
Muhammed Siad Barre	Somalia
Jean Bokassa	Central African Republic
Yaukubu Gowon	Nigeria
Sese Seko Mobutu	Zaire
Antonio Neto	Angola
Julius Nyerere	Tanzania
Kwame Nkrumah	Ghana
Leopold Senghor	Senegal

Figure 9.3

Many of these leaders rejected violence, while some used it to further their power. Select one leader for further study and report your findings to the class. You can search the Internet, typing the leader's name into your favourite search engine.

INTERNATIONAL SUPPORT FOR INDEPENDENCE

Strong leadership and popular support at home were not enough to ensure the success of Africa's nationalist movements. African independence needed the support in principle of the United Nations (UN). It received it in the form of the Universal Declaration of Human Rights, adopted by the General Assembly on 10 December 1948. This historic document, often cited as the first major achievement of the UN, not only emphasized personal rights and freedoms, but also propelled the world toward "a common standard of achievement for all peoples and all nations."

African nationalism also needed the support of the two superpowers, the United States and the Soviet Union. The United States had both a philosophical and an economic motive for supporting African nationalism. Having staged a revolution for its own independence from the British Empire in 1776, the US was naturally sympathetic to the African colonies' desire to end the injustice of colonialism. It also recognized that newly independent countries would be interested in establishing political and economic relationships with the US. These relationships could provide American industries with valuable raw materials and new export markets.

The Soviet Union also had its own motives for supporting African independence. Philosophically, the USSR supported liberation movements. It also saw independence as a way of weakening the European powers and counteracting the spread of American influence. Without the support of the United States and the Soviet Union it would have been more difficult for African states to break free from European domination.

WWW.UNHCHR.CH/UDHR

This is the official Universal Declaration of Human Rights Home Page. To read the Declaration, go to the site and select your language of choice. Background information on this historic resolution is also provided.

Within Europe itself, there was considerable support for African independence. The African colonies had made tremendous contributions to the European countries during the Second World War. Many Europeans felt that the reward for such support and loyalty should be independence. These sentiments were reinforced by a growing liberalism that favoured nationalist ambitions. Yet in Europe, too, the promotion of African nationalism was not without self-interest. The high cost of postwar reconstruction meant few resources could be spared for the colonies. In addition, Africa was facing severe social and economic problems. The Second World War had stripped the European powers of the economic and military strength needed to enforce their rule over their overseas possessions.

INDEPENDENCE

The imperialist nations of Europe professed to support African independence. Yet racism continued to play a role in colonial policy-making. The Western nations still viewed themselves as a "civilizing" force for African peoples. From their point of view, **self-determination** should be granted to the colonies through a slow and deliberate transition. The African nationalists had a different timetable, however. They were determined to gain their freedom and independence more quickly— even if it meant dealing with the myriad of social and economic ills that colonialism had left on the continent.

"As long as we are ruled by others we shall lay our mistakes at their door, and our sense of responsibility will remain dulled."

— Dr. Kwame Nkrumah, first prime minister of Ghana, 1953

The Organization of African Unity, 2002

Algeria*	Ethiopia*	Nigeria*
Angola	Gabon	Rwanda*
Benin*	Gambia	Sahrawi (Saharan Rep.)
Botswana	Ghana*	São Tomé and Principe
Burkina Faso*	Guinea*	Senegal*
Burundi*	Guinea-Bissau	Seychelles
Cameroon*	Kenya	Sierra Leone*
Cape Verde	Lesotho	Somalia*
Central African Republic*	Liberia*	South Africa
Chad*	Libya*	Sudan*
Comoros	Madagascar*	Swaziland
Congo	Malawi	Tanzania*
Côte d'Ivoire*	Mali*	Togo*
Dem. Rep. Congo	Mauritania*	Tunisia*
Djibouti	Mauritius	Uganda*
Egypt*	Mozambique	Zambia
Equatorial Guinea	Namibia	Zimbabwe
Eritrea	Niger*	

* Original members

Figure 9.4
Morocco was an original member of the OAU but resigned in protest in 1984 when Sahrawi (Saharan Republic) was admitted. In recent years this organization has mediated several border and internal disputes in Africa. In 2002, the OAU began a process to change its name to the African Union.

"The wind of change is blowing through this continent."
— British prime minister Harold Macmillan, 1960

"It is no ordinary wind, but a raging hurricane."
— Dr. Kwame Nkrumah, prime minister of Ghana, 1960

TRANSITION TO INDEPENDENCE

There were two very different roads to independence—through peaceful negotiation or through violent confrontation. The first peaceful transition took place in the British colony of Gold Coast when a group of African lawyers and businesspeople formed a nationalist movement in 1947. Kwame Nkrumah, the leader of the National Gold Coast Convention, was a political activist educated in the United States.

Inspired by India's Mahatma Gandhi, Nkrumah organized non-violent protests and boycotts against British rule. Eventually, British authorities jailed him for treason, but this only served to enhance his popularity. In elections to a new legislative assembly in 1951, Nkrumah's party won 34 of 38 available seats. Bowing to the public's support of Nkrumah, Britain released the jailed leader and asked him to form a new government. For six years the Gold Coast existed under limited self-rule. In 1957, Britain withdrew from the colony altogether. The new country of Ghana served as a model for peaceful independence movements across the continent.

Figure 9.5
Left, Kwame Nkrumah led the former British colony of Gold Coast to independence as the country of Ghana. He became prime minister of Ghana in 1952, and president in 1957. Right, two women pause before huge pictures of Queen Elizabeth II and Kwame Nkrumah. The occasion was the queen's impending trip to Ghana in 1961. Why would the government of Ghana honour the queen after declaring its independence from Britain?

Not all transitions were peaceful, however. A number of colonies erupted in violence and bloodshed during their drives for independence. In Kenya, the secret society known as the Mau Mau launched violent attacks against colonial institutions. A war of independence raged in Algeria between 1954 and 1962. The Belgian Congo (now the Democratic Republic of Congo) was granted independence in 1960, but civil war erupted almost immediately. Racial violence flared in the colony of Southern Rhodesia after it declared unilateral independence from Britain. Majority rule was established in 1980, when the country became Zimbabwe. Guerrilla warfare broke out against Portuguese forces in Angola until Portugal granted that colony independence in 1974.

Uganda gained independence in 1962, but the new nation was plagued by famine and violence; conditions only became more dangerous and chaotic during the tyrannical rule of Idi Amin from 1971 to 1985. Amin, a former lieutenant in the British Colonial Army, solidified his power base by appealing to his own Kakwa tribe. After seizing power in 1971, he murdered hundreds of thousands of civilians from rival tribes and placed his own military tribunals above the rule of law.

MAP STUDY

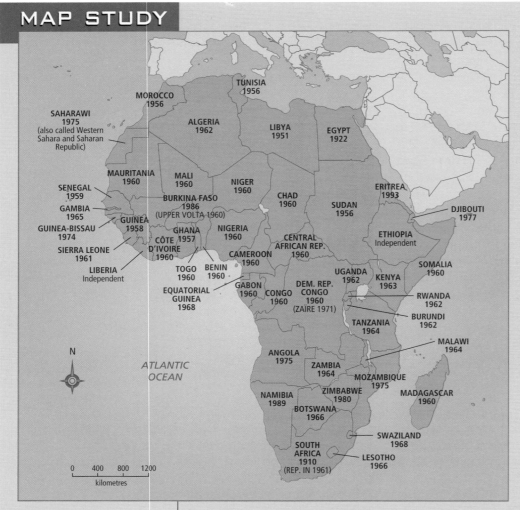

Figure 9.6
Africa, 2003

This map depicts the national boundaries within the continent of Africa as of 2003, along with the dates that nations reached their independence.

Interpreting

1. During which decades did most of the countries of Africa achieve their independence?
2. Identify three instances where boundaries could create problems for the countries of Africa. For example, tiny Gambia is surrounded on three sides by the larger Senegal. What impact might this have on Gambia?
3. Identify all the landlocked African countries. Using an encyclopedia or fact book, find the Gross National Products per capita (GNP/capita) for these countries. Does being landlocked pose a problem for African countries?

ECONOMIC CHALLENGES

Optimism for the future in Africa's newly independent countries was high in the 1960s and 1970s. Leaders believed that rapid industrialization was the key to economic success. To achieve this goal, many countries took control of their resources and nationalized key industries. Yet they lacked the management expertise to run state-owned operations, and many of these businesses quickly failed.

Foreign Debt

In time, most African nations had to borrow heavily from the developed world and international agencies such as the World Bank. Crushed by debt, African nations found it hard not only to pay back loans, but also to attract new investment. Today, most Africans are poorer in material terms than they were at the time of independence. On the United Nations' Human Development Index, African countries occupy the bottom 28 rankings.

The foreign debt crisis is one of the greatest obstacles to African development. For many countries, interest payments alone on foreign debts exceed the total value of exports. Money that leaves a country as debt payment is lost as investment capital at home. On a national level, this means there is little money to spend on improving the quality of life. On the local level, it means that consumers have little money to spend, and businesses have few customers.

Most governments are required to adopt economic programs established by international lending organizations as a condition of continued support. Often, however, these programs are ill-suited to the economies of these developing nations. In many countries, for example, governments are required to cut government spending as part of their international loan agreement. Wages are cut and the number of government employees is reduced. Health, education, and other social services are devastated as a result.

Church groups and non-governmental organizations (NGOs) have helped to publicize the impact of foreign debt. They have tried to persuade lending agencies to reduce or eliminate these debts. These campaigns have done little, however, as the institutions argue that shareholder or voter interest is more important than the conditions in developing countries. Foreign debt could cripple development for many years to come.

Hunger and Food Production

Another serious problem faced by African nations is hunger. In the decades leading up to the end of the century, famine plagued 22 countries; in 2000, it was estimated that 70 per cent of Africans did not have enough food to eat. The lack of fertile land led farmers to overuse the land, and excessive grazing and planting caused soil erosion. Forests were laid bare as the trees were removed to provide fuel wood for heating and cooking. Combined, these factors led to **desertification**. Recurring drought created even greater losses of vegetation.

Acute shortages of food have also led to its use as a political or military weapon. For example, during Sudan's prolonged civil war in the 1990s, the government regularly prevented international food aid from getting to rebel-held parts of the country. In 2002, observers of Zimbabwe's national election accused President Robert Mugabe of starving those communities that did not support him. In Angola, where a civil war raged from 1975 to 2002, people were forced to flee their homes in search of food because the fields and crops had been destroyed by government troops.

Figure 9.7

By the 1980s, chronic food shortages in Somalia had become commonplace, the result of environmental conditions, war, and government policies concerning food production.

"No private investors—not the most far-sighted multinational corporation, nor yet the most patriotic African—are going to risk their hard-won capital in a chronically insecure neighbourhood."

— Kofi Annan, Secretary-General of the UN, 1998

Some African nations turned to producing cash crops, such as bananas, sugar, and peanuts, for export. These remained the foundation of the African economy throughout the twentieth century. Countries relied on these exports to generate foreign currency to buy everything from energy supplies and pharmaceuticals to machines and military equipment. But prices for these crops are highly variable and are tied to the boom-and-bust world economy. Thus, a modest drop in world demand can cause the market price of a crop to plummet. Moreover, the land dedicated to these uncertain global markets could have been used to produce food for local consumption. For many African nations, the shift to crops for export only weakened economic growth.

Some African nations import food to deal with their domestic food shortages, thereby intensifying economic problems. These imports have increased as desertification has spread. With few resources to pay for these imports, many countries have amassed even greater foreign debt in their efforts to maintain the food supply.

Globalization

The **globalization** of the economy has not helped Africa deal with its economic challenges. Some observers claim that unfair trade practices have actually weakened developing economies while increasing profits for European, Japanese, and American corporations. African businesses have been largely shut out of global economic expansion. The poor state of Africa's economy has hindered foreign investment, and widespread poverty and disease have caused labour shortages. The brutal struggle for survival has often resulted in civil unrest and war—forces contrary to growth and expansion.

Voices The Causes of Underdevelopment

Despite the political strides made by the African nations, Africa faced many difficulties in the twentieth century. Many experts have tried to explain the lack of development and continued poverty in Africa. Some blame the impact of European colonialism for the conditions in Africa today. Others argue that those countries with closer colonial ties are actually the more prosperous nations. Still others blame not the political imperialism of the past, but the economic imperialism that replaced it.

As you read the following excerpts, consider which one seems to have the most merit, and why.

YULI M. VORONSTOV, FORMER SOVIET AMBASSADOR TO THE UN

"A serious and comprehensive analysis of the economic difficulties prevailing in Africa indicates that their real causes are rooted in the ills inherited from colonialism, in the merciless plunder and selfish polices pursued by the colonial powers towards African countries. Today there is an abundance of studies demonstrating convincingly that the root causes of the African crisis originated in colonial times...."

Source: Statement to the United Nations General Assembly, 27 May 1986. © Copyright United Nations, 2000-2003.

CARLOS RANGEL, POLITICAL THINKER AND AUTHOR

"The Third World's poorest countries are not those that have had longer and closer exchanges with the West, but, significantly, those whose exchanges had been weaker and shorter—Ethiopia, for instance.... In sharp contrast is Nigeria, where, prior to 1890, there was no cultivation of cocoa, peanuts or cotton. Due to the British development and commercialization of their cultivation, however, Nigeria today exports an enormous proportion of the world supply of these products."

Source: Reprinted by permission of Transaction Publishers. Excerpt from *Third World Ideology and Western Reality* by Carlos Rangel. Copyright © 1986. All rights reserved.

MICHAEL PARENTI, PROFESSOR AND AUTHOR

"In a word, the Third World is not 'underdeveloped' but overexploited. The gap between rich and poor nations is not due to the 'neglect' of the latter by the former as has often been claimed.... [T]he gap between rich and poor only widens because investments in the Third World are not designed to develop the capital resources of the poor nations but to enrich the Western investors...."

Source: Michael Parenti, *The Sword and the Dollar: Imperialism, Revolution and the Arms Race* (St. Martin's Press, 1989).

Responding

1. Which views are similar? Which opinion is at odds with the other two views?
2. Do you think that Voronstov, Rangel, and Parenti would have common points of discussion if they were to meet and share their views? Why or why not?

SOCIAL CHALLENGES

At the turn of the twenty-first century, the most difficult problem faced by the countries of Africa was the HIV/AIDS **pandemic**. It has been compared to "a powerful storm or war that lays waste to a nation's physical infrastructure...[and] damages a nation's social infrastructure, with lingering demographic and economic effects." (Worldwatch Institute Sept/Oct 1999)

In 2000, more than 25 million Africans had AIDS, and 2.4 million people died of the disease. The loss of parents and family members has created a generation of orphans who face insurmountable odds. The disease has also diminished the labour force. The poor state of health care in the continent, and the high cost of medicine, which African states can ill afford, means that AIDS will continue to erode the economic vitality of the continent for many years to come.

Countries Where HIV Infection Rate Is Greater than 10%, 2001

Country	Total Population (millions)	Proportion of Adult Population Infected (%)
Botswana	1.6	38.8
Zimbabwe	12.9	33.7
Swaziland	0.9	33.4
Lesotho	2.1	31.0
Namibia	1.8	22.5
Zambia	10.7	21.5
South Africa	43.8	20.1
Kenya	31.3	15.0
Malawi	11.6	15.0
Mozambique	18.6	13.0
Central African Republic	3.8	12.9
Cameroon	15.2	11.8

Estimated People Living with HIV/AIDS, 2001

Sub-Saharan Africa	28 500 000	North America	950 000
South and Southeast Asia	5 600 000	Western Europe	550 000
Latin America	1 500 000	North Africa and the Middle East	500 000
East Asia and the Pacific	1 000 000	Caribbean	420 000
Eastern Europe and Central Asia	1 000 000	Australia and New Zealand	15 000

Figure 9.8

Over the next decade, countries like Botswana and South Africa will lose at least 20 per cent of their adult populations to AIDS. What impact will this have on these countries? After gathering population statistics, compare the percentage of people living with AIDS in Africa with the percentage living in North America. (Source: Compiled from The Joint United Nations Programme on HIV/AIDS. © Joint United Nations Programme on HIV/AIDS [UNAIDS] 2001. All rights reserved.)

POLITICS IN INDEPENDENT AFRICA

Many of Africa's new nations adopted some form of parliamentary democracy once independence was achieved. Yet democracy did not always seem to be a good fit. As former colonies, many African nations had been ruled by highly centralized administrations that were anything but democratic. However, Kofi Annan, Secretary-General of the UN, has observed the following:

There is a saying among my people in Ghana: One head alone is not enough to decide.

I often think of that when I hear people say that democracy is alien to Africa, or that Africans are "not ready" for democracy. In reality, African communities from the village upwards have traditionally decided their course through free discussion, carefully weighing different points of view until consensus is reached. So Africans have much to learn from their own traditions, and something to teach others, about the true meaning and spirit of democracy.

Source: *The International Herald Tribune,* 5 December 2000.

Politics has been made more difficult by the ethnic diversity within countries. When boundaries were carved out by the imperial powers, little consideration was given to traditional tribal, ethnic, and cultural divisions and territories. These borders often split cultures among different colonies and placed different ethnic groups under common rule. The new governments often faced the task of trying to unite diverse cultural groups that may have had little or no attachment to the nation state.

Political instability frequently resulted in military **coups** in which governments were overthrown by force. The new military regimes promised to end political conflict and economic instability through rigid discipline and control. Yet these governments proved to be ineffective in improving the quality of life. Military rule was often followed by revolution or civil war as dissatisfied social groups and political factions reacted against repressive regimes.

For example, in its first 40 years of independence, Nigeria had six military coups. These conflicts have produced millions of refugees and internally displaced people. By the end of 2000, there were an

Figure 9.9

UN Secretary General Kofi Annan is shown here during a visit to a Displaced Person's Centre in Angola. Angola has one of the highest number of displaced people in the world due to the civil war that had engulfed the country since it gained independence from Portugal in 1975. This war ended in April 2002, just a few months prior to Annan's visit. Do some research to discover the different sides that were fighting the war and the reasons for their conflict.

estimated 3.3 million refugees on the continent, displaced by conflicts in places like Sudan, Rwanda, Democratic Republic of the Congo, and Sierra Leone. This political instability has served to make social and economic progress difficult.

AFRICA'S FUTURE

The people of Africa are both optimistic and pessimistic about their future. The population is young and has yet to reach its full potential. Literacy rates are rising. More opportunities are available for people seeking secondary and higher education.

More people are receiving medical care. As a result, infant mortality rates, while still high, are declining and life expectancies are rising.

However, these positive achievements have added to a growing population problem. In 1994, Africa's population was 701 million; by 2010 it is expected to exceed 1.1 billion. Rapid population growth creates greater demand for health care and social services. Education costs rise annually because of the growing number of children. The need for more food increases the stress placed upon

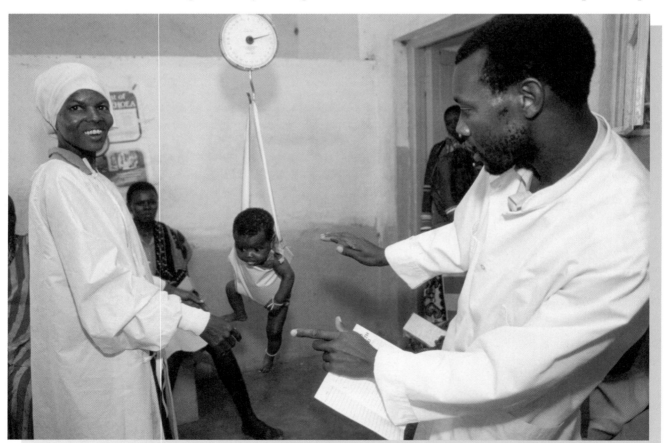

Figure 9.10

A doctor weighs a baby during a checkup at a clinic in Kenya. Post-natal health clinics have helped to reduce infant mortality rates in much of Africa. What might be the impact of a lowered infant mortality rate?

already fragile ecosystems. Growing populations place pressure on the basic infrastructure of water supplies, transportation facilities, and other essential services.

Africa is rich with abundant natural resources. The continent produces large volumes of chromium, plutonium, manganese, and cobalt, and there are still vast mineral resources to be explored. But the mining industry is primarily foreign-owned. The raw materials are often exported for processing, thereby limiting the opportunities for economic growth in Africa itself. Manufacturing and service sector industries have been slow to develop, and the continent suffers from chronic unemployment and under-employment.

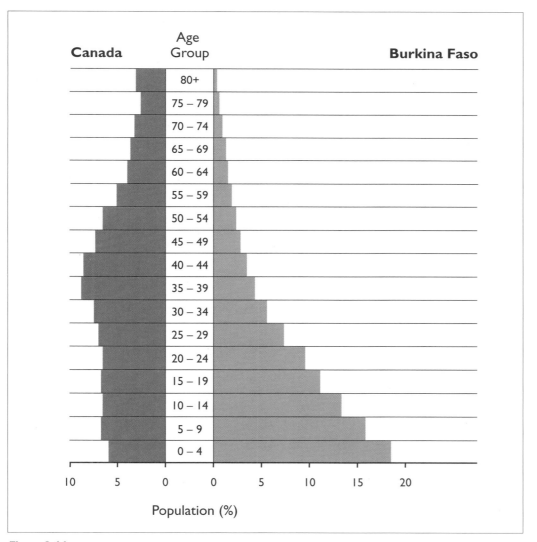

Figure 9.11

Population Pyramids for Canada and Burkina Faso, 2000. For what reasons might such differences exist in the shapes of the pyramids? (Source: US Census Bureau, International Data Base)

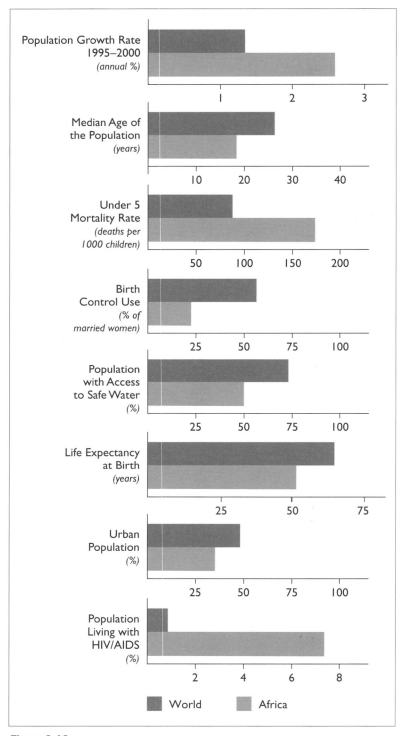

Figure 9.12

Population Comparisons: Africa and the World, 2000. Explain how each graph illustrates Africa's tenuous conditions.

AFRICAN INITIATIVES

The end of the Cold War has created a new order in Africa. The United States and the former Soviet Union are no longer jockeying for political advantage in the region. Instead of relying on international programs to direct their economic development, many Africans are now looking for African solutions to African problems. In almost every country in Africa, there are new human rights organizations monitoring activities without assistance from international agencies. A conference convened by African ministers of health in 1992 brought together grassroots groups with government officials and health care specialists to address the pressing health concerns in Africa.

Many countries are looking at ways to relieve chronic food shortages through long-term reconstruction programs rather than internationally sponsored relief programs. Environmental groups are actively protesting environmentally destructive projects and policies in an effort to reduce the damage being inflicted on this diverse land. In Kenya, for example, the Greenbelt Movement mobilized 50 000 women in a tree-planting project. There is also talk of placing more long-term emphasis on hardy crops, such as maize and millet, for local consumption and moving away from export crops for cash. Across the continent, the people of Africa are looking for their own solutions to their unique problems.

In 2002, the leaders of the **G-8**—the eight most powerful industrialized democratic nations—met at Kananaskis, Alberta, to support a new economic plan for Africa. It was the first time African leaders had been invited to attend a G-8 summit. Here, the Africans drafted a new plan—NEPAD (New Partnership for Africa's Development). It won G-8 support, with the promise of $6 billion in aid by 2006. The plan urges Western nations to increase African aid, investment, debt relief, and trade opportunities. In return, African nations hoping to benefit from this support must commit themselves to democracy, good governance, and peace.

Though drafted by African leaders such as South African president Thabo Mbeki, NEPAD was promoted vigorously by Canadian prime minister Jean Chrétien, who hosted the G-8 summit.

Voices Voices of Africa 2002

In 2002, Johannesburg, South Africa, was the site of a 10-day UN World Summit on Sustainable Development. This event drew more than 40 000 delegates from around the world, including approximately 100 heads of state. The summit focused the world's attention on the plight of African countries and the challenges that they face in the twenty-first century.

As you read the following quotations from African leaders, take note of the issues being addressed.

THABO MBEKI, PRESIDENT OF SOUTH AFRICA

"A global human society based on poverty for many and prosperity for a few, characterized by islands of wealth, surrounded by a sea of poverty, is unsustainable…. We do not accept that human society should be constructed on the basis of a savage principle of the survival of the fittest."

MU'AMMER GADDAFI, DICTATOR OF LIBYA

"It is quite hard and difficult for an African man to believe he will be treated on an equal footing by the colonizers and the racists. I don't believe they have changed their racist mentality."

AMARA ESSY, SECRETARY-GENERAL OF THE ORGANIZATION OF AFRICAN UNITY

"The new globalization, and profound advances in technology it has brought in, have left some in Africa handicapped and frightened that our continent is being disconnected from the movement which is forging new international relationships. If there is no significant improvement in conditions enabling us to participate properly in the new international trading systems, the marginalisation of our continent can make it the source of serious dangers for stability, security and development."

KOFI ANNAN, SECRETARY-GENERAL OF THE UNITED NATIONS

"In this age of globalization, even the richest and most powerful countries ignore the challenges and crises of other parts of the world at their own peril. At the same time, opportunities for growth and innovation exist everywhere…"

FESTUS G. MOGAE, PRESIDENT OF BOTSWANA

"Using aid as an instrument of promotion of economic activity in donor countries themselves distorts development policies in recipient countries. Aid policies should be flexible and forward looking and ensure equitable access by developing countries at various stages of development."

Responding

1. Identify the top three themes emerging from these comments. What do they tell you about the priorities of African leaders?
2. Which issue do you think is most critical to the future of Africa? Briefly state why.

In Review

1. a) What were (i) the benefits and (ii) the costs of colonialism for the imperial countries?

   b) What were (i) the benefits and (ii) the costs of colonialism for the colonies?

2. What factors led to the independence movements in Africa after the Second World War?

3. What economic problems exist in many parts of Africa?

4. In what ways is AIDS eroding the potential of the people of Africa?

5. What reasons are there to be optimistic about Africa's future?

6. What initiatives are African groups taking to solve the problems on their continent?

7. What might be a good way for the developed countries of the world to help African countries solve their own problems? Explain your answer.

South Africa

The Dutch were the first Europeans to arrive in the southern tip of Africa. They came to the area in 1652, followed by the French in 1688. Britain took possession of the Cape Colony in 1815, after a war with France. When Britain outlawed slavery in the colony in 1834, angry Dutch Boers (farmers) left the Cape to form their own republics in the interior—the Republic of Natal, the Orange Free State, and the Transvaal. But the British also expanded into the interior, annexing Natal in 1843 and dominating the locals through the use of military force.

With the discovery of diamonds in 1867 and gold in the 1880s, many Britons and Europeans flocked to the Orange Free State and the Transvaal. Here, they immediately came into conflict with the Boers. War was declared between the two sides in 1899 (see Chapter One, pages 21 to 23); it ended in 1902 with the defeat of the Boers by the British. An act of the British Parliament in 1910 joined the British and Boer colonies in the Union of South Africa. In 1926, South Africa became an independent dominion within the British Empire.

The ruling white minority of the new union was outnumbered by the native black population by more than ten to one. To ensure that white rule would continue, the new government enacted a series of laws and regulations. The Urban Areas Act of 1923 established separate residential areas for blacks and whites. Under **pass laws**, non-whites were required to carry documents that proved their residence in special reserves or resettlement camps that had been established for them; they were required to present these passbooks on demand. Over the years the number of restrictions on non-whites increased. As nationalist movements swept across the continent following the Second World War, the white South African government moved to tighten its grip over the largely non-white population.

APARTHEID BECOMES LAW

Apartheid was introduced in South Africa in 1948. This racial policy classified all residents of South Africa into four categories: white, black, coloured (people of mixed ancestry), or Asian. The purpose was to create two separate and distinct classes—a privileged white ruling class and an exploited, dependent, and subservient underclass. Whites controlled the political, educational, and economic institutions. Racial groups were forced into separate schools, workplaces, and residential areas. It was illegal for people of different races to marry or even to mix together in public places.

Apartheid was supported by the majority of the white population and by the country's social institutions. The Dutch Reform Church declared that "God divided humanity into races, languages, and nations.... Those who are culturally and spiritually advanced have a mission to leadership and protection of the less advanced." This "leadership and protection" included laws restricting blacks to menial and low-paying jobs and forcibly moving them to resettlement camps. To constrain native opposition to apartheid, the government limited the number of blacks who could live in urban areas where they could organize their resistance more easily. Many blacks were forced to live in native homelands. While these regions were granted some degree of self-rule, they were not free of South African control.

Figure 9.13
At the height of apartheid, this telephone booth in Cape Province, South Africa, proclaims that only whites may use it.

MAP STUDY

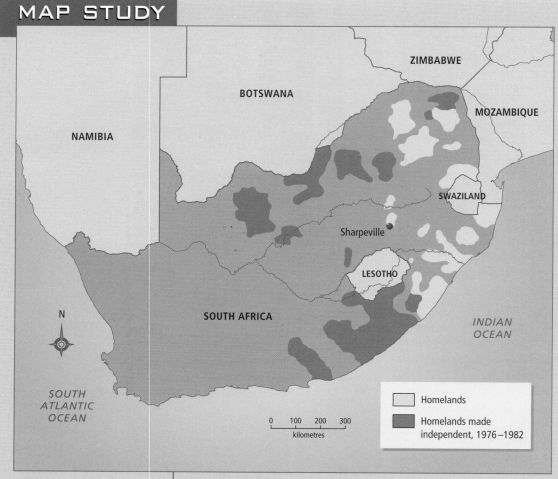

Figure 9.14
Black Homelands in South Africa, 1985

This map illustrates the black homelands of South Africa in 1985. "Homelands" for black South Africans were created when apartheid became the official policy. They were always located in areas of poor farmland. The high population densities of the homelands resulted in poor living conditions.

Interpreting

1. What generalization can you make about the locations of black homelands in South Africa?
2. What roles do you suppose the neighbouring countries of Botswana, Zimbabwe, and Mozambique played in the opposition to South Africa's racist policies?
3. Swaziland and Lesotho were given some autonomy as independent countries, but were still controlled by South Africa. What conditions allowed South Africa to dominate these places?

Figure 9.15

Sixty-nine people were killed in the Sharpeville massacre. The incident created an international furor. Many foreign companies withdrew their investments in South Africa, and the country withdrew from the Commonwealth.

OPPOSITION TO APARTHEID

After the Second World War, nationalist groups such as the African National Congress (ANC) began to attack racial discrimination in South Africa using non-violent resistance. They used boycotts, strikes, and demonstrations and openly defied segregation laws by entering "whites only" areas and using facilities designated for use by whites.

The government's response included arresting leaders such as the ANC's Nelson Mandela. Tensions reached a violent climax on 21 March 1960 during a demonstration outside a police station in Sharpeville. The police opened fire on the demonstrators; 249 people were shot, 69 of them fatally. In response, a crowd of 30 000 Africans marched into the heart of white Cape Town. A state of emergency was declared and 18 000 people were later arrested. In April, other repressive measures were introduced: all public meetings were banned, suspected dissidents were arrested and held indefinitely without warrants, black nationalist organizations like the African National Congress were banned and their leaders were arrested. It seemed that political change through non-violent protest had its limits.

Following the government ban on nationalist organizations, resistance groups

> "I...thought this apartheid was most stupid. We peel the European's potatoes, we bring up their children...but when it come to wages, to employment, we are called kaffirs."
>
> — Lilian Ngoyi, political activist, 1952

set up their headquarters in neighbouring countries. From there, they launched their violent attacks against the government. South African armed forces repeatedly raided Mozambique, Botswana, Zambia, and other border countries in search of the rebels.

During the 1970s and 1980s the violence escalated. Hundreds of demonstrators were killed in clashes with police and army forces. In response to the growing unrest, the white government eased some of the apartheid laws. The ban on inter-racial marriages was lifted and black labour unions were legalized. In 1984, coloureds and Asians were granted the right to vote for representatives to their own parliaments, although these bodies had little authority. Blacks, however, who made up 67 per cent of South Africa's population, were still denied voting rights. They responded with riots, strikes, violence and acts of sabotage against the white rulers. Moreover, different groups were openly divided on the most effective means of obtaining equality. The ANC, for example, had abandoned passive resistance as an ineffective method of producing change. In 1985, South African president P.W. Botha declared a state of emergency. Police now had sweeping powers to arrest hundreds of black nationalist leaders.

NETSURFER

WWW.MECCA.ORG/~CRIGHTS/DREAM.HTML

This site contains the text of the "I Have a Dream" speech delivered by Martin Luther King Jr. in 1963. Read the speech and reflect on why it is known as such a famous speech.

Civil Rights in the United States

Opposition to apartheid in South Africa was paralleled by another movement far away. In the years following the Second World War, the United States was racially segregated under a "separate but equal" policy. Blacks had separate facilities in all aspects of life, but they were rarely equal to those facilities enjoyed by the white population. This inequity was especially visible in schools; black schools were poorly funded compared to schools for white children.

Finally, in 1954, the Supreme Court demanded an end to segregation of schools. However, due to resistance to the decision, only 1 per cent of black students were attending racially integrated schools by the mid-1960s. During this time, black activists were working hard to change attitudes—by signing up black voters and demonstrating against unfair laws.

Martin Luther King Jr., a Baptist minister and native of Atlanta, Georgia, emerged as the leader of these non-violent protests. His "I Have a Dream" speech in the summer of 1963 remains one of the most powerful and evocative statements of the civil rights movement. King was assassinated in 1968. Riots and violence swept the nation throughout the mid- and late 1960s, but the process to end legally sanctioned discrimination could not be stopped. By the late 1980s, civil rights for blacks in the United States were guaranteed by law, and organizations such as the National Association for the Advancement of Colored People (NAACP) were organized and ready to protect the rights of black Americans in every sphere of life.

Figure 9.16
Thousands gathered to watch Martin Luther King Jr. deliver his "I Have a Dream" speech in Washington on 28 August 1963.

International Sanctions

In spite of the state of emergency, the South African government continued to ease some apartheid laws after 1985. In 1986, the pass laws were ended, and signs identifying separate facilities by race were removed. Non-white workers were no longer forced to pay more taxes than whites, and blacks were allowed to hold skilled jobs. More money was allocated to black education, although the school system remained segregated and unequal.

Much of this reform was the result of pressure by the international community. Many countries, including Canada, imposed **sanctions**—actions directed at a nation to force it to meet its legal obligations—against South Africa. Canada restricted business loans and investment in South Africa and reduced trade with the country as a means of applying pressure on the government. Several multinational corporations, such as General Motors and Kodak, withdrew their operations. Sanctions were supported by some African leaders, including Archbishop Desmond Tutu, the head of the Anglican Church in South Africa. As reforms increased, international sanctions were gradually lifted.

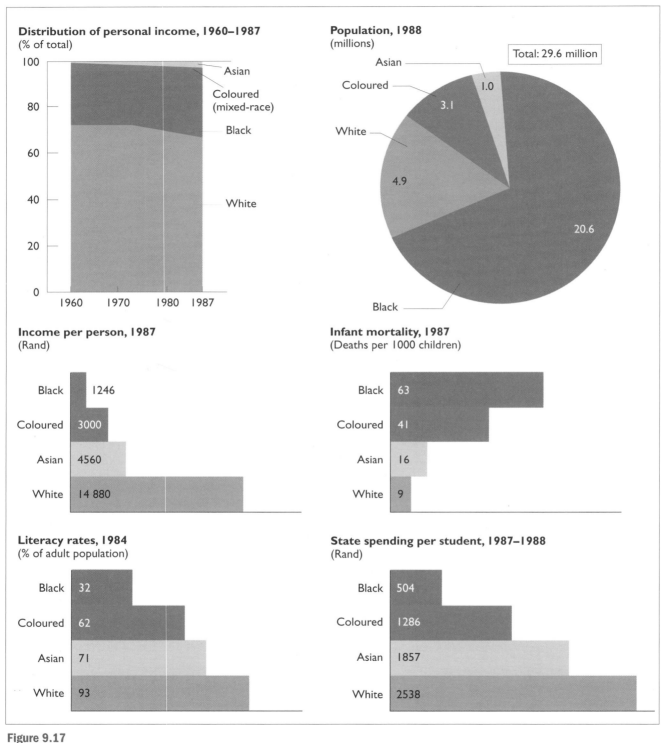

Distribution of personal income, 1960–1987
(% of total)

Population, 1988
(millions)

Total: 29.6 million

Income per person, 1987
(Rand)

Black	1246
Coloured	3000
Asian	4560
White	14 880

Infant mortality, 1987
(Deaths per 1000 children)

Black	63
Coloured	41
Asian	16
White	9

Literacy rates, 1984
(% of adult population)

Black	32
Coloured	62
Asian	71
White	93

State spending per student, 1987–1988
(Rand)

Black	504
Coloured	1286
Asian	1857
White	2538

Figure 9.17

Apartheid Statistics: Selected Data on Racial Inequality in the 1980s. Explain how each of these graphs illustrates the racial inequities that existed in South Africa at this time in its history. (Source: *The Economist*)

Profile

Lilian Ngoyi (1911-1980)

Figure 9.18
Lilian Ngoyi

As a young person growing up in Pretoria, South Africa, Lilian Masediba was aware of the poverty endured by black South Africans—it was the poverty that she, her family, and their black neighbours endured daily. After only one year in high school, Lilian went to work to support her parents and brother. She married, but her husband died, leaving her to raise a three-year-old daughter.

> *"I said to myself that we are definitely a nation…. But something must be done, not prayers alone."*
>
> — Lilian Ngoyi (as a young woman)

> *"I will fight for freedom to the bitter end. I am determined. It does not matter what. I am determined to fight for a multi-racial South Africa where we can live in peace."*
>
> — Lilian Ngoyi, 1954

Lilian Ngoyi's life as a worker and mother began to change in 1952 when she joined the Garment Workers' Union and saw the great impact of the African National Congress (ANC) on South African workers. She joined the ANC and, within a year, was elected to that organization's National Executive.

She also became president of the ANC's Women's League and, later, president of the Federation of South African Women. Her leadership style was simple and uncomplicated—a manner born out of harsh experience and a keen intelligence. As an orator, she had few equals. She always advocated a peaceful end to apartheid, denouncing violence as "stupid and impractical."

Lilian Ngoyi's political activities did not make for a calm and peaceful life. In 1956, she led 20 000 women in a protest against the pass laws, an action that resulted in her being charged with high treason. She was still out on bail for that case when the state of emergency was declared in 1960 following the Sharpeville massacre; Ngoyi was arrested and spent the time in prison in solitary confinement. On her release in 1961, she was placed under an order that prohibited her from attending meetings, restricted her to her immediate community (Soweto), and forbade her to speak to the press or anyone about apartheid or the situation in South Africa. Each time the ban ended, her activities immediately gave rise to a new ban. She became a symbol of resistance and an inspiration to young revolutionaries, especially young women.

When Lilian Ngoyi died in 1980, the black newspapers of the day reflected on how her life had symbolized black women's struggle for human rights and the struggle of women for a better life everywhere.

Responding

1. Would being a black woman in South Africa during apartheid make one more or less likely to be a revolutionary? Explain your answer.

2. Lilian Ngoyi was a powerful speaker who was described as having the ability to "toss an audience on her little finger." What are the characteristics of effective orators?

3. Lilian Ngoyi died about 14 years before the ANC formally took power in South Africa. How would you describe her contributions to the end of apartheid and white-rule in that country? Explain your ideas.

Canada's Opposition to Apartheid

In the years following the Second World War, Canada supported independence movements in non-white countries around the world. In South Africa, however, a policy of "constructive engagement" remained in effect. Officially, Canada's rhetoric denounced apartheid, yet trade between the two countries continued to grow. In 1977, conditions began to change. Canada was elected to the UN Security Council and felt obligated to apply different standards in its relationships with other countries. Limited economic sanctions were imposed on South Africa, including an arms embargo and restricted sports contacts.

The election of Prime Minister Brian Mulroney in 1984 brought about more significant change. The government responded to the stories of brutality in South Africa and imposed tough economic sanctions on that country, including closing trade offices, adopting a Code of Conduct for Canadian companies operating in South Africa, and preventing South African athletes and officials from entering Canada. In addition, the Mulroney government placed South Africa on the international agenda by raising the issue of apartheid at international meetings and conferences. These actions helped to stir international outrage against apartheid and to bring about the election of a new leader—one who promised reform.

THE REFORM MOVEMENT

In 1989, F.W. de Klerk became president of South Africa. He promised a program of gradual reforms aimed at reducing black grievances and ending the civil strife that gripped the country. Within a year, de Klerk repealed laws that maintained racial segregation in public facilities. He lifted the ban on the African National Congress and freed its leader, Nelson Mandela, who had been jailed for 27 years. In June 1991, the government ended the hated Population Registration Act, which officially segregated South Africans, and introduced new laws to end the partitioning of South Africa into separate racial states. In return, the ANC agreed to suspend its violent activities and to work toward a negotiated settlement of racial issues.

Many whites opposed de Klerk's initiatives. They feared that democracy, which would place the black majority in a powerful position, would lead to retaliation by blacks against whites. Fears of violence were magnified in the early 1990s when rival black groups clashed, leaving many black Africans dead. In response, extremist white groups launched their own violent campaigns designed to intimidate the reformers.

In 1993, against a background of continuing violence and bloodshed, the de Klerk government and the ANC reached an historic agreement. The country's first democratic elections, with voting privileges for all citizens regardless of colour, were announced for April 1994. The international community supported the decision and took the first steps toward lifting all economic sanctions. In January 1994, Nelson Mandela launched an historic campaign for the presidency of South Africa against the incumbent de Klerk. Voting began on April 26. Over the next three days all people of South Africa were free to cast their ballots. More than 300 observers from other nations monitored the election and declared it free and fair.

The results of South Africa's elections were announced on May 6. Mandela's African National Congress captured 63 per cent of the vote, while de Klerk's National Party received 20 per cent. On May 9, the 400-member National Assembly chose

"[I]f there is no progress in the dismantling of apartheid, relations with South Africa may have to be severed absolutely."

– Canadian prime minister Brian Mulroney, speaking at a meeting of the Commonwealth Heads of Government, 1985

Nelson Mandela as the new president.

Not all blacks recognized the ANC as the legitimate voice of black South Africa. Violence broke out between the ANC and the Inkatha Freedom Party, another black, primarily Zulu, nationalist group. The animosity threatened to undermine South Africa's transition to democracy. However, public support for Mandela was overwhelming. Heads of state and other dignitaries from around the world joined the celebrations at his inauguration on May 10. In a spirit of co-operation and harmony, Mandela formed his cabinet, including former president de Klerk as a vice-president. Apartheid no longer existed. Now the challenge was to build a new South Africa.

Figure 9.19
This woman is voting in Transkei, South Africa, in her nation's first post-apartheid election, which took place in 1994.

Profile   Nelson Mandela (1918-)

Figure 9.20
Nelson Mandela

Nelson Mandela was once known as "the most famous prisoner in the world." From 1963 until 1990, Mandela was imprisoned in South Africa for leading the black majority's fight against apartheid. During his incarceration, he became an international figure with a worldwide following of supporters.

After reading about Nelson Mandela, decide which of his qualities contributed most to his stature as a world leader for democracy and human rights.

"The white government must legalize us, treat us like a political party and negotiate with us. Until they do we will have to live with the armed struggle. It is useless to simply carry on talking."

— Nelson Mandela, 1960

"I do not deny that I planned sabotage. We had to either accept inferiority or fight against it by violence. When my sentence has been completed...I will still be moved to take

up again, as best I can, the struggle for removal of injustices until they are finally abolished once and for all."

— Nelson Mandela, to the court upon his conviction, 1963

"No serious political organisation will ever talk peace when an aggressive war is being waged against it. No proud people will ever obey orders from those who have humiliated and dishonoured them for so long."

— Nelson Mandela, in response to offers of a political deal in exchange for his release from prison, 1989

Nelson (Rolihlahia) Mandela was born a member of the Tembu people of South Africa, the son of a Tembu chief. He attended university in Johannesburg, where he earned a degree in law and set up South Africa's first black legal practice.

Mandela's battle against racial injustice began when he joined the African National Congress in 1944. He helped to co-ordinate the 1952 Defiance Campaign of passive resistance against the white regime's apartheid laws. When the Defiance Campaign was brutally suppressed by authorities, Mandela was arrested. His nine-month sentence was suspended, but he was banned from attending public meetings or taking part in ANC activities. In 1956, Mandela participated in the Congress of the People's Freedom Charter, which declared that "South Africa belongs to all who live in it, black and white." Mandela, along with 156 other South Africans, was arrested and tried for treason. He mounted his own eloquent defence and was acquitted, along with his co-defendants.

Following the Sharpeville massacre in 1960 (see page 295), Mandela and other ANC leaders decided that non-violent protest was ineffective in the face of such government brutality. Mandela organized the Spear of the Nation movement and led a series of violent acts of sabotage and guerrilla activity. He was forced to go underground but was eventually arrested and imprisoned for five years for incitement of violence. In 1964, after a second trial, he was convicted of sabotage and treason and sentenced to life in prison.

Mandela spent the next 27 years in captivity. While in prison, he fought against abuse and brutality, defended prisoners' rights, and confronted authorities. He repeatedly refused offers of freedom in exchange for a political deal with the government. His convictions elevated him to mythical status among many black South Africans.

During Nelson Mandela's incarceration, his wife Winnie, whom he had married in 1958, carried his message to the world. In 1982, an international campaign was launched to free Mandela. The United Nations Security Council demanded his freedom. World leaders applied diplomatic and political pressure for Mandela's release. Musicians, writers, and dramatists championed his cause. Bowing to the pressure, the government offered to release Mandela, but on their terms. Again Mandela refused.

In 1988, the year of Mandela's seventieth birthday, demands for his release escalated amidst much international publicity. Mandela was moved to more comfortable facilities as his health began to deteriorate. Finally, in 1990, in the face of mounting civil unrest and external pressure, President F.W. de Klerk ordered the release of the man who had come to symbolize the future freedom of millions of black South Africans. The government pledged reforms to create an equal and democratic South Africa. Mandela committed his leadership to negotiating a new order for the country. As a result of their efforts, Mandela and de Klerk were jointly awarded the Nobel Peace Prize in 1993.

In 1994, Nelson Mandela was elected the first black president of South Africa. His autobiography, *Long Walk to Freedom*, written during the years he was in prison and smuggled out by friends, was published the same year. Mandela led the government during its first years in power.

Responding

1. How might Mandela's education have led him toward the political path he chose?
2. Why do you think Mandela chose the path of peaceful resistance? Explain your answer.
3. What kinds of qualities are necessary to endure imprisonment and not give up hope for one's cause? What would you have done, faced with such circumstances?

Skill Path

Delivering an Oral Presentation

Expressing your ideas orally may be one of the most useful communication skills you ever develop. As with written material, oral communication entails some basic steps — researching, writing, organizing, rehearsing, delivering the presentation, and responding to audience feedback.

Step One: Research Your Topic

The more prepared you are for an oral presentation, the more confident you will likely feel. Preparation involves becoming completely familiar with your topic and the issues it raises. As with any research paper or position paper, the first step is research. You must first select a topic, then locate sources of information from which to draw your facts. The Skill Path features in Chapters Five and Six (pages 166 and 195) will give you guidance on writing a thesis statement and developing research strategies.

Step Two: Write Your Script

The content of an oral presentation is often called a "script." Its structure is similar to that of a position paper. You state your thesis in the opening paragraph; offer your supporting arguments, with substantiating evidence, in the following paragraphs; and conclude by summarizing your main points.

However, oral presentations offer more flexibility than do most position papers. For example, you could begin with a dramatic quotation, a statistic, or a personal story. All these devices help to seize and hold your audience's attention. For example, if your thesis is that nationalist movements must never resort to violence, you could open with an arresting quotation from poetry or fiction that underscores this point. You could conclude by appealing to the audience for a response or action, or by reinforcing your argument with a prediction or a challenge. Structure your script so that you can recall it easily by referring to cue cards containing key words, phrases, and concepts.

Step Three: Create Visual Aids

Use visual aids to complement your oral presentation — to add interest or to clarify and punctuate the points of your argument. For example, a presentation on the US civil rights movement or on the emergence of South African leader Nelson Mandela would be enhanced by photographs from the period.

Use your visuals at key points in your presentation to vary the pace. Practise with each image to ensure that it will inform the audience and convey the message you intend.

Step Four: Rehearse and Present

Rehearse your script using the equipment you plan to use on the day of the presentation. Rehearse until you feel completely comfortable with the material and have committed most of it to memory. This will help you to avoid simply reading from your cue cards. Time your presentation to ensure it is within the limits set by your teacher. (Also, make sure you account for a short period of time at the end for questions from the audience.)

Arrive early for your presentation so that you can set up the equipment you plan to use. When it is your turn to present, make sure you stand in a position where everyone can see you. Face your audience when you speak, and project clearly and loudly so that even the people at the back can hear. Make eye contact with the audience members to engage them in the presentation. Smile and show enthusiasm for your topic. Respond to questions politely, returning to some of your main points for emphasis.

Practise Your Skill

1. In pairs, research, plan, prepare, and orally present one of the following events, using some combination of reference notes, visuals, and technology. Include information on the major participants, the main issue or cause, the course of action, any resolution(s), and the present situation.

- The Boer War, 1899
- Ghana's declaration of independence from Britain, 1957
- Martin Luther King Jr.'s "I Have a Dream Speech," 1963
- N. Mandela elected as president of South Africa, 1994

2. Select one individual discussed in Chapter Nine and prepare a three-minute presentation outlining that person's main accomplishments. Include information about where the person was born, early influences, and the impact of his or her achievements.

Figure 9.21

Johannesburg, South Africa. Conditions in larger cities in South Africa deteriorated in the years following democratization in 1994—there were simply not enough jobs to go around.

BUILDING A NEW SOUTH AFRICA

Mandela's ANC government faced some difficult challenges. About 33 per cent of blacks were unemployed, whereas the unemployment rate for whites was only 3 per cent. Moreover, average incomes for whites were nine times higher than for blacks. Clearly, major restructuring of the economy was required. The government sought to ease the fears of white South Africans and international investors by trying to balance plans for reconstruction and development with financial restraint. Their Reconstruction and Development Plan allotted large amounts of money to the improvement of basic health care—desperately needed in the former homelands—and to the creation of jobs and housing. Providing electricity to 350 000 homes, and water services to 3.5 million people, were seen as important steps in moving toward equality in living standards.

Mandela's government also had to deal with animosities created by decades of apartheid. The government set up the Truth and Reconciliation Commission to consider the widespread allegations of human rights violations and atrocities committed by former governments under apartheid. Presided over by Archbishop Desmond Tutu, the 17-member commission conducted hearings and investigated victims' accounts of incidents. In the hopes of fostering healing within the nation, the commission generally provided amnesty for those who confessed. The commission released its report in 1998 and condemned actions of all the political organizations during apartheid, including the ANC.

In spite of the best efforts of the ANC government, social and economic progress in South Africa did not match the expectations of the population. Blacks had flocked to urban areas seeking jobs; shantytowns appeared on the outskirts of major cities like Johannesburg and Cape Town, crime rates soared, and social services became overloaded. HIV/AIDS infection rates in South Africa were the highest in the world. The country has the highest incarceration rates of all countries. In 1999, the disillusionment led to attacks against white farmers who had resisted an ambitious land reform scheme designed to put more land under black ownership.

Mandela, who had announced that he would not run for re-election in 1999, stepped down as party leader of the ANC in late 1997 and was succeeded by Deputy President Thabo Mbeki. Mandela's presidency came to an end in June 1999 when the ANC won legislative elections and selected Mbeki as South Africa's next president. One hundred years had passed since the start of the Boer War. In the intervening years, the challenge to build a new South Africa had been met and surpassed.

In Review

1. Explain the policy of apartheid in South Africa.

2. Why did the African National Congress abandon its policy of non-violent protest against apartheid in the 1960s?

3. What reforms were introduced in the mid-1980s? What prompted their introduction?

4. a) What was the purpose of sanctions imposed by the international community?

   b) Why were sanctions gradually eased?

5. What measures did F.W. de Klerk take to end the civil unrest in South Africa?

6. What were the results of South Africa's first free elections?

7. In your opinion, has the democratization of South Africa made any real difference in the lives of the ordinary people of the country? Explain your answer.

Summary

In the late 1800s, Europe's systematic colonization of Africa was gathering force. By 1914, seven European nations controlled most of Africa, and its political boundaries bore no resemblance to its ancient past. Nationalism finally swept the continent in the years following the Second World War, when a new generation of Africans began fighting to return Africa to African rule. The movement toward independence was supported by the United Nations, the United States, the Soviet Union, and even by Europe itself. By 1957, Ghana had declared its independence from Britain. Other independence movements followed—some peaceful, some bloody.

In South Africa, black activists led one of the most important human rights battles in the twentieth century. There, a system of institutionalized racism known as apartheid had been in effect since 1948. Most members of the black majority lived in poverty, with few rights, while the white minority enjoyed full political rights, mobility, and a comparatively high standard of living. International pressure on South Africa forced it to dismantle apartheid in the 1980s. In 1994, the nation held its first free elections, and the anti-apartheid African National Congress captured the majority vote. Its leader, Nelson Mandela, became South Africa's first black president.

As a continent, Africa continues to face social, political, and economic challenges. Hunger remains a problem, AIDS has taken a huge toll, and Africa still has a poorer standard of living than most areas of the world. As the twenty-first century opened, Africans were engaged in meeting these challenges—and steering their own course to the future.

Viewpoints

ISSUE: Is colonialism responsible for Africa's problems?

Background

Africa is a continent mired in poverty. Much of the region is politically unstable. Repeated droughts threaten the survival of many of Africa's people. Widespread environmental destruction is a constant danger. AIDS is destroying whole generations of people. Africa's continuing crises threaten the region's prospects for long-term economic development.

Debate continues to rage about the origins of Africa's problems. Many experts believe the lasting effects of colonialism are to blame. In the first reading, Charles O. Chikeka, an African-American Associate Professor of history, argues that colonialism created the economic dependency that remains with Africa to the present day. In the second reading, Finnish scientist Mai Palmberg—a supporter of black liberation groups in southern Africa—continues this theme by exploring the role of "development aid" in perpetuating dependence. In the third reading, P.T. Bauer, a professor at the London School of Economics and Political Science, argues that colonial rule is not the cause of African poverty.

Read these three viewpoints carefully, and answer the questions that follow. (You may want to refer to the Skill Path "Analysing a Reading" on page 14 before beginning.)

Remnants of the colonial heritage

At the present time, most African states have achieved flag or legal independence but not real or genuine independence. The colonial heritage, which in the past divided the African continent into spheres of influence for European hegemony, has continued and, in effect, has undermined the efforts of Pan-Africanists to achieve regional as well as continental unity and cooperation. The structures of economic dependency, which were established in the colonial times, have endured longer than the European powers' actual presence.

Foreign interests still control major sectors of African economies. Expatriate administrators, bureaucrats, businessmen, scientists, and technical experts continue to make vital decisions that affect the economic and political destinies of African states. In many fields of economic activity, such as trade, investment capital, marketing, monetary and fiscal management, and distribution,

European states still exercise their dominance over African economies. ...the plight of the underdeveloped countries ... is doubly vulnerable because of the two-fold concentration of their exports in terms of commodities and in terms of markets.

For example, not only is each African country dependent on the fortunes of a very narrow range of export products, so that a serious decline in market demand for any one product is likely to become a major problem, but in addition, the prosperity of most of these states is very much bound up with that of one or two principal industrial powers to which they sell the bulk of their exports. The critics of these continued ties between the ex-imperial powers and the new states have expressed legitimate concerns over African states' dependence on European states for markets, aid, capital, technology, and defense. The term dependency syndrome has been used to characterize this situation. After examining the impact of foreign influence in general and the dominant presence of the former colonizers in their former colonial preserves, one alarmed African intellectual commented:

We are undergoing a second colonization: our present leaders are just like the old tribal chiefs who signed pacts with colonizers for a few beads.

Friendship and military pacts are now penciled up in return for guns, aid, or cash loans. Africa is up for grabs.

Source: Charles Ohiri Chikeka, *Decolonization Process in Africa During the Post-war Era, 1960-1990.* Queenston: The Edwin Mellen Press, 1998, pp. 247-248.

The exploitation of Africa

The then Prime Minster of England, Harold Macmillan, in a speech in Cape Town on 3 February 1960, said that "a wind of change" was blowing over the continent and that the main question now was whether the peoples of Asia and Africa would turn to the East or to the West, to Communism or to "the free world." In December of the same year Charles de Gaulle, then President of France, spoke to army officers in Blida in Algeria. He asked them to try to understand what was happening in the world, to understand that the old methods of direct control, based on arms and the colonial state apparatus, had become impossible to practice, the new way had to be found so that "the activities of France in Algeria can continue." In March 1961 the US President John F. Kennedy launched what was called "The Alliance for Progress" for the Latin American states. To prevent the revolutionary example of Cuba becoming contagious the Latin American states were to embark on some social and economic reforms with the aid of US dollars.

These three speeches show how the leaders of the Western world understood that new forms for imperialism had to be created when direct colonial control was no longer politically possible. The question was how to continue the exploitation of the Third World as cheaply and as easily as possible, and also to prevent the "loss" of more countries than China, that is, a change in Socialist direction. Independent Africa became a field of experiments for neo-colonial policies....

Economic dependence

The independent African states got their own national flags but they inherited economic dependence. This dependence should be used by the imperialist forces to further their aims. The dependence rests on two pillars, a continued colonial division of labour and foreign control of key sectors of the economy.

But investments and trade are not the only form of dependence. "Development aid" has become an important instrument for the neo-colonial policies. The words "development aid" give an impression that it is an unselfish sacrifice from the rich to the poor. But only if we look at it as part of the total economic relations between underdeveloped countries and industrialized capitalist states can we judge the real function of development aid....

An overwhelming part of all development aid goes to infrastructure, that is, to the preconditions for modern production. Infrastructure means, on the one hand, economic investments, such as communications, telecommunications, airports, harbours, energy supply, irrigation projects etc., and, on the other hand, social investments such as schools, hospitals and administrative buildings. Of course, such projects need not be worthless for the receiving country. But, in the first place, they are designed to reinforce export dependence instead of furthering domestic use of the raw materials. In the second place, these investments are, to quote [L.D. Black], a North American spokesman for development aid, "an indispensable precondition for the capacity to attract foreign private investment"....

Unequal exchange

To all this must be added the losses incurred by the Third World countries from deteriorated terms of trade. This means that most raw materials, which we have seen make up the major share of the exports from underdeveloped countries, have decreasing prices on the world market, whereas the prices of manufactured goods, which the underdeveloped countries import, steadily rise....

This "unequal exchange" means that for the Third World the loss is often more than what is "given" in development aid. Another difficulty for the economy of Third World countries is the fact that they do not control the sale of their raw materials, but this is subject to speculation on the raw materials exchanges in New York and London....

As long as the majority of the Third World countries believe that changes can be made in co-operation with those industrialized countries which have created and maintained the Third World's underdevelopment, the neo-colonial policies have not completely lost the day....

Political organization is decisive for development in the progressive states. Only through a popular basis and control of political life can the people decide what will be produced and for whom.

Source: *The Struggle for Africa* by Mai Palmberg, published by Zed Books, 1983, London. Reprinted with permission of Zed Books Ltd.

Colonialism is not to blame

About ten years ago a student group at Cambridge published a pamphlet on the subject of the moral obligations of the West to the Third World. The following was its key passage:

We took the rubber from Malaya, the tea from India, raw materials from all over the world and gave almost nothing in return.

This is as nearly the opposite of the truth as one can find. The British took the rubber to Malaya and the tea to India. There were no rubber trees in Malaya or anywhere in Asia (as suggested by their botanical name, Hevea braziliensis) until about 100 years ago, when the British took the first rubber seeds there out of the Amazon jungle. From these sprang the huge rubber industry—now very largely Asian-owned. Tea-plants were brought to India by the British somewhat earlier; their origin is shown in the botanical name Camilla sinensis, as well as in the phrase "all the tea in China"....

Far from the West having caused the poverty in the Third World, contact with the West has been the principal agent of material progress there.

Large parts of West Africa were...transformed...as a result of Western contacts. Before 1890 there was no cocoa production in the Gold Coast or Nigeria, only very small production of cotton and groundnuts and small exports of palm oil and palm kernels. By the 1950s all these had become staples of world trade. They were produced by Africans on African-owned properties. But this was originally made possible by Westerners who established public security and introduced modern methods of transport and communications. Over this period imports both of capital goods and of mass consumer goods for African use also rose from insignificant amounts to huge volumes. The changes were reflected in government revenues, literacy rates, school attendance, public health, life expectation, infant mortality and many other indicators.

Massive transformation

Statistics by themselves can hardly convey the far-reaching transformation which took place over this period in West Africa.... For instance, slave trading and slavery were still widespread at the end of the nineteenth century. They had practically disappeared by the end of the First World War. Many of the worst endemic and epidemic diseases for which West Africa was notorious throughout the nineteenth century had disappeared by the Second World War....

The role of Western contacts in the material progress of Black Africa deserves further notice. As late as the second half of the nineteenth century Black Africa was without even the simplest, most basic ingredients of modern social and economic life. These were brought there by Westerners over the last hundred years or so. This is true of such fundamentals as public security and law and order; wheeled traffic (Black Africa never invented the wheel) and mechanical transport (before the arrival of Westerners, transport in Black Africa was almost entirely by human muscle); roads, railways and man-made ports; the application of science and technology to economic activity; towns with substantial buildings, clean water and sewerage facilities; public health care, hospitals and the control of endemic and epidemic diseases; formal education. These advances resulted from peaceful commercial contacts.

Wherever local conditions have permitted it, commercial contacts with the West, and generally established by the West, have eliminated the worst diseases, reduced or even eliminated famine, extended life expectation and improved living standards....

Colonialism is not at fault

Whatever one thinks of colonialism, it cannot be held responsible for Third World poverty. Some of the most backward countries never were colonies, as for instance Afghanistan, Tibet, Nepal, Liberia. Ethiopia is perhaps an even more telling example (it was an Italian colony for only six years in its long history). Again, many of the Asian and African colonies progressed very rapidly during colonial rule, much more so than the independent countries in the same area. At present one of the few remaining European colonies is Hong Kong—whose prosperity and progress should be familiar. [Note: Since 1997, Hong Kong has been a special administrative region of China.] It is plain that colonial rule has not been the cause of Third World poverty.

Nor is the prosperity of the West the result of colonialism. The most advanced and the richest countries never had colonies, including Switzerland and the Scandinavian countries; and some were colonies of others and were already very prosperous as colonies, as for instance North America and Australia. The prosperity of the West was generated by its own peoples and was not taken from others. The European countries were already materially far ahead of the areas where they established colonies....

The allegations that external trade, and especially imports from the West, are damaging to the populations of the Third World reveal a barely disguised condescension towards the ordinary people there, and even contempt for them. The people, of course, want the imports. If they did not the imported goods could not be sold. Similarly, the people are prepared to produce for export to pay for these imported goods. To say that these processes are damaging is to argue that people's preferences are of no account in organizing their own lives....

Source: *Equality, the Third World* and *Economic Delusion* by P.T. Bauer, George Weidenfeld & Nicolson Limited, London, 1981.

Analysis and Evaluation

1. What specific evidence does Chikeka offer to support his contention that Africa has suffered from economic dependence?

2. According to Palmberg, what is the other form of dependence?

3. What benefits did the West provide Africa, according to Bauer?

4. Identify examples in any of these readings of what we would consider racist language, and describe why you feel it should be identified as such.

5. In Bauer's view, why is colonialism not a cause of African poverty?

6. Decide which of the viewpoints you tend to support, and explain why. If you agree with neither, state the position you do support and explain it. Be sure to use specific information from this textbook, the readings, and other sources to support your position.

Chapter Analysis

MAKING CONNECTIONS

1. What were some similarities between colonialism in Africa and in North America? What were some important differences?

2. What are the most important problems facing Africans? Brainstorm a list of 10 significant problems, rank the problems, and provide justification for the top three on your list.

3. For a number of years, South Africa was shunned by the rest of the world. Conduct research to investigate South Africa's role in the world today, looking at its contributions in such areas as sports, culture, international politics, and business. Prepare a report to communicate your findings.

DEVELOPING YOUR VOICE

4. Is the colonial history of Africa responsible for the poverty and economic problems the continent faces today? If so, what obligations do the former imperial powers have toward these countries? Discuss this issue in class.

5. Debate the statement: "Nothing has really changed in Africa. Political imperialism has simply become economic imperialism."

6. Create a role-playing situation in which several students act as government officials in an imperial country, and an equal number of students act as African nationalist leaders in a colony. Working together, propose a plan for a smooth transition of power from imperial rule to African self-government.

RESEARCHING THE ISSUES

7. Research an African country of your choice to determine the major issues in its history since the Second World War. Prepare a case study based on your findings.

8. Do enough research to find two examples of African nations (other than Ghana) that experienced peaceful independence processes. Describe what happened in each case.

9. Find several photographs of places and people in Africa in magazines, newspapers, and books. What impressions are created by these photos? Write a one-page essay on the impact of the media on our perceptions of Africa.

10. Research one of the problems facing the countries of Africa today. Possible topics include population growth, desertification, urbanization, and AIDS. Prepare a three-page essay detailing the nature of the problem, its impact on countries and people, and possible solutions.

11. Research Canada's role in helping to dismantle apartheid in South Africa, beginning with the work of John Diefenbaker, who was prime minister from 1958 to 1963.

12. Find out more about the history and activities of the National Association for the Advancement of Colored People. List its top five contributions to race relations, explaining why you think each contribution has been important.

13. Investigate the progress of the New Partnership for Africa's Development (NEPAD) by visiting the official Web site at www.nepad.org and completing a brief profile of one of the member nations.

CHAPTER TEN

Asia at the Crossroads

Fireworks light up the sky over Victoria Harbour as Hong Kong is returned to Chinese control on 1 July 1997. For more than 150 years, the island had been a British territory. What emotions might spectators be feeling at such an event?

"What I did was a very ordinary thing. I declared that the British could not order me around in my own country."

— Mahatma Gandhi, 1947

"In the process of changing itself, Asia will change the world."

— David Crane, *The Toronto Star*, 26 July 1996

Overview

In the aftermath of the Second World War, many nations of the South Pacific and Southeast Asia were left with shattered economies and unstable governments. Out of the chaos emerged a handful of dynamic and prosperous industrial economies, along with some of the poorest nations in the world.

As the twentieth century closed, Japan remained the most powerful economy in Asia—despite its economic downturn in the early 1990s. It led a string of newly industrialized powers that were reshaping the economy of the region and of the world. Manufacturing nations such as Taiwan and Singapore gained international prominence as they challenged the economic supremacy of the West. China also gained economic momentum as its leaders embarked on a path of state-controlled capitalism and encouraged entrepreneurs for the first time.

Yet prosperity is only one aspect of such a diverse continent as Asia. Many nations remain mired in poverty, their economic development hampered by rapid population growth, political instability, and internal conflicts. China's treatment of Taiwan, as well as its poor human rights record, are still heavily criticized in the West. When the International Olympic Committee awarded China the 2008 Summer Games, the move was applauded by some as the start of a new era in global relations. Others viewed it as an outrage. As the twenty-first century opened, Asia was at a crossroads. No one, however, doubted that its role in the twenty-first century would be significant.

Focus Questions
1. In what ways did the Second World War affect economic development in Asia?
2. What was the role of nationalism in the independence movements in Asia after 1945?
3. Why have some Asian nations experienced economic success while others have not?
4. What characteristics of China suggest that it could be a world superpower?

The End of Imperialism

The struggle for political and military power has been an overriding theme in the recent history of Asia. During the age of imperialism, all of South and Southeast Asia, with the exception of Thailand, was under the control of European powers. Japan had its own imperialist ambitions, expanding into Formosa and Korea in the nineteenth century. During the 1930s, Japan renewed its intentions to dominate the region. By 1942, during the height of the Second World War, Japan controlled most of Southeast Asia until its surrender to the Allies in 1945.

NATIONALIST MOVEMENTS
The end of the Second World War signalled the end of European colonial rule. The Italian and Japanese Empires disappeared as a result of their military defeats. Over the next 30 years, the remaining empires of Britain, France, Spain, Portugal, the

Netherlands, and Belgium were dissolved as their colonies gained independence and became sovereign states.

There were several reasons for the dramatic events. Many colonial regiments served alongside the Allies in the war. Their participation raised the hopes of colonial peoples for political freedom in the postwar world. Hope was also fuelled by the promises of the Atlantic Charter drafted by Winston Churchill and Franklin Roosevelt in 1941, which promoted sovereignty and self-government for all nations. This coincided with strong nationalist movements in the colonies. Led by a new generation of European-educated leaders, the colonies demanded the right to rule themselves.

Many European leaders supported these independence movements. The experience of the Second World War led many people in Europe to oppose imperialism philosophically; they were also unable to justify it economically as they struggled to rebuild their own countries after six years of war. Britain was prepared to grant independence to new pro-Western governments. The other European colonial powers were in similar economic positions, although France and the Netherlands did not give up their colonies without a struggle.

Following the war, the United States and the Soviet Union emerged as the dominant world powers. Both countries wanted to see the breakup of the European empires. The United States, having waged its own war of independence against the British Empire in 1776, supported independence movements. But the US was also motivated by political and economic interests: if Europe lost its empires, the United States would have greater access to the former colonies' markets and resources. The Soviet Union, too, opposed European imperialism in principle, but it also recognized that a weakening of European power in Asia would provide greater opportunities for establishing communist rule in the new nations.

INDEPENDENCE GAINED

As nationalist movements gained momentum after 1945, the colonies in Asia became independent. Britain, which had the largest empire, withdrew from its empire without serious conflict. In 1947, under the provisions of the Indian Independence Act, India was partitioned and the independent states of India (primarily Hindu) and Pakistan (primarily Muslim) were formed. Ceylon (renamed Sri Lanka in 1972) and Burma (renamed Myanmar in 1989) gained their independence in 1948. Internal struggle in Malaya delayed its independence until 1957. In 1963, Malaya merged with other colonies to form the Federation of Malaysia.

France was less co-operative in dismantling its empire. After seven years of fighting in Vietnam against nationalist forces, France was defeated in 1954. At the Geneva Conference that year, France lost control of all of Indochina.

The Netherlands had controlled the Dutch East Indies since 1799, but the islands were abandoned to the Japanese in 1942. After the war, the Netherlands tried to re-establish colonial rule. But after four years of armed conflict, the Dutch government recognized the independent republic of Indonesia in 1949. Nationalist movements continued throughout Asia, Africa, and the Middle East. By the 1970s, most of the European empires had disappeared.

MAP STUDY

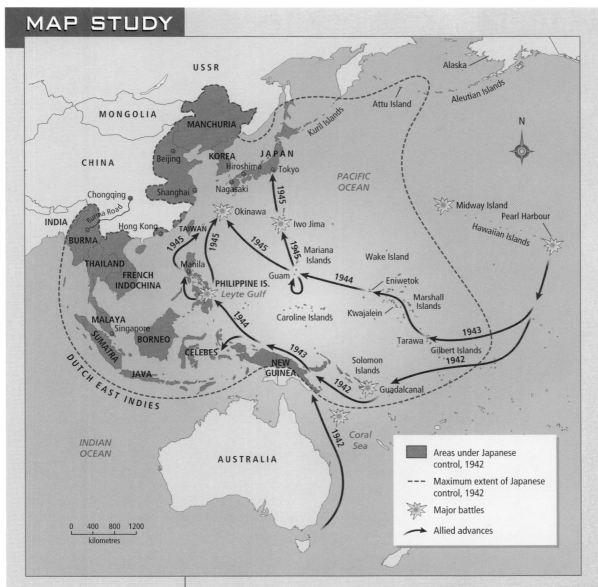

Figure 10.1

Areas Under Japanese Control during the Second World War

This map shows the Japanese-controlled regions of Asia in 1942. On June 4 of that year, the Americans defeated the Japanese in the Battle of Midway. It was considered a turning point in the Second World War, leading to the eventual Japanese surrender.

Interpreting

1. Describe the distribution of Japanese-controlled territories in 1942.
2. Using an atlas, identify the current countries that were once part of the Japanese Empire.
3. Using the map for ideas, speculate on why the Japanese attacked Pearl Harbor in 1941.
4. When you examine the progress of the Allied forces from 1942 to 1945 and look at the locations of the major battles, what military strategy did the Allies appear to be using?

MAP STUDY

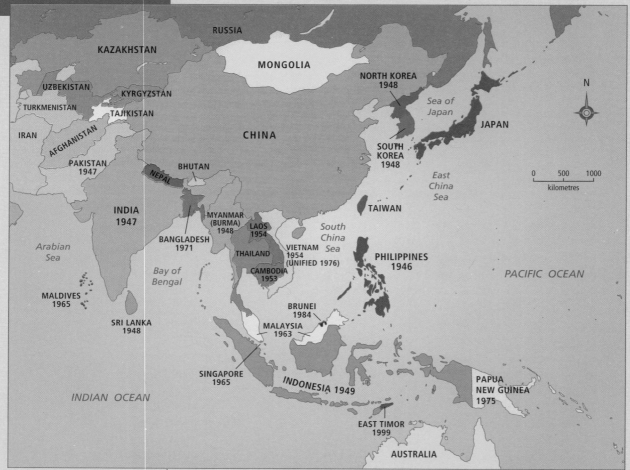

Figure 10.2
Asia, 2002

This map depicts Asia today. The dates represent the year each nation in the region gained independence from colonial rule.

Interpreting

1. A number of nations of this region are composed of islands united under one flag, such as Indonesia and Malaysia. What special problems might this create for these countries?

2. China and India are the two most populous countries of the world. What impact might these large populations have on nations such as Nepal, Bhutan, and Myanmar?

3. Vietnam was the focus of a great deal of international conflict between 1954 and 1973. Research the war in Vietnam to determine how it affected the other countries of the region. You could begin by revisiting Chapter 5.

THE PROBLEMS OF INDEPENDENCE

While independence marked the end of European political domination and economic exploitation, it created its own set of problems. Many of the boundaries of the former colonies had been arbitrarily determined by the colonial powers, without consideration to race, culture, or religion. In countries such as India, Ceylon, and Vietnam, civil wars erupted from the tensions that lay hidden beneath the blanket of colonial rule. In addition, many of the new nations inherited weak economies with limited resources. Most countries exported raw materials and agricultural products and imported manufactured goods from the home country. Raw materials were at the mercy of fluctuating world prices. Most countries faced declining revenues for the raw products they exported and increasing prices for the finished goods they imported.

Although the Asian nations had a new generation of educated leaders and trained administrators, the challenges of managing a new economy, society, and government often proved difficult. Most countries were experiencing the opportunities and responsibilities of democracy for the first time. In some cases inefficient, unstable, or corrupt democracies were replaced by military dictatorships.

Revolution and Conflict

Most revolutionary movements in Asia were rooted in nationalist campaigns against existing governments. In China, Indochina, the Philippines, and Malaysia, these governments were supported by the West. Nationalist forces, whether or not they were communist, often sought Soviet support in their opposition to these pro-Western governments.

As the Cold War developed, communist expansion in Asia became a source of great anxiety for the United States. American leaders feared that the Soviet Union and China were planning to spread communism throughout Southeast Asia. The US decided that a military alliance similar to NATO was needed to halt communist expansion in Asia. In 1954, the United States founded the **Southeast Asia Treaty Organization** (SEATO). Members included the United States, France, Great Britain, Australia, New Zealand, Thailand, Pakistan, and the Philippines.

While the Americans supported independence, they were concerned about the movement of some Asian nations toward communism. Determined to prevent this, the United States attempted to solidify its influence through direct intervention in Asian affairs.

Conflict in South Asia: India

For 200 years Britain had ruled the subcontinent of India as one nation in spite of the region's deep ethnic, linguistic, and religious diversity. Britain was reluctant to relinquish its hold on this jewel of the British Empire, but it did grant India limited self-rule between the two world wars. When the Second World War broke out, Britain promised full autonomy to India at the war's end in return for India's help in defeating the Axis powers.

Once the war was over, Britain began negotiating an independence agreement between the two main political organizations, the Muslim League and the Indian National Congress. The main obstacle was the fundamental difference between the Muslim minority, which wanted a separate Muslim state, and the Hindu majority, represented by the Indian National Congress, which opposed the partitioning of India.

Efforts at compromise failed. In 1946-1947, waves of violence swept the country. This convinced the British that

MAP STUDY

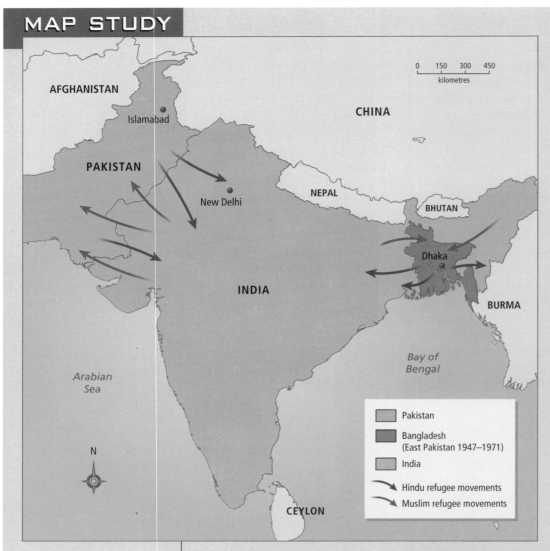

Figure 10.3
The Partitioning of the Indian Subcontinent

This map shows the partitioning of India and Pakistan in 1947 and the flow of people across the new borders. East Pakistan declared independence as Bangladesh in 1971. Bangladesh, an independent Islamic republic, is one of the world's poorest countries. It is constantly plagued by natural disasters.

Interpreting

1. What might be some effects of the migration of so many people?
2. Why might the state of Pakistan, comprising East and West Pakistan, not be a viable nation?
3. Consult an atlas to find out why Bangladesh is subject to so many natural disasters. How would the poverty of Bangladesh hinder its response to natural disasters?

India should be partitioned and that the date for independence should be moved forward from 1948 to 1947 in order to avert further violence. Under the provisions of the Indian Independence Act of 1947, India was partitioned and two republics were formed. The new Muslim state of Pakistan was created by separating two Indian provinces with large Muslim populations, the Punjab and Bengal, into West and East Pakistan.

Mass migrations of more than 12 million people followed the partitioning of India. Muslims in India fled to Pakistan while Hindus and Sikhs in Pakistan fled to India. The migrations were not peaceful, however. Approximately one million people were killed in the violence; still more died of disease and starvation brought on by the disruption. Conflicts continued throughout the 1950s and 1960s. In 1971, East Pakistan declared its independence from Pakistan as the new state of Bangladesh. Civil war followed in which thousands were killed and 10 million people were forced to flee to India. Later that year, India intervened to help Bangladesh and quickly defeated Pakistan.

Profile — Mahatma Gandhi (1869-1948)

Figure 10.4
Mahatma Gandhi

Mahatma Gandhi was one of this century's most powerful leaders. His words and deeds mobilized millions of people, yet he remained a humble man. From 1925 to 1948, Gandhi led India to independence. A lawyer by training, Gandhi held religious and political beliefs that powerfully blended Western and Indian thought.

"Non-violence is the first article of my faith. It is also the last article of my creed."

— Mahatma Gandhi, 18 March 1922

"The British Government in India has not only deprived the Indian people of their freedom but has based itself on the exploitation of the masses, and has ruined India economically, politically, culturally, and spiritually. We believe, therefore, that India must sever the British connection and attain Purna Swaraj, or complete independence...."

— Mahatma Gandhi, in a speech to the Congress Party, 31 December 1931

Mohandas Karamchand Gandhi was born to a prosperous Hindu family in India in 1869. At the age of 18, he went to England to study law. Soon after graduating and returning home, Gandhi was offered an assignment in South Africa, which had a large Indian population. Almost immediately he experienced racial discrimination, which led him to mobilize Indians to protest against oppression.

On his return to India in 1915, Gandhi was welcomed as a champion of Indian rights. He became a leader in the National Congress and a prominent activist in the struggle for independence. He abandoned Western clothing, preferring to identify with the Indian masses by wearing a loincloth and living a spiritual life of fasting and meditation. The great Indian poet, Raindranath Tagore, winner of the Nobel Prize for Literature in 1913, called Gandhi "Great Soul (Mahatma) in peasant's garb."

When British troops fired on unarmed demonstrators at Amritsar in 1919, killing or wounding more than 1500 people, Gandhi insisted that his followers not respond with violence. He believed that the British would be defeated not when they had no strength (which was limitless) but when they had no heart to continue the fight against moral, nonviolent people who simply would not submit to them. This commitment to peaceful change earned Gandhi respect worldwide.

In 1928 and 1929, nationalism reached a peak in India. Violent protests became common as people grew impatient with the lack of progress toward independence. Gandhi took action by protesting the Salt Laws, which required that salt be purchased from the government salt monopoly. On 12 March 1930, Gandhi and 78 followers set off on a long trek to the sea where they could illegally obtain salt. They reached the Indian Ocean on April 5, having marched nearly 500 km.

Along the way, their band of protestors had grown to several thousand. At the ocean Gandhi picked up some of the salt from the beach, thereby officially infringing on the government monopoly. Peasants took Gandhi's cue. All along the coast they began collecting salt for sale in the cities. More than 60 000 people were jailed. Despite the arrests, the protest remained peaceful, but civil disobedience increased. The British were forced to back down and release Gandhi and many other Indian leaders.

In 1935, Winston Churchill proclaimed that "Gandhism and all it stands for must ultimately be grappled with and finally crushed." Gandhi stood for an independent India; Churchill stood for the British Empire. In 1940, Churchill became prime minister and announced his refusal to "preside at the liquidation of the British Empire." However, when Japan attacked British colonies in Asia, Britain sought to secure Indian loyalty by offering independence following the war.

In 1947, the new states of India and Pakistan were created. Ongoing conflict between the Hindus and the Muslims, however, resulted in violent confrontations. Gandhi tried to quell the violence as he travelled tirelessly throughout India convincing rioters to practise love and tolerance. In January 1948, at the age of 78, he went on a hunger strike to bring about peace and universal compassion. The disorder in India diminished amidst promises of tolerance, and Gandhi ended his fast. Later that month, only five months after independence, Gandhi was assassinated by a group of militant Hindu conspirators who opposed Gandhi's acceptance of Muslims.

Gandhi's funeral was attended by a million mourners. World leaders paid homage to the man who inspired India. The United Nations lowered its flag to half-mast. Indian Prime Minister Jawaharlal Nehru said, "The light has gone out of our lives and there is darkness everywhere." But Gandhi's message continues to inspire humanitarians and seekers of peace.

Responding

1. What qualities of Mahatma Gandhi seem the most inspiring? Explain why.
2. Why do you think it was impossible for Winston Churchill to respect Gandhi's vision of an independent India?

ECONOMIC PATTERNS

The nations of Asia have chosen radically different paths in their political and economic development. These choices have created vast differences among them in their current economic realities and their prospects for the future. These economic patterns fall into four categories: industrialized economies, resource-based economies, centrally planned economies, and developing economies.

Industrialized Economies

The industrialized economies of Asia are Japan and the "Four Dragons"—Taiwan, Singapore, South Korea, and Hong Kong, which is now a Special Administrative Region (SAR) of China. These economies demonstrate the rapid economic change that has swept through some parts of Southeast Asia. In just a few decades these economies have been transformed from agrarian societies to important manufacturing entities.

The Four Dragons modelled their development on postwar Japan, achieving rapid growth by targeting high-tech industries. They have worked to create an attractive environment for export-oriented industries by encouraging their banking systems to provide maximum support for industry and by sponsoring research and development. The positive attitude toward business and industry has encouraged foreign investment. The results have been impressive. Singapore's annual economic growth rate through the 1990s averaged an impressive 7.8 per cent, while South Korea's growth rate was 5.7 per cent per year. The growth rate for Canada during the same period was 2.9 per cent.

People in each of these nations also share a strong work ethic, placing considerable value on hard work and loyalty to employers and employees. It is common for employees in these countries to work long hours six days a week and for workers and industries to place long-term financial rewards above short-term gain. Because of this, wage rates for skilled workers are lower than in competing countries. Workers also save more of their incomes than North Americans do, creating large capital resources for business ventures.

> "Singapore's social order is rather good. Its leaders exercise strict management. We should learn from their experience, and we should do a better job than they do."
>
> — Deng Xiaoping, Chinese Communist leader, 1992

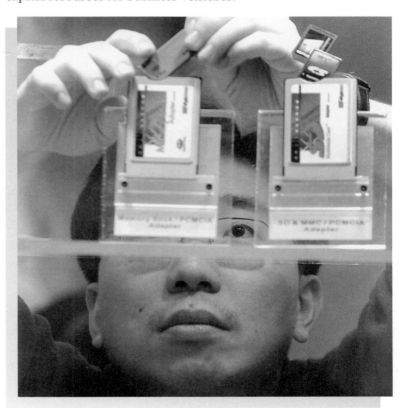

Figure 10.5

The Four Dragons have targeted manufacturing in high-tech industries to achieve their economic success. Here, a man sets up a display of flash memory adapters at the US International Consumer Electronics Show in 2002. Taiwan is one of the world's leading producers of electronic goods.

Japan: Woes of a Powerhouse

Japan is the economic powerhouse of Asia. Following the Second World War, Japan rebuilt its industrial base, relying on a combination of its own ingenuity and American aid and incentives. Its post-war recovery was hailed as nothing short of a miracle.

Yet Japan struggled to maintain its competitive position in the 1990s. In the years immediately following the war, the Japanese economy grew at an astounding rate—an average growth rate of 9.2 per cent from 1955 to 1973. Even in the years of the global recession that began in 1973, the Japanese economy had an average growth rate of 3.8 per cent, well above other industrialized nations. Between 1987 and 1991, the economy surged forward, a time that has since been labelled "the bubble."

Since 1992, however, the Japanese economy has faltered—even shrunk— much to the consternation of Japanese leaders. The economic downturn in the 1990s was due to several factors. The cost of houses in Japan had tripled from 1985 to 1991 because of **speculation**—the rapid buying and selling of homes in order to take advantage of rising prices. But by the end of 2001, housing prices were lower than 1985 levels, locking many families into homes that cost much more than they were actually worth.

Industries had over-invested in the late 1980s because the government's monetary policies favoured low interest rates, and corporations were unable to generate the income to pay back the loans. These "non-performing loans" threatened the financial stability of the banking system in the country. Efforts by corporations to pay back loans usually involved some sort of restructuring that caused unemployment rates to jump to record levels. Faced with financial uncertainty, consumers—who were the driving force for the Japanese economy—began to hold on to their discretionary income, putting further downward pressure on the economy.

In 2002, Japan's leaders implemented emergency measures to counter the deflation in the economy. Included in the reform packages were programs to eliminate non-producing loans, tax cuts to stimulate the economy, and reforms to government to prevent such situations from occurring again. The prognosis for Japan's economic performance for 2003 to 2006 was described as "guarded."

Resource-Based Economies

Not all nations in Asia have achieved the economic success of the Four Dragons. Indonesia has substantial oil and natural gas reserves, but has been plagued by political instability and ethnic rivalry. Combined with weak global markets for energy, political corruption, and rapid inflation, Indonesia has endured widespread unemployment and persistent food shortages. India has a significant natural resource base that could be used to expand its economy. But its rapid population growth, averaging 2 per cent a year, negates the country's economic gains. While harvests have improved due to better agricultural practices, food and other resources must be shared among a growing number of people. About half the population of India lives in poverty.

Centrally Planned Economies

The centrally planned economies of Vietnam, Myanmar, and North Korea are founded on government control of all aspects of the economy. In a centrally planned economy, there is usually emphasis on heavy industry and agriculture. Often, the economic policies isolate the countries by restricting foreign interaction, investment, and tourism. As a result, per capita incomes remain low in these nations, and they continue to be mired in out-of-date and inefficient technologies. Through much of the 1990s, North Koreans struggled with famine, in spite of government insistence that no such condition existed.

China is also a centrally planned economy, yet in the 1990s China made far-reaching modifications to its system—all with an eye to encouraging trade and tourism. China's leaders worked hard to promote, adopt, and integrate capitalism into the nation's existing political structure. China's **state capitalism** represents a new form of political and economic partnership. In this system, government industries and agencies co-exist with vibrant, privately owned enterprises. However, new businesses must be approved by the government.

In the last decades of the twentieth century this new economic freedom spawned millions of entrepreneurs and hundreds of multi-millionaires, sometimes called "red capitalists." It was estimated that nearly one-fifth of Chinese entrepreneurs were members of the Communist Party. Fully 113 000 Communist members ran private enterprises by 2002. So great was this alliance of Communists and capitalists that the Communist regime promised special protection for private property in the constitution.

Figure 10.6

An indoor movie theme park in Beijing in 1999. Who helped to build this indoor theme park? How does it represent the new sensibilities of China?

Developing Economies

A number of countries in Asia lack any real economic opportunities. Countries like Bangladesh, Laos, and Mongolia count as some of the poorest nations in the world. Their economic plight is usually further hampered by forces beyond their control. Natural disasters such as floods, typhoons, droughts, and earthquakes frequently devastate these countries. The cost of rebuilding over and over again consumes financial and human resources that might otherwise be used for economic development. These nations are forced to rely on foreign assistance for their very survival.

Other Factors in Economic Development

Ethnic strife is another factor hindering economic development. Sri Lanka, for example, is divided along ethnic lines, with the Tamils concentrated in the north and the Sinhalese in the south. Since independence from Britain in 1948, the minority Tamils have fought for recognition of their separate cultural identity while the Sinhalese have asserted control over the nation. Intense ethnic violence has gripped the country since 1985. Similar circumstances exist in other countries where political boundaries have not recognized ethnic divisions, such as Indonesia.

Figure 10.7

A mother and child cross a makeshift bridge over a polluted canal in the Muara Baru slum of north Jakarta, Indonesia. The photo was taken in 1998, during the worst economic crisis to hit the country in three decades. Do some research to find out if the situation has improved in this area since that time.

Political instability also limits economic growth. Papua New Guinea, for example, achieved independence from Australia in 1975 and adopted a parliamentary system of government. But the government has faced a series of no-confidence votes, uneasy coalitions, civil unrest, and violence. Unable to wield real power, the government has been unsuccessful in dealing with the problems facing the nation, including a lethargic and corrupt bureaucracy, a weak global economy for mineral exports, ethnic conflicts, and increasing violence.

PROSPECTS FOR THE FUTURE

As the nineteenth century was the age of Europe and the twentieth century was the age of the superpowers, many observers predict the twenty-first century will be the age of the Pacific. The Asian region accounts for more than 20 per cent of the world GNP, roughly equal to that of Europe and North America. In January 1992, the leaders of the **Association of Southeast Asian Nations** (ASEAN) signed an agreement to create a regional free trade zone by 2008.

Yet obstacles to economic prosperity in Asia remain. While economic issues may be the top priority for many nations, military conflicts cannot be ruled out, particularly in sensitive areas such as Korea, Taiwan, and India and Pakistan. Trading blocs in other regions, such as an expanded North American Free Trade Agreement (see Chapter Eight), may hurt those Asian economies that rely on their exports to consumer nations like the United States and Canada. As in the past, much of the economic development in

Selected Asian Countries Compared

Country	GNI/PPP per capita (US$)*	Average Annual Growth in Services 1990-2000 (%)	Average Life Expectancy (Years)
Industrialized Economies			
Japan	25 170	2.5	81
South Korea	15 530	5.7	74
Taiwan	–	2.6	75
Resource-Based Economies			
India	2 230	8.0	61
Indonesia	2 660	4.0	67
Centrally Planned Economies			
China	3 550	9.0	71
Vietnam	1 860	7.7	66
Developing Economies			
Bangladesh	1 530	4.5	59
Papua New Guinea	2 260	3.0	56

*Gross National Income/Purchasing Power Parity. It is a measure of what the average national income would buy in the United States.

Figure 10.8

There is a wide range in conditions throughout Asia. If you were hoping to invest in the consumer market, which group of countries would you most likely target? Why?

Asia will depend on the continuing prosperity and investment of Japan, although that country faces its own economic uncertainties. The direction of China's role in the region remains uncertain, although this huge nation will undoubtedly have a significant influence on the nations of Asia.

In Review

1. In what ways did the Second World War both help and hinder Asian efforts to gain independence?

2. Why did violence and unrest often accompany the move to independence in Asia?

3. What were the problems associated with independence in India?

4. Identify the factors responsible for the economic diversity in Asia.

5. What caused the economic downturn in Japan in the 1990s?

6. Why is China moving toward a system of controlled capitalism?

7. List the positive and negative factors that may affect economic development in Asia in the future.

China

During the Second World War, Japanese forces controlled most of the coastal areas and the major cities of eastern China. They were opposed by a fragile coalition of China's two most important military-political forces—the Chinese Communists, led by Mao Zedong, and the **Kuomintang**, led by Jiang Jie Shi (Chiang Kai-shek). When Japanese forces withdrew from China following their defeat in 1945, the Communists and the Kuomintang turned on each other in a bloody and brutal civil war. When the war ended in 1949, China—the world's most populous nation—was a bastion of communism.

THE KUOMINTANG AND THE COMMUNISTS

In 1912, after years of rebellion and bloodshed, China ceased to be an empire and became a republic. The National People's Party, or Kuomintang (also referred to as the Nationalists), was organized that year as a political party under the leadership of Dr. Sun Yat-sen. The goals of the new party were to defeat the warlords who controlled China, to unite China under a democratic government, to help the peasants obtain land, and to eliminate foreign control in China.

When Dr. Sun died in 1925, Jiang Jie Shi assumed the leadership of the Kuomintang. Jiang did not share Sun's commitment to democracy and socialism, and unlike Sun he was opposed to the Communist Party, which had emerged in 1921. The Soviet Communists had been supporting the Kuomintang, which by 1924 included many Chinese Communists who were helping to organize the workers. Jiang wanted to eliminate the Communist influence in the Kuomintang and in China.

In 1927, Jiang launched a campaign to destroy the Communists. In Shanghai, Communists, trade unionists, workers, and anyone suspected of being a Communist sympathizer were attacked by supporters of Jiang. An estimated 330 000 people were killed in battles and extermination campaigns waged by the Kuomintang during the 1920s. The Communists came close to being annihilated. Hundreds of thousands of peasants starved to death or were killed as a result of the Kuomintang's actions.

The remaining Communists under

Mao had the support of China's peasants; they treated the peasants fairly and redistributed land wherever they gained power. Jiang's corrupt military bureaucracy, on the other hand, operated for its own enrichment and was seen as not serving the interests of the people.

In 1937, the Kuomintang was unable to defend China from Japanese invasion and was forced to retreat to a remote province of China. During the Second World War, both groups fought the Japanese, but the Communist forces, who employed guerrilla tactics and adhered to a strict code of behaviour, were the superior fighting force. While the Kuomintang was backed by the United States and the Soviet Union, the Communists had to resort to capturing their arms and supplies from the enemy.

As the war drew to a close, Jiang expected to assume the leadership of China once the Communists were defeated. Soviet leader Joseph Stalin and US president Harry S. Truman also expected that Jiang would defeat Mao, but no one had anticipated the strength, discipline, organization, and popular support of the Communists. Jiang's Kuomintang army numbered more than three million soldiers. It was supported by the United States, which instructed the Japanese to surrender to the Kuomintang and not to the Communists. The US even airlifted Kuomintang troops to Japanese-held areas in northern China to try to prevent the Communists from liberating those regions. In spite of these advantages, Jiang quickly lost ground to the Communists, who rushed to liberate Japanese-held territory. While Mao's People's Liberation Army was smaller, it was supported by the peasants. In addition, many Kuomintang troops, disillusioned with the corruption of Jiang's army, defected to the Communist side.

Figure 10.9
Civilians in Shanghai pack their belongings and prepare to flee the advancing Communist forces in April 1949. What aspects of the photo suggest that people are leaving in a hurry?

The peace that came with the end of the Second World War was extremely short-lived in China. Civil war erupted almost immediately as the Kuomintang and the Communists fought for control. By 1949, the remnants of the Kuomintang had taken refuge on the island of Taiwan, driven from mainland China by Mao's forces. The victorious Communists proclaimed the establishment of the People's Republic of China in 1949. From his base in Taiwan, Jiang Jie Shi continued to claim sovereignty over all of China. The Nationalist government of the Republic of China in Taiwan was recognized by the West as the official government of China, a situation that continued until 1971. To this day, the Communist government of China claims that Taiwan is legitimately a part of China and not an independent nation.

CHINA AND TIBET

Mao's ambition to put all Chinese territories under direct control was not limited to Taiwan. In 1949, Chinese troops invaded Tibet, claiming it was Chinese territory. Most leaders around the world agreed that there was no legal basis for China's claim of sovereignty, but they were reluctant to stop the aggression. The government of Tibet and its spiritual leader—the Dalai Lama—were forced to sign a treaty that declared the region part of China, but with a large degree of autonomy. That autonomy proved to be a sham, and the Tibetans rebelled in 1959. Hundreds of thousands were killed in the subsequent crackdowns and the Dalai Lama fled the country.

In the years that followed, any form of Tibetan protest was brutally quashed by China. The International Commission of Jurists also concluded that China had committed **genocide** on the Tibetan nation. As the twentieth century drew to a close, China still controlled Tibet and placed many restrictions on the Tibetan people.

CHINA UNDER MAO

In 1950, the Korean War began when North Korea decided to unite North and South Korea by force. The United Nations condemned the action and sent American-led troops to defend South Korea. The UN troops pushed the North Koreans back to the Chinese border; in response, Mao warned that China would attack if the UN did not pull back. When his warning was ignored, Mao sent an army to North Korea. By the time the war ended in 1953, China had lost more than one million soldiers, and China and the United States had become confirmed enemies.

Following the Korean War, Mao set out to strengthen China from within and make it impervious to outside forces. A Ministry of Public Security was established to find and punish "enemies of the people." Denunciations, arrests, confessions, and punishments allowed Mao to rule with an iron grip. But it was the propaganda campaigns that were Mao's most effective method of control. The media were subjected to intense censorship. Children were taught to love Mao and to study his writings. They were also taught to spy on their parents and inform on them if they failed to embrace Mao's teachings.

In 1958, Mao launched the Great Leap Forward to expand and modernize industries. Iron and steel plants were constructed and citizens were directed to boost steel production by building backyard smelters. These initiatives created short-term increases in steel output, but the long-term consequences proved to be less desirable. Agriculture suffered as crops were left to rot in the fields while workers laboured to produce inferior steel in inefficient smelters. The Great Leap Forward ended in widespread famine and economic chaos. Estimates of deaths from starvation between 1959 and 1961 ran as high as 30 million people, although officially the famine was attributed to natural disasters. In 1959, in the face of mounting criticism, Mao retired as official leader of the People's Republic, but he continued to strongly influence policy as chairperson of the Chinese Communist Party.

"Letting...a hundred schools of thought contend is the policy for promoting progress in the arts and the sciences and a flourishing socialist culture in our land."

— Mao Zedong,
27 February 1957

Profile Mao Zedong (1893-1976)

Figure 10.10
Mao Zedong

Mao Zedong, the leader of the People's Republic of China, was one of the twentieth century's most radical and successful revolutionaries.

"Every Communist must grasp the truth. 'Political power grows out of the barrel of a gun.' "

— Mao Zedong, 6 November 1938

Born in Hunan province to a peasant family in 1893, Mao became a revolutionary early in life. In 1911, he joined the revolutionary army during the first rebellion against the Manchu dynasty. He already supported nationalist movements when he enrolled in Beijing University in 1919. There Mao became a Marxist, and in 1921 he co-founded the Chinese Communist Party.

Mao publicly supported a united front with the nationalist Kuomintang to defeat the warlords who sought to control China. When Jiang Jie Shi assumed the leadership of the Kuomintang in 1925, however, he wanted no connection with Mao's Communists. Jiang's bloody campaign against the Communists forced Mao's army to retreat to the countryside.

From there Mao trained his supporters in the tactics of guerrilla warfare.

Mao disagreed with the Marxist-Leninist view that revolution must be based on the class struggle of industrial workers. He believed that since China was an agricultural society, it was the power of the peasants that would bring about revolution. In 1929, he established the Chinese Soviet Republic in southern Kiangsi province, winning the support of the peasants by redistributing land, reducing taxes, and establishing schools.

In 1934, the Communists were forced to evacuate Kiangsi. Enduring cold, hunger, and attacks from warlord troops and bandits, the Communist army marched for more than a year. The epic Long March, as it came to be known, covered nearly 10 000 km, crossed 18 mountain ranges and 24 rivers, and ended at the mountain fortress of Yenan in the northern province of Shensi. Almost 90 000 people set off on the march but only 8000 survived. Those who made it to Shensi were a hardened and dedicated military force.

In 1937, the Japanese began a full-scale war in China. They overran the north and by 1938 had taken several cities, including Shanghai, Guangzhou, and Hangzhou. From his stronghold in Yenan, Mao launched daring guerrilla attacks against the Japanese. He agreed to an alliance with the Kuomintang during the Second World War in order to combat Japanese forces. But with the collapse of Japan in 1945, Mao and Jiang squared off in battle over China once again. In the next four years, the Kuomintang was crushed, Jiang fled to Taiwan, and Mao proclaimed the People's Republic of China in 1949. He would continue to be the dominant force in Chinese politics until his death in 1976.

Responding

1. Why do you think Mao is considered one of the most important figures of the twentieth century?
2. Why did Mao believe that China's agricultural base was the key to its revolution?

THE CULTURAL REVOLUTION

By the mid-1960s, Mao believed his revolution was being threatened by capitalist forces. In 1966, he called upon China's youth to lead a great proletarian **Cultural Revolution** to rid China of the "Four Olds"—old ideas, old culture, old customs, and old habits—and purge the Communist Party of elitists and **revisionists**, people who favoured gradual change. It was a desperate act to regain control of his revolution and pass on the revolutionary zeal that had fuelled his own career.

> Dare to struggle,
> Never stop making
> revolutionary
> rebellion.
> We will smash the
> old world ...
>
> — Excerpt from Battle Song
> of the Red Guards

Millions of young people, known as the **Red Guards**, were released from schools and factories to criticize, beat, exile, and murder political leaders, government officials, scientists, musicians, writers, teachers, and other **bourgeois** elements. One of Mao's prime targets was his revisionist successor as head of the People's Republic, Liu Shao-chi. He was removed from office and imprisoned until his death from pneumonia in 1969.

The Red Guards destroyed priceless antiquities, libraries containing precious books and scrolls, monasteries, statues, foreign-made goods—anything that offended their revolutionary sensibilities. They were allowed to travel freely carrying the Cultural Revolution throughout China. A collection of Mao's writings, known as the *Little Red Book*, was carried by every Red Guard and came to symbolize the Cultural Revolution.

Eventually the Cultural Revolution took on the semblance of civil war as workers, farmers, and soldiers armed themselves in opposition to the Red Guard. In July 1968, Mao called upon Red Guard leaders to curtail their chaotic activities. In only a few months, the political, educational, and economic systems of the country had been shattered and the lives of thousands of people had been destroyed. The forces of the Cultural Revolution that Mao unleashed did not completely disappear until Mao's death in 1976.

Figure 10.11
In a photo taken in 1966, Mao has a smile for this young member of the Red Guard. The Red Guard marched throughout China spreading the word of the Cultural Revolution. Are there any current equivalents to Mao's Red Guard?

CHINA, THE SOVIET UNION, AND THE UNITED STATES

China and Russia had been traditional rivals for centuries. But after both countries adopted communism, it was expected they would establish closer ties. Instead they vied with one another for leadership of the world communist revolution.

During the Second World War, the

United States believed that if China fell to Mao's Communists the country would become a puppet of the Soviet Union. What they failed to realize was that Mao and Soviet leader Joseph Stalin distrusted each other. Stalin resented Mao's independence, and Mao was wary of Stalin's ambitions in China. Not wishing to see a strong, united China, Stalin withheld Soviet support for the Chinese Communists in their struggle against the Kuomintang and later the Japanese. Instead, he supported the Nationalists, and in 1949 he urged Mao to settle for control of northern China and leave the rest of the country to Jiang Jie Shi.

Mao, of course, disregarded Stalin's advice. When he achieved victory over the Kuomintang in 1949, Mao asked Stalin for help in rebuilding China. But their talks in Moscow ended in argument, and Chinese-Soviet relations declined rapidly thereafter.

In the 1950s, the Soviet Union refused to share its nuclear weapons technology with China. In response, China conducted its own nuclear research and in 1964 exploded its first atomic bomb. Three years later China tested its first hydrogen bomb.

Tensions between China and the Soviet Union continued throughout the 1960s. Mao was critical of the Soviets for straying from what he considered to be the pure form of communism—that practised by the Chinese. The Soviet invasion of Czechoslovakia in August 1968 further heightened Chinese suspicions that the Soviet Union was bent on ruling the communist world. When Soviet premier Leonid Brezhnev announced the Brezhnev Doctrine, which asserted the Soviet Union's right to invade rebellious communist countries, Chinese officials were convinced they had much to fear from their neighbour.

An outright confrontation between China and the Soviet Union was ignited in the spring of 1969 over an island in the Ussuri River, which forms part of the long boundary between the two countries. Violent skirmishes continued until September when both sides agreed to negotiate a peaceful settlement of the dispute. But the issue remained unresolved and by the early 1970s there were more than one million troops amassed on each side of the border.

The hostilities between China and the Soviet Union prompted Mao to make overtures of friendship to the United States. The first move came in 1971 when China invited an American table tennis team to China for a tournament. Official political visits began shortly thereafter, including the historic visit by US president Richard Nixon in February 1972. Around this time, China—no longer internationally isolated—was admitted to the UN, replacing the Nationalist Chinese republic in Taiwan on such important bodies as the Security Council.

The American government was eager to develop stronger ties with China to create a counterbalance to Soviet influence in Asia. In 1979, the United States and China entered into formal diplomatic relations and the US terminated its recognition of the Republic of China in Taiwan as the legal government of China. With their political disagreements set aside, the way was cleared for economic co-operation between the two nations.

CHINA AFTER MAO

When Mao died on 9 September 1976, his legacy was considerable. He had built a communist revolution based on poor peasants rather than urban workers. China had emerged as one of the world's great military powers. The Communist Party was firmly in control of China's destiny. How long Mao's revolution would survive the challenge of economic growth and political reform now rested in the hands of his successors and with the Chinese people themselves.

Immediately following Mao's death, two factions sought to fill the power vacuum his death created. One was the radical group known as the Gang of Four, which included Mao's widow, Jiang Qing. The other was a group of political moderates headed by Deng Xiaoping, a former premier. Less than a month after Mao's death, Jiang Qing and the remaining Gang of Four were arrested for plotting to seize power. In 1980, they were blamed for the excesses of the Cultural Revolution and were found guilty of crimes against the state.

Deng Xiaoping emerged as the most powerful figure in the country. He earned a reputation as a pragmatic leader, willing to bend communist ideology to achieve results. The China that Deng inherited was in a state of disarray. The agricultural sector was inefficient, and much of the food supply had to be imported. Industrial productivity was hopelessly low. Lawlessness born of a frustration with poverty and hunger was sweeping the land. To turn the country around, Deng pursued the Four Modernizations, a program to achieve real development in agriculture, industry, science and technology, and defence.

Farming communes were broken up and the land was distributed to the workers. Increased production was encouraged through incentives and decentralized control. Private enterprise was permitted in certain areas, and local managers were given greater decision-making authority. Food and housing subsidies were reduced to allow prices to better reflect market conditions. To improve industries, foreign investment was encouraged, as was the transfer of technologies from other countries. Small- and medium-sized industries were emphasized instead of heavy, capital-intensive projects. Thousands of students were sent abroad to study to help achieve these goals.

China also started to come to grips with its growing population problem. A "one-child" policy was instituted in 1979, which restricted urban couples to having only one child. Chinese parents in rural areas were still allowed to have two children. The policy was highly controversial and sometimes enforced through compulsory abortion, sterilization, and infanticide. Couples who violated the policy were fined, sometimes heavily, or they lost job-related perquisites such as bigger apartments. Yet the Chinese government argued that economic development was hampered by rapid population growth and that the policy was essential.

In general, China's reforms opened the country to the international community and loosened its ties to socialist doctrine. The changes were welcomed by some but resented by others. Deng had to balance the need for economic reforms with resistance to political change on the part of the Communist establishment. Some pro-democracy forces began to advocate a Fifth Modernization—greater political freedom.

THE TIANANMEN SQUARE MASSACRE

As political change swept across the Soviet Union and Eastern Europe in the late 1980s, many Chinese citizens were eager for similar reforms in their country. Student demonstrations for democracy culminated in a massive protest in Tiananmen Square in Beijing in April 1989. When the government failed to meet the protestors' demands, many students began a hunger strike. This launched a vast popular movement that united the students with intellectuals, professionals, workers, and peasants against the Communist regime.

On May 20, **martial law** was declared. Within the government, a power struggle was developing between Communist hardliners and a more conciliatory wing of the party. Ultimately, the hardliners gained the upper hand. On June 3, the army moved into Tiananmen Square. More than 100 000 citizens tried to block the troops and tanks. When tear gas failed to move the human barricade, the killing began. Students and other demonstrators were shot down or crushed by army tanks. Thousands were killed and even more were injured.

Following the massacre, 300 000 troops occupied Beijing. There were mass arrests throughout China as the government initiated a crackdown. Official statements branded the students as counter-revolutionaries trying to over-throw the government. But the massacre at Tiananmen Square had been witnessed around the world via television. The international community reacted with horror at the brutal tactics used to put down a peaceful demonstration. Some countries, including Canada, withdrew their ambassadors from China and adopted economic sanctions. But most of these actions were short-lived and had little impact on China.

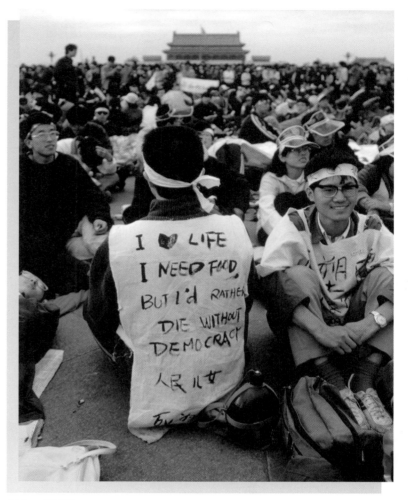

Figure 10.12

Pro-democracy demonstrations in Beijing's Tiananmen Square were quashed by the Red Army on 3 June 1989. What is your response to the demonstrator's message? Why do you think the demonstrators wrote their signs in English?

CHINA AND HONG KONG

In 1842, China was forced to cede part of Hong Kong to Britain and in 1898 to lease additional lands on a 99 year lease. With its excellent port facilities, convenient access to the rest of Asia, and efficient labour force, the British colony flourished economically to become the world's third largest financial centre. In 1997, Britain's lease on this bastion of capitalism expired and Hong Kong reverted to the People's Republic of China.

When it began negotiating for the return of Hong Kong in the 1980s, the Chinese government agreed that existing capitalistic economic and social systems would be left intact for 50 years. Despite these assurances, many Hong Kong entre-preneurs chose to emigrate rather than live under communist rule. Throughout the 1980s and 1990s, a steady flow of peo-ple and capital left Hong Kong, a signifi-cant part of the flow destined for Canada.

Faced with their own slow economic

growth, the Chinese government hoped to use the wealth and expertise of Hong Kong to improve the economy of the whole nation. Cities close to Hong Kong were granted status as Special Economic Zones (SEZ) with greater economic freedoms and tax incentives to encourage foreign investment. Cities such as Shenzhen, Zhuhai, and Shantou experienced economic booms as a result of their SEZ status. In 1992, Deng Xiaoping called for the country to build "several Hong Kongs." Chinese officials seem willing to bend communist ideas of state ownership and central planning to achieve economic progress.

The shift in control of Hong Kong to China took place with much fanfare but little immediate economic disruption as China promoted a "one country, two systems" policy. Over the next few years the economy did slow down, in part because integration with mainland China's economy tended to sap some of the entrepreneurial spirit from the former colony, in what some labelled "a culture of compliance." Fortunately for China, the presence of Hong Kong had stimulated significant economic activity in nearby regions, to the point where Chinese officials were considering special aid programs to help out the recession-beleaguered Hong Kong.

Politically, the transition to Chinese rule occurred with little conflict. The territory's chief executive, Tung Chee-hwa, moved slowly on such constitutional issues as prohibiting crimes such as subversion and banning local groups from having links with foreign organizations. It appeared that the Chinese government was concerned about Hong Kong's international image. Overall, the transition of Hong Kong to Chinese control was not as bad as the pessimists had predicted, nor as good as the optimists had boasted.

CHINA AND HUMAN RIGHTS

A major issue to emerge in recent years is China's dismal record on human rights.

Figure 10.13
Even after being handed back to China, Hong Kong remains an important commercial centre in the Pacific.

Many have noted the Tiananmen Square massacre and the one-child policy as indicative of China's weak regard for human rights. There are many stories of protesters being jailed for speaking out against the government and its slow progress on social change. This 2001 *Report on China* from Amnesty International details some of these concerns:

Thousands of people remained arbitrarily detained or imprisoned across the country for peacefully exercising their rights to freedom of expression, association or belief. Thousands of others were detained during the year. Some were held without charge or trial under a system of administrative detention; others were sentenced to prison terms after unfair trials under national security legislation. Torture and ill-treatment remained widespread and appeared to increase against certain groups. A "strike hard" campaign against crime led to a massive escalation in death sentences and executions. ...[F]reedom of speech and religion continued to be severely restricted.

Source: Adapted from *Amnesty International Report 2001*. © Copyright Amnesty International Publications 2001.

Some have sought to enlist the international community in pushing for human rights improvements. Canadian human rights advocates have tried to link trade policies to human rights improvements. They argue that economic sanctions should be applied to China until it makes significant improvements in its treatment of dissidents and citizens in general.

> "One casualty of the SAR's economic integration with the mainland could be Hong Kong's unique, quasi-independent identity, as well as its proud tradition of hacking out a path of its own."
>
> — Zheng Yongnian, Singapore-based China analyst, 2002

NETSURFER

WWW.AMNESTY.ORG

To learn more about human rights violations in China and other countries, visit the official Web site of Amnesty International. To search the site by country, click on "Find information on specific countries."

Figure 10.14

On 13 July 2001, China celebrated after being awarded the 2008 Olympics (left). However, many human rights activists protested Beijing's candidacy as host for the games. Right, members of the Tibetan Women's Association protest in New Delhi. They cited human rights violations in Tibet and throughout China.

The government of Canada, on the other hand, has argued that punitive sanctions would only serve to isolate China and that positive, long-term relationships that improve economic conditions are the best way for other countries to influence human rights policies in that country. The question of human rights and the role of the international community was widely debated in 2002 when Toronto competed with Beijing to host the 2008 summer Olympics. Beijing was awarded the games, a move applauded and criticized around the world (see Viewpoints, pages 340 to 342).

CHINA AND TAIWAN

When Kuomintang leader Jiang Jie Shi fled to Taiwan in 1949, he vowed to return and reclaim the mainland from Communist rule. While he never came close to defeating his enemy, he agreed with Mao that Taiwan was a part of China. The mainland Chinese government continues to hold this attitude today and claims that Taiwan is simply a rebellious part of China.

In the years following the Second World War, the United States propped up the government in Taiwan to prevent the spread of communism, and supported the island's claim as the legitimate representative of the Chinese people in the United Nations. The thaw in the relationship between China and the United States in 1971, however, led to China joining the UN and replacing Taiwan on key agencies such as the Security Council. This new relationship obligated the United States to accept Beijing's "one China" claim over Taiwan. However, the United States continued to have economic ties to Taiwan.

Within Taiwan, democratic movements began to agitate for independence. These pressures came to a head in 1996 when Lee Teng-hui was seeking re-election

as president of the island's National Assembly. A native islander who had not fled from China, Lee worked hard to gain international support for independence. In an effort to influence the election, China conducted military exercises in the Taiwan Strait, including firing missiles over the island of Taiwan. The United States responded by sending into the strait aircraft carrier battle groups that represented the largest US naval force since the Vietnam War.

In the end, Lee won a decisive victory. He proposed a "special state-to-state relationship" between Taiwan and China in 1999, an idea that was quickly rejected by the government in Beijing. Over the past decade, Taiwan has increased its military strength and now has a modern air force with the technological capacity to challenge China. Clearly Taiwan is not interested in a "one China" future.

INTO THE TWENTY-FIRST CENTURY

China showed an impressive ability to reinvent itself in the twentieth century. It is now poised to become the tiger of the twenty-first century. After the dark days of the Tiananmen Massacre, the Chinese leadership led another sort of cultural revolution. Fearing the disintegration that came to the Soviet Union and other communist powers in Eastern Europe, a new leader, Jiang Zemin, presided over a remarkable transformation of the world's most populous nation. Although political freedom was still sharply curtailed by Western standards, the Chinese state and the Communist party itself underwent wholesale reform.

From 1989 until the revolutionary 16th Party Congress in 2002, the Chinese government steadily withdrew its once famous intrusion into the private lives of its citizens. Greater social freedom and mobility became the norm. The response to the age-old challenge of capitalism was even more startling. Far from trying to erase capitalism, China's leaders worked hard to promote, adopt, and integrate capitalism into the existing political power structure.

The result of accepting private enterprise was a red-hot Chinese economy and an entirely new "look" to the nation. Chinese cities surged with the building of new skyscrapers. Men and women flocked to Western styles. Instead of relying solely on agriculture and heavy industry, China made a great leap forward and became a leader in a broad array of high-tech, new-economy industries. China kept pushing ahead in foreign relations, establishing freer trading links to most of the world's nations. When China won the 2008 Olympics, its new status in the world as an economic powerhouse—and

a player in the world community— seemed more assured than ever.

Yet China still faces serious challenges. Its citizens experience minimal political freedom and a great deal of religious suppression. Moreover, there has been an unequal sharing of the nation's economic progress. While party leaders and capitalists have grown wealthy, there is evidence that workers and farmers are feeling very unhappy with, even betrayed by, the party that was supposedly their protector. There are increasing reports of strikes, even riots, in some centres. Finally, there is a growing rivalry between China and its traditional Asian rival, Japan.

As the first years of the new century unfolded, China looked forward to greater prosperity and a more important role in the world. Japan may have been the first Asian economic giant in the modern world. China would clearly be the next.

Skill Path

Working Effectively in Groups

Throughout your reading of *Twentieth Century Viewpoints*, you have seen that political leaders often co-operate to find solutions to problems. For example, when Japan suffered an economic downturn in the early 1990s, its leaders met to plan emergency measures to save the economy and to prevent such a catastrophe from happening again. These leaders listened to each other, discussed the problems, and tried to reach solutions that would be acceptable to everyone.

You don't have to be a world leader to benefit from working in a group. Many everyday situations require group discussion and group solutions. For example, what if you and your friends wanted to ban junk food from the school cafeteria? No doubt, you would have to meet as a group to plan your strategy. Similarly, if residents in a neighbourhood were protesting the opening of a strip mall, they would have to meet to decide on their approach with the mall developer. No matter what the group discussion is

about, or who is involved, the participants must be able to set goals, listen to and respect the opinions of others, and accurately communicate the outcomes.

The following steps will help guide you in becoming an effective group participant.

Step One: Set the Goals

Why is the meeting necessary? What exactly do you want to accomplish? The answers to these questions will tell you what the group's goals are. It is important for all members of the group to have a common understanding of the group's goals before the issue is examined. Someone in the group can write down these goals on a chalkboard or flip chart so that they are visible throughout the meeting.

Step Two: Set the Agenda

How can the group accomplish its goals? Before the group meets, someone can draw up a list of topics to be discussed in a particular order. But what if your group doesn't know what the topics are yet? In that case, you might need to meet and discuss the research that must take place before a meaningful discussion can occur. If a number of people are coming to the meeting with information, then the agenda might consist of a series of presentations followed by questions. Whatever the format, everyone in the group should have a clear idea of how the meeting will unfold and how they will contribute to the discussion. The agenda should be in writing, should reflect the topics or tasks to be addressed, and should be made available to each member.

Step Three: Assign Roles and Outline the Responsibilities

To keep your group work organized, it may help to assign specific roles to individual members. Below is a list of some of the possible roles that could be assigned (or chosen) by group members to help the debate along and keep everyone involved.

- *Chairperson:* manages the meetings and keeps the group moving forward according to the agenda; also reminds members of the set goals when necessary
- *Recorder:* records the group's ideas, decisions, and plans
- *Encourager:* supports, motivates and encourages other members of the group
- *Reflector:* helps group members look back on the progress of the discussion
- *Question commander:* checks to see if anyone in the group has questions and tries to obtain a response from another group member
- *Spokesperson:* presents the group's work to others (e.g., to a class, community, media, and so forth)

Each group member also has certain responsibilities to maximize the effectiveness of the meeting:
- Each member should ensure that he or she is informed and prepared for the discussion. If members were asked to read pertinent documents (e.g., chapters, articles, and so forth) or to conduct specific research, that work should be completed before the meeting begins.
- Each group participant should consider the rights of all other participants. Group members should feel that they are being listened to, that their views and comments are valued, that they are respected, that they are free to present their own opinions without fear of insult.

Step Four: Present Your Group Work

One person may act as spokesperson and present the group's findings, or individual members can present their own findings. However, before any presentations are begun, group members should present to each other. This will give the group the opportunity to catch any errors, or answer any last-minute questions.

As with any oral presentation, it is often a good idea to use visuals to help the audience understand your topic and to help keep them engaged in the discussion. For more information on the types of visuals that could be used, see the Skill Path "Delivering an Oral Presentation" in Chapter Nine, page 303.

Practise Your Skill

Your group is charged with the task of planning a class trip to China for the 2008 Summer Olympics, or a later Olympics if after 2008.

1. The goal is to determine whether such a trip is reasonable. Within two weeks, your group will report back to class with the following information:
- airfares to China for the 2008 Olympics, including any discounts
- hotel accommodation during the Olympics, including any discounts
- available staff or parents to act as chaperones
- passes to the games—when and how to book and obtain them
- other tourist attractions within China and their distance from Beijing
- medical information for travellers to China

As a group, meet to discuss the execution of these tasks. Assign one task to each member of the group. At this first meeting, you could also choose to assign each member a role (see above). Reconvene with the information you have gathered and determine whether the trip is a reasonable proposition. Report your findings to the class.

2. As a group, select one of the tasks noted in Question 1. Determine how to gather the information requested, for example, on the Internet, through personal interviews, or by consulting the general telephone directory or Yellow Pages.

In Review

1. Outline the struggle between the Kuomintang and the Communists up until 1949.

2. Explain the Great Leap Forward.

3. a) What was the purpose of Mao's Cultural Revolution?

   b) What was the result of the Cultural Revolution?

4. a) What was the relationship between China and the Soviet Union?

   b) How did this relationship influence China's foreign policy toward the United States?

5. What reforms were introduced by Deng Xiaoping following Mao's death?

6. What led to the massacre in Tiananmen Square?

7. What was the overall effect of Hong Kong's reversion to Chinese control?

8. What is China's relationship to Taiwan? What has been the main conflict in that relationship?

Summary

The end of the Second World War set in motion many changes that would have great consequences for Asia. Independence came quickly for many new nations, beginning with the partitioning of the Indian subcontinent. Leaders emerged who had been inspired by nationalist movements in the inter-war years and now sought futures free of European control. Unfortunately, for some of these countries, economic conditions created by years of imperialism have made development difficult—and poverty, political turmoil, and violence common.

Certain nations, such as Singapore and South Korea, have been able to parlay their resources and strengths into thriving economies. These will lead the economic transformation of the region over the next decades. China will play an increasingly important role in the Asian region as its economic reforms shape the economy to match the political and military influence of the giant nation. Its international status, however, will be tarnished by questions of human rights and social justice.

Other issues loom in Asia. India and Pakistan continue to experience rivalry; there are border disputes between North and South Korea; and religious and ethnic conflicts in Central Asia may all command attention in the first decade of the twenty-first century.

Viewpoints

Background

On 13 July 2001, China was awarded the 2008 Olympic Summer Games. The final vote was Beijing 56, Toronto 22, Paris 18, and Istanbul 9. China had lost by only two votes in its last bid for the 2004 Games, so many people thought it was China's turn. The International Olympic Committee (IOC) claimed this was a "new era for China," and that the Olympics would be a positive step for improvement of human rights in China. Others were shocked that a repressive nation should be awarded the Olympics.

In the transcript that follows, US Congressman Tom Lantos and visiting professor Wang Jian Wei tackle the issue in a debate broadcast by the Public Broadcasting Station (PBS) on 12 July 2001. Tom Lantos argues against giving the Olympics to China, whereas Wang Jian Wei argues that the Olympics could make a positive contribution to improving human rights in China. Read these two viewpoints carefully, and answer the questions that follow. (You may want to refer to the Skill Path "Analysing a Reading" on page 14 for guidance before you begin.)

Tom Lantos and Wang Jian Wei

GWEN IFILL (Host of the TV program): Now, two opposing views. Congressman Tom Lantos, a Democrat from California, is the ranking member of the House International Relations Committee, co-chair of the Human Rights Caucus, and Wang Jian Wei is a visiting scholar at George Washington University, and a citizen of the People's Republic of China. Congressman Lantos, why should China be denied the right, the opportunity, to host the Olympics in 2008?

REP. TOM LANTOS: Because China's human rights record is an unmitigated disgrace. They persecute people for religious reasons. There is no political freedom. There is no media freedom. American scholars are arrested. A little while ago we had our reconnaissance plane forced down, our service people were kept against their wishes for 11 days in Chinese captivity. It is a totalitarian police state. It would be the ultimate outrage to have the

International Olympic Committee give them this opportunity of basking in the reflected glory of the Olympics. Police states are excellent at staging pageantries. Hitler benefited enormously from the 1936 Olympics in Berlin. And we know what happened in the years following. The Soviet Union had the Olympics in 1980, and there came nine years of Soviet suppression. I would love to see the Olympics in China...once their human rights record is cleaned up.

GWEN IFILL: Dr. Wang, those are strong words. What's your response?

WANG JIAN WEI: Yes, with all respect, I think that I disagree with some of the points raised by the Congressman. I agree that China has a lot of human rights problems, but the...question here is not whether...China has a human rights problem, but rather, whether China deserves to have these games and whether giving China the opportunity to have these Olympic games will improve human rights in China or make it worse.

GWEN IFILL: You think these are two separate issues, about whether China actually has reasonable human rights protections and whether this event should come to Beijing? You see those as two separate things?

WANG JIAN WEI: Yes, I see these as two separate things because I have a problem with the logic of the Congressman's argument. He seems to say that because China has serious human rights problems, China should not get the Olympic games. And well, you can extend that logic to other issues, too; you can argue that China probably should not be a member of the WTO because of human rights issues. Probably the United States should not do any trade with China because of human rights issues. So basically, if...you apply this logic consistently, then you are talking about shutting China out of the international community. I don't think this is the right way to improve the human rights situation in China.

GWEN IFILL: What about that, Congressman Lantos, the situation of China on the verge of being accepted into the WTO with a lot of American business working there, doing business and in fact paying for this bid. This is different from what happened with Germany in 1936.

REP. TOM LANTOS: Well, it's not very different. It's a totalitarian police state that tortures citizens who freely express their views—religious, political or otherwise. It is certainly not different from Moscow in 1980, which was a totalitarian police state. ...That the Olympiad, which in its very charter calls for respecting the dignity of the individual, that that should be ignored is simply preposterous. We are not living in a purely commercial world. We are living in a world where young men and women—the athletes from all over the world—should be competing in a free society. Now just imagine the Olympics go to China in 2008 and the Chinese perpetrate outrages similar to the ones we

had at Tiananmen Square just a decade ago. What would be our reaction?

We have some excellent choices. We have Canada and we have France—both democratic states fully prepared to host the Olympics. I think one of the most remarkable things about the Chinese plan is that they have public executions with mass audiences in places where they plan to build Olympic stadiums. Well, I don't think American athletes want to compete in stadiums which today are used for mass executions.

GWEN IFILL: Dr. Wang, how do you respond to that?

WANG JIAN WEI: Well, I'm not sure what the Congressman says about the public executions is still prevailing practice in China.

REP. TOM LANTOS: It's in today's paper on the front page....

WANG JIAN WEI: It used to be the case during the heyday of the Cultural Revolution, you know, when the human rights situation was at its worst in the history of the PRC [People's Republic of China]. So another point I want to raise is that while China does have human rights problems..., on the other hand we have to look at things in the long term. For example, we have to look at the whole picture—the development over the last 20 years compared to the 1960s and 1970s—whether the human rights situation in China has become better or worse. I think that the answer is pretty self-evident.

GWEN IFILL: Why couldn't they just say, aha, we have the Olympics—we don't have to do anything now.

WANG JIAN WEI: There are a couple of things that will benefit China moving towards the direction of betterment. First of all I think that the Olympics will facilitate China's further integration into the international community, together with membership in the WTO, and China has to adapt more to the international standards and norms in doing things. Secondly, I think that the Olympics will also diffuse the writhing nationalism in China. As you know, the Chinese were not very happy with their failed Olympic bid in 1993, and so that will give the Chinese some feeling that it looks like...they are part of the international community and they are accepted by the world.

GWEN IFILL: What is at stake for China economically because of the Olympics?

WANG JIAN WEI: I think in economic terms that probably the membership in the WTO is much more important to China than the Olympics. Of course, the Olympic games will bring more investment and opportunities to China. But I think that with or without the Olympics China's economic development will continue.

GWEN IFILL: Dr. Wang and Congressman Lantos, thank you both for joining us.

Source: Adapted from *PBS NewsHour*, 12 July 2001. <www.pbs.org/newshour/bb/sports/july-dec01/olympics_7-10.html>. Copyright © 2003 MacNeil/Lehrer Productions. All rights reserved.

Analysis and Evaluation

1. Why does Lantos feel that China should not be awarded the Olympic Games?
2. How does Wang Jian Wei view the issue of China, human rights, and the 2008 Olympics?
3. Which of the commentators do you think is assessing the situation more accurately? Why?
4. Decide which of the viewpoints you tend to support, and explain why. If you agree with neither, state the position you do support and explain it. Be sure to use specific information from this textbook, the readings, and other sources to support your position.

Chapter Analysis

MAKING CONNECTIONS

1. In your opinion, what are the most significant forces affecting events in Asia?
2. Widespread instability occurred in Asia after the Second World War and again in the late 1980s and the 1990s with the rapid rise in economic importance of a handful of Asian countries. Compare these two periods in chart form under the following headings: Major Forces, Key Countries, Important Issues.
3. Compare conditions in Canada and China. Record your points in a comparison chart under the following headings: Economic Conditions, Political Conditions, Important Problems, Possible Future Developments.

DEVELOPING YOUR VOICE

4. a) In a small group, brainstorm the problems facing the countries of Asia. After you have prepared your list, select the three most important problems.
   b) If you were a leader in one of these countries, what policies would you propose to try to solve these problems?

5. Compare and contrast the ideas of Mao Zedong and Mahatma Gandhi. Which leader's philosophy do you think is more appropriate in today's world? Why?

6. In small groups, discuss this statement: "As the twentieth century ended, the era of North America was on the wane while that of Asia was on the rise."

RESEARCHING THE ISSUES

7. Have human rights in China improved over the past few years? Research this topic using sources such as Amnesty International, and produce a report that can be shared with others.

8. Maintain a media watch of press clippings and magazine articles on the 2008 Olympics in Beijing. What are the important issues being discussed?

9. Select one country in Asia and prepare a case study outlining the major issues this country has faced since 1945. Discuss the present situation and the prospects for the future.

CHAPTER ELEVEN

The Middle East: Conflict or Co-operation?

Peace activists rally in Jerusalem on 13 September 2000 to call for a final deal that would grant Palestinian autonomy. Do peace rallies in the Middle East get enough media coverage in North America?

"We have to try to build a new Middle East.... Resolving the Palestinian-Israeli conflict and building economic hope for the future is the only solution."

— Shimon Peres, *World Press Review*, September 1991

"If all conditions were secure we wouldn't need a peace process.... [Y]ou do not make peace when everything is fine and everybody's secure and we're living happily as next door neighbors.

— Hanan Ashrawi speaking at Beloit College, Wisconsin, 6 December 1999

Overview

As the birthplace of three of the world's great religions—Islam, Judaism, and Christianity—the lands of the Middle East are sacred to many people. Culturally, the region is largely Arabic, except for Israel, which is Jewish, and Iran, which is Persian. Politically, authoritarian regimes surround the hereditary monarchies of the Gulf states. Economically, the contrast between wealthy oil countries, such as Saudi Arabia, and poor countries, such as Sudan, is stark. These differences have created intense political and religious conflicts between and within states.

A major issue of Middle East politics is the Arab-Israeli conflict. The fear and distrust felt by Arab states toward a Jewish state have shaped international relations for more than a century. Unless Israelis and Arabs can reach a lasting compromise to coexist in peace, terrorism and war will continue.

Focus Questions
1. What factors have made the Middle East so volatile?
2. What factors led to the creation of the state of Israel?
3. How has the Arab-Israeli conflict affected the region and the world?
4. What are the prospects for lasting Middle East peace?
5. Will the Palestinians ever have their own sovereign territory?

Region of Conflict

Historically, the Middle East has long had contact with Europe. For much of that time, the region's technological capabilities and cultural achievements equalled or exceeded those of Europe. While European and Middle Eastern cultures occupied parts of one another's territories at various times, their civilizations remained separate and distinct.

In the nineteenth century, the balance shifted. The Ottoman Empire had ruled much of the Islamic world since the 1500s, but began to lose power and influence to Europe as Britain, Russia, France, and Italy expanded their empires. However, European expansion into the Middle East was less successful than in other parts of the world. The long history of interaction between the two civilizations and the unity of Islamic culture created a strong resistance to Western influence. By 1914, Turkey, Palestine, Syria, Iraq, and part of the Arabian peninsula were still under Ottoman control.

In the aftermath of the First World War, the Ottoman Empire collapsed. A new political order emerged as Britain and France divided the territories of the Middle East into **mandates** (regions controlled by other states), a move that angered many Arabs, since Britain had promised to create an independent Arab state following the First World War. The League of Nations, however, declared these former colonial holdings to be unprepared for self-rule. The mandates were placed under the administrative control of a League member, but were not owned by that country.

MAP STUDY

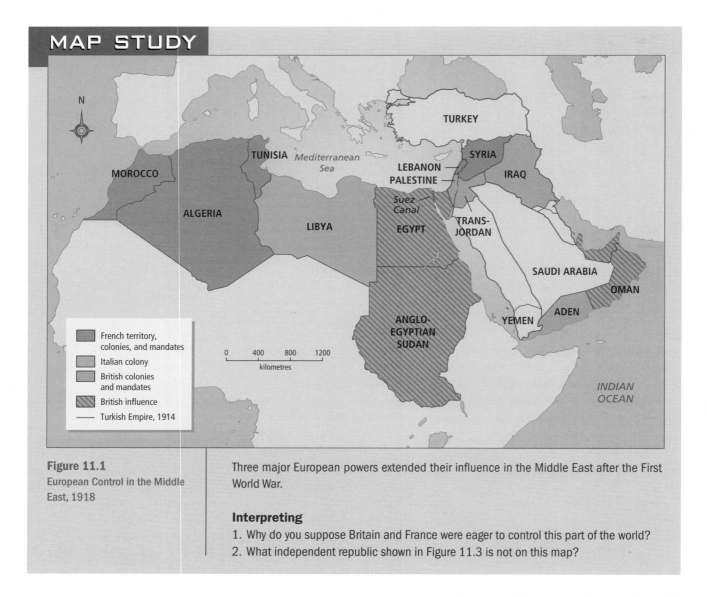

Figure 11.1

European Control in the Middle East, 1918

Three major European powers extended their influence in the Middle East after the First World War.

Interpreting

1. Why do you suppose Britain and France were eager to control this part of the world?
2. What independent republic shown in Figure 11.3 is not on this map?

INDEPENDENCE AND REVOLUTION

Britain and France drew political boundaries in the Middle East with little regard for local societies. These artificial borders disrupted the lifestyles of many people, which led to cultural and economic upheavals and extreme hardship. The colonial powers established political systems, but they proved incapable of governing the diverse jurisdictions they had created.

Between the First and Second World Wars, discontent with European rule spread throughout the region. Nationalist movements spread and gained in popularity. By the end of the Second World War, local leaders challenged British and French authority. In the 1950s, independent states began to emerge in the Middle East, often giving rise to violent retaliation by the colonial rulers.

Many of the newly independent countries became monarchies still largely influenced by Western interests. In some countries, revolutionary movements overthrew the monarchies to establish republican governments. For example, in 1952, Colonel Gamal Abdel Nasser led the Free Officers Revolution that ousted Egypt's unpopular ruler, King Farouk. The new government launched a reform program to end foreign control and improve the quality of life in the desperately poor country. In spite of Nasser's criticism of royal regimes and his promotion of **republicanism** (government by the people), democracy remained uncertain in the region, and many of the new governments evolved into authoritarian regimes.

In neighbouring Libya, Colonel Mu'ammer Gaddafi deposed King Idris in a military coup in 1969. He believed that colonialism was the root of all problems in the Arab world, and steadfastly opposed both capitalism and communism. He used his country's oil wealth to improve social services and raise living standards.

In Iran, the monarch, Shah Pahlavi, forged an alliance with the United States and introduced Western-style reforms in the Muslim nation. While the Shah tried to modernize his nation—spending money on infrastructure, promoting literacy, and introducing rights for women—he was also a repressive, corrupt ruler. In 1979, he was ousted by the *Ayatollah* (from the Persian language, meaning "token of God") Khomeini, who led an Islamic **fundamentalist** revolution that banished Western influences and introduced a strict version of Islamic rule.

Even with independence, the artificial boundaries remained. Sometimes this placed diverse peoples within the borders of a single country, as in Lebanon and Sudan. At other times, boundaries splintered a single culture. The Kurds, for example, were split among Iran, Iraq, and Turkey. These political divisions created instability and still feed many conflicts in the region today.

Figure 11.2

Left, the Shah of Iran, pictured with his children at his Swiss villa in 1970. Right, the Ayatollah Khomeini is greeted by his followers in Tehran in 1979. While both of these rulers can be considered repressive, what contrasts are apparent in these images of them?

MAP STUDY

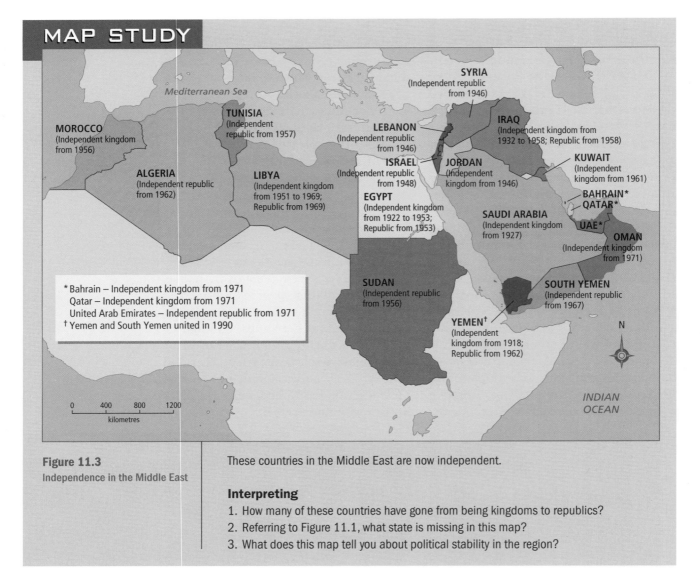

Figure 11.3

Independence in the Middle East

These countries in the Middle East are now independent.

Interpreting

1. How many of these countries have gone from being kingdoms to republics?
2. Referring to Figure 11.1, what state is missing in this map?
3. What does this map tell you about political stability in the region?

FLASHPOINTS

The Iran-Iraq War

After succeeding in Iran in 1979, Khomeini tried to export the fundamentalist revolution to neighbouring Iraq. Khomeini proclaimed it a Holy War, or *jihad*, and conscripted hundreds of thousands of civilians to fight for the cause. Iraq's leader, Saddam Hussein—who also coveted Iran's oil fields and the Shatt al-Arab Waterway—responded by attacking Iran.

During the bloody war that followed, Iraq was supported by moderate Arab nations, and also by Western countries, including the United States and the Soviet Union. To keep Islamic fundamentalism from spreading, Iraq obtained the latest weaponry, including technology for chemical and nuclear weapons. Iran, on the other hand, became even more economically and diplomatically isolated.

Iraq and Iran fought intermittent battles throughout most of the 1980s. With help from the West, Iraq gained air superiority in 1985. In 1987, Iran started attacking commercial shipping in the Persian Gulf. The United States and other nations provided naval escorts, but confrontations continued. Meanwhile, bombs and missiles bombarded cities on both sides. Both Iran and Iraq used chemical weapons, killing countless innocent civilians.

In 1987, the UN Security Council called for a ceasefire, and Iraq agreed. Iran, however, refused. UN Secretary-General Javier Pérez de Cuéllar organized more negotiations, which finally led to a peace settlement in August 1988. More than 1.5 million people had died in the long and bloody conflict.

Conflict in Lebanon

Lebanon is composed of Muslims and Christians, with distinct religious groups within the two faiths. When Lebanon gained independence in 1944, Christians outnumbered Muslims, and the balance of power in government gave the Christian majority an edge. That ratio collapsed, however, when Muslim Palestinian refugees fled to Lebanon after Israel was created in 1948, and the Christians became a minority. As refugees continued to pour in, tensions increased. Finally, in 1958, civil war erupted. American troops restored political order, but religious conflicts continued to simmer, causing two decades of unrest.

In 1975, war again erupted in Lebanon when Palestinian guerrillas in southern Lebanon launched raids against Israel. Israel retaliated by attacking Lebanon. The presence of the Palestinian guerrillas heightened tensions between Muslims and Christians within Lebanon. Most Muslims supported the Palestinians, while Christians objected to their presence and activities. Civil war broke out, until Syria intervened to restore a degree of order.

In June 1982, Israel invaded and occupied Beirut, Lebanon's capital. This only added to the chaos. American, British, French, and Italian troops were deployed to contain hostilities and oversee the evacuation of Palestinian guerrillas. But then terrorists attacked the Western forces. In October 1983, a terrorist bombing killed 241 American and 31 French troops in their barracks. Shortly thereafter, the international troops withdrew. Israeli forces withdrew in 1985 but kept a "security zone" in southern Lebanon—in defiance of a United Nations call for withdrawal. The bloody civil war continued.

By 1987, the worst violence centred in southern Lebanon. Confrontations between Christians and Muslims were interrupted only by brief ceasefires. In 1989, under pressure from Syria, Saudi Arabia, and the Arab League, the Lebanese government agreed to constitutional changes. In the 1990s, a semblance of peace ended the bloody civil war. Israel's occupation of "security zones" in the south, however, remained a sore point. Lebanese guerrilla groups continued to use Lebanon as a base for raids into Israel. Israel retaliated, but its military actions drew increasing condemnation from the international community. In May 2000, under pressure from the UN Security Council and its own allies, Israel withdrew from Lebanon completely.

The Persian Gulf War

Before Iraq gained independence from Britain in 1932, Kuwait had been part of its southern territory. To ensure its own access to the Persian Gulf and the Indian

MAP STUDY

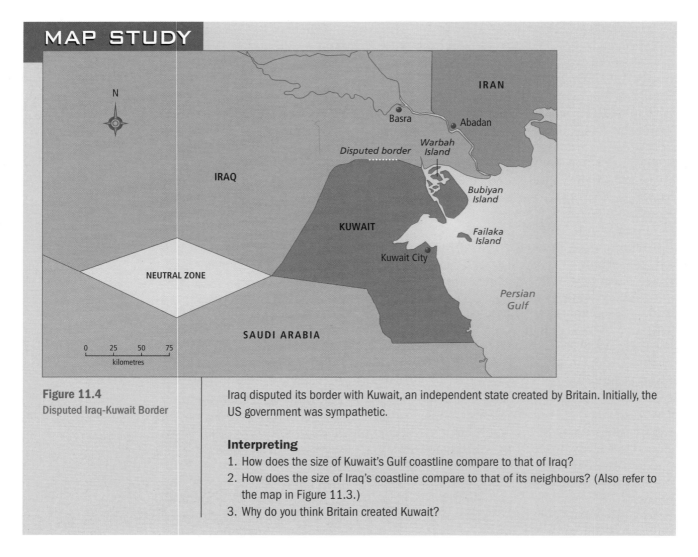

Figure 11.4
Disputed Iraq-Kuwait Border

Iraq disputed its border with Kuwait, an independent state created by Britain. Initially, the US government was sympathetic.

Interpreting
1. How does the size of Kuwait's Gulf coastline compare to that of Iraq?
2. How does the size of Iraq's coastline compare to that of its neighbours? (Also refer to the map in Figure 11.3.)
3. Why do you think Britain created Kuwait?

Ocean, however, Britain created the separate state of Kuwait as a British protectorate. (Kuwait gained independence in 1961.) Kuwait's boundary limited Iraq's access to the Persian Gulf to a 10 km stretch of coastline, which Iraq disputed. On 1 August 1990, negotiations between Iraq and Kuwait over boundaries, payments for oil shipments, and oil quotas broke down, and Iraq invaded Kuwait.

The United States, anxious to maintain its own oil supply, condemned the invasion and demanded that Iraq withdraw. Within days, an economic boycott was imposed on Iraq and a massive US-led international military coalition was established. A deadline for Iraq's withdrawal from Kuwait was set, but Iraqi leader Saddam Hussein adamantly rejected it. The day after the deadline passed, coalition forces attacked.

For 38 days, air units from the United States, Britain, France, Saudi Arabia, Canada, and other countries pounded Iraqi targets. Once Iraqi defences were shattered, coalition tanks and troops went in. The ground war lasted only 100 hours before US president George Bush ordered a cease-fire. By this time, an estimated 120 000 Iraqi soldiers were dead, while only 200 coalition personnel had been killed.

UN forces drove Iraqi troops out of Kuwait but stopped short of a full-scale invasion of Iraq. At the time, it hardly seemed necessary: Iraq's economy and infrastructure were in ruins; Iraq had to pay war reparations to Kuwait; and the UN trade embargo on Iraq remained intact. The UN Security Council also set strict conditions for sanctions to be lifted: Iraq must destroy its chemical and bio-logical weapons, end its nuclear weapons programs, and accept international inspections to ensure that conditions were being met. Saddam Hussein resisted UN demands, and in the years after the war Iraq repeatedly challenged the condi-tions of the peace treaty. At times, Britain and the United States replied with mili-tary force.

The economic sanctions against Iraq were widely unpopular. Reports from within Iraq documented deepening poverty and crumbling health care and social facilities. It became clear that chil-dren, women, and the elderly were the real victims of the sanctions. In 1995, the UN Security Council voted to allow lim-ited sales of Iraqi oil, with revenues to be used for humanitarian purposes. Sales levels were allowed to increase in 1998.

Saddam Hussein remained defiant. In the West, he was labelled a villain. The United States government suspected that Iraq was developing nuclear and other weapons of mass destruction. The war in the Persian Gulf seemed anything but over.

Figure 11.5
Saddam Hussein fires a rifle during a military parade in Baghdad on 31 December 2001. The parade demonstrated Iraq's support of the Palestinian uprising against Israel. Why would Hussein support the Palestinian cause?

Skill Path

Analysing a Current Issue

Canadian society is virtually bursting with minute-by-minute news. Cable-news TV channels and high-speed Internet can transport events and issues to Canadians as they happen. Instant commentary usually follows, in the form of "expert interviews" and "in-depth analysis." But how much does this wide-ranging coverage of events really contribute to your knowledge of an issue? Hearing a headline, or even what someone thinks about the headline, is a far cry from understanding an issue. To do that, you need strategies to state the issue clearly, determine the players, and draw your own conclusions about it.

For example, in the fall of 2002, US president George Bush strongly indicated that the United States would invade Iraq if UN weapons inspectors were thwarted in their search for Iraqi weapons of mass destruction. Many headlines followed the president's announcement, as various groups scrambled to react. The Canadian government immediately announced that it would not support American military action against Iraq unless it had stronger evidence of an imminent threat of danger. However, many Americans and Canadians supported the president's stance, saying that Iraqi leader Saddam Hussein was an extremely dangerous individual who had to be removed from power.

How can you understand this issue?

Step One: State the Issue
You must be clear about exactly what aspect of a given issue you are analysing. Therefore, state the issue in the form of a concise question. For example, "Is the Canadian government correct in refusing to endorse American military action in Iraq without further information?"

Step Two: Identify Possible Answers
What answers to your question immediately spring to mind? If you don't know what the possible answers might be, you should do some initial research to find out. Newspaper editorial pages are a good place to begin, since columnists often offer alternative views on the issues of the day. (Most newspapers also operate an Internet site, so reviewing papers from across Canada and the world is a simple process.) Construct an organizational chart and write each alternative in a separate column across the top. For the question stated above, some potential answers might be:

1. Yes, the Canadian government is correct. Saddam Hussein is not an imminent threat. There has been no credible evidence linking him to the events of September 11, and military action would only create more hardship for Iraqi civilians, who have suffered too long under economic sanctions.
2. No, the Canadian government is incorrect. Saddam Hussein is a leader who gassed his own people and has shown a great interest in obtaining weapons of mass destruction, including biological, chemical, and nuclear weapons. He is a threat and must be removed from power for the safety of the world.
3. Maybe. This situation should be watched closely, and military action should not be ruled in or out at this point.

Step Three: List Criteria to Evaluate Each Alternative
By what criteria are you going to judge each possible answer to your question? Brainstorm a list of criteria, then choose the most important and list these down the side of your chart, as in the following example:

Issue: Is the Canadian government correct in refusing to endorse American military action in Iraq?

Criteria	Alternatives		
	Answer #1	Answer #2	Answer #3
Who will benefit?	Canada benefits by avoiding a messy conflict and loss of Canadian lives.	Bush's popularity could increase, and he could avoid dealing with some domestic issues. The people of Iraq could benefit if Saddam is deposed.	Canada benefits from reviewing the facts as they emerge and refusing to make a hasty decision.
Who will suffer?	Canada's relationship with the US will suffer if it does not support its ally.	Canadian soldiers will die in Iraq and many Iraqi citizens will be maimed and killed. The US could suffer if it tries and fails to depose Saddam by military force.	Perhaps no one will suffer if Canada has time to review the facts and refuses to be pressured into action. On the other hand, Canada's dithering may turn into a negative.
Who offers this answer, and why?	A growing number. Polls indicate that support for military action in Iraq is waning, even among Americans. This position is also endorsed by religious groups and peace activists.	This position is supported by most American and Canadian conservatives, as well as some terrorism experts who believe that Saddam poses a special threat.	This position is supported by many Canadians who believe that caution is advisable. Support for the wait-and-see approach could shift in the future, though.

Step Four: Fill in Your Chart

Conduct additional research to evaluate each alternative answer according to the list of criteria. Your inquiry strategy will require that you establish relationships between some historical events and present circumstances. General sources, such as recent world almanacs and serial publications that summarize developments in countries of the world can be found at your local library. You could also consult Web sites such as Country Watch (www.country-watch.com) that briefly detail a nation's political, economic, and social histories and current events. If the issue is local, you might conduct personal interviews with municipal politicians and businesspeople.

The idea is to learn as much as you can about all sides of the issue so that you can effectively analyse each alternative in an unbiased manner. If you have lots of points under each criterion (some issues will yield more points than others), record them in point form.

Step Five: Draw Your Conclusions

Study the chart and weigh all the points under each column. Which possible answer has the strongest points? Decide on the best alternative, in your opinion, and write out your conclusion in a paragraph.

Practise Your Skill

1. Choose an issue that you have been following in your local newspaper, and use the steps outlined above to analyse it. Once you have reached your conclusion, write a letter to the editor of the paper explaining your view or "solution" to the issue.

2. Add one more criterion to the chart on US military action in Iraq (above) and fill out the rest of the columns as required. Why did you select this criterion?

Figure 11.6
A Kuwaiti worker prays near a burning oil field in 1991. At the end of the Persian Gulf War, retreating Iraqi troops set oil fields ablaze. Why did Saddam Hussein want to destroy Kuwait's oil production?

OIL AND ECONOMIC DEVELOPMENT

Following the Second World War, oil became the Middle East's most valuable commodity. As Western nations rebuilt after the war, the need for oil steadily increased.

Prior to the war, most oil fields in the Middle East were operated and controlled by British and American oil companies, which held **concession rights** on the land. Such agreements usually resulted in poor profits for Middle East governments. The independence movements sweeping across the region brought demands to nationalize foreign oil operations. Fearing outright takeover, Western oil companies conceded more control over oil resources and distributed greater oil profits to Middle Eastern governments.

Oil-rich nations channelled their bigger share of the oil wealth into industrial development and social programs. Agricultural reforms were also introduced, including land redistribution and irrigation projects. By the 1970s, living standards in the oil-producing nations had increased substantially, especially in countries like Saudi Arabia, United Arab Emirates, and Kuwait.

Development brought new schools, hospitals, and transportation and communications networks. The percentage of educated people, both men and women, doubled in some countries and increased 10 times in others. New opportunities in industry lured rural workers away from farms and into cities. Literacy rates skyrocketed from an average below 10 per cent to between 50 and 70 per cent.

Improved health care enhanced the quality of life and increased life expectancy.

Modernization and industrial development also created problems. In many countries, only the elite and the middle class reaped the benefits. Rapid urbanization overwhelmed many cities, which could not keep pace with the demands of growing populations. Many people came to the cities seeking a better life, but found themselves mired in poverty.

Modernization also strained traditional values. The process of **Westernization,** which accompanied economic development, disrupted some social customs. Many younger Arabs, for example, admired Western ideas, entertainment, and clothing. This created conflicts with parents who held traditional values.

Many Arabs still believe that Western innovations must be scrutinized. In their view, those that benefit society, such as many scientific and technological innovations, should be adopted, whereas those that seem to challenge traditional values, for example, flexible gender roles, should be rejected. The challenge for many countries in the Middle East, as elsewhere in the world, is to blend modern concepts with traditional values.

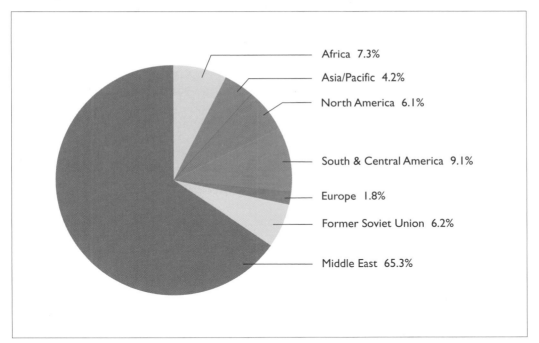

Figure 11.7
World Oil Reserves by Region, 2001. This graph depicts the world's oil reserves by region. Reserves are bodies of oil known to exist through exploration. In what ways might the distribution of oil reserves concern the world's rich, developed countries? (Source: Adapted from *The Changing Geopolitics of Energy–Part II*, Anthony H. Cordesman, Center for Strategic and International Studies, 1998, p.20. Copyright Anthony H. Cordesman, all rights reserved.)

Islamic Fundamentalism

Increased Western influence in the Middle East led to a revival of religious values in some Middle Eastern societies, including forms of Islamic fundamentalism rejected by many Muslims. Fundamentalists argue for a return to the "fundamentals" of religion, emphasizing the purity of Islam in the time of the Prophet Muhammad, and arguing that the Muslim world has lost its way.

Some extreme political and fundamentalist religious leaders have called for Holy War as a way of serving their own ambitions. For example, the terrorist organization **al-Qaeda**, led by Osama bin Laden, has justified its attacks on United States targets—including the 11 September 2001 attacks—as a religious war. Most Muslims condemned the September 11 attacks and this use of religion to justify violence.

FUTURE PROSPECTS

Most Middle East countries have vast oil reserves, but some, like Jordan, have little or no oil. The economies of stable, oil-rich countries such as Kuwait, Saudi Arabia, and United Arab Emirates have flourished—with some of the highest incomes in the world. Other countries have remained trapped in poverty. Extreme economic disparity is one of the major sources of discontent and instability in the region.

It is estimated that the region's total population will double in less than 25 years, creating increased demand for food, water, and land. Populations in the poor countries are also growing rapidly, which has further burdened social systems and development. Countries like Iran, Iraq, and Libya have oil reserves, but have missed opportunities to improve the lives of their people because of military ambitions or economic isolation.

Politically, the Middle East remains one of the world's most volatile regions. Progress has been made toward peace on some fronts in recent years, but religious, ethnic, and political rivalries remain, threatening to ignite a number of Middle Eastern "powder kegs."

In Review

1. What was the fundamental reason behind revolutionary movements in the Middle East?

2. a) Why did Iraq invade Kuwait?

   b) What was the outcome of the Persian Gulf War?

3. How did oil transform the economies of the oil-rich nations?

4. What problems did development create?

5. What situations continue to be flashpoints in the Middle East?

6. Suggest a few ways in which Middle Eastern issues and conflicts might influence Canada and Canadians.

Israel and Palestine

Palestine has been a land of hope and despair, miracles and massacres. Over thousands of years, this Middle Eastern territory has endured many invasions which have uprooted its people and left them dispossessed. In the twentieth century, Jews and Arabs fought tenaciously to possess what both have claimed as holy land. The bitter struggle inflamed all of the Middle East and at times threatened to engulf the entire world.

A RELIGIOUS BATTLEFIELD

Palestine, and its holy city of Jerusalem, is the home of three world religions: Judaism, Christianity, and Islam. In the course of history, Jews, Egyptians, Persians, Syrians, Greeks, Romans, Muslims, and Christian Crusaders have fought over this small strip of the Mediterranean coastline. The Ottoman Turks controlled the region from 1517 to 1918.

The Zionist Movement

The Romans expelled the Jews from Palestine in 135 CE. This began the **Diaspora**, the dispersal of Jewish people around the world. For centuries, Jews dreamed of returning to Palestine, their "Promised Land." In the late nineteenth century, the dream became a political movement known as **Zionism**. Theodore Herzl's 1896 book, *The Jewish State*, helped to shape the early Zionist movement. The next year, the World Zionist Organization was formed.

In 1916, Britain made promises of Arab independence. Then, in 1917, with the Balfour Declaration, it gave its support to the establishment of a Jewish homeland in Palestine. When Palestine became a British mandate in 1920, the Zionist movement grew. Jews, anxious to escape rising European fascism—and increasingly confident that the new Jewish state would become reality—began to migrate to Palestine. The Arabs who lived in the area, and could trace their roots for thousands of years, denounced the Jewish claim of a homeland.

The conflict between Arab independence and the establishment of a Jewish state was intense. Riots broke out in Jaffa in 1920 and in Jerusalem in 1921 and again in 1929. Jewish immigration to Palestine increased, fanning the fires of Arab nationalism. In 1936, violent riots broke out, with participants blocking roads and sabotaging trains. Britain sent in 20 000 troops and imposed martial law to restore order.

In 1939, the Palestinian Conference held in London failed to resolve the dispute. During the Second World War, both Jews and Arabs supported Britain, yet the conflict continued.

Growth of the Jewish Population in Palestine

Year	Jews	%	Total Population
1882	24 000	na	na
1922	83 790	11.1	753 048
1928	151 656	16.9	935 951
1937	395 836	28.2	1 401 794
1945	554 329	30.6	1 810 037

(Note: Illegal immigrants not included.)

Figure 11.8

This table shows Jewish population growth in Palestine. As Jewish immigration swelled, Arabs became more hostile. What might they have learned? (Source: Adapted from S. Hadawi, *Bitter Harvest: A Modern History of Palestine*. New York: Olive Branch Press, 1991.)

THE PARTITION OF PALESTINE

When the war ended in 1945, Britain again focused its attention on Palestine. In the eyes of the Western Allies, the horrors of the Holocaust had made a Jewish homeland a necessity. To the dismay of Arabs in Palestine, the West seemed ready to give Holocaust survivors their land. They resisted the very principle that their land could be taken from them and assigned to the Jewish people. To protect and promote the interests of Arab peoples, the **League of Arab States** was formed in 1945. It organized opposition to the creation of the independent state of Israel in Palestine. As Jewish immigration to Palestine increased, violent clashes escalated. Frustrated by the deepening conflict, Britain agreed to a United Nations Commission in 1947.

Pressured by the United States, the United Nations established a plan to partition Palestine into a Jewish state and an Arab state. (See Figure 11.11.) Zionists accepted the plan reluctantly, but the Palestinian Arabs rejected it outright. Palestine, they said, belonged to them. Moreover, Palestinian Arabs comprised the majority of the population and held most of the land. As the 15 May 1948 deadline for British withdrawal neared, the Jewish-Arab conflict escalated. It was clear the UN plan would be decided on the battlefield.

Figure 11.9

Most Western countries, including Canada, rejected Jewish refugees fleeing anti-Semitism in Europe. This increased immigration to Palestine. In 1935 alone, more than 60 000 Jews fled Germany and Poland seeking safe haven in Palestine. What impact might this have had on the government of Palestine?

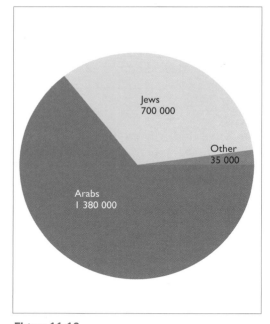

Figure 11.10

Ethnic Breakdown of Palestine, 1948. By 1948, the number of Jews living in Palestine had increased. This chart shows the ethnic makeup of Palestine at that time. How might the UN Commission on Palestine have used such information?

TWO DECADES OF CONFLICT

The First Arab-Israeli War, 1948-1949

As British forces withdrew from the region, neighbouring Arab states gave the Palestinians military support to drive out the Israelis. War raged on for more than a year. As it drew to a close, Israel's superior military strategy and weaponry placed most of Palestine under its control. Hundreds of thousands of Palestinians fled from their homes into nearby Arab states, such as Egypt, Jordan, Syria, and Lebanon. The United Nations responded to the refugee crisis and established camps near Israel's borders. Faced with the problems created by huge numbers of refugees, Arab nations pledged to "liberate Palestine" and, in the process, destroy Israel. The stage was set for decades of conflict.

MAP STUDY

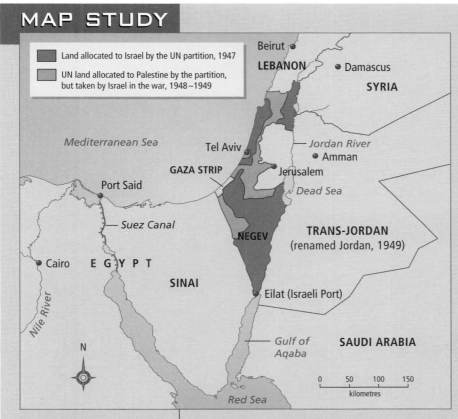

Land allocated to Israel by the UN partition, 1947

UN land allocated to Palestine by the partition, but taken by Israel in the war, 1948–1949

Figure 11.11

Israel, 1947 to 1949

The UN partitioned Palestine in 1948, creating the new state of Israel and immediate armed conflict with Arab forces in the region. By 1949, when an armistice was reached, Israel had taken control of more territory.

Interpreting

1. Estimate the proportion of the land mass that was allocated to Palestine and to Israel. Compare those figures to the proportion of the population indicated in Figure 11.10.
2. If you had been either a Jewish or Arab leader during partitioning, what concerns might you have had about land allocation?

The Suez Crisis, 1956

The next major flashpoint was the Suez Crisis. Riding a wave of Arab nationalism, Gamal Abdel Nasser seized control of Egypt in a military coup in 1954. In July 1956, he nationalized the Suez Canal. In October, under a secret agreement with Britain and France, Israel invaded Egypt. Britain and France then attacked Egypt to take control of the canal, but international pressure forced them to withdraw. This crisis heightened Arab distrust of Israel's intentions in the region. (See pages 191-194 in Chapter 6 for details on the Suez Crisis.)

The Six-Day War, 1967

In May 1967, Egypt was putting pressure on UN forces to withdraw from the Israeli frontier in the Sinai. At the same time, it was amassing troops in the Sinai and blockading the Israeli port of Eilat. In response, Israel launched a surprise pre-emptive attack on 5 June 1967. Within two days, Israeli troops crossed the Suez Canal and advanced south into Egypt. At the same time, more Israeli troops encircled the Egyptian army in the Sinai. Israel's superior air force destroyed the Egyptian air force on the ground and bombed airfields in Syria, Iraq, and Jordan. Israeli forces seized Old Jerusalem and the West Bank. On June 7, Jordan accepted a UN ceasefire, followed by Egypt on June 8, and Syria on June 9. On June 9 and 10, Israeli tanks occupied the Golan Heights and advanced into Syria. Israel agreed to a ceasefire on June 10, ending its most remarkable victory over its Arab neighbours.

Israel's defensive position was better than ever before. Its forces occupied Egypt's Sinai Peninsula, the Gaza Strip, all of Jerusalem, Syria's Golan Heights, and the West Bank of the Jordan River. In six days, Israel had gained control of an area three times larger than it had in 1949.

Figure 11.12
Israeli tanks rumbled into the Jordanian section of Jerusalem on 7 June 1967. Israel's defence minister said, "[W]e have returned to Jerusalem never to part from her." How would you view this statement as (a) an Israeli and (b) a Jordanian?

MAP STUDY

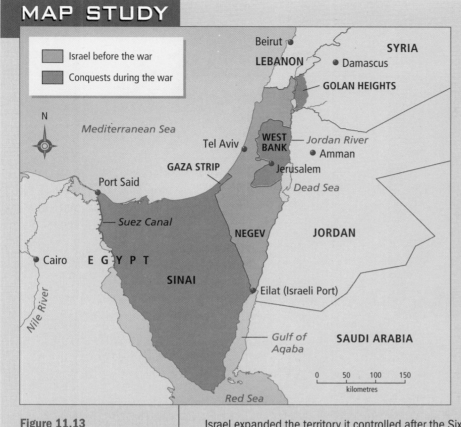

Figure 11.13
Israeli-Controlled Territory after the Six-Day War, 1967

Israel expanded the territory it controlled after the Six-Day War in 1967.

Interpreting

1. How would control of the Sinai Peninsula improve Israel's defensive position?
2. What difficulties might this create for the government of Israel in terms of the ethnic makeup of areas under its control?
3. Speculate on the impact this would have on Arab-Israeli relations in the region.

The Yom Kippur War, 1973

As Israelis observed the religious holiday of Yom Kippur on 6 October 1973, rearmed Egyptian and Syrian forces launched a surprise attack. After the 1967 war, the Soviet Union had supplied Egypt and Syria with more modern, sophisticated weaponry. They quickly captured Israeli positions in the Sinai and the Golan Heights. Caught off guard, Israeli forces suffered serious losses but launched a successful counterattack. By the time a ceasefire was reached three weeks later, Israel had crossed the Suez Canal and encircled the Egyptian Third Army.

After the Arab states had been pushed back beyond the 1967 ceasefire lines, the Soviets came to their aid. This almost ignited a global conflict. To counter direct Soviet involvement, the United States placed its nuclear forces on full alert. Intense negotiations defused the standoff, but these events clearly showed that war in the Middle East was a threat to global security.

Profile   Golda Meir (1898-1978)

Figure 11.14
Golda Meir

Golda Meir was born Goldie Mabovitch in Ukraine. As a young girl in 1907, she immigrated with her family to the United States. She married Morris Meyerson in 1917, and in 1921 they immigrated to Palestine to live on a kibbutz, or communal farm. (She Hebraized her surname in 1956.) Meir was active in the Women's Labour Council and became head of the Political Department of the Jewish Agency. She worked to free Jewish activists detained by British authorities in the troubled days before Israel was founded.

"There is a type of woman who cannot remain at home. In spite of the place her children and family fill in her life…she cannot divorce herself from the larger social life…. For such a woman, there is no rest."

— Golda Meir, 1928

"We only want that which is given naturally to all peoples of the world, to be masters of our own fate, only of our fate, not of others, and in co-operation and friendship with others."

— Golda Meir, 1957

"A leader who doesn't hesitate before he sends his nation into battle is not fit to be a leader."

— Golda Meir, 1970

"Our generation reclaimed the land, our children fought the war, and our grandchildren should enjoy the peace."

— Golda Meir, 1977

In 1948, Meir was a signatory to the Israeli independence declaration. She served as ambassador to the Soviet Union, where millions of Jews were eager to claim Israeli citizenship. As minister of labour and minister for foreign affairs, she achieved a highly visible profile in world politics.

Meir held a seat in the Israeli parliament, the Knesset, from 1949 to 1974. She helped mould one of Israel's strongest political organizations, the Labour Party. In 1969 she became prime minister, in a coalition government. Meir defended Israel and attacked its enemies with determination. She was particularly skilled at building support for Israel against the attacks of Palestinian terrorists.

Even though the 1973 Yom Kippur War ended in victory for Israel, it suffered a high number of casualties and many early losses. Meir was held responsible and resigned in 1974. A year later, she published her autobiography, *My Life*. She died of leukemia in 1978.

Meir had spent 50 years in the turbulent world of Zionist and Israeli politics. She was a driving force behind the Zionist dream of a Jewish homeland in Palestine. She was also seen as a guiding force for peace in the Middle East, even though she did not hesitate to send Israeli troops into battle when necessary.

Responding

1. Explain how Meir could both support peace in the Middle East and defend Israel with military attacks.

THE PALESTINE LIBERATION ORGANIZATION

The Palestinian refugee camps around Israel became hotbeds of Arab resistance. But the resistance groups lacked organization and supplies. In 1964, the Arab states created and funded the **Palestine Liberation Organization** (PLO). Arab countries saw it as a voice for the Palestinian people, but also as a way to prevent the Palestinians from drawing the Arab world into a war with Israel.

The PLO assumed a degree of sovereignty over some refugee camps. However, militant guerrilla groups used these as bases to launch raids into Israel—and Israel retaliated. It also increased tensions between the Palestinians and their host nations, especially Lebanon and Jordan.

In 1969, Yasser Arafat was elected head of the PLO, a position he held for more than 30 years. Arafat had been the head of Al Fatah, a guerrilla group that had been waging military operations against Israel.

ISRAEL AND EGYPT

In the late 1970s, the United States took the lead in efforts to find peace in the Middle East. Dr. Henry Kissinger, US secretary of state, met separately with Arab and Israeli leaders to encourage them to soften their positions. This was called **shuttle diplomacy**, and it gradually led to small amounts of land in the Sinai being returned to Egypt.

Negotiations continued under US president Jimmy Carter. In March 1979, Egyptian president Anwar Sadat and Israeli prime minister Menachem Begin signed the Egyptian-Israeli Peace Treaty. This agreement reaffirmed each party's adherence to the historic Camp David "Framework for Peace," or Camp David

Accord, agreed to one year earlier. The conflict had been costly to both countries. Egyptian leaders wanted to reduce poverty and improve living standards. They knew that maintaining a huge military to defend against Israel would drain their efforts. Under Sadat, they tried a new tactic: peace. Israel agreed to withdraw from the Sinai in stages, and the two countries established formal relations. Israeli hardliners—a minority of citizens—opposed the accord, as did the PLO. And the Arab League expelled Egypt.

> "Armed Struggle is the only way to liberate Palestine. Thus it is the overall strategy, not merely a tactical phase...."
>
> — Article 9, The PLO Covenant, 1968

WWW.YALE.EDU/LAWWEB/AVALON/MIDEAST/ART9

To read the Palestinian National Charter (July 1-17, 1968) go to this Web site for Yale Law School's Avalon Project. You will find other historic documents there as well.

Figure 11.15
Egyptian president Anwar Sadat (left) embraces Israeli prime minister Menachem Begin as US president Jimmy Carter looks on in Washington during the Camp David Summit in 1978. Three years later, Sadat was assassinated by Islamic extremists. What had each leader hoped to gain by signing the peace agreement?

TERRORISM

As the situation of Palestinian refugees worsened and organizations such as the PLO were created, violence escalated in the Middle East. Arab nations continued to support organizations whose goal was to liberate Palestine—and destroy the state of Israel.

Israel and much of the West viewed the acts of violence against Israel as terrorism. But many Palestinians and Arab supporters viewed the attackers as freedom fighters courageously battling for the rights of a dispossessed people. The battles and conflicts of the Middle East could not be contained by borders; they spread, affecting nations and citizens around the globe.

Terrorist attacks, however, failed to liberate a single metre of Palestinian soil or to gain concessions from Israel. The terrorists did draw world attention to the volatile Middle East and the plight of the Palestinians. By the late 1980s, there was a growing realization that terrorism had only hardened Israel's resolve to survive and damaged the image of the Palestinian cause.

Figure 11.16

Middle East terrorism spread to Europe. At Rome's international airport in 1985, terrorists attacked people waiting at the check-in area of Israel's El Al airline. Fourteen people died and 60 were injured. Why would terrorists attack these travellers?

THE OCCUPIED TERRITORIES

In March 1978, Israel invaded southern Lebanon and destroyed bases the PLO had established there. In June 1982, Israel launched a full-scale military operation against Palestinian bases, and Beirut, Lebanon's capital, became a war zone.

Several months later, Palestinian guerrillas fled from Beirut to sympathetic countries such as Libya. With the PLO rendered relatively ineffective, Israel moved to increase Jewish settlements in the **Occupied Territories**.

MAP STUDY

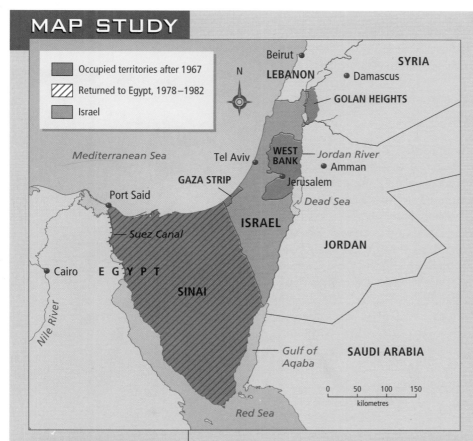

Figure 11.17
The Occupied Territories,
1967 to 1982

Israel maintained control of most of the Occupied Territories. Settlement of the Occupied Territories signalled that it intended the control to be permanent.

Interpreting

1. Why do you suppose Israel would want permanent control over the Occupied Territories?
2. Describe how the size of Israel compares in 1947, 1949, and 1982. (Refer to the map of Israel, 1947 to 1949 on page 359.)
3. How might this affect future Arab-Israeli relations?

The territories Israel had captured in the Six-Day War of 1967 were ruled by military law. Palestinians living there had no citizenship rights, and many lived in refugee camps. Jews who chose to settle in the Occupied Territories, however, had full Israeli citizenship. The number of Jewish settlements grew quickly, from 36 in 1977, with 5000 people, to more than 120 in 1987, with 70 000 settlers. By 1987, half of the West Bank was occupied by Israelis. By and large, the international community considers these settlements on Palestinian lands to violate international law.

The First Intifadah

Through the mid-1980s, Palestinians demonstrated against Israeli domination of the Occupied Territories. In December 1987, an outbreak of clashes led to a Palestinian uprising known as the **Intifadah**. Violent demonstrations tore apart the Gaza Strip and the West Bank in early 1988, with Palestinians hurling rocks and gas bombs at Israeli soldiers and citizens. Israeli troops responded to the protestors with force, arresting and deporting Palestinians suspected of being involved in the violence. The unrest continued for months. By July, 300 Palestinians had been killed. Israel's response brought harsh international criticism, even from Israel's staunchest supporter, the United States.

Then in December 1988, under pressure from the US and moderate Arabs, Arafat formally recognized Israel's right to exist on condition that Palestine also have a right to exist. Israeli defence minister Itzhak Rabin responded by proposing elections in the Occupied Territories, provided the Intifadah ceased. The uprising, however, continued unabated. By 1993, 950 Palestinians had been killed and more than 100 000 had been injured in confrontations with Israelis, and about 15 000 people were being held in detention camps. Peace eluded the Middle East once again.

Figure 11.18

Masked Palestinian youths fight in the Intifadah against Israeli occupation in the West Bank in 1988. How effective do you think slingshots would be as weapons?

> **With petrol bomb and stone
> I will build my state...
> Strike with the stone.
> Burn, burn the tyre,
> Put up barriers.
> Revolution, revolution, do not fade.**
>
> — Lyrics from *Intifadah*, a popular Palestinian song

Voices The Creation of a Palestinian State

Central to the Palestinian-Israeli conflict is the issue of whether an independent Palestinian state should be created out of Israeli-occupied land. In the extract below, Salah Khalaf, a former PLO member assassinated in the 1990s, argues that it is time for the Arab world to recognize the legitimacy of the state of Israel and for Israel to allow a homeland for the displaced Palestinian people. This view is not shared by all Arabs. Sheikh Ahmed Yassin, for example, is the spiritual leader of the opposition group Hamas, and argues that Palestinian rights have been violated.

Israeli David Bar-Illan, head of an anti-terrorist foundation, argues that an independent Palestine would pose an unacceptable threat to Israel. Yossi Beilin represents a more moderate view of the proposed Palestinian state. As you read their opinions, consider ways in which this complex issue might be resolved.

SALAH KHALAF

"Strange as it may seem at first glance, Israel and the Palestinian people have similar and compatible goals. Israel wants to be master of its own fate—an independent state, secure, and at peace with its neighbors. We ask for nothing more than the same rights for ourselves. The Israeli government believes the two nations' objectives are mutually exclusive. Its view is that the independence, security, and peace of Israel are attainable only if the Palestinians' right to those same privileges is denied or at least severely restricted. The Palestinians now believe that the two peoples' separate quests for independence, security and peace will either fail together or succeed together. The Palestinian peace plan is built on that conviction. The plan itself is simple.

The state of Israel would live in peace with the state of Palestine, which would be established in the West Bank and Gaza Strip, with East Jerusalem as its capital. This final settlement would be part of a comprehensive Arab-Israeli agreement that would establish peace between the Jewish and Arab states, thus allaying Israel's security concerns."

Source: Reprinted with permission from *Foreign Policy 78* (Spring 1990). Copyright 1990 by the Carnegie Endowment for International Peace.

SHEIKH AHMED YASSIN

"...[T]he Israelis will never give the Palestinians back their legitimate rights. The only language Israel understands is the language of power, resistance and Jihad... Our struggle with Israel will continue until we remove this entity from our land. Our position is clear—there is an Israeli entity occupying our lands and there are Palestinian displaced and refugees. What we are struggling for is to end the occupation of our lands and get the refugees back home... Establishing a Palestinian state requires only two conditions—first, the state needs borders and sovereignty, and second, [there should not be any] concession or compromise on the legitimate and historical rights of our Palestinian people. If these two conditions are present, our position concerning the establishment of the state will be positive. Hamas can stop its military activities if they give us all of our legitimate rights."

Source: From an interview published in *Palestine Report*, Volume 7, No. 7, 2 August 2000. © 2000 Palestine Report. All rights reserved.

DAVID BAR-ILLAN

"Israel is in a bad situation. Not because it won the 1967 war and, as a result, added a million hostile Arabs to the population under its control; not because it suffers universal calumny for allegedly mistreating them; not because the higher Arab birth rate poses a demographic threat; and not even because the territory of the land of Israel is also claimed by [Arabs].... [W]hat makes Israel's situation truly bad is that 170 million Arabs consider the very existence of Israel an offense to their sense of history and destiny.... A Palestinian state in Judea-Samaria [the West Bank] and Gaza would cut through Jerusalem and flank the city on three sides, touch on Tel Aviv's suburbs, and have a long border, nine to fifteen miles [15 to 24km] from the sea, with Israel's most thickly populated areas. Palestinian militias...would have Israeli pedestrians within rifle range.... Real peace can only come in the event...that a very large number of Jews from the Soviet Union, South and North America, and Europe immigrate to Israel. A massive settling of Judea and Samaria would then make Israel's presence there irreversible...and finally convince the Arab states to resign themselves to the existence and indestructibility of Israel and give up the war they have been waging against it since the day of its birth."

Source: David Bar-Illan, "Can Israel Withdraw? No!" *Commentary*, 1988. Reprinted from COMMENTARY, April 1988, by permission; all rights reserved.

YOSSI BEILIN

"Israel currently faces two major threats.... By 2010 there will be a Palestinian majority in the area Israel controls (Israel, the West Bank and Gaza). Israel must choose between remaining a democracy or be a Jewish but undemocratic state, with a minority of Jews controlling a majority of Arabs. Both of these options are devastating. We must have a border in place by 2010.

There are only two options: (1) to reach peace with the Palestinians who are ready to negotiate, or, if this is impossible, (2) to unilaterally withdraw to the 1967 borders—the only internationally recognized and accepted border. Only a negotiated settlement will allow Israel a more secure border that includes Jerusalem and most of the settlers than the June 1967 border. The idea that we can wait and see, without negotiating or withdrawing, cannot be accepted and it is not in Israel's national interest."

Source: Excerpted from a speech given by Yossi Beilin at the Center for Middle East Peace and Economic Cooperation, Washington, DC, 21 May 2002.

Responding

1. Summarize each viewpoint in your own words.
2. With whom do you agree and why?
3. If you were involved in a diplomatic mission, how would you convince David Bar-Illan and Ahmed Yassin to take part in peace talks?

MOVEMENTS TOWARD PEACE

The Arab-Israeli wars from 1948 onward shed blood and created bitterness on all sides. Israel won on the battlefield, but it faced revenge from Arab neighbours and lethal attacks from Palestinian terrorists. Maintaining a large, state-of-the art military drained Israel's economy. The Occupied Territories, with hundreds of thousands of Palestinian refugees living in misery, were a continuous security threat. Conditions were so bad in the 1980s that many thousands of young Israelis were emigrating each year.

Apart from the Egyptian-Israeli peace accord, however, the combatants in the Middle East remained polarized. The best peace efforts of moderate politicians and diplomats on all sides achieved nothing more than vague promises and temporary ceasefires.

In the early 1990s, the situation began to change. Moderate Israelis and Palestinians appeared to be gaining power. The Cold War had ended, and the United States pursued peace initiatives in the Middle East with renewed vigour. Terrorism seemed to be on the wane as a new generation of Palestinian leaders presented their case to the international community. World opinion had also changed: the notion of Israel as the courageous underdog had been battered because of its response to the Intifadah and its military actions in Lebanon.

THE OSLO PEACE PROCESS

In 1991, the Soviet Union and the United States organized a conference in Madrid that was attended by delegates representing Israel, the Palestinians, Egypt, Lebanon, Syria, and Jordan. It was the first time that Israel and its foreign neighbours, except for Egypt, had met face to face to negotiate anything. The talks resolved nothing, but they laid the foundations for a series of talks and negotiations.

Those talks culminated two years later in a series of agreements negotiated secretly in Oslo, Norway. In September 1993, US president Bill Clinton presided as Israeli and PLO representatives signed what became known as the **Oslo Accord**. Israel agreed to withdraw from the Occupied Territories of Gaza and the West Bank town of Jericho. It also accepted limited self-rule for the 1.8 million Palestinians living in the Occupied Territories. Israel accepted the PLO as the legitimate representative of the Palestinians. And the PLO formally recognized Israel's right to exist for the first time, renouncing terrorism and threats to destroy Israel.

Figure 11.19

Professor Hanan Ashrawi is the highest-ranking woman to speak for the Palestinian cause and the cause of peace in the Middle East. Commenting on the unfolding peace process in the Middle East, Ashrawi once noted: "Any peace process has to have clearly defined objectives. You cannot enter a process as a fishing expedition; you have to know where you're heading... Peace means that you really have the courage to tackle the causes of the conflict, to address them, to disentangle them, and to solve them."

Most of the world community welcomed the Oslo Accord and peace process. But in their respective communities, both Arafat and Israeli prime minister Itzhak Rabin faced extremist opposition—including death threats. Regardless, the peace process continued.

In October 1994, Israel and Jordan signed a peace treaty. They had technically been at war since the founding of Israel.

> **"Today marks a shining moment of hope for the Middle East; indeed, of the entire world."**
>
> — US president Bill Clinton, Washington, 13 September 1993

Profile   Yasser Arafat (1929-)

Figure 11.20
Yasser Arafat

Yasser Arafat was born in Cairo to a middle-class family that opposed Zionism. From an early age, he knew all about the bitter, brutal world of Palestinian politics. In the early 1950s, while studying engineering at Cairo University, he became leader of the League of Palestinian Students, which called for the destruction of Israel. During the Suez Crisis in 1956, Arafat served briefly in the Egyptian army.

> "We seek true independence and full sovereignty: the right to control our own airspace, water resources and borders; to develop our own economy, to have normal commercial relations with our neighbours, and to travel freely. In short, we seek only what the free world now enjoys and only what Israel insists on for itself: the right to control our own destiny and to take our place among free nations."
>
> Source: Yasser Arafat, Op-Ed, *The New York Times*,
> 3 February 2002.

In 1963, Arafat helped to found Al Fatah, an Arab guerrilla group pledged to wage war on Israel. Al Fatah joined the PLO in 1964. Within five years, Arafat was leader of the PLO, and Al Fatah was its major force. A wave of guerrilla attacks brought the PLO global recognition and recrimination. In 1974, however, the UN granted the PLO observer status and Arafat was invited to address the General Assembly.

In spite of its political initiatives, the PLO was responsible for a wave of attacks against Israel. In 1982, Israel invaded Lebanon and defeated Arafat's forces. Arafat's leadership was openly challenged by PLO hardliners, but he remained leader and set up PLO headquarters in Tunisia.

In the face of Arab division and Israel's military successes, Arafat's leadership declined throughout the 1980s. In the 1991 Gulf War, he and the PLO co-operated with Iraqi leader Saddam Hussein. This weakened Arafat and the PLO even more in both Arab and Western eyes, but Arafat continued working behind the scenes. In 1993, he negotiated an agreement with Israel that would allow him to return to Palestinian soil. In the same year, he shared the Nobel Peace Prize with Israeli foreign minister Shimon Peres and Israeli prime minister Itzhak Rabin for their efforts in the Middle East.

Yet Arafat was beloved and despised. His return in 1994 was greeted as both triumph and travesty. As leader of the PLO, his goal had been clear: creation of an independent Palestine out of Israeli-occupied territories. To some Palestinians, he was a proud symbol of hope, a courageous freedom fighter. To others, he was corrupt and ineffectual—his time had passed. To many Israelis, Arafat was a deadly terrorist whose real purpose was to destroy Israel, not bring peace.

Responding

1. How would you classify Arafat—as a freedom fighter or terrorist? Explain.

FROM ACCORD TO INTIFADAH

As the peace process continued, so did extremist threats. In May 1994, an agreement was signed to initiate Palestinian self-rule in Jericho and the Gaza Strip and to end the Intifadah. On July 1, Arafat crossed from Egypt into the Gaza Strip, stepping onto Palestinian soil for the first time in 27 years. On July 5, he became head of the new Palestinian Authority (PA). In August, Israel agreed to shift administrative functions in the West Bank. The PA gained control over health, welfare, education, tourism, and taxation. Israel kept control of its armed forces and Israeli citizens living in Palestinian-controlled areas.

In September 1995, the second part of the Oslo Agreement, "Oslo II," was signed. This implemented the next stages in the process toward Palestinian self-rule. It also created more conflict, especially around the question of Jewish settlements in the Occupied Territories. At a student peace rally a few weeks later, a young Jewish ultranationalist shot and killed Israeli prime minister Itzhak Rabin.

Regardless, the peace process continued. On 9 January 1996, Palestinians voted in elections for the first time since Israel had been formed. They were voting for the Palestinian Authority (PA), the 88-member legislative council that would administer the Palestinian areas of the Occupied Territories. With the support of 87 per cent of voters, Yasser Arafat became president of the PA.

In early 1996, Israel suffered a series of deadly suicide bombings organized by

Figure 11.21

US president Bill Clinton walks away as Israeli prime minister Netanyahu (left) shakes hands with Palestinian leader Yasser Arafat in December 1998. The meeting was held in Gaza to restart the peace process, but it failed. What does this photograph say to you about the relationship between Arafat and Netanyahu?

> "We must return to a peace based on the concept of deterrence: a strong Israel that is prepared to defend itself and use its power when necessary."
>
> — Benjamin Netanyahu, former prime minister of Israel, 2001

the terrorist group Hamas. It then bombarded bordering areas of south Lebanon, where terrorist groups like Hamas and Hezbollah ("Army of God") had established bases. Viewpoints hardened. In May 1996, Israeli voters narrowly elected Benjamin Netanyahu, of the conservative Likud Party, as their new prime minister. Netanyahu, a hardliner, promised to re-examine the peace agreement. This won support from Israelis but angered Palestinians.

In September 1996, despite international criticism, Israel completed an underground tunnel near one of Islam's most sacred shrines in Jerusalem. It was also a sacred site for Jews. What followed was the worst gunfight between Israelis and Palestinians since the Six-Day War in 1967. After three days, more than 70 Palestinians and Israelis had been killed.

Tensions increased in the West Bank as Netanyahu allowed construction to resume in the Jewish settlements. In March 1997, violence erupted at an Israeli construction site in mostly Arab East Jerusalem. The housing development signalled that the Israeli government had returned to a policy of building Jewish settlements in the Occupied Territories.

Alarmed by growing violence, Netanyahu accused Arafat of doing nothing to stop terrorist attacks and refused to take part in further peace talks. In October 1998, prompted by US president Bill Clinton, Netanyahu and Arafat did sign an accord. Israel would continue to withdraw from the West Bank. Palestinians agreed to improve security measures against terrorist attacks on Israel and to remove calls for Israel's destruction from their national charter. Citing Palestinian violations of the accord, however, Israel froze implementation of the accord in December.

The Second Intifadah

In 1999, Netanyahu's government collapsed, and Ehud Barak, of the Labour Party, was elected the new prime minister of Israel. Barak resumed negotiations, but they bogged down in disagreements. In May 2000, US president Bill Clinton pressured Barak and Arafat to resume peace talks. They met at Camp David for three weeks, but no new agreements were reached. The peace process was stalled. In the wake of this setback, a wave of violence broke out in Israel and the Occupied Territories.

In September 2000, Ariel Sharon, new leader of the Likud Party, visited a sacred Islamic site in Jerusalem. Sharon had been defence minister during Israel's invasion of Lebanon in 1982. Hundreds of Palestinian refugees had been killed by Lebanese Christian militiamen in camps that were under Israeli control. In 1983, Sharon was found indirectly responsible for the massacre and removed from office. In 2000, he was a figure despised by many Palestinians. Riots broke out during his visit to the shrine and escalated into the second Intifadah.

Violence increased on both sides. The terrorist group Hamas was responsible for a series of gunfights and suicide bombings. This uprising was far more deadly than the first Intifadah, and the group operated outside the control of the Palestinian Authority or the PLO. The bombers, usually young males, worked their way amongst groups of Jewish Israelis on buses, in markets, at prayer, in clubs, at checkpoints. Then they detonated explosives strapped to their bodies.

HRW.ORG/PRESS/2002/11/ISRL-PA1101.HTM

Visit this page on the Human Rights Watch Web (HRW) site to read a report by the internationally respected agency on the deployment of suicide bombings. Which four groups are directly addressed by HRW? What is the basic message to each group?

In January 2001, elections were held again in Israel. Sharon, who promised military action, was swept to power. Israeli forces closed off Palestinian areas. They set up military checkpoints in the Occupied Territories that made movement to jobs, food, or medical care very difficult. Israel assassinated known Palestinian militants, used tactical air strikes, and sent tanks and troops into Palestinian-ruled areas where it suspected terrorist activities. Violence worsened through 2001 and 2002.

In 2002, the world watched as Israeli tanks isolated Arafat in his Ramallah headquarters for four months. Israeli prime minister Ariel Sharon blamed Arafat of harbouring terrorists and of being "irrelevant."

By the end of 2002, little remained of Palestinian autonomy. Many of the Palestinian refugee camps had become even more cramped and squalid after the military actions. In the face of this, construction in the settlements continued, and Israelis faced yet another election. Periods of relative peace had become disquieting. Moreover, the death toll continued to rise. Between September 2000 and August 2002, Israeli sources reported 607 Israeli deaths due to ongoing violence. Over the same time period, Palestinian sources reported 1552 Palestinian deaths.

"The people who carry out suicide bombing are not martyrs, they're war criminals, and so are the people who help to plan such attacks."

— Kenneth Roth, Executive Director, Human Rights Watch

Figure 11.22
Members of Force 17 (Palestinian leader Yasser Arafat's elite presidential guard unit) present their arms during Arafat's arrival in the West Bank town of Ramallah on March 2001. Several Force 17 facilities, in Ramallah and the Gaza Strip, were attacked by Israeli army helicopter gunships prior to his arrival. Israel alleges the 3500 member Force 17 unit, widely regarded as the best trained and the one most trusted by Arafat, is responsible for a spate of deadly attacks against Israeli civilians, but Arafat denies its role.

In Review

1. a) What immediate impact did the creation of the state of Israel have on the Palestinians?

   b) What were the long-term consequences?

2. What did the PLO hope to accomplish? Was it successful?

3. What were the chief consequences of the Arab-Israeli wars from 1948 to 1973?

4. How did the Egyptian-Israeli Peace Treaty split the Arab world?

5. a) What prompted the first and second Intifadahs in the Occupied Territories?

   b) What was Israel's response in both cases?

6. Outline the steps taken toward negotiating Palestinian self-rule after 1988.

7. What forces or factors seem to have undermined attempts at Palestinian self-rule?

8. If you were in a position to advise either the Israeli government or the Palestinian Authority on a peace process, describe three actions that you would recommend it take. Explain your recommendations.

9. Comment on the tactic of suicide bombings used by Palestinians. Why might this strategy be used? How successful does it appear to have been?

10. Conduct research to determine who is currently leading the Palestinians. Is Arafat still in power? If so, how solid is his leadership? If there are other leaders, do they have the support of Palestinians? Produce a one-page report on this topic.

Summary

The Middle East is a region of deeply held religious beliefs and cultural values. Historically, it has been exploited, divided, and fought over by competing imperial powers. When the state of Israel was created as a homeland for Jews in Palestine after the Second World War, it ignited many longstanding conflicts. Wars and peace agreements followed, but the peace was short-lived and precarious.

At the end of the twentieth century, the Oslo Accords set in motion a process meant to bring peace and to lead to Palestinian self-rule and a Palestinian state. It seemed that hardened attitudes were softening. By the beginning of the twenty-first century, the peace process had collapsed in terrible violence. With rumbling Israeli tanks and Palestinian suicide bombers, a peaceful resolution hangs in the balance.

Viewpoints

ISSUE: Does the US have a role in the Middle East peace process?

Background

The Middle East has been a focus of conflict for most of the twentieth century. Throughout the 1990s, the United States intervened to introduce a peace in the region, with limited success. In the excerpts that follow, Rabbi Sherwin Wine, founder of the Humanist Institute, and Palestinian legislator Hanan Ashrawi examine the priorities in the region. Rabbi Wine argues that peace must be politically imposed by a superpower such as the United States, whereas Ashrawi argues that the Palestinian government must first reform itself—without US interference.

Read these two viewpoints carefully, and answer the questions that follow. (You may want to refer to the Skill Path "Analysing a Reading" on page 14 for guidance before you begin.)

Rabbi Sherwin Wine, founder of the Humanist Institute

The failure of the Oslo peace process is as much the result of intense hatred and suspicion as it is the incompatibility of vested interests. The issues of boundaries, Jerusalem, and refugees are shrouded by such levels of distrust that the normal compromises that negotiations bring can never emerge. No arrangements can provide the security that most Israelis want. And no "deal" can yield the sense of honor and vindication that most Palestinians and Arabs seek.

Jews and Arabs, Israelis and Palestinians by themselves cannot achieve peace—or even an effective truce—by relying on negotiations alone; the cycle of vengeance has its own logic. Every terrorist action incites retaliation; every retaliation incites counter-retaliation. No antagonist can allow itself to be seen as weak. Revenge is a necessary tactic in maintaining credibility. The cycle cannot stop itself without outside intervention.

A binational Israeli-Palestinian state—a dream of many peaceniks—is not politically viable even though it would be economically desirable. Jewish and Arab nationalism are realities; they cannot be wished away. Mutual hatred and suspicion are realities; they cannot be dismissed. Arguing against nationalism may work a hundred years from now but it doesn't fly today. A Jewish state—in which Jewish national culture is the dominant culture and most people speak Hebrew—is no more racist than would be an Arab state whose dominant culture and language reflected its people. Three million Palestinian refugees cannot return to the Jewish state without destroying the Jewish national character of the Jewish state.

Because outside intervention is required, the only superpower capable of orchestrating it successfully is the United States. Since September 11, George W. Bush has mobilized an effective coalition of world powers, including Europe, Russia, China, and India—as well as many allies in the Muslim world. The war between the Israelis and the Palestinians has begun to undermine the coalition, especially with Bush's perceived support of the Ariel Sharon government in Israel. Joint intervention with the approval of the United Nations and with the support of moderate Muslim powers could restore the coalition. This intervention is no different from the intervention that the United States initiated in Bosnia and Kosovo.

What would be the elements of such an intervention? The United States controls the process. The Israelis don't trust the United Nations and won't cooperate with an effort managed by the hostile nations of the developing world.

The United States acts as a neutral "parent." It doesn't always praise one side and condemn the other; it creates a setting for negotiations, with the presence of major members of the coalition. The format of such negotiations is only a pretense. In the "back room" the United States dictates the settlement and everybody knows that the United States has imposed the settlement. Both antagonists protest, but they yield because they have no choice.

All that can realistically be achieved at this time is an effective truce. Peace will have to await a reduction in the fury of hatred and suspicion. For now, an imposed settlement should include the following:

- the removal of all Jewish settlements from the West Bank and Gaza, except those settlements which function as contiguous communities for Tel Aviv and Jerusalem
- the digging of a ditch and construction of a fence between the Jews and Arabs along the adjusted 1967 boundaries
- the policing of this fence by the United States and its European allies
- the granting of Arab East Jerusalem to the Palestinians as their national capital
- the demilitarization of the new Palestinian state, with periodic inspections by the United States and its coalition partners

- compensation for Palestinian refugees who cannot return.

Such compensation may cost over $30 billion and would be covered by the United States, Japan, and European allies. If the compensation helps to bring about an effective truce, it would be worth the investment. Rescuing the global economy for peace justifies the expense.

Israel needs to be compensated for its "willingness" to shrink and to confront the wrath of its right-wing extremists. Since it won't in the foreseeable future be accepted by the Arab and Muslim worlds, it needs to be regarded as the European power it is. Israel's high-tech economy needs the European market, just as its European culture needs a European support system. The price that Europe pays for this necessary peace is that it accepts Israel as a member of the European Union. Such acceptance is no different than acceptance of Cyprus or Turkey, and Israelis will be better off trading in euros than shekels.

After this settlement is imposed, terrorist violence will likely continue. The war against Muslim fundamentalist terrorists will also continue. For the extremists in the Arab and Muslim world—and even in the Jewish world—hatred is a way of life. For moderates, an effective truce will enable them to join the forces of peace.

Source: *The Humanist*, September-October 2002. Reprinted with the permission of the publisher, American Humanist Association, copyright 2002.

Hanan Ashrawi, member of the Palestinian Legislative Council

The current push for changes in the Palestinian political process is neither new nor externally motivated. Rather, there is a call to implement a home-grown, authentic programme of structural, legal and procedural reform which has been gathering steam in Palestinian society for years. Political reform must come from the Palestinians. Foreign interference will not help the process.

Average Palestinians have become increasingly frustrated with the repressive and extra-legal security services, and with the inept administra-tion in the occupied territories. Throughout the deeply flawed Oslo peace process, many elected officials stood beyond the reach of their voting constituencies. These matters came to a head after the latest round of Israeli sieges. With much of Nablus, Bethlehem and Ramallah in ruins, Palestinians began asking: how was this allowed to happen? Where was the protection? Can things be put back together?

The only way to close the gap in confidence between Palestinians and their leaders is to overhaul the political process. A mere reshuffling of the deck will not do. Reform is also needed to strengthen international support and streamline domestic mechanisms for confronting the challenges raised by the ongoing occupation.

Making constitutional changes in the middle of a war, or in the wake of the sort of physical destruction recently inflicted by the Israeli military, will not be easy. Though Palestinian will is not broken, the civil infrastructure of the Palestinian Authority is in shambles. The World Bank conservatively estimates the damage of recent Israeli incursions throughout the West Bank at $361m. This is nothing compared to the suffering and loss of life.

New presidential, legislative council and municipal elections are needed immediately and will require the registration of more than a million voters. All mismanagement, abuse of authority and misuse of public funds must be weeded out. The bloated cabinet should be trimmed to become efficient and accountable. Four-year term limits should be imposed on security officials. There must be equality before the law and a clear separation of powers.

The new draft legislation which would bar the president or the security forces from interfering with judicial decisions—for example, keeping those who have been ordered to be freed behind bars—is a step in the right direction. The application of the new legislation would spell the end of the state security courts, notorious for their lack of due process and rapid-fire convictions. It would also require trials for those involved in extra-judicial killings, including the murder of alleged collaborators.

The call for Palestinian political reform belongs only to the Palestinian people, and it deserves sharp skepticism when made by others. In the hands of the Israeli government the call for reform is both disingenuous and self-serving. The intention is to appropriate grassroots frustrations in order to undermine the credibility of larger Palestinian political demands.

The Israeli government also hopes to divert international criticism and increase Palestinian factionalism in order to delay military withdrawal from the occupied territories. Coming so soon after the war crimes committed in Jenin and other Palestinian towns and camps, Ariel Sharon is the last person to be advising others on democratic transition. More importantly, however, Sharon has latched on to "reform" as a precondition for negotiations in order to avoid anything that would foil his unilateral expansion plans.

Coming from the American government, the call for reform is generally counterproductive. American involvement has been far from principled or even-handed, and Palestinian trust of US influence is at an all-time low. Historically, the US administration has been more than willing to turn a blind eye to abuses within the Palestinian system so long as the Palestinian Authority discharged its "security" obligations towards Israel and maintained its commitment to the "process."

Civil society organisations and average citizens have presented the Palestinian government with an invaluable opportunity to correct deep-seated problems. To succeed, the movement for fundamental change must be proactive and steered internally by and for the benefit of Palestinians. Otherwise, it will end up being reactive and forced externally for the benefit of others. Such neo-colonial interference can only backfire.

Source: "Reforming from Within," by Hanan Ashrawi, *The Guardian* (London), 7 June 2002. © Hanan Ashrawi.

Analysis and Evaluation

1. Why does Wine think that the Israelis and the Palestinians cannot negotiate peace by themselves?

2. Why does Ashrawi think that Palestinian reform is necessary? What does she think must change?

3. Decide which of the viewpoints you tend to support and explain why. If you agree with neither, state the position you do support and explain it. Be sure to use specific information from this textbook, the readings, and other sources to support your position.

Chapter Analysis

MAKING CONNECTIONS

1. Outline the major sources of conflict in the Middle East, both past and present.

2. What useful role might Canada play in the reduction of Middle East tensions? Be specific.

3. Reviewing Arab-Israeli relations from the birth of Israel to the present, can you say that peace in the Middle East is closer or further away today? Explain your answer.

DEVELOPING YOUR VOICE

4. Imagine you are a spokesperson for the Palestine Liberation Organization. Write a brief speech in which you present your case for a Palestinian homeland to a Canadian audience.

5. Canada joined the UN coalition in the Gulf War in 1991 and participated in several air offensives against Iraqi targets. Canada also contributed forces to free Afghanistan from Taliban forces in 2001-2002. Do you think Canada should have become involved in these conflicts? Give reasons for your answer.

6. Given the level of violence in the Middle East, do you think the United States should continue to support Israel? Give reasons for your answer.

RESEARCHING THE ISSUES

7. Create and keep a file on peace and violence in Israel. Summarize your findings over a period of a few weeks or months.

8. Syria and Jordan suffered greatly following the creation of Israel and the hostilities between Arabs and Israelis. Research to find out the political, economic, and social impact on one of these countries.

9. During terrorist and Middle East crises in 2001-2002, anti-Semitic and anti-Arab incidents increased in Canada and other Western countries. Synagogues and mosques were threatened and defaced in many cities. Research any recent incidents of this type. How have they been dealt with by police and the community involved? Create a newspaper report based on your findings.

10. Following the 11 September 2001 attacks on the US, Muslims living in Canada experienced increased hostility. Extremists blamed all Muslims for the attacks. Research the current situation for Muslims in Canada. Have the accusations continued? Have the human rights of Muslims been eroded? Present your findings in a one-page summary.

UNIT FOUR

The Contemporary World

CHAPTER TWELVE:

Learning Goals

By the end of this unit students will be able to:
- Explain the international war on terrorism and describe the events that have shaped it
- Give examples of different forms of international co-operation, including governmental and non-governmental organizations
- Understand the motives for international co-operation, e.g., humanitarian aid, protection of the environment
- Identify the role of the UN Declaration of Human Rights in fostering international co-operation
- Demonstrate an understanding of the importance of human rights in the twentieth century
- Distinguish between nationalism and supranationalism and describe the motives for each
- Describe the reach of US culture around the world and form an opinion about it
- Analyse the benefits and disadvantages of globalization from the standpoint of different players
- Critically evaluate a message in a poster and identify its purpose and intended audience
- Propose some solutions to international problems and explain their advantages
- Communicate your opinions clearly, effectively, and respectfully
- Describe the role of international organizations such as the G7/G8 Nations and the World Bank

1990-2003

ECONOMY

- North American Free Trade Agreement links Canada, the United States, and Mexico by gradually eliminating tariffs and other barriers to investment and trade (1994)
- UN report notes that the 10 largest transnational companies have a total income greater than that of the world's 100 poorest countries (1997)
- Fair Labour Association formed to minimize exploitation of labour through globalization (1998)
- Quebec City hosts the 2001 Summit of the Americas economic conference; many anti-globalization protests occur (2001)
- There is a worldwide market slump, caused by the collapse of major companies such as Enron and WorldCom; corporate corruption is the culprit (2002)
- The Free Trade Agreement of the Americas—affecting 34 countries of the Western Hemisphere—is in its second draft (2002)

ENVIRONMENT

- 17 science academies worldwide—from Europe, Canada, China, and Australia—urge policy makers to ratify the Kyoto Protocol (May 2002)
- Kyoto Protocol ratified by the Canadian government (December 2002)

HUMAN RIGHTS AND QUALITY OF LIFE

- Augusto Pinochet, former dictator of Chile, is detained for human rights violations (1998)
- Slobodan Milosevic, leader of the former Yugoslavia, is arrested by the UN War Crimes Tribunal (1999)
- New Convention on the Worst Forms of Child Labour (2000)
- Sima Samar, an advocate for women in Afghanistan, receives the John Humphrey Freedom Award (2001)
- The UN warns that 38 million people in Africa face the prospect of famine (2002)

WAR AND PEACE

- PLO-Israel peace agreement (1993)
- Arusha Peace Agreement in Rwanda (1993)
- UN authorises the restoration of order and democracy in Haiti (1994)
- Civil war in Rwanda (1994)
- Operation Desert Fox—America and British bombing of Iraq (1998)
- War between Ethiopia and Eritrea (1998)
- UN presence in Timor to quell violence in civil strife (1999)
- The British government formally transfers power to the government of Northern Ireland (2000)
- Terrorists attack the World Trade Center in New York and the Pentagon in Washington (September 2001)
- United States launches retaliatory war on Afghanistan for September attack (October 2001)
- United States sends troops to the Persian Gulf in preparation for a possible war with Iraq (2003)

CHAPTER TWELVE

The Challenges at the Turn of the Twenty-First Century

Carrying a huge banner, anti-war demonstrators pack London's core one day in February 2003. They were on their way to a rally in Hyde Park to protest against a possible war between the United States and Iraq. Many similar protests took place in countries around the globe as US President George Bush amassed his troops in the Persian Gulf. Why were so many people opposed to this war? Do you believe that massive demonstrations such as this seriously influence the decisions made by our leaders?

"…[T]he US government is unjust, criminal and tyrannical … it is our duty to make jihad [holy war] … so that we drive the Americans away from all Muslim countries."

— Osama bin Laden, leader of al-Qaeda, in a CNN interview, March 1997

"Every nation, in every region, now has a decision to make. Either you are with us, or you are with the terrorists."

— US president George W. Bush, address to Congress, 21 September 2001

Overview

As the twentieth century closed, a new world order seemed to emerge. The end of the Cold War and the revitalization of the United Nations offered hope for a world that had gone to war too many times. Technology and free trade seemed to make borders disappear and increase productivity. Advancements in science, medicine, and biotechnology offered many the promise of a longer, healthier life. World stock markets enjoyed a dizzying boom. No doubt the height of the exuberance was reached on New Year's Eve, 2000, when the whole world ushered in the new century.

Within a year, the horrific attacks on New York and Washington had exploded much of the hope and global unity expressed during those celebrations. Now fear and insecurity dominated the headlines and the political agenda. Instead of promoting peace, progress, and global security, the Western world entered into a conflict that had no precedent—one known as the "international war on terrorism." Once again, the twin themes of confrontation and co-operation set the tone for the new century. A new generation of leaders and citizens faced an era of deepening uncertainty. A generation of young people watched uneasily as the new century—their century—unfolded.

Focus Questions
1. What were the origins and major events of the "war on terrorism"?
2. What evidence is there that co-operation is an ongoing goal in the new century?
3. Compare and contrast the roles of women in this chapter. What challenges did they face?
4. What are some of the positive and some of the negative signs for the future of the world in the twenty-first century?

Global Interactions: Confrontation and Co-operation

SEPTEMBER 11 AND THE NEW WAR ON TERRORISM

On 11 September 2001, at 8:45 a.m., an airliner crashed into one of the twin 110-storey towers of New York's World Trade Center. Television crews rushed to the scene of what seemed to be a terrible accident. As black smoke poured from this massive icon of US global economic power, the unthinkable happened. Live on TV, as millions of people around the world watched, another airliner filled with passengers banked, turned, and slammed into the other tower, bursting into an enormous ball of flames. In that instant, world history changed.

In the chaotic moments that followed, news reporters scrambled. Terrorists had hijacked other planes and seemed to be piloting them toward vital targets—perhaps even the White House, Camp David, or the Pentagon. For the first time,

US airspace was closed down, and incoming flights were diverted to Canada. From Florida, where he had been reading to children in a schoolroom, newly elected US president George W. Bush vowed that those responsible would be "hunted down."

Within a few hours, the World Trade Center had collapsed, killing thousands, and the Pentagon's west wing had been destroyed. Another airliner had crashed in a field near Pittsburgh after passengers overpowered the hijackers. Political and religious leaders around the world condemned the attacks and offered the US sympathy and support. In capital cities, flags flew at half-mast and crowds gathered to lay flowers at US embassies. That evening President George W. Bush addressed the US and the world on television: "America and our friends and allies join with all those who want peace and security in the world, and we stand together to win the war against terrorism."

The "first war of the twenty-first century" had been declared; but it would take on clearer form in the following days as the US sought broad international support. But who, exactly, was the enemy? US intelligence immediately zeroed in on Osama bin Laden and his Islamic fundamentalist terrorist network, al-Qaeda.

The Persian Gulf War of 1991 had been launched by President George Bush, the father of the new president. Saudi Arabia was bin Laden's birthplace and home to Islam's two most sacred sites. Bin Laden saw the ruling Saudi regime as corrupt, and when it allowed the US to establish bases on Saudi soil from which to attack Iraq, bin Laden, al-Qaeda, and similar terrorist groups were enraged. This was a sacrilege to them, a blow to the Muslim world they dreamed of unifying. So was Israel's very existence, and US support of Israel. They vowed revenge.

Figure 12.1

The Capitol building rises above the ruins of the Pentagon's west wing at sunrise after the 11 September 2001 terrorist attacks. The Pentagon is the heart of the US military-industrial complex. What message would this image send to you as an American? As a civilian victim of a US cruise missile?

Al-Qaeda, in fact, had been linked to an earlier bombing of the World Trade Center, in 1993. It was also suspected in a series of increasingly deadly attacks against US targets (see Figure 12.2). In a

1997 interview on CNN, Osama bin Laden denied any responsibility for this and other attacks. He said Americans were weak and feared casualties. He warned: "[I]f the American government is serious about avoiding the explosions inside the US, then let it stop provoking the feelings of 1250 million Muslims."

In the days ahead, as its economy stumbled, the US sought broad international support for its new "war on terrorism." On September 12, NATO for the first time invoked Article 5 of its charter, under which a military attack on one member is regarded as an attack on all members. That meant the attacks of September 11 were seen as an attack on all 19 member states. On September 15, President Bush identified Osama bin Laden as the prime suspect for the first time. As he told Americans to prepare for war, tens of thousands of Afghans tried to escape from their country. Osama bin Laden was in Afghanistan as a protected guest of the ruling Taliban government. They refused to hand him over to the United States.

The War in Afghanistan

In Chapter Seven, you learned that the Soviet Union withdrew from Afghanistan in the late 1980s. Shortly after this, the Soviet Union collapsed, and the Cold War was over. The US had spent billions of dollars supporting and training Mujahidin forces (also supported by Pakistan and Saudi Arabia) to fight the Soviets. Among those receiving US support had been Osama bin Laden and al-Qaeda, heroes of the war.

Figure 12.3
This 1999 poster of Osama bin Laden was a bestseller in Pakistan. It reads: Osama bin Laden— Warrior of Islam. Bin Laden was a Muslim hero after the Soviets were forced out of Afghanistan. What visual elements make him appear to be mythic and heroic?

Terrorist Attacks Attributed to Al-Qaeda

Year	Bombing Location	Casualties
1993	World Trade Center	6 killed, more than 100 injured
1996	US Air Force Base, Saudi Arabia	19 killed, hundreds injured
1998	US Embassies in Kenya and Tanzania	Hundreds killed, hundreds injured
2000	*USS Cole*, Yemen	17 US sailors killed, 19 injured
2001	World Trade Center, Pentagon	2 823 killed

Figure 12.2
This table lists attacks linked to Osama Bin Laden and al-Qaeda. In 1998 and 2000, the US launched cruise missiles at al-Qaeda training camps and sites in retaliation. What effect would this have on bin Laden?

With the Soviets gone, the US disengaged from Afghanistan and the country plunged into ethnic and rebel conflicts. In 1997, the Taliban seized control, but the UN would not recognize it as the official government. No countries did, except Pakistan and Saudi Arabia. The Taliban intended to create a pure Islamic state. It banned music, movies, and television. The preaching of any religion other than Islam was punishable by death. Education for girls was outlawed. Women were forbidden to appear uncovered in public or to hold jobs.

MAP STUDY

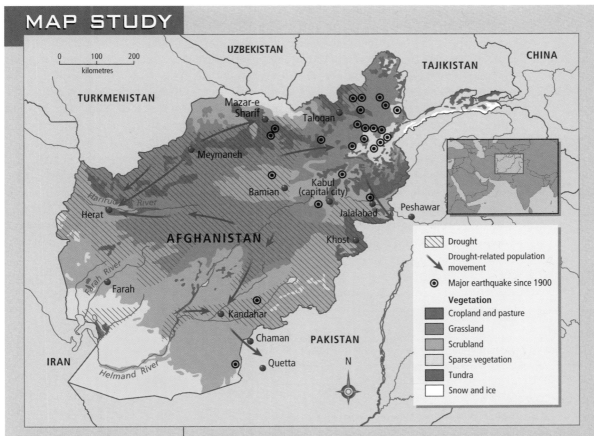

Figure 12.4

Vegetation Map of Afghanistan (a nation of semi-arid to arid conditions)

Afghanistan is a mountainous country in south-central Asia. Approximately half its land is subject to the risk of desertification. Within the mountain ranges, there are many fertile valleys and plains, but its rivers are almost impossible to navigate.

Interpreting

1. Use this map and other resources to determine which physical features may have contributed to the slow industrialization and economic progress of Afghanistan.
2. Make another observation about Afghanistan's geographic position and its impact on the nation.
3. What features about Afghanistan might suggest it would be a difficult country to invade and control?

During the war in Afghanistan, the Taliban had forged close ties with bin Laden. After the war, it played protective host to him and the al-Qaeda training camps, regardless of international protests. In 1999, and again in early 2001, the Taliban refused to hand bin Laden over to the United Nations to be tried for terrorist attacks. The UN imposed strict sanctions against Afghanistan.

After the September 11 attacks, the Taliban not only refused to hand bin Laden over to the US, it threatened to declare a holy war against America and its allies if attacked. With strong support from British prime minister Tony Blair, President Bush gathered allies for a "global war on terrorism." As NATO countries joined the coalition, Canada made its largest military commitment since the Korean war. Under pressure, Pakistan severed ties with the Taliban and aligned with the US. Russia also gave its support: it had been fighting Muslim rebels in Chechnya for years. Saudi Arabia also cut relations with the Taliban.

A US-led multilateral force was in place for the war on terrorism. Its goals: to topple the Taliban regime, capture bin Laden, and destroy al-Qaeda's leadership and training camps.

Opponents declared that attacking Afghanistan would breach international law, the very instrument meant to preserve world order. They feared that such an attack would create a humanitarian disaster. Others said a war would only create more terrorists and get bogged down in guerrilla fighting. Some critics pointed to decades of US support for corrupt regimes in the region that had supported US interests. To prevent future attacks, they argued, the US should adopt a more humane foreign policy. Support for development and democratic reform would bring lasting peace; troops and high-tech bombs would not.

Prime Minister Jean Chrétien outlined his view that it is not enough to wage war on terrorism. Western countries must help poorer counties, such as those in Africa, in order to stop terrorist attacks from recurring in the future. During a speech in New York City, he said, "We have to focus our resources and our budgets on more than simply defence against possible attacks. We must not, and cannot, ignore our obligations to the rest of the world—not only because it is right but because it is in our own longer term self-interest."

On October 7, the US-led coalition launched a rain of high-tech air strikes against the Taliban and al-Qaeda targets. Ground troops were sent in to work closely with Afghan opposition forces. This military strategy was used throughout the

Information on Al-Qaeda

What	a loose network of autonomous terrorist cells
Where	50 countries, in the Americas, Europe, Middle East, and Asia
Training camps	Afghanistan, Yemen, Sudan, Somalia, Chechnya, and others
Links	Islamic Jihad (Egypt), Abu Sayyaf Group (Philippines), Armed Islamic Group (Algeria), militant Kashmiri groups, among others
Membership	estimates vary widely, from 10 000 to 50 000
Goal	to free Muslim nations of Western dominance
Methods	attack Western targets—military and civilian; suicide bombings; sophisticated co-ordination; mass destruction, mass murder

Figure 12.5

This table outlines a few facts on al-Qaeda. It has been said that terrorism revealed a new face on 11 September 2001. In what ways do you think this terrorism was "new"?

Figure 12.6
Afghan girls were allowed to go to school for the first time in six years on 31 December 2001. The Taliban closed this girls' school in Kabul after seizing power. What else in this picture says the Taliban was no longer in control?

war and succeeded more quickly than anyone had predicted. By December, the Taliban government had fallen and an interim government of Afghan groups was in place. Al-Qaeda strongholds and training camps had been destroyed. Thousands of al-Qaeda fighters had been killed and many were taken prisoner, but it appeared that Osama bin Laden had escaped.

By January 2002, peacekeepers, known as the International Security Assistance Force, were in place under UN mandate. In June, Afghanistan's *Loya Jerga* (grand council) elected Hamid Karzai interim head of state. In a clear departure from the Taliban rule, the rights of women were acknowledged, when two women were appointed to the cabinet (see Voices on page 388). It became clear that peace was precarious. In July, the vice-president of the interim government was assassinated, and attempts were made on Karzai's life. The tensions that had torn Afghanistan apart remained. At the end of 2002, the UN reported that new al-Qaeda volunteers were making their way to mobile training camps in eastern Afghanistan and near Peshawar, on the border with Pakistan. Reports indicated there was no proof al-Qaeda had nuclear material, but there were concerns it could obtain such material.

Voices   The Future for Women in Afghanistan

Sima Samar was named minister for women's affairs and vice president of the interim government in Afghanistan in January 2002. She was later accused by members of the Loya Jerga of "insulting Islam" during an interview she gave to a Vancouver newspaper. As a result, her ministry was abolished. President Karzai immediately appointed her president of the Human Rights Commission of Afghanistan. Samar received the 2001 John Humphrey Freedom Award (named in honour of Canadian John Peters Humphrey, who prepared the first draft of the Universal Declaration of Human Rights) for her work in Afghanistan, which she describes in these excerpts from her acceptance speech:

SIMA SAMAR

"As I speak today, the future of Afghanistan is at a crossroads, particularly the future of women. With the removal of the Taliban from control, women finally may be able to regain our rights and Afghanistan may at long last have a chance for a peaceful future. But none of this is a certainty.

"Finally the world is becoming aware of the plight of Afghan women. The media is now paying attention to the suffering that women have endured under the Taliban's restrictions. More people now know about the starvation and disease that have come from the drought, the fighting, and the overall lack of humanitarian assistance. The situation of women in Afghanistan has been deteriorating for the past two decades. It could not get much worse.

"Under the Taliban, women in Afghanistan were banned from attending school, prohibited from working outside their home, and not allowed to leave their homes without the company of a close male relative or without wearing the full burqa. The punishment for violating these decrees has been harsh and included among other punishments public beatings, imprisonment, and even execution.

"… The exclusion of women from public life under the Taliban has taken its toll not only on women whose lives were destroyed, but also on society as a whole. Before the Taliban took over, women were the majority of teachers and the majority of health care workers. With the restrictions on women, the education system collapsed and the healthcare system was severely damaged, and the whole population suffered.

"Despite the Taliban's restrictions, my organization—the Shuhada Organization, which I founded in 1989—continued to provide health care services and educational opportunities to girls. I run 45 schools in Central Afghanistan, currently educating some 20 000 students. My high school for girls is the only formal girls' high school that continued to function under the Taliban. Because of our dedication and support within the community, the Taliban could not close the girls' schools in this part of Afghanistan. Their harassment was constant, but we kept the schools open and kept teaching the girls math, science, and other courses.

"My organization also has 11 clinics and 4 hospitals in Afghanistan. … My clinics and hospitals continued to provide health services to women, including reproductive health services such as contraception, despite the Taliban's prohibition and at great risk.

"In Pakistan, I operate a hospital, clinic, and 4 schools for Afghan refugees. I also run a co-educational Science Institute that provides post-secondary training to become physician assistants, paramedics, and science teachers.

I began this program to prepare young women and men to go back to Afghanistan to provide desperately needed health and education services. I hope now that my students can aid in the rebuilding of our country.

"One of the reasons for the chaos, destruction, and oppression that followed the Soviet withdrawal was that the United States and the international community abandoned Afghanistan after funding and training the most radical extremists.

"We hope that the United States and the international community will not forget Afghanistan again. We hope the US and other countries will keep their new promises and provide substantial relief and development assistance to rebuild the whole system and economy in Afghanistan....

"We have much work to do. We will not be able to do it alone. We need the support of the international community, including Canada. We need multi-national troops in order to disarm the different factions, to maintain stability and security, and to allow the government system to be re-established.

Whatever government structure is in place, women's rights must be restored. We need the commitment of Canada and the international community to make gender issues central in the reconstruction of Afghanistan.

"I am honored to accept this prestigious award on behalf of the millions of Afghan women and children who are hungry, homeless, and traumatized. I will continue my work so that women's rights in Afghanistan will be counted as human rights and that girls will no longer be punished for having a notebook and pen in their hands."

Source: International Centre for Human Rights and Development, <www.ichrdd.ca>. 10 December 2001.

Responding

1. Why might Samar's views not be welcomed by some members of the interim Afghan government? Quote two or three statements from her speech as evidence.
2. Why does Samar think Afghanistan needs the international community to rebuild itself? What does she say happened in the past?

THE QUESTION OF IRAQ

Iraqi leader Saddam Hussein defied the West and the UN after the Gulf War. For years, he played a game of cat and mouse with UN weapons inspectors, whose mission it was to ensure that Iraq was not producing weapons of mass destruction. In late 1998, Saddam blocked UN inspections entirely, and the US bombed Iraqi targets. No-fly zones were imposed to limit Iraq's air power. US and British forces bombed Iraqi sites in disputes over these zones several times, and just one week before the September 11 terrorist attacks in New York.

President George W. Bush declared that the new war on terrorism would not be limited to Afghanistan. It would be a long war, one fought on many levels and many fronts. Together, Bush said, the countries of Iraq, Iran, and North Korea formed an "axis of evil" that promoted terrorism and possessed weapons of mass destruction. Many international leaders were disturbed by the rhetoric, but the US insisted: Iraq was a threat to US and global security.

With support from Britain, the US increased pressure on Iraq to open up. The US also threatened to attack Iraq unilaterally, and it met with Iraqi representatives in London who could form a new government if Saddam were overthrown. Saddam Hussein threatened that any attack by the "forces of evil" would result in catastrophe. By August, Iraq began negotiating on inspections.

"And all nations should know: America will do what is necessary to ensure our nation's security."

— President George W. Bush, State of the Union address, 29 January 2002

Many countries, including Canada, demanded proof of the US claims against Iraq and questioned the legality of any attack. After two months of turbulent debate, the UN Security Council passed Resolution 1441 in November 2002. It laid out a specific inspections plan and demanded that Iraq disarm. If Iraq did not comply, military action would be justified. In mid-November, UN weapons inspectors entered Iraq for the first time in four years. The US, however, maintained that it had a right to self-defence, and could attack Iraq unilaterally at any time.

UN inspectors made slow progress in finding and destroying some weapons. However, the US and Great Britain felt Iraq was hiding biological and chemical weapons. They advocated military action to disarm Iraq. France, China, and Russia urged patience. Canada failed to effect a compromise at the badly divided Security Council and declared that it would not support a war without UN approval. Finally, on 17 March 2003, President Bush gave Saddam Hussein an ultimatum to leave Iraq within 48 hours or face invasion. The deadline came and went without compliance from Saddam, and the American led attack began.

Figure 12.7

What effect was the cartoonist trying to create by juxtaposing the two men in this way? What is he saying about the relative threat of each? What is your opinion of this cartoon?

"There are lots of countries around the world that have weapons of mass destruction. We can't presumably attack them all."

— Canadian foreign minister Bill Graham, September 2002

Figure 12.8

An Iraqi woman holds her child as a UN inspection team arrives in December 2002 in her town about 30 km north of Baghdad. How might she view the presence of the UN?

Voices   A Dangerous World

In 2002, former US president Jimmy Carter won the Nobel Peace Prize. Carter was president for only one term, from 1977 to 1981. He was an active promoter of peace and development in the world, both in and out of office.

Excerpts from Carter's acceptance speech follow. As you read it, consider whether Carter's comments are still relevant today.

JIMMY CARTER, FORMER US PRESIDENT

"The world has changed greatly since I left the White House. Now there is only one superpower, with unprecedented military and economic strength. Instead of entering a millennium of peace, the world is now, in many ways, a more dangerous place. There is a plethora of civil wars…and recent appalling acts of terrorism have reminded us that no nations, even superpowers, are invulnerable.

"It is clear that global challenges must be met with an emphasis on peace, in harmony with others, with strong alliances and international consensus. Imperfect as it may be, there is no doubt that this can best be done through the United Nations.

"Today there are at least eight nuclear powers on earth, and three of them are threatening to their neighbours in areas of great international tension. For powerful countries to adopt a principle of preventive war may well set an example that can have catastrophic consequences. For more than half a century following the founding of the state of Israel in 1948, the Middle East conflict has been a source of world-wide tension.

"United Nations Resolution 242 calls for withdrawal of Israel from the occupied territories, and provides for Israelis to live securely and in harmony with their neighbours. There is no other mandate whose implementation could more profoundly improve international relationships.

"Perhaps of more immediate concern is the necessity for Iraq to comply fully with the unanimous decision of the Security Council that it eliminate all weapons of mass destruction and permit unimpeded access by inspectors to confirm that this commitment has been honoured.

"The world insists that this be done.

"I am not here as a public official, but as a citizen of a troubled world who finds hope in a growing consensus that the generally accepted goals of society are peace, freedom, human rights, environmental quality, the alleviation of suffering, and the rule of law.

"During the past decades, the international community, usually under the auspices of the United Nations, has struggled to negotiate global standards that can help us achieve these essential goals.

"I am convinced that Christians, Muslims, Buddhists, Hindus, Jews and others can embrace each other in a common effort to alleviate human suffering and to espouse peace.

"At the beginning of this new millennium I was asked to discuss, here in Oslo, the greatest challenge that the world faces. I decided that the most serious and universal problem is the growing chasm between the richest and poorest people on earth.

"The results of this disparity are root causes of most of the world's unresolved problems, including starvation, illiteracy, environmental degradation, violent conflict and unnecessary illnesses that range from Guinea worm to HIV/AIDS.

"War may sometimes be a necessary evil. But no matter how necessary, it is always an evil, never a good. The bond of our common humanity is stronger than the divisiveness of our fears and prejudices. God gives us the capacity for choice. We can choose to alleviate suffering. We can choose to work together for peace. We can make these changes—and we must."

Source: Excerpts from Nobel Prize acceptance speech
© The Nobel Foundation 2002.

Responding

1. What does Carter suggest about the position of the United States in the modern world? Is he accurate in your view? Explain.
2. In general, would you judge this speech as optimistic or pessimistic about the world in 2002? Why?
3. Quote phrases/sentences from Carter that support his position as a promoter of peace and development in the world.

NETSURFER

WWW.NOBEL.NO

Visit the official Web site of the Nobel Peace Prize for more information about this significant prize and those who have won it. Who won the Nobel Peace Prize in 1957?

In Review

1. Create a brief chronological timeline to detail the events of 11 September 2001.

2. What was the result of the US-led invasion of Afghanistan?

3. Why were the US and the UN concerned about Iraq?

Skill Path   Answering Multiple-Choice Questions

Most people agree that writing an exam is a stressful event. While knowing and understanding the material is the best defence against anxiety, it also helps to have specific strategies for dealing with different question *types*. This feature examines the skill of exam writing and, specifically, strategies for dealing with multiple-choice questions. This type of question appears often on high school, college, and university exams and on entry exams for professional schools.

Step One: Study for Your Exam

The best preparation for any exam, including one featuring multiple-choice questions, is a firm knowledge base in the subject. This includes knowing not only the facts— the *who, what, where,* and *when* of history—but also understanding the *how* and *why* of events. How did that leader arrive at that decision? Why was that government overthrown? Studying for a test or exam in twentieth-century history will entail more than memorizing dates, names, and ideologies; it will mean understanding key concepts and being able to apply them, analysing data, and making connections between events.

But how can you study "analysing data" and "making connections"? Pre-test yourself by reciting or writing definitions of key terms, organizing significant events chronologically in timelines, and associating as many related facts as you can into patterns or themes. You could use the Skill Paths "Interpreting Graphs and Timelines" (page 42) and "Creating Concept Maps" (page 84) to practise these strategies. Use acronyms, mnemonics, and word association to assist memorization. While studying, ask yourself "Why?" and "What has A got in common with B?" As you are reviewing the material, list any questions that arise and make sure you find the answers. This is why it's best to study material as you progress through the term, rather than just in the week leading up to the exam. Only then will you have the time to find the answers and clarify any points you do not fully understand.

Step Two: Prepare for Different Types of Multiple-Choice Questions

Most multiple-choice exams will include different types of questions to challenge you. A percentage of questions will test your knowledge and comprehension of the content and will require accurate recall. Another type of question will move you into higher-order thinking and skill application to interpret and analyse information and ideas. You will be asked to make a judgment about relationships between historical events and present circumstances. Other questions will be more complex still, requiring you to synthesize and evaluate data and concepts.

Example of a basic knowledge question

1. During the 1990s, international multilateral military initiatives directed against Iraq have taken the form of
   a) United Nations weapons inspection programs
   b) the institution of economic sanctions
   c) coalition forces mounting air and ground campaigns
   d) American invasions, victory, and withdrawal

(C is the correct answer. Inspections programs and economic sanctions are not "military" initiatives; American action against Iraq is "international" but not "multilateral." "Coalition" does imply "international multilateral involvement," and "air and ground campaigns" are "military" initiatives.)

Example of a question requiring application, analysis, interpretation

Use the following list of "Events of the 1990s" to answer Question 2.

- Civil War in Somalia, 1988-1995
- Attempted Genocide in Rwanda, 1990-1996
- Civil War in Serbia, 1989-1999

2. An examination of these events would be most useful to a person preparing to write a position paper on which of the following issues:
   a) Should national governments use collective security rather than diplomacy to resolve disputes?
   b) Should national disputes be addressed internationally?
   c) To what extent was the United Nations justified in its participation in these conflicts?
   d) To what extent is the International War Crimes Tribunal a success?

(B is the correct answer. The list of events includes several of the conflicts of the 1990s that required international involvement of either UN peacemaking/peacekeeping forces or NATO coalition forces to reach resolution.)

Example of a question entailing evaluation and judgment

3. Tasked with intervention in over 45 hostile situations during one decade, the United Nations peacemaking/peacekeeping operations came under heavy scrutiny. Which event during the last decade of the twentieth century is least supportive of this hypothesis?
   a) Invasion of Kuwait by Iraq, 1990
   b) Operation Restore Hope in Somalia, 1992
   c) Deployment of UN Peacekeepers in Rwanda, 1992
   d) Ceasefire agreements in Bosnia, 1993

(A is the correct answer. The intervention of UN peacemakers/peacekeepers forced the withdrawal of the aggressor nation, Iraq, from the sovereign nation of Kuwait. In each of the other events, involvement of the UN was either ineffective or unsuccessful. While UN sanctions against Iraq continue to be scrutinized, this is not at issue here.)

Step Three: Write Your Exam

When you first receive your exam, take the time to briefly orient yourself to its contents. Determine how the exam is organized; highlight, underline, or circle specific vocabulary, concepts, and main ideas in the questions.

Most multiple-choice questions have four possible answers. Of the four alternatives, you are to choose the *best* answer. Be sure to read each question and all alternative responses thoroughly before answering. You may find it effective to read each question twice, underlining key words and ideas.

- Questions that depend on text excerpts, quotations, charts, political cartoons, and maps require you to read and interpret the information carefully before you attempt the accompanying questions. Be sure to read any footnotes—these supply context by shedding light on the source of the information (e.g., who said it, when, and under what circumstances) or alerting you to any possible bias. Titles, legends, and borders on maps may help you determine the time period(s) examined.

- Multiple-choice questions that contain qualifying words such as "mainly," "primarily," "best," "most," and "least" ask you to judge among the alternatives presented. When answering these questions, be sure to understand the context of the question—which answer is most strongly supported by the information provided? "Generally," "often," "frequently," and "seldom," are qualifiers, which are often found in correct answers. Absolutes—broad statements that contain words such as "all," "always," never," and "none"—appear rarely in correct answers. Watch for negative terms such as "not," which can reverse the meaning of a question. Sometimes the presence of a single word

can help you distinguish between a correct and an incorrect answer.

- If you cannot quickly locate the correct answer, change your strategy and eliminate the answers that seem most wrong. This strategy will work in most cases, and you will be left with only two alternatives from which to choose. At this point, go back to the question and analyse it to pick up the subtlety of the phrasing used. This will help lead you to picking the right answer from two seemingly "correct" answers. However, if you still cannot decide, leave the question and return to it later because you may learn the correct answer from the rest of the examination.

- Pace yourself throughout the examination so that you can orient yourself, answer all questions, and review all your answers in the time allotted. Don't allow distractions to interrupt you, but do take short breaks occasionally to breathe deeply and relax before continuing.

Practise Your Skill

1. Locate copies of recent examinations similar to the exam you will be facing at the end of your course, and use them as practice pre-tests. You may be able to acquire past examinations through the school board or the provincial agency that produces them. Independent publications, which may contain entire copies of examinations, are particularly useful because they often analyse each multiple-choice question to explain the reasoning for the correct answer.

Global Interactions: Co-operation

For many, the events of the twentieth century had revealed the high cost of rivalry and global conflict—ideas that were explored in Chapter Eight. The emergence of regional co-operative models such as the European Union, and the growing sense that nations could achieve more through co-operation than through conflict, signalled the winds of change.

The terms *internationalism* and *globalization* are often used interchangeably to describe this momentum. In general, internationalism refers to international trade and relations, and the common ventures undertaken by groups of nations acting together. Globalization refers to the integration of many national economies. It has been called the "effective erasure of national boundaries" for economic purposes, made possible through free trade and free-flowing capital across borders.

The New NATO

Since the collapse of communism in Eastern Europe and the Soviet Union, NATO (North Atlantic Treaty Organization) has been evolving along with the political landscape. Over the last decade, NATO's membership has changed dramatically, as has its role and agenda in an attempt to meet the challenges of the twenty-first century.

One important change that took place in NATO was the establishment of a discussion forum known as the Euro-Atlantic Partnership Council (EAPC) in 1997. The 46 members of the EAPC—19 NATO nations and 27 partner countries—meet regularly to discuss political and security issues. Currently, EAPC meetings focus on arms control, peacekeeping, defense, economic issues, civil emergency planning, and scientific and environmental issues. However, in the wake of the terrorist attacks on the United States in September 2001, EAPC discussions will concentrate to a greater extent on the measures needed to combat international terrorism.

In 2002 Bulgaria, Slovenia, Slovakia, Romania, Estonia, Latvia, and Lithuania were invited to join NATO. They will be made official members in 2004. This marks the fifth expansion of the membership, which began with Greece and Turkey in 1952; Germany in 1955; Spain in 1982; and the Czech Republic, Hungary, and Poland in 1999. These additions bring the total current membership to 19 and, according to NATO Secretary General Lord Robertson, the expansion will not end there. During the 2002 Summit meeting he told aspiring NATO members, "Through the MAP [Membership Action Plan] process, we will continue to help you pursue your reform process, and we remain committed to your full integration into the Euro-Atlantic family of nations."

In the last decade, NATO faced new instabilities in Europe, which drew into question the organization's strictly defensive mandate. Former Soviet Union states were developing into fledgling independent countries amidst weak economies and bloody ethnic conflicts. In Yugoslavia, as the organization quietly celebrated its fiftieth anniversary, NATO took on the new task of promoting peace in a non-NATO sovereign state. The aggressive action NATO took against the regime of Slobodan Milosovic in Serbia in 1999 (see Chapter 7) demonstrated its willingness to militarily intervene in civil conflicts where human rights were being abused. The use of this type of intervention moved NATO into a controversial new role, that of peacemaker.

The most recent statement on the evolution of NATO's role came during the "Transformation" Summit of member nations in Prague in 2002. During the meeting, a commitment was made to enhance NATO's military capabilities so that it would be able to deal with the modern threat of terrorism and rogue states. For example, the organization decided to create a cutting-edge NATO Response Force. This force, including air, land and sea elements, would be technologically advanced, flexible, and ready to move quickly wherever it was needed. As well, individual members agreed to

"This is not business as usual, but the emergence of a new and modernized NATO, fit for the challenges of the new century."

— NATO Secretary General Lord Robertson, 2002

strengthen their air-to-ground surveillance and to enhance defensive strategies to suit the current threat of nuclear, chemical, and biological attacks.

THE ROLE OF THE UNITED NATIONS

As the century closed, many hoped that the United Nations would continue to play an important role in enhancing the well-being and security of all peoples around the world. Since its creation in 1945, the UN had

- deployed peacekeeping forces and observer missions around the world
- negotiated peaceful settlements to end regional conflicts
- handed down judicial settlements through its International Court of Justice
- promoted democracy in many nations, enabling more men and women to participate in free and fair elections
- promoted development and human rights
- provided humanitarian aid to refugees and victims of war
- provided health care and reduced child mortality rates
- protected the environment

As the new century opened, the role of the United Nations was still widely debated. While many observers thought that the UN's priorities should continue to be human rights and peacekeeping operations, others believed that it had a major role to play in combating international terrorism. In the past, the UN had experienced considerable challenges when serving in the more aggressive role of peacemaker, for example, in Korea (see page 187) and Somalia (see page 201). Terrorism was clearly an international problem and threatened innocent people all over the globe. However, the UN did not have a permanent force to deal with this kind of subversive, often underground, activity. More powerful nations such as the United States and Britain seemed prepared to "go it alone" if the UN could not act decisively.

The UN was still struggling to define its path. However, the UN still possessed considerable moral authority, intellectual clout, and diplomatic expertise. UN support, if not its leadership, remained important; without it, international action would prove difficult.

GOVERNMENTAL AND NON-GOVERNMENTAL ORGANIZATIONS

Governmental organizations (GOs) provide another example of co-operation among nations. These government-based groups work to achieve the political, economic, social, and cultural goals of groups of nations.

The European Union and the Organization of African Unity are examples of political GOs. Economic GOs include the Organization for Economic Co-operation and Development (OECD) and the Organization of Petroleum Exporting Countries (OPEC). Sometimes economic GOs are formed to enhance the investment opportunities of the member nations (OECD). At other times, nations simply gain more economic clout by presenting a united front. OPEC, for example, was formed in 1960 by five large oil-producing nations—Iran, Iraq, Kuwait, Saudi Arabia, and Venezuela. In the early 1970s, the OPEC nations came together to raise the price of oil from $3 a barrel to $12 a barrel. The increase hit many industrialized nations hard, including Canada. Cultural GOs—those that promote social and cultural initiatives—include such groups as the Organization of the Islamic Conference and the South Asian Association for Regional Co-operation.

Non-governmental organizations (NGOs) are local, national, and international organizations that operate independently of any government. The United Nations considers NGOs to be "vital partners of governments" in pursuing peace and development. By and large, NGOs raise money for their work in the developed world and distribute the funds in developing nations. They work closely with grassroots organizations in these nations (such as women's co-operatives and farmers' associations) to undertake local initiatives. Many NGOs advocate for development concerns—a job that demands NGO workers voluntarily give up the comforts of industrialized nations to work and live in places where human survival is a challenge.

NGOs also participate in international lobbying and education programs to affect important changes. For example, the first call to ban anti-personnel land mines came from six non-governmental organizations that launched an international campaign in 1991. Insidious and potentially lethal, anti-personnel land mines (APLs) threaten soldiers and non-military

Figure 12.9

Members of the NGO Amnesty International demonstrate in favour of extraditing former Chilean dictator Augusto Pinochet to Spain on charges of crimes against humanity. What advantage might such a demonstration have over action taken by a governmental organization such as NATO?

populations in at least 64 nations today. Eighty-five to 110 million land mines of various types—plus millions more unexploded bombs, shells and grenades—remain hidden around the world, waiting to be triggered by the innocent and unsuspecting. The International Committee of the Red Cross initiated a second campaign in 1995. Later in the decade, the United Nations General Assembly passed three resolutions related to land mine issues.

The Ottawa Convention, which banned the production, sale, use, and stockpiling of anti-personnel land mines, came into force in 1998. The treaty also pledged signatory nations to clear their lands of landmines within 10 years, and to destroy existing stockpiles within four years. Many states—Angola, Bosnia-Herzegovina, Cambodia, Croatia, El Salvador, Ethiopia, Mozambique and Sudan—blighted with millions of land mines, signed the treaty. Non-signatory nations included the world's principal producers and exporters of armaments—China, Russia, and the United States. Other nations such as Egypt, Iran, Iraq, India, Israel, Libya, Pakistan, North Korea, South Korea, Sri Lanka, Syria, and Turkey also did not elect to sign the treaty because their governments consider land mines to be essential to their defense.

By May 2002, the issue originally brought to the world's attention by NGOs saw substantial international support. A total of 139 nation states had signed, ratified, or acceded to the treaty. Canada, Bosnia-Herzegovina, Germany, France and the United Kingdom have completed destruction of their stockpiles of APLs more than three years ahead of schedule.

Some well-known NGOs are the World Council of Churches, the International Committee of the Red Cross, Doctors Without Borders/Médecins Sans Frontières, Amnesty International, CARE, OXFAM, World Vision, and the World Wide Fund for Nature (WWF). These are just a few of the thousands of non-governmental organizations that exist today and actively promote humanitarian aid.

Some NGOs have been criticized for imposing Western views on vulnerable societies. In some cases, a high percentage of NGO revenues is used to pay for administration and fundraising activities, and only a small amount of money raised actually reaches developing countries. In other cases, NGO programs have been well-intended but poorly matched to local needs. By design, many NGO development projects are small-scale and are not easily transferred to other locales.

In spite of such criticisms, however, billions of dollars annually are invested in developing nations through the efforts of NGOs. It is estimated that more than 15 per cent of total overseas development aid is dispersed through international NGOs. In an era of increasing international co-operation, NGOs are able to provide basic assistance to improve global standards of living.

UNITING TO SAVE THE ENVIRONMENT

At the end of the century, there was growing concern for the environment, and a will to address the problems that had been caused by industrialization—holes in the ozone layer, global warming, toxic chemical pollution, and the destruction of the tropical rainforest.

WWW.MSF.ORG

Learn more about Doctors Without Borders by visiting the organization's international home page. The Canadian branch can be visited at www.msf.ca. Summarize their activities in a paragraph.

Figure 12.10
A member of Doctors Without Borders with Ethiopian children at the Tug-Wajale refugee camp

A report issued by the World Commission on Environment and Development in 1987 spurred a number of environmental proposals, among them, the 1988 Montreal Protocol. This treaty was signed by 47 nations, including Canada, to control the use of chemicals that destroy atmospheric ozone. The environmental movement of the 1980s came to the conclusion that development must continue but in environmentally responsible ways.

In 1997, the nations of the world cooperated once more to try to reduce environmental damage. Delegates representing more than 160 nations met in Kyoto, Japan, to discuss and sign an international agreement on global warming. The agreement, known as the **Kyoto Protocol** on Climate Change, committed delegates to

a step-by-step reduction in the emissions of greenhouse gases caused by the burning of fossil fuels such as coal, natural gas, and crude oil, and believed to be the main cause of global warming. It established target dates for meeting these reductions, and offered nations alternative means of achieving them.

Businesses were required to reduce the level of their industrial production and/or install costly equipment that can filter out greenhouse gases and other pollutants from their waste emissions. Individual citizens were asked to cut back on their level of energy consumption and to explore alternative, renewable forms of energy, such as wind and solar power, for providing heat and electricity for their homes. They were encouraged to use their cars less, switch from energy-guzzling sport-utility vehicles (SUVs) to smaller models, and possibly consider purchasing new kinds of automobiles that do not run on gasoline.

In May 2002, 17 science academies worldwide (from Europe, Canada, China, India and Australia) issued a joint statement urging policy-makers to ratify the Kyoto Protocol. Their counterparts in the United States and Russia, however, did not sign the statement, citing the economic consequences of implementation.

In December 2002, the Canadian government ratified the Kyoto Protocol. However, there continues to be disagreement about the effects implementation of Kyoto could have on the Canadian economy. The Alberta government under Ralph Klein, for example, stated that, while it supports reductions in greenhouse gas emissions, it is concerned that the agreement could cost that province billions of dollars and thousands of jobs.

TRADE BLOCS AND FAIR TRADE

In Chapter Ten, you learned that economies of Southeast Asia have become the most dynamic in the world, with Japan, South Korea, and Taiwan leading the way. As the century drew to a close, there was a sense that only the strongest economies—the wealthiest and the most entrepreneurial—would survive.

Trade blocs such as NAFTA and the Southern Common Market (see Chapter Eight) are one way for nations to expand their markets and reduce barriers to trade. Individual countries set aside some of their national economic interests in order to take advantage of the benefits of co-operation. "Free trade" is the current model for economic growth. As you have learned, NAFTA—the North American Free Trade Agreement of 1994—economically linked Canada, the United States, and Mexico by gradually eliminating tariffs and other barriers to investment and the movement of goods and services among the three countries. NAFTA provides for the complete removal of all trade tariffs between the member countries. Ultimately, NAFTA will create a vast open market—more than 370 million people and more than $6 trillion in annual output.

International trade organizations were also created to ensure that trade is conducted fairly among member nations. Two are of particular interest—the World Trade Organization (WTO) and the G-7/G-8. The Geneva-based WTO has 144 member states. Representatives meet periodically to facilitate and liberalize multilateral trade. The G-7 (Canada, France, Germany, Italy, Japan, the United Kingdom, and the United States), more recently known as the G-8 (the G-7 plus Russia and the European Union), is an international association of the world's most influential market economies. The G-8 holds an annual economic summit to discuss common objectives and issues, co-ordinate economic policies, and encourage international co-operation and global economic stability.

The globalization of national economies is not limited to trade blocs and free trade zones. Globalization also includes the growth of transnational corporations—companies that design, manufacture, assemble, and distribute products in different locations all over the world, taking advantage of cheap labour every step of the way. One criticism of globalization is that the wealth that is generated remains concentrated in the hands of large multinational corporations, and that employees often have fewer opportunities than before (see Viewpoints on page 415). However, both the WTO and the G-8 are proponents of globalization, claiming that it will eventually offer more people a chance to share in the wealth.

In Review

1. Note at least three achievements of the UN since 1945. In your view, which is most important? Why?

2. In your view, what should be the chief role of the UN in this century? Explain.

3. Explain the difference between a GO and an NGO.

4. How would you assess the current impact of the Kyoto Protocol? Why?

5. Do you consider yourself a supporter or an opponent of globalization? Explain.

Progress and Uncertainty

THE ENDURING PROBLEM OF MILITARISM

The end of the Cold War brought an end to the bipolar world that had been dominated by the two superpowers—the USA and the USSR. Some world leaders and political thinkers were hopeful this change would allow for global relationships that did not depend on military threats, but rather on the fact that all nations would be mutually vulnerable. They predicted the fall of the Iron Curtain would open the door for greater co-operation among nation states. To some extent, they were right. The years leading into the twenty-first century saw many countries promoting world peace and security through international agreements designed to end the production and stockpiling of weapons of mass destruction. Treaties were signed to renew the International Non-Proliferation Treaty, create nuclear-free zones, eliminate global stocks of chemical weapons, and reduce major conventional weapons and armed forces in Europe (see chart in Figure 12.11).

Other political analysts, however, took the viewpoint that the Cold War acted as a deterrent to military conflict.

The bipolar world was stable because neither superpower could dominate the other. Nor could they risk provoking each other into a large-scale confrontation,

Disarmament Agreements of the 1990s

Year	Treaty	Countries Involved
1990	Chemical Weapons Destruction Agreement	US-Russia
1990	Conventional Armed Forces in Europe	30 nations
1991	START I	US-Russia
1992	Lisbon Protocol	5 nations
1992	Open Skies Treaty	27 nations
1993	UN Register of Conventional Arms	85 nations
1993	START II	US-Russia
1993	Chemical Weapons Convention	160 nations
1995	Wassenaar Arrangement on Export Controls	28 nations
1995	Inhumane Weapons Convention	56 nations
1996	Comprehensive Test Ban Treaty	44 nations
1996	African Nuclear Weapon Free Zone Treaty	57 nations
1998	Inter-American Convention Against Illicit Manufacturing and Trafficking	OAS nations
1998	UN Convention for the Suppression of Terrorist Bombings	189 nations
1999	Inter-American Convention on Transparency	OAS nations
1999	Convention on Prohibition of Anti-Personnel Mines	133 nations

Figure 12.11

Choose three of these treaties and research them on the Internet or at your local library. Describe the circumstances that led to the agreement. What were the terms of the treaty?

since it could end in nuclear war. Smaller nations were discouraged from military action because of the threat that the superpowers might become involved.

Once the balance of terror and power the Cold War had created disappeared, some previously unarmed countries took the opportunity to militarize. Individual republics of the former Soviet Union competed over control of the nuclear weapons that had been stockpiled in their territories. With the breakup of the USSR, Ukraine suddenly became the third largest nuclear superpower.

Although the treaties outlined in Figure 12.11 eliminated some of the potential threat, they could not solve the problem of the existence of nuclear weapons technology and the desire of some countries to use it. As certain nations disarmed, others such as Iraq and North Korea began shopping to buy the materials and expertise needed to estab-

lish their own nuclear arsenals. India and Pakistan both acquired nuclear capabilities. The world's newest nuclear powers have claimed justification in development of their own nuclear weapons because China, Russia, and the United States still have theirs. In May 2002, Pakistan tested three different nuclear-capable ballistic missiles for the first time. The will and capacity to use nuclear weapons provides both India and Pakistan with political and diplomatic importance, and raises the stakes in their conflict over Kashmir.

Because tight control over nuclear weapons by the two former Cold War enemies was lost, in some ways, security from the threat of nuclear war became more elusive in the twenty-first century.

LIVING IN THE SHADOW OF A GIANT

Prime Minister Wilfrid Laurier famously said, "The twentieth century belongs to Canada." An objective look at the history of the troubled twentieth century would suggest otherwise.

At the end of two devastating world wars, the United States stood as a global superpower, challenged only by the might of the former Soviet Union. From 1945 to 1990, much of the world was divided into two armed camps led by these ideological, military, and political rivals. Although they avoided direct military conflict, their "cold war" shaped global politics and caused nations to rise and fall. The result was a costly arms race, heightened international tensions, and the threat of catastrophic nuclear war. When the Soviet Union was finally dismantled, the United States stood alone as the dominant world power.

In the early years of the twenty-first century, the US stood poised to play a powerful and active role in world politics.

Figure 12.12

These Indian soldiers were sent in a convoy to bolster forces at the India-Pakistan border in Kashmir in 2002. What impact do you think the fact that both sides have nuclear capabilities will have on this conflict?

The United States was now prepared to use its enormous military, economic, and political muscle to shape and direct world affairs. In some ways, the United States achieved a stature that no other power had ever achieved in absolute global terms.

The position of the United States has important implications for all nations of the world. Because Canada lives next to this solitary superpower, American influence pours across its long border. Inevitably, the priorities of the US government bear heavily on the lives of Canadians. In the ongoing war against terrorism, for example, Canada has been pressured to upgrade its military capacity and play a more active role alongside its American allies. And despite the benefits of NAFTA, Canada continues to fight the United States for unfettered access to American markets.

In the future, the ability of Canadians to pursue an independent Canada—to build a unique national identity—will likely be constrained by these close ties with the United States. To outside observers, Canadians and Americans seem to share the same general culture. The struggle to remain unique is experienced by more nations than just Canada.

THE CULTURE WARS

A dominant United States cannot help but challenge the smaller nations of the world. It is especially difficult to maintain a unique national or ethnic culture when American commercial symbols—such as McDonald's, Coca-Cola, and Disney—flood the international media and extend their influence everywhere. Many people react negatively to what has been called the "Disneyfication" of the world. At the same time, American pop culture—whether it be blue jeans, Hollywood superstars, or pop music—has found a global following. Much of the world harbours a love-hate relationship with the United States.

Figure 12.13

Euro Disney in France, Coca-Cola in Tokyo, and McDonald's in Russia: These photographs reveal the influence of American culture around the world. Why do you think some people react negatively to these symbols? Explain.

National identity is central for many people. Their language and religious and cultural traditions are core aspects of their identity. Communities want to share and pass on traditional values and experiences, unique histories and religions. Some of the tensions felt by the Muslim nations, for example, reflect their desire to resist American influence and to ensure protection and promotion of their social and religious institutions. Conflicts between rebel and revolutionary groups and state governments in Latin America, Africa and Asia are evidence of many peoples struggles to gain a national identity.

There is a huge range of social, cultural and political national expressions around the world, but American pop culture has a very strong financial backing, which makes it difficult for other nations to avoid. Diversity and tradition are equally challenged by the impact of **consumerism** and pervasive technology. Maintaining "uniqueness" amid strong external influences and a world that is changing so quickly is a challenge.

NATIONALISM VERSUS SUPRANATIONALISM

The history of the twentieth century reveals two very different tendencies. In one sense, the world appears to be a smaller place. Today, global communications are virtually instantaneous, and inventions and news sweep across borders. Earlier marvels, such as the telegraph and telephone, seem quaint compared to the power of the Internet. Problems such as HIV/AIDS, international terrorism, and global warming and pollution cannot be confined to one region—they are the world's problems.

In such a connected world, old borders and frontiers seem dated. Many people

"Nationalism is an infantile disease. It is the measles of mankind."

— Albert Einstein

Figure 12.14

The success of space exploration encouraged people to view the world as a single entity. In the vastness of space, Planet Earth appeared small, and borders appeared arbitrary.

now travel to other countries to pursue a career, for recreational purposes, or to create new family ties.

By the end of the century, international migration—the movement of people from their native country to another country—was at an all-time high. About 150 million people lived outside their countries of origin and the number continued to increase by two- to four million each year. According to the Population Reference Bureau, the most significant immigration flows were from Latin America and Asia into North America; and from Eastern Europe, the countries of the former Soviet Union, and North Africa into Northern and Western Europe.

In such a fluid world, the nationalist ties of the pre-First World War years seemed hopelessly out of date. Observers began to note a growing sense of **supranationalism**—an allegiance to or identification with a structure larger than one's nationality. This new spirit of internationalism was reflected in successful models of regional co-operation such as the European Union and NAFTA, and in humanitarian efforts such as Doctors Without Borders/ Médecins Sans Frontières. The United Nations also survived the divisions of the Cold War and the rise of the United States to offer a more global vision for humankind. Was the world more united at the end of the century? Certainly, the idea of "supranationalism" suggested that the world could transcend national, territorial limits and become a more inclusive place.

A SMALLER, MORE HOSTILE WORLD?

While the world appeared to be shrinking, there was a countertrend to supranationalism. The rise of ethnic nationalism and racism based on narrow allegiance to religion, race, language, and ethnicity was clearly evident. As the Communist regimes fell, some (like Yugoslavia) dissolved into civil war based on the narrowest of identities. In Africa, in spite of the surge to independence, the forces of tribalism threatened to tear apart nations such as Somalia and Rwanda. In Germany, a neo-Nazi movement arose in reaction to the country's diverse population mix, the result of massive immigration following the Second World War.

The new century may well see the continued battle between the broader forces of internationalism and the narrower allegiances of nationalism and ethnic and religious identity. For many nations—perhaps for many individuals— the challenge will be to marry the forces of globalization with the need to belong to a smaller, more defined community.

Figure 12.15

In late 2002, the Miss World pageant had to be moved from Nigeria to London, England, after violence erupted between Christians and Muslims over the role of women and the legitimacy of the pagent. Is it unusual for an international event to spark local violence?

Profile   Aung San Suu Kyi (1945-)

Figure 12.16
Aung San Suu Kyi (in framed photo, with microphone) inspired human rights activists all over the world. Here, citizens of Myanmar living in Japan demonstrate for her release on International Human Rights Day, 2000.

Aung San Suu Kyi was awarded the Nobel Peace Prize in 1991. Under house arrest and confined to her home, she led a non-violent struggle for democracy in her home country of Burma (Myanmar). (The military government has renamed the country Myanmar, but Aung San Suu Kyi and her supporters continue to use the name Burma.)

"Violence is simply the symptom of hate."

— Aung San Suu Kyi, 1988

"We believe we shall have democracy because the people of Burma want democracy and they deserve it and they know how to cope with it. It is not new to our country. We have had it before and we shall have it again."

— Aung San Suu Kyi, 1996

"…[T]o protect the spirit of liberty is to protect something that is worthwhile, so no one will set it aside or throw it away on the street if it is so truly worthy…. Only if we are able to protect liberty will it be long lasting."

— Aung San Suu Kyi, 2003

At first glance, Aung San Suu Kyi seems an unlikely revolutionary. Born into a politically prominent family in Burma, she spent her early years in Rangoon and Delhi, India, where her mother was the Burmese ambassador. She moved to Britain for her university education, studying at Oxford; there she married a British academic. Over the next few years she worked for the United Nations in New York and held academic positions in Japan and India.

This tranquil life ended suddenly in April 1988, when Aung San Suu Kyi returned to Rangoon, Burma, to support her dying mother. Protests against the repressive military government were rocking the city. The month before, police had killed 200 demonstrators, but the people continued to demand free multiparty elections and a democratic government. Many of the demonstrators carried pictures of Suu Kyi's father, General Aung San, a nationalist leader whose resistance to colonial rule resulted in Burma's independence in 1948. He was assassinated when Suu Kyi was only two years old. Compelled by the intensity of the protesters' convictions, Aung San Suu Kyi spoke at a rally of several hundred thousand people. This act thrust her into the forefront of the pro-democracy movement.

The Burmese pro-democracy movement evolved into a political party, the National League for Democracy. It won an overwhelming majority in national elections in 1990. The military regime was not prepared to give up its power, however. The military had placed Suu Kyi under house arrest without charge or trial the previous year and refused to recognize the results of the election.

The world was outraged by the repression of the Burmese non-violent democratic movement. In December

1990, then-UN Secretary-General Javier Pérez de Cuéllar called for Suu Kyi's release. In 1991, Suu Kyi was awarded the Nobel Peace Prize for her outstanding work for human rights and democracy. The public opposition to her sentence did little good, however, and Suu Kyi remained under house arrest until the end of her sentence in 1995. In the following years, her movements were carefully restricted by the military government. Because of her continuing opposition to the government, she was again placed under house arrest in September 2000. On 6 May 2002, she was released again— this time unconditionally. The event marked "a new page for the people of Burma and the international community," according to a government press release.

Burma's human rights record continues to be regarded as one of the worst in the world.

Responding

1. What attributes made Aung San Suu Kyi an able spokesperson for the pro-democracy movement in Burma?

2. In spite of widespread publicity and international condemnation, the military regime has never allowed a democratically elected government to take power in Burma. What could Aung San Suu Kyi and her party do to counteract this resistance?

3. What action could people around the world take to support the movement for democracy in Burma?

HUMAN RIGHTS AROUND THE WORLD

At the turn of the century, uncertainty and progress also marked the status of human rights. During your reading of *Twentieth Century Viewpoints* you have seen that protection of human rights was formally entrenched in 1948 by the United Nations in the Universal Declaration of Human Rights. This declaration includes many important articles, including the following:

- All human beings are born free and equal in dignity and rights. (Article 1)
- Everyone has the right to life, liberty and security of person. (Article 3)
- No one shall be subjected to torture or to cruel, inhuman or degrading treatment or punishment. (Article 5)
- No one shall be subjected to arbitrary arrest, detention or exile. (Article 9)
- Everyone has the right to freedom of opinion and expression … (Article 19)
- Everyone has the right to take part in the government of his or her country, directly or through freely chosen representatives. (Article 21)

While these principles seem firm and sound, they have yet to be realized globally. Nevertheless, by the start of the twenty-first century, there was a growing demand for all nations to respect human rights. The dismantling of oppressive systems such as apartheid in South Africa (see Chapter Nine, pages 292-304) showed the world that change could occur. Here, and in other parts of the world, pressure was brought to bear in the form of trade sanctions and public demonstrations, often with startling results. In 1998, Augusto Pinochet, the former dictator of Chile, was detained for human rights abuses and accused of mass torture and genocide. In 1999, Slobodan Milosevic, leader of the former Yugoslavia, was arrested by the United Nations War Crimes Tribunal and indicted for war crimes and crimes against humanity.

In the last decades of the century, many political prisoners were released as a result of pressure from monitoring groups such as **Amnesty International** and Human Rights Watch. Others received more humane treatment while in prison

"Where, after all, do universal human rights begin? In small places, close to home—so close and so small that they cannot be seen on any map of the world. Yet they are the world of the individual person."

— Eleanor Roosevelt, author, diplomat, and former First Lady

Figure 12.17
Former Yugoslav president Slobodan Milosevic is led into the courtroom of the UN War Crimes Tribunal on 3 July 2001. He represented himself at his hearing.

because of the harsh glare of the world spotlight. When China won the 2008 Summer Olympics, the world's attention was focused on its poor human rights record (see Chapter Ten, Viewpoints, page 340). China and other nations, including Afghanistan, Colombia, Iraq, and North Korea, continued to be monitored for human rights abuses as the century closed.

Children suffered some of the worst human rights violations in the twentieth century. Currently, between 200 million and 250 million children under the age of 14 work for wages. In a few South Asian countries, the number of working children is as high as 60 per cent of the workforce—and some are as young as five years old. These children do not have a choice; they must either work or starve.

For most of the world, child labour is the result of poverty. Parents cannot afford to feed and house their families, so children must contribute to the family income. Wages paid to children are far lower than those paid to adults, and many children work for less than a dollar a day. Hours are usually long and working conditions can be hazardous.

Working children are often trapped in the cycle of poverty because they lack the opportunity to receive an education or any skilled training. The new Convention on the Worst Forms of Child Labour came into effect in late 2000. It required that nations abolish child slavery, trafficking, debt bondage, child prostitution and pornography, and child labour (including the forced recruitment of children as soldiers). NGOs also monitor child labour issues, often asking North Americans to refuse to buy goods produced by nations that disregard child labour standards.

Not only are children being forced to work in industry, they are also being drawn into military service at unprecedented rates. According to UNICEF, during the period of 1990 to 2000, over 300 000 children were forced to fight in at least 36 conflicts worldwide. In 2002, over 50 countries were actively engaged in the recruitment of children under the age of 18. In Afghanistan, Burundi, Columbia, Congo, Ethiopia, Eritrea, Myanmar, Pakistan, Sierra Leone, Sri Lanka, and Uganda, children as young as 8 years of age were recruited by rebel groups to be soldiers and into national armed forces.

On 12 February 2002, a new international treaty sponsored by the High Commissioner for Human Rights and approved by the UN General Assembly was passed to try to halt the recruitment of child soldiers around the world. By mid 2002, this treaty, called the "Optional Protocol to the Rights of the Child on the Involvement of Children in Armed Conflict," was signed by 99 nations, but only 16 of these had ratified it.

Figure 12.18
A former child labourer protests against child labour in New Delhi. What does it mean to "save childhood"?

Figure 12.19
Samboo, a 12-year-old soldier in the Karen rebel army fighting against Myanmar's military government, poses with his gun in a jungle camp near the Thailand border in this photo taken in January 2000. It was the 51st anniversary of Karen revolution day. More than 300 000 child soldiers are fighting for national and guerrilla armies around the world, according to the Coalition to Stop the Use of Child Soldiers.

Voices Child Soldiers

The use of child soldiers is common in nations of Asia and Africa, and in some countries of Latin America and Europe. In 1998 Afghanistan was estimated to have 108 000 soldiers and rebels under the age of 18—more than twice as many young soldiers as any other country. In Colombia, the Armed Revolutionary Forces of Colombia and the National Liberation Army are known to have recruited children younger than 15 years of age. Youths have participated in European conflicts in Bosnia-Herzegovina, Chechnya, Kosovo, and the Former Yugoslav Republic of Macedonia in recent years; mostly with armed opposition groups, but sometimes with government-aligned paramilitaries. In 2002, in Uganda, children aged 13 to 16 made up 90 per cent of the Lord's Resistance Army (LRA), an armed rebel opposition force.

"I was recruited by force, against my will. One evening while we were watching a video show in my village, three army sergeants came. They checked whether we had identification cards and asked if we wanted to join the army. We explained that we were under age and hadn't got identification cards. But one of my friends said he wanted to join. I said no and came back home that evening but an army recruitment unit arrived next morning at my village and demanded two new recruits. Those who could not pay 3000 kyats had to join the army, they said. I (my parent) could not pay, so altogether 19 of us were recruited in that way and sent to Mingladon (an army training center)."

— Zaw Tun, 15, Burmese ex-army soldier

"When I get older, I will organize a gang and seek my father's revenge."

—Asif, 12, Afghan refugee

"We were drugged and ordered to move forward on the battlefield. We did not know what sort of drug or alcohol we were given but we drank it because we were very tired, very thirsty and hungry. We had walked for two whole days under very hot burning sun. The hill (battlefield) had no shade, trees were burnt and artillery shells were exploding everywhere. We were so scared, very thirsty and some of us collapsed due to over-tiredness. But we were beaten from behind (by the officers) and had to move forward. One got killed."

— Myo Win, 12, Burmese ex-army soldier

"I joined the army when I was young (at 15) without thinking much. I admired soldiers, their guns and crisp, neat uniforms. I just wanted to fight the way they did in the movies and so I joined the army."

— Htay, 21, Burmese ex-army soldier

'They abducted me but still they went ahead to kill my mother and father that night."

— Richard, 12, Rwandan refugee

Responding:
1. Why would certain governments and rebel groups recruit child soldiers?
2. Determine your own point-of-view on the use of child soldiers. Write one argument to defend your point-of-view using current examples to support your argument.

A STANDARD OF LIVING

You may not give much thought to your standard of living, but for much of the world, poverty is a constant companion. By the end of the century, the tension between the "haves" and the "have-nots"—alluded to by former US president Jimmy Carter (see Voices on page 391)—had reached a critical level. Not only are people in the developed world better fed, housed, educated, employed, and entertained—they also use far more of the Earth's resources than do the people of Africa, Asia, and Latin America.

The facts are chilling: people in nations with developed, diversified economies represent less than 20 per cent of the world's total population but use more than 80 per cent of the world's resources. To ensure their own standard of living, such nations are 30 times more destructive to the global environment than are their African, Asian, and Latin American neighbours.

Population growth is another important variable. By the end of the century, overpopulation was still a problem in many regions of the world, and this combined with other factors to create even more hardship. Rapid population growth in Africa, Asia, and Latin America taxed the environment through increased demand for land, food, and water.

In June of 2002, five million people across southern Africa faced the worst food crisis in a decade. Severe weather brought drought to Malawi, Zambia, and Zimbabwe; heavy rains and hailstorms to Lesotho; and extensive flooding to Mozambique. Maize and sorghum crops—staples in the diet of South Africa—failed. Crop failures and critical food shortages are typical of nations that face chronic food insecurity, and they often lead to famine and starvation. While the populations of many developed nations have stabilized or are decreasing, population growth in these regions continues to place a strain on the planet's resources and environments.

The economies of developing nations are often dependent upon the success of food crops, which are vulnerable to weather, and on the income derived from cash crops such as coffee, sugar, tea, and tobacco, which are subject to changing world prices. If economic expansion within a developing nation cannot keep pace with the population growth, family incomes decline, unemployment

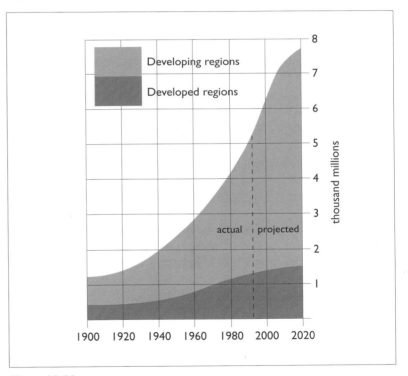

Figure 12.20

Population Growth, Actual and Projected to 2020. Which is greater cause for concern: Projected population increases in developed or developing regions by 2020?

Figure 12.21
Not all campaigns aimed at curbing the population have been benign. In China, the government program promoting the one-child family has involved coercion and punishment.

increases, and everyone experiences a lower standard of living. The poverty cycle continues, extending itself into the next generation.

Many experts consider economic development to be the most effective means of eliminating poverty. However, in developing nations, economic development often comes at the price of environmental degradation. Local initiatives often work better than large-scale projects organized by international aid programs.

Another solution is to reduce the rate of population growth in certain areas of the world. Educating families about family planning methods, and offering incentives designed to reduce family size, have proven to be successful methods. Redistributing populations within nations and reversing the trend toward urbanization are other strategies. However, all of these methods bring with them a host of complex social problems. There are no easy answers.

While few people are prepared to sacrifice their own quality of life, many see the need to work toward a better global standard of living. There are many ways to achieve this end without sacrificing the world's environment. Some of these solutions are

- tapping environmentally-friendly energy resources such as such as wind and solar power
- providing emergency food aid during times of famine and starvation
- ensuring that project aid meets real local needs
- providing "intellectual capital"— trainers and teachers who can help people in developing nations to better utilize their own resources

THE TWENTY-FIRST CENTURY

The twentieth century began with technological, scientific, cultural and social innovations and visions that opened many nations to greater international opportunities and interactions. Economic and political changes have taken place to transform how peoples and nations interact at home and abroad.

Technological improvement has changed and shaped the industrialized and, to some extent, the industrializing world. A great many of the world's peoples are better educated, live longer, and are more productive than ever before. The world produces more of everything—faster and more cheaply—than it ever has before. For millions, one constant has been the continued increase in the productive capacities of humankind.

Science is on the verge of producing wonder drugs and dream technologies that may successfully defeat cancer and AIDS. The Human Genome Project is poised to revolutionize our understanding of human life and increase our capacity to direct human development. Space and deep-sea exploration have become everyday realities—no longer even meriting mention on the front pages of newspapers.

Regional agreements and economic unions are clearly the order of the day. Trade within international economic blocs and organizations is becoming freer. Through the European Union, NAFTA, the Mersocur, and the Andean Community, trade organizations have been created as regional covenants to generate advantages for members.

The United Nations has succeeded where the former League of Nations faltered. There is growing support for the spirit of internationalism. However, addressing the nationalist goals of numerous cultural and ethnic groups within nations will continue to take centre stage in the years ahead. "Local" (as opposed to "regional") conflicts are those that erupt within a single nation, often within a sub-region of that single state, and have led to wars in Asia, Africa, and Eastern Europe in the past decade. Not only have these wars affected the nations surrounding the warring localities, they have also had an impact internationally, to the extent that both UN peacekeeping/peacemaking and NATO forces have interceded to reduce or end the conflict.

Many countries have evolved, or are evolving, into more progressive democratic nations, with expanded opportunities and rights for their citizens. While there remains much scope for increased parity, the rights of women have been improving, slowly but dramatically, across the globe. Concern for children has risen much higher on the political agenda of the world's nations. On many levels, it would appear that the history of the twentieth century has been one of progress. The twenty-first century offers probabilities and possibilities for the future opportunities and challenges that lie ahead.

In Review

1. Describe the position held by the United States at the opening of the twenty-first century. How does US power affect Canada?

2. What evidence is there that national identity is still important in the world?

3. In your view, is the world more, or less, united than in 1900? Explain.

4. In your opinion, what are the most important human rights? Why?

5. What evidence is there that prosperity is not shared equally around the globe?

6. What challenges continue to face the developing nations of the world?

7. Briefly describe the major positive and negative features of the world today.

8. In general, has the world become a better or a worse place in the last 100 years? Explain.

Summary

The end of the century is usually an occasion for reflection. At the close of the twentieth century, there was much to celebrate—scientific progress, technological innovation, expanded health care, a growing commitment to human rights, and a new spirit of co-operation among nations. Models of regional co-operation such as the EU, the Organization of African Unity, Mercosur, and NAFTA illustrated that nations had much to gain from putting their heads together and leaving their animosities behind.

But the world was also shaken. It had survived two world wars and the collapse of many social, political, and economic systems, replacing them with models that had yet to be tested — such as globalization. In the last decades of the century, there was deep resentment over the dominant position of the United States. Then, just 20 months after the festive New Year's Eve celebrations on 31 December 1999, there was a brand new threat—international terrorism on a scale never before witnessed. Following the attacks on 11 September 2001, the US—not the United Nations—declared itself a leader in the international war on terrorism, invaded Afghanistan, and immediately targeted Iran, Iraq, and North Korea as "the axis of evil." The twenty-first century began with challenges of conflict management that were truly global and that would require co-operation within the international community to resolve.

Viewpoints

ISSUE: To what extent do people benefit from globalization?

Background

Globalization of the economy can be viewed as both a solution and a problem. Since the end of the Cold War at the end of the twentieth century, the drive to develop market economies has accelerated around the world. Former Soviet bloc nations have rushed to embrace capitalism, and Western-based multinational corporations were more than happy to expand into new markets. While market economies promote wealth and freedom, they have a dark side—the concentration of wealth and power in the hands of a few at the expense of the poor.

Do people benefit from economic globalization? Shanti Zachariah is a writer. She argues that the global economy has hurt the ordinary working people of the poor countries. Jagdish Bhagwati says people do benefit in the long term. He is a professor of economics and political science at Columbia University. He served as the economic policy advisor to the Director-General of GATT and advised India's finance minister on economic reforms.

Read these two viewpoints carefully, and answer the questions that follow. (You may want to refer to the Skill Path "Analysing a Reading" on page 14 before beginning these articles.)

Shanti Zachariah

Even as the media, economists and governments speak of the "new" global economy, and "new" ways to compete in it, globalism has pushed to the forefront the oldest of battles within our capitalist system—the ongoing and unresolved struggle for workers' rights. The globalization and decentralization of manufacturing has meant the creation of 850 Export Processing Zones, or EPZs, that employ 27 million people worldwide. The International Labour Organization (ILO) defines EPZs as "industrial zones with special incentives set up to attract foreign investors, in which imported materials undergo some degree of processing before being exported again."

According to a 1998 ILO report, very low wages are commonplace for EPZs, as much of the work performed there is low skilled and worker turnover is high. "Employers are generally loath to invest in training and social security benefits because they assume that workers will leave after a few years," states the report, and "industries see labour as a cost to be contained rather than as a resource or asset to be developed."

The push for low wages raises the question of who benefits the most from this system. A 1997 UN report makes that clear: the 10 largest transnationals have a total income greater than that of the world's 100 poorest countries; and two-thirds of international trade is accounted for by 500 transnationals.

"You have to ask," says Greg Degroot-Maggetti, the socio-economic concerns coordinator for Citizens for Public Justice, "what is the purpose of an economy? It should be for the well-being of the people."

The key to the challenge of organizing workers in EPZs can be found in the very term "transnational corporation." These companies are highly mobile because many don't actually own the factories where their goods are manufactured. They contract out to smaller companies who own the factories and determine the workplace rules. If workers from one factory attempt to organize for better conditions, the transnational can pull out and settle in another area. Making a transnational legally accountable is tricky: technically, it employs the middle manufacturer who, in turn, is the legal employer of the workers.

Dr. Woodhead says: "We're not calling for a universal wage. We're calling for the right to unionize, so the (EPZ workers) can determine their own wage. If you have a union, you can eliminate most sweatshop conditions. There's enough wealth in the world today that transnational corporations can pay a living wage, have acceptable working conditions and still be profitable."

Linda Yanz is a coordinator with the Maquila Solidarity Network (MSN) in Toronto. She says her organization takes great care to say that factories shouldn't pull out, due to media and public pressure, but should work to improve conditions. "Whether in El Salvador or China, the workers want and need their jobs, and they definitely resent it when anything puts their jobs in jeopardy. Any wage is better than no wage, but their wages right now are not legitimate and need to go up so they can support themselves."

When GAP allowed one of its factories in El Salvador to be inspected in 1996, Mark Anner helped coordinate the Independent Monitoring Group, made up of church and social activists. He saw workers almost "killing themselves" to exceed already tough quotas to top off their daily wage of approximately $4.50 U.S. From talking to workers in El Salvador's maquila zone, he knows they want to improve their conditions but "until a way can be found to form unions without getting fired, they're going to stay away. We have to rethink strategies behind organizing drives," he says.

Boycotting a company's goods to exact change is not a popular choice with EPZ workers, according to Gretchen Ferguson, coordinator of the Trade Union Group for International Solidarity, which promotes worker solidarity between Canada and Latin America. She has worked and spoken with EPZ workers who tell her boycotting does not help their cause because it simply puts them out of work.

There are some corporations that have introduced limited regulations into the factories that make their goods. In 1998, the Fair Labour Association was formed, with members including Liz Claiborne, Levi Strauss, and Nike. The FLA charter creates an industry-wide code of conduct and monitoring system, where companies, suppliers and contractors will be held accountable for work conditions and rights. Both internal and independent monitoring of factories will be ongoing.

Before the GAP factory in El Salvador was inspected, Anner says, "there wasn't proper drinking water...locks were on the bathroom door, and women had to ask permission to go.... There was forced overtime and women had to get pregnancy tests to get a job." After the agreement with GAP, these conditions were rectified, but he admits that "we can only achieve so much in one isolated factory." GAP still will not allow independent monitoring of its other 50 contract factories. And the FLA agreement only calls for 30 per cent of its companies' factories to be independently inspected.

Real and lasting change will require state intervention, along with industry self-regulation, to remedy the worst excesses of capitalism. This intervention can take the form of international labour standards, including comparable living wages, and the right to organize. If many countries adapted such standards to their situation, the mobility of transnationals would be restricted, which would ultimately mean stability for the workers and better health and training.

It is interesting, and disconcerting, to hear and read the perfect logic of economists who defend cheap labour as the way it has to be right now. But justice, too, makes sense. People get it, across cultures and generations, whether they be strikers in Winnipeg in 1919, or women in 2000 sewing khakis on the Mexican-U.S. border.

"We want a system," says Yanz, "where countries can compete with ethical standards and labour rights—where a competitive edge is gained by living up to ethical standards."

Source: Excerpted from Shanti Zachariah, "Old fight is 'new' global economy," *Catholic New Times*, 6 February 2000, Vol. 24, No. 2, pp.10-11.

Jagdish Bhagwati

GINA KRAMER: Would you consider international regulations or sanctions intended to enforce or discourage some particular domestic policy, such as child labor, as inappropriate?

JAGDISH BHAGWATI: You can't blame US policymakers for thinking that somehow, trade sanctions are the way to spread goodness around the world. In a way, that is a cultural notion; Americans seem to adopt the Superman model very quickly. They forget that the rest of the world could think of us as Lex Luthors instead. Trade sanctions are useful only when really egregious [bad] kinds of abuses exist and when you can work up a substantial enthusiasm for sanctions from many nations.

If you simply put a child-labor standard into WTO regulations, it automatically becomes a trade sanction. This is not productive, however, because if child labor were just a feature of one sector or one firm, you could target it and that would be the end of the matter—freeze it out. But child labor is just one of billions of activities, because child labor is a reflection of poverty. If child labor is regulated through WTO rules, then children are likely to be bumped down into other forms of occupation, such as prostitution. You cannot just move some children away from employment. We can wear a button on the lapels of our jackets and say we're against child labor; it sounds good, it's good for the heart, but it's really counterproductive and morally obtuse [unclear].

When many developing countries see legislation in the United States against child labor, they view it as protectionism intended to prevent competition. We devalue our own moral agenda by trying to use the wrong instruments. We must not undermine the ability to advance trade liberalization; trade is an engine of prosperity and in the end does push people into gainful employment. Prosperity generates revenue, and there is a good chance that increased revenue will be spent on liberal programs like public health for the poor.

GINA KRAMER: What role will globalization play in the relationship between trade and social issues?

JAGDISH BHAGWATI: Increasingly, people who want to act in their own self-interest will use global competition as an excuse. This isn't a compelling argument. Major firms, thanks to NGOs, thanks to CNN, and thanks to modern international civil society networks, can't afford to indulge in environmentally unfriendly practices just because there are no laws to prevent them from doing so. For multinationals today, reputation plays a large role. I am known for a proposal, which makes me very unpopular with the business world, that it should be mandatory for an American firm abroad to act as if it were at home in matters of minimum safety requirements and environmental friendliness, although not necessarily wages. I call it: "in Rome, do as New Yorkers do, not as the Romans do."

GINA KRAMER: What is the relationship between democratization and development?

JAGDISH BHAGWATI: There is a traditional argument that as a population becomes more gentrified [economically secure] and a middle class emerges, demands for democracy will grow.

GINA KRAMER: In light of the increased competition and a world economy moving toward freer trade, what strategies should developing countries pursue?

JAGDISH BHAGWATI: World Bank funds should be used to make it possible for us to live in a modern economy. At the same time, some progressive social agendas ought to be handled by appropriate institutions and governance. We have a lot to gain from the bulk of globalization, but we have to embed it in institutional changes. We have to think in threefold terms: growth, prosperity, and then appropriate governance at the international level and internal institutional frameworks. But ultimately, you're only protected from bad economics by your good judgment.

Source: Excerpted from Jagdish Bhagwati, "Economic sense and nonsense: Misconceptions of the global economy," *Harvard International Review*, Fall 2000; Volume 22, No. 3, pp.78-81.

Analysis and Evaluation

1. Who does Shanti Zachariah say benefits most from globalization?

2. What "checks" on the effects of globalization does Jagdish Bhagwati seem to envision? Do you agree with his analysis?

3. Decide which of the viewpoints you tend to support, and explain why. If you agree with neither, state the position you do support and explain it. Be sure to use specific information from this textbook, the readings, and other sources to support your position.

Chapter Analysis

MAKING CONNECTIONS

1. Briefly review Chapter One and note what you feel are the biggest changes from 1900 until today. For each change, indicate whether it is positive or negative.

2. As you consider the previous chapters in this textbook, indicate what you think have been the best and the worst features of the previous century.

3. Will the UN continue to succeed or is it doomed to fail, as did the League of Nations? Explain fully.

DEVELOPING YOUR VOICE

4. Working with a partner, prepare a *Youth Manifesto for the Twenty-First Century*. In it, outline your hopes, aspirations, and demands for the future development of the world in this century. Be prepared to share your views with your peers.

5. Participate in a small-group discussion to examine the photographs in this chapter. To what extent do you think that "a picture is worth a thousand words"?

6. Write a letter to the future child that you may parent. In your letter, outline what you think will be the future of the twenty-first century. Reread your letter when and if that child is born.

7. Invite your local Member of Parliament to come to your school to discuss current world affairs. Prepare a list of excellent questions.

8. In your view, who was the greatest figure in the twentieth century? Explain your choice. Be prepared to support your views in discussion with your peers.

RESEARCHING THE ISSUES

9. Review the format used to write the Profile features in this textbook. Now research at least one humanitarian agency active in the world today and write a "Profile" of that agency's work in the world.

10. Use a reference such as *The Statesman's Yearbook*, published annually in Great Britain since 1864, or the Internet to find out more about one of the GOs or NGOs mentioned in this chapter. Using word-processor technology, design a "fast facts" data sheet to offer information on these aspects of the organization:

    • Origin and history
    • Membership
    • Aims and activities
    • Achievements
    • Headquarters
    • Web site

Glossary

agreement of mutual non-aggression: A pact signed in 1939 between Germany and the USSR stipulating that neither country would attack the other.

Alliance for Progress: A US assistance program for Latin America created to counter the appeal of revolutionary politics such as those in Cuba. The Alliance called for ambitious programs to end poverty and social inequities in the region.

alliance system: The division of Europe into two rival camps, the Triple Alliance and the Triple Entente, which resulted in the escalation of the international tensions that led to the First World War.

alliances: A formal treaty or agreement of co-operation between nations.

al-Qaeda: An international terrorist organization based in the Middle East and headed by Osama bin Laden.

Amnesty International: An organization that monitors human rights violations around the world and exerts pressure on repressive governments through public awareness.

anarchist: A person who rebels against any authority, established order, or ruling power.

apartheid: A racial policy introduced in South Africa in 1948 classifying residents into two separate and distinct classes: white and non-white. The policy resulted in racial segregation and restrictions on marriages, residences, and education.

appeasement: The policy of making concessions to satisfy the demands of Nazi Germany prior to the Second World War.

armistice: A temporary truce between two opposing parties.

arms race: The competition between rival states to gain superior military weapons and technology.

Aryans: A term used by Nazi Germany to describe non-Jewish people, especially of Nordic heritage.

Association of South East Asian Nations (ASEAN): An organization established in 1967 to promote peace, economic and cultural growth, and free trade within its membership.

authoritarian: Relating to a leader or government that holds absolute power and is not constitutionally responsible to the people.

autonomy: Self-governing and independent of the control of others.

balance of power: An distribution of power, such as military and economic power, among nations or groups of nations.

bias: A prejudiced opinion or predisposition for or against something or someone. The existence of bias in sources of information can distort facts and create an unbalanced view.

biculturalism: Relating to or including two distinct cultures.

bipolar: A state of two diametrically opposed forces.

Black Hand: The name of a Serbian secret society formed in 1911 that sought the union of Serb minorities in Austria-Hungary and Turkey with Serbs living in independent Serbia.

Blackshirts: An organization of the unofficial Italian militia created by Mussolini in 1921 to intimidate opponents.

blitz: The intensive German bombing of Britain during the Second World War, specifically during the Battle of Britain in which an estimated 30 000 civilians died.

blitzkrieg: A German term for "lightning war," a sudden and rapid military offensive designed to cripple the enemy before they can defend themselves.

Bolsheviks: An extremist wing of the Russian Democratic Party that opposed participation in the First World War. Led by Lenin, the party seized power during the Russian Revolution in 1917 and later became the Russian Communist Party.

bourgeoisie (bourgeois): The middle class (or relating to the middle class) of a capitalist society.

Boxer Rebellion: The armed rebellion of a secret Chinese society opposed to foreigners and Christianity in 1900; the Boxers were defeated by American, Japanese, and British troops.

Brezhnev Doctrine: A policy used by Leonid Brezhnev to protect communism from outside influences and to secure the centralized power of Moscow over its satellite states. This policy was used to justify the Soviet invasion of Czechoslovakia in 1968.

brinkmanship: The pushing for a negotiated settlement of a dangerous situation to the very limits of safety before giving ground.

buzz bombs: Unguided jet-propelled missiles used by Germany against Britain during the Second World War.

capitalism: An economic system characterized by private or corporate ownership of capital goods, production, and distribution. A free-enterprise system with relative absence of economic control by the government.

Central Treaty Organization (CENTO): A mutual defence policy between Turkey, Iraq, Iran, Pakistan, Britain, and the US against the USSR in 1958.

Cold War: The period after the Second World War until 1990 when increasing diplomatic and political tension between the United States and the Soviet Union created constant threat of war.

collective security: A group of nations acting together to preserve peace through mutual defense and security.

collectivization: The Soviet plan to create an agricultural co-operative through consolidation of peasant villages into state-controlled collective farms.

colonial domination: Control exerted by an imperial power over its colonies in such aspects of life as the economy, culture, and politics.

Cominform: The Communist Information Bureau established in 1947 to coordinate Communist Party activities and strengthen the position of the Soviet Union in Europe.

Cominterm: An organization founded by Lenin and the Soviet Communist Party in 1919 to encourage worldwide communism.

command economy: An economy in which production and distribution of goods are controlled by a central power.

Common Market: See European Economic Community.

Commonwealth: An association of nations that were once subject to the imperial government of the United Kingdom.

communism: A system based on the principle of communal ownership of all property.

concentration camps: A prison system established by the Nazis in the Second World War for the confinement, slave labour, and mass execution of political prisoners. More than 6 million Jews were killed in these camps.

concession rights: A lease of land granted by the state for purposes of profit.

conscription: A law requiring mandatory military service.

constitutional monarchy: A king, queen, or emperor whose powers are limited by the constitution.

containment: The defensive American foreign policy in 1947 to contain the spread of communism through economic and technical assistance to threatened countries. The policy later included military force.

contras: A guerilla group opposed to the Sandinista government in Nicaragua.

co-operative federalism: A policy in which provinces are consulted on a wide range of federal matters.

Council of Ministers: The major decision-making body of the European Union. It issues directions to the European Commission for implementation.

counterculture: A culture with values in conflict with those of established society.

coup: The sudden and often violent overthrow of a government by a group, such as the military.

cruise missile: A self-guided, low-flying missile that could deliver a nuclear weapon over thousands of kilometres and hit a specific target.

Cubism: An art style of abstract structure that displayed several aspects of the same object simultaneously in fragmented form.

Cultural Revolution: The political upheaval in China between 1965 and 1968 that called for a return to Mao's revolutionary ideals and the abandonment of liberal practices.

Dawes Plan: A plan presented by a committee headed by American Charles G. Dawes to deal with Germany's lagging payments on its First World War reparation debt of almost 20 billion marks. The plan went into effect in 1924.

debt recycling: A program in which a developing nation pays off a portion of its debt to a foreign bank with the agreement that the bank will reinvest the money into the local economy.

Declaration of Human Rights: Passed on December 10, 1948, the Declaration by the United Nations set a common standard on human rights for all peoples and all nations.

demilitarized zone: An area that is prohibited from military use.

desertification: The process of land being transformed into desert as a result of mismanagement of natural resources.

détente: The relaxation of international tensions, specifically between the Soviets and the Americans in the 1970s.

deterrence: The act of restraining or preventing an action through fear of the consequences. During the Cold War, the West sought to prevent an attack by the Soviet Union by expanding its military might.

Diaspora: The dispersal of Jews around the world.

Diet: The Japanese parliament.

domino theory: The fear that if communism is not contained, as one country falls to communism its neighbours will fall soon after. This theory was used to justify American involvement in South-East Asia in the 1960s.

draft dodger: A person who evades compulsory military service. For example, young Americans who did not support the Vietnam War fled to places like Canada to avoid military service.

draft: Compulsory enrolment of eligible citizens for military service.

dreadnought: A battleship introduced by Britain in 1906 that represented a revolution in naval shipbuilding.

economic imperialism: Control of a nation through foreign investment in which the foreign government dictates development policies and projects that benefit its interests rather than those of the host country or its people.

economic rivalry: Competition between nations to produce the greatest economic growth.

enclave: A separate or distinct area surrounded by another territory.

enfranchisement: The right to vote in elections and to be recognized as a citizen of society.

enterprise culture: An attitude that values the entrepreneurial spirit of a population and discourages public sector involvement.

ethnic cleansing: The displacement or murder of one ethnic group by another.

ethnic federalism: A governing structure in which a central government shares power with a variety of political and ethnic parties.

ethnic nationalism: The desire of an ethnic group to preserve its own language, religion and traditions through a strong political or geographic unit; the desire of an ethnic group for national independence.

European Commission: The body that takes care of the day-to-day functioning of the European Union, under the direction of the Council of Ministers.

European Community (EC): The term for three European Communities that merged in July 1967: the European Economic Community, the European Coal and Steel Community, and the European Atomic Energy Community. The EC's objective is to create a free and unified market. In 1994, the EC became the European Union (EU).

European Economic Community, or Common Market (EEC): An economic association of nations formed in 1958 to promote free trade among members, joint social and financial policies, and free movement of capital and labour.

European Parliament: An elected body of representatives of the member countries of the European Union. Its role is advisory or consultative to the Commission and Council.

European Union: A deeply integrated political and economic union of European countries to form a large trading bloc.

fascism: A movement emphasizing national and racial superiority and a centralized, autocratic government headed by a dictator.

feminization of poverty: The condition in which women are disproportionately represented among the poor. Discrimination against women in education and job opportunities pushes them into the lower classes.

final solution: Hitler's plan for the systematic murder of all European Jews between 1941 and 1945. More than 6 million Jews were killed during this period.

flashpoints: A moment or event that triggers sudden action that may result in conflict.

Fourteen Points: US president Wilson's statement of principles that he believed should be the basis of the peace settlement at the end of the First World War.

fundamentalist: A person who believes that a religious doctrine should be believed and followed literally. Fundamentalists do not accept any teachings that conflict with their understanding of their faith.

General Assembly: The body of the United Nations in which each member country has one vote and all nations are given the opportunity to express their views.

genocide: The extermination of a race by deliberate and systemic means.

Gestapo: The secret state police of Nazi Germany that was notorious for its brutality.

ghettos: Sections of a city where Jews were forced to live in Nazi Germany.

glasnost: A policy of openness and increased freedom in social and cultural matters in the Soviet Union, introduced by Gorbachev in 1986.

global collective security: The notion that security for all nations and peoples can be achieved through international efforts such as the United Nations.

Global South: The name given to the developing countries of the world.

globalization: To make world-wide in scope or application, especially in reference to international trade, investment, and production. It can result in the restructuring of the global economy.

governmental organization: An organization, supported by governments, whose aim is to effect positive social, economic, or political change in their member nations.

Great Depression: The prolonged period of economic decline, including decreased production and high unemployment, that followed the American stock market crash of October 29, 1929.

guerrilla warfare: Military activity that relies on surprise raids and unconventional military tactics.

hotline: A direct telephone line between the heads of state in Washington and Moscow for immediate emergency communication and to prevent nuclear war.

human rights: The freedom granted to all people protecting them from unlawful arrest, torture, or execution.

humanitarian: Helpful to humanity or the welfare of others.

hyperinflation: A period of exceedingly high inflation.

imperialism: The policy of extending the authority of a nation over foreign countries through the acquisition of colonies.

industrialization: The development of large industries in a country or region.

inflation: A persistent rise in the prices of consumer goods resulting from too great an increase in the supply of credit or the issuing of too much paper money.

infrastructures: The system of roads and communication networks of a country, state, or region.

intercontinental ballistic missile (ICBM): A missile capable of travelling between continents.

Intifadah: Violent demonstrations by Palestinians against Israeli rule in the Gaza Strip and on the West Bank of Jordan that began in 1987.

isolationism: A national policy of abstaining from political or economic relations with other countries.

juntas: A group of persons controlling a government after a revolutionary seizure of power.

kamikaze: The suicide missions of Japanese air force pilots who crashed their aircraft into enemy targets during the Second World War.

Kellogg-Briand Pact: Also known as the Pact of Paris, this 1928 agreement among 15 countries (including Canada) called for the end of war. The countries agreed that settlement of all disputes would be done by negotiation and diplomacy. The Pact made no meaningful contribution to international order.

kibbutz: A communal farm or settlement in Israel.

Kristallnacht (9 November 1938): The attack by German Nazis on Jewish communities across Germany; also known as "The Night of Broken Glass," the violence marked an escalation in the Nazi plan of Jewish persecution.

kulaks: Russian peasants who became prosperous farmers of mid-size farms as a result of agrarian reforms in 1906 and who were eliminated in 1929 by Stalin because of their opposition to collectivization.

Kuomintang (the Chinese Revolutionary Party): A political party that ruled all or part of mainland China from 1928 to 1949 and subsequently ruled Taiwan.

Kyoto Protocol: This international accord states that developed countries should commit to reducing collective emissions of greenhouse gases by an average of at least five per cent by 2008-2012. Canada ratified Kyoto in 2002.

Lateran Treaties: A series of agreements in which Italy recognized the sovereignty of the Vatican City State and the role of the Catholic Church within the Italian state.

League of Arab States: An organization formed to promote Arab unity and co-operation that opposes the creation of an independent state of Israel in Palestine.

left: A political view advocating reform in the established order to better represent the people.

liberalism: A political philosophy centred on individual freedom, a belief in democracy, and a desire for progress.

limited war: The waging of war in a way that does not require the full involvement of all aspects of society. The US presence in Vietnam was meant to be a small war or police action—a limited war.

Locarno Pact: A treaty among the European powers in 1925 that guaranteed the boundaries of Belgium, France, and Germany as specified by the Treaty of Versailles of 1919. The Pact included mutual defense agreements between France and Poland and France and Czechoslovakia.

mandates: Former colonial territories of the Ottoman Empire that were consigned by the League of Nations to other nations to administer.

Manhattan Project: The code name of the US research project charged with developing the atomic bomb.

Marshall Plan: A proposal by US secretary of state George Marshall in 1947 to offer American financial aid to countries devastated by the Second World War. It resulted in the growth of industrial Western Europe and the stimulation of the US economy through exports.

martial law: Enforced military law, introduced by government, to maintain public order and safety.

McCarthyism: A campaign led by US senator Joseph McCarthy and the House Un-American Activities Committee to search for communist infiltrators in American society.

Mensheviks: A wing of the Russian Social Democratic Party during the Russian Revolution that believed that socialism should be gradually achieved through parliamentary methods rather than revolution.

Mercosur Agreement: A 1995 trade alliance between Argentina, Brazil, Paraguay, and Uruguay to eliminate tariff barriers among the signatories.

military-industrial complex: A state's armed forces, including technology and product suppliers.

mixed economy: An economy that contains elements of both private and state enterprise.

Molotov Plan: The Soviet plan to create a bilateral trade agreement with the Soviet bloc in 1947 in response to the US Marshall Plan.

monarchist: A person who believes in a constitutional king or queen as hereditary head of state.

Munich Pact: In 1938 this act of appeasement allowed Germany to occupy the Sudetenland, a part of Czechoslovakia. Britain's Prime Minister Neville Chamberlain announced that the Pact had secured "peace in our time."

national security: National policies and actions taken in an effort to guarantee a country's own safety.

national self-determination: The free choice of a nation to establish its own political affairs.

National Socialist German Workers Party (Nazi): The political party, led by Adolf Hitler, that ruled Germany from 1933 to 1945.

national sovereignty: The power and authority of a nation over its own affairs.

nationalism: A sense of national consciousness that fosters loyalty to the country.

nationalization (nationalize): The transfer of private ownership and control to the state.

New Deal: The policy of social and economic reforms introduced by US president Roosevelt to relieve the Great Depression.

New Economic Policy: A policy introduced by Lenin in 1921 following food shortages and peasant riots in which communist economic practices were relaxed to allow limited private commerce and internal trade.

noble destiny: The belief that a course of events is predetermined by superior status and ideals.

Non-governmental organizations (NGOs): Organizations that operate independently of any government and draw resources from the developed world to assist in the economic and social development of developing countries.

North American Aerospace Defence Command (NAADC): See North American Air Defence Command.

North American Air Defence Command (NORAD): A joint American-Canadian organization established in 1957 to monitor nuclear tracking, warning, and control stations across the northern Arctic. In 1981 the name was changed to North American Aerospace Defence Command.

North American Free Trade Agreement (NAFTA): The treaty creating a North American trading bloc and a common market among Canada, the United States, and Mexico. The agreement may be expanded to include other countries in Latin America, such as Chile, which has applied for membership.

North Atlantic Treaty Organization (NATO): A mutual defence pact, established in 1949 to counter the threat of the Soviet bloc. Members include the United States, Canada, Britain, France, Belgium, the Netherlands, Denmark, Norway, Iceland, Italy, Portugal, Greece, Turkey, and Spain.

nuclear age: The era following the Second World War that produced the threat of nuclear war.

nuclear arms race: The competition between nations for the superior build-up of nuclear weapons.

Nuremburg Laws: Nazi legislation in 1935 that reduced all Jews in Germany to second-class citizens.

Occupied Territories: The West Bank and the Gaza Strip (taken over by Israel after the 1967 Six-Day War), the Golan Heights (annexed by Israel in 1981), and East Jerusalem (annexed by Israel in 1967). The Sinai Peninsula was also taken in the Six-Day War but it was returned to Egypt in 1979 as terms of a peace treaty.

Organization for African Unity (OAU): An agency established in 1963 to promote African unity and solidarity, to coordinate political, economic, defence, and social policies of all members, and to eliminate colonialism.

Organization of American States (OAS): An agency founded in 1948 to promote co-operation and security among American nations and to discourage European intervention in the Americas.

pacifism: A policy of opposition to war and violence.

Palestine Liberation Organization (PLO): An umbrella political organization formed in 1964 to centralize Palestinian leadership and create a democratic Palestinian state.

pandemic: A disease that affects a large proportion of the population spread over a large area.

Pan-Slavism: The movement by Russian nationalists to gain influence and power over Serbia by calling on the Slavic people in the Balkans to unite under their leadership against Austria-Hungary.

pass laws: Legislation in the apartheid state of South Africa that required non-whites to carry identification passbooks for presentation on demand to authorities.

Pax Britannia: A period of general international peace under the military power of Britain.

peace dividend: The benefits of redirecting funds once designated for military expenditures into domestic spending.

peacekeeping: The activities, mediation, and deployment of UN forces in civil or international wars to help maintain peace between two conflicting parties.

peacemaking: The activities, mediation, and deployment of UN forces in civil or international wars to establish peace or provide a settlement between two conflicting parties.

perestroika: Gorbachev's policy of restructuring economics and government in the Soviet Union in the 1980s.

plebiscite: A vote by the entire voting community on a major issue.

policy of containment: The policy of keeping the expansion of a hostile power or ideology in check. This policy was used by the United States to prevent the Soviet Union from expanding beyond its borders beginning in the late 1940s.

privatization: The change of businesses from public to private control or ownership.

purges: The removal of suspected enemies from the Communist Party and the Soviet Union by Stalin. Between 1935 and 1938, an estimated 11 million people were sent to labour camps or were executed in the purge known as the Great Terror.

racial superiority: Discrimination based on the belief in the relative superiority of one race over other races.

radar: A technology used to detect the nature, position, and movement of an object using electromagnetic waves.

Reagan Doctrine: A US program that called for American moral and material support for movements seeking to oust socialist regimes in developing countries.

Red Guards: A youth organization in China created to help Mao combat revisionists.

Reichstag: Germany's parliament.

reparations: Compensation in money or materials paid to the victorious country by the defeated country for the damage inflicted by war.

republic: A state in which the citizens or their democratically elected representatives hold supreme power.

republicanism: A form of government in which the citizens elect representatives to manage the government. Governments of this type are usually led by a president.

revisionists: Communists who favour evolutionary reform rather than revolutionary change.

right: A conservative political view that opposes change to the established government and advocates traditional attitudes and practices.

sanction: An action taken by nations working together to force another nation to obey international laws. Sanctions can take the form of economic restrictions, blockades, travel restrictions, etc.

scapegoating: Shifting the blame for a problem to some other person or group.

Schlieffen Plan: Germany's military strategy in 1914 for attacking France through its unprotected Belgian border.

Secretary-General: The principal administrator of the United Nations.

Security Council: The UN council charged with the duty of maintaining international peace and security.

Selective Service Act: A conscription act passed by US president Harry Truman in response to the Soviet-backed communist takeover of Czechoslovakia.

self-determination: The free choice of a people of a nation for their own political future.

shuttle diplomacy: A diplomatic arrangement in which a third party intermediary shuttles back and forth between negotiating nations.

skinheads: Youth gangs, usually white male, with shaved heads who are violent in their promotion of white-supremacist beliefs.

social democrats: A moderate political philosophy that tends to support social values and tolerance.

socialism: A political and economic system of the moderate left in which the means of production and distribution are owned and controlled by the public.

South East Asia Treaty Organization (SEATO): An alliance established in 1954 among the United States, Australia, New Zealand, the Philippines, Thailand, Pakistan, Britain, and France providing for collective action in the event of an attack or internal subversion.

speculation: Buying and selling when there is a risk in the hope of making a profit from future price changes.

sphere of influence: A major power's domination over a geographic area.

squatter settlements: Regions in which people have claimed unused plots of land to create makeshift lodgings and villages.

state capitalism: An economic system in which public control and private enterprise are blended together. In China, for example, the state establishes the direction or context for entrepreneurial activity.

state socialism: A system of government in which the state controls most of the means of the production and distribution of goods.

structural unemployment: A state that is created when significant changes in demand or technology occur, creating long-term unemployment because workers' skills cannot be easily transferred to the new technologies.

suffrage: The right to vote in an election.

supranationalism: The linking of nations having a common bond or experience.

sustained development: The development of natural resources for long-term use that aims to conserve it as a renewable resource.

total war: Total war is war in which all citizens, whether in combat or not, are involved with the war effort.

totalitarianism: A form of government with a centralized state authority that permits no competing political group and has strict control over economic, social, and political aspects of life.

Treaty of Brest-Litovsk: The treaty, signed in March 1918 between Germany and the Russian government under Vladimir Ilyich Lenin, that brought an end to the fighting between these two countries near the end of the First World War.

Treaty of Versailles: The peace settlement negotiated at the Paris Peace Conference that ended the First World War. Its terms included reparation payments, limitations on Germany's military force, the surrender of German colonies, and the establishment of the League of Nations.

Triple Alliance: The alliance in 1882 of Germany, Austria-Hungary, and Italy in an attempt to isolate France.

Triple Entente: The 1907 alliance of Britain, France, and Russia in response to the rising powers of Germany, Austria-Hungary, and Italy (the Triple Alliance).

Truman Doctrine: US president Harry Truman's policy to fight the spread of communism around the world through US military and economic aid.

U-boat (*Unterseeboot*): A German submarine introduced during the First World War.

ultimatum: A final proposal of terms which, when rejected, may end negotiations and result in a war.

Uniting for Peace resolution: A United Nations resolution passed in 1950 that gave the General Assembly power to deal with issues of international aggression if the Security Council is deadlocked.

universal suffrage: The right to vote extended to all citizens of a society despite social class.

veto power: The right to reject a proposal or forbid an action. The five permanent members of the UN Security Council have veto power over all resolutions.

war by proxy: Rather than confront each other and risk the use of nuclear weapons, the superpowers supported wars involving smaller allied nations, using their forces to accomplish broader goals.

war communism: The period following the Russian Revolution in 1917 in which the Bolsheviks attempted to establish communist rule in the face of foreign military intervention in the civil war.

Warsaw Pact: A mutual defense pact signed by the Soviet Union, Albania, Bulgaria, Czechoslovakia, East Germany, Hungary, Poland, and Romania, as a communist counterpart to the North Atlantic Treaty Organization.

welfare state: A social system based on government-sponsored social welfare programs, including health plans, unemployment insurance, and social security programs.

Westernization: The influence of Western ideas and customs on a country and its culture.

Young Plan: An American program for settlement of German reparations that was put in place after it became apparent that Germany could not meet the conditions of the Dawes Plan. The Young Plan reduced the payments appreciably and extended them over a longer period of time.

zaibatsu: Large family-owned businesses in Japan prior to the Second World War.

Zionism: An international movement for the establishment of a Jewish state in Palestine.

Index

Text Credits

11 Excerpts from Nellie McClung, *In Times Like These*, 1915. (Toronto: University of Toronto Press), 1972; **15** Excerpts from Valerie Bryson, *Feminist Debates: Issues of Theory and Political Practice*. (New York University Press: Washington Square), 1999. © 1999 NYU Press. All rights reserved; **28** Cecil Rhodes "Confession of Faith" (1877), quoted in Marvin Perry, ed. *Sources of the Western Tradition, Volume II: From The Scientific Revolution To The Present*, pp. 178-179, Copyright © 1987 by Houghton Mifflin Company; **29** John Atkinson Hobson, "Imperialism" (1902) quoted in Marvin Perry, ed. *Sources of the Western Tradition, Volume II: From The Scientific Revolution To The Present*, pp. 186-188, Copyright © 1987 by Houghton Mifflin Company; **43** Roger Graham, Canadian historian, quoted in Andrew H. Malcolm, *The Canadians* (Markham, ON: Fitzhenry and Whiteside, 1979); **44** Quote from Modris Eksteins, historian, *The Rites of Spring: The Great War and the Birth of the Modern Age* (Toronto: Key Porter © 1989]; **47** Excerpts reprinted from *The First Day on the Somme* by Martin Middlebrook. Copyright © 1972 by Martin Middlebrook. Reprinted by permission of Curtis Brown, Ltd.; **124** Figure 4.19 from Hans Jacobsen, *Der Zweite Weltkrieg*, 1965; **127** Excerpt from NIGHT by Elie Wiesel, translated by Stella Rodway. Copyright © 1960 by MacGibbon & Kee. Copyright renewed © 1988 by The Collins Publishing Group. Reprinted by permission of Hill and Wang, a division of Farrar, Straus and Giroux, LLC; **132-133** "A.J.P. Taylor" reprinted from *Past and Present* (April 1965), by permission of the author and *Past and Present* (Article: "War Origins" p. 110); **133** "H.R. Trevor Roper" from E.M. Robertson (ed.), *The Origins of the Second World War: Historical Interpretations*, 1978, Macmillan Press Ltd., pp. 83-104 reproduced with permission of Palgrave Macmillan; **164** Quotes from Hanson W. Baldwin excerpted from Hanson W. Baldwin, "We Must Choose (1) 'Bug Out', (2) Negotiate, (3) Fight" from *New York Times Magazine*, 21 February 1965. Copyright © 1965 by The New York Times Company. Reprinted by permission; **170** Quotes from George F. Kennan from *Russia and the West Under Lenin and Stalin* by George F. Kennan. Copyright © 1960 by James Hotchkiss, Trustee. By permission of Little Brown and Company / Quotes from Ronald Reagan reprinted with the permission of Simon & Schuster Adult Publishing Group from AN AMERICAN LIFE by Ronald Reagan. Copyright © 1990 by Ronald W. Reagan; **174-175** "The sincerity of the American's alarm" from THE LONG PEACE: INQUIRIES INTO THE HISTORY OF THE COLD WAR by John Lewis Gaddis, copyright © 1987 by John Lewis Gaddis. Used by permission of Oxford University Press, Inc.; **175-176** "The exaggeration of the Soviet threat" from MEETING THE COMMUNIST THREAT: TRUMAN TO REAGAN by Thomas G. Paterson, copyright © 1988 by Thomas G. Patterson. Used by permission of Oxford University Press, Inc.; **198** Q & A excerpted from "We Need New Concepts, A New Approach," by Richard Gwyn, *Toronto Star*, 23 March 1993, A17. Reprinted by permission of the Toronto Star Syndicate; **206-207** "Useful roles of the UN" excerpted from Gerald Segal, *The Stoddart Guide to the World Today*, Stoddart Publishing Co. Limited, Don Mills, Ontario; **207-208** "Limitations of the UN" adapted from Ted Galen Carpenter, "Pruning the United Nations," November 18, 1997; **213** Figure 7.2 from *Preparing for the 21st Century* by Paul Kennedy. Copyright © by Paul Kennedy. Published in Canada by HarperCollins Publishers Ltd.; **217** Excerpt from a poem by Evgenii Evtushenko that appeared in a Soviet literary magazine in September 1985; **220** Quotes from Madelaine Drohan excerpted from Madelaine Drohan, *The Globe and Mail*, 4 July 1992. Reprinted with permission from The Globe and Mail / Quotes from Flora Lewis reprinted from Flora Lewis, "A European Germany or a German European?" *New Perspectives Quarterly*, Winter 1993, by permission; **239-240** "The case for opening up NATO to the East" and "Why Spain should have been NATO's last member" from *The Future of NATO: Enlargement, Russia, and European Security*. Eds. Charles-Philippe David and Jacques Levesque, McGill-Queens University Press, Montreal & Kingston. (Published for the Centre of Security and Foreign Policy Studies and the Teleglobe+Raoul-Dandurand Chair of Strategic and Diplomatic Studies). 1999; **259** Figure 8.12: Candidate Countries for EU Membership from *World Guide 2001/2002*, New Internationalist Publications. © Copyright 2002 New Internationalist Publications Ltd. All rights reserved; **270-271** "Enlargement: Frequently Asked Questions" from Europa: The European Union Online, March 2002. <europa.eu.int/comm/enlargement/faq/index.htm#Why> © European Communities, 1995-2002; **271-272** "Europe's Eastern Enlargement: Who Benefits?" adapted from John Hall and Wolfgang Quaisser, "Europe's Eastern Enlargement: Who Benefits?" *Current History*, November 2001, pp. 389-393. Reprinted with permission from *Current History* magazine (November 2001), © 2001, Current History, Inc.; **285** Quote from Yuli M. Voronstov in a statement to the United Nations General Assembly, 27 May 1986 © Copyright United Nations, 2000-2003 / Quote from Carlos Rangel reprinted by permission of Transaction Publishers. Excerpt from *Third World Ideology and Western Reality* by Carlos Rangel. Copyright © 1986. All rights reserved / Quotes from Michael Parenti from Michael Parenti, *The Sword and the Dollar: Imperialism, Revolution and the Arms Race* (St. Martin's Press, 1989); **286** Figure 9.8: Information compiled from The Joint United Nations Programme on HIV/AIDS. © Joint United Nations Programme on HIV/AIDS (UNAIDS) 2001. All rights reserved; **287** Quote by Kofi Annan from *The International Herald Tribune*, 5 December 2000; **289** Figure 9.11 from U.S. Census Bureau, International Data Base; **291** Quote by Amara Essy from "African Leaders blast UN Security Council," BY ROMAN ROLLNICK © Earth Times News Service / Quote by Festus B. Mogae from a statement by His Excellency Mr. Festus G. Mogae, President of the Republic of Botswana, at the International Conference on Financing for Development, Monterrey, Mexico, 18-22 March 2002. © Copyright United Nations, 2000-2003; **307-308** "The exploitation of Africa" from *The Struggle for Africa* by Mai Palmberg, published by Zed Books, 1983, London. Reprinted with permission of Zed Books Ltd.; **308-309** "Colonialism is not to blame" from *Equality, the Third World and Economic Delusion* by P.T. Bauer, George Weidenfeld & Nicolson Limited, London, 1981; **335** Report on China excerpt adapted from *Amnesty International Report 2001*. © Copyright Amnesty International Publications 2001; **340-342** "Tom Lantos and Wang Jian Wei" adapted from *PBS NewsHour*, 12 July 2001 www.pbs.org/newshour/bb/sports/july-dec01/olympics_7-10.html. Copyright © 2003 MacNeil/Lehrer Productions. All Rights Reserved; **355** Figure 11.7 adapted from *The Changing Geopolitics of Energy – Part II*, Anthony H. Cordesman, Center for Strategic and International Studies, 1998, p. 20. Copyright Anthony H. Cordesman, all rights reserved; **357** Figure 11.8 adapted from S. Hadawi, *Bitter Harvest: A Modern History of Palestine* (New York: Olive Branch Press, 1991); **366** Lyrics from *Intifadah*, a popular Palestinian song; **367** Quote by Salah Khalaf reprinted with permission from *Foreign Policy* 78 (Spring 1990). Copyright 1990 by the Carnegie Endowment for International Peace / Quote by Sheikh Ahmed Yassin from an interview published in *Palestine Report*, Volume 7, No. 7, 2 August 2000. © 2000 Palestine Report. All rights reserved; **368** Quote by David Bar-Illan from David Bar-Illan, "Can Israel Withdraw? No!" *Commentary*, 1988. Reprinted from COMMENTARY, April 1988, by permission; all rights reserved / Quote by Yossi Beilin excerpted from a speech given by Yossi Beilin at the Center for Middle East Peace & Economic Cooperation, Washington, D.C., 21 May 2002; **370** Quote by Yasser Arafat from Yasser Arafat, Op-Ed, *The New York Times*, 3 February 2002; **375-376** "Rabbi Sherwin Wine, founder of the Humanist Institute" from *The Humanist*, September-October 2002. Reprinted with the permission of the publisher, American Humanist Association, copyright 2002; **376-377** "Hanan Ashrawi, member of the Palestinian Legislative Council" from "Reforming from Within," by Hanan Ashrawi, *The Guardian* (London), June 7, 2002. © Hanan Ashwari; **388-389** Sima Samar, 2001 John Humphrey Freedom Award Recipient: excerpts from acceptance speech, December 10th, 2001. Source: International Centre for Human Rights and Development www.ichrdd.ca; **391-392** Jimmy Carter, Former US president, excerpts from Nobel Prize acceptance speech © The Nobel Foundation 2002; **396** Quote by George Bush from speech to the General Assembly of the United Nations, September 12, 2002. © Copyright United Nations, 2000-2003; **415-416** "Shanti Zachariah" excerpted from Shanti Zachariah, "Old Fight is 'new' global economy," *Catholic New Times*, 6 February 2000, vol. 24 no. 2, pp. 10-11; **417** "Jagdish Bhagwati" excerpted from Jagdish Bhagwati, "Economic sense and nonsense: Misconceptions of the global economy," *Harvard International Review*, Fall 2000; Volume 22, No. 3, pp. 78-81.

Photo Credits

t=top; b=bottom; c=centre; l=left; r=right
AP=Associated Press CP=CP Picture Archive

4 © Archivo Iconografico, S.A./CORBIS/MAGMA; **8** MARY EVANS PICTURE LIBRARY; **9** © Museum of London/Heritage Images; **10** Hulton Archive/Getty Images; **11** Cyril Jessop / National Archives of Canada / PA-030212; **17** The Granger Collection, New York; **20** Picasso, Pablo (1881-1973). Woman sitting in an armchair, 1910. AM 4391 P. Photo: Adam Rzepka. CNAC/MNAM/Dist. Réunion des Musées Nationaux/ Art Resource, NY. © Estate of Pablo Picasso / SODRAC (Montreal) 2003; **22 tc** Courtesy of the Canadian Forces, **bl** Reproduced by permission of Punch, Ltd., **br** Illustration by Bruno Paul in Simplicissimus/MARY EVANS PICTURE LIBRARY; **32** Alfred Bastien, "Over the Top" (CN8058). © Canadian War Museum (CWM); **35** © Hulton-Deutsch Collection/CORBIS/MAGMA; **40** The Granger Collection, New York; **49** William Rider-Rider/Canada Dept. of National Defence/National Archives of Canada/PA-002156; **52** Hulton Archive/Getty Images; **53** Zeno Diemer in 'Jugend' November 1918 page 939/MARY EVANS PICTURE LIBRARY; **59** © Bettmann/CORBIS/MAGMA; **66** The Persistence of Memory, 1931 (oil on canvas) by Salvador Dali (1904-89). Museum of Modern Art, New York, USA/Bridgeman Art Library. © Salvador Dali/ Fondation Gala-Salvador Dali/Sodart, Montreal 2003; **71** The Granger Collection, New York; **73** © Hulton-Deutsch Collection/CORBIS/ MAGMA; **74** © Yevgeny Khaldei/CORBIS/MAGMA; **78** The Granger Collection, New York; **79** Hulton Archive/Getty Images; **89** The Granger Collection, New York; **90** © Bettmann/CORBIS/MAGMA; **97** Alex Colville, "Infantry, near Nijmegen, Holland" (CN12172). © Canadian War Museum (CWM); **100** © Hulton-Deutsch Collection/CORBIS/MAGMA; **102** Hulton Archive/Getty Images; **104** "Rendezvous" by David Low, *Evening Standard*, September 20, 1939, Centre for the Study of Cartoons, University of Kent, http://library.ukc.ac.uk/cartoons/. © Atlantic Syndication; **108** Hulton Archive/Getty Images; **111 tr** © Bettmann/CORBIS/ MAGMA, **bl** The Granger Collection, New York; **112** © Bettmann/ CORBIS/MAGMA; **116** The Granger Collection, New York; **118 t** Hulton Archive/Getty Images, **b** © Bettmann/CORBIS/MAGMA; **121 t** © Bettmann/CORBIS/MAGMA, **b** Hulton Archive/Getty Images; **122** STEVE BENSON © UFS. Reprinted by Permission; **125** © Bettmann/CORBIS/MAGMA; **129** The Granger Collection, New York; **138** © Bettmann/CORBIS/MAGMA; **140** © Bettmann/CORBIS/ MAGMA; **143 bl** Library of Congress, Prints and Photographs Division, LC-USZ62-86602. Used by permission of the Marcus family, **br** © CORBIS/MAGMA; **146** © Bettmann/CORBIS/MAGMA; **149** © Bettmann/CORBIS/MAGMA; **152** CP; **154** © Bettmann/ CORBIS/MAGMA; **156** © Bettmann/CORBIS/MAGMA; **158** Hulton Archive/Getty Images; **159** Hulton Archive/Getty Images; **162** © Bettmann/CORBIS/MAGMA; **163** © Jonathan Blair/CORBIS/ MAGMA; **165** © Bettmann/CORBIS/MAGMA; **171** © Bettmann/ CORBIS/MAGMA; **172** Copyright © Geoff Hook. All rights reserved; **178** United Nations/Department of Public Information Photo; **180** CP(Kevin Frayer); **181** "A fine team but could do with a dash of unity" by David Low, *Evening Standard*, June 4, 1945, Centre for the Study of Cartoons, University of Kent, http://library.ukc.ac.uk/ cartoons/. © Atlantic Syndication; **182** © Reuters NewMedia Inc./ CORBIS/MAGMA; **183** AP/Wide World Photos; **186** Hulton Archive/Getty Images; **193** United Nations/Department of Public Information Photo; **197** Hulton Archive/Getty Images; **202** © Peter Turnley/CORBIS/MAGMA; **203** © Reuters NewMedia Inc./ CORBIS/MAGMA; **210** © Alfred/Sipa Press/PONOPRESSE; **212** © Reuters NewMedia Inc./CORBIS/MAGMA; **214** © Shepard Sherbell/CORBIS/MAGMA; **215** © Jacques Langevin/CORBIS SYGMA/MAGMA; **218** © Rex Features/PONOPRESSE; **219** © Reuters NewMedia Inc./CORBIS/MAGMA; **222** Richard Ellis/Getty Images; **223** © Shone/Gamma/PONOPRESSE; **224** © Gamma URSS/PONOPRESSE; **227** CP; **231** CP(Hidajet Delic); **232** © Gamma/ PONOPRESSE; **233** © AFP/CORBIS/MAGMA; **246** © Derek Grant; **250** Copyright © Geoff Hook. All rights reserved; **251** © Jerry Bergman/Gamma/PONOPRESSE.; **253** Reprinted by permission of the Audiovisual Library of the European Commission; **254** © SIE Productions/CORBIS/MAGMA; **256** © Owen Franken/CORBIS/ MAGMA; **257** © William Whitehurst/CORBIS/MAGMA; **259** © David Turnley/CORBIS/MAGMA; **262** CP/Victoria Times-Colonist (Ian McKain); **263 t** CP(Richard Sobol), **b** CP(Mark Cowan); **266** CP(Fred Chartrand); **274** © Peter Turnley/CORBIS/MAGMA; **276** The Queen's Empire vol 4 page 269/MARY EVANS PICTURE LIBRARY; **281 tl** © Bettmann/CORBIS/MAGMA, **tr** © Bettmann/CORBIS/ MAGMA; **284** © Peter Turnley/CORBIS/MAGMA; **287** © AFP/ CORBIS/MAGMA; **288** © Liba Taylor/CORBIS/MAGMA; **293** © Martin Jones/CORBIS/MAGMA; **295** © Hulton-Deutsch Collection/ CORBIS/MAGMA; **297** © Bettmann/CORBIS/MAGMA; **299** Eli Weinberg/UWC-Robben Island Museum Mayibuye Archives; **301 tr** © David Turnley/CORBIS/MAGMA, **bl** © David Turnley/CORBIS/ MAGMA; **304** © David Turnley/CORBIS/MAGMA; **312** © Catherine Karnow/CORBIS/MAGMA; **319** © Bettmann/CORBIS/MAGMA; **321** © Reuters NewMedia Inc./CORBIS/MAGMA; **323** © AFP/CORBIS/ MAGMA; **324** AP/Wide World Photos; **327** © Bettmann/CORBIS/ MAGMA; **329** © Bettmann/CORBIS/MAGMA; **330** © Bettmann/ CORBIS/MAGMA; **333** © Peter Turnley/CORBIS/MAGMA; **334** © Royalty-free/CORBIS/MAGMA; **335 bl** © Reuters NewMedia Inc./CORBIS/MAGMA, **br** © AFP/CORBIS/MAGMA; **344** © AFP/ CORBIS/MAGMA; **347 bl** © Bettmann/CORBIS/MAGMA, **br** © Bettmann/CORBIS/MAGMA; **351** CP(Jassim Mohammed); **354** CP(Michel Lipchitz); **358** © Bettmann/CORBIS/MAGMA; **360** © Bettmann/CORBIS/MAGMA; **362** © David Rubinger/CORBIS/ MAGMA; **363** CP; **364** © Reuters NewMedia Inc./CORBIS/MAGMA; **366** © Peter Turnley/CORBIS/MAGMA; **369** © AFP/CORBIS/ MAGMA; **370** CP(Vadim Ghirda); **371** CP; **373** AP/Wide World Photos; **381** CP/PA(Kirsty Wigglesworth); **383** CP(Stephen Boitano); **384** CP(B. K. Bangash); **387** CP(Kevin Frayer); **390 t** © Joe Heller/ Green Bay Press-Gazette, **b** © Reuters NewMedia Inc./CORBIS/ MAGMA; **397** © AFP/CORBIS/MAGMA; **399** © Peter Turnley/ CORBIS/MAGMA; **402** © Brabazon / Gamma-FSP / PONOPRESSE; **403 bl** © Peter Turnley/CORBIS/MAGMA, **bc** © Ken Straiton/ CORBIS/MAGMA, **br** © Peter Turnley/CORBIS/MAGMA; **404** © Royalty-Free/CORBIS/MAGMA; **405** CP(Boris Heger); **406** © AFP/CORBIS/MAGMA; **408** © AFP/CORBIS/MAGMA; **409 t** © Reuters NewMedia Inc./CORBIS/MAGMA, **b** © Reuters NewMedia Inc./CORBIS/MAGMA; **412** © Owen Franken/CORBIS/MAGMA.